Second Edition

Administration of Intercollegiate Athletics

Second Edition

Administration of Intercollegiate Athletics

Robert H. Zullo, PhD
Slippery Rock University

Erianne A. Weight, PhD, MBA
University of North Carolina at Chapel Hill

Editors

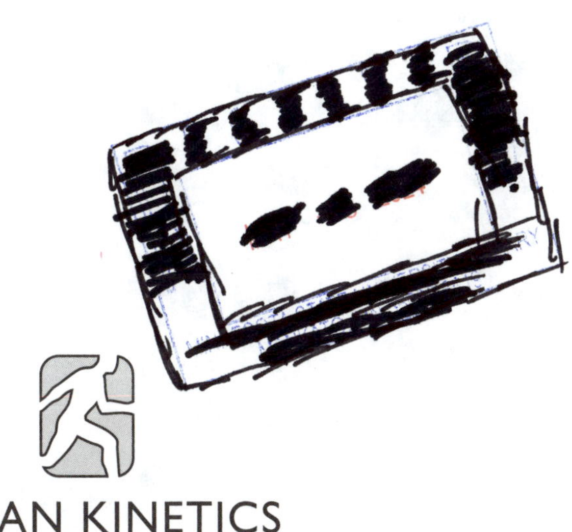

HUMAN KINETICS

Library of Congress Cataloging-in-Publication Data

Names: Zullo, Robert H., 1975- editor of compilation. | Weight, Erianne A., 1981- editor of compilation.
Title: Administration of intercollegiate ahletics / Robert H. Zullo, PhD, Slippery Rock University, editor, Erianne A. Weight, PhD, MBA, University of North Carolina at Chapel Hill, editor.
Description: Second [edition] | Champaign, IL : Human Kinetics, [2025] | First edition: 2015. | Includes bibliographical references and index.
Identifiers: LCCN 2023028865 (print) | LCCN 2023028866 (ebook) | ISBN 9781718213012 (print : alk. paper) | ISBN 9781718213029 (epub) | ISBN 9781718213036 (pdf)
Subjects: LCSH: College sports--United States--Management. | National Collegiate Athletic Association. | National Association of Intercollegiate Athletics. | BISAC: SPORTS & RECREATION / Business Aspects | SPORTS & RECREATION / Reference
Classification: LCC GV351 .A36 2025 (print) | LCC GV351 (ebook) | DDC 796.04/30973--dc23/eng/20230828
LC record available at https://lccn.loc.gov/2023028865
LC ebook record available at https://lccn.loc.gov/2023028866

ISBN: 978-1-7182-1301-2 (print)

The web addresses cited in this text were current as of August 2023, unless otherwise noted.

Acquisitions Editor: Andrew L. Tyler; **Managing Editor:** Anna Lan Seaman; **Copyeditor:** Laura Magzis; **Proofreader:** Rebecca L. Emanuelsen; **Indexer:** Dan Connolly; **Permissions Manager:** Laurel Mitchell; **Graphic Designer:** Joe Buck; **Cover Designer:** Keri Evans; **Cover Design Specialist:** Susan Rothermel Allen; **Photograph (cover):** Lindsey Wasson/NCAA Photos via Getty Images; **Photographs (interior):** © Human Kinetics, unless otherwise noted; **Photo Production Manager:** Jason Allen; **Senior Art Manager:** Kelly Hendren; **Illustrations:** © Human Kinetics, unless otherwise noted; **Printer:** Sheridan Books

Printed in the United States of America

10 9 8 7 6 5 4 3 2 1

The paper in this book is certified under a sustainable forestry program.

Human Kinetics
1607 N. Market Street
Champaign, IL 61820
USA

United States and International
Website: **US.HumanKinetics.com**
Email: info@hkusa.com
Phone: 1-800-747-4457

Canada
Website: **Canada.HumanKinetics.com**
Email: info@hkcanada.com

E8604

Contents

Preface

As we approach a new era of intercollegiate athletics, this second edition addresses cutting-edge issues that affect stakeholders across the industry. Governing bodies explore their purpose. Student-athletes pursue name, image, and likeness (NIL) opportunities and utilize the transfer portal, toeing the line of employee status, unions, and collective bargaining. Coaches seek to increase their staff sizes with quality control assistants, graphic designers, and support staff in the areas of nutrition, psychology, and more. Athletics directors strive to work with NIL collectives and third-party multimedia rights and ticketing partners and continue to generate new revenue while assessing return on investment as salaries escalate and buyouts become the norm. University and college presidents work with their boards and influential major donors to consider changing athletic conferences. Consulting firms arise to help with searches for head coaches. Postseasons expand in the pursuit of larger television contracts, while also balancing the growing influence of agents who advise their clients to opt out for fear of injury and to better prepare for their professional pursuits. Compliance officers adjust to continuous rule changes and strive for adherence to Title IX legislation as athletic departments engage in diversity, equity, and inclusion (DEI) advancements. Senior leadership teams at enrollment-driven institutions rely on athletics to balance their operating budgets while exploring the addition of new sports programs, including esports. Senior leadership teams at other schools examine the potential for cutting some sports programs to lower costs, while continuing to increase expenditures in revenue sports. All of this continues to evolve in the aftermath of the COVID-19 pandemic, which has affected policies, pushed sports medicine expectations to unprecedented heights, and required continuous assessment of best practices in facility and event management.

Intercollegiate athletics is poised for a renaissance. This updated book comes to press amid a steady stream of tumult in the media, where headlines are dominated by community-shaking scandals, passionate reform commentaries, league-altering court cases, spikes in expenses for facilities and coaches' salaries, conference realignment announcements, and concerns about athletes' health and safety. These media emphases provide a very narrow representation of intercollegiate athletics as being founded on a win-at-all-costs mentality in a multibillion-dollar industry.

However, when one looks beyond the headlines and game-day stadium scenes into the actual corridors of athletics departments, the overtones of scandal and greed quickly fade into the shadows. Here, we see administrators working long hours, generally for very modest pay, and striving to facilitate educational growth opportunities for their student-athletes and service to their community.

We also see student-athletes determined to balance the demands of their complex lives. They often rise from bed far earlier than other college students. They face grueling training sessions at the mercy of coaches who wield power over their time, their bodies, and sometimes even their minds. They attend a full day of classes, often while physically exhausted; participate in additional extracurricular activities required of athletes; and, in many cases, work part-time jobs to help cover their expenses. And they meet these demands in addition to all the demands faced by typical full-time college students, yet with the added stresses of scrutiny from the media, fans, and sometimes even their classmates, professors, and friends.

It is for these athletes that the industry of intercollegiate athletics exists. It is for them that most athletics administrators, coaches, and staff members choose to devote their professional (and much of their personal) lives to creating positive life-changing experiences. Indeed, given that athletics is a facet of our educational system—and a department within our colleges and universities designed to provide opportunities for educational growth—it is troubling to witness the growing divergence between the narrow public perception and the general private reality. It is, in fact, heartbreaking to witness the extravagance, hypocrisy, and mentality of the few who perpetuate the ills in the industry and take advantage of the power that can be so easily wielded over a population of extraordinary collegiate athletes.

Collegiate athletics needs a revolution, and the revolution it needs is you. We need well-trained leaders who understand the purpose of intercollegiate athletics and care about the athletes whom the educational model should sustain. We need leaders who understand how critical money is to the operation of college sport, who think strategically about how it is disbursed, and who are selective and innovative in its attainment. We need leaders who passionately strive to fulfill the missions of their universities through faculty–athletics partnerships, who act as responsible stakeholders of their university's brand, and who strive to use the power of athletics to benefit their communities. We need leaders who embrace diversity and understand how valuable, and essential, it is to involve multiple perspectives in both critical and everyday decision-making. We need leaders who challenge the status quo, challenge the media, prepare for the future, and believe in the transforming power of intercollegiate athletics. If this sounds like a challenge you want, then read on, because we need you to be at the forefront of the intercollegiate athletics revolution.

To help you prepare to take part in such a transformation, this text provides you with an overview of the daily operations and inner workings of intercollegiate athletics departments. The text focuses on larger NCAA-governed institutions but also includes examples of policies and procedures for governance and management structures that vary depending on the resources and objectives of a school, including those at Division II, Division III, and other levels. We pair this foundational knowledge with chapter-by-chapter leadership lessons, discussion questions, and learning activities, including case studies, to help you prepare for the active role you will soon play in the industry. This updated edition includes industry profiles, technology tools, and professional development resources for aspiring athletics administrators. It also adds a new chapter devoted to diversity, equity, and inclusion.

A presentation package, a test package, and chapter quizzes are available for instructors at www.HumanKinetics.com/AdministrationOfIntercollegiateAthletics. The presentation package includes a comprehensive series of more than 250 PowerPoint slides that can be used directly in PowerPoint or printed to make transparencies or handouts for students. The test package includes questions that instructors can use to create customized tests, and the chapter quizzes include ready-to-use 10-question quizzes, which are automatically graded.

In chapter 1, we begin this journey with a historical foundation written by Dr. Ellen Staurowsky, a beloved champion of student-athletes' rights, a former director of athletics, and a leading scholar of intercollegiate athletics. Chapter 2 contains a discussion of governing bodies by Barbara Osborne, a sport law expert and former senior woman administrator and associate athletics director, and editors Erianne A. Weight and Robert H. Zullo. The third chapter, contributed by Weight and Zullo, covers leadership and management principles from both scholarly literature and popular works, infused with personal insights and examples from a variety of leaders in intercollegiate athletics. Chapter 4, by Molly P. Harry, Weight, and Zullo, explores compliance and the continuous challenges and updates relative to rules and regulations of intercollegiate athletics, and chapter 5—added especially for this edition—spotlights the increasing attention being paid to diversity, equity, and inclusion at institutions of higher education. The young rising scholars Joseph N. Cooper and Harry, along with Osborne and editor Weight, have contributed their knowledge and research to help develop tomorrow's leaders.

The remaining eight chapters examine various aspects of administration—academics and eligibility for student-athletes, media relations, financial operations, marketing, corporate sponsorship, facility management, development, and support services—highlighting intradepartmental synergies and opportunities for leadership. These chapters have been carefully crafted by academic and professional leaders to provide a foundation from which you can confidently practice, lead, and innovate in this industry that we care about so deeply.

Acknowledgments

This second edition is dedicated to my favorite "student": my son, Cameron Zullo. Faculty are not supposed to have favorites, but I think an exception can be made in this case. A blessing to his mother and me from day one, Cam loves the college campus experience and finds joy in his interaction with students. We look forward to many years of campus exploration, sporting events, the arts and sciences, and making lifetime memories.

I also need to acknowledge my students, who provide so many wonderful relationships and lifelong friendships. My students: Continue to open doors and shatter glass ceilings, because our identities are not defined by sports alone. Extend your comfort zones and get comfortable being uncomfortable as you grow, each day of your life. Be the change you seek in the world. Nothing works unless you do.

I also need to thank such wonderful resources as Nathan LaRiccia, Jared Benko, Kyle McMullin, Jackie Wallgren, Amanda Braun, Brian Johnston, Mike Montoro, Leland Barrow, Patrick Gray, Joel Coleman, Dan Jankoski, Chris Morales, Alan Thomas, Claude Felton, Thomas Stepp, Loran Smith, Maura Murphy, Dan Gale, Jon Jaudon, Damian Salas, Tony Schmidt, Aaron Epstein, Kirk Gatlin, Sarah Ratchford, Robyn Felton, Bethany Hawkins, Zack Lassiter, Stephen Foshee, Travis White, Ervin Lewis, Brad Purvis, Davis Babb, Jed Castro, Brad Vickers, Charles Bloom, John Bateman, Ryan Trichel, John Meshad, and Mike Curtis. Inspirational coaches, including Debbie Ryan, Jim Thompson, Sylvester Croom, Bart Bellairs, Kenny Brooks, Bruce Arena, George Gelnovatch, Matt Chulis, Brian Novotny, Isaac Collins, Courtney Grove, Brian Tucker, Mark Katarski, Tyler Bratton, Shane Beamer, Dawn Staley, Beverly Smith, Girish Thakar, Tammy Swearingen, Kevin Siroki, Rosanne Scott, Jan Reddinger, Pat Smith, Krista Archambeau, Mark Richt, Jack Bauerle, Brooke Lyczek, DJ Cannon, Maggie Kuhn, Andy McNab, Cameron Evans, Tyler Greene, Chris Ilse, Erik Hultgren, Marquase Lovings, Zack Walters, and so many others who continue to shape the lives of many student-athletes through their teaching. Thank you to my wonderful colleagues at Slippery Rock University: Brian Crow, Robertha Abney, Frank Tsai, Jim Dombrosky, Diane Robbins, and many others who set the bar high in your rigor, expectations, and collegiality.

This book could not have been completed without the support of mentors, including Audrey Quinlan, Mary Ann Gawelek, Bibiana Boerio, Victoria Marie Gribschaw, and Westminster College colleagues, including Jeffrey Coker, Jesse Ligo, John Geidner, Keith Bittel, Jen Hough, Kara Montgomery, Jim Dafler, Rachel Burns, Sam DiVitto, Linda Travers, Joe Onderko, Kevin Fenstermacher, Eric Gaber, Brian Petrus, and many other great coaches and friends in New Willy. To Doctors Hawkins, Fields, Billing, Mueller, Shields, and Schempp, thank you for your continuous support and push for knowledge.

I also need to acknowledge great men and friends in Matt Chelap, Brian Thornburg, Scott Poveromo, Mike McKinney, Richard Orr, Eric Roedl, John Mark Adkison, David Ridpath, and Roger Zullo; my brothers, Nick Zullo, Dan George, and Billy Josay; my sisters, Jessica George and Jessica Zullo; and my beautiful nieces and nephews. My parents continue to be amazing role models each day, and I must thank my amazing in-laws and my Crown Point relatives, Big Mike and Terry. Finally, I need to recognize those who have passed but continue to be an inspiration, especially my grandparents, Robert Gruver, Elise Gruver, and Rosaria Zullo; great mentors and academic leaders Ming Li, Ronald Hyatt, Doug Toma, and JoAnne Boyle; and stellar athletic administrators Mark Fletcher, Terry Holland, Jim Weaver, and Vince Dooley.

Many thanks to the contributors to this second edition, including a dear friend and mentor, Barbara Osborne, as well as Ellen Staurowsky, a guide and advisor to so many of us. Special thanks to David Shonk and Alyssa Bosley, two wonderful colleagues at James Madison University, in addition to Brendan Dwyer and Stephen Shapiro. To rising stars Joey Cooper, Molly Harry, and Lisa Rubin, your contributions here only hint at the many impacts you will make on this field and society. I would also like to acknowledge Landon Huffman and Coyote Cooper for their past contributions. Most importantly, thank you dearly to coeditor Erianne Weight as we complete round two. Continue to soar on and off the field, as you are proof that nice people can finish first.

In closing, thanks to Adam Gardner, Brian Rosenworcel, and especially Ryan Miller from the band Guster for providing humor, wonderful music, and uplifting inspiration, decade after decade. Their lyrics inspired writing, research, and working with the great team at Human Kinetics, especially Andrew L. Tyler and Anna Lan Seaman. Be calm. Be brave. It'll be okay.

And most importantly, thank you to my wife. You are my rock, my copilot, and the person who makes each day better than the one before.

—Robert H. Zullo, PhD

My primary thanks goes to my incredible collaborator Rob Zullo, whose passion for the field of intercollegiate athletics and sport management education is continually inspiring. I would like to thank my students, colleagues, and mentors at the University of North Carolina at Chapel Hill, Bowling Green State University, and Indiana University. I have learned so much from each of you and am so grateful for the guidance, inspiration, and challenges that inspire me to continually seek knowledge and work to improve every day in every facet of my professional expedition. I am grateful for the countless professionals who contributed to the book.

At the outset, Rob and I determined to have the content of each chapter be driven largely by what administrators told us they wished they had known and what they wished their new hires knew. Toward that end, we conducted many interviews to gather this valuable information. Special acknowledgment goes to Richard Baddour and Scott Palanjian, in particular, for their tremendous help in the foundational stages of the text. Their insights, research, and encouragement were paramount to this project coming to fruition. In addition, I would like to thank my high school and college track coaches and officials for fueling my passion.

I would not be in this field, nor would I have a passion for intercollegiate athletics, had I not experienced how transformational education through athletics can be. Coaches Jones, Caviness, Boyack, and Archer, thank you for being my mentors, advocates, and teachers. Finally, I would like to express my gratitude to my incredible parents for instilling a foundational hunger for education and appreciation of hard work, and for being a constant source of support and encouragement in every aspect of my life; my sisters, Chelsea, Megan, and Lindsay, for being my eternal best friends; my husband for being my primary research partner, source of joy, fount of wisdom, and absolute perfect companion in life; and my daughters, Aleah and Lillian, for providing a completely new lens through which to see the world, for making me smile and laugh continually, and for reminding me what really matters in life.

—Erianne A. Weight, PhD

Matt Riley/UVA Athletics

A Brief Historical Perspective on Intercollegiate Athletics

Ellen J. Staurowsky, Ithaca College

In this chapter, you will explore

- higher education and student experience in 19th-century America,
- the early years of college sport as a student-led enterprise,
- the emergence of the NCAA and the evolution of college sport governance,
- the distinct history of women's college sport as an integrated part of the educational enterprise,
- the role of historically Black colleges and American Indian boarding schools in providing athletics opportunities for students of color, and
- concluding thoughts about how these threads combine to form a backdrop for what we understand about college sport today.

HISTORICAL PERSPECTIVES IN THE LIVES OF COLLEGE SPORT ADMINISTRATORS

As a director of athletics, the daily demands of your job loom large. As much good will and enthusiasm as your program may have engendered in the community and among constituencies on your campus (i.e., administrators, alumni, athletes, donors, faculty, fans, media, and parents), you cannot help but notice that there is a constant wave of dissatisfaction manifest in persistent calls for reform, concerns about athlete health and well-being, questions about whether athletes are receiving a legitimate education while pursuing their sports, and frustration with the perception that coaches are paid too much and the athletic department spends excessively.

In confronting those issues as a leader, how do you educate yourself and how do you approach these problems? To know an industry is to know what forces have shaped its present and future. The only way to do that is by looking to the past. In college sport, there is a certain reverence for some aspects of history. Traditions, as embodied in school colors, the school song, certain rituals associated with your particular school and conference, and storied rivalries, all speak to connections with the past. Yet the scripts that you enact daily may have been set in motion generations ago. Unnoticed, they may guide you in directions unknown. The greater appreciation you have for the historical roots of the college sport enterprise, the more you can understand problems as they exist today and the more you will be able to identify ways to address those problems. You do not want to be bound by the past, but you also do not want to approach problems from a position of ignorance. Balancing the past, present, and future may be one of the biggest challenges for anyone seeking to lead college sport programs effectively in the 21st century. To be better prepared, read on.

Poll a dozen people about their perspectives on the value of college sport to higher education and you are likely to get a dozen different answers. Some will extol the virtues of participation in college sport: the camaraderie, the tests of courage and will. Others will point to the benefits of college sport in creating avenues to education, inspiring work ethic, goal orientation, and focus that predicts success in academic settings. And there will be still others who celebrate the capacity of college sport to serve as an anchor for institutional identity, pride in place, a generator for publicity, and a bridge between higher education and broader communities.

Though the value of college sport may be obvious to some, its shape and contours have been forged out of controversy and ongoing calls for reform. Today, the intense media scrutiny that is characteristic of 21st-century society highlights an array of issues for Americans to contemplate related to college sport. Yet this broadcast and journalistic analysis bears a remarkable resemblance to concerns expressed generations earlier and dating back as far as 150 years or more. For example, a college president faced with the challenge of attracting a student body and meeting enrollment demands in the early 1900s was as likely to fret then as they are today about the threats posed by athletics to academic integrity. Indeed, more than 100 years ago, Woodrow Wilson, then president of Princeton University and later the 28th president of the United States, observed that the centerpiece of higher education often competed for attention with other offerings that both students and the general public found more alluring: "The sideshows are so numerous, so diverting—so important, if you will—that they have swallowed up the circus, and those who perform in the main tent often whistle for their audiences, discouraged and humiliated" (Wilson, 1909, p. 576).

These tensions were revisited by Scott Carlson (2013), who explored the evolution of the "country club" college. At such institutions, administrators invest more and more in "consumption amenities," such as athletics complexes and other kinds of entertainment facilities, that lend the air of a resort community to the experience of campus residential life as a way to maintain market share and garner publicity (College Ranker, 2021; Jacob et al., 2018). In fact, regardless of whether we are talking about small, selective institutions in the least competitive arena of what the National Collegiate Athletic Association (NCAA) refers to as Division III—where athletics is viewed as critical to the overall admissions process because of its power to bring tuition-paying students to campus (Stevens, 2007)—or about large public universities with multimillion-dollar athletics programs that draw more than 100,000 fans to football games, the relationship between athletics and academics has rarely been harmonious (Desrochers, 2013).

Indeed, one encounters an almost parallel universe when comparing today's headlines with those that appeared in earlier years when the structure of college sport was being put into place. For example, a diary maintained by Harvard football coach Bill Reid in 1905 indicates the preoccupations that accompanied the job (Smith, 1994). For one thing, the media had to be managed, and deception was not out of the question. In addition, as the highest-paid coach in the country at the time, Reid became the focal point for discussions about excessive compensation for coaches, much like Louisiana State University's Brian Kelly, Michigan State's Mel Tucker, and Penn State's James Franklin, who were signed by their respective institutions in 2021 to 10-year contracts worth US$100 million, US$85 million, and US$75 million respectively (Schad & Berkowitz, 2021).

In his diary, Reid chronicled the instability that characterized coaching football at the college level, the tenuous job security, and pressures of coaching under heavy scrutiny and high expectations from a demanding and impatient fan base (Smith, 1994). More than a century later, the rate of turnover in college football has only escalated, as compensation packages rise alongside increasing media scrutiny, insistence on producing winning teams, and persistent pressure to generate revenue (Blinder, 2021).

Reid also faced other challenges—such as keeping athletes eligible and managing relationships with faculty—that resonate with current discussions regarding the sincerity of the NCAA's efforts to address academic fraud (Schuster, 2019), recent investigations into academic misconduct (Lederman, 2019), and ongoing concerns about academic clustering within college teams (Miller, 2021). Academic clustering is when a high percentage of an athletic team pursues a similar major. Reid pondered how to deal with players who exhibited too great a preference for strong drink, womanizing, and altercations with the law (Smith, 1994). These themes of legal altercations are all too familiar today, as evidenced by the mishandling of sexual misconduct cases at Louisiana State University that came to light following an investigation by *USA Today* in 2020 and a 148-page report completed by Husch Blackwell the following year (West, 2021).

In the area of campus politics, Reid undermined university president Charles Eliot's efforts to ban football by going to Harvard's governing board. In the present day, power struggles involving coaches who make more than the college president (and in some cases more than any other public official in their state) continue to raise concern that college presidents are not in charge of athletics (Staurowsky, 2011) or are conspicuously absent from the national dialogue on the future of college sports because of political expediency (Thelin, 2021).

Despite these similarities, some dramatic differences have also emerged in the evolving American educational landscape. Colleges and universities once dominated by male students are now populated by coeducational student bodies, and on many campuses female students are in the majority. Similarly, racial segregation has given way to integrated campuses. As these changes have occurred, athletics programs have also changed. As a result, grounding our approach to intercollegiate athletics in an appreciation of its historical roots offers insight into how issues arise and develop, what happens when issues remain unresolved, and where potential pathways to progress might be uncovered.

HIGHER EDUCATION AND STUDENT EXPERIENCE IN 19TH-CENTURY AMERICA

In the modern consciousness, it would be difficult to dispute the notion that football serves as the center of the solar system of college sport. In the December 2012 IMG Intercollegiate Athletics Forum (presented by *Street & Smith's SportsBusi-*

ness Daily/Global/Journal), the tone for the two-day discussion of the business of college sport was set when it was announced that "college football owns Saturdays," meaning that college football drew the highest Saturday-night ratings among network television programs seven times during the 2012 season (Elfman, 2012). Emblematic of this status, ESPN devoted more than 100 hours of programming to college football media days and kickoff events across 16 conferences between July 14 and August 4, 2021, alone (Brooks, 2021). Furthermore, college football ranked just behind professional football and professional baseball as being most Americans' favorite sports (OH Predictive Insights, 2021). However, for all of football's dominance today, it was not always this way.

In fact, in the years before the American Civil War, football was decades away from being crowned king, and other sports were pursued as occasional pastimes. Institutions of higher learning were small. Typically known as "Old Main" were large central buildings imbued architecturally with the hopes and aspirations of the founders. These edifices housed the administration, served as the location for classrooms, and provided a space for social activities (Dober, 2007). Dormitories offered spartan conditions (Mendenhall, 1993). Fraternity life emerged out of literary and secret societies, and students made their homes in fraternity-sponsored lodges or houses (Birdseye, 1907).

A day in the life of a college student in the 1850s would likely include rising early and attending chapel. A good portion of the morning and early afternoon would be dedicated to lectures and recitations, and the evening would be devoted to studying. The afternoons, however, presented students with free time—time to escape faculty demands and the monotony of a curriculum that was sometimes boring, dry, or unchallenging and instead pursue their own interests and activities (Mendenhall, 1993; Smith, 1988). Often living in rural communities that offered few amusements, students made their own fun and gravitated at times toward the rebellious.

Indeed, though campuses may have been pastoral, the atmosphere often was not. To the contrary, collective student unrest was a hallmark of early campus life (Allmendinger, 1973), and it could be

King Football

The term "King Football," which has been used to describe the power and money associated with college football, comes from the title of a book written in 1932 by Reed Harris, a student editor of the Columbia University school newspaper. Harris' attacks on football as overly commercial and anti-intellectual eventually resulted in his dismissal from the university. When he was readmitted after an appeal, he declined and wrote the book instead.

As Michael Oriard (2001) reports in his book on the evolution of college football from 1920 to 1950, the expression "King Football" was used by others who either decried its vulgarity or celebrated its expression of what they saw as the boldness of the American spirit. (See the cover of Oriard's book in figure 1.1.) Also, here are two *New York Times* headlines from stories dealing with alleged corruption in the college game; the first was published in 1932, the second, nearly 80 years later, in 2011.

King Football: Racket or Sport? (Kiernan, 1932)

The Dangerous Cocoon of King Football (Vecsey, 2011)

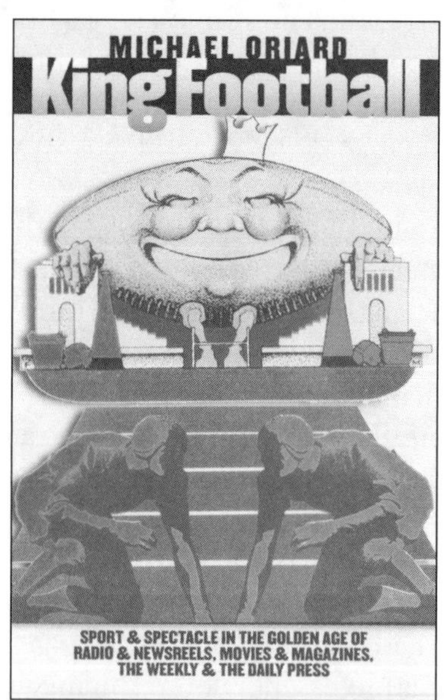

Figure 1.1 ***King Football* by Michael Oriard.**

triggered by any of a number of motivations, some of the worst involving bad food (Ireland, 2012). Between 1766 and 1834, for example, Harvard was the site of no fewer than eight rebellions, which resulted in property damage, physical clashes between faculty and administrators, and mass student suspensions and expulsions (Ireland, 2012).

Male students' physical pursuits were also areas of ambivalence and protest. Faculty and college administrator efforts to manage the engagement of male students in sport activities eventually distilled into two complementary but often competing models of sport participation—one being the eventual foundation for the intercollegiate athletics team model and the other being "the collegiate gymnastics model." While male students pursued rough team games such as shinny, a form of hockey that inspired faculty members to ban it as "low and unbecoming of gentlemen and scholars" (Rudolph, 1990, p. 151), gymnast-physicians advocated physical training regimens based on German and Swedish gymnastics to promote overall health and well-being (Soares, 1979).

As a result of that advocacy, schools in the Northeast United States started to build gymnasiums to support these programs, beginning with Harvard in 1820 (Seidentop & Vandermars, 2011). In 1860, Amherst College added a department of hygiene and physical education (Sweet, 2011) to address concern about student health and the increased interest in team sports. As the 19th century wore on, however, students balked at the "mechanical," "business-like" approach to movement professed by their instructors (Rudolph, 1990, p. 153). As a result, the tide began to turn: "While pre–Civil War educators thought gymnastics foster[ed] self-control and were superior to most team sports, postwar students began to argue that athletics assuaged the monotony of the industrial-era curriculum" (Ingrassia, 2012, p. 22).

It is something of an irony, then, given the focus educators placed on student health concerns, that intercollegiate athletics owes its start to the exhaustion of a quite serious young man who was wearing himself thin studying for the Junior Exhibition at Yale University in 1852, where he delivered a speech titled (in Latin) "*Roma Disrepta*" (Mendenhall, 1993; Whiton, 1901). James Whiton had brought honor to himself and his family by placing second in his class that May, missing out on the top spot by a mere fraction of a point. The effort left him "out of sorts," and a decision was made for him to return to New Hampshire with his family to rest and rejuvenate. On that trip home, Whiton met with a business associate of his father's, James Elkins, an agent with the Boston, Concord, and Montreal (BC&M) railroad. In the course of their conversation, the idea for a rowing regatta was born (Mendenhall, 1993; Smith, 1988), and "the assurance of a free excursion and a jolly lark" was persuasive enough to get four teams (three from Yale and one from Harvard) to sign on (Mendenhall, 1993, p. 16).

Patterned after the Oxford and Cambridge regatta in England (Ingrassia, 2012), this one featured three teams from Yale and one from Harvard competing on New Hampshire's Lake Winnipesaukee in front of an audience of roughly 1,000 spectators. The crowd included a future U.S. president, as well as local dignitaries and politicians, members of the "fairer sex" waving their handkerchiefs, enterprising vendors making the most of the occasion, and curious townspeople (Mendenhall, 1993; Smith, 1988). An original handbill promoting the event (figure 1.2) documents both the expense associated with building the boats and the discipline of the men who crewed them. A training race in the morning was followed by lunch, mineral water, ale, brandy, and cigars—a

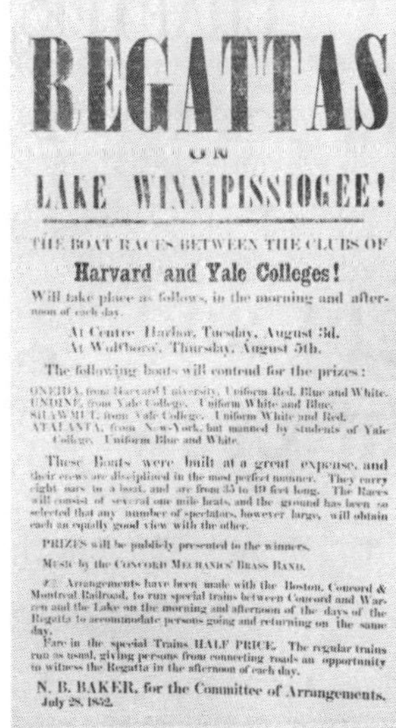

REGATTAS

ON

LAKE WINNIPISSIOGEE!

THE BOAT RACES BETWEEN THE CLUBS OF

Harvard and Yale Colleges!

Will take place as follows, in the morning and afternoon of each day.

At Centre Harbor, Tuesday, August 3d.
At Wolfboro', Thursday, August 5th.

The following boats will contend for the prizes:

ONEIDA, from Harvard University, Uniform Red, Blue and White.
UNDINE, from Yale College. Uniform White and Blue.
SHAWMUT, from Yale College. Uniform White and Red.
ATALANTA, from New-York, but manned by students of Yale College. Uniform Blue and White.

These Boats were built at a great expense, and their crews are disciplined in the most perfect manner. They carry eight oars to a boat, and are from 35 to 40 feet long. The Races will consist of several one mile heats, and the ground has been so selected that any number of spectators, however large, will obtain each an equally good view with the other.

PRIZES will be publicly presented to the winners.

Music by the Concord Mechanics' Brass Band.

☞ Arrangements have been made with the Boston, Concord & Montreal Railroad, to run special trains between Concord and Warren and the Lake on the morning and afternoon of the days of the Regatta to accommodate persons going and returning on the same day.

Fare in the special Trains HALF PRICE. The regular trains run as usual, giving persons from connecting roads an opportunity to witness the Regatta in the afternoon of each day.

N. B. BAKER, for the Committee of Arrangements.
July 28, 1852.

Figure 1.2 Promotional handbill for the 1852 Harvard-Yale regatta.

menu that apparently agreed with the members of the Harvard crew, who went on to victory in the afternoon, collecting a set of silver-tipped black walnut oars for their trouble (Mendenhall, 1993; Smith, 1988).

At a gala dinner and dance later that day, "toasts were drunk, and the oarsmen passed resolutions thanking their hosts and particularly the committee for the treatment they had received" (Mendenhall, 1993, p. 20). Collecting their free passes, they then boarded the BC&M and returned to their institutions, having taken part in an event that, despite one skeptic's prediction that it would be a "frolic without sequel," became a model for other regattas and contributed to the growth of intercollegiate athletics on college campuses (Sack & Staurowsky, 1998).

From that point on, as intercollegiate athletics grew, questions arose about who should run them and how they should be run. Through the early part of the 20th century, intercollegiate athletics for men were run by students in an entrepreneurial fashion, similar to the approach taken by James Whiton at Yale. Organizers experimented with a range of financial models—creating student organizations and associations for the purpose of collecting dues to support their athletic endeavors, approaching businesses for sponsorship of teams and events, selling tickets to contests, and promoting fundraising campaigns.

These developments happened alongside the rapid expansion of educational institutions (as a result of the Morrill Land-Grant Acts of 1862 and 1890) into states whose populations had not yet grown enough to support them (Sack & Staurowsky, 1998, p. 19). In this context, institutions faced greater competition for students and increasing pressure to move away from a classical curriculum in favor of programs that focused more on practical skills to appeal to an increasingly business-minded public. In turn, college administrators began to use advertising as a means of selling their institutions. "What they needed more than anything was a bridge that could link the high culture of the university with the mass culture of the broader society. . . . In the late 1800s few campus activities could better meet that need than intercollegiate sport" (Sack & Staurowsky, p. 20).

In particular, football—with its flair for spectacle, its assurances of masculine superiority, and its tests of valor, made for and by the sport pages (Oriard, 2001)—assumed a new status among the sports that were taking hold on college and university campuses. Though baseball, basketball, tennis, track and field, wrestling, and other sports also commanded interest among students, football's star was ascending. This development was aided in no small measure by increasing commercialism, which took the form of building stadiums for the purposes of generating gate receipts and drawing large numbers of people to campuses, cultivating media attention, and forging relationships with boosters and sponsors (Sack & Staurowsky, 1998; Smith, 1988). Amid these changes, student leadership gave way to professional coaches hired to bring a scientific approach to coaching and performance. Schools that hired professional coaches, such as Yale and Harvard, would dominate the intercollegiate athletics scene well into the 20th century—but not without a price to be paid (Sack & Staurowsky, 1998; Smith, 1988).

While administrators fed the growth of intercollegiate athletics and student interest carried it forward, faculty members opposed the incorporation of athletics as mass spectacle. They warned of the dangers of increasing commercialism and professionalism and labeled the model a threat to the academic mission of higher education (Chu, 1989). Faculty strongly opposed the recruiting of "tramp athletes" who were "subsidized" (in other words, paid to play) and did not attend classes, as well as the "smash mouth" nature of football, where formations such as the flying wedge set the stage for bloodshed and occasionally death (McQuilkin & Smith, 1993).

Concern about threats to academic integrity, as well as students' health and well-being, served as rallying points around which faculty mobilized to exert influence over college sport during this era. Indeed, according to Barr (1998, p. 5), "the high point of faculty control in intercollegiate athletics" occurred between 1895 and 1914, as college faculty worked to form faculty-led conferences. These efforts contributed to the creation of the National Collegiate Athletic Association.

THE NCAA AND THE FOUNDATIONS OF A COLLEGE SPORT GOVERNANCE STRUCTURE

As faculty attempted to assert their voice against an expanding tide of support from students, alumni, governing boards, and the public, college presidents were caught in the middle—trying to respond to the requirements of institutions with uncertain financial futures while working to mediate disputes on all sides. Meanwhile, slippage in the status of athletics was becoming ever more problematic. Not all constituencies bought into the notion of college athletes as unpaid amateurs. Boosters who believed athletic talent should be rewarded offered payments under the table. In addition, with a touch of creativity from team loyalists who had deep pockets, athletes were hired into jobs for which they were paid to do nothing (Sack & Staurowsky, 1998). In a 1905 article in *Collier's*, Stanford president David Starr Jordan laid responsibility at the feet of faculty members and declared that the standards of colleges should exist "in fact as well as in name."

> *The professor who neglects his duty to escape the execrations of the bleachers is an accessory in fact to whatever the bleachers may demand. Nine-tenths of the athletic parasites remain through neglect on the part of the individual professors or through the scholarship committees to do their own duty in the matter of upholding standards.*
>
> David Starr Jordan, president, Stanford University, 1905

Professors who understood Jordan's point were organizing and attempting to provide oversight to safeguard college sport from the professional and commercial influences that were increasingly taking it away from the mandates of higher education. Most significantly, in 1895, a group of faculty members started the process of forming the Intercollegiate Conference of Faculty Representatives, which would later become known as the Western Conference and eventually the Big Ten (Sack & Staurowsky, 1998). In 1898, seven of the eight schools that now make up the Ivy League sought to exert similar control, when faculty, students, and alumni from all but Yale attended a conference on college sport reform at Brown University. Seeking to create an interinstitutional governance structure, the participants addressed agenda items that included athletics scholarships, undergraduate and graduate eligibility, summer baseball for pay, commercialism, and the role of faculty in athletics governance (Sack & Staurowsky, 1998).

In 1906, these attempts to control athletics and respond to calls for reform led to the creation of the NCAA—the first in a long line of college sport reform efforts that continue today. For a timeline of major athletics reform efforts, see figure 1.3.

Though noble in intent, the report from the 1898 conference at Brown reads as if it were written by people who—despite understanding the high purpose of an amateur approach to college sport—were somehow unaware that commercial forces and the ever-expanding complex of support for college sport were moving it to the center of higher education rather than the periphery. The point was not lost, however, on R. Tait McKenzie, a renowned physician,

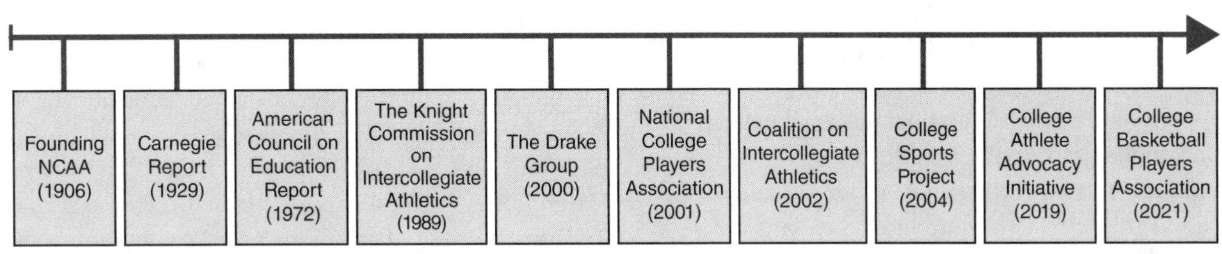

Figure 1.3 Major athletics reform efforts.

Reprinted from E. Staurowsky, *Reclaiming Our Inheritance as Faculty: Understanding Academic Freedom in Relationship to College Sport,* Paper Presented at the Meeting of the North American Society of Sociology and Sport Conference (Greensboro, NC, 2005). By permission of E. Staurowsky.

physical therapist, physical educator, and sculptor who taught at the University of Pennsylvania. In a 1910 address to the NCAA convention, McKenzie mapped out an exhaustive history of 1,200 years of Greek athletics before observing that college sport was dangerously close to abandoning the amateur model and operating at a level of professionalism that marked the end of the Greek athletic model, in which sport was valued for its entertainment appeal (Crowley, 2006).

Faculty efforts did periodically slow the rising tide of professionalization during certain windows of opportunity. For example, at the 1918 NCAA convention, faculty delegates approved a de-emphasis of campus sport in light of personnel and resource shortages related to World War I. They believed that this step would allow them to rein in college sport (Sperber, 1993). A similar moment occurred in 1926, when the American Association of University Professors issued a bulletin decrying excesses associated with college football and the building of large stadiums, which were perceived as menaces to higher education (Smith, 2001).

Crisis in Football: Player Safety

Another seminal moment of potential opportunity for reform presented itself during the 1904 college football season, which was distinguished by 21 player deaths and more than 200 serious injuries. In response, "muckraking newspapers . . . focused on the brutality and alleged corruption of the game, and editorials began to appear demanding athletic reform" (Sack & Staurowsky, 1998, p. 32). In fact, calls to reform or abolish the game reverberated across the United States, and they found special resonance in the White House.

Moved by public outrage, President Theodore Roosevelt, an outdoor sport enthusiast who extolled the virtues of a strenuous life in response to his own periodic struggles with ill health, took the side of reform. In 1905, Roosevelt convened members of the football power elite who made up the American Intercollegiate Football Rules Committee to discuss the future of the game. When the committee failed to address the problem, a second meeting, and then a third, called by New York University chancellor Henry MacCracken, resulted in the formation of the Intercollegiate Athletic Association of the United States, which in 1912 was renamed the National Collegiate Athletic Association.

Athlete Eligibility and Amateurism

Despite the fact that football reform catalyzed the formation of the NCAA, the commercial market drove the rule-making process even during those first meetings. This reality was evidenced in concerns about fair competition and equal opportunity to share in the profits of this emerging industry. At the same time, the NCAA, upon its birth, espoused a definition of amateurism borrowed liberally from British universities such as Oxford and Cambridge. Consistent with that standard, members were expected to avoid practices that violated amateurism principles, especially "the offering of inducements to players to enter colleges and universities because of their athletic abilities or supporting or maintaining players while students on account of their athletic abilities, either by athletic organizations, individual alumni, or otherwise, directly or indirectly" (Intercollegiate Athletic Association of the United States, 1906, p. 33). Member institutions were expected to abide by these rules, though enforcement was left to individual institutions, which were supposed to act in accordance with a code of honor (Crowley, 2006; Sack & Staurowsky, 1998).

Over the years, the NCAA membership continued to define amateurism. Within a decade of the organization's founding, it developed a definition of the amateur athlete. According to Article VI(b) of the 1916 bylaws, an amateur was "one who participates in competitive physical sports only for the pleasure, and the physical, mental, moral, and social benefits directly derived therefrom" (National Collegiate Athletic Association, 1916, p. 118). By 1922, the definition was revised to read as follows: "An amateur sportsman is one who engages in sport solely for the physical, mental, or social benefits he derives therefrom, and to whom the sport is nothing other than an avocation" (National Collegiate Athletic Association, 1922, as quoted in Sack & Staurowsky, 1998, p. 35).

This emphasis on athletic activity as an "avocation" (i.e., diversion or hobby) obscured the fact that male athletes in this era received remuneration in the form of room, board, and financial compensation to play for college teams. With an enforcement structure that relied on "home rule"—in which individual institutions made their own determina-

What Awaits the NCAA?

The NCAA's mechanism for enforcing rules has been the subject over many years of criticisms and complaints, most notably that punishments meted out often hurt athletes and coaches who were never involved in the wrongdoing to begin with. In 2018, following a Federal Bureau of Investigation (FBI) probe into improper payments made by an Adidas executive to direct men's basketball players or family members and associates to certain schools, and subsequent convictions of several runners and former basketball coaches as well as the Adidas executive, the NCAA instituted what it called the Independent Accountability Resolution Process (IARP). The IARP was intended to be part of the NCAA's enforcement process that handled what were classified as "complex" cases. Criticisms arose, however, when cases went unresolved for years and sentiment rose that the IARP needed to be "sunsetted."

In November 2021, a group known as the LEAD1 Association, representing 130 Football Bowl Subdivision (FBS) athletic directors, recommended that IARP cases should be subject to appeal until such time as the process itself was abandoned and that changes should be made to the enforcement program. Part of the momentum for this push for changes stemmed from the NCAA Infractions Committee on Appeals to uphold what has been described as unprecedented penalties against the Oklahoma State University men's basketball team for the misconduct of one of their former employees, then associate coach Lamont Evans, who accepted payments of US$18,000 to US$22,000 to direct athletes to the Oklahoma State program dating back to 2017. As expressed by Oklahoma State head men's basketball coach Mike Boyton:

> *I invite members of the NCAA enforcement staff, its Committee on Infractions, and appeals panel involved in our case to meet with my team, to look each of them in their eyes and explain why illicit conduct committed by a rogue assistant coach five years ago—conduct which led to no competitive advantage for our program, and for which the coach was fired immediately upon discovery by our administration—should serve as a basis for denying them the opportunity to experience postseason tournament play. (The Athletic Staff, 2021)*

The LEAD1 recommendations included applying a more consistent standard to the credit schools are given when they come forward and admit that the rules were violated; clarifying rules pertaining to coach responsibility and academic fraud; instituting checks to control for investigator bias; assigning penalties to the bad actors in such a way as to avoid punishing innocent athletes; and giving hiring preference to individuals who have worked as athletic directors and compliance officers at member institutions (Dodd, 2021).

tions of how to abide by NCAA rules—schools took liberties. As the NCAA itself notes in retrospect,

> *"home rule" was both sensible and attuned to the political and philosophical realities of the time, but it carried a built-in tension between the NCAA's commitment to amateurism and its reliance on the member institutions to honor that goal. That "trust factor" became the root of the Association's early enforcement challenges and it continues as a primary driver of enforcement issues today" (National Collegiate Athletic Association, 2013, para. 3).*

Home Rule and the Sanity Code

The NCAA amateur code of the 1920s through the 1940s, which embraced, in theory but not practice, sport participation as an avocation, was rendered unenforceable internally by factions in the membership and externally by publics that did not fully endorse it. The problems arising from this lack of universal agreement about the code were compounded by the fact that home rule left the monitoring of rule violations up to individual institutions. Not surprisingly, this era of college sport was marked by the emergence of an underground economy in which college athletes were paid under the table in the form of jobs, loans, athletics scholarships, and money. In the 1929 Carnegie Report on American College Athletics, a detailed study of the practices of coaches and administrators running intercollegiate athletics programs, 81 of 112 colleges and universities were found to have offered subsidization (financial support) to athletes because of their ability to compete on teams (Savage, 1929). When publicly questioned about the state of intercollegiate athletics, college presidents lauded the merits of the amateur code, even as they overlooked the transgressions on their own campuses. Meanwhile, they argued that concerns about hypocrisy in college sport were overblown and merely anecdotal.

Recognizing the need to replace home rule with an effective enforcement mechanism, NCAA members issued an executive regulation in conjunction with the Sanity Code (see sidebar) to create a constitutional compliance committee and a fact-finding committee. The compliance committee was authorized to make rulings about interpretations of constitutional language and to answer inquiries about whether or not certain practices were forbidden by the NCAA constitution. The penalty for an institution that failed to comply with rules was termination of NCAA membership—if approved by a two-thirds vote.

No sooner had the Sanity Code been inserted into the NCAA constitution and the compliance committee put in place than allegations arose that the code was unenforceable. In opponents' views, this half-measure would still allow the underground economy to flourish. In particular, schools in the Southern, Southeastern, and Southwestern conferences took exception to the Sanity Code because they had grown accustomed to offering full athletics scholarships. In fact, they threatened secession from the NCAA.

The crisis continued to mount when the compliance committee announced that 20 institutions were violating rules. Thirteen came off the list within a year, but the other seven—Boston College, the Citadel, Villanova, Virginia Military Institute, Virginia Polytechnic Institute, the University of Maryland, and the University of Virginia—remained to force the issue. By 1950, schools opposed to the Sanity Code, which they viewed as hypocritical and contradictory to the definition of amateurism, stood their ground, forcing a confrontation at the NCAA convention. When it came time to vote on expelling schools for failing to comply with the Sanity Code, the membership was unable to muster the needed two-thirds majority.

Thus, the experiment of the Sanity Code came to a de facto end, leaving the membership to hammer out another arrangement about the subsidizing of athletes. By 1957, NCAA rules permitted universities to pay athletes' room, board, tuition and fees, and even laundry money as an inducement to sign on. Within the rules that governed these athletics scholarships, some vestiges of the amateur ideal

Sanity Code

Efforts by NCAA members to resolve the differing viewpoints about subsidizing athletes eventually led to the passage of the Principles for the Conduct of Intercollegiate Athletics, which later became known as the Sanity Code. The measure was intended as a compromise between southern schools (e.g., Maryland, Virginia, and the Citadel, in South Carolina) that wished to offer athletes full athletics scholarships and northern schools (e.g., Harvard, Princeton, and Yale) that were opposed to such provisions. The Sanity Code of 1948 conceded the awarding of financial aid for athletic talent but required that awards be need-based, meaning that recipients had to demonstrate financial need. In order to sidestep the fact that athletes were being paid for services provided on the field or court, a clause from earlier constitutions was used: "No athlete shall be deprived of financial aids [sic] . . . because of failure to participate in intercollegiate athletics" (Sack & Staurowsky, 1998, p. 34). This stipulation allowed the awards to be viewed as gifts, thus presumably averting potential problems associated with "pay for play."

continued to operate; for example, an athletics scholarship was to be given to an athlete for four years with the expectation that the award would remain available regardless of the athlete's contribution on the field or court.

In 1972, another change in the rules turned the athletics scholarship into a one-year renewable award, which increased the pressure on athletes to perform. That contractual change altered the relationship between college athletes, their coaches, and institutions. Coaches now had the power to terminate scholarship agreements with athletes after one year. Indeed, "within a half century, the concept of amateurism had become a convenient label that the NCAA could arbitrarily define to suit its needs" (Sack & Staurowsky, 1998, p. 47).

Big-Time College Sport and the Influence of Television

From its beginning, college sport has been viewed by its developers and supporters as a form of entertainment. Students enjoyed playing sports, of course, but comparisons between college sport and other forms of entertainment hinged on the capacity of some sports to draw a crowd, garner media attention, and be promoted as events where people wanted to be—and be seen.

The disputes that threatened to break apart the NCAA—over the management of programs and the terms and conditions under which athletes were recruited and compensated in the 1950s—were fueled in part by questions about how television would either enhance or interfere with the money-making potential of football. Under home rule, some schools, such as Notre Dame (three-time national champion in the 1940s) and perennial powerhouse Penn, negotiated television contracts independently in the belief that this new commercial medium offered exposure and financial possibilities not yet fully appreciated (Smith, 2001). The remainder of schools in the East, however, feared that television would negatively affect game attendance; more specifically, they subscribed to the idea that "radio aroused curiosity while television satisfies" (Smith, 2001, p. 60).

Under pressure from the Big Ten and various NCAA institutions, Notre Dame lost its advantage in negotiating its own television deal due to the NCAA's decision to put forward an experimental national television plan designed to control football telecasting nationally. In the experimental year of 1951, Penn notified the NCAA that it would continue with its own plan, only to be labeled a "member not in good standing." With expulsion on the horizon and other schools refusing to play Penn, the NCAA took over national control of football television contracts. In assessing the NCAA's decision at the time, the assistant attorney general of the Department of Justice's antitrust division, H. Graham Morison, commented that "if the colleges commercialize football they must expect commercial rules to be applied to them. If they compete for gate receipts, they should expect to be governed by the laws of free competition" (Smith, 2001, p. 72).

The seeds of discontent sown during this dispute eventually came to fruition in multiple ways. For one thing, the pressure to acquiesce to the NCAA's vision of national television control led Notre Dame president John Cavanaugh to envision a "super conference" of football powers. "Cavanaugh's insights, though not accepted in 1951, eventually were put into practice by the College Football Association (CFA)—a now-defunct group of 63 football colleges formed in 1977 to negotiate television deals—

"Big-Time" College Sport

The term "big-time" is not an accidental or random descriptor of the mass-mediated spectacle of college sport. To the contrary, as Ingrassia (2012, p. 5) notes,

> *at the turn of the [20th] century, the same time when college football emerged, diverse crowds flocked to entertaining vaudeville variety shows. The companies that sponsored these popular events were dubbed either big-time or small-time, depending on how far they traveled, the size of the cities or theaters where they performed, and the number of tickets sold.*

in 1984 and by some of the major conferences in the 1990s" (Smith, 2001, p. 65).

In addition, the antitrust challenge to the NCAA television policy that had been anticipated by Morison, the assistant attorney general, came in 1984 in the form of a lawsuit brought by the boards of regents of the University of Oklahoma and the University of Georgia. One day after the U.S. Supreme Court found in favor of the boards, the NCAA Division I-A television committee moved to pass a less restrictive plan. Within a month, Notre Dame received a multiyear, US$20 million contract offer from the NBC television network, which it declined. By 1990, however, Notre Dame reached an agreement with NBC that created controversy because of damage done to the CFA's television contract. These events set the stage for the evolution of the Big Ten Network, the Texas Longhorn Network, the Pac-12 Network, and the SEC Network and spurred controversies regarding the management of postseason bowl games.

The increased financial independence of the college football powers did not leave the NCAA without significant financial resources. In fact, retaining rights to its postseason men's Division I basketball tournament, the NCAA negotiated its first billion-dollar television deal in 1989 with CBS. By 1995, that agreement had doubled in value (Byers, 1995; Dunnavant, 2004).

For their part, the college football powers created a unique structure to foster postseason competition that optimized access of the very top teams to the most lucrative bowl games while establishing a national championship on the basis of selection or voting by numerous parties (sportswriters and coaches' associations) using numerous methodologies, rather than through a single end-of-season tournament. With a process open to interpretation, controversy followed for decades. In 1985, the head coach of the University of Michigan referred to the selection of a national champion in NCAA Division I-A football as a "mythical national champion" because the final decision was made by those voting, not based on the performance of two teams in a final championship game (Moran, 1989).

In 1992, after two years when two teams were declared national co-champions, the Bowl Coalition was formed among NCAA Division I-A bowl games and conferences. This eventually evolved into the Bowl Alliance (1995-1997), the Bowl Championship Series (1998-2013) and ultimately the College Football Playoff (2014-present). In its current iteration, the College Football Playoff (CFP) is an invitational tournament that hosts four teams playing in semifinal matchups, with the winners of those semifinal games moving to the national championship game. Teams for the CFP are selected by a 13-member committee and the games themselves rotate among the top six major bowl games, including the Cotton Bowl, Fiesta Bowl, Orange Bowl, Peach Bowl, Rose Bowl, and Sugar Bowl. Efforts to expand the CFP have fueled ongoing discussion without yielding a clear pathway forward. In the summer of 2021, a proposal was revealed that called for a 12-team expansion model with six automatic berths going to the highest-ranked conference champions, with the remainder of the field comprising at-large selections. The four highest-ranked conference teams would receive a bye in the first round, with the remaining eight teams playing in the first round (Shapiro, 2021). In a December 2021 discussion regarding where major conferences stood on the prospect of expanding beyond a four-team bracket, questions were raised as to the likelihood that an agreement on CFP expansion would occur before the end of the existing contract in 2025 because the Atlantic Coast Conference was in favor of an eight-team model; the Big Ten only supported a model that would offer automatic berths to the Power Five conference champions, and the Pac-12 was open to an 8- or 12-team model, with or without qualifiers (Dellenger, 2021). After numerous schools departed the Pac-12 in August 2023, the 12-team playoff model, which was announced in December 2022 and starts in the 2024 season, will need evaluating into the number of automatic qualifiers and at-large berths.

DEMOCRATIZATION OF COLLEGE SPORT

The democratization of the higher education system in the United States can be traced, in part, through the opportunity for people of various racial and ethnic groups, religions, and (eventually) genders to play college sport. For example, the Golden Dome and the statue of Mother Mary at

College Athletes, Activism, and Organizing

Through a convergence of events and circumstances, college athletes in the 2020s are mobilizing in numbers and ways that have not been seen since the late 1960s and early 1970s. If there is a time in recent memory when rumblings signaled that the NCAA and its member institutions were ignoring or failing to respond to college athlete concerns, it was the signing of union cards by Northwestern University football players in 2014. While the National Labor Relations Board (NLRB) never denied the fact that the players were in fact employees nor denied that they had the right to collectively bargain, the NLRB sidestepped the issue by claiming that recognizing Northwestern players as employees would disrupt the rest of the market.

That action was followed with a favorable ruling on behalf of former and current college athletes in *O'Bannon v. NCAA* (2015), which resulted in a change in NCAA rules to allow for college athlete compensation to exceed the cost of a full scholarship and include a stipend to cover the full cost of attendance. In the same window of time, University of Missouri football players pledged to boycott practices and games in solidarity with members of the university community calling for their president, Tim Wolfe, to resign in the aftermath of racist incidents on that campus. Following the death of George Floyd in May 2020, in the burgeoning COVID-19 pandemic, college athletes around the country organized to call for racial justice and to challenge athletics administrations to respond to these issues. In 2019, the NCAA's restrictive policies on athletes being able to earn money from endorsement deals was challenged in the state of California when the legislature, by a wide majority, passed the Fair Play to Pay Act, an act that became a model for 27 other states to introduce and/or pass similar laws, forcing the NCAA to relent in 2022 when the first of those laws went into effect, ushering in what has come to be known as the NIL (names, images, and likenesses) era.

Described as a game changer, current NCAA rules regarding NIL deals require that there be a quid pro quo (an exchange in return for the compensation); compensation is not contingent on an athlete attending a particular school; athletic performance is not a consideration in the compensation offer (athletic performance can amplify an athlete's value but they may not be paid for their performance); and institutions are prohibited from entering into NIL deals with their athletes. Since July 2021, when the first state laws went into effect and the NCAA announced its policy, all manner of athlete endorsements have been publicized. Some have raised questions around whether athletes and the third parties they are contracting with are abiding by NCAA regulations. As a case in point, Caleb Williams, a quarterback who had competed one season with Oklahoma in the fall of 2021, entered the transfer portal. In turn, Charlie Batch, a former Eastern Michigan football player who had also played in the NFL, now CEO of an investment firm, published a post indicating that if Williams agreed to play at Eastern Michigan, Batch would give him US$1 million. As lawyer Darren Heitnor (2022) points out, Williams could go to Eastern Michigan on his own and play there. An NCAA violation threatening Williams' athletic eligibility would not occur unless Williams actually took the money. As this era continues to unfold, cases like this one and others will fuel further conversation.

In the aftermath of the athletes asserting their rights to promote and endorse products and receive payment for doing so (within limits established by various states and NCAA rules), the NCAA has indicated that it is elevating athlete voices and including athletes in more levels of NCAA decision-making. How legitimate those efforts are remains to be seen. Put another way, if athletes are outnumbered at the negotiating table and one athlete is tasked to represent entire divisions across all sports, how effective can such representation be? One of the issues facing the college sport industry is the question of whether athletes need their own players' associations to best represent them at the table.

While it is difficult to know, given the NCAA's history, whether substantive changes will be made in terms of relationships between athletes, their athletic departments, and the association itself, there are numerous examples of athletes exercising the power they have. A notable example is the documentation of the gender inequities that existed when the NCAA hosted its men's and women's

(continued)

COLLEGE ATHLETES, ACTIVISIM, AND ORGANIZING *(continued)*

basketball tournaments in 2020. In what became known as the "post heard 'round the world," Sedona Prince's post illustrates the power athletes have to mobilize public sentiment when the system is failing them. Prince, a member of the University of Oregon women's basketball team, used video evidence and oral commentary in her post to show the disparity in the weight room resources between the men's and women's basketball programs competing in the 2021 March Madness.

As college athletes continue to realize their economic value in tandem with a growing appreciation for how to use the platforms they have available individually and collectively, this may be signaling that athlete associations may be evolving in the future. At present there are several groups that are evidencing such a shift, including the longest-standing college athlete association, the National Collegiate Players Association (NCPA), an organization that has lobbied state legislatures and the U.S. Congress on matters pertaining to college athlete health and safety, education, and compensation; United College Athlete Advocates, a group that focuses on building grassroots athlete advocacy organizations to make changes within athletic departments to racial justice, gender equity, mental health, LGBTQIA+ issues, and economic rights; the College Football Players Association, which advocates on behalf of college football players in areas of health, safety, and welfare; Athlete Ally, an organization that advocates on behalf of LGBTQ athletes; and the Hidden Opponent, which assists college athletes through education, advocacy, and support in terms of mental health.

the University of Notre Dame came to symbolize a place where the Catholic faith was treasured and diverse traditions were shared and valued (About ND, 2013). Indeed, Notre Dame became home to students from immigrant families who would not have been admitted to elite schools due to their background and social standing (Sperber, 1993).

Strikingly, the university took root in a state where three of four white males were members of the Ku Klux Klan and where anti-Catholic and anti-immigrant sentiments were a regular part of the worldview of most Indianans. These tensions came to a head in a 1924 riot pitting Notre Dame students against members of the Ku Klux Klan, who espoused anti-Catholic views. In this difficult climate, Notre Dame teams played a role in changing attitudes and providing opportunities (Tucker, 2004), and the "fighting Irish" became a representative term for disenfranchised persons seeking a better life in America.

The complicated tensions involved in issues of inclusion and exclusion are seen perhaps most clearly in the contributions made by football teams at American Indian boarding schools, including the Carlisle and Haskell schools. These schools were formed as part of a U.S. government policy intended to solve the "Indian problem" through either assimilation or extermination. In other words, American Indians were either to be stripped of their language, customs, culture, traditions, and dress or face the prospect of imprisonment or death.

The boarding schools themselves were military installations. In them, American Indian children were removed from family and strictly disciplined; thus they suffered the stress and trauma of leaving the security of their homes to make their way in a white world (Bear, 2008). For the role played by American Indian football teams in this difficult situation, see the sidebar titled The Rattling of the Bones.

The cultural spaces of college sport were equally contested for African Americans. Historically Black colleges and universities (HBCUs) were often required by law to compete among themselves. As a result, a rich tradition of rivalries developed between these schools, such as Johnson C. Smith University (North Carolina), Grambling State University (Louisiana), Howard University (Washington, DC), Lincoln University (Pennsylvania), Livingstone College (North Carolina), and Tuskegee University (Alabama). According to Grundy (2001), "[O]fficials at black colleges had looked to sports to build race pride and solidarity . . . at the same time [that] athletic contests gave community cultural endeavors a place within the symbolically potent sphere of education pursuits" (pp. 179-180).

For African Americans at previously all-white institutions, their place on college football teams inspired attention, was the subject of periodic racial

Peer-Reviewed Research With Publications and Conferences

The College Sports Research Institute (CSRI), based at the University of South Carolina, is led by its mission of encouraging and supporting interdisciplinary and interuniversity research, serving as the research consortium for college sport researchers across the United States. CSRI provides opportunities for independent, organized, and focused cross-disciplinary research regarding college sport in the United States. A national clearinghouse for college sport inquiry and research, CSRI increases the ability of students, faculty, and college sport practitioners to explore issues in college sport. Its objectives are threefold:

- Investigate issues on college sport and conduct cooperative, collaborative research with affiliated faculty and universities.
- Provide opportunity for faculty to develop research activities.
- Encourage the presentation of research results to colleagues and the general public by hosting a national conference and publishing a peer-reviewed scholarly journal on college sport.

CSRI hosts its annual conference in Columbia, South Carolina, each spring and also publishes the peer-reviewed *Journal of Issues in Intercollegiate Athletics*. The conference and journal help CSRI to further the following goals:

- Create public awareness of sociocultural, economic, and political issues in college sport.
- Provide a forum for open discussion of relevant issues within the college-sport community.
- Build relationships within local, regional, and national communities to generate funding for independent critical research into college sport.
- Generate local, regional, and national awareness of the College Sport Research Institute and The University of South Carolina in Columbia as a leader in college sport research.
- Educate students, scholars, athletic administrators, college athletes, coaches, and the general public on college sport.

To learn more about CSRI, including its annual conference and peer-reviewed journal, visit its website or follow the institute on social media.

Website: www.CSRI.org

X (formerly known as Twitter): @CSRIConference

Instagram: CSRI_Conference

Additional peer-reviewed publications devoted to intercollegiate athletics include *Journal of Intercollegiate Sport*, *Journal for the Study of Sports and Athletes in Education*, *Journal of Amateur Sport*, *Journal of Contemporary Athletics*, *Journal of Physical Education and Sports Management*, and *Journal of Athlete Development and Experience*, among others. *The Sports Business Journal* also hosts an annual forum on intercollegiate athletics, and the NCAA Convention and National Association of Collegiate Directors of Athletics (NACDA) Convention offer opportunities to learn of new research directly from industry practitioners.

unrest, and served as a focus of political debate. In addition, from the late 19th century through the 1970s, African American players on integrated teams were barred from playing against some teams in the South, who refused to play against integrated teams. Resistance to recruiting African American players by all-white teams led to a migration of African American players further north to schools such as Michigan State in the early 1960s. Gene Washington, a native of La Porte, Texas, has spoken of the decisions that African American players of that era had to make in leaving home to pursue their dream of playing college football:

The Rattling of the Bones

One of the most famous teams to emerge out of the American Indian boarding school system was the Carlisle Indians, a football team credited with introducing innovations into the game, including the forward pass, the flea-flicker, the end-around, and the reverse (Jenkins, 2007). The team included All-Americans Jim Thorpe (Sac and Fox, Oklahoma), Albert Exendine (Delaware and Cherokee, Oklahoma), and Joe Guyon (White Earth and Ojibwe, Minnesota) and compiled a record of 38 and 3. This achievement was even more remarkable considering that Carlisle was one of the most-traveled teams of the time, playing all major games at away venues (Oxendine, 1988).

In a telling 1912 confrontation with the team from the United States Military Academy, Carlisle debuted an offense that had not been seen before and executed it in a way that left the soldiers without doubt as to who had won the day. Carlisle won 27 to 6 in a game described by Carlisle player Gus Welch as the most satisfying contest he ever won (Jenkins, 2007). Welch described the experience of the win as "the rattling of the bones." For all of the efforts to assimilate American Indians, the Carlisle teams used sport as a vehicle to preserve their identity and oppose the oppression inherent in the system.

> *All the Southern players, we were outcasts from our own states. All of the states where we were from, they would not take black athletes. We bonded at Michigan State because we all had similar stories. We could make a contribution. That was very important to us. We didn't talk about that all the time, but we knew we had something to prove, and this is our opportunity. (Rittenberg, 2013)*

The notion of white players competing with and against Black players on the same field fueled political debate among segregationists, particularly in the South. In 1956, when the Georgia Institute of Technology was slated to play in the Sugar Bowl against the University of Pittsburgh, whose team included African American star Bobby Grier, Georgia governor Marvin Griffin ignited a student protest when he sought to bar the team from playing. Tech students took to the streets of Atlanta and eventually won a concession that the team could go, but not without the Georgia legislature passing a law banning interracial contests within state boundaries (Watterson, 2000).

As a measure of the talent level in the HBCU football ranks, Jackson State alone had 11 players drafted by the National Football League in 1968 (Oriard, 2009). Over time, however, as segregation gave way, both in higher education generally and on the playing field in particular, the HBCU talent pool was drained, which resulted in long-term negative consequences for those programs. For example, some of the most accomplished HBCU football programs (Grambling, Florida A&M, Southern, and Morgan State) lost prized recruits to schools such as Auburn and Alabama.

WOMEN'S COLLEGE SPORT: ENTREPRENEURS VERSUS EDUCATORS

Rebellion can take many forms. As noted earlier in this chapter, the all-male enclaves of Harvard and Yale in the 1800s were places where students tested authority in physical ways. Sport itself was a form of protest, and interclass conflicts played out on the football field. At Harvard, for example, "Bloody Mondays" were the scene of violent competitions organized between members of the lower and upper university classes to determine who would dominate in the hierarchy of the school. This practice was carried out in blatant defiance of concerns expressed by faculty members and administrators.

Women who sought to be educated were engaging in a rebellion of their own by defying social conventions dictating that women were to be seen and not heard and a common belief that women and girls did not "need" higher education. Indeed, the mere act of going to college raised concerns about female health, as acknowledged in 1875 by L. Clark Seelye, the first president of Smith College:

Professional Development

National Association of Collegiate Directors of Athletics (NACDA)

NACDA, founded in 1965, fosters networking, the exchange of ideas, and professional development. It allows athletics administrators and others in senior leadership positions to share their experiences and their expertise about current issues, challenges, and best practices through publications, workshops, and an annual convention. NACDA includes smaller groups that focus on marketing, development, business, licensing, compliance, academics, and facility and event management. The organization also promotes diversity initiatives. Whereas the NCAA convention addresses legislative issues, the NACDA convention better serves individuals within their specific professions in intercollegiate athletics through breakout sessions and guest speakers.

The organization addresses issues in NCAA Divisions I, II, and III and in the National Association of Intercollegiate Athletics (NAIA), two-year colleges along with conference commissioners and other stakeholders in college sport through various subassociations including the Football Championship Series Athletic Director Association (FCS ADA); Division I-AAA Athletic Directors Association (DI-AAA ADA), D2 Athletic Directors Association (D2 ADA); D2 Conference Commissioners Associations (D2 CCA); National Association of Division III Athletics Administrators (NADIIIAA); National Association of Intercollegiate Athletics Athletics Directors Association (NAIA ADA); and the National Association of Two-Year College Athletics Administrators (NATYCAA).

Further, as a testament to the magnitude of the commercial stakes involved in big-time college sport as part of a global multibillion-dollar sport and entertainment enterprise, the LEAD1 Association, formerly known as the Division IA Athletic Directors Association, comprises 133 athletic directors representing the interests of Football Bowl Subdivision (FBS) athletic departments. With former U.S. Congressman Tom McMillen (D-MD) as the executive director, the LEAD1 Association develops policy positions on a range of issues that affect the top tier of schools in NCAA Division I and brokers influence on Capitol Hill in efforts to preserve the corporate interests that operate in their sector of the college sport enterprise (Libit & Cyphers, 2019).

> *We admit it would be an insuperable objection to the higher education of women, if it seriously endangered her health. . . . With gymnastic training wisely adapted to their peculiar organization, we see no reason why young ladies cannot pursue study as safely as they do ordinary employments. (Sack & Staurowsky, 1998, p. 55)*

This preoccupation with the health of women college students in the late 1800s and into the early years of the 20th century created an opening for women's sport to take hold in a formally developed women's physical education curriculum. However, just as there was ambivalence about women being educated, so too was there concern about women participating in strenuous physical activity.

The "Weaker Sex"

Because women were cast as the "weaker sex"—frail in both body and psyche—prohibitions were installed to insulate female college students from the supposed potential for harm when devising rules of play for a variety of games. For example, Senda Berenson, director of physical education at Smith College, and Clara Baer, her contemporary at H. Sophie Newcomb College, each set out to adapt the rules of basketball to suit female players. Confronted with the belief that women jeopardized their capacity to have children if they participated in activities that were too physically demanding, Berenson and Baer reworked the dimensions of the court to prevent women from running full court, confining them instead to small sections (offense, defense, middle).

In addition, emphasis was placed on teamwork and passing rather than scoring. Players were discouraged from becoming overly excited or exerting themselves too much; in fact, they were penalized if they bumped into one another, fell down, or were too enthusiastic about the idea of winning. When games were "got up," they were intended to be held in front of all-female audiences—free from any additional pressure that might result if males were present.

These rules have often been interpreted as indicating that women are anticompetitive, but in point of fact they speak to the realities of women's lives at the time. If the women physical educators navigating this delicate territory had advocated too strongly, they themselves might have been out of a job. As for the players, if they had gotten hurt, the games might have been taken away from them.

Letting go of the belief that a woman's destiny was determined by her biology and that she would forever be thought of as the weaker sex became the substance of discussions about the appropriateness of women participating in sport throughout the 20th century. Women were also keen observers of what was happening in men's sport. With this perspective, while women physical educators were systematic and careful in challenging prohibitions against strong physical exertion by women, they were not prepared to accept the commercial, professionalized model of men's athletics as the ideal. To the contrary, they were hesitant to lend their support to a system that so blatantly contradicted the mission of higher education in its payment of athletes (either formally or under the table), that emphasized winning over education, that opened the door for corruption due to the financial stakes involved, and that led to public scandal.

In 1924, the Women's Division of the National Amateur Athletic Federation issued guidelines for women's sport to "stress enjoyment of the sport and the development of sportsmanship, and to minimize the emphasis placed on individual accomplishments and the winning of championships" (Suggs, 2005, p. 25). Referred to as the Women's Division platform, these guidelines "emphasized that sport for women should be inclusive and based on democratic and educational principles; in balance with other aspects of life; and unmotivated by profit, spectator, or commercial interests" (Sack & Staurowsky, 1998, p. 67). The platform also firmly put forward the notion that women's sport was to be coached by women (Sack & Staurowsky, 1998).

The preferred format for women's college sport emerging from the platform was the "play day." In this approach, groups of women from various colleges would converge on one campus to participate in a variety of sports that they had most likely learned in their physical education classes, including field hockey, basketball, and volleyball (Gerber et al., 1974). Women would not, however, play for their own schools but would be placed on mixed teams through a lottery system.

A few progressive institutions—such as Bryn Mawr, Ursinus College, and others in the Philadelphia area—did not subscribe fully to the belief that women should be prevented from playing varsity sports. Ursinus, for example, offered varsity sports for women in 1923. These institutions, however, were clearly in the minority (Sack & Staurowsky, 1998).

By 1957, the Division for Girls and Women's Sport (DGWS)—a division of the American Association for Health, Physical Education and Recreation—acknowledged the necessity of meeting the needs of highly skilled female athletes with competitive opportunities. The opportunities were limited, however, because they "deprived others [girls and women] of the many different kinds of desirable activities which are inherent in well-conducted sports programs" (Sack & Staurowsky, 1998). Still, momentum from the women's movement and the second wave of feminism in the 1960s chipped away at the societal hesitation to allow women to participate in varsity competition. As that shift occurred, women physical educators felt increasing concern about how to handle championship competition.

In an attempt to get a handle on the issue, the DGWS created the Commission on Intercollegiate Athletics for Women (CIAW) in 1967. Five years later—in the same year that Title IX of the Education Amendments of 1972 was enacted to protect students from discrimination on the basis of sex in federally funded schools—CIAW became the Association for Intercollegiate Athletics for Women (AIAW). Still seeking to carve out a space for an educationally sound and student-centered model of college sport, the AIAW issued a policy statement

The AIAW–NCAA Struggle Over Women's Athletics

Christine Grant (1981), former president of the AIAW and longtime women's athletics administrator at the University of Iowa, remembers what it was like at the 1981 NCAA Convention, where the association voted to sponsor Division I women's championships, thus effectively undermining the AIAW. She issued the following statement:

> *I rise in symbolic opposition to the motion before you.*
>
> *It is difficult to describe the actions taken in the last three days.*
>
> *I, and many other women, came here convinced that a desire for mutual accommodation between AIAW and NCAA would far outweigh any thirst for precipitous action.*
>
> *Obviously, I was in error. Obviously, it was not persuasive to you that by your actions women in athletics—students and professionals—were losing control of their own destinies. Obviously, it was not persuasive to you that it was the conviction of those most closely associated with women's athletic programs that your actions will do untoward damage to those programs. And finally, it is obvious that our appeal to your sense of fair play had little effect upon your actions.*
>
> *I find it somehow fitting that Father Joyce's same pleas on behalf of football coaches, however, were persuasive to and prevalent in this assembly. [Earlier in the day, Father Edmund Joyce, representing the University of Notre Dame, had spoken on behalf of the football powers arguing against legislation that would have placed financial limits on athletic scholarships (UPI, January 13, 1981)]. I would hope in the future that you might be as considerate of women's athletics, and those involved in it, as you have demonstrated you can be to football coaches.*
>
> *My three days here have not been pleasant. As 1980 AIAW president, I was privileged to meet a large majority of those directly involved in administering women's athletic programs and female student-athletes. In the last three days, I have seen their hopes and aspirations to chart a new and innovative course for intercollegiate athletics severely damaged. I believe we will all live to regret the actions you have taken. I believe our institutions and our students will suffer in the coming years from the loss of a viable option to NCAA governance.*
>
> *I am not angry at what has occurred, but I am profoundly sad. Mainly, I'm sad that I have found very little sincere interest in the preferences of the women in athletics, or in seeking a mutually agreeable alternative governing structure for men's and women's athletics. Instead, I and many of the other women who have spoken have sensed aggression and hostility toward our views, and an unbridled desire for the precipitous extension of this association's authority into women's athletics.*
>
> *You have spoken of options, yet with motion after motion you have [en]sured that women will have no options. The realities of women in subordinate positions and the practicalities of conflicting noncompetitive rules systems have left very little option indeed. You have bought your way into women's athletics with the lure of big money and other luxuries, but you haven't bought it from those most directly affected.*
>
> *As certainly as I stand before you, you will find that you have also bought the philosophy and expectation of organizational responsiveness that those in women's athletics have held dear. AIAW is not only a governance organization, but it is also an idea. And, while I do not know what the future may hold for that organization, I do know that the idea will never die.*

Leadership Lesson

Paradigm

A paradigm is a framework of ideas, beliefs, values, and experiences through which an individual interprets and responds to reality. In essence, a paradigm is an individual's worldview. As we study the history of intercollegiate athletics in relation to the present and future of the industry, pay attention to the paradigm or framework that you use when perceiving issues involved in intercollegiate athletics. To get an idea of the difference that a perspective can make, look at figure 1.4. Do you see an old woman or a young woman? Similarly, how does your lens affect the way you interpret or react to the latest sport industry news?

For example, do you view a scandal as a repeat of history, a consequence of an overregulating governing body, or a result of ineffective leadership? Any one of these conclusions—and many others—can provide clues to the paradigm that affects your perceptions. It is important to actively analyze how you perceive the world and understand that your view may be very different from that of the person sitting next to you. Your reality is not *the* reality. Effective leaders know this, and they strive to gain a broad perspective by continually stretching themselves to seek greater understanding of differing paradigms and surrounding themselves with individuals who see things differently than they do. The study of history is particularly important in this quest, because many of the issues we face today are eerily similar to issues that plagued the college sport industry in past decades.

Much of the interpersonal conflict that arises within an organization can be attributed to differing paradigms. Just as some see an old woman and others see a young woman in figure 1.4, it is not uncommon for members of a department to see issues, policies, tactics, and decisions very differently. In an effort to understand and appreciate the differences within our organizations, many consultants and leadership teams use the Myers-Briggs Type Indicator (MBTI). The MBTI is a refined questionnaire designed to measure psychological preferences in how people make decisions and perceive the world.

Figure 1.4 Depending on perspective, a person may see an old woman or a young woman.
Library of Congress Prints and Photographs Division, LC-DIG-ds-00175.

The MBTI's four pairs of preferences address the following factors:

1. How you get energy (extrovert versus introvert)
2. How you get information (intuitive versus sensing)
3. How you use information to make decisions (feeling versus thinking)
4. How you take action (judging versus perceiving)

MBTI assessment results may help individuals gain better understanding of what approaches are more natural or more difficult, both for themselves and for their colleagues. Such understanding can help people communicate more effectively, better understand unique perspectives, and defuse tension. The MBTI should be administered by someone who has been trained and understands MBTI theory. If you are interested in identifying your MBTI preferences, you can do so by visiting www.myersbriggs.org or by exploring a variety of online adaptations of the test.

As we begin our journey of exploring administration in intercollegiate athletics, we do so with a belief that you, the reader, will soon shape the governance of intercollegiate athletics for future generations of students, spectators, and stakeholders. Therefore, it is critical to acknowledge that leadership begins at the individual level and that your paradigm will affect both the decisions you make and, as a result, the future of the industry.

Throughout this text, you will be faced with ethical dilemmas as you strive to balance financial realities, commercial enticements, and educational priorities. As these moments of power arise in your career, it will be critical for you to make decisions based on principles that remain unchanged in the heat of the moment. For now, in *this* particular moment, as you read these words, begin thinking about the principles that you will rely on to guide you through these inevitable challenges. How will your paradigm affect your leadership? What MBTI preferences will help or hinder you in your leadership journey? What is the purpose, in your view, of intercollegiate athletics, and how can you facilitate this purpose in your future leadership roles?

> *The significant problems we face cannot be solved at the same level of thinking we were at when we created them.*
>
> Albert Einstein

in 1974 advocating "separate but comparable sports for female and male athletes" and arguing that the centerpiece of a college sport experience should be "the enrichment of life of the participant" (Holland, 1974, p. 12).

This unique stance on the part of the women's athletics community—which sought autonomy in fostering a model of college sport different from the one already in place for men—ended up serving as a point of contention for those who believed that the requirements of Title IX would not allow such a distinction. Having sought to avoid the pitfalls of men's intercollegiate athletics, the AIAW had cautioned against the adoption of athletics scholarships, believing that they distorted the educational experience of athletes, were prone to manipulation by coaches, and served as the basis of a pay-for-play system. However, under pressure from a lawsuit brought by Fern Kellmeyer (a junior college coach) and female tennis players, the AIAW acquiesced on the issue of athletics scholarships and reversed course in 1973 (Staurowsky, 2012). By 1980, the NCAA effectively took over the AIAW in a power play designed to undermine women's leadership in athletics by moving to offer championships in Divisions II and III. The following year, the takeover was completed when the NCAA committed to hosting women's championships in Division I as well.

As Michelle Hosick (2011) of NCAA News wrote, the decision was a difficult one for those committed to the idea of women forging their own way in college sport. Christine Grant, a former AIAW president who served with distinction for many years as the University of Iowa's director of athletics for women, described the impact on AIAW leaders as follows: "We were fighting for our lives. And we lost. It was a very difficult and emotional situation" (Hosick). Speaking to the all-male NCAA membership that was deciding the fate of the women in the AIAW, Grant evoked a sentiment that had been expressed years before by women suffragists. She implored, "This is an opportunity for you to send a message to the leadership of this organization, and to the hundreds of women who cannot speak for themselves, that you will not take the women against their will" (Hosick).

AIAW leaders speaking that day recall being booed, something NCAA officials deny, and finding scraps of paper with mocking caricatures left for them by male delegates. While some believed that separate athletics associations for men and

Industry Profile

CANDICE STOREY LEE

Vice Chancellor for Athletics and Student Affairs, Vanderbilt University

Of the 65 schools in the Power Five conferences, only 6 of them are led by women. Candice Storey Lee is one of them. She is also the first African American woman to serve as athletic director for a Southeastern Conference (SEC) school. The manner in which Dr. Lee ascended to the rank of vice chancellor for athletics and student affairs and athletic director is reflective of a rare and singular journey. By any measure, she has unusually strong and deep ties to Vanderbilt and to the city of Nashville, Tennessee.

Her affiliation with Vanderbilt began as an undergraduate. She was a member of the women's basketball team between 1997 and 2000, serving as captain in her senior year. She also holds three degrees from Vanderbilt, the highest being a doctorate in higher education administration. She started out as a university intern, entering into the field of athletics administration by first serving as an athletics academic advisor. With time and increased responsibility, she was named senior woman administrator (a role she held from 2004 through 2020), compliance director, associate athletics director, and deputy athletics director.

Over the years, she progressively developed a deeper understanding of how the college sport business works, emerging in 2019 as one of the *Sports Business Journal's* "Power Players." That recognition followed her selection for the John McLendon Scholarship for Black Administrators in 2017 and her selection by Adidas for its "Next Up" list in 2018.

In February 2020, Dr. Lee was tapped by the university to take on the critical role of interim athletic director at a time of transition and change. Her mentor, beloved former Vanderbilt athletic director David Williams, had retired in February of 2019. The position was filled by Mason Turner, an executive with background in the NBA who stayed for just over a year and left abruptly (Stephenson, 2020). By May 2020, Dr. Lee was placed into the permanent position.

Vanderbilt Athletics

In 2021, she served alongside Chancellor Daniel Diermeier to oversee the ambitious Vandy United Fund, a US$300 million campaign to realize her vision of Vanderbilt as one of the world's finest academic institutions located in one of the nation's best cities that thrives in the most competitive athletic conferences (Athletic Communications Staff, 2022). That effort will include a renovation of the football stadium, a new basketball practice facility, a new football practice facility, and more (Weinstein, 2021).

Speaking at the Harpeth Hall School, a college preparatory school for girls, in November 2021, Dr. Lee emphasized leadership and "encouraged students to hold each other accountable, [to] call out inequity, to show others what is possible, and to be the champions for the people who cannot be champions for themselves" (Staff, 2021).

women would not be permitted because of Title IX, there was a sense among AIAW leadership that the NCAA had literally "bought" agreement from some women leaders and that those women had sold out. In other words, some women leaders felt trapped, forced to vote to dissolve the AIAW in the absence of litigation. Others blamed the NCAA and the women who aligned with it. In either case, the NCAA's decision to bring women's athletics under its governance structure led to the merger of men's and women's athletics departments nationwide, which was followed by the demotion of hundreds of women physical educators and administrators. The legacy of that decision and the loss of women's leadership in college sport remains more than 40 years later.

Case Study

The Case of Liberty University and Challenges Associated With Moving Into a Higher Division

Where a school fits within the larger college sport universe is a function of institutional vision, aspiration, resources, timing, and access. An institution that wishes to move up a division may be willing to make the financial investment to upgrade facilities and expand staffing to support such a move, but their efforts might be put on hold or quashed entirely if they are unable to find schools to compete against. Such appeared to be the case for Liberty University. Having set a course to become a force within NCAA Division I, Liberty had established itself as an institution and athletic department with ambition. In 2017, its application to be recognized as an FBS institution was approved by the NCAA contingent on Liberty being accepted into an FBS conference. As per the NCAA transition process, schools are typically given two years to make the full transition to FBS. Liberty encountered some turbulence in landing an FBS conference. In 2017, Liberty's bids to be welcomed into Conference USA (CUSA) and the Sun Belt were both declined, despite the fact that Liberty offered to pay a sum of money that was much greater than the US$2 million initial admission fee. Competing accounts offer different perspectives on why Liberty was turned down at that time. The then president of Liberty, Jerry Falwell Jr., alleged that CUSA's rejection reflected religious bias against Christian evangelicals. Karl Benson, commissioner of the Sun Belt, indicated that the decision was based on geographic location, thus Coastal Carolina was chosen over Liberty (Johnson, 2017). In 2021, Liberty was admitted into CUSA along with three other institutions: Jacksonville State, New Mexico State, and Sam Houston State. This move ended Liberty's status as an independent in football and represented the overall athletic department's transition to its third conference since moving up to NCAA Division I in 1988. Liberty is scheduled to compete under the umbrella of CUSA during the 2023-2024 academic year.

The Liberty University saga provides an opportunity to explore numerous questions associated with how decisions are made to elevate an athletic department to a new division, the risks involved, and the factors that come into play in assessing whether a move up is a worthwhile decision.

Questions to Consider

1. Compare Liberty's move up to FBS with that of the University of Connecticut and Rutgers University, schools that have struggled since making the decision to move up. What are the challenges that confront schools wishing to move to FBS? What are Liberty's prospects based on what is known about FCS schools moving to FBS?
2. Do research on CUSA and consider why that conference admitted four institutions, including Liberty. What contributed to those decisions and does this bode well for Liberty moving forward?
3. Does Liberty lead us to think that successful transitions are all about having more financial resources than your competitors?

CONCLUSION

With the benefit of a historical perspective, we can better appreciate the origins of key issues in intercollegiate sport and the complexities of potential resolutions. The age of the "super conference" (meaning the current state of affairs in big-time college sport), for example, was set in motion more than 60, perhaps more than 100, years ago, and the legacy of those early tensions related to the earning power of football persists today. Indeed, the century-old insight of Penn's R. Tait McKenzie, who saw signs of professionalism in the college sport system that grew out of male-only institutions, remains relevant today in light of the continuing escalation of coaches' salaries and the ongoing questions about appropriate compensation for revenue-producing athletes. The "tramp athlete" of yesteryear who did not receive a college degree may have a counterpart in the here and now.

The history also remains relevant on various other fronts. For example, the NCAA's efforts to address issues of diversity and inclusion have been expanded recently to include creating a more welcoming environment for lesbian, gay, bisexual, and transgender athletes. In addition, a 2013 letter of clarification from the U.S. Department of Education's Office for Civil Rights outlines athletics departments' obligation to provide opportunities for disabled athletes. And just as threats to football players' health contributed to the creation of the NCAA in the first place, concerns about traumatic brain injuries among players now threaten the financial viability of the college sport enterprise. With an eye toward these issues and others, this text gives you an opportunity to learn more about the mechanisms in place to govern athletics and to shape the future through a responsive mobilization of creative decision-making and problem-solving.

DISCUSSION QUESTIONS

1. Reflect on the chapter's opening scenario and the varying broad sentiments that people express about intercollegiate athletics. Why do you think these differences in perspective exist? Where do you fall in this range? What are your current views about the value of college sport?
2. Explain the notion of a "country club" college. When you were considering which college to attend, did "consumption amenities" influence your choice? How might the "country club" mindset affect university administrators' views of intercollegiate athletics?
3. If you could go back in time to the period when intercollegiate athletics was just beginning, what might you tell faculty reformers to help facilitate greater balance between athletics and academics in the industry for years to come?
4. What are the similarities and differences between "tramp athletes" and current NCAA full-scholarship athletes?
5. Outline the evolution of the concept of amateurism in the NCAA. What has driven this evolution?
6. Explain the role played by college sport in facilitating access to higher education and American society more generally for American Indians, African Americans, and women in the late 20th century.
7. The 1974 policy statement by the AIAW advocated "separate but comparable sports for female and male athletes" and argued that the centerpiece of a college sport experience should be "the enrichment of life of the participant." Can you envision the possibility of separate programs for men and women today? Would there be a benefit to having programs separated in this manner today? Why or why not?
8. After researching the AIAW and reading Christine Grant's statement to the NCAA (included in full in this chapter), reflect on the events that transpired in 1981 when the NCAA took over college women's sport.

LEARNING ACTIVITIES

1. In the chapter, you encountered Stanford University president David Starr Jordan, who offered leadership regarding college sport in 1905. Do some research to identify a college president who is providing leadership in college sport today.
2. Columbia student Reed Harris was so passionate in his view that out-of-control commercial interests were distorting "King Football" in 1932 that he not only endured being expelled from school but also declined an invitation to return because he preferred to speak out publicly. Are you aware of students who have challenged the status quo in college athletics? Have any student newspapers put a spotlight on detrimental behavior in college sports? If so, what issues they have raised? What do you think of Harris?
3. The chapter's conclusion highlights parallels between past and present-day intercollegiate athletics. Choose one of the issues discussed and research its current status.

Governing Bodies

Barbara Osborne, University of North Carolina at Chapel Hill

Erianne A. Weight, University of North Carolina at Chapel Hill

Robert H. Zullo, Slippery Rock University

In this chapter, you will explore

- the variety of intercollegiate athletics governance structures in the United States,
- the principle of institutional control,
- internal and external stakeholders who influence athletics governance,
- conference governance,
- NCAA association-wide and federated governance, and
- NCAA Division I governance.

THE CONFERENCE REALIGNMENT DOMINO EFFECT

Two West Coast Power Five universities announce they are leaving their Power Five conference to join a Power Five conference with members from the East Coast through the Midwest. This stunning move would have been unimaginable just a few years ago, but college athletics is currently in an unprecedented state of flux, driven not only by promises of television revenue but by legal challenges and athlete activism. The chain reaction of conference-hopping began in 2010, with all 11 Football Bowl Subdivision (FBS) conferences gaining or losing football members. This new alignment creates a divide among the Power Five conferences, making the Big Ten and the SEC the power brokers of college football and leaving the ACC, Big 12, and Pac-12 reeling to discuss survival—a state that was previously reserved for conferences outside of the Power Five. A Big Ten source said, "[E]veryone has to be nimble. One day, you might be saying one thing, and you mean it from the bottom of your heart. And the next day you have to flip, based on economics, based on governance, based on something" (Adelson et al., 2022).

Presidents and athletics directors emphasize the ways in which such moves give their schools opportunities to improve their academic image (Forde, 2010). Other reports assert the primary motives involve conference television revenues. Meanwhile, many stakeholders wonder whether the governance structures of intercollegiate athletics are broken, whether the money filtering through this industry is being handled wisely, and who the key decision-makers are in the administrative chain. As student-athletes advance through gaining NIL rights and schools utilize NIL collectives that could potentially alter the recruiting landscape, is the highest level of intercollegiate athletics evolving so that students are becoming employees and negotiating as one unit through the formation of labor unions?

The governance of intercollegiate athletics in the United States is based on three levels of control: institutional, conference, and national. An institution holds authority over the level and scope of athletic competition that it wishes to sponsor on its campus or campuses. Based on its institutional mission and scope of athletic competition, it can choose membership in a national governing body that helps it accomplish its organizational athletics goals.

The institution also decides whether or not conference membership will help it meet its athletics goals. Based on these decisions, athletics at the institution can cover a wide range of purposes, from opportunities for athletes to participate casually in recreational sport to athletics competition on an elite national scale, with the institution hoping to leverage athletics as a vehicle to market and brand their university. Thus, institutional goals for athletics vary tremendously, which leads to a variety of related governance structures.

At the base of the intercollegiate athletics hierarchy reside the athletes who compete on the field, track, mat, and court, or in the pool or other setting. The education of these athletes is the reason that the endeavor exists; as a result, each level of the governance structure is charged with facilitating optimal experiences for this foundational population. Athletes receive the majority of their instruction from—and are governed directly by—their coaches, who are responsible for the competitive direction, athlete development, and overall day-to-day operation of their teams.

The next level of institutional administration is implemented by athletics administrators, who are typically responsible for budget management, facility oversight, fundraising, marketing and promotions, operations, rules compliance, and other management functions. Ultimately, the director of athletics is responsible for all personnel and management decisions, as well as the integration of athletics, university, conference, and national governing body regulatory influences.

The highest level of *individual* authority at the campus level resides with the president (or chancellor, depending on the institution's preferred nomenclature). However, even presidents themselves are accountable to a board of trustees (or board of governors). This hierarchy of responsibility at an institution represents the foundational principle of NCAA athletics governance—that of institutional autonomy and control.

Although colleges and universities function independently, sport competition is a cooperative venture. Indeed, intercollegiate athletics could not exist if schools did not agree on rules or dates and locations of competition. Historically, schools formed alliances with other similarly situated schools and created athletics conferences—a middle layer of regulatory governance. Athletics conferences are voluntary membership associations whose members come together for a specific purpose. Historically, similarities between institutions—such as geographic proximity, type of institution (e.g., public or private; liberal arts, vocational, or technical; large or small), academic standards, and intercollegiate teams sponsored—have motivated schools to band together to develop rules and regulations that facilitate a level playing field and ease burdens such as scheduling and assigning officials.

More recently, however, conference membership appears to be driven by economic incentives, as these organizations pool the inventory of their members to maximize television and marketing revenues. While the members of a traditional athletics conference compete in all conference-sponsored sports (and postseason championships—another revenue opportunity), some conferences administer only one sport. Examples include Hockey East and the East Atlantic Gymnastics League. The largest intercollegiate athletics conference in the country is the Eastern College Athletic Conference, which operates as a regional governing body with postseason championships for member institutions offered in Divisions I, II, and III.

A college or university may also choose to become a member of a national governing body. The purpose of such bodies is to provide postseason championship opportunities, establish a level playing field through rules and regulations, and promote and supervise intercollegiate competition. The first national athletics organization was the National Collegiate Athletic Association (NCAA), which was founded in 1906 to develop safety rules to protect football players; it subsequently began sponsoring national championships in 1921. It has grown to be the largest national intercollegiate athletics governing body, with about 1,100 member institutions providing competitive opportunities for

Professional Development

Women Leaders in Sports

The National Association of Collegiate Women Athletic Administrators (NACWAA) rebranded as Women Leaders in College Sports in 2017 to facilitate the advancement and growth of all women in all levels of intercollegiate athletics, and then rebranded again to Women Leaders in Sports in 2023 to encompass the growth and impact on all fields. Founded in 1979, the group advocates for more women at the senior level of athletic administration and consists of over 3,500 members from the conference level and school level, including coaches and even students. Educational programming is targeted at entry-level, midlevel, senior-level, and executive-level women. There are mentoring opportunities as well as a dedicated effort to assist women of color. With a presence on Facebook, X (formerly known as Twitter), Instagram, and LinkedIn, the organization promotes networking and hosts an annual convention for greater educational opportunities. Other events, such as happy hours, align with the NCAA Convention, the Final Four, and other, larger industry gatherings. The group is a valuable opportunity for women to enhance their careers, learning from peers and especially those with greater experience in the industry. A student/intern membership rate is available and the organization offers a membership scholarship for those in need of financial assistance.

approximately 500,000 intercollegiate student-athletes participating in 24 sports.

Four other national organizations provide additional options for institutions seeking postseason national championships. Although the NCAA is well known for its March Madness basketball tournament, the National Association of Intercollegiate Athletics (NAIA) sponsors the longest-running national basketball tournament in the United States. The NAIA held its first men's basketball tournament in 1937, and the association became formally established in 1938. NAIA was also the first national intercollegiate athletics governing body to invite historically Black institutions into membership (in 1953) and to sponsor both men's and women's national championships (in 1980). Currently, there are 241 member institutions with more than 83,000 student-athletes competing in 28 different NAIA championship sports. Conference membership is based on geography, and only 24 NAIA member colleges remain independent of the 20 affiliated conferences (National Association of Intercollegiate Athletics, 2023).

Another national organization, the National Junior College Athletic Association (NJCAA), was established in 1938 to promote competition between institutions granting two-year or associate's degrees. Today, the NJCAA boasts over 500 member institutions competing over multiple divisions across 44 states in 28 sports. The divisions are based on the amount of scholarship funding the member school may provide to student-athletes: Division I schools may award full athletics scholarships, Division II schools may grant scholarships that are limited to the cost of tuition, and Division III schools do not offer athletics scholarships (National Junior College Athletic Association, 2022).

In 1968, the National Christian College Athletic Association (NCCAA) was incorporated. It currently includes over 90 member schools and promotes Christian outreach and ministry through sponsorship of over 20 national championships (National Christian College Athletic Association, 2023).

The newest national governing body for intercollegiate athletics is the United States Collegiate Athletic Association (USCAA), established in 2009 to provide national competition experiences for small-enrollment schools and nontraditional programs. The association's almost 70 member institutions offer four-year degrees, associate's degrees, or trade programs. The USCAA offers nine men's championships and nine women's championships (United States Collegiate Athletic Association, 2023).

With this context in mind, the remainder of this chapter focuses on governance within the framework of the NCAA as the largest and most influential of the national governing bodies for intercollegiate athletics in the United States.

INSTITUTIONAL CONTROL

Although the governance and regulation of intercollegiate athletics may appear to be top-down endeavors, the voluntary nature of membership and enforcement necessitates individual compliance from the bottom up. Rules compliance starts with the student-athlete. Individual student-athletes may be recruited, but ultimately the student-athlete chooses to participate and in so choosing agrees to follow the rules of all school, conference, and national governing bodies. The failure of individual athletes to adhere to the rules jeopardizes, not only their individual eligibility but also the success of the team, the coaches, the athletics administrators, and everyone on up through the institution's administrative ranks, all of whom may also be subject to sanctions by the conference, the national governing body, or both. Student-athletes can contribute to governance on their own campus through student-athlete advisory committees (SAACs), which are discussed in chapter 6.

Coaches also have a responsibility to follow the rules and to monitor their assistants, staff members, and student-athletes for rules compliance. In fact, NCAA rules require the head coach to monitor assistant coaches and staff members, and penalties are enforced against head coaches for recruiting violations and academic violations committed by anyone in their programs. This role of oversight involves understanding the rules and completing many institutional compliance forms, but it is also critically important that coaches buy into the governance philosophy of intercollegiate athletics. Coaches serve as role models for playing fair and balancing the demands of athletics and academics, and they *must* lead by example.

Larger athletics programs include various internal units with layers of middle managers who play supervisory (and therefore rules-enforcement) roles. Over the past 20 years, the typical compliance unit in an athletics department has grown in both staff size and importance. The compliance staff's primary responsibility is to educate all members of the athletics program—from student-athletes to alumni—about the rules. This education is generally carried out through informational meetings and the distribution of instructional and reference materials.

In addition to increasing awareness of the rules and identifying areas of risk, the compliance staff work with coaches to provide forms and tools to monitor, assist with monitoring, and supervise rules compliance. When violations or other problems occur, the compliance staff investigates to determine what happened and whether it could or should have been prevented. The staff then reports the violation to the conference and/or the NCAA, self-imposes a penalty (if necessary) on the institution, and works to prevent recurrence.

The size and sophistication of the compliance staff depends on institutional priorities and resources. The largest compliance unit in an athletics department includes more than a dozen full-time staff, whereas the smallest consists of a single coach or administrator for whom compliance is listed as one of many responsibilities. Regardless of the size or scope of the compliance department, rules compliance is really the responsibility of every individual involved in the athletics department—not just those who work in the compliance unit. This is discussed more thoroughly as we explore compliance as a functional unit in chapter 4.

The athletics director (AD) bears ultimate responsibility for everything that goes on in the athletics program. As the leader of the athletics department, the AD establishes the program's internal compliance culture and also serves as the face of the program for all other institutional and external constituencies. An athletics director's job description can vary widely, depending on the type of institution. At smaller institutions with fewer athletics administrators, the AD is tasked with specific duties as well as general supervisory responsibility, whereas the AD of a larger program typically assumes a general supervisory role. The AD usually holds approval authority over all athletics depart-

Technology Tools

USA Today and Salary Databases

Through its tenacious and dedicated research, *USA Today* has worked aggressively to provide data to its readers on the salaries of FBS head coaches. In recent years, the database extended to include head coaches for Division I men's and women's basketball programs. Led by Steve Berkowitz, the research team reaches out to schools individually and gathers information that administrators find useful in benchmarking. The research has even extended to the escalating salaries of assistant football coaches and strength and conditioning coaches.

In addition to the database, Berkowitz and his colleagues examine game contracts for unique clauses and incentives, taking readers into the complex world of negotiations between agents, the schools, and opponents. In recent years, the research staff has begun to examine the complexities of Division I football and basketball scheduling, poring over contracts to examine fair market value, unique scheduling arrangements, and innovative ideas hidden from the casual fan. For example, a smaller Group of Five school that might lose its successful head coach to a Power Five school that can pay more and offer more resources might include a traditional buyout clause, but might also note in the contract that the Power Five school must schedule the Group of Five school at a future date as well. Berkowitz's investigative journalism is useful for aspiring athletic administrators, and he utilizes X (formerly known as Twitter) to keep his readers informed of current events associated with contracts, especially as it relates to finances, including bonuses and buyouts.

ment policies and procedures and represents the institution at the conference and national levels.

The president of the academic institution is the final authority in the structure of institutional control. The athletics department is only one part of the educational institution, but intercollegiate athletics may generate more attention than most other university departments combined. Therefore, it is up to the president to retain a holistic view of the institution's mission and determine what role the athletics department plays in achieving that mission. In theory, the president occupies the best position from which to establish the culture and set the rules and limits for the athletics program. On the other hand, because the president is responsible for the entire academic institution, they may not be particularly interested in devoting much time to the athletics department or may not be sufficiently educated about relevant issues to make informed athletics policy decisions. Presidential authority is discussed further in the sections addressing internal and external stakeholders and the NCAA governance structure.

> *If you're running a school that has big-time sports, if there's a problem, it can overwhelm you . . . when you look at all the problems we're having as I see my colleagues around the country struggling, it just makes me wonder whether [presidential control of athletics] was a good idea.*
>
> H. Thorpe (qtd. in Stancill, 2013)

In general, the philosophy of institutional control provides autonomy for the institution to make its own decisions and control its own destiny in matters such as offering teams, allocating resources, and determining the appropriate balance between academics and athletics. However, because intercollegiate sport cannot exist without rules, institutional autonomy is somewhat problematic in the context of athletics competition. From a governance perspective, sport organizations must balance the need of every institution to chart its own course with the need for all competitors to follow the same rules and achieve a standard of fairness on the playing field. In a narrower view of rules compliance, institutional control involves the ability of the college or university to operate the athletics department in a way that abides by the spirit and the letter of the governing rules.

INTERNAL AND EXTERNAL STAKEHOLDERS

Authority over the administration of athletics at the institutional level is continually challenged by both internal and external forces. Though faculty members generally possess an important voice in the governance of an academic institution, they have had varying degrees of success in controlling or influencing athletics program policy. Local and national faculty groups calling for reform have proliferated as concerns have risen about the commercial and academic aspects of college sport at the "big-time" level. Examples include the Coalition on Intercollegiate Athletics, the Drake Group, and the American Association of University Professors.

Similarly, varying degrees of influence on athletics administration are wielded by governing boards (e.g., boards of trustees) at the institutional level and by state-level boards (e.g., boards of regents) for public colleges and universities. Powerful influence is also exerted on athletics programs by other external stakeholders, including alumni and other fans, members of the media and entertainment industries (e.g., broadcasters), the sporting goods manufacturing industry, and governmental entities.

Faculty

As one former University of Michigan president recounted, "Many members of the faculty believe that the true control of intercollegiate athletics should be their responsibility, either through specific bodies such as faculty athletics boards or through more general faculty governance" (Duderstadt, 2003, pp. 105-106). The rationale for faculty governance hinges on the educational foundation of intercollegiate athletics and on overarching faculty concern for the students, for whom the enterprise exists. However, the role and authority of faculty members on their individual campuses varies depending on institutional structures.

This variance was examined in a study of faculty governance across 32 institutions in three major athletics conferences (the Big Ten, SEC, and what was then the Pac-10), which analyzed formal governing documents detailing the role and authority of faculty governing bodies. The study reported minimal faculty participation and authority; in fact, participatory faculty committees assumed responsibility for the quality of athletics programs and operation at only two schools (Minor & Perry, 2010). However, though few athletics programs appear to operate with mandatory faculty governance in the form of a faculty advisory committee, many athletics departments do voluntarily include faculty members on a variety of athletics department committees to help bridge the gap between athletics and the academy. Examples include student-athlete academic support advisory committees, Title IX committees, and committees related to student-athlete admissions.

Faculty also play a formal role in athletics governance at all NCAA member institutions through the role of the faculty athletics representative (FAR). Article 6.1.3 of the NCAA constitution describes the FAR as a faculty member or an administrator with faculty rank who does not hold a position in the athletics department. The FAR formally represents the view of the faculty in advising the institution's president on athletics-related issues. The FAR also plays a key communication role on campus by informing the faculty about athletics issues, policies, and procedures. Other duties of the FAR vary, depending on the academic institution, but most FARs are involved in academic oversight of the athletics program and in ensuring the welfare of student-athletes. The role requires substantial knowledge of university, conference, and NCAA rules because the FAR represents the university on various conference and NCAA committees and may serve as the institution's voting delegate if the president is unavailable.

Governing Boards

Internal pressures also arise from university governing boards, which often exert an unusual amount of oversight with regard to the management of intercollegiate athletics. The primary reasoning behind this level of control hinges on the visibility of collegiate athletics programs on many campuses and the political pressures and acclaim that can result from being associated with such programs. Regardless of the motives for intervention, the reality remains that institutional control of intercollegiate athletics is not ultimately held by these internal bodies. Though their concern may be broad and well intentioned, most faculty or board members have limited knowledge of the system's intricacies and are not in a position to accept or be held accountable for governance in the final analysis (Duderstadt, 2003).

External Stakeholders

External stakeholders range in power and organization, and they are a constant presence among the forces that create intercollegiate athletics governance. These stakeholders include fans and alumni, the media, the entertainment industry (e.g., broadcasters), the sports apparel industry, and the government. Only the government can exert direct authority over an institution, yet each of these external stakeholders wields powerful influence over college sport.

This power was explored in a study—conducted by the Knight Commission on Intercollegiate Athletics (KCIA)—related to the costs and financing of intercollegiate athletics within FBS institutions. The research involved nearly 80 percent of NCAA Division I FBS university presidents, and the majority indicated a feeling of possessing only limited power to effect financial change in athletics on *their own* campuses. As one president commented, "The real power doesn't lie with the presidents; presidents have lost their jobs over athletics. Presidents and chancellors are afraid to rock the boat with boards, benefactors, and political supporters who want to win, so they turn their focus elsewhere" (Knight Commission, 2009, p. 16).

Thus, while presidents may reside at the top of the organizational hierarchy, for many of them their power (or belief in their power) has been limited by the strength of external forces. A follow-up study to the KCIA presidential study examined the power felt by conference commissioners in regard to the athletics "arms race." This study found similar results, as the commissioners collectively disagreed with the notion that they held the power to enact change (Weight et al., 2013). The NCAA has also made adjustments based on the impact of external stakeholders. The new NCAA governance structure includes two independent members who are not affiliated with NCAA member schools or conferences. Similarly, the NCAA's recent loosening of restrictions related to student-athlete name, image, and likeness (NIL) earnings was driven by external stakeholders and state legislation.

CONFERENCE GOVERNANCE

While the concept of a level playing field is attractive in theory, it quickly became apparent to leaders in intercollegiate athletics that not all programs are created equal. To create a more level playing field, schools naturally gravitated toward competing against similar institutions. This self-selection eventually led to the formation of athletics conferences. Initially, intercollegiate athletics conferences were formed by institutions that were similar in the size of their student body, their academic offerings and standards, their status as public or private institutions, their geographic location, and the quality and quantity of competitive opportunities they sponsored. Over time, the conferences became independent organizations with constitutions and bylaws defining their purpose and mission and their members' responsibilities.

The organization of a conference can vary tremendously. Some smaller NCAA Division III conferences operate as voluntary cooperatives in which athletics administrators from member programs carry out leadership and administrative tasks on an assigned or rotating basis. At the other end of the spectrum, most NCAA Division I FBS conferences employ a conference commissioner and a large staff of administrators to provide a wide range of services and generate additional revenue for conference members. The original appeal of conference membership included ease of scheduling and the opportunity to compete in a season-culminating conference championship. Now, the largest conferences still facilitate scheduling and conference championships but have expanded to handle officiating bureaus, legislative services, rules compliance, education, and interpretation.

Conferences also actively promote themselves and their championships through marketing, public relations, media relations, and athletics communication. Conference games and championships are broadcast through a variety of television, radio, and digital communication platforms that are either produced or procured by the conference. Some conferences even own dedicated television networks. Additional revenues are generated through the sale of conference-licensed merchandise and apparel, through either online stores or physical storefronts—for example, ACC (Atlantic Coast Conference) stores and restaurants in malls and airports.

Conferences also provide leadership, governance, and professional development opportunities for athletics administrators and student-athletes of member institutions. Various parties—including presidents, athletics administrators (e.g., ADs and senior woman administrators [SWAs]), faculty athletics representatives, coaches, athletic trainers, sports information and athletics communication directors, and other athletics administrators or personnel—meet regularly to discuss possible or proposed legislation, issues and concerns related to scheduling and conference championships, and various hot topics in intercollegiate athletics. These meetings promote the exchange of ideas and best practices, determine conference policy, and provide networking opportunities.

Conference governance is generally determined through member representation, and the conference commissioner and administrators execute the wishes of the membership on a daily basis. However, as the face of the conference, the commissioner generally also possesses a strong voice in discussions about conference policy and may represent conference members in NCAA governance matters. The voice of athletes is represented at the conference level through the conference-sponsored student-athlete advisory committees (SAACs), through which student-athletes share ideas, discuss issues, and vote on whether to support proposed legislation. Conferences may also support students by providing postgraduate scholarships or internship opportunities.

NCAA GOVERNANCE STRUCTURE

The basic purpose of the NCAA is "to support and promote healthy and safe intercollegiate athletics, including national championships, as an integral part of the education program and the student-athlete as an integral part of the student body (NCAA

Constitution, 2022, p. 1). The operations of the association are managed through the national office, located in Indianapolis, Indiana. The highest-ranking employee of the national office is the president, who is advised by a senior management group that includes a chief policy advisor; a general counsel; a chief operations officer; and vice presidents of communication, membership, student-athlete affairs, championships, and alliances.

The NCAA staff is organized by functional units, providing services in membership and student-athlete affairs, enforcement, communication, finance and operations, championships, and administrative services. Contrary to popular media-driven perception, the national office does not independently dictate an NCAA agenda. Rather, the staff handles general promotion of intercollegiate athletics under the NCAA brand, facilitates national championships, helps interpret NCAA rules, and supervises rules enforcement.

Association-Wide Governance

Historically, the NCAA was a democratic membership organization with each member institution having equal representation and equal voice in the

Industry Profile

JAMES J. PHILLIPS

Commissioner, Atlantic Coast Conference

James J. (Jim) Phillips began his tenure as commissioner of the Atlantic Coast Conference (ACC) in 2021. Before becoming commissioner, he served as the athletics director and vice president for athletics and recreation at Northwestern University (2008-2021), where he was recognized as the 2018 *Sports Business Journal* Athletic Director of the Year. Prior to Northwestern, the Chicago native and youngest of 10 children was an AD at Northern Illinois University (2004-2008); associate director of athletics and senior associate director of athletics for external affairs at Notre Dame (2000-2004); assistant athletic director for annual giving and major gifts at the University of Tennessee (1998-2000); graduate assistant coach and assistant basketball coach at Arizona State University; and team manager and student assistant to the basketball team at the University of Illinois.

Commissioner Phillips is known for his focus on students and commitment to giving his stakeholders a voice. Individuals who work for him speak of how inclusive and accessible he is as a leader—how valued they feel and how he genuinely cares about them and their perspectives. This leadership style is not always easy. He was heavily criticized in 2021 for not supporting the expansion of the College Football Playoff (CFP) because he felt the proposal did not contain sufficient details. His head football coaches were unanimously unsupportive of the playoff expansion at the time due to such issues as the length of the season, the academic calendar, athlete healthcare, NCAA governance structure, federal legislation, and other concerns (Dodd, 2022). The following year, CFP leaders brought forward the proposal with more detail and it was supported.

Courtesy of Northwestern University.

Given that football media rights are the lifeblood of conference financial health, Phillips has focused on challenging the status quo in football and finding innovative paths toward competitive equity and revenue streams throughout the Football Bowl Subdivision. These discussions, building from the empowered voices of his coaches and ADs, will undoubtedly shape the future of college sport governance.

governance process. In 1973, the NCAA federated into three divisions, self-determined by the members according to their institutional philosophy. The association and each division operated under a democratic one-school/one-vote rule. In 1997, association-wide governance was changed to a representative structure that eliminated the one-school/one-vote approach. Instead, Division I, II, and III voting issues were separated, and the composition of the association-wide executive committee was altered to heavily favor Division I.

In 2022, the NCAA membership adopted a new constitution. The NCAA Constitution is the defining organizational document, so all association rules, policies, and procedures must be consistent with its overarching principles. The new constitution clearly establishes the autonomy and responsibility of each member institution for the management of its athletics program. It also provides a new association-wide governance framework and gives greater autonomy to each of the three NCAA membership divisions.

The core NCAA principles include

- the primacy of the academic experience,
- the collegiate student-athlete model, which does not permit "pay for play,"
- integrity and sportsmanship, which promotes the ideals of higher education and human development, including respect, fairness, civility, honesty, responsibility, academic integrity, and ethical conduct,
- protecting, supporting, and enhancing the physical and mental health and safety of student-athletes,
- reinforcing the responsibility of the members to monitor and control the athletics program and ensure rule compliance,
- a commitment to diversity, equity, and inclusion to create environments that promote an atmosphere of respect for and sensitivity to the dignity of every person,
- conducting programs free of gender bias in athletics activities, hiring, leadership, and advancement, and
- establishing divisional recruiting standards to promote informed decisions and balance the interests of student-athletes, their educational institution, and intercollegiate athletics overall (NCAA Constitution, 2022, pp. 1-4).

The Board of Governors

In restructuring the association-wide governance of the NCAA, the highest oversight is provided by the Board of Governors. This board consists of nine voting members who serve two-year terms: four representatives from Division I, including "at least one member institution president or chancellor and one conference commissioner"; one member *each* from Division II's and Division III's Presidents Council; two "independent" members, who may not be paid by any member institutions; and one recently graduated NCAA student-athlete. Ex officio, nonvoting members of the board include

- the NCAA president,
- the chairs of each of the three divisions' councils,
- the president of a historically Black college or university (HBCU) selected by the divisional representatives among the voting members, and
- one recently graduated NCAA student-athlete from each of the two divisions not represented by the voting student-athlete board member.

The duties and responsibilities of the Board of Governors include approving and overseeing the association budget, hiring and supervising the association president, and approving contracts related to media rights and revenue production. The board is also responsible for adopting and implementing legal strategy, risk mitigation, and government relations for the association. When issues affect the association as a whole, the board holds the authority to convene a joint meeting of the presidential and legislative bodies for all divisions. Similarly, if a constitutional amendment is required, or if a division has enacted legislation that may violate the association's constitution, the board holds the authority to call for a vote of the entire membership. Neither the Board of Governors nor the association's president may enact NCAA rules.

The Role of the NCAA President

Mark Emmert served the NCAA as president from 2010 to 2023. In April 2022, his resignation was announced. Charlie Baker, former governor of Massachusetts, assumed the role of president in March 2023. The role of the president is to oversee the national office under the guidance of the Board of Governors and divisional leadership bodies. The president is the signatory for all association contracts (including those that require Board of Governors approval), with additional responsibility for administering and enforcing those contracts. The president attends board meetings and holds the responsibility for casting a tie-breaking vote: given that the board numbers nine members, this role will likely be needed only in the event of abstention or absence of one voting member.

The Role of the Membership

The NCAA membership has a reduced role in overall association-wide governance. Only amendments to the constitution, which may be proposed and adopted at annual or special conventions, will require a two-thirds supermajority of all members in order to pass. At the 2022 NCAA Convention, the chairs of each divisional SAAC also voted on these matters for the first time (Media Center, 2022). Association-wide issues were rare under the past governance structure, with only four special conventions in the history of the NCAA.

Divisional Autonomy and Obligations

When the NCAA separated into three competitive divisions in 1973, divisional governance (federation) was also established. Each division has a unique operational philosophy and a separate NCAA manual of rules and regulations governing participation. A primary identifying distinction between the three divisions is the distribution of athletics scholarships. Division I institutions provide the most funding across all sports, Division II provides more limited funding, and Division III athletes receive no athletics-related scholarships. Other differences include the number of sports each division member must have, scheduling considerations, and financing sources (see table 2.1).

Division I is the most widely publicized and highly visible of the NCAA divisions. Many Division I schools are athletics powerhouses with elaborate facilities and large budgets. Built on financial inputs such as conference football television contracts, ticket sales, alumni donations, student fees, institutional subsidies, NCAA basketball tournament shares, and other NCAA allocations (Finances of Intercollegiate Athletics Database, 2022), Division I institutions offer the most financial aid to student-athletes. The amount of aid falls

Table 2.1 NCAA Divisional Differences

	Division I	Division II	Division III
Number of schools*	350 (32%)	310 (28%)	438 (40%)
Median undergraduate enrollment	8,960	2,428	1,740
Students who are athletes	1 in 23	1 in 10	1 in 6
Average number of teams per school	19.2	15.9	18.8
Percentage of NCAA student-athletes in division	37%	25%	39%
Athletics scholarship	Multiyear, cost-of-attendance athletics scholarship available; 57% of student-athletes receive athletics aid	Partial athletics scholarship model; 60% of student-athletes receive athletics aid	No athletics scholarships; 80% of student-athletes receive nonathletic aid

*Numbers are from 2019-2020. All other numbers are from 2018-2019.

Data from "Our Three Divisions," National Collegiate Athletics Association, 2022, https://ncaaorg.s3.amazonaws.com/about/ncaa/101/NCAA101_Our3Divisions.pdf.

within a range bracketed by a division-specific minimum and maximum.

The importance of football as a revenue sport in Division I was highlighted in 1978, when Division I was further subdivided based on competitive emphasis and funding for football. As of this writing, FBS schools provide a maximum of 85 full football scholarships and strive for postseason bowl bids; Football Championship Subdivision schools offer only 63 full scholarship equivalencies, which may be shared among no more than 85 student-athletes; and the remaining Division I members do not sponsor football teams, instead focusing their competitive emphasis and budgets on other sport offerings. These schools fall under the Division I-AAA category.

In 2014, the NCAA board voted to allow 64 schools in the richest five leagues (the ACC, Big 12, Big Ten, SEC, and Pac-12) further federation or autonomy to write many of their own rules. Some of the issues that will continue to evolve as this autonomy unfolds include cost-of-attendance stipends, staff sizes, recruiting rules, four-year-scholarship guarantees, agency rules, opportunities for athletes to pursue paid career opportunities, provisions and financial support for family members to attend postseason tournaments, and mandatory hours spent on individual sports. Regulations that will not be affected by the autonomy of these schools include rules governing on-field play, postseason tournaments, scholarship limits, transfer policies, and signing-day dates.

Division II offers an intermediate-level philosophy, providing limited athletics scholarships and emphasizing an appropriate balance between athletics participation and academics. Community service is also emphasized as an additional educational opportunity to develop productive, socially conscious citizens. Division II athletics programs include few students on full athletics scholarships, but a majority receive some sort of financial assistance for their athletics participation.

Division III is the NCAA's largest and most diverse division in terms of total membership, but 80 percent of the members are private institutions according to the 2022-23 Division III Facts and Figures (National Collegiate Athletics Association, 2022). Division III is philosophically set apart by its financial aid policy, wherein no athletics-based aid is offered. Still, almost 38 percent of all NCAA athletes compete at the Division III level. The emphasis in Division III is on the participation experience of student-athletes as an extension of their educational experience.

A college or university interested in becoming a member of the NCAA must complete a multistep, multiyear process before it is granted full membership privileges. Each division has unique requirements and slightly different processes and timelines for full membership. An institution must first self-evaluate to determine which division's philosophy most closely aligns with its own, then complete a membership application for that division. In the following candidacy or exploratory period, applicants are familiarized with NCAA rules and regulations, engage in self-study, and determine what changes need to be made in the athletics program in order to be compliant.

If a candidate institution is accepted for provisional or reclassification status, the school must pay a fee and membership dues. Depending on the division, provisional members are expected to engage in more rules education, comply with all NCAA rules, and undergo formal review of their programs for compliance. When the institution has met all requirements for membership, it is granted full membership status, which includes the privilege of qualifying for participation in NCAA postseason championships.

Schools can move their membership from one division to another by completing the membership process for reclassification. More schools have moved to a more competitive division, but some members have reduced the competitive emphasis and financial commitments in their athletics program by moving to a lower division. Similarly, institutions have sometimes chosen to change their affiliation from one national governing body to another. The same membership process applies regardless of whether an applicant was formerly independent or affiliated with another association. Much of the increase in NCAA membership at the Division II level has been from schools that were previously associated with the NAIA.

The new NCAA constitution provides the divisions with a broad right to self-governance, "including creation of sub-divisions or creation of a new division and determination of membership eligibility for these new organizations" (NCAA Constitution, 2022, p. 10). Each division's leadership—D-I's Board of Directors and the DII and DIII Presidents Councils—must have at least one student-athlete representative with voting power.

With the adoption of the new constitution, each NCAA division is now required to review and revise its division manual to ensure consistency with the governing principles in the NCAA constitution. Each division has autonomy to define the role of conferences, determine membership eligibility for institutions, and determine academic eligibility for student-athletes. Divisions are required to establish guidelines regarding student-athlete benefits, including those related to name, image, and likeness (NIL), with a focus on preventing exploitation by individuals or organizations not controlled by the member institution.

While the national office is responsible for conducting national championships, the divisions may collectively decide to create a national (interdivisional) championship. Each division also has expanded powers to determine which sports will be sponsored. Division II was the first to exercise this power by voting to expand its softball championship to six days effective in spring 2022. Similarly, the divisions hold the power to assess whether an institution may reclassify, or switch divisions, for a sport.

Going forward, much about the future of divisional governance is unknown. Each division has an assigned committee responsible for restructuring its governance in the context of its newfound autonomy: D-I has a Transformation Committee, D-II has an Implementation Committee, and D-III has a Constitution Advisory Council. Although the NCAA constitution tasked the divisions with implementing changes by August 1, 2022, little has been shared publicly regarding new policies and rule changes.

The Role of Conferences

Under the current constitution, each division has exclusive power to set policies for and oversee the conferences within them. The divisions may choose to relinquish these powers to their subdivisions, conferences, or even to the member institutions. Broadly, the constitution requires conferences to comply with and propagate the broad principles in the NCAA constitution. Multisport conferences must meet divisional membership criteria, including sport sponsorship minimums and regular-season competition requirements. If conferences create policies pertaining to their use of student-athletes' NIL, they are required by the NCAA constitution to disclose such policies to the athletes. See additional information about the Power Five Division I conferences in the sidebar Autonomy Economics and Division I Implications in the Power Five Conference.

The Role of NCAA Member Institutions

Article 6 of the NCAA Constitution confirms the principle of institutional control (NCAA Constitution, 2022, pp. 19-20). Each institution is responsible for the conduct of its athletics program, while adhering to guidance in the NCAA Constitution, which emphasizes the physical and mental health of student-athletes; student-athlete well-being; and diversity, equity, and inclusion. Members are required to submit annual reports for compliance with the constitution's principles, student-athlete eligibility and progress toward degree, and the financial data reports that the association maintains. Institutions must establish and maintain written policies regarding their usage of student-athletes' name, image and likeness, which must be provided to both the athletes and the public.

Member institutions are required to designate individuals to serve in the following roles: faculty athletics representative (FAR), senior woman administrator (SWA), athletics healthcare administrator, athletics diversity and inclusion designee, and senior compliance administrator. The faculty athletics representative and senior woman roles were previously required. The athletics healthcare administrator role is a new designation that appears consistent with the increased responsibility of each member institution to enhance student-athlete well-being and with the constitutional requirement to provide independent medical care for student-athletes. Similarly, the new athletics diversity and inclusion designation appears consistent with the constitutional principle to create inclusive athletics environments. Senior compliance administrator is a newly created designation, and it is assumed that designation will be given to the institution's

Autonomy Economics and Division I Implications in the Power Five Conference

Consider this 2021 data addressing the financial inequalities between the Power Five (major conferences plus Notre Dame) and the remaining Division I institutions as well as the data comparing the Power Five (major conferences plus Notre Dame) and the Group of Five institutions:

	Power Five (65 institutions)	All other Division Is (286 institutions)
Total enrollment (FTE)	1,785,000	3,515,000
Average enrollment	27,500	12,300
Athletic budgets (combined)	US$5.85 billion	US$5.73 billion
Athletic budgets (average)	US$90 million	US$20 million
Athletic subsidies (total)	US$380 million	US$3.7 billion
Athletic subsidies (average)	US$5.85 million	US$12.94 million
% Athletic subsidies	6.5%	65%
Athletic subsidies (per student)	US$210	US$1,050

Knight-Newhouse College Athletics Database

Revenue	Power Five	Group of Five
Other Revenue Revenue from the following categories: compensation and benefits provided by a third party; game program, novelty, parking, and concession sales; sports camps and clinics; athletics-restricted endowment and investments income; other operating revenue	6.93%	2.90%
Corporate Sponsorship, Advertising, and Licensing Revenue generated by the institution from royalties, licensing, advertisements, and sponsorships	10.57%	4.54%
Donor Contributions Funds contributed by individuals, corporations, associations, foundations, clubs, or other organizations external to the athletics program above the face value for tickets	22.39%	10.65%
Competition Guarantees Revenue received from participation in away or neutral-site games	0.07%	0.85%
NCAA/Conference Distribution, Media Rights, and Postseason Football Revenue received from the NCAA (including championships) and athletics conferences, media rights, and postseason football bowl games	47.36%	11.19%
Ticket Sales Revenue received from ticket sales for all NCAA-sponsored sports at an institution	3.30%	1.22%
Institutional/Government Support Revenue received from governments, direct funds from the institution for athletics operations, and costs covered and services provided by the institution to athletics (and for athletics debt) but not charged to athletics	7.02%	45.54%
Student Fees Fees paid by students and allocated for the restricted use of the athletics department	2.36%	23.11%
Excess Transfers Back Positive net revenues generated by athletics and transferred to the institution for nonathletics purposes: these funds are in excess of the transfers subtracted from the institutional and governmental funds allocated to athletics.	0.31%	0.00%

Expense	Power Five	Group of Five
Other Expenses Expenses related to the following categories: sports equipment, uniforms and supplies, fundraising, marketing and promotion, sports camps, spirit groups, direct overhead and administrative expenses, indirect institutional support, membership and dues, student-athlete meals, and other operating expenses	8.83%	7.21%
Medical Medical expenses and medical insurance premiums	2.44%	2.46%
Competition Guarantees Amounts paid to visiting participating institutions, including per diems and/or travel and meals	0.43%	0.62%
Recruiting Spending on transportation, lodging, meals, and other personnel and administrative expenses relating to recruitment of prospective student-athletes	0.44%	0.40%
Game Expenses and Travel "Game expenses" relate to competition expenses other than travel. "Travel" relates to spending on transportation, lodging, meals, and incidentals related to preseason, regular season, and postseason competition.	7.29%	7.64%
Facilities and Equipment Facility expenses include debt service, leases, and rental fees for athletics facilities. This includes overhead and administrative expenses. Equipment expenses include spending for items provided to teams, including in-kind equipment.	23.35%	20.81%
Coaches' Compensation Coaches' compensation includes bonuses and benefits, but not severance payments. This category includes direct payment and bonuses to coaches from the institution and from a third party.	22.39%	22.10%
Support and Administrative Staff Compensation Support and administrative staff compensation includes bonuses and benefits paid to all administrative and support staff. This category includes direct payment from the institution and payment from a third party. Severance payments for former coaches and administrators are also included.	21.30%	17.46%
Athletic Student Aid Total expenses for athletic student aid, including tuition and fees, room and board, books, summer school, tuition discounts, and waivers, including aid given to student-athletes who have exhausted their eligibility or who are inactive due to medical reasons	13.22%	21.29%

Knight-Newhouse College Athletics Database

Compared to the Group of Five revenue, a significant amount of Power Five revenue comes from external sources, such as other revenue, corporate sponsorship, advertising, licensing, donor contributions, conference distributions, media rights, and postseason football bowl games. The Group of Five members rely more heavily on institutional and government support and student fees. Within expenses, the Power Five members spend more on facilities and equipment and support staff and administration compensation with severance than their Group of Five peers.

(continued)

AUTONOMY ECONOMICS AND DIVISION I IMPLICATIONS IN THE POWER FIVE CONFERENCE *(continued)*

Proposed Solution for Enervated 1s: A Five-Year Plan

1. Restructure conferences by sports and regions, not universities or colleges.
2. Allow institutional choice of sports and competition level.
3. Limit institutional subsidies.

This new model of federation allows room for cost containment at the schools that desperately need to refocus on their academic mission and institutional affordability, rather than allowing the Power Five to direct their destiny. The implications of their financial models have minimal impact on their students. Their financial issues are centered on lawsuits (e.g., the O'Bannon case [see chapter 1], players' unions) and payment of players. Possibly they will evolve to a market-driven model of organization through regions or divisions and thus improve the benefits to the student-athletes, students, alumni, and institutions.

The Path of NCAA Division I Legislation

1. Schools or conferences propose legislation to the legislative council.
2. The legislative council discusses, revises, accepts, or rejects proposed legislation.
3. The board of directors discusses, revises, accepts, or rejects proposed legislation.
4. Approved legislation is posted for comment.
5. Members who oppose legislation may submit a request to override.
6. The working group on rules provides documentation of its discussions and draft proposals and requests feedback from the membership in order to address concerns as new legislation is adopted in the Division I manual.
7. The working group on enforcement provides documentation of its discussions and draft proposals and requests feedback from the membership in order to facilitate the enforcement or infractions process of this new legislation.
8. Legislation is implemented.

The Division I Board of Directors, Leadership Council, and Legislative Council are assisted by myriad committees and cabinets with very specific roles. This structure enables experts to evaluate issues, inform decision-making bodies, and carry out organizational tasks. Standards have been established to maintain gender, racial, and positional diversity on virtually all NCAA committees; however, all major leadership positions in Division I are based on conference appointments. Thus the representation of various positions is, for instance, limited to the responsibility that any given conference feels comfortable giving to a faculty athletics representative, athletics director, president, or conference official.

highest-ranking athletics administrator responsible for NCAA compliance. Additionally, all members are still required to have a SAAC. All of these roles are required, but the NCAA constitution grants each institution autonomy to determine how that role will serve its unique needs.

The Role of Student-Athletes in Governance

For the first time in the NCAA's history, the new constitution, approved in January 2022, provided student-athletes the right to voting representation on the Board of Governors, Division I Board of

Leadership Lesson

No Excuses

Intercollegiate athletics is founded on the principle of institutional autonomy—the premise that individual institutions govern athletics. Through their presidents (who are influenced by numerous stakeholders), individual schools are responsible for making the decisions that govern the industry. This reality contradicts the popular notion that the NCAA is an all-powerful entity led by a dictatorial czar. Certainly, the NCAA president holds a tremendous amount of power in determining initiatives and areas of emphasis, but in the end, industry-guiding legislation rests in the hands of individual institutions.

Until we acknowledge this reality and take responsibility at the institutional level, the many ills described in chapter 1 will likely continue. In the worst-case scenario, an author writing a similar text 150 years from now might marvel that the same issues remain. The leadership lesson in chapter 1 notes that leadership begins at the individual level and that your paradigm affects your own decisions and the future of the industry. The leadership lesson presented here emphasizes that such leadership comes with responsibility and accountability.

Sociologists have estimated that even the most introverted people influence 10,000 others in an average lifetime (Elmore, 2010; Maxwell, 2011). Given the public admiration and fandom associated with athletics departments, imagine the lifetime influence you might have as a leader in this industry. As challenges arise, will you be a thermometer or a thermostat? A thermometer measures the temperature around it, and its action is determined by its environment. A thermostat, on the other hand, sets the temperature. It affects the environment. As human beings, we may find it easy to blame our environment, history, colleagues, predecessors, government, or any number of other external influences that affect our circumstances. By doing so, however, we forgo the empowerment that comes from realizing our fundamental freedom to choose.

Viktor Frankl, a Jewish psychiatrist, was held prisoner in four Nazi concentration camps between 1942 and 1945. His family was killed, and he experienced cruelty, humiliation, misery, and suffering through the daily trials of life in the camps. Surviving this experience, he wrote *Man's Search for Meaning*, in which he said, "Everything can be taken from a man but one thing: the last of the human freedoms—to choose one's attitude in any given set of circumstances, to choose one's own way" (1963, p. 66). In every circumstance we arrive in, we can choose to focus our energies on what we can influence. We have the ability to choose how we respond. We have "response-ability" (see figure 2.1).

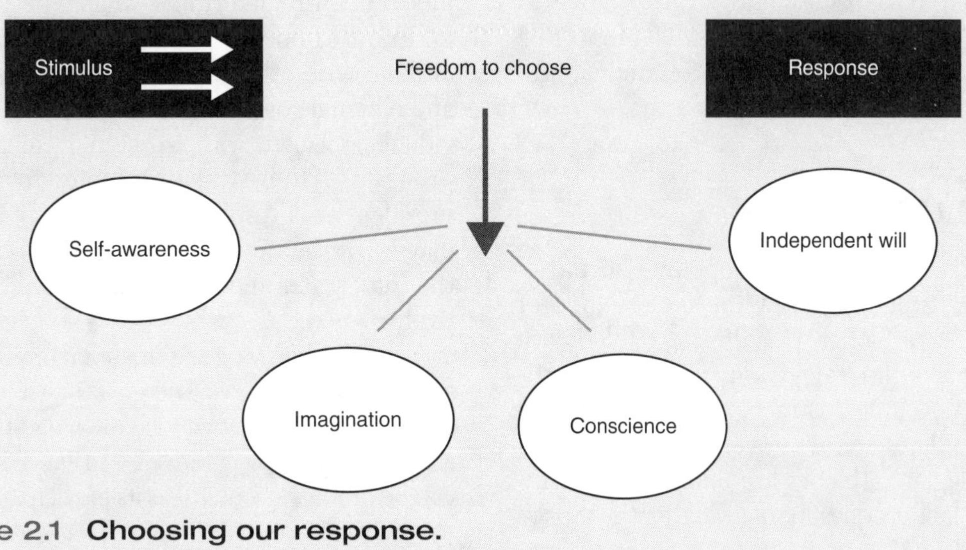

Figure 2.1 Choosing our response.

(continued)

LEADERSHIP LESSON *(continued)*

Contrast this frame of mind with a reactive approach. People who are reactive allow circumstances to determine their frame of mind. They are at the mercy of stimuli because they do not choose their response. Reactive people focus their energies on what they cannot control. They blame others, highlight the weaknesses of their peers, find external excuses and causes for their own circumstances, and ultimately feel trapped as victims of their environment.

> *I know of no more encouraging fact than the unquestionable ability of . . . man to elevate his life by conscious endeavor.*
>
> Henry David Thoreau

Putting into practice the wisdom of Viktor Frankl, on the other hand, can foster tremendous personal power. Similarly, the business and personal growth author Stephen Covey wrote, "Until a person can say deeply and honestly, 'I am what I am today because of the choices I made yesterday,' that person cannot say, 'I choose otherwise'" (Covey, 2004, p. 72). Within this proactive paradigm, there are no excuses. We cannot be bullied by external stimuli, and we cannot accept the passivity of a reactive paradigm. Covey urges individuals who find themselves taking an irresponsible position to use their resourcefulness and initiative (their "R and I").

Whatever the stumbling block or confounding issue, accept responsibility and choose how you respond. You may not be able to change the environment—you may not even be able to influence, for example, your president's vote on governance issues—but you will always have the power to choose your response. And as you focus on what you can influence, your circle of influence will grow.

Directors, and Division II and Division III Presidents Councils (NCAA Constitution, 2022, p. 16). The constitution also identifies the faculty athletics representative as the person for student-athletes to contact if anyone associated with the athletics department engages in behaviors inconsistent with the NCAA principles, particularly the principle of student-athlete health and well-being. It is important to note the faculty athletics representative, as defined in the constitution, is merely a reporting contact and not a legal advocate for student-athletes.

CONCLUSION

As discussed in the chapter-opening scenario, criticism is growing about the governance of intercollegiate athletics. Headlines are filled with multibillion-dollar television deals, multimillion-dollar coaching contracts, lawsuits, and calls for reform. The current governance structures in intercollegiate athletics are under attack, with many stakeholders questioning whether the money filtering through this industry is being handled wisely and who the key decision-makers really are in this administrative chain.

In this chapter, you have learned about the principle of institutional control. You have also learned how conferences serve their member institutions while also facilitating rules compliance and acting as intermediaries with the NCAA. Institutions independently determine what type of athletics program to operate and then choose how they affiliate with others through playing conferences and national governing bodies. In turn, each individual associated with an intercollegiate athletics program—from student-athletes to institution presidents—is responsible for understanding and playing by the rules of the governing bodies. Thus the integrity of intercollegiate athletics is collectively owned.

You now have a greater understanding of how the NCAA functions. The governance of intercollegiate athletics is not a top-down dictatorship but a bottom-up representative governance system that can be only as successful as its participants make it.

Case Study

Intercollegiate Athletics as an Enrollment Tool at DIII Schools

Elizabeth A. Gregg and Robert Zullo

While Division I athletics are the most visible, high-profile programs in the United States, Division III (DIII) athletics departments are the most prevalent within the NCAA. DIII athletics are unique because no athletic scholarships specifically for student-athletes are allocated. According to Bandre (2011), "Schools participating at this level must offer at least 10 programs, five each for men and women, of which a minimum of two for each gender are of the team sport (e.g., basketball or soccer as opposed to golf or tennis) variety" (p. 40). DIII athletics exist because college presidents believe that athletics contribute to the personal development of those participating and enhance the academic experience of all (Feezell, 2009; Miller & Kerr, 2002).

Typically, DIII schools do not profit from media rights or ticket sales like their DII and DI counterparts. To generate enough revenue to rationalize hosting athletic programs, DIII schools must be creative in their methods of making money. According to Bruder (2017), "NCAA Division III institutions often use intercollegiate athletics to increase enrollment in response to the challenges they face such as rising tuition, changing demographics, and economic struggles throughout the years" (p. 119).

During the 1990s and 2000s, one relatively prevalent way for a school to generate revenue was to add sports. Because of its roster sizes of 80-100 students, football has been one of the most popular additions to DIII athletic programs. Beaver (2014) iterated, "Players may receive grants and non-athletic scholarships, but almost all will finance their education at least in part through loans and parental support. A danger is that schools will spend too much on athletic facilities, staffing, and other costs, negating any financial benefit to the institution and diverting funds from academic needs" (p. 38). Schools also frequently add junior varsity football teams, rowing programs, and marching bands to boost enrollment. Coaches face pressure to maintain rosters capable of bolstering enrollment and thus producing tuition revenue. If a coach consistently fails to achieve roster target sizes, the coach could face termination.

There is data that demonstrates DIII athletes complete more credit hours and have higher graduation rates than their nonathletic peers (Todd & Brown, 2003). The addition of football players and junior varsity football teams also helps to offset gender imbalances at many institutions. There are downfalls, however. The College Sports Project determined that men entering DIII schools often have lower GPAs than their nonathletic peers and underperform during college. That said, there is no indication at this time that these men receive more money than traditional students. Thus, the NCAA has declined to intervene in athletics as an enrollment tool.

With this information in mind, how would you address the following scenarios if you were the Director of Intercollegiate Athletics at a DIII institution?

Questions to Consider

1. An incoming student is going to play two sports. Which coach gets credit for that recruit?
2. Aside from junior varsity games, what other types of activities or programs could an athletics department develop to attract student-athletes?
3. What resources does a school need to invest in if it accepts incoming student-athletes who may be at risk academically?
4. Is the use of DIII athletics as a recruiting tool an ethical strategy? Explain your response in detail.
5. At DIII institutions, coaches often have more than one job. Select a DIII university and examine the various titles of employees in the athletics department. Explain whether or not having more than one job title would be appealing to you.
6. What are hidden costs to adding DIII athletic programs beyond hosting teams and paying coaches?

DISCUSSION QUESTIONS

1. What are the limitations of institutional control in intercollegiate athletics?
2. Some argue that the NCAA has grown too big and powerful. Given the purpose of a national governing body as discussed in this chapter, how might you refute or support this argument?
3. The Drake Group, the Coalition on Intercollegiate Athletics, and the American Association of University Professors are faculty groups that have called for reform in intercollegiate athletics. Visit the web pages of these groups and explore some of the reforms they suggest. Do you support these suggested reforms? Why or why not?
4. Initially, conferences were organized to help facilitate competition between similarly situated schools with geographic proximity. How have conference missions changed, and what has spurred this change?
5. The top two levels of NCAA governance involve college presidents. What are the strengths and weaknesses of this structure?
6. Explain the differences between NCAA Division I, II, and III institutions. What are some strengths and weaknesses of each division?
7. Given the current NCAA Division I "top-down" legislative process (with override authority residing with the schools), is it possible for individual schools to enact change? How might a president, athletics director, FAR, or athletics administrator pursue a cause that he or she feels is important?

LEARNING ACTIVITIES

1. Research the rules passed by the Power Five conferences that were granted autonomy in 2014. What legislation has been adopted and how have these changes affected intercollegiate athletics?
2. Interview one of the following administrators to gain perspective about their role in the NCAA governance process: institutional compliance director, senior woman administrator, athletics director, faculty athletics representative, conference compliance administrator, or conference commissioner.

Leadership and Management

Erianne A. Weight, University of North Carolina at Chapel Hill

Robert H. Zullo, Slippery Rock University

In this chapter, you will explore

- the importance of vision in modern-day intercollegiate athletics administration,
- effective strategies for optimizing resource management,
- tools to help formulate information-driven decisions,
- the importance of effective communication throughout the organization and beyond, and
- strategies for effective personnel leadership.

LEADING WITH VISION

A new athletics director (AD) prepared for her first senior staff meeting. After working in the corporate world for 20 years, she had gotten a job as AD at her alma mater, a Division I Football Bowl Subdivision (FBS) school with an annual budget of US$90 million. The budgetary demands of the position were familiar—a fact that she had clearly articulated throughout the interview process—but balancing the budgetary demands and the academic mission of the department was going to be a new challenge.

As she approached her first week in this new position, she hoped to be guided by the vision, mission, and philosophy statements she had presented during the interview process. She had been attracted to this position with a desire to give back to the institution that had given her so much—as a fan, student-athlete, and alumna. But as the emails, phone calls, and appearance requests piled up on top of the budget cuts and the day-to-day demands of leading 18 teams and a 350-person staff, it became evident that the position would involve a continual battle to maintain vision and perspective through all the day-to-day operations.

As governmental and institutional financial constraints have led to an expectation for athletics departments to become more self-sufficient, modern-day athletics directors have absorbed many of the responsibilities and challenges typically faced by CEOs, educators, and politicians. As a result, ADs need to be well versed in identifying and building both revenue streams and relationships while maintaining a focus on their role as educators. In fact, they must play a diverse range of roles, as summarized eloquently in the following quotation:

> *Major-college ADs are expected to find ways to keep shoes on hundreds of athletes who will never make the pros while still investing heavily in traditional revenue-generating sports. They have to be fans and dispassionate observers. They must have creativity, imagination and vision, but they better know NCAA rules to the letter. They must lead, follow and get out of the way. They must be contrarians with deft conflict resolution skills. They must make deals and friends (wealthy ones, especially). They must hire and fire. They must understand contracts and contractors, traditions and academicians, Twitter and glitter (Berkowitz & Upton, 2011).*

An athletics director's responsibilities may include elements of being a lobbyist, designer, or fundraiser for new facilities; a legal expert when making decisions surrounding Title IX, liability, contracts, and other issues; a publicist, for promoting the good in an era in which bad news sells; and a strategist, making both long-term and short-term management decisions and financial plans. Whether an AD manages a staff of more than 400 people at the Ohio State University athletics department or a staff of 5 at a smaller school, many of the leadership demands of the position are the same. Issues range from competitive coaches vying for scarce departmental resources to persistent public commentary about departmental decisions. In this complicated context, the tasks of allocating fiscal, physical, and human resources can be challenging indeed.

LEADERSHIP

The job descriptions of a corporate CEO and a "big-time" athletics director are similar in many respects. They differ considerably, however, in the purpose and structure of their respective organizations. Most corporate CEOs pursue a general organizational purpose of creating value and are charged with maximizing returns for shareholders. In contrast, the purpose of an intercollegiate athletics department should be to facilitate educational opportunities for its athletes. As a result, the athletics director's role is to strengthen the philosophical, financial, and organizational structure necessary to create optimal experiences within the parameters defined through the university's own organization and its national governing body. (For information about divisional philosophies, see chapter 2.) ADs should clearly define, differentiate, and inspire departmental stakeholders, which requires them to delineate a vision, a mission, and core values.

Vision

A vision is a clear, concise, and inspiring statement defining what the athletics department wants to be or what it should look like in the future. This statement should be easy to remember and should provide a sense of direction and pride for the organization's stakeholders. A powerful vision can motivate and inspire staff members and athletes to accomplish extraordinary feats in an effort to reach for this image of the future. The following list gives a sampling of powerful visions from the corporate sector:

- To solve unsolved problems innovatively (3M)
- To make people happy (Disney)
- Making tools for the minds that advance humankind (Apple)
- Refresh the world, inspire moments of optimism and happiness, create value, and make a difference (Coca-Cola).

An athletics department might conceive of a vision statement like this: "To transform our athletes into world leaders."

Mission

An organizational mission is a unique statement of purpose describing why an athletics department exists and what distinctive competences or competitive advantages it uses in striving to achieve its vision. Mission statements can be used to frame SMART (specific, measurable, achievable, realistic, and time-bound) objectives that guide an organization toward its vision. Many organizations have confused their vision and mission statements or melded them into one statement of purpose, and some have used broad terms rather than unique processes and expected performance levels that can set the department apart from others. In doing so, they can lose the "big picture" inspiration underlying why the organization does what it does from a wider perspective, as expressed in the vision statement. As you peruse the following examples, you will note that many of the mission statements could be used as either a mission statement or vision statement. The differentiation between the two types of statements is far less important than the guiding purpose and inspiration they can bring. Here are some powerful mission statements from the corporate sector and intercollegiate athletics.

- To bring inspiration and innovation to every athlete in the world (Nike)
- Apple is committed to bringing the best personal computing experience to students, educators, creative professionals, and consumers around the world through its innovative hardware, software, and Internet offerings.
- 3M is committed to actively contributing to sustainable development through environmental protection, social responsibility, and economic progress.
- To be the world's best fast-food restaurant that gives excellent service, is clean, provides quality food, and puts a smile on every customer's face (McDonald's)
- To bring students, faculty, and staff together in educational activities that promote healthy lifestyles, enhance a sense of community, foster growth in leadership and teamwork skills, and encourage the pursuit of excellence (Massachusetts Institute of Technology Department of Athletics, Physical Education, and Recreation)
- To provide student-athletes with the opportunity to compete at the highest level while making progress toward completion of a degree of their choice in an environment consistent with high academic standards, a commitment to equity and diversity, sportsmanship, personal growth and development, and ethical conduct (University of Tulsa Athletic Department)
- We educate and inspire through athletics (University of North Carolina at Chapel Hill Athletics).

An athletics department might conceive of a mission statement like this: "To facilitate unmatched educational experiences for student-athletes through holistic training in the classroom, on the field, and throughout their university experience."

Core Values

Departmental values are shared beliefs about desired behaviors and outcomes that provide a framework in which decisions are made. Values drive the culture and priorities of an athletics department; therefore, identifying these shared beliefs can allow organizations to create a culture that embraces common goals and outcomes (Abreu et al., 2009; Berings et al., 2004). As a result, they should form the underlying current in the development of vision and mission statements.

The core value of candor, for instance, can improve organizational efficiency by encouraging employees to be honest with each other (Welch & Welch, 2005). Alternatively, a core value of excellence can emphasize the importance of process and doing things the right way in every departmental decision or challenge. The stated core values of the NCAA include belief in and commitment to the following ideals:

- The collegiate model of athletics in which students participate as an avocation, balancing their academic, social, and athletics experiences
- The highest levels of integrity and sportsmanship
- The pursuit of excellence in both academics and athletics
- The supporting role that intercollegiate athletics plays in the higher education mission and in enhancing the sense of community and strengthening the identity of member institutions
- An inclusive culture that fosters equitable participation for student-athletes and career opportunities for coaches and administrators from diverse backgrounds
- Respect for institutional autonomy and philosophical differences
- Presidential leadership of intercollegiate athletics at the campus, conference, and national levels

Value Culturalization

In 1994, Jim Collins and Jerry Porras released their influential book *Built to Last*, which described a core ideology common to many high-performing organizations. In the wake of this wisdom, corporations around the globe have adopted organizational statements of vision, mission, and values (Lencioni, 2002). In doing so, corporate leaders have sought to attain the purported benefits of a core ideology, including inspiration, motivation, empowerment, organizational effectiveness, and fulfillment of personal aspirations (Berry, 1999; Collins & Porras, 1994; Harmon, 1996; Pattakos, 2004; Van Rekom, Van Riel, & Wierenga, 2006). A clearly defined mission also brings external benefits, including the ability to attract well-qualified personnel (Brown & Yoshioka, 2003), to define a niche in the industry (Bolon, 2005) that can facilitate brand equity, and, for institutions of higher learning, to "attract the best recruits, garner the most donations, earn the most revenue, and reflect best upon their universities" (Meyer, 2008, p. 72).

Scholars have cautioned, however, that value, mission, and vision statements that are insincere or lack organizational buy-in and infusion can be detrimental and ultimately undermine leadership action. In particular, dissonance between stated and practiced values can lead to mistrust, cynicism, and skepticism because the effort is interpreted as a dishonest approach used simply to maximize productivity. The result can be more detrimental to the culture of an organization than not having defined values at all (Ferguson & Milliman, 2008; Ind, 2007; Milliman & Clair, 1995; Sull & Spinosa, 2007).

The challenge of creating buy-in through an organizational ideology may be more complex for modern-day athletics directors because the sanctity of college sport in its current form at the big-time level is continually questioned by scholars and the media (Branch, 2011; Deford, 2011; Splitt, 2011; Vedder, 2011). Indeed, the combination of commercial and educational values that often seem at odds with each other can leave stakeholders searching for direction. However, this tumultuous climate can also create an opportunity for leadership as stakeholders search for guidance (Kotter, 1996). Because the NCAA is a member-driven organization, these issues fall within the sphere of influence of ADs through their college presidents, and a powerful vision can facilitate tremendous buy-in, hope, and inspiration for members of an athletics department.

As ADs strive to overcome negative media reports and inspire their employees, they must realize that creating and communicating values constitutes only one step in the process of maximizing organizational efficiency. Research has

Industry Profile

DICK RASMUSSEN

Executive Director, University Athletic Association

When asked about Division III sports, many sports enthusiasts would think of the absence of athletic scholarships at regional colleges and universities whose athletes are competing for the love of the game. These students would travel by bus to their area competitions and avoid overnight trips as a cost-cutting strategy. One Division III athletic conference is uniquely different from its peers in that the University Athletic Association (UAA) features eight major research universities in competition. The schools include: Emory University (Atlanta, Georgia), Case Western Reserve University (Cleveland, Ohio), Washington University in St. Louis (Missouri), University of Rochester (New York), Brandeis University (Boston, Massachusetts), University of Chicago (Illinois), New York University (New York City), and Carnegie Mellon University (Pittsburgh, Pennsylvania). Dick Rasmussen has served as the conference's executive director since 1987, promoting athletic and athletic excellence across the geographically expansive conference. His leadership has promoted over 45 national championships, over 3,200 All-American honors, and over 670 Academic All-American honors. The former baseball coach and business manager at the University of Rochester, Rasmussen was instrumental in his role as part of the planning group to initiate the conference in 1985. This included preparing briefing material, financial projections, and presentations.

> *"There are few commissioners in the history of the NCAA—at any level—that are more closely identified together with their conference than Dick Rasmussen and the University Athletic Association. In his 30 years as the only executive the UAA has ever known, the conference stands out not only for its incredible academic reputation and its numerous athletic success stories, but also for Dick's consistent vision and professionalism. Throughout his career, he has also given back selflessly to college athletics in his leadership roles with the Division III Commissioners Association (DIIICA) and the National Association of Division III Athletic Administrators (NADIIIAA). As a young commissioner, I personally learned a great deal from him simply by observing his interactions with others and watching how he handled himself in professional settings, and I remain grateful for the guidance and mentoring he has provided me over the past 10 years. The current position of the UAA as one of the flagship conferences in NCAA Division III is a direct reflection of Dick's wisdom and steady leadership." Joe Onderko, Commissioner, Presidents' Athletic Conference (University Athletic Association, 2017)*

He has served on the NCAA council responsible for the overall governance of the NCAA and the NCAA Division III Management Council (responsible for the overall direction of championships and programs); chaired the NCAA Division III Membership Committee, which develops regulations and educational programs for institutions seeking membership, and was a member of the NCAA Committee on Women's Athletics. He also served as a member of a focus group that facilitated the initial NCAA Diversity Education Program with the Minority Interest and Opportunities Committee and in 1994 helped to found the National Association of Division III Athletic Administrators (NADIIIAA). A chemistry major, he played both football and baseball as an undergraduate at the University of Rochester before earning his master's degree in science education and his doctorate in higher education from the school. He has been nationally recognized numerous times for his service to intercollegiate athletics, especially at the Division III level, and continues to be a tremendous influence on all around him.

demonstrated that the most successful results come from defining values and imparting them to an organization through value creation, consistent communication, and synergistic rewards systems (Van Rekom et al., 2006). "From the first interview to the last day of work, employees should be constantly reminded that core values form the basis for every decision the company makes" (Lencioni, 2002, p. 117). This process starts with the example set by upper-level administrators and continues through the integration of these values in all of the organization's processes—a process known as "culturalization." This type of leadership empowers employees to make effective situational decisions through ingrained organizational principles (Ouchi, 1979; Sull, 2010).

Most intercollegiate athletics departments have defined vision, mission, or value statements, but they vary in the extent to which they are unique (Meyer, 2008; Ward & Hux, 2011) or effectively used and ingrained in the organization (Cooper & Weight, 2012; Cooper et al., 2014). In a study examining Division I athletics directors' perceptions of core values, Cooper et al. (2014) explored the presence of a leader–value continuum in intercollegiate athletics departments. On one end of the continuum, they uncovered efficient administrators who fully embraced departmental core values and proactively rooted day-to-day decisions in values. On the other end of the spectrum, however, they found evidence of administrators who embraced a hypocritical approach in which they professed to believe (or proclaimed) values to be important yet did not act in accordance with these values.

Undoubtedly, the majority of administrators fall somewhere in the middle of the continuum. They aspire to create efficient organizations driven by culturalized values yet have not fully achieved buy-in and therefore leave untapped potential in their sphere of influence (Cooper et al., 2014). Ultimately, effective leaders must "create a vision, articulate the vision, passionately own the vision, and relentlessly drive it to completion" (Jack Welch as qtd. in Tichy & Charan, 1989, p. 173).

Situational Vision and Decision-Making

In *Developing the Leader Within You* (2005), John C. Maxwell explained that one of the most common questions from people in leadership is

Technology Tools

Staying Current With Online Resources

Athletics administrators can and should stay abreast of current events and interact with colleagues by attending local, regional, and national conferences regularly. Administrators must also keep up to date with relevant publications, both popular and academic. Many administrators utilize the D1 Ticker, CollegeAD, and similar tools that automatically email current headlines to your inbox. (There is also a D2 Ticker, a D3 Ticker, and a D3 Playbook.) Other sources include job boards, podcasts, and industry-specific profiles and research. In addition, there are sport-specific websites and social media to follow, like FootballScoop.com, Hoop Dirt, Women's Hoop Dirt, and Skippers Dugout, among others, for current events and industry updates. Many of the resources are free to students.

Additionally, there has been an explosion of name, image, and likeness (NIL) deals with student-athletes since 2021, when the NCAA legalized this activity. The Business of College Sports website, developed by Kristi Dosh, provides a page dedicated to NIL news, deals, policies, marketplaces, and tax implications. This web page is a great financial resource for anyone researching or working in the NIL sector, and the weekly newsletter offers current news and analyses. It also includes podcasts and social media resources for current events and headlines.

NIL for Student Athletes

https://*businessofcollegesports*.com/name-image-and-likeness/

how to develop a vision for their organization. This question is crucial because, until it is answered, a person will be a leader in name only.

Throughout the day-to-day demands of an athletics director, decisions and situations arise that may carry long-term or far-reaching implications. In these situations, a leader can avoid viewing the problem from the weeds by stepping back for a moment to reflect and then composing a vision specific to the situation. In some instances, a situational vision may naturally surface, but more often than not, an effective leader needs to consciously create a process to guide the department through each unique circumstance. Whether facing a contract renegotiation, a personnel problem, an outsourcing decision, or a new initiative, leaders can use certain strategies to navigate any given complex circumstance. These strategies include beginning with the end in mind (Covey, 1989), pondering the hoped-for result of the decision 2 (or 10!) years down the road, examining the most significant stakeholders affected, and formalizing a decision-making process.

When confronted with a challenging decision, it is crucial to gather high-quality information. Yet in our increasingly fast-paced communication environment, administrators often feel pressure to make decisions quickly. In reality, this is a reckless approach perpetuated by the notion that a powerful organizational "quarterback" will be able to assess the field and make snap judgments in order to lead the team to victory. Some intercollegiate athletics administrators who have acted rashly later find themselves being questioned about irresponsible decisions that clearly contradicted federal law and legal precedent (Ridpath et al., 2008; Yiamouyiannis & Lawrence, 2009).

Instead, scholars have urged administrators to use rationality in their decision-making (see figure 3.1) and to optimize decisions rather than simply "satisficing" (i.e., making an inadequate compromise between satisfying and sufficing) (Simon, 1977). The practice of satisficing reflects the limits of human decision-making based on available information, time, and information-processing ability, which is often referred to as "bounded rationality" (Simon, 1977). Certainly, there are limits, and in some situations, it is acceptable to "satisfice" and make a "good enough" decision rather than overthinking it. Too often, however, people jump to the good-enough approach too early and make grave mistakes that could have been easily avoided through a more systematic decision-making process.

Another approach, the Delphi method, can be used to capitalize on the skill of experts in forecasting or decision-making. In this process, 8-10 experts who remain anonymous are presented with an issue or question. They respond in writing, and a summary of all the experts' opinions is compiled and sent back to each expert. The experts can then modify their position based on the feedback of the others. Respondents whose opinions deviate from the median are asked to defend their positions. After multiple rounds, a final summary report is sent to management.

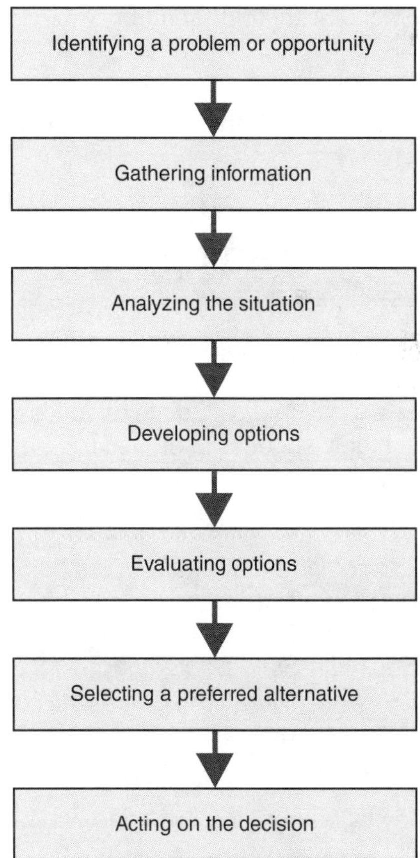

Figure 3.1 The rational decision-making model.

Reprinted by permission from "Rational Decision Making," *The Happy Manager* (Chester, United Kingdom: Apex Leadership). Available: www.the-happy-manager.com/rational-decision-making-model.html

Whether one uses a formal decision-making model such as the Delphi method or another approach, gathering high-quality information increases the likelihood of optimizing a decision rather than merely satisficing. These methods also provide data to justify decisions. This data can be particularly useful if a decision turns out to be less than ideal.

In moments of turmoil, when you receive troubling information, ask yourself, "What is the other side of the story?" Empower those around you to have patience in the face of criticism and to take the time to gather the information needed in order to make an informed decision. After all, you simply don't know what you don't know. The situational vision that led the University of North Carolina at Chapel Hill (UNC–Chapel Hill) through the challenge of a major infractions case in 2010 and 2011 provides a glimpse of the structure that this approach can bring to difficult organizational circumstances.

One of the most significant challenges faced in intercollegiate athletics administration is compliance. No amount of policing or departmental staffing seems to be enough. Instead, compliance needs to be built on a culture of accountability emphasized by each departmental stakeholder. In order for an organization to feel congruence in this and other facets of its mission, it helps to have a leader at the helm who champions the cause. In other words, compliance comes from the top. Athletics directors must embrace the responsibility of challenging the status quo within their organizations and governance structures to inspire positive change.

Considerable research has been conducted to examine how an individual can lead an organization to accomplish extraordinary feats by inspiring dedication, loyalty, and admiration in subordinates. Throughout the 1970s and 1980s, several theories founded upon the importance of a leader's ability to express a compelling vision, display charismatic behavior, and lead through personal example arose (Bass, 1985; Bennis, 1984; Burns, 1978; Graeff, 1983; House, 1971; Vroom & Yetton, 1973). One philosophy that emerged during this era was the

Embry-Riddle University Jumps From NAIA to NCAA Division II

In summer 2013, ideas and talk that had begun the year before turned into action as Embry-Riddle Aeronautical University, located in Daytona, Florida, began the process of moving from the National Association of Intercollegiate Athletics (NAIA) to the NCAA. Embry-Riddle's Eagles athletics department, highly successful at the NAIA level, completed a feasibility study of joining either the Peach Belt Conference or the Sunshine State Conference, added a softball program, and committed to adding women's basketball for 2015-16 (Woronoff, 2013). Then athletics director Steve Ridder said:

> *I think many individuals on our campus agree that the Sunshine State Conference with other private institutions in our own backyard is a great choice for us. I think for the first time in a number of years there is some real interest for growth and expansion, particularly in the Sunshine State Conference. That's what we're seeing and hearing. We can't control what they're thinking and what they're going to decide, but hopefully by end of summer some things are going to materialize. We're having some dialogue and interaction. I think we just have to be patient. (Woronoff, 2013)*

The invitation from the Sunshine State Conference ultimately arrived and Embry-Riddle competed its final NAIA season in 2014-15. The 2015-16 and 2016-17 academic years were provisional years for most Eagles sports, meaning no postseason play. The transition, a three-year process, required formal approval from the NCAA Division II Management Council (Dean, 2017). The school was a full Division II member for the 2017-18 academic year. The move enhanced the school's athletic reputation, according to Ridder, because "everyone recognizes the NCAA" (Dean, 2017). The school concluded the 2021-22 academic year with a Top 30 finish in the Division II LEARFIELD Directors' Cup standings, their best since moving up (Mayfield, 2022).

theory of transformational or visionary leadership (Bass, 1985; Bennis, 1984; Burns, 1978). This theory describes the ability of a leader to inspire an organization by expressing a determined vision that leads to positive organizational change or rebirth as employees are motivated and empowered (Bass, 1985; Conger & Kanungo, 1987). Theorists have described the effects that can be achieved by a transformational leader, including the metamorphosis of followers into leaders and creating an intrinsic desire of subordinates to surpass the leader's expectations (Yukl, 1989). Specific dimensions of a transformational leadership approach are listed in table 3.1.

Many transformational leaders have shaped intercollegiate athletics. Jeremy Foley, for example, is known as a man with great vision who has applied a top-to-bottom team approach in his 25-year tenure as director of athletics at the University of Florida, which concluded in 2016. The mission of the department under his leadership was to produce good citizens, to graduate the athletes who come through the program, and to win with grace and integrity (Mondello, 1997). Throughout his tenure, he led the department to a perfect record of top-10 finishes in the National Association of Collegiate Directors of Athletics all-sport standings, and he is respected for his support of all programs in the department—not just the most visible sports (Smits, 2016). Indeed, in an era in which the vast majority of Division I athletics departments engage in deficit spending, Foley added three women's sports and oversaw a budget responsible for contributing more than US$55 million to help fund University of Florida academic endeavors (Floridagators.com, 2010). He helped to increase the budget from US$30 million in the 1991-92 academic year to US$119.3 million in his last year and remains in an emeritus role with the athletics department (Smits, 2016). Kent Fuchs, the University of Florida president, praised Foley:

> *Jeremy's amazing accomplishments as Athletics Director are well known, and the university is very grateful to him for the national championships, a winning sports program that is highly ranked year after year, and the growth of women's sports. Jeremy also has a well-deserved reputation for recruiting the nation's most talented coaches and building an athletic association that is recognized among the best in the country. What I especially appreciate about Jeremy, however, is his integrity and his commitment to our students. Success to Jeremy is a student athlete who graduates and wins championships the right way. That is the culture he created over his 25-year career and it is what we will remember about his remarkable tenure as athletics director. (Smits, 2016)*

Responding to Foley's gutsy decision to hire 39-year-old Texas defensive coordinator Will Muschamp as the football head coach, successor to the very successful Urban Meyer, columnist Gene Frenette (2010) commented, "He's not afraid to think outside the box or risk being bombarded down the

Table 3.1 Transformational Leadership Dimensions

Dimension	Description
Vision	"The expression of an idealized picture of the future based around organizational values" (p. 332)
Inspirational communication	"The expression of positive and encouraging messages about the organization, and statements that build motivation and confidence" (p. 332)
Supportive leadership	"Expressing concern for followers and taking account of their individual needs" (p. 333)
Intellectual stimulation	"Enhancing employees' interest in and awareness of problems, and increasing their ability to think about problems in new ways" (p. 333)
Personal recognition	"The provision of rewards such as praise and acknowledgement of effort for achievement of specified goals" (p. 334)

Reprinted by permission from A.E. Rafferty and M.A. Griffin, "Dimensions of Transformational Leadership: Conceptual and Empirical Extensions," *The Leadership Quarterly* 15, no. 3 (2004): 329-354, with permission of Elsevier.

road by an orange-and-blue legion of second-guessers" (p. 94). Foley also did not hesitate to make a change later, when Muschamp won only 57 percent of his games in four years, became less competitive in conference play, and lost national relevance. Foley valued such criteria in his coaches as integrity and commitment to NCAA rules, respect for other sports in the department, a strong work ethic, and a high level of passion and energy (Newell, 2008). Foley stated, "In the competitive world, you have to outwork people. I like people who will work very hard and who will focus on the positives rather than the negatives" (qtd. in Mondello, 1997, para. 14). In keeping with this approach, Foley encourages athletics administrators to talk about the positives in intercollegiate athletics, which he feels are never as broadly reported as the negatives (Mondello, 1997).

Other examples of transformational athletics directors include Ron Wellman and Peter Roby. Wellman, athletics director of Wake Forest University, one of the smallest schools to compete at the NCAA Division I FBS level, led the school to tremendous achievement over 27 years, until his retirement in 2019. Former Atlantic Coast Conference Commissioner John Swofford has commented on Wellman's success and respect in the industry: "I think he has earned it by the consistency he has had over the years, by the standards he sets for himself and those around him, by his capabilities administratively, which are enormous, by the manner in which he treats people, and the manner in which he conducts himself" (qtd. in Collins, 2009).

Roby was the former athletics director at Northeastern University from 2007 to 2018 and is a vocal leader for social change through sport education and values-driven leadership. He freely shares his vision of being in the business of "people development." Roby modeled his emphasis on education in his athletics department by instituting various programs to help athletes stay on top of their studies. One such program was "lecture-capture," wherein the athletics department supported the recording and uploading of lectures for students who miss class due to athletics competition (Roby, 2012). Roby, who served as interim athletics director at Dartmouth College from 2021 to 2022 to assist the department during the COVID-19 pandemic and to move past Title IX challenges, encourages athletics administrators to be led by values of conviction rather than values of convenience and urges leaders to hold themselves accountable to the students they serve (Wykes, 2022).

Regardless of the strategy used in leading an organization, the message must be communicated powerfully and frequently in order for a new vision, mission, culture, initiative, or set of values to take root and flourish. The message can be disseminated formally (e.g., through meetings, memos, and official departmental lines of communication) and informally (e.g., through discussions during casual lunches, modeling through example, and distribution of unique reminders featuring highlighted keywords). For more on this topic, see the sidebar titled Culture Is the Shadow of the Leader: Embedding Culture Within an Organization.

In most situations where organizational change is needed, buy-in is difficult to achieve without a sense of urgency or need for the change, as well as support for the change from powerful leaders in the organization. John Kotter has outlined an eight-step change management model that details how to implement organizational change (see table 3.2). When pursuing a cultural initiative, it is important to remember that an athletics director's time is one of the most valuable resources in the department. Therefore, how ADs choose to spend their time sends the clearest message about departmental priorities and sets the tone in the department about what is important.

MANAGEMENT

Although a visionary leader can make a good organization great by inspiring stakeholders, a solid management structure is also necessary for optimal organizational effectiveness. Management functions include leading, planning, staffing, organizing, and evaluating in an effort to accomplish a goal. Thus far in this chapter, we have discussed leading and planning; this section focuses on staffing, organizing, and evaluating.

For an employee, few things are more frustrating than running into bureaucratic roadblocks that do not make sense. Whether it is the structure of a department within a larger unit or a policy that seems to hinder progress, the "way things are done" often impedes forward momentum. Athletics directors can be constrained by the overall university structure in which they function, but there is

Culture Is the Shadow of the Leader: Embedding Culture Within an Organization

Primary Embedding Mechanisms

- What leaders pay attention to, measure, and control on a regular basis
- How leaders react to critical incidents and organizational crises
- How leaders allocate resources
- Deliberate role modeling, teaching, and coaching
- How leaders allocate rewards and status
- How leaders recruit, select, promote, and communicate

Secondary Articulation and Reinforcement Mechanisms

- Organizational design and structure
- Organizational systems and procedures
- Rites and rituals of the organization
- Design of physical space, facades, and buildings
- Stories about important events and people
- Formal statements of organizational philosophy, creeds, and charters

Reprinted by permission from E.H. Schein, *Organizational Culture and Leadership,* (San Francisco, CA: Jossey-Bass, 2010), 36, permission conveyed through Copyright Clearance Center, Inc.

Table 3.2 Kotter's Eight-Step Change Management Model

1. Create urgency.	In order for stakeholders to buy in to the change and the strategy, they need to believe that change is needed.
2. Form a powerful coalition.	Change will be facilitated if you create a team of influential people who believe in the strategy. Their power may come from longevity, status, expertise, or political clout.
3. Create a vision for change.	Simplify the strategy into a form that encapsulates its potential and is easily understood by all stakeholders.
4. Communicate the vision.	Communicate the strategy frequently and powerfully. Demonstrate the type of behavior that is integral to the plan and openly address ideas and potential concerns.
5. Remove obstacles.	Alter any structures or processes that can impede the implementation of the plan. Eliminate any barriers to progress.
6. Create short-term wins.	Success breeds success and can be a strong motivator. Set short-term targets that can be celebrated along the journey toward complete implementation of the marketing plan.
7. Build on the change.	Be careful not to declare success too soon. After each victory, analyze what was done right and what could be better. Strive for continuous improvement.
8. Anchor the changes in corporate culture.	In order for the strategy to stick and remain grounded in the organization over time, communicate progress often and emphasize ideals of the strategy in hiring and training new staff members.

Reprinted by permission from E.A. Weight and M. Walker, "Ensuring Strategic Sport Marketing Success," in *Sport Marketing: Winning Strategies for Sport Business Success,* edited by B. Turner et al. (Dubuque, IA: Kendall Hunt, 2012).

Professional Development

Graduate Programs in Intercollegiate Athletics

Graduate programs exist in sport management and sport administration, but some programs focus on intercollegiate athletics. Ohio University started the first sport administration program in 1966, and the University of North Carolina established the initial graduate program with an emphasis on college sports in 1982. Subsequent programs have been launched at the University of Washington, the University of Oklahoma, the University of Virginia, Coker University (South Carolina), Mississippi College, Springfield College (Massachusetts), Messiah University (Pennsylvania), and California University of Pennsylvania. Other schools, including Northeastern University (Massachusetts); the University of Mississippi; and the University of Nevada, Las Vegas, have added certificate programs at the graduate level. Students are encouraged to search online for the latest programs as schools are consistently making updates to their academic offerings.

often a fair amount of latitude in what can be done in the department itself. Specifically, the athletics director can exert considerable control over the *who* (staffing) and the *how* (organization, evaluation, and communication) of athletics department management.

Staffing

The importance of staffing is easily understood by anyone who has fielded an athletic team. You may be the best coach in the world with a highly trained and well-prepared team, but if your athletes average a 6-inch (15-centimeter) or 50-pound (23-kilogram) deficit compared to the competition, it will be difficult to win. Successful Penn State University lacrosse coach Jeff Tambroni explained how he attracts great players and builds winning a team year after year: "We know who our type of player is. We have identified what we are looking for. We tell them that we will work and train harder than any other team in the country . . . so if they don't have a strong work ethic they are not our type of player" (qtd. in Gordon, 2009).

In the best-selling book *Good to Great,* Jim Collins explained that a critical element of successful organizations is the competence to get the right people on the bus and put them in the right seats (2001). In other words, it is critical for administrators to build a team that shares the organization's guiding philosophy. It is also wise for leaders to focus on key responsibilities rather than job titles. Collins recommends that leaders list key positions, roles, and duties and then determine what percentage of them are currently handled by the right people. Increasing this figure to 100 percent is one of the most difficult tasks that leaders need to be willing to address. Some longtime traveling companions may need to be asked to get off the bus before the newly charted route can be traveled, and some duties may be best fulfilled through outsourcing.

In a different approach toward the same staffing goals, Jon Gordon (2009), consultant for numerous professional and college coaches and teams, recommends an exercise of identifying several people in the organization whom you wish you could clone. Write down their characteristics and create benchmarks for identifying the right person for each position. Gordon reminds leaders to hire the right kind of people—those who fit the organizational culture. If you want a creative culture, hire creative people; if you want a positive culture, hire positive people. "Remember," he emphasizes, "the people you surround yourself with will often determine the kind of ride it's going to be" (p. 6).

One pitfall of this approach that should be consciously avoided is hiring staff who all think alike or who have similar cultural backgrounds and similar worldviews. Although Gordon uses "cloning" as a metaphor to illustrate attributes to replicate, administrators should seek as much diversity as possible. Research has demonstrated that the more perspectives, experiences, empathy, and education are collected within an organization, the greater an

Jared Benko on Hiring and Firing Coaches

Jared Benko became Georgia Southern University's director of athletics in March 2020, when the COVID-19 pandemic began. He was instrumental in leading the department and student-athletes through the pandemic, helping the football program to play all of its regular season games. He has escalated fundraising to new heights, implemented significant facility upgrades, and added numerous head coaches, including football and men's basketball. A University of Georgia double graduate with a bachelor of science in sport studies and a master of public administration, Benko worked at his alma mater, the University of Arkansas, Auburn University, and Mississippi State University prior to his move to Georgia Southern.

Scrutiny and second-guessing—by the media, by an institution, and now even by researchers—are heaviest at the time of a firing rather than at the time of a hiring. What aspect of the process (such as ticket sales, fundraising, recruiting) does the media not see?

Terminating a coach without cause (e.g., by convenience) is a decision that is not taken lightly. From a best practice standpoint, this decision takes into account several areas: a team's competitive performance, academic record, recruiting, and interest/support of program from an internal and external constituent. The competitive success (or lack of) is the most outward-facing metric that the media observes. Working relationships, academic performance, revenue impact, etc., are a few items often not considered.

Given the dollar amounts involved in firing a coach and then hiring a new coach, what process do you use to examine the new coach's ability to achieve more success than their predecessor?

Often when hiring a new coach (on the heels of dismissing your previous coach), one looks to address deficiencies from the last staff. Regardless of the sport or change in personnel, I look for the following attributes for coaches I hire: integrity, intelligence, leads with optimism, relentless recruiter (student-athletes and staff), excellent communicator (demonstrated ability to manage difficult conversations), embraces being visible in the community, accessibility and approachability, supports complete student-athlete experience (ensures right fit for your school), relentless focus on culture, has a "good" edge about them, proven track record of making each program better, and coached/played in a great program(s)/mentored by great coaches. Taking these attributes into consideration during the hiring process mitigates risks related to performance.

When determining the length of a contract for a new coach, how do you balance the need for long-term job security (recruiting perception) against a possibly shorter time line to get results on the field?

Personnel contracts for coaches can be structured in many ways. Often, the state by which the contract is drafted and executed has various rules (e.g., one-year contract) by which you must adhere. Sometimes, universities and/or foundations established to support athletics can draft an income guarantee contract that supplements a coach's university contract. Regardless, liquidated damages as a result of terminating a contract for convenience are often at the forefront of the decision-making process an administrator must consider while finalizing a personnel contract. These damages can often impact the term of the agreement. Additionally, while longer-term contracts help with messaging to recruits, administrators must always balance fiscal responsibility.

Interview with Benko, July 2022.

organization's creativity, productivity, and quality (e.g., Earley & Mosakowski, 2000; Ely & Thomas, 2001; Swann et al., 2003).

Use of Search Firms in Athletics Staffing

At the Division I level, the use of search firms has become increasingly common in high-profile recruitment of athletics directors and coaches of football and men's basketball. Each year, Division I schools conduct roughly 35 to 45 searches through the use of an outside agency (Smith, 2011). Dave Brandon, former University of Michigan athletics director and former CEO of Domino's Pizza, generally disliked using search firms in the corporate world but sees tremendous advantages in using them in intercollegiate athletics because of the highly specialized nature of the position.

> *You're dealing with a compressed period of time, and you need to be as efficient as possible. To be productive, you've got to know the agents, the coaches. You've got to set up meetings and move around the country, all while maintaining confidentiality . . . [O]ur football search was done in six days, and if I had done it on my own, it would have taken two to three weeks, and there would have been a lot of frustrating moments in the process. (qtd. in Smith, 2011)*

Search firms offer an array of services that can be tailored to fit a university's needs (see figure 3.2), including developing a candidate profile, meticulously screening résumés, developing a pool of candidates, enticing candidates to the institution, and negotiating and developing contracts (Ammons and Glass, 1988).

Organizing

In order to maximize an organization's potential, a leader must also create a clear and efficient structure with defined channels of communication and divisions of labor. If effective people are placed in ineffective structures, they experience frustration, demotivation, and confusion. Putting it in terms of athletics, coaches must not only recruit the right athletes but also give them proper coaching and training. A group of phenomenal athletes with minimal direction may be able to compete against a well-trained opponent for a while, but as the competition continues, the team with superior conditioning and coaching is likely to win. In a departmental setting, all the effort spent to get the right people on the bus can quickly unravel in the face of bureaucratic minutiae. The best people will then begin to peruse NCAA job listings in search of alternative professional homes. As with most leadership challenges, departmental organization requires both science and art.

An athletics department is typically housed within the larger university organizational structure, and the athletics director usually reports either to the university president or to the vice president of student affairs. The department itself is generally led by the AD with help from a senior staff comprising associate and assistant ADs who are each responsible for unique functional responsibilities (e.g., compliance, marketing, finance, student affairs, operations). A few athletics departments operate as separate men's and women's programs, each with its own director, and some departments are housed with recreation or exercise and sport science departments that administer intramurals, recreational sports, and related educational programs in addition to varsity athletics.

Within the department's senior staff, the NCAA has mandated that one woman hold the designation of senior woman administrator (SWA). In addition, a faculty athletics representative (FAR) represents the institution's faculty in its relationship with the NCAA and its conference. The FAR is designated by the university president or chancellor and does not hold a coaching or administrative position in the athletics department (NCAA Division I Manual, 2022).

Other NCAA regulations related to organizational structure include limits on the number of coaches and graduate assistants per sport. Bylaw 11.7.4 in the Division I manual, for instance, limits the number of football staff within Football Bowl Subdivision institutions to one head coach, ten assistant coaches, and four graduate assistant coaches. Similarly, bylaw 11.7.6 limits the number of coaches and off-campus recruiters for each sport. Division I men's and women's basketball programs, for example, are each limited to four coaches and three off-campus recruiters (NCAA Division I Manual, 2022).

Beyond meeting these requirements, the department should be structured in such a way as to create an efficient chain of command and day-to-day functionality. Learning activity 2 at the end of this chapter encourages you to search online for various athletics department organizational charts to gain an understanding of the lines of communication and authority, as well as possible career paths. Searching organizational charts can also illuminate the multiple levels that are integral to the operation of an athletics department.

One of the best ways to create efficiency in a complex organization is to assign responsibility and delegate authority. With this in mind, effective management has been compared to conducting an orchestra. The conductor is the only person in an orchestra who does not make a sound. They are judged by how well they inspire the musicians to perform. Similarly, an athletics director empowers the department's staff to make decisions—to push issue resolution down the organizational chain and eliminate the potential for upper-level bottlenecks.

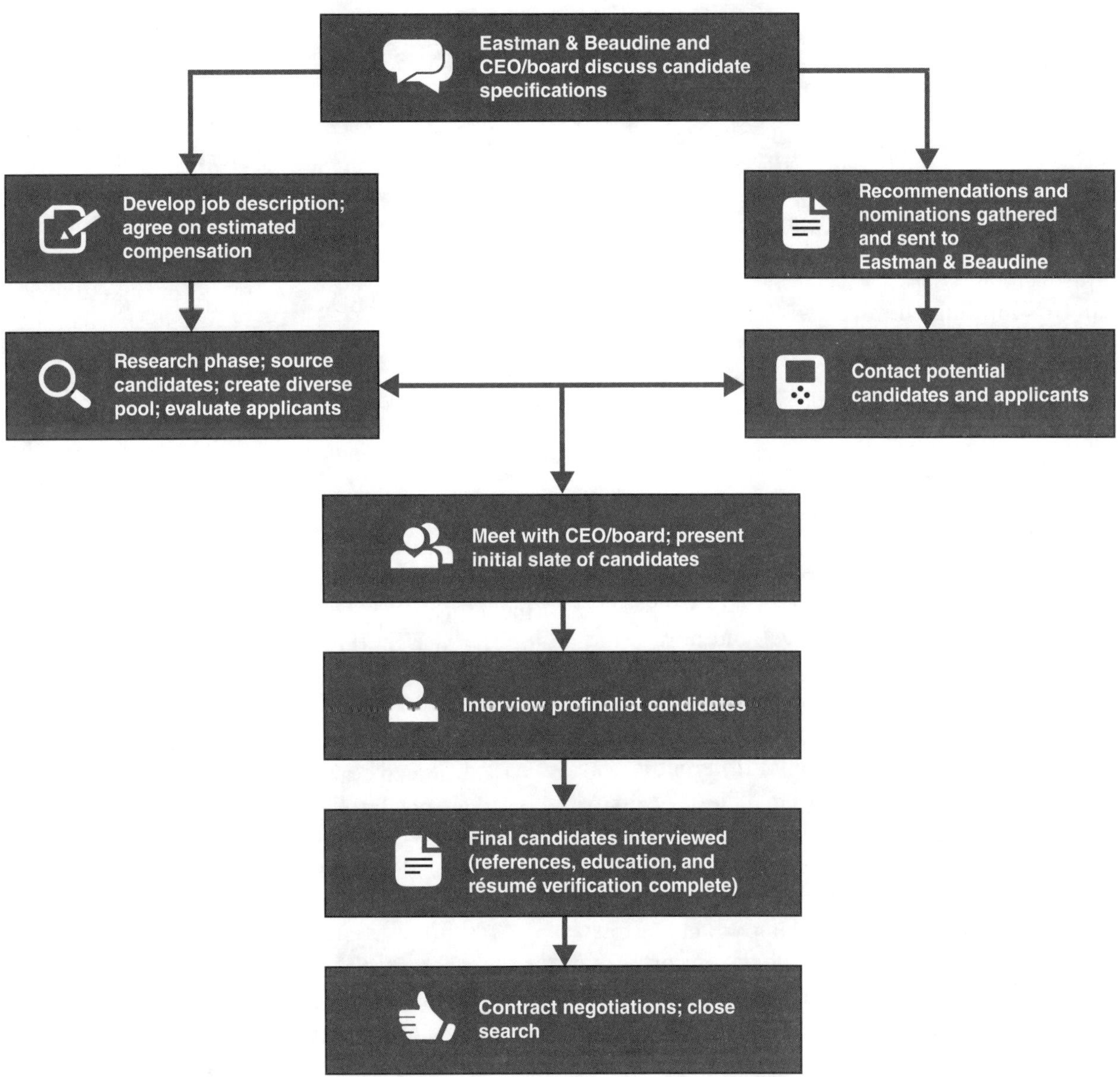

Figure 3.2 The Eastman & Beaudine search firm process.

Reprinted by permission from Eastman and Beaudine. Available: http://eastman-beaudine.com/our-approach/our-process-timeline/.

Because of the highly visible nature of athletics departments, employees who have not been effectively empowered often get nervous about making decisions. They question whether they will receive support and therefore are often slow to make decisions. In contrast, establishing a strong vision—coupled with clear support, evaluation, and communication—allows coaches and other staff members to build a sense of what is important and what authority and responsibility they have to act. Over time, everyone should know what issues to handle themselves, what issues might be best addressed by the senior staff, and when it might be best to involve a task force to investigate an issue at length. Building this strong organizational structure allows the athletics director to focus on the most important leadership functions and maintain a balanced approach to personal and organizational management.

> *[As] the first Black female to be an athletic director at this level, [I had] no one else that I could look to and say, "That's what I wanted to do." So I knew I would be the first when it happened. It is an awesome blessing to be in this position because you can chart a path for others to follow . . . and I get to mentor a lot of people of color, a lot of women, and I get great satisfaction in that. There are plenty of Black women working in senior positions in athletic departments that are well-qualified to be athletic directors. They need opportunities.*
>
> University of Virginia AD Carla Williams (qtd. in Brennan, 2022), who started in October 2017

Vanderbilt University hired Candice Storey Lee as its athletics director in May 2020 and Duke University hired Nina King to lead its athletics department in May 2021.

We have all felt the difference between a frazzled leader who carries a high level of stress and one who seems to be composed and always far ahead of deadlines. The difference between these two people likely hinges on the way in which they prioritize and manage their time. Stephen Covey created a visual representation of different types of demand faced by individuals in their day-to-day lives and divided the tasks into four quadrants based on importance and urgency (see figure 3.3). Covey urges leaders to live their lives in quadrant II. Certainly, many urgent and important matters will arise, but habitually spending a majority of time in a quadrant I crisis-management mode leads to stress, burnout, and inefficiency. On the other hand, planning and carving out maximal time in quadrant II creates a life led by vision, control, balance, and perspective. Therefore, leaders are advised to delegate all matters that are urgent but not important to trusted support staff and to avoid doing activities that are neither important nor urgent, because they result in irresponsible use of time (Covey, 1989).

Evaluating

Returning to the sport analogy of developing and fielding a competitive team, it is difficult to pinpoint the strengths and weaknesses of an offense or of a particular player without some type of metric, whether it be a game, a time trial, or a strength test. Just as hundreds of auditioning singers learn for the first time that they might not be cut out for stardom when they receive feedback from a panel of judges, so too are many employees completely unaware of their shortcomings in the workplace until they receive proper feedback.

The best evaluation mechanisms are used every day, in every interaction. Athletics directors should view employee interactions as a microcosm of the educational mission of the athletics department. Just as opportunities for life lessons can occur on the mat, on the track, or in the training room, they can also be found in meetings, projects, and crises faced in the organization. To ensure a base level of formal appraisal, it is wise to institute at least an annual evaluation system that can be tied to position-specific objectives based on the unique job function of each individual. Beyond the educational and motivational roles that evaluations can play, an additional reason for performing them involves the possibility of legal liability. Consistent and equitable practices in personnel decisions—including salary allocation, promotion, and hiring and firing, to name a few—must be documented in order to provide legal support for those decisions.

As noted earlier, Peter Roby, former athletics director at Northeastern University and interim athletics director at Dartmouth College, prides himself on being in the "people development"

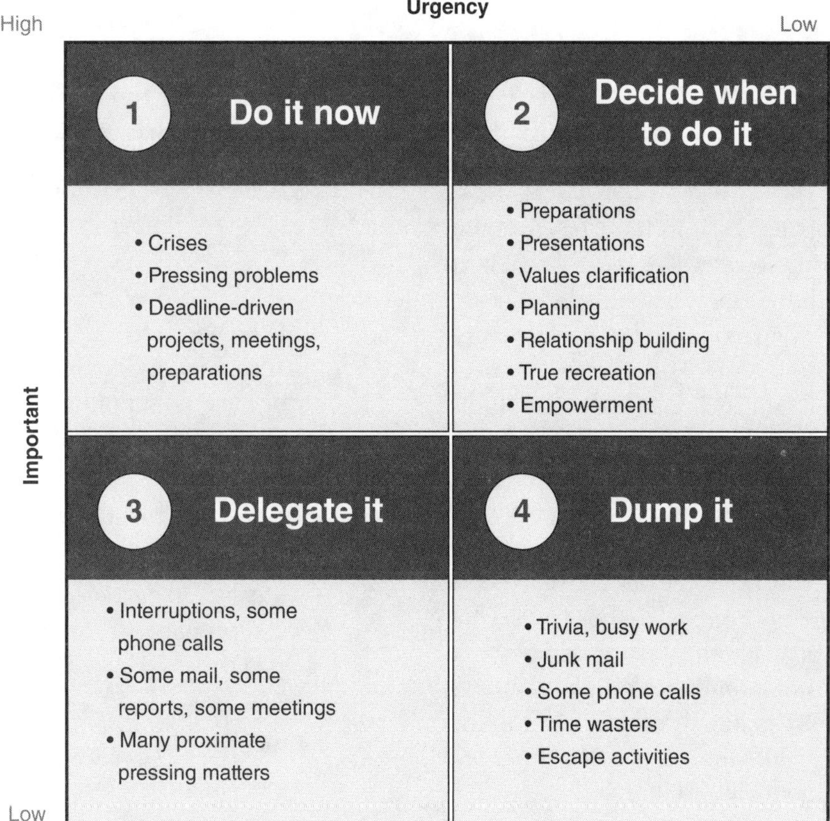

Figure 3.3 **Four-quadrant time management paradigm.**

Showing Initiative Without Taking Liberties

As a new intern or employee, one of the most difficult challenges is that of taking initiative without overstepping your span of control. The best way to address this challenge is by facing it head on through conversation. One of the first conversations you should have with your supervisor is about how much authority or responsibility he or she hopes for you to wield. Ask your supervisor when he or she wants to see you and when you are being a burden. Explain that you are a person of initiative but you also want to make sure not to overstep the expected boundaries.

If you are the leader in this situation—if you have a subordinate trying to find their way—there is generally no simple prescription. Begin the relationship by erring on the side of caution. Have the person see you often, encourage them to run ideas by you, and strive to build their confidence in the process. If they are struggling with a challenge, ask what they plan to do. If they are on track, you can say, "You're right—now go do it!" If they are not on track, the oversight necessary to facilitate their success will need to remain until they are able to take the reins. In this way, the gap between manager and subordinate responsibility is closed over time. One of the greatest ways to inspire confidence in your subordinates is by clearly articulating the goal of a project and setting checkpoints from the beginning. When the subordinate understands the ultimate purpose of a project and realizes the supervisor's role as the facilitator of success, you can unleash tremendous potential.

Wise individuals also take the time to sit back and debrief after each meeting. Contemplate what the manager or subordinate questioned or learned in this particular instance and how it might be valuable for future interactions. If implemented effectively, situational communication coupled with honest evaluation can help both the manager and the subordinate develop their ability to anticipate each other's thoughts, thus leading to greater self-efficacy, a sense of what is important, and a knowledge of how the other would respond in various situations. If no feedback is sought or given, no learning occurs, and the potential for synchronicity is squandered.

business. He emphasizes this philosophy not only with his coaches, who are held accountable as educators, but also in his interactions with other staff members. He meets with all new hires and asks them to share their career aspirations. He then commits to supporting them in their professional pursuits and provides evaluation and feedback as they strive to fulfill their professional objectives.

In the athletics department at the University of North Carolina at Chapel Hill, the annual performance appraisal and review process has traditionally involved a formal evaluation of significant accomplishments and areas of focus over the past year for each employee. In addition, supervisors share their thoughts about each staff member's strongest professional traits and areas that need attention. The review process is concluded by creating a game plan for the future. Employees are encouraged to continually seek evaluation and strive to improve professionally as they accomplish clear, specific, and measurable job assignments with associated time lines and budgets.

COMMUNICATION AND LEADERSHIP

Athletics directors spend the vast majority of their time hiring, firing, managing, motivating, inspiring, evaluating, solving problems, and building relationships. To succeed in these activities, the AD must practice effective communication both within and beyond the organization on the basis of a strong organizational structure and vision. We have already discussed in this chapter the process of developing an inspiring vision. In this section, we review the relevant communication mechanisms.

One of the primary methods of direct communication within the organization is through meetings. While this method of communication has tremendous potential, most individuals have experienced the frustration that can result from sitting through unnecessary or inefficient meetings. In order to combat this very common practice and run efficient and productive meetings, administrators can use several rules of thumb. (For additional insight on meetings, see the leadership lesson sidebar in chapter 9.)

1. Preparing for the meeting:
   a. Determine the meeting purpose.
   b. Determine the desired meeting outcomes.
   c. Ask: Do we need to have a meeting? Is it necessary for people to come together, or are there more efficient alternatives to accomplish the same result?
   d. Who needs to participate in the meeting? If some individuals are not on the agenda or have no input in the work, allow them the option to be informed through the minutes.
   e. Select the meeting place.
   f. Provide a thoughtful agenda and distribute it to all participants in advance so they can prepare for the meeting.
   g. Delegate an individual to record minutes of key action items discussed in the meeting.
   h. Consider the equipment needed.
   i. Prepare your state of mind to accomplish the desired outcomes in the most efficient manner.
2. Participating in the meeting:
   a. Greet people as they enter the room.
   b. Explain the meeting purpose and allow the agenda to be modified if necessary.
   c. Keep the meeting moving by staying on task and using the agenda as a guide. Use a "parking lot" to respectfully capture ideas that can lead the group off onto tangents.
   d. Close the meeting by reviewing the parking lot, assigning tasks with specific follow-up dates, and providing direction for any open items.
   e. End on time and on a positive note.
3. Following up after the meeting:
   a. Prepare and distribute the minutes within 24 hours in order to allow review while the meeting is still fresh in participants' minds. The minutes also serve as an immediate assignment reminder.

Leadership Lesson

Building a Strong Team and Avoiding Turf Wars

Have you ever heard track-and-field coaches compare their budget or facilities with those of women's soccer, women's basketball, or even football? Similarly, how often do those in internal marketing look at those in ticketing, external marketing, or sports information with an "us versus them" mentality? "*We* work harder than *they* do, but *they* were able to take their whole team to the convention and *we* only got to send two." "If *they* would read the material *we* sent them about promotions, *we* wouldn't have so many complaints." "*They* get preferential treatment because *they* went on the basketball trip with the AD." And so on.

As is the case in most organizations, intercollegiate athletics departments include a number of units that should work together to accomplish a common mission. All too often, however, individual units become myopic in their pursuits and care far more about their own success than about the success of the department as a whole. The result of these divisions is infighting between heavily reinforced "silos," which causes people to compete against each other rather than working together (Lencioni, 2006). Silos develop when leadership teams either do not understand the importance of their interdependence or fail to communicate that importance to the people in their chain of command (Lencioni, 2006).

In order to foster unity from the top down, Lencioni recommends issuing a rallying cry—a single, temporary, qualitative goal that all members of a leadership team (and organization) can share. This "thematic goal" should identify the single most important priority of the organization for a time frame of 3-12 months. The objective should capture equal attention from everyone in the organization and rise above the functional specializations and teams (e.g., finance, marketing, operations). The thematic goal should support the vision and mission of the organization while helping all the teams focus on current priorities. Each thematic goal should also include several supporting objectives that can be measured (i.e., a quantifiable metric or a date by which a supporting activity will be completed). The biggest key, however, is for each department to have a stake in each objective and an understanding of how critical interdependence is to achieving the goal (Lencioni, 2006). The goal should also be distinct from common operating objectives, such as revenue generation, conference finishes, and customer satisfaction; it should capture the most important focus of the organization unique to the current time period.

A great way to establish a thematic goal is to have teams write down an answer to one of the following questions:

- "What is one thing we must achieve during the next nine months?"
- "We will fail if we do not achieve ________ in the next nine months" (Lencioni, 2002).

An appropriate rallying cry for an athletics department following a scandal, for instance, might be to reestablish credibility, whereas an athletics department with limited local support might choose to focus on building community partnerships for a set time period, with each member of the athletics department able to buy in and hold responsibility for specific objectives related to the thematic goal of the period.

Defining the rallying cry and shared objectives are important first steps toward achieving organizational unity, but it is also vital to implement the process through a fully functional team. Members of a truly cohesive team implement the following key practices:

- Trust one another. Team members are willing to be vulnerable within the group and are genuinely open about their mistakes and weaknesses.
- Engage in unfiltered discussion about ideas. Team members are willing to engage in passionate ideological debate in order to extract the best from everyone.
- Commit to decisions and plans of action. After expressing their opinions and hearing an unguarded discussion of others' perspectives, they are able to fully buy into decisions.

(continued)

LEADERSHIP LESSON *(continued)*

- Hold one another accountable for delivering according to plan. Committed team members challenge and hold one another to clearly defined standards.
- Focus on achieving collective results. Team members put the needs of the team above divisional or individual needs in an effort to achieve predefined, time-bound, measurable results.

> *Politics is when people choose their words and actions based on how they want others to react rather than based on what they really think.*
>
> Lencioni, 2002, p. 88
>
> *Talent wins games, but teamwork and intelligence wins championships.*
>
> Michael Jordan

Each of these crucial team functions is listed in figure 3.4, along with the role of the leader. Again, the leadership team sets the tone for the organization. When egos and turf wars prevail among the senior staff, the stage is set for discord and silos are created throughout the athletics department. Similarly, when meetings are boring, when consensus comes too easily, when discussions and decisions seem to resurface over and over, when team members focus on individual rather than collective goals, and when deadlines are missed and mediocrity abounds, there is clearly room for improvement. Though many of these issues need to be addressed from the top down, you can also focus on your role as a team member, regardless of whether you are the AD or an intern. There is always someone within your sphere of influence; therefore, you can help your team function effectively.

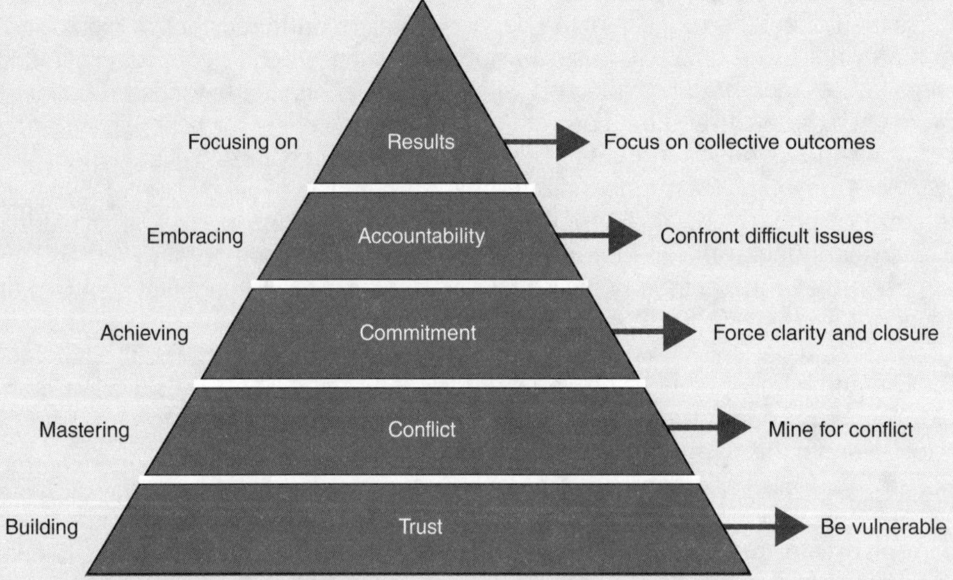

Figure 3.4 Characteristics of High-Performing Teams.
Reprinted by permission from The Table Group.

b. Follow up on any action items that you have been assigned.

c. Evaluate the success of the meeting through reflection. Ask yourself, and occasionally others, what went well and what could be improved.

d. Develop an agenda for the next meeting. (Earnest & Cugliari, 2009)

In a study of core values in Division I, II, and III athletics departments, the majority of senior-level administrators cited meetings as the primary mechanism for infusing core values, but a vocal minority voiced concern about dissonance between stated values and leaders' actions (Cooper & Weight, n.d.). As discussed in an earlier chapter, such dissonance can carry damaging organizational consequences (a lack of value culturalization). In order to avoid this treacherous organizational pitfall, administrators need to "walk the walk" and examine informal mechanisms of communication.

Edgar Schein, a noted organizational development expert, explained that leaders embed culture through what they "pay attention to, measure, and control on a regular basis" (2010, p. 236). In other words, if leaders purport to value all sports equally within the department but attend only football games, their credibility comes into question and the climate of the department morphs into one driven by a football-is-king mentality. Conversely, athletics directors who emphasize the role of department personnel in fostering educational experiences for athletes and model this mission—for example, by supporting them in leadership development activities, thanking them for their positive representation of the university, and maintaining an open-door policy—will create a departmental culture driven by athlete education.

Communicating values through action (or inaction) can be particularly powerful during times of turbulence. In fact, sometimes the most important method of communication is the art of listening. In all situations, the leader should not rush to judgment but rather should assess the situation, seek and hear all sides of the story, and contemplate whether this is a moment that requires vision. A secondary culture-embedding mechanism mentioned by Schein is the way in which leaders "react to critical incidents and organizational crises" (2010, p. 236). Though an athletics director does not directly report to shareholders, there are hundreds, thousands, and sometimes hundreds of thousands of stakeholders invested in the output of an athletics department. In this high-pressure climate, addressing problems directly paves the path for progress.

Often in these times of trial, the media is particularly hungry for a story. Therefore, when athletics leaders are approached by the media, they are well advised to take a moment to reflect on what message needs to be delivered—and to whom. Most often, the communication should be directed toward the organization's stakeholders. They need to be touched, and they often need a reason to keep believing in the organization.

As mainstream media sources seem to focus on news that sells, many intercollegiate athletics leaders have turned to social media as an alternative way to engage the public. Whether driven to this channel of communication out of frustration, in a desire to take charge of communication, or as an alternate marketing vehicle, athletics directors can consciously develop an online personality and draw allegiance through direct communication with fans. These lines of communication facilitate a more intimate view of the administrator's life than traditional modes of public communication, which usually took the form of interviews or media conferences during times of crisis and often left the administrator looking rehearsed. Social media options, such as blogging and posting, can provide effective ways to let people know what the department is all about. Some examples of social media communication from athletics directors are presented in the sidebar titled Stakeholder Engagement Through Social Media. Take some time with the learning activities at the end of this chapter to learn more about how athletics directors use social media. For information about social media as an element of departmental marketing initiatives, see chapter 7.

Stakeholder Engagement Through Social Media

School	Athletics director	Number of X (formerly known as Twitter) followers
University of Alabama	Greg Byrne	77.7k
Arizona State University	Ray Anderson	9.3k
University of Arkansas	Hunter Yurachek	74.5k
Clemson University	Graham Neff	7.2k
University of Florida	Scott Stricklin	79.7k
University of Georgia	Josh Brooks	15.7k
Iowa State University	Jamie Pollard	40.8k
University of Kentucky	Mitch Barnhart	53.3k
University of Miami	Dan Radakovich	25.4k
University of Nebraska	Trev Alberts	32.1k
University of North Carolina	Bubba Cunningham	18.8k
University of Notre Dame	Jack Swarbrick	10.4k
Ohio State University	Gene Smith	34.9k
University of Oklahoma	Joe Castiglione	54.4k
University of Pittsburgh	Heather Lyke	12k
University of South Carolina	Ray Tanner	69.3k
Stanford University	Bernard Muir	3.6k
University of Tennessee	Danny White	67.2k
University of Texas	Chris Del Conte	52.2k
Texas A&M	Ross Bjork	54.9k
Vanderbilt University	Candice Storey Lee	9.4k
University of Virginia	Carla Williams	11.2k
Virginia Tech	Whit Babcock	21k
Louisiana State University	Scott Woodward	NA
University of Michigan	Warde Manuel	NA
University of Oregon	Rob Mullens	NA
Penn State University	Patrick Kraft	NA
University of Wisconsin	Chris McIntosh	NA

Athletics Directors at 2022-23 NACDA LEARFIELD Directors' Cup Winners

School	Athletics director	Number of X (formerly known as Twitter) followers
Grand Valley State University (Division II)	Keri Becker	1,633
Johns Hopkins University (Division III)	Jen Baker	322
Indiana Tech University (NAIA)	Jessie Biggs	1,194

Case Study

Turmoil in Tennessee: Securing the Next Football Head Coach

In fall 2017, Butch Jones, the head football coach for the University of Tennessee Volunteers, was nearing a losing record that included zero conference wins. Despite winning over 64 percent of his games in the past three seasons—including three bowl wins and two recent second-place finishes in the competitive East Division of the Southeastern Conference—and achieving national rankings in 2015 and 2016, the coach was let go. What followed was a tumultuous search process that included the suspension of the athletics director (AD), the return of an iconic football coach, and a month-long search that played out in front of the national sports audience and was affected by the fans' displeasure with numerous candidates.

Tennessee AD John Currie announced the firing with two home games remaining in the regular season. Two wins would have led the Volunteers to finish with a .500 record and a likely fourth consecutive bowl bid. However, a 0-6 conference record with lopsided losses to Georgia, Alabama, and Missouri was too much for the passionate fan base. The University of Georgia and the University of Alabama were national sports powers, but losing to the University of Missouri in a lopsided contest was the tipping point. Jones' firing on November 12 allowed Currie to get an early start on his national search for a new football coach. Jones, who had been hired from the University of Cincinnati by the previous Tennessee AD, would later join head coach Nick Saban's staff at the University of Alabama.

Currie started as Tennessee's AD in February 2017. He had previously worked in athletic development at Tennessee from 1997 through 2009, so he was familiar with donors and donors knew of him. Before coming to Tennessee, Currie had been AD for eight years at Kansas State University. While at Kansas State, Currie earned national recognition with the *Sports Business Journal* 40 Under 40 honor and was named the Under Armour AD of the Year, presented by the National Association of Collegiate Directors of Athletics (NACDA). He was established in his field and returning to the school where he earned his master of science in sport management. He elected not to use a search firm in replacing Jones.

The University of Tennessee's fan base, notorious for filling up Neyland Stadium with over 100,000 attendees at home games, wanted former NFL coach Jon Gruden to lead their program. Shortly after the search began, social media reported that Gruden was seen in Knoxville with former Tennessee great Peyton Manning, further exciting the Volunteer Nation (Rittenberg, 2017). Another possible candidate was Chip Kelly, a highly successful coach at the University of Oregon, who did not win as much in the National Football League. However, the University of Florida was also looking for a head football coach and was considering Kelly as well as Dan Mullen, the head coach at Mississippi State University and a former Florida offensive coordinator. The University of Nebraska and the University of California, Los Angeles (UCLA), were also searching for head coaches.

UCLA hired Chip Kelly and Florida hired Dan Mullen, taking two top Tennessee candidates off the board. Nebraska hired Scott Frost from the University of Central Florida, increasing the perception that Tennessee was now a second-tier job. Tennessee then contemplated Matt Campbell, the young head coach at Iowa State, but also considered two experienced coordinators: Joe Moorhead (Penn State University offensive coordinator) and Greg Schiano (Ohio State University defensive coordinator and former head coach at Rutgers, the State University of New Jersey). Neither of these coordinators excited the fan base, who deemed the Volunteers program—the national champions in 1998—to be an elite college football destination.

Schiano was considered the front-runner for the position, with many reports alleging he had accepted the job. Schiano had been a finalist for the head coaching job at the University of Oregon the previous year and was impressive in leading Rutgers, a perennial football doormat, to winning seasons, including five bowl

(continued)

CASE STUDY *(continued)*

wins, in seven of his past eight years. However, on November 26, fans, business owners, and politicians took to social media and other platforms to express their displeasure with Currie's alleged choice. Currie was in Columbus, Ohio, to secure Schiano with a signed memorandum of understanding while Tennessee supporters revolted (Murray, 2018). The deal was never finalized, and Currie had to identify more candidates after missing out on Gruden, Kelly, Mullen, and Schiano.

In the following days, two more candidates, Mike Gundy, the head coach at Oklahoma State University, and Matt Campbell, received raises from their employers after considering the Tennessee football program. Tennessee then reached out to Duke University football coach David Cutcliffe and Purdue University coach Jeff Brohm. Neither was interested, so the search moved to David Doeren, the head coach at North Carolina State University (NCSU). Doeren, the ninth candidate, turned down Tennessee on November 30 and received a new contract from NCSU. Later that afternoon, Currie was reportedly in talks with Washington State University coach Mike Leach. Open-records requests enabled local reporters to see and verify text messages and email correspondence between Currie, candidates or their representatives, and Currie's supervisors (Murray, 2018).

Currie was suspended by University of Tennessee Chancellor Beverly Davenport on December 1, and Phillip Fulmer, the former head football coach of the 1998 Volunteers football team, was named AD (Toppmeyer, 2021). The school attempted to fire Currie "with cause" to avoid a buyout in excess of US$5 million. Butch Jones' buyout was in excess of US$15 million. Currie and UT eventually reached a separation agreement of US$2.5 million (Staples, 2019). In March 2019, Currie returned to his alma mater, where he was named the athletics director. At the 2022 NACDA Convention, he was honored as Cushman & Wakefield Athletics Director of the Year.

Fulmer, a candidate for the AD job when Currie was hired eight months before, led the football coach search that resulted in hiring University of Alabama defensive coordinator Jeremy Pruitt on December 7, 2017. Pruitt, previously a defensive coordinator at Florida State University and the University of Georgia, was fired in his third season, on January 18, 2021, after a 3-7 season and 16-19 overall record, including 10-16 in the Southeastern Conference. Eleven wins from the 2019 and 2020 seasons were later vacated by the NCAA. The school cited significant recruiting violations as the rationale and also terminated two assistant coaches and seven support staff. Days later, Fulmer retired, though he reportedly would be compensated each month through the end of 2023 (WBIR Staff, 2021). Parker Executive Search helped find a new coach, and Josh Heupel was hired on January 27, 2021, by new AD Danny White, his former boss at the University of Central Florida (Toppmeyer, 2021). Tennessee paid Central Florida a buyout of US$3.45 million to secure Heupel's release from his contract with the school as well as a buyout of US$2.5 million to secure White (West, 2021). Pruitt pursued legal action to secure his US$12.6 million buyout from Tennessee, which claimed the firing was "with cause" (Estes, 2021).

Questions to Consider

1. What criteria would you use to assess your head coaches? Would your response change depending on the sport? Would your response change depending on whether your athletics department was in Division I, Division II, Division III, or NAIA?
2. What would your priorities be in firing a coach or a coaching department? What would the timeline look like, up to and including bringing in a new coach?
3. How would you identify candidates for your head coaching positions?
4. In negotiating with candidates, do you think you could prevent the candidate from using the interview as financial leverage with their current employer? How?
5. Given the power and influence of traditional media and social media, what strategies could you implement to reduce speculation and rumors but still communicate with stakeholders?
6. What would your argument be for using a search firm? For not using one?
7. What are the tangible and intangible costs associated with searches, especially at the Power Five level?

CONCLUSION

Peter Drucker, the father of modern-day management, eloquently defined the difference between leadership and management: "management is doing things right," whereas "leadership is doing the right things" (qtd. in Covey, 1989, p. 101). As leaders in intercollegiate athletics guide the industry through the challenges of the 21st century, it is increasingly important for athletics directors to do the right things—to lead through vision and focus on the mission of their organization. Once this approach is established, leaders can build a strong organizational structure and team and inspire them to their greatest effectiveness.

DISCUSSION QUESTIONS

1. In 2020, the athletics director at the University of Iowa announced the elimination of four sports in an effort to offset a budget shortfall attributed to the COVID-19 pandemic. Research this decision and its reverberations to decide what type of decision-making framework may have been used. Describe the reasoning behind your conclusions.
2. Select a leader with whom you have had contact. How does that leader spend their time? What does this time usage reveal about the leader's values?
3. Take a moment to review the time management quadrants presented in Stephen Covey's *The 7 Habits of Highly Effective People* (see figure 3.3). In which quadrant do you focus the majority of your time? What adjustments to your time management could you make to become more effective?
4. Imagine that you are a new AD coming into an institution. In gathering information for strategic planning, you were told by multiple stakeholders that a certain coach is "bad news" and should be fired. What is the best way to handle this situation considering any potential legal, communication, and departmental morale effects?
5. What type of organizational culture will be created by an athletics director who does the following?
   a. Purports to value all sports equally yet attends only football games
   b. Attends only women's sporting events
   c. Associates with the male head coaches in a weekly workout that is understood to be unwelcoming to female head coaches
   d. Touts the importance of academic focus but recognizes students and coaches only for athletics performance

LEARNING ACTIVITIES

1. Write a unique vision and mission for the athletics department at your school or an athletics department where you hope to work. Utilizing this vision and mission, write down characteristics of people you might wish to hire as a director of marketing or a director of compliance.
2. Search the web for two athletics department organizational charts. What can you learn about the organizations? Do the charts include all levels (coaches, graduate assistants, and support staff)? Why are organizational charts important? How many steps might it take to advance from an intern position to the role of athletics director? Do any of the individuals seem overloaded with responsibility? What jobs look interesting to you?
3. The National Association of Collegiate Directors of Athletics (NACDA) offers a variety of support services and opportunities for professional growth. Explore the group's website (www.nacda.com) to learn about its convention, upcoming events, and affiliated professional organizations. After exploring the site, find two current job postings that you might be interested in pursuing at some point in your career.

4. Ask an athletics department employee if they feel that collaboration between functional units (e.g., marketing and ticket sales) is as strong as it could be. Ask the person to discuss the reasons that this collaboration is currently strong or weak. Drawing on the leadership lesson from this chapter, decide what areas could be focused on to strengthen the departmental collaboration.
5. Ask two colleagues or former employers to identify two areas in which you are strong and suggest two ways in which you could improve your professionalism.
6. Search X (formerly known as Twitter) for some athletics administrators who post frequently. Select a month's worth of posts from one athletics director to analyze. What do their posts reflect about their priorities?

Compliance

Molly P. Harry, University of Arkansas–Fayetteville

Erianne A. Weight, University of North Carolina at Chapel Hill

Robert H. Zullo, Slippery Rock University

In this chapter, you will explore

- the logic behind NCAA regulations,
- the primary responsibilities of compliance personnel,
- changes to NCAA compliance purposes and principles,
- recruiting and rules education, and
- outlets for finding additional compliance information in order to learn more and stay informed as changes arise.

COMPLIANCE AS A CULTURE

While attending a meeting about NCAA compliance issues, an exasperated Football Bowl Subdivision (FBS) athletics director mentioned he was spending more than US$2 million per year on compliance efforts at his institution. Despite this tremendous investment, a rogue coach who chose to bend some rules had brought the entire department into question. The ensuing discussion revolved around the tremendous pressure placed on ADs to oversee actions taken within their departments and the challenge of covering all compliance bases through a single compliance unit (regardless of size).

Indeed, in the face of increasing competitive pressure, media scrutiny, and public skepticism, the importance of compliance oversight in intercollegiate athletics administration has become paramount to long-term success in this ever-changing industry. To avoid facing allegations, sanctions, and a tarnished brand, administrators need to be informed, involved, and heavily invested in NCAA rules compliance. As the discussion among ADs concluded, the sentiment shared by most was that in order to maximize departmental functionality, compliance must be everyone's responsibility—and therefore an integral part of the department's culture.

Throughout the last decade, news headlines trumpeted scandals involving athletics personnel who chose to ignore or tried to bend rules and regulations designed to ensure a level playing field. From the days of paid nonstudent ("tramp") athletes in early intercollegiate athletic competitions to the academic, agent-related, booster-recruiting, point-shaving, administrative, and pay-for-play issues we have seen in more recent years, the temptation to skirt the rules in order to gain a competitive advantage has been a constant presence in collegiate athletics. For this reason, the NCAA manual has grown thicker year after year, as more and more rules have been adopted. In fact, the 2022-2023 Division I manual published by the NCAA spanned 464 pages.

However, with significant changes in 2021—among them name, image, and likeness (NIL) rules, allowance of a one-time transfer rule, and athletes' abilities to capitalize on academic-based funding as ruled in *Alston v. NCAA*, which prohibited the NCAA from limiting education-related benefits for student-athletes—the NCAA voted to adopt a new constitution in January 2022 (Witz, 2022). This new constitution updated the purposes, meaning what the organization does, and principles, meaning how the organization operates.

The previous constitution provided 16 principles for the NCAA and its member schools to comply with, covering the following areas: institutional control, student-athletes' well-being, gender equity, good sporting behavior and ethical conduct, sound academic standards, nondiscrimination, diversity in governance structures, rules compliance, amateurism, competitive equity, recruiting governance, eligibility governance, financial aid governance, governance of playing and practice seasons, governance of postseason competition, and governance of economic program operation. Within its new constitution are only eight key principles:

- The Primacy of the Academic Experience
- The Collegiate Student-Athlete Model
- Integrity and Sportsmanship
- Student-Athlete Well-Being
- Institutional Control
- Diversity, Equity, and Inclusion
- Gender Equity
- Recruiting Standards

As you can see, there is some consistency between the old and new principles. For example, the principles of nondiscrimination and diversity within governance structures in the 2021-2022 constitution align with the diversity, equity, and inclusion principle in the 2022-2023 constitution. Additionally, institutional control is consistent as both a principle and its own bylaw. However, there are some key differences. The 2022-2023 constitution does not discuss amateurism, the NCAA's foundational principle (Smith, 2021), in this section or in any part of the new document. Additionally, the principles concerning financial aid and the economy of athletics have also been removed from the constitution. More information about the structure of the new constitution and NCAA manual is provided in the sidebar titled Organization of the NCAA Manual.

The new NCAA constitution is for all levels of competition; however, the NCAA provides a different manual for each of its three divisions. Division I in the NCAA has the most complex regulations of any governing body, so for this reason, we focus primarily here on NCAA Division I athletics, although we address other divisions and governing bodies throughout the chapter as well. As we explore the association and its compliance principles and bylaws, be mindful of how a thorough understanding of current practices and regulatory rationales can facilitate cultures of buy-in and compliance throughout your future athletics departments. Furthermore, informed and invested administrators are equipped to shape future legislation in an effort to sustain the integrity of intercollegiate athletics. As your understanding deepens, your power to effect change grows.

The NCAA manual outlines the association's constitution and the operating and administrative bylaws to be followed by each member institution. Athletics administrators are responsible for understanding the manual and other applicable regulatory materials in addition to ensuring compliance by all staff members, athletes, boosters, and any others representing the institution's athletics interests. This is no small task, and as bemoaned by the athletics director in this chapter's opening scenario, even a fully staffed compliance department leaves room for error.

INSTITUTIONAL CONTROL

Institutional control is perhaps the most important area of compliance as it undergirds all other principles and policies of the NCAA and its membership. This is perhaps why it is both a principle of the association (Article 1E) and its own bylaw. The principle of institutional control in Article 1E states that it is "the responsibility of each member institution to monitor and control its athletic programs and to provide education and training to ensure compliance with the rules established by the Association, its division and conference" (NCAA Division I Manual, 2022-2023, p. 2). Similarly, it is up to each member school to report any and all violations of the bylaws to their conference and division in a timely and cooperative manner. While the athletics director is responsible for the day-to-day operations of the athletics department, the ultimate responsibility for institutional control—per the association's governance structure—is with the institution president or chancellor.

One of the harshest violations in the NCAA is a breach of institutional control. This occurs when one or all of the following is uncovered by the NCAA enforcement staff: (1) inadequate compliance measures in place, (2) inappropriate education on compliance measures that led to the violation, (3) insufficient monitoring of compliance to ensure that regulations are followed, or (4) the institution was slow to take action after it discovered the violation.

RULES, COMPLIANCE, AND ACCOUNTABILITY

Article 4 of the NCAA manual discusses rules, compliance, and accountability. In following institutional control, each member "holds itself accountable to support and comply with the rules and principles approved by the membership" (NCAA Division I Manual, 2022-2023, p. 9). Further, schools must also agree to follow specific division, conference, and institutional policies as they manage their athletics departments. This is done to ensure fair play and integrity, not only on the courts and fields of competition but also in the adjudicatory process. More recently, the NCAA and member schools have attempted, in the case of penalties, to avoid punishing teams or athletes who were not involved or implicated in infractions. Of course, this is sometimes challenging and the goal cannot always be achieved.

Compliance may look slightly different, depending on the division. This becomes evident when looking at the NCAA's website. For example, the NCAA simply notes that Division I schools must "conduct their athletics programs with integrity and in compliance with conference and NCAA rules and regulations" (Division I Compliance, n.d.,

Organization of the NCAA Manual

The separate manuals for Divisions I, II, and III each contain legislation specific to the relevant division. Since this chapter focuses on Division I, some bylaws may have gaps in their numbering.

Constitution

Articles 1 through 6 address the governing body's principles, structure, and legislative processes.

Article 1: Principles

Article 2: Organization

Article 3: Finance

Article 4: Rules, Compliance, and Accountability

Article 5: Amendments to the Constitution

Article 6: Institutional Control

Operating Bylaws

Articles 8 through 21 are the operating bylaws, which consist of legislation adopted by the division membership to promote the principles enumerated in the constitution and to achieve the association's purposes.

Article 8: Institutional Control

Article 9: Legislative Authority and Process

Article 10: Ethical Conduct

Article 11: Conduct and Employment of Athletics Personnel

Article 12: Amateurism and Athletics Eligibility

Article 13: Recruiting

Article 14: Academic Eligibility

Article 15: Financial Aid

Article 16: Awards, Benefits, and Expenses for Enrolled Student-Athletes

Article 17: Playing and Practice Seasons

Article 18: Championships and Postseason Football

Article 19: Infractions Program

Article 20: Division Membership

Article 21: Governance Structure and Committees

Administrative Bylaws

Article 31, Executive Regulations, is the administrative bylaw that sets forth policies and procedures for implementing NCAA championships and lays out regulations for bid sites, qualifying athletes, and other logistical concerns. This administrative bylaw can be adopted or modified by the Division I board of directors or the legislative council for the efficient administration of the activities that they govern. Similarly, Article 31 may be amended by the membership through the regular legislative process.

To download a free PDF of the comprehensive NCAA manual, visit www.ncaapublications.com.

Industry Profile

JACKIE WALLGREN

Senior Associate Athletic Director, University of Akron

Jackie Wallgren is the senior associate director of athletics at the University of Akron in Ohio and possesses over 15 years of senior athletics administrative experience. A graduate of the University of Wisconsin–Superior and the University of North Carolina, Wallgren serves as the school's senior woman administrator and provides oversight in the areas of compliance, academic support services, and student-athlete advisory council, in addition to oversight of the sports of women's golf, women's lacrosse, rifle, men's and women's soccer, softball, swimming and diving, and volleyball.

After graduating from Chapel Hill, she was an assistant to the commissioner for the Wisconsin Intercollegiate Athletic Conference, helping with the processing of NCAA eligibility, conference championships and postseason events, and social media. She also worked in the life skills department at the University of Nebraska, leading a senior retreat and networking night for student-athletes, as well as pursuing community outreach efforts and guiding student-athletes and staff to best practices in social networking.

Before moving to the University of Akron, Wallgren was the deputy athletics director at Colorado State University at Pueblo, where she contributed to the leadership, strategic planning, budget management, and oversight of over 20 sports. She also helped with the areas of compliance, strength and conditioning, sports medicine, and Title IX as well as diversity and inclusion. She was the specific sport supervisor for men's and women's soccer, men's and women's lacrosse, and softball. Additionally, Wallgren has worked in compliance at Texas A&M University–Commerce and Texas A&M University–Kingsville, leading efforts to comply with NCAA and conference rules through continuous monitoring and educational programs. This included certifying the eligibility of student-athletes, oversight of the drug-testing program, and handling issues related to reinstatement, relief waivers, violation reports, financial aid, and amateurism.

Jackie Wallgren

Wallgren provided the following recommendations for students interested in the field of compliance:

Compliance is frequently overlooked by students as a great career opportunity. How would you, as a veteran athletics administrator, give a "sales pitch" for that sector of college sports administration?

Compliance can be something that many folks overlook when thinking about careers in athletics. I think it is one of the hidden gems in athletics because you get to experience virtually every part of the athletics department—we educate boosters, work with student affairs administrators across campus, interact closely with student-athletes, analyze marketing initiatives, et cetera. It gives you a taste of everything, which is an excellent foundation for building a diverse career in college athletics.

What is the best part of working in compliance?

My favorite thing is that no two days are the same. I've always loved solving puzzles, and I enjoy trying to find permissible ways within our legislation to say yes as often as possible to our coaches, student-athletes, and other constituents. Sometimes we [cannot] get there the way they wanted to, but we can usually find a path that leads to the outcome they want if we work together.

(continued)

INDUSTRY PROFILE *(continued)*

What areas are growing or changing the most with respect to compliance?

NIL and the Transfer Portal have certainly changed the game in recent years. Really, though, the entire industry is changing rapidly and frequently now, just like most sectors. Our rules are adapting and transforming to accommodate the needs of a new generation of student-athletes, technology, and modernization. The need to be nimble and up to date has never been more important!

With constant change in the field, what do you see on the horizon as a big issue?

While it is not really "on the horizon"—it is already here—mental health is the biggest issue I can think of in today's world. The challenges with managing mental health of our student-athletes and the coaches and staff that work with them is growing every day. We are all working a lot, the world is stressful, and athletics is a competitive arena by nature. We need to continually find ways to make work-life more manageable for everyone involved in college athletics.

Other than volunteering in a school's compliance office, what other opportunities would shine on a student's resume if they are interested in compliance?

Project management is huge. Finding ways to manage projects from start to finish, even if they are not specific to athletics and/or compliance, and then being able to articulate how those skills transfer into the compliance realm, would set you apart from many applicants. Additionally, there are excellent professional development resources out there—attend an NCAA Regional Rules Seminar, join and attend NAAC [National Association for Athletics Compliance], et cetera.

How do you stay up to date with the most current changes from the conference standpoint and the national standpoint?

I primarily get my information through emails from the NCAA and our conference office. Additionally, the NCAA will often put out resources and information through their social media sites, so I make sure I have alerts set up for key profiles (@InsidetheNCAA). (Wallgren, 2022)

Jackie Wallgren

para. 1). This language is a little more ambiguous than that used for Divisions II and III, which gives Division I schools more flexibility for compliance.

For Division II, the language is slightly different, stating that members must run programs with integrity but also "in a *welcoming* manner that complies with conference and NCAA rules and regulations" (Division II Compliance, n.d., para. 1; emphasis added). The Division II manual continues on to stress the importance of institutional control and the importance of compliance in ensuring education is at the center of Division II athletics participation.

The Division III manual notes the importance of "integrity" and a "welcoming manner" in a way that is similar to the Division II manual. Additionally, the Division III compliance manual highlights institutional control and the responsibility of the president or chancellor regarding sport oversight. Interestingly, the NCAA expands on Division III compliance, stating: "Division III also encourages compliance to have a teamwork approach in which all members of the athletics department and other personnel across campus who are associated with athletics conduct the program with the highest levels of integrity and fairness" (Division III Compliance, n.d., para. 3). The importance of teamwork is stressed by countless compliance officers, but, interestingly, is included as a kind of best practice only on Division III's compliance web page.

Compliance Office Overview

As with many positions in intercollegiate athletics, there is no typical day for compliance staffers. Depending on the time of year, their day may consist of entering data and generating reports with Compliance Assistant (CAi) (discussed later in the Compliance Resources section), referring to the NCAA Legislative Services Database (LSDBi) to find case precedents and rules interpretations, reviewing new NCAA legislation, preparing coaches for their annual certification exam, administering the athlete opportunity fund, ordering NCAA manuals for staffers, organizing compliance forms, conducting eligibility meetings, monitoring schedules for playing or practice seasons, reviewing coaching designations, compiling athlete book-purchasing forms, reviewing recruiting logs, self-reporting an infraction, conducting rules education, or approving official or unofficial visits. Each of these tasks requires a strong understanding of the rules, appropriate forms and procedures to follow, and the ability to promote understanding and adherence among departmental stakeholders.

A compliance officer is often an athletics department's most important—and perhaps most resented—employee (Rhoden, 2009). As big-time athletics departments are increasingly scrutinized, a violation can tarnish the reputation of an entire university and affect hundreds of athletes and thousands of fans (see cases such as the University of Louisville pay-for-play scandal, discussed later in this chapter). With these risks in mind, the compliance officer's primary responsibility is to protect the university, and doing so often creates departmental tension as coaches strive to maximize their competitive advantage. This "cordial but often contentious relationship" was explained by compliance director Amy Herman: "There will always be that inherent tension; really it's probably better that way for the protection of the institution. If that tension were to go away, I think you would have trouble" (qtd. in Rhoden, 2009).

Traditionally, compliance has been handled as an internal function in the athletics department with an external reporting obligation. However, in response to the scrutiny associated with major infractions, several new models of compliance have emerged. Ohio State University moved its compliance office out of the athletics department with the stated purpose of maximizing objectivity. This adjustment was made in order to centralize all university compliance offices, including those that address research and medical practices (Infante, 2011; Ludlow, 2011). The University of Oregon advertised a position on its compliance staff for an individual with law enforcement or investigative experience. The position is intended to serve as a liaison between the athletics department and the law enforcement community, and encompasses responsibilities including cyberspace surveillance and athlete self-defense training. Finally, West Virginia University added an employee with experience working for the NCAA, the U.S. government, and legal entities to help with compliance measures, but rather than working in the compliance office, the employee works specifically for the football team (Infante, 2011). As the stakes continue to escalate in intercollegiate athletics, new approaches will likely emerge. Indeed, with the adoption of NIL in 2021, some athletics departments tasked compliance officers with handling NIL training and regulations (such as the University of Florida), while others created new departmental units focusing solely on NIL (such as the University of Arkansas–Fayetteville).

> *For athletics compliance, as in life, stagnation leads to routine and routine leads to mistakes.*
>
> Jacob Fricke, University of Notre Dame compliance assistant (2022)

Rules Education

Because of the depth and detail of NCAA legislation, it is rare to find any coach, athlete, or even compliance officer who claims full understanding of all areas for which universities are held strictly accountable. As a result, education is a fundamental area of emphasis for compliance personnel. Most universities require coaches and athletes to participate in workshops reviewing compliance basics, and many distribute weekly newsletters with compliance reminders to help administrators, athletes, and coaches understand the repercussions of their actions, the philosophy behind the rules, and the accountability they each carry. Educational efforts must also extend beyond the walls of the department to include boosters, prospective athletes, and any others who promote the interests of the athletics department. The NCAA has mandated education for each of these groups.

Pursuant to NCAA bylaw 11.1.1.1, head coaches are responsible for creating an atmosphere of rules compliance and monitoring the activities of their staff. Therefore, a coach can be held responsible for the actions of the individuals within the program. Informing coaches of this responsibility should facilitate an understanding between compliance personnel and head coaches in which coaches have an ongoing desire to create efficient monitoring systems, learn more about legislation that affects their processes, and ask questions when in doubt. If red flags do arise, coaches should clearly understand that it is their responsibility to immediately report suspected and actual rule violations. Building strong relationships and facilitating an atmosphere that encourages continuing education are critical to efficiency in a compliance system.

Four important components to fostering a coach culture of compliance include: (1) demonstrating that compliance is a shared responsibility through transparent expectations of coaches and their staffs, (2) showing that the responsibility for a team's integrity rests with the head coach, (3) creating a team that will immediately report potential concerns to the compliance office and allow an investigation into said concerns, and (4) providing frequent and timely compliance training for coaches and their staffs. To facilitate these four components, the compliance officers must actively look for issues, ask coaches questions, consult with conference and NCAA compliance officials, and regularly ask for feedback.

Compliance director Amy Herman addressed the dynamic between coaches and compliance officers: "We don't expect them to know all the rules, because we don't know all the rules, and we deal with it on a daily basis. What we expect of them is that they know enough of the rules to know when to ask. If they have a question about something or if something raises even a tiny red flag, that they know to pick up the phone and make the call to us" (qtd. in Rhoden, 2009, para. 8).

Recruiting

Article 1H of the constitution focuses on the recruiting standards for member institutions. This article notes that division recruiting bylaws should help prospective athletes make informed decisions while also finding an equilibrium between the athlete and their potential institution. Still, recruiting is a vital—and volatile—step in the pursuit of competitive excellence in intercollegiate athletics. This importance has led coaching staffs to work long hours reviewing junior films and senior recruiting lists in order to narrow a class of 1,000 prospects down to 25 signees (Feldman, 2007). Because of the need to bring in a top class year after year, staffers feel constant pressure to entice athletes by demonstrating bigger and better facilities, unique selling points specific to a program, and anything else that might convince an up-and-coming superstar to sign a national letter of intent. Successful Michigan State University basketball head coach Tom Izzo described recruiting as the worst part of his job.

> *It has gotten to the point where there are too many people involved. There are too many people that do not have anyone's best interest in mind, and I struggle with that. I also struggle with being able to go into a kid's home and telling the kid what he wants to hear instead of what he needs to hear. I'm not a very good used car salesman, and I don't want to be a good used car salesman (qtd. in Hemminger & Bensch, 2007, p. 59).*

Now, with the adoption of NIL legislation, recruiting is an even more precarious endeavor. While interim NCAA rules prohibit coaches, administrators, and boosters from using potential NIL deals to persuade a recruit to choose an institution (NIL Interim Policy, 2021), many in athletics have come forward to say that coaches are inappropriately using NIL as a recruiting incentive. In a tiff that went viral in summer 2022, University of Alabama head football coach Nick Saban even accused Texas A&M University's head football coach, Jimbo Fisher, of "buying" his recruits since the NIL era began in the summer of 2021 (Daniels, 2022). This spat clearly demonstrates the tensions present in NIL and recruiting compliance. However, NIL is still new, so we do not yet know its full ramifications on the NCAA recruiting landscape.

Each year, college coaches, graduate assistants, and other staff members involved in the recruiting process are required to pass an exam demonstrating knowledge of NCAA bylaws in order to become certified to recruit off campus. These exams serve

Recruiting Definitions

Contact

A contact occurs any time a coach has face-to-face contact with an athlete and/or their guardians off the college's campus and says more than hello. A contact also occurs if a coach has any contact with an athlete or their parents at the athlete's high school or any location where they are competing or practicing.

Contact Period

During this time, a college coach may have in-person contact with an athlete and/or their parents on or off the college's campus. The coach may also watch the athlete play or visit their high school. The athlete and their parents may visit a college campus and the coach may write and telephone during this period.

Dead Period

The college coach may not have any in-person contact with an athlete or their parents at any time in the dead period. The coach may write and telephone the athlete and/or their parents during this time.

Evaluation

An evaluation is an activity by a coach to evaluate an athlete's academic or athletic ability. This would include visiting an athlete's high school or watching them practice or compete.

Evaluation Period

The college coach may watch an athlete play or visit their high school but cannot have any in-person conversations with them or their parents off the college's campus. The athlete and their parents can visit a college campus during this period. A coach may write and telephone the athlete and/or their parents during this time.

Official Visit

Any visit to a college campus by an athlete and their parents paid for by the college. The college may pay the following expenses:

- Athlete and parents' transportation to and from the college;
- room and meals (three per day) while visiting the college; and
- reasonable entertainment expenses, including three complimentary admissions to a home athletics contest.

Before a college may invite an athlete on an official visit, the athlete will have to provide the college with a copy of high school transcript (Division I only) and SAT, ACT, or PLAN score and register with the NCAA Eligibility Center.

Prospective Student-Athlete

A high school athlete become a "prospective student-athlete" when

- they start ninth-grade classes; or
- before they begin their ninth-grade year, a college gives the athlete, their relatives, or their friends any financial aid or other benefits that the college does not provide to students generally.

Quiet Period

The college coach may not have any in-person contact with an athlete or their parents off the college's campus. The coach may not watch them play or visit their high school during this period. An athlete and their parents may visit a college campus during this time. A coach may write or telephone an athlete and their parents during this time.

(continued)

RECRUITING DEFINITIONS *(continued)*

Unofficial Visit

Any visit by an athlete and their parents to a college campus paid for by the athlete and/or their parents. The only expense an athlete may receive from the college is three complimentary admissions to a home athletics contest. An athlete may make as many unofficial visits as they like and may take those visits at any time. The only time an athlete cannot talk with a coach during an unofficial visit is during a dead period.

Verbal Commitment

This phrase is used to describe a college-bound athlete's commitment to a school before he or she signs (or is able to sign) a national letter of intent. A college-bound athlete can announce a verbal commitment at any time. While verbal commitments have become very popular for both college-bound athletes and coaches, this "commitment" is NOT binding for either the college-bound athlete or the school. Only the signing of the national letter of intent accompanied by a financial aid agreement is binding on both parties.

National Letter of Intent

A National Letter of Intent or (NLI)—not to be confused with name, image, and likeness or NIL—is an official document from the Collegiate Commissioners Association used by member schools to establish the commitment of a prospective athlete to attend an institution. Thus, the letter acts as an agreement between the athlete and the school, not an athlete and a coach. Athletes may sign the NLI if there are requirements to do so in other documents, such as their financial aid agreement form. However, athletes are not always required to sign the NLI. Athletes may sign to demonstrate commitment to a school and/or end their recruiting process.

as an educational tool to inform coaches of new legislation and to verify their knowledge of the bylaws. Theoretically at least, this process should negate the possibility of violations deriving from lack of knowledge about the bylaws. The exam is 30 questions long, and in order to pass it a test taker must correctly answer 80 percent of the questions and complete the exam within an hour. If a person fails, they are allowed to retake the test an unlimited number of times with a minimum of 30 days between attempts.

Each division and each sport has unique contact periods and specific rules; however, similar language is used in all recruiting bylaws (see the Recruiting Definitions sidebar). Each year, the NCAA releases the recruiting calendars for Division I and Division II sports. The calendars have specific recruiting time periods and designate dates for contact, evaluation, quiet, and dead (no-contact) periods. It is important for prospective athletes to be guaranteed certain times without coach contact so they are not overwhelmed, anxious, or experiencing other distressing symptoms. Having quiet and dead periods helps to ensure prospective athletes' mental well-being, while allowing them to focus on important areas outside of athletics, such as academics and social endeavors.

Division III institutions are allowed to begin recruiting through unlimited telephone calls and recruiting material as early as a prospect's first year in high school. In general, the recruiting calendar for most Division I and II sports notes that coaches can begin contacting prospective athletes beginning on June 15 after the athlete's sophomore year of high school. See bylaw 13 in the three divisions' NCAA manuals for more specific regulations for each sport and appropriate recruiting methods. Additional recruitment rules and processes are covered in this book in chapter 6.

Violations and Infractions

Despite a compliance officer's best efforts, most institutions commit several violations a year. These are generally innocent mistakes, referred to as "secondary violations," and they typically involve an isolated or inadvertent breach that does not or is not intended to provide a significant recruiting or other type of benefit. These secondary violations often stem from a lack of knowledge about intricate legislation, a miscommunication between personnel, or an oversight. Most secondary violations are self-reported through a standard form and resolved administratively, often through self-imposed minor penalties.

Repeated secondary violations, however, may be elevated to major infraction status, in which case the institution becomes subject to the process and penalties associated with such infractions. Major

The Committee on Infractions and the Independent Accountability Resolution Process

The Committee on Infractions (COI) is part of the NCAA's enforcement staff and is present at each level of NCAA competition. As discussed in Article 19, the COI operates as an independent body tasked with deciding infractions cases involving NCAA schools or their representatives (e.g., administrators, coaches, athletes, boosters). The COI has the authority to find facts, conclude violations, dole out penalties, monitor institutions on probation, and conduct follow-up inquiries as needed. The committee also may hear appeals should schools or their representatives object to the decision. The COI includes a host of potential representatives making these decisions, including current and former presidents and chancellors, ADs, former coaches, persons from the general public with legal training, conference leaders, and more.

In 2018, based on recommendations from the Commission on College Basketball after the Federal Bureau of Investigation (FBI) looked into a men's basketball pay-for-play scandal involving multiple schools, the NCAA created the Independent Accountability Resolution Process (IARP) (McGavic, 2021). This body served as an alternative to the COI and was reserved for particularly contentious and complicated cases in Division I. There were four key components to the IARP that institutions had to traverse before receiving their final ruling. These included: (1) the Independent Accountability Oversight Committee, (2) Infractions Referral Committee, (3) Complex Case Unit (CCU), and (4) Independent Resolution Panel (IRP). Steps 1 through 3 were designed to weed out the less egregious cases and were also where the investigations occurred.

Once a case reached the fourth step of the IRP, it was examined by a 15-person committee whose members had legal, sports, and/or higher education–related backgrounds. The IRP examined the facts as found by the CCU and the facts according to the school with the alleged violations. A hearing was held and penalties were administered if appropriate (McGavic, 2021). An important difference between the IARP and COI was that once a ruling was handed down by the IARP, a school could not appeal it.

However, in 2022, the NCAA voted to disband the IARP, in favor of a more streamlined investigative approach (Durham, 2022). The IARP failed for two key reasons. First, the panel received a larger than anticipated number of referrals from programs being investigated, creating a backlog of cases. Second, the IARP's inquiry process was not as quick as originally planned, raising scrutiny and causing disdain in the association, particularly in men's basketball. Critics asserted that the oversight body was nothing more than a "failed infractions experiment" (Tait, 2022, para. 1).

Going forward, the NCAA is slated to change its review and appeals processes (Durham, 2022). When reviewing cases, the investigative body plans to (1) provide more clearly defined violation standards, (2) clarify how school leaders should be involved in investigations, (3) enforce a new standard for head coach responsibility requirements, and (4) establish a public-facing dashboard for current cases. For appeals, the goal is to (1) reduce the number of appeals, (2) decide the majority of appeals in writing rather than oral arguments, (3) limit appeal extensions unless extenuating circumstances arise, (4) overturn COI decisions only if the appealing institution or representative can show that the decision is unreasonable, (5) remove the automatic stay for appealed penalties, and (6) allow the Infractions Appeals Committee to offer summary affirmations of COI findings without further comments (Durham, 2022).

infractions are those that provide an extensive recruiting or competitive advantage. Institutions accused of major infractions are investigated by the NCAA enforcement staff, like the Committee on Infractions (COI) or the Independent Accountability Resolution Process (IARP). An investigation is generally launched because the staff has reason to believe that an institution has intentionally broken rules in a way that yielded a significant competitive advantage (NCAA Rules Enforcement, 2014).

When sufficient information is discovered to warrant an investigation, the enforcement staff provides a letter of inquiry to the university president or chancellor. At this point, the enforcement staff conducts an investigation to determine whether rule violations occurred. Primary methods used in the investigation typically include interviews and information collection through documents such as telephone records, bank records, and academic transcripts. If a major violation is discovered, a notice of allegations (NOA) is sent to the member school's president or chancellor, with copies sent to the athletics director, the executive officer of the conference, and the institution's faculty athletics representative. At this point in an investigation, the school must respond to the allegations, and a hearing date is set with the relevant NCAA infractions committee.

The enforcement committee compiles a case summary outlining the allegations, the individuals involved, and any other relevant information. All parties receive the information at least two weeks before the hearing date. If all parties accept the allegations in the report, a summary disposition may be conducted in which the school, the individuals involved, and the enforcement staff cooperate to confirm the violations and propose penalties in an effort to bypass an in-person hearing. The committee on infractions then reviews the report to decide whether the terms are acceptable or a hearing is needed. If a hearing is necessary, penalties are announced six to eight weeks after the hearing.

Each NCAA division has a COI. The number of members on the committee ranges from 5 (Division III) to 10 (Division I), and the membership includes lawyers, member-school law professors, and individuals from the general public. The committees serve as independent groups responsible for assessing penalties against institutions and individuals who break NCAA rules (NCAA Rules Enforcement, 2014).

Professional Development

National Association for Athletics Compliance (NAAC)

NAAC provides professional development through an annual conference and online resources. It strives to push the industry standards to the greatest heights, ensuring ethical behavior and integrity in intercollegiate athletics regardless of member institution, conference affiliation, or division. NAAC membership facilitates networking and provides access to educational sessions, such as best-practice education and roundtables at the summer conference. Rules information, education, compliance forms, certification and recruiting, and booster guidelines continue to evolve and NAAC helps members stay current. Officers and committees steer the group and select annual award winners and keynote speakers. The leadership also holds question-and-answer sessions and fosters diversity among compliance professionals. Online resources available throughout the year, including data and trends analysis, educational webinars, *Athletics Administration* magazine, and the NACDA Daily Review email, address current events, explore new strategies, and provide continuing education. Reduced-price memberships are available to help students engage in professional development early in their career. Students can also follow NAAC on social media platforms, including X (formerly known as Twitter): @naacconnect

Penalties for major violations vary depending on the severity of the case, but generally involve termination of the guilty staff member's employment, preclusion of postseason competition, forfeiture of wins throughout the time frame of the noncompliance, fines, and limits on scholarships or recruiting visits. The most significant penalty, often referred to as the "death penalty," can include eliminating a sport for at least one year, eliminating athletic scholarships for two years, and eliminating NCAA voting privileges for four years. This penalty is applicable only to repeat offenders, and to date it has been implemented only once—at Southern Methodist University in 1987, after a series of major violations.

The NCAA has been criticized for what some see as punitive and unfair enforcement. The effort to govern is complicated by the fact that the association's investigative and enforcement power is limited. An institution or individual who commits a major infraction has not committed a crime addressable by the legal system but rather a violation for which the response is limited to NCAA sanctions on member institutions, staff members, and athletes. Therefore, the penalties for past violations are often shouldered by future administrators and athletes.

The burdens associated with the investigation process—and the negative publicity and financial implications that can come with a postseason ban or other penalty—have caused many institutions to employ outside legal counsel to regularly self-investigate. This action can head off an NCAA investigation and the associated strife.

Institutional Response to Major Infractions

For an administrator involved in an investigation, it is wise to seek outside legal counsel and create a guiding vision for the investigation. Several firms that specialize in addressing infractions employ highly experienced lawyers, some of whom have served on infractions committees. Seeking advice, experience, and insight from outside counsel in a major infractions case can help tremendously, and it has become a common practice in major NCAA infractions cases.

Under its previous director of athletics Dick Baddour, the University of North Carolina at Chapel Hill developed a situational vision as a guide for handling a major NCAA infractions case. At difficult times during the process, the philosophical approach adopted at the beginning of the investigation helped administrators make effective decisions and keep the process in perspective. Such a vision also helps employees muster the courage to bring forward information that is potentially damaging. Indeed, if a director of athletics does not lay out a clear philosophical approach in such a situation, it might be wise for an employee to suggest doing so. Administrators are often so inundated with intense day-to-day operational demands that they fail to step back and devise an approach that looks at the big picture in order to help them best navigate a difficult situation.

The "Death Penalty"

The NCAA has always had the power to prevent an institution from participating in athletics if it has violated principles and bylaws. However, it was not until 1985 that the association passed its repeat violator rule due to a host of schools committing repeated violations of rules for which they had already been sanctioned. The repeat violator rule states that if a second major violation occurs at a member school within five years of being sanctioned or on probation for that same violation, the school can be barred from competing in the sport involved in the second violation for one or two seasons. The harshness of the rule led to the media nicknaming the rule the "death penalty."

Selected Major and Secondary Violations

Major Violations

Violation summary: Violations of NCAA legislation in the men's lacrosse program involving ineligible participation, failure to maintain squad lists, and lack of institutional control. Violations of NCAA legislation in the football program involving impermissible inducements and extra benefits, inconsistent financial aid packages, and lack of institutional control.

Penalty summary: Public reprimand and censure; three-year probation; NCAA regional rules seminar required for the directors of admissions, athletics, compliance, and financial aid, as well as the vice president for institutional advancement and head coach; vacation of lacrosse wins while the ineligible student-athlete competed; lacrosse postseason ban for the following year; limit of five official paid football visits for the following two years; vacation of football wins in which two athletes competed while ineligible; financial penalty of US$70,000; and required annual compliance reporting.

Violation summary: Violations of NCAA legislation involving impermissible recruiting of a prospect by a representative of the institution's athletics interests; impermissible phone calls and text messages; impermissible inducements; impermissible entertainment; unethical conduct; failure to promote an atmosphere of compliance; and failure to monitor by the institution.

Penalty summary: Public reprimand and censure; three-year probation (the institution had proposed a two-year period); reduction by one (from 13 to 12) of the permissible number of grants-in-aid in men's basketball for the following academic year; reduction by 40 (from 130 to 90) of the permissible number of "recruiting person days" for the following two academic years; limit of no more than five official paid visits in men's basketball for the following two academic years; show-cause order placed on the former operations director for a period of three years; suspension of the head coach from all coaching duties for the first three conference games of the following season; informing of all prospective men's basketball athletes about the term of probation for the institution; requirement that the institution permanently disassociate the representative of the institution's athletics interests involved in this case; and required annual compliance reporting.

Violation summary: Academic fraud by four baseball athletes and a women's tennis athlete.

Penalty summary: Public reprimand and censure; one-year probation; athletes ruled ineligible for competition for the remainder of the current baseball season and the entire following season; athletes ruled permanently ineligible for and removed from the baseball and women's tennis teams; vacation of records.

Secondary Violations in Football

Violation: During the fall semester, an assistant football coach had telephone contact with two prospective athletes on two occasions, each during the same week. The coach misunderstood what constituted a recruiting week.

Institutional action: Letter of admonishment issued to involved assistant coach; rules education for entire coaching staff; preclusion of entire staff from using next permissible calling opportunities with both involved prospective student-athletes.

Enforcement action: Preclude the entire football coaching staff from having telephone contact with prospective athletes for the next two calling opportunities.

Violation: An institution paid for additional hotel charges incurred by the parents and siblings of prospective student-athlete (PSA) 1 and PSA 2 while accompanying the prospective student-athletes on their official visits. Specifically, PSA 1 and PSA 2 had their parents and siblings accompany them on their official visit, which resulted in a US$40 hotel charge for a rollaway bed for two nights on each PSA's bill. The violation was discovered when the director of compliance reviewed all travel reimbursement documents related to the football program. PSA 1 promptly repaid the US$40, and when reported, the institution was waiting on PSA 2's payment.

Institutional action: Prior to the next official visits, compliance will meet with hotel staff to educate them about rules regarding what the institution can pay for and the fact that any room charges for a PSA other than those for parents are the responsibility of the PSA's parents. Football coaches have been informed that they must educate PSAs' parents regarding additional charges incurred by bringing other family members.

Enforcement action: No further action. However, please note that PSA 2 is ineligible for intercollegiate competition at the institution until restitution is made to a charity of his choice or until his eligibility is restored by the NCAA athlete reinstatement staff.

Violation: During the spring semester, an assistant coach (AC) sent one text message to a PSA. Specifically, the PSA was preparing for his official visit to the institution and sent a text message to the AC to inform him of his SAT score. The AC responded to the text message without realizing his mistake. The AC subsequently reported the violation to the compliance office.

Institutional action: Entire football coaching staff prohibited from initiating phone calls or correspondence with involved PSA for a two-week period; rules education provided to all coaches at next rules education meeting.

Enforcement action: No further action.

Violation: Two football athletes participated in one countable athletics-related activity prior to completing the compliance paperwork.

Institutional action: A letter of admonishment was issued to the head football coach. The institution is required to conduct a rules education session about the applicable NCAA legislation with the involved staff member(s). The student-athletes are ineligible for further practice and competition at the institution until completion of the forms.

Enforcement action: No further action.

Compliance Resources

Compliance administrators can find a wealth of information in two NCAA resources: the Legislative Services Database (LSDBi) and the Compliance Assistant (CAi). The LSDBi fulfills two main functions: to provide a comprehensive collection of information about NCAA bylaws and processes and to serve as a resource regarding prospective athletes' eligibility. One of the main purposes of the LSDBi is to allow compliance administrators to search for NCAA bylaws, interpretations, and legislative proposals. This capacity is especially valuable when administrators are asked rules questions by coaches and staff members, because it means the compliance administrator has the relevant information at hand. The LSDBi also allows administrators to search for all major and secondary infractions committed by NCAA institutions, which can provide points of comparison if a similar situation arises at a particular institution.

In addition, the LSDBi is one of the sources where administrators may access educational materials and compliance forms and check the status of various submitted waivers—for example, initial eligibility, progress-toward-degree, legislative relief, and athlete reinstatement. The LSDBi is also the home of the NCAA Eligibility Center. This resource focuses on information relevant to prospective and current athletes. Compliance administrators use this site for a variety of purposes, including adding a prospective student-athlete to their institutional request list (IRL) once a coach has decided to pursue the athlete. The site also contains guidelines, checklists, and instructions for completing an NLI. These documents may be sent to prospects in order to increase their awareness of the NLI process.

Administrators can also view an NLI report that contains a list of all signees in a certain sport in a particular year and check the status of an NLI. Finally, the Eligibility Center allows administrators to view information about current student-athletes. A detailed report is kept for each prospect and includes demographic information, academic qualifier status, amateurism status, IRL and NLI information, transcripts and test scores, and a list of items needed by the NCAA to complete the prospect's initial eligibility evaluation.

The Compliance Assistant (CAi) website is another resource that allows compliance administrators to keep detailed records regarding their institution's current athletes and athletic teams. Administrators can upload or input each team's playing and practice season, including such items as start and end dates of practice, competition days, and required days off. The institution's academic calendar can also be added to provide a comprehensive view of a team's schedule for a specific year. The site provides a recruiting calendar for each sport by specifying what type of period (i.e., contact, evaluation, quiet, or dead) is in effect for the sport on any given day. Administrators can also input information regarding each prospective athlete being recruited by the institution and thereby house all data in one location.

CAi can be used to run a multitude of reports on topics such as eligibility and financial aid, and the reports can be customized for each institution. Each student's profile contains information about enrollment, recruitment status, seasons of competition used in the applicable sport, financial aid received, eligibility status, degree progress, waivers applied for and received, forms completed, and transfer information (if applicable). Administrators are not required to fill out every possible piece of information on CAi, and some institutions input data for certain sections but leave others blank. The site simply provides a centralized location that administrators can use for managing information about their student-athletes and teams. Though CAi is used primarily by compliance administrators, some coaches have purchased their own software to prevent violations and manage information. Leading software options in this category include Jump Forward and FieldLevel.

As an administrator, it is critical to remain informed about changes or potential changes in compliance. The NCAA often uses social media to communicate changes and updates related to compliance. Consider following @NCAACompliance on X (formerly known as Twitter) for information such as releases of the yearly manuals, discussions on waivers, and information concerning recruiting policies.

Technology Tools

ARMS Software

ARMS is a monitoring platform for compliance officers and other athletics administrators. It is currently being used across more than 100 NCAA campuses. ARMS offers built-in compliance monitoring systems for college athlete recruitment, countable athletics-related activities, eligibility, and academic progress rate. ARMS claims that in some instances it can even flag potential violations to prevent sanctions. Additionally, the software also can provide support in the areas of development, business operations, and team management.

Other comparable monitoring platforms utilized by compliance officers include Teamworks, ACS/FrontRush, and Jump Forward, as well as INFLCR and Opendorse to assist with name, image, and likeness (NIL). Both of the NIL platforms include monitoring and educational aspects.

Leadership Lesson

The Importance of a Vision Framework

Responding to tremendous criticism related to perceived overregulation, complexity, and legislation thought to be unfriendly to athletes, the NCAA Division I board of directors adopted a set of 25 proposals in 2013 aimed at creating "a more flexible manual based on common sense" (Hosick, 2013, p. 1). This move was the first step toward deregulation in several areas, which, as then NCAA president Mark Emmert noted, "refocuses our attention on things that really matter, the core values of intercollegiate athletics" (Hosick, p. 4). Indeed, "things that matter" can sometimes be lost in the seemingly never-ending onslaught of administrative tasks to complete, recruiting materials to prepare, fires to put out, and legislative changes to absorb. This type of focus, one might argue, is what produced a 464-page Division I rulebook. The complexity of the rules was such that "patches" were created to help control problems in a system that had lost sight of what was truly important.

In the famous book *Alice's Adventures in Wonderland*, Alice comes to a fork in the road and politely asks the Cheshire Cat which road she should take. "'Where do you want to go?' responded the Cheshire Cat. 'I don't know,' Alice answered. 'Then,' said the Cat, 'it doesn't matter'" (Carroll, 1865). As we pursue the tasks that fill our days, it is easy to become busy—very, very busy. We might work from sunup to sundown, trudging along a path, only to realize when we reach the end that we took the wrong one. If we don't know where we hope to go, it is extremely difficult to get there. In chapter 3, we discussed the importance of vision in an organization. In this leadership lesson, we explore the concept a bit more, on an organizational and individual level.

While they may differ somewhat in their approach to composition and scope, virtually all leadership experts emphasize the importance of this long-term, big-picture approach to organizational leadership. Kotter (1996) called it "setting a direction," Covey (2004) referred to it as "beginning with the end in mind," and Drucker (1967) asked, "What needs to be done?" Collins and Porras (1994) defined a vision framework as something that preserves the core ideology, purpose, and values of an organization while stimulating progress and envisioning a future through a 10- to 30-year "big hairy audacious goal (BHAG)."

Collins and Porras (1994) also referred to the yin-yang concept from Chinese philosophy, which is used to describe how seemingly contradictory or opposing forces are often complementary and interconnected (see figure 4.1). With this in mind, they urge leaders to "embrace the 'genius' of the *And*'" by simultaneously preserving the core while stimulating progress; holding a long-term focus while also effectively focusing on the short-term; and, possibly for our purposes here, pursuing excellence both in athletics *and* in academics. In this way, the core of a business or department can remain constant with a clear vision and core values

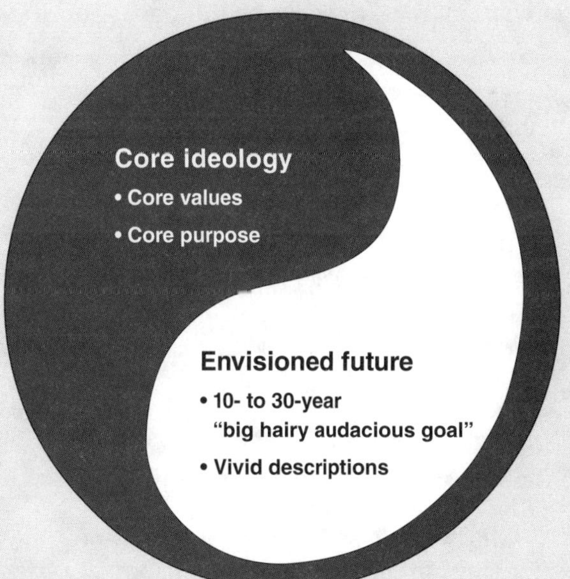

Figure 4.1 The yin-yang symbol can represent a vision framework that focuses on both core values and future progress.

(continued)

LEADERSHIP LESSON *(continued)*

amid continual change in the NCAA rulebook as the organization maneuvers in the competitive marketplace to drive toward progress and the future vision (Collins & Porras, 1994).

With this concept of the yin-yang vision framework in mind, let's transition now from an organizational paradigm to a personal one. As explored in chapter 1, all leadership begins with the individual. But how does vision play out on the individual level? The importance of a vision framework in organizational health is apparent. Indeed, you should soon be able to recite the vision or mission statement of the organization where you intern, work, or hope to work. Perhaps the department is even working toward a "big hairy audacious goal." But what is *your* mission? What is your envisioned future? Do ***you*** have a firm grasp on a core ideology that will stay constant as you move toward your envisioned future? If not, we urge you to forge one now. Just as vision is important in the direction of an organization, it is also important in your path as a leader.

Covey argues that all things are created twice—first mentally, then physically. He urges individuals to begin with the end in mind, to have a clear idea of their destination and the steps necessary to get there. Toward this end, it is helpful to write personal mission statements to guide you through life. In order to envision our "end," we must start by understanding our core. Echoing the yin-yang philosophy, Covey noted that "people can't live with change if there's not a changeless core inside them. The key to the ability to change is a changeless sense of who you are, what you are about and what you value" (2004, p. 108).

Change, as the saying goes, is the only constant in life. Understanding our desired destination makes it possible to maintain a proactive approach—to act, rather than to be merely acted upon—through all of the changes and curveballs that we may encounter (Covey, 2004). Taking the time to write a personal mission statement allows you to reap the rewards on an individual level that have been well documented on an organizational level. If you are struggling with what you might write in a mission statement, or what your core is made of, try the following exercises to help solidify the values and principles that are most important to you.

> *If you want to build a ship, don't drum up people to collect wood and don't assign them tasks and work, but rather teach them to long for the endless immensity of the sea.*
>
> Antoine de Saint-Exupéry

- Visualize your own funeral, the people who might attend, and the things that you hope might be said. How do you hope to be remembered? What will you wish you spent more—or less—time doing?
- Imagine that you have only one semester to live and that during this semester you must remain in this course as a standout student. What might you do differently? What would you do the same?
- List the differing roles you currently hold and the goals you hope to achieve in each role. (Covey, 2004)

When you walk into a visionary company—a company with a strong core and an envisioned future—you should be able to feel the culture and sense the vision as it emanates from everyone and from everything that is done. Can your coworkers sense your core and your vision? Take some time to ponder, write a personal mission statement, and then review it often. Take time first to create mentally what you intend to accomplish physically. Stay true to your core while continually stimulating personal progress, and begin with the end in mind . . . for if you know where you're going, it's a whole lot easier to get there!

Case Study

Louisville Lawyers: Worth the Price?

The University of Louisville was part of the FBI's 2017 investigation into pay-for-play in Division I men's basketball. In 2020, the institution received its notice of allegation (NOA) from the NCAA, claiming significant violations, including a Level I allegation—the most severe—and Level II allegations. The Level I violation alleged that the men's basketball program provided improper recruiting inducements, up to US$100,000, to the family of a men's basketball athlete. The Level II violation charged that the former coach failed to create a culture of compliance and that the school athletics department failed to monitor staff. The school released a statement that it would appeal these allegations. However, the University of Louisville and the NCAA are still entangled in this enforcement process. Most recently, in the summer of 2022, the institution retained a lawyer charging almost US$2,500 per hour to appeal the NCAA's NOA and punishment. As noted earlier in the chapter, hiring outside counsel in major infractions cases can work to limit NCAA punishment. However, US$2,500 per hour is a significant amount of money that can add up quickly, depending on the length of the appeal.

Questions to Consider

1. Should the university retain such an expensive attorney to help fight the NCAA's punishment? Why or why not?
2. Where does one find attorneys skilled in litigation within intercollegiate athletics?
3. How does retaining a lawyer influence the tensions of athletics within the academy?

CONCLUSION

The collegiate model of athletics participation is founded on an ideal of education through participation in athletics. The proliferation of compliance rules and regulations speaks to the ever-present temptation for commercial and competitive interests to outweigh the pure purpose of athletics within the academy. For this reason, administrators should remember the student-focused foundation of all rules as they lead the association and their departments into the future. Although NCAA compliance procedures can be intimidating at first glance, the common themes of fair play and opportunity enhancement should serve as the foundation for each bylaw.

DISCUSSION QUESTIONS

1. Why are the relationships between coaches and compliance staff so important? If you were a director of compliance, how might you suggest strengthening these relationships?
2. What does a "culture of compliance" mean? How might you help instill a culture of compliance as an athletics director, a coach, or an intern?
3. Do you agree with the NCAA maintaining the "death penalty" as a potential punishment for repeat violations for an athletics program? Why or why not?
4. With all the complexities associated with NCAA compliance, how could institutions or the association make athletics compliance education and training easier for coaches and administrators in order to prevent future violations?
5. What major shifts do you see from the NCAA's 2021-2022 constitution to its 2022-2023 constitution? Why do you think these changes are important for athletics managers to understand?
6. How does your vision statement align with the purpose and goals of athletics compliance?

LEARNING ACTIVITIES

1. The NCAA has been criticized for seemingly punitive and unfair methods of rules enforcement. Search the web for a specific example of such criticism. In your chosen situation, why do you think the NCAA acted as it did? Was there an alternative approach that might have been better for the individuals and institutions involved? How might this alternative action have affected other individuals and institutions?
2. Using the NCAA Legislative Services Database (LSDBi), find an example of a secondary violation. If you had been an administrator at the involved school, how might you have prevented this violation? What would you have done immediately upon finding out about it? How might you have addressed your stakeholders once the sanction or self-imposed penalty had been decided?
3. Take an NCAA Coaches Recruiting Practice Exam to test your knowledge and ability to search the NCAA manual for answers: https://web1.ncaa.org/coachesTest/exec/practiceexam?division=1.

Diversity, Equity, and Inclusion

Joseph N. Cooper, University of Massachusetts–Boston

Molly P. Harry, University of Arkansas–Fayetteville

Erianne A. Weight, University of North Carolina at Chapel Hill

Barbara Osborne, University of North Carolina at Chapel Hill

In this chapter, you will explore

- the evolution of diversity, equity, and inclusion in intercollegiate athletics;
- the importance of diversity, equity, and inclusion;
- the implications of Title IX in fostering diversity, equity, and inclusion;
- Title IX compliance; and
- how to use critical theories to understand and improve diversity, equity, and inclusion in intercollegiate athletics.

WHERE ARE THE WOMEN IN MEN'S SPORTS?

Intercollegiate athletics has long been divided into "men's sports" and "women's sports." The doors have been open for men to coach a women's program, such as the iconic Jack Bauerle leading the University of Georgia women to numerous swimming and diving championships, or Mike Drahos leading the University of Pittsburgh at Johnstown women's basketball program, or Girish Thakar serving as the head coach of the Westminster College women's soccer program. But what about the opposite? What about women running men's athletic programs in the head coaching role?

Bernadette Mattox gained national attention in 1990 when she became an assistant coach at the University of Kentucky under Rick Pitino before eventually becoming the head coach of the women's basketball program at the school. Kim Wyant, the head coach of the men's soccer program at New York University (NYU), led her team to six postseason bids in her first seven seasons. While Wyant's team was knocked out of the 2022 NCAA Tournament in the first round, her coaching counterpart at the University of Chicago, Julianne Sitch, would eventually lead her team, the Maroons, to win the national championship. Sitch, from 2015 to 2017 an assistant coach for the women's soccer program, became head coach of the men's program on April 20, 2022. Her first team finished 22-0-1, outscoring its opponents 14-3 in its six wins in the NCAA Tournament. Only once during the season did her team give up two goals, and the Maroons won their conference title as well. The team's only tie came at the hands of Wyant's NYU squad, in an unusual encounter between two women leading men's soccer programs.

Sitch replaced a male head coach of a program that reached the national semifinals in three of the past four seasons. Her leadership took a great team to the highest level possible. Her expectations are for a strong culture, strong standards, and strong expectations as she recruits in pursuit of another national title. A 2020 study by the U.S. Department of Education found that less than 5 percent of men's teams are coached by women, yet those positions tend to be in golf, tennis, and track at the Division III level (Wetzel, 2022). The same study found that men serve as head coach for approximately 50 percent of women's programs. At what point will women see greater inclusion in the head coaching ranks? What will effect that change?

Intercollegiate athletics has historically failed to provide meaningful opportunities for people of color and women. Critics of intercollegiate athletics have called for advancements toward racial and gender equity, particularly as it relates to the experiences of racial and gender groups facing structural marginalization (Associated Press, 2021; Cooper, 2019; KCIA, 2021). The Institute for Diversity and Ethics in Sport (TIDES) at the University of Central Florida releases an annual report grading the NCAA conferences and schools on their racial and gender hiring practices. The 2021 report gave college sports a B in racial hiring and a C+ in gender hiring, indicating an overrepresentation of white male leaders in intercollegiate athletics. This is problematic, given that one-third of NCAA athletes are persons of color and that almost half of the NCAA athletes compete on women's teams (NCAA Demographic Database, n.d.). Clearly, there is much room for improvements in diversity, equity, and inclusion in college sports. It is up to the next wave of college athletics administrators and practitioners to push these causes forward and enact meaningful change to improve representation of and equitable treatment for groups that have historically been subjected to marginalizing conditions.

HISTORY AND EVOLUTION OF DIVERSITY, EQUITY, AND INCLUSION IN INTERCOLLEGIATE ATHLETICS

Higher education and intercollegiate athletics are microcosms of the broader society whereby gender and racial stratification have been deeply embedded in institutional structures, arrangements, and cultures. Prior to the Morrill Land-Grant Act of 1890, a vast majority of colleges and universities were exclusively reserved for whites (Cooper et al., 2014). The eight Ivy League schools (Brown University, Columbia University, Cornell University, Dartmouth College, Harvard University, Princeton University, University of Pennsylvania, and Yale University), viewed as the most prestigious higher education institutions in the United States, were founded prior to the passage of the Emancipation Proclamation of 1863 and the ratification of the Thirteenth Amendment to the U.S. Constitution, which abolished slavery and involuntary servitude except as a punishment for crime. Hence, the founding principles of these institutions emerged while Native Americans were subjected to genocide and land displacement and African Americans were subjected to dehumanization and enslavement (Sage, 2007). In 1906, the National Collegiate Athletic Association (NCAA) was established in response to President Theodore Roosevelt's call for more governance over college athletics competitions, particularly with regard to safeguarding white male football players (Thelin, 1996). Mattheessen (2016) documented how the NCAA was largely composed of white males from its inception until the early 1970s.

The American Physical Education Association created the Committee on Women's Athletics in 1917 due to the exclusion of women in all levels of sport (interscholastic, intercollegiate, and professional). Nearly 50 years later, in 1964, that committee led to the creation of the Commission on Intercollegiate Athletics for Women, and subsequently this organization led to the formation of the American Intercollegiate Association for Women (AIAW) in 1971 (Mattheessen, 2016). The founders of the AIAW sought to create a female-centered and education-first sport organization that did not grant athletic scholarships, which was starkly different from the male-centered and competitive focus of the NCAA, which did grant athletic scholarships to male athletes. Title IX, which prohibits discrimination on the basis of sex in educational programs, was passed in 1972. The NCAA initially opposed it, but five years later, the NCAA created compelling incentives for programs that were previously affiliated with the AIAW to transfer their membership (Mattheessen, 2016; Westerhaus, 2007).

Clearly, institutionalized sexism and racial segregation were commonplace when the NCAA was founded. Cooper et al. (2014) outlined how historically Black colleges and universities (HBCUs) were not permanently granted access to NCAA membership in the mid-1960s. Similar to Black athletes themselves, HBCU athletic programs were allowed only limited access to intercollegiate competition during the early 20th century. The increased racial and gender diversity within the NCAA occurred as a result of external pressure associated with the midcentury Civil Rights and women's rights movements (Cooper et al., 2014; Mattheessen, 2016).

Along the same lines, Native Americans are another group that has experienced widespread exclusion and mistreatment in intercollegiate athletics; hence, the establishment of the Native American Athletic Association in 1973 (King, 2015). The NCAA did not ban racist "Indian" mascots for its

Diversity in the United States

Diversity remains one of the most important considerations for leaders working in intercollegiate athletics. Although the TIDES reports reveal the slow pace of diversity and inclusion in athletics, the United States is diversifying quickly. By 2040, less than half of the U.S. population will be white (Frey, 2018). With the representation of people of color on the rise in American society, athletics departments should seek to mimic this representation on their teams and staffs. However, diversity goes beyond representation. Having members on teams and staffs from diverse backgrounds may be a competitive advantage as those with diverse backgrounds bring different perspectives to issues and more creative solutions to those issues (Cunningham, 2007; Lussier & Kimball, 2013). In January 2020, NCAA voted to establish the position of Athletics Diversity and Inclusion Designee (ADID) (Dent, 2020). The NCAA Constitution now requires all NCAA members to appoint an employee in this role.

First Athletes of Color to Participate in College Athletics

Native American involvement in Indigenous sports predates the 19th century; however, one of the most recognizable Native American institutions of the late 19th century, when modern-day college sport was forming, was the Carlisle Indian Industrial School. The most famous athlete in Carlisle history was the legendary Jim Thorpe, a multisport athlete (football, baseball, and track and field) who earned Olympic gold in the pentathlon and decathlon in the 1912 Olympics (Buford, 2010). Moses Fleetwood Walker is credited as the first African American to participate in college baseball, at Oberlin College in 1878 (Ashe, 1988). Joe Kapp and Anthony Muñoz are recognized as among the early pioneers in college football, dating back to the late 1950s and 1970s (Harrison et al., 2013). Walter Achiu is recognized as one of the Asian American sport pioneers as a standout athlete in football, baseball, track, and wrestling at the University of Dayton (Ohio) in the early 1920s (Franks, 2016). These pioneers, along with their same-race peers, paved the way for current college athletes from diverse backgrounds.

members until 2006, reflecting the pervasive commodification and objectification of Native Americans (SPLC, 2005). The NCAA allows exceptions when institutions have formal agreements with and permission from specific Native American tribes. Although this policy change was a progressive step in terms of diversity, equity, and inclusion, the lack of land-acknowledgment statements and failure to redistribute resources (i.e., land) reflect the perpetuation of settler colonialism by the NCAA and its member institutions (Chen & Mason, 2019; Staurowsky, 2007). However, some athletics facilities have undergone name changes to avoid honoring whites who terrorized Native Americans, and there have been coordinated partnerships with tribal colleges and universities.

Diversity efforts in higher education and intercollegiate athletics have been propelled by court cases and legislation. Some of the most important milestones were *Brown v. Board of Education of Topeka, Kansas* (1954), which mandated racial desegregation of public schools; Title VI and Title VII of the Civil Rights Act of 1964, which prohibits employment discrimination on the basis of race, color, religion, sex, or national origin as assessed by disparate treatment or impact (Davis, 2008; Flowers, 2015); and Title IX of the Education Amendments of 1972, which prohibits discrimination on the basis of sex in educational programs. Each of these laws was instrumental in providing increased access and protection from discrimination for people of protected classes.

Throughout the 1980s and 1990s, diversity issues continued, as the passage of supposedly race-neutral and gender-neutral policies had a disparate impact on the athletic eligibility of underrepresented groups such as African Americans. For example, Proposition 42 and Proposition 48 denied scholarships and limited eligibility of high school athletes whose GPAs and standardized test scores fell below a specific standard. However, decades of research indicate that standardized tests measure test-taking ability rather than aptitude or knowledge and are fundamentally racist, classist, and sexist (Au, 2016; Garrison, 2009), thus limiting opportunities for education.

Responding to pressure built on social recognition of oppression, the NCAA established the Committee on Women's Athletics (CWA) in 1989 and the Minority Opportunities and Interests Committee (MOIC) in 1991 (Westerhaus, 2007). Both committees created demographic reports to examine diversity in athletic participation, leadership, and staffing. Data from these initial reports to the more recent diversity reports (such as those produced by TIDES) reveal racial and gender disparities whereby African Americans and women are more likely to be hired for entry-level and mid-level positions, such as academic advisors and life skills coordinators, as opposed to upper-level administration positions. Data also revealed that African Americans, Latinos, and Asian Americans were consistently underrepresented in coaching positions compared to their representation as athletes (Westerhaus, 2007). Numerous initiatives, such as the former Advanced and Expert Coaches Academies, the Dr. Charles Whitcomb Institute Program (formerly the Leadership Institute for Ethnic Minority Females and Males), Academic Performance Program, Supplemental Support Fund, the Presidential Pledge to Commit to Diversity and Inclusion, and the establishment of Athletic Diversity and Inclusion Designees (ADID), have contributed to nominal (albeit debatable) improvements in terms of experiences and outcomes for underrepresented groups at the athlete, coaching, staff, and administrator levels (Cooper et al., 2014; Davis, 2008; Keaton, 2021; Weight et al., 2020a; Westerhaus, 2007).

> *Black male college athletes' "collective athletic prowess, intellect, and mighty presence on campuses and in athletic departments across historically white US institutions of higher education has literally and figuratively changed the face and trajectory of college sport over the past several decades."*
>
> J.N. Singer (2019)

In 2003, the NCAA established the Office of Diversity and Inclusion to supplement member institutions' efforts to foster environments where diversity, equity, and inclusion were optimized (Brooks & Althouse, 2007; Westerhaus, 2007). The progressive Dr. Bernard Franklin was appointed as the first Executive Vice President of Education and Community Engagement and Chief Inclusion Officer in 2003 (Keaton, 2021; Rietmann, 2017). Franklin established the diversity hiring presidential pledge, official NCAA inclusion statement, Accelerating Academic Success Program for limited resource institutions, and the annual NCAA Inclusion Forum (Newton, 2021; Rietmann, 2017). By 2021, the NCAA had established the Board of Governors Committee to Promote Cultural Diversity and Equity, CWA, Gender Equity Task Force, and MOIC (NCAA, 2021a).

Notable legal cases against the NCAA and its member institutions have increased diversity and inclusion of underrepresented groups. Cases such as *O'Bannon v. National Collegiate Athletic Association* (2015) and *National Collegiate Athletic Association v. Alston* (2021) as well as California Senate Bill 206 (also known as the Fair Pay to Play Act) have resulted in major changes in terms of college athletes' rights within the NCAA structure. Despite these advances, serious, persistent diversity and inclusion issues include inequitable recruitment, hiring, retention, and promotion practices, and overall lack of inclusivity (Newton, 2020). It is also worth noting another significant NCAA omission: the lack of adaptive sport offerings. Adaptive, or para, sports are sports that have been adapted or modified to accommodate individuals with disabilities. These sports are designed to allow people with a wide range of physical, sensory, or intellectual impairments to participate in athletic activities and compete at various levels. Adaptive sports provide a range of physical and mental health benefits, including improved fitness, self-esteem, and social interaction, and they also contribute to breaking down barriers and changing perceptions about disability. Although antiracism and antisexism efforts are demonstrated by the formation of the current NCAA inclusion committees and task forces, anti-ableism is another important yet often overlooked aspect of diversity initiatives within athletics (Fay & Wolff, 2009).

BLACK ATHLETE EXPERIENCES

Scholarship notes that due to power structures in place within the NCAA and its member institutions, athletes of color can have very different experiences than white athletes. This is particularly true for athletes of color in the revenue-generating sports of football and men's basketball (Beamon, 2008; NCAA Student Athletes and NIL Rights, 2021; Nocera & Strauss, 2016; Rubin & Moses, 2017; Van Rheenen, 2011). Using survey data from revenue-generating and non-revenue-generating athletes (n = 581), Van Rheenen (2011) explored athlete feelings of exploitation. Participants rated their agreement or disagreement with the following three statements: (1) "Sometimes I feel that I am being taken advantage of as an athlete," (2) "I give more to the university than it gives to me," and (3) "This university makes too much money off its athletes, who see very little of it" (Van Rheenen,

2011). While 25 percent of non-revenue-generating athletes expressed feelings of being exploited, 71 percent of revenue-generating athletes noted such feelings. When it came to race, Black athletes were five times more likely to feel exploited than were white athletes and those of other racial groups (Van Rheenen, 2011).

Feelings of exploitation often result from the commercialization and professionalization of Black college athletes in football and men's basketball (Beamon, 2008; Nocera & Strauss, 2016; Van Rheenen, 2011). The economic structure of athletics predominantly favors white men (Branch, 2011). For example, while head coach salaries for football and men's basketball continue to rise, athletes are limited in their compensation to their athletics scholarship and cost-of-attendance stipends (Clotfelter, 2019). It was not until summer 2021 that athletes could profit from their name, image, and likeness (NIL) and receive supplemental compensation from outside the institution (NCAA Student Athletes and NIL Rights, 2021). The majority of head coaches for football and men's basketball identify as white, while the majority of athletes in these sports are Black (NCAA Demographic Database, n.d.). With the commercialization of college football and men's basketball, particularly through media rights contracts, Black athletes have become increasingly professionalized and commodified (Comeaux, 2018; Harper, 2018): They dedicate more hours to their athletics and fewer to academics and serve as public relations and branding symbols for the institutions they represent (Clotfelter, 2019; Hawkins et al., 2015).

Because the majority of NCAA schools are predominantly white institutions, it is important to understand how the campus environment can influence the experiences of athletes who do not identify as white (Gayles et al., 2018). For example, Harper's (2018) report titled *Black Male Student-Athletes and Racial Inequities in NCAA Division I College Sports* states that Black men are 2.4 percent of undergraduates at the 65 universities in the Power Five. However, Black men make up 55 percent of football teams and 56 percent of men's basketball teams at these 65 institutions. Thus, Black men are overrepresented on their athletics teams but underrepresented in the classroom. This reality, that a Black man is 23 times more likely to be an athlete than a traditional student, fuels racist campus stereotypes about scholarly merit and can have negative effects on athletes' self-efficacy, motivation, and academic performance (Gayles et al., 2018; Weight et al., 2020b; Wininger & White, 2008).

Using NCAA data from 7,703 Division I athletes, Gayles and colleagues (2018) examined differences in athletes' sense of belonging across race, gender, and sport profile. The authors found that: (1) athletes of color were significantly more likely to report lower levels of sense of belonging than their white counterparts, (2) men reported significantly lower levels of sense of belonging than women, and (3) athletes in revenue-generating sports reported significantly lower levels of sense of belonging than athletes in non-revenue-generating sports. Importantly, Gayles et al. (2018) found that positive climates—such as those bolstered with diversity,

WCC's Bill Russell Rule

In 2020, the West Coast Conference (WCC) adopted the Bill Russell Rule to advance the conference's commitment to diversity hiring. The rule was named after Bill Russell, a men's basketball athlete at the University of San Francisco from 1953 to 1956. During his collegiate career, Russell won two national championships and led calls for racial equity. Then, while playing for the Boston Celtics in the National Basketball Association, Russell led many racial justice protests and, in 1966, became the first Black head coach in the four major sports in the United States. Russell's influence on sports' relationship to race and inclusion cannot be overstated. The "Bill Russell Rule" requires that each WCC athletics department include a member of a historically underrepresented group in its final pool of candidates for full-time assistant coach, head coach, senior administrator, and athletics director.

equity, and inclusion—increased all athletes' feelings of belonging. Thus, this research highlights the significance of diversity, equity, and inclusion in intercollegiate athletics.

RECENT TRENDS IN ATHLETE SOCIAL JUSTICE ACTIVISM

The summer of 2020 saw a surge of athlete advocacy and activism across all levels of sport,

Industry Profile

DR. CARLA WILLIAMS

Director of Athletics, University of Virginia

Carla Williams was appointed as the director of athletics at the University of Virginia (UVA) in 2017, making her the first African American female AD at a Power Five institution. Prior to this position, she was an athletics administrator at the University of Georgia for 13 years, serving as associate AD (2004-2008), senior associate AD (2008-2011), executive associate AD (2011-2015), and deputy AD (2015-2017).

This pattern of hard work, impact, and internal ascension started young. Williams was recruited to play basketball for the University of Georgia. She excelled as a player, then a graduate assistant, then assistant coach, then assistant director of compliance. Next she moved to Florida State University, where she completed her PhD in sport administration and worked as a graduate assistant for athletic academic support (1998-2000). She then worked at Vanderbilt University as an assistant AD (2000-2003) and associate AD (2003-2004), overseeing 11 sports and the CHAMPS/Life Skills program.

Williams is known for her passion for athlete development and academic excellence through sport. She often shares her path wherein the ability to attend college and have a successful career would not have been possible were it not for her basketball skills. She wants these same opportunities to be available for all the athletes and administrators in her sphere and she supports innovative programs to make this happen, including UVA's Pathways program. The Pathways program connects university, community, and alumni resources with student-athletes to help launch their careers.

Williams is also passionate about inclusion, learning, and growth through adversity. Commenting on the COVID-19 pandemic, social justice movement, and return-to-play discussions that occurred in 2020 and 2021, she shared her belief that they all happened at the same time for a reason: "We were separated physically from our student-athletes, and we were forced to use . . . technology to connect. . . . Then everything else happened in our community, in our country related to social justice, and it gave us another opportunity to have even more meaningful connections to our student-athletes. This situation was primed for there to be a disconnect between coaches, staff, administrators, student-athletes, but ironically because of everything that's happened, we're actually closer, I believe. There's been more interaction and more connection, more substantive conversations, which I think has been really helpful" (qtd. in White, 2020).

Matt Riley/UVA Athletics

Extending her influence nationally, Williams serves on the executive committee of the Black AD Alliance, the NCAA NIL Legislation Solutions Group, and the ACC Football Subcommittee. She was recognized as Women Leaders in College Sports 2019 Administrator of the Year and was a 2021 finalist for *Sports Business Journal*'s Division I Athletics Director of the Year.

including intercollegiate athletics. In fall 2020, the NCAA administered the Student-Athlete Well-Being Survey, which included questions about student athletes' perceptions of and involvement with social justice advocacy and activism (NCAA, 2021b). Across all three divisions, 24,974 student-athletes completed the survey. Key findings revealed Black student athletes were more likely to indicate a willingness to take a stance on a social issue (60 percent) compared to Latinx (49 percent), other student-athletes of color (49 percent), and white student-athletes (41 percent). Across all racial groups, a majority (over 75 percent) of all student-athletes expressed the importance of being an active and engaged citizen (voting, for instance). Given the focus on racism in the wake of the police killings of George Floyd of Minneapolis, Minnesota; Breonna Taylor of Louisville, Kentucky; and Ahmaud Arbery of Brunswick, Georgia, the involvement of Black student-athletes reflects their socioemotional, cultural, and personal connection to the vulnerability of Blacks in the United States. Additional findings from the survey revealed that student-athletes requested support from coaches and administrators to offer more social and racial justice education sessions, communicate more definitive public stances against injustices when they occur, diversify athletic programs through recruitment, hiring, and promotion, and listen to and support student-athletes who experience racial injustice (NCAA, 2021b).

GENDER EQUITY

As mentioned previously in this chapter, institutionalized sexism, racism, and segregation were legal and common in college sport until external pressure associated with the midcentury Civil Rights and women's rights movements spurred legislation to protect women and people of color (Cooper et al., 2014; Mattheessen, 2016). Title IX of the Education Amendments of 1972 is the federal law that prohibits sex discrimination in any educational program or activity at any institution that receives federal funds. The 37 words that form this law—along with supplementary regulations, policy interpretations and guidance from the Office of Civil Rights in the U.S. Department of Education, and case law—form the basis upon which the law is interpreted and applied. The following discussion

UVA Groundskeepers

In 2017, white supremacists descended on Charlottesville, Virginia, challenging the removal of a statue of a Confederate general from the city's downtown mall (Spencer, 2018). While counterprotestors remained peaceful, one white supremacist drove his car into a crowd of counterprotestors, injuring 19 and killing one, a young woman named Heather Heyer. A few years later, in 2020, the murder of George Floyd by a police officer sparked increased attention on racial injustice in America. Floyd, a Black man who allegedly used a fraudulent check at a store, was restrained by a white police officer. The officer put a knee to Floyd's neck, restricting oxygen flow to Floyd's brain, killing him (Hill et al., 2020). Feeling called to action based on these two events, football players and coaches at the University of Virginia founded the Groundskeepers. This group mobilized to bring increased awareness to hatred and racism, while also trying to protect the Charlottesville community from a repeat of what happened in 2017 (Adelson, 2020). One way the group has brought awareness to racial justice concerns is through a three-mile walk around the city and school grounds. The walk begins at Heather Heyer Way—a street renamed to honor the woman killed at the white supremacy march—and moves toward the university's Memorial to Enslaved Laborers, which honors the enslaved people who helped build the University of Virginia. The football team and other athletics teams complete this walk a couple of times each semester as a reminder of those who have made sacrifices for racial equity and to continue discussions about racism in society and in sports. The Groundskeepers hope to establish other initiatives to achieve their racial equity goals, including discussions with campus and local police and creating mentorship programs (Adelson, 2020).

provides an overview of the law with particular focus on current interpretation and application in college sport.

Title IX Time Line

- 1963—Hourly women workers are included in the Equal Pay Act.
- 1964—Title VII of the Civil Rights Act prohibits discrimination in employment based on race, color, sex, national origin, or religion.
- 1969—Bernice Sandler files complaints of gender-based discrimination in university admission, hiring, and promotion practices against more than 200 universities.
- 1970—U.S. Congresswoman Edith Green, chair of the U.S. Subcommittee on Higher Education, holds the first congressional hearings on women in education and hires Bernice Sandler to compile the findings of the hearings.
- 1971—Senator Birch Bayh introduces a proposal to ban sex discrimination in schools. The legislation is not approved because it would open The Citadel, a military college, to women.
- 1971—U.S. House of Representatives approves an amendment to the Higher Education Act authored by Congresswoman Patsy Mink that includes Title IX.
- 1972—U.S. Congress approves Title IX, which is enacted into law.
- 1974—Tower Amendment to exempt revenue-producing sports from Title IX is rejected.
- 1975—U.S. Department of Health, Education, and Welfare issues final regulations banning sex discrimination and establishing a three-year time frame for institutions to become compliant with Title IX.
- 1975—Bills to alter Title IX athletics coverage die in committee.
- 1975 and 1977—U.S. Senate rejects bills to curtail Title IX enforcement.
- 1978—Mandatory Title IX compliance date arrives.
- 1980—Title IX enforcement is assigned to U.S. Department of Education's Office for Civil Rights.
- 1984—Title IX is suspended after the Supreme Court rules in *Grove City College v. Bell* that Title IX is applicable only to programs receiving specifically targeted federal funding.
- 1988—Civil Rights Restoration Act of 1987 is approved by Congress over the veto of President Ronald Reagan). The act renders the *Grove City College* ruling obsolete, restoring Title IX's institution-wide coverage in any program or activity in an educational institution receiving federal funding.
- 1992—Private right of action is established in *Franklin v. Gwinnett.* Title IX plaintiffs can recover monetary damages and attorney fees for intentional discrimination.
- 1993—*Favia v. Indiana University of Pennsylvania* establishes that budgetary difficulties are not an excuse for noncompliance with Title IX.
- 1994—Equity in Athletics Disclosure Act is passed, requiring disclosure of compliance data.
- 1996—Office for Civil Rights (OCR) issues Clarification of Intercollegiate Athletics Policy Guidance, explaining how schools can comply with each prong of the three-part test of the participation requirements of Title IX.
- 1996—Validity of the three-part test is confirmed in *Cohen v. Brown University.*
- 1997—OCR issues Sexual Harassment Guidance.
- 2000—OCR issues Revised Sexual Harassment Guidance, reaffirming standards described in 1997 guidance.
- 2001—U.S. Department of Justice issues the Title IX Legal Manual.
- 2003—OCR issues further clarification: Title IX does not encourage limiting men's opportunities.
- 2005—Additional clarification issued by OCR introduces controversial survey method approach to three-prong test of Title IX participation compliance. It is rejected by the NCAA and will be rescinded by OCR in 2010.
- 2005—U.S. Supreme Court rules in *Jackson v. Birmingham Board of Education* that Title IX prohibits schools from retaliating against those who protest sex discrimination.

- 2010—OCR rescinds the 2005 "additional clarification."
- 2011—U.S. Department of Education issues policy guidance clarifying that Title IX's protections against sexual harassment and sexual violence apply to all students, including athletes. It requires schools to use the same procedures that apply to all students to resolve sexual violence complaints involving student-athletes.
- 2016—Administration of President Barack Obama cites Title IX and issues guidance saying that transgender students at public schools should be allowed to use the bathroom or locker room that matches their gender identity.
- 2016—Hillary Clinton becomes the first woman to win a major party nomination for president.
- 2017—Administration of President Donald Trump revokes the Obama administration's guidance on transgender public school students and bathroom usage.
- 2020—U.S. Supreme Court holds that discrimination based on sexual orientation and gender identity is discrimination based on sex that is prohibited under Title VII.
- 2020—New Title IX regulations are promulgated addressing sexual harassment in schools.
- 2022—Acknowledgments of progress and calls for action are heard around the United States, celebrating 50 years of Title IX.

From Carpenter and Acosta (2014); DeJulio et al. (2008); National Coalition for Women and Girls in Education (2008); Women's Sports Foundation (2014).

The landscape of educational equality prior to the passage of Title IX is clearly illustrated by the following scenario. Throughout a three-year period in the 1960s, more than 20,000 female applicants were denied admission to colleges and universities in the state of Virginia. In that same time frame, no men were denied admission. Until the passing of Title IX, there was no legal precedent for preventing sex-based discrimination in educational institutions. The Fourteenth Amendment to the U.S. Constitution provides all persons "equal protection of the laws," but the Supreme Court applies an intermediate level of review for cases involving sex, so cases concerning discrimination against women in education have never prevailed. Title VII of the Civil Rights Act prohibited discrimination in employment on the basis of race, color, religion, national origin, or sex, but this law was not applicable to admissions in educational institutions. Similarly, the Equal Pay Act prohibited salary discrimination on the basis of sex, but again required an employment relationship. Finally, Title VI prohibited discrimination in federally assisted programs, but only on the basis of race, color, and national origin—not sex.

After years of determined effort by early pioneers, Title IX of the Educational Amendments of 1972 was adopted, and the following 37 words became law: "No person in the United States shall, on the basis of sex, be excluded from participation in, be denied the benefits of, or be subjected to discrimination under any education program or activity receiving Federal financial assistance" (Title IX of the Education Amendments of 1972, 44 Fed. Reg. at 71413). While often recognized as the law that requires gender equity in athletics, Title IX was passed primarily to address discrimination in education. The law addresses discrimination in admissions and counseling, discrimination against pregnant or married students, sexual harassment, sexual assault, and inequities in extracurricular activities. Broadly, Title IX offers legal protection from any form of sex discrimination in public or private educational programs receiving federal funding. As a result, even private colleges and universities are required to comply with Title IX when they accept federal financial aid packages for students.

From its inception, Title IX's application to intercollegiate athletics has been attacked. Critics have labeled Title IX an unfair quota system that limits men's opportunities. A growing body of scholarly research and legislative interpretation, however, supports the conclusion that many administrators are using Title IX as a scapegoat for lavish expenditures in football and men's basketball that deplete resources and opportunities for both men and women in athletics departments (e.g., Roessner & Whiteside, 2016; Staurowsky & Weight, 2013). Though many administrators choose to limit opportunities for men rather than expand opportunities

Leadership Lesson

Allyship

Allyship is defined as intentional efforts enacted to support an individual or group who identifies with a different identity or identities than oneself (Cooper, 2022). This can happen when a member of a privileged group works in unity, partnership, and solidarity with a marginalized individual or group to break down systems and disparities that challenge the group's right to thrive. Acts of allyship can be as small as speaking up in opposition to a man who presents his thoughts as though they were more important than a woman's (known as "mansplaining"). An ally in this situation would interrupt the man and invite the woman to finish her thoughts. Allied partnerships help to strengthen marginalized groups and encourage recognition, voice, inclusion, consideration, access, and equity.

Acts of allyship can also be more public. Before a basketball game between Knox College and Fontbonne College on November 28, 2014, Ariyana Smith of the Knox College women's basketball team engaged in a symbolic protest of the killing of Michael Brown of Ferguson, Missouri. During an altercation with a police officer on August 9, 2014, Brown was shot by the officer, allegedly while his hands were in the air. His body remained in the street for four and a half hours after the killing. In her protest, Smith walked around the court with her hands up and lay on the court for four and a half minutes to draw attention to Brown's death. Knox College initially suspended but later reinstated Smith. An example of allyship would have been for her coaches, teammates, and administrators to respect Smith's protest and use their agency and platforms to show support for her protest.

Allyship could have involved teammates' kneeling in solidarity with her, coaches and administrators issuing a statement that they support Smith's First Amendment rights, a statement from the athletics department that it supports any action by a college athlete that seeks to redress social injustices, or creation of a petition by the athletics department to demonstrate support for the Brown family and hold the police officer accountable for these actions. Allyship demonstrates a pronounced commitment to and support for those who have suffered from injustices and marginalization in any context, irrespective of whether the ally shares the identities associated with the person or group most directly affected.

Allyship involves conscious action to support a group that is discriminated against—to recognize the systemic struggles they face and to authentically partner with the group to break down barriers. To become an ally, try the following:

1. Educate yourself about the systems of oppression that hinder equity in the workplace. Do not ask those from marginalized communities to educate you, but rather seek out resources on your own.
2. Listen to colleagues from marginalized groups when they want to talk about their experiences. Acknowledge their struggles and be open to feedback about your own behavior.
3. Endorse and promote their ideas and use your name and connections to advocate for their opportunities.
4. Use your privilege to speak up. For instance, instead of being a passive nonracist, become an active anti-racist.

As you find your way as an ally, it is often tempting to be bold and outspoken in the quest. There is certainly a place for this, but balance it with care. Remember that the lived experiences of marginalized groups may be a new discovery to some, but they are not new to the oppressed. As you navigate difficult conversations, remember it is often best to address issues of oppression in private, rather than in public forums, and to be sure you are respecting the wishes of the person for whom you wish to be an ally.

Adapted from Cooper (2022).

for women, the spirit of the law reflects a hope for equality and increased opportunity for both sexes.

TITLE IX COMPLIANCE

In 1979, the U.S. Department of Health, Education, and Welfare issued a policy interpretation to help colleges and universities understand Title IX compliance measurement in athletics. This document outlined three areas of compliance: (1) participation, (2) scholarships, and (3) other benefits. For a visual representation of this policy interpretation, see figure 5.1. For each area of compliance, the document defined in detail key factors to be measured. Since then, the foundation set by this policy interpretation has been supplemented by clarifications and judicial decisions. These intricacies—and the ways in which they are viewed by the current regulatory body charged with enforcing Title IX, the U.S. Office for Civil Rights (OCR)—are discussed in the following sections.

In order to most effectively comply with the requirements of Title IX, an athletics department should rely on an institutional Title IX policy or a plan led by an institutional Title IX coordinator. In addition to following university guidance, most athletics departments maintain a Title IX committee that is consulted regularly.

Participation

The 1979 policy interpretation outlines the method through which institutions can demonstrate effective accommodation of students' interests and abilities. This method has become known as the three-part or three-prong test. This method of demonstrating participation compliance has been supported time and again in legal cases because it provides flexibility for an institution in how it chooses to demonstrate effective accommodation. Despite a pervading belief that *prong 1* is the only method for achieving participation compliance, institutions have successfully demonstrated compliance in OCR reviews and in the courts by using any one of the three prongs:

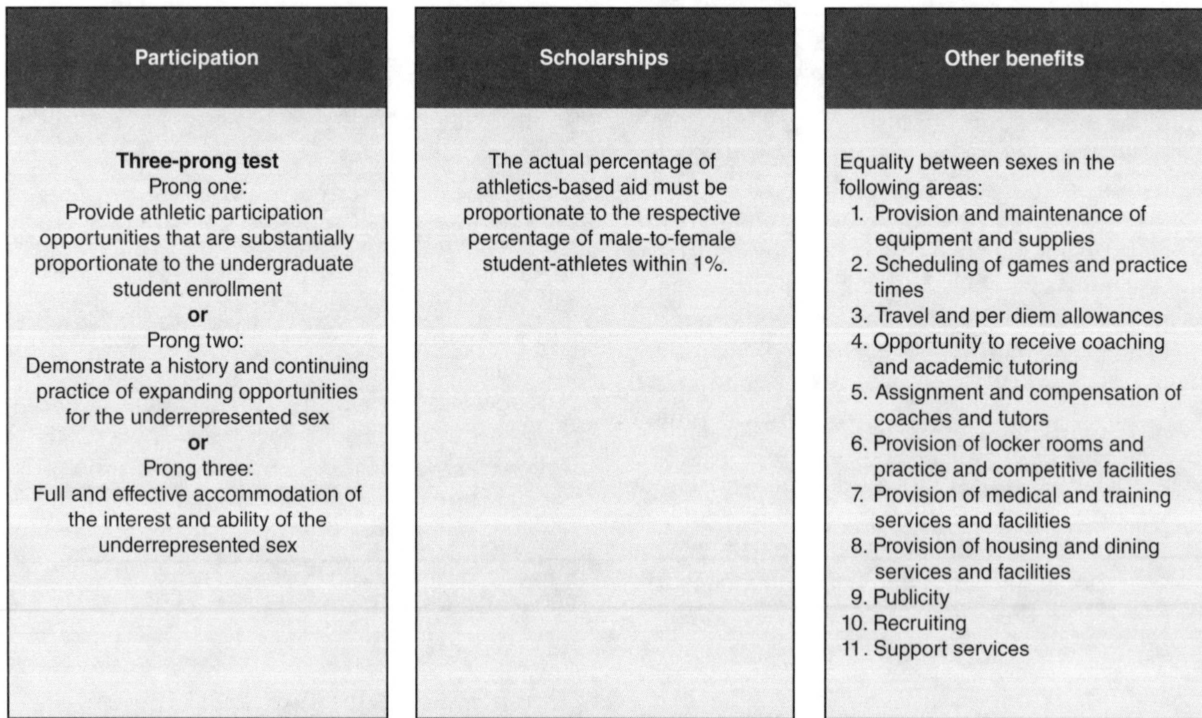

Figure 5.1 **1979 policy interpretation of compliance measures.**

- *Prong 1.* Providing athletics participation opportunities that are substantially proportionate to the undergraduate student enrollment
- *Prong 2.* Demonstrating a history and continuing practice of expanding opportunities for the underrepresented sex
- *Prong 3.* Accommodating in full the interest and ability of the underrepresented sex

In 1996, the OCR issued a clarification of the three-part test, and the document's introductory letter referred to *prong 1* as a "safe harbor." Nevertheless, the 1996 clarification and each subsequent one have upheld each of the prongs as a method of participation compliance. Let us now take a closer look at each of these compliance methods.

Prong 1: Proportionality

The proportionality prong recognizes that women are entitled to equal opportunity, and adopts the common-sense principle that schools can comply with Title IX when they provide their female students with the same number of athletics opportunities they provide their male students (Samuels, n.d.). An institution can establish compliance with prong 1 by providing athletics participation opportunities to a substantially proportionate percentage of the underrepresented sex as compared with its percentage of the school's full-time undergraduates. Thus, if women make up 60 percent of the undergraduate population, approximately 60 percent of the athletics participation opportunities in the athletics program should be provided for women. The OCR defined "substantial proportionality" in its 1996 clarification as one of the following: (1) exact proportionality; (2) a disparity of less than 1 percent caused by an increase in the current year's enrollment after a year of exact proportionality; or (3) an institution's pursuit of proportionality over a five-year period.

The OCR and courts have allowed schools to comply with this prong as they see fit. In practice, this freedom has allowed many schools to use practices that are detrimental, and even fundamentally opposed, to the spirit of the law. One such practice is roster management, in which the number of participants in men's sports is artificially capped by limiting the number of walk-ons and eligible athletes, while coaches of women's sports are pressured into increasing their roster size, thus leading to a less-than-optimal experience for all athletes on the team. This practice at the Division I level has altered the competitive landscape of the other divisions, as men who previously would have been able to compete at the Division I level now seek opportunities in the other divisions (Staurowsky & Weight, 2011). Although this practice may be legal in some cases, it is not encouraged.

Prong 2: Program Expansion

An institution can establish compliance with prong 2 by demonstrating a history and continuing practice of expanding opportunities that are responsive to developing interests and abilities of the underrepresented sex. Administrators determining whether this method of compliance is sufficient should gather detailed records of institutional decisions to add programs. These records should indicate the timeline of program expansion, how the expansion affected the male-to-female ratio of participants, and how these additions were responsive to interests and abilities of the underrepresented sex.

In assessing an institution's participation compliance through the lens of history and a continuing practice of program expansion, the OCR examines the following factors:

- Record of adding intercollegiate teams by sex
- Record of upgrading teams to intercollegiate status by sex
- Record of increasing the number of participants of the underrepresented sex
- Affirmative responses to requests by students or others to add or elevate sports
- Current implementation of a policy or procedure for requesting the addition of sports that include the elevation of club or intramural teams
- Effective communication of that policy or procedure to students
- Current implementation of a plan or program expansion that is responsive to developing interests and abilities of the underrepresented sex
- Demonstrated efforts to monitor developing interests and abilities and timely reaction to the results of those efforts

Opportunity expansion requires a definitive increase in the participation opportunities for the underrepresented sex in the athletics department's offerings. Therefore, expansion of opportunity for the underrepresented sex cannot be demonstrated by reducing opportunities for men or by upgrades to facilities designated for women's athletics.

> *Under the second prong, schools that do not currently provide equal opportunity can show that they have made, and are still making, progress toward equality. This prong is lenient in a way that is unprecedented in the history of civil rights law. For example, an employer would not be allowed to continue paying women less than men on the basis that it was moving toward equality. (Samuels, n.d.)*

Prong 3: Accommodation of Interests and Abilities

Under the third prong, schools can show that they are fully meeting the actual athletics interests and abilities of women on their campuses, even if they are not giving women the same opportunities to play as their male students. An institution can establish compliance with prong 3 by demonstrating full and effective accommodation of the interests and abilities of the underrepresented sex. This prong is often overlooked as a legitimate method of participation compliance, yet an institution can add participation opportunities for the overrepresented sex as long as it can also prove a good-faith effort to conclusively demonstrate that there is no interest, demonstrated ability, or reasonable expectation of competition by the underrepresented sex in the institution's competitive environment.

The Office of Civil Rights determines whether schools can justify compliance with prong 3 utilizing the following measurement criteria (2020):

- Whether an institution uses nondiscriminatory methods of assessment when determining the athletics interests and abilities of its students
- Whether a viable team for the underrepresented sex was recently eliminated
- Multiple indicators of interest
- Multiple indicators of ability
- Frequency of conducting assessments
- Competitive opportunities offered by other schools against which the institution competes
- Competitive opportunities offered by other schools in the institution's geographic area, including those offered by schools against which the institution does not now compete

A primary indicator of interest is the ongoing assessment of club and intramural participation. If substantial participation and competitive experience in an interscholastic sport has the potential to sustain it as a varsity sport—and if participants have an interest in competing at the varsity level—the OCR would likely determine that the interests and abilities are not being accommodated. Proactive methods of ascertaining interest levels such as surveying applicants for admissions to the institution and the undergraduate student body are also necessary for this method to suffice in participation compliance.

Title IX Literacy

A series of studies conducted by Staurowsky and Weight (2011, 2013, and 2014) found that a majority of NCAA coaches were lacking in basic Title IX knowledge. In addition, nearly 30 percent of coaches indicated hesitancy in raising Title IX issues, and more than 10 percent feared losing their job if they were to bring up concerns related to Title IX. Administrators were slightly better off but still demonstrated limited knowledge and moderate fear in some areas. The study findings reveal that training and education related to Title IX is needed so that coaches and administrators may be fiscally responsible and creative to make decisions that are in the best interest of the overall athletics program. Ongoing educational efforts will create the greatest buy-in as institutions strive to provide equitable educational opportunities for all student-athletes.

From Cook (2010); Staurowsky and Weight (2011).

Participant Defined

A common misunderstanding in compliance determination involves the definition of a participant. A primary reason for this confusion lies in the unfortunate reality that a participant is defined in three ways in three gender-equity analyses—Title IX participation, financial aid, and the Equity in Athletics Disclosure Act (EADA). For purposes of Title IX participation analysis, a participant is defined in the 1996 OCR clarification as someone

1. who receives the institutionally sponsored support normally provided to athletes competing at the institution involved (e.g., coaching, equipment, medical, and training room services on a regular basis during a sport's season);
2. and who participates in organized practice sessions and other team meetings and activities on a regular basis during a sport's season;
3. and who is listed on the eligibility or squad lists maintained for each sport;
4. or who, because of injury, cannot meet 1, 2, or 3 above but continues to receive financial aid on the basis of athletics ability (Office for Civil Rights, 1996).

The 1996 clarification specifies that participant count should be based on the number of athletes listed on the NCAA roster on the first day of competition. Despite this specificity, OCR routinely checks for significant changes in roster count after the initial competition, and in at least one court case a broader definition has been used that views a participant as one who participated for the majority of a season. In participation analysis (not to be confused with Title IX financial aid or EADA accounting), multisport athletes count as participants for each sport in which they participate. For instance, an athlete who runs cross country and indoor and outdoor track counts as three participants (see figure 5.2).

Scholarships

Thus far in our Title IX discussion we have focused on the participation requirements of the legislation. The 1979 policy interpretation also addresses equity in athletics financial assistance as a necessary area in which to demonstrate compliance. The OCR's assessment of compliance in this area is very clear. Institutions that provide financial assistance to student-athletes must demonstrate that the percentage of athletics-based aid given (not just budgeted) is proportionate to the respective percentage of male and female student-athletes. Therefore, if an institution's male participants comprise 60 percent, then the men should receive 60 percent of the scholarship dollars awarded, including the real-dollar amount of tuition, room, board, fees, supplies, summer tuition, cost of attendance, and post-eligibility aid. There is an assumption that a difference of less than one percent is sufficient to indicate compliance.

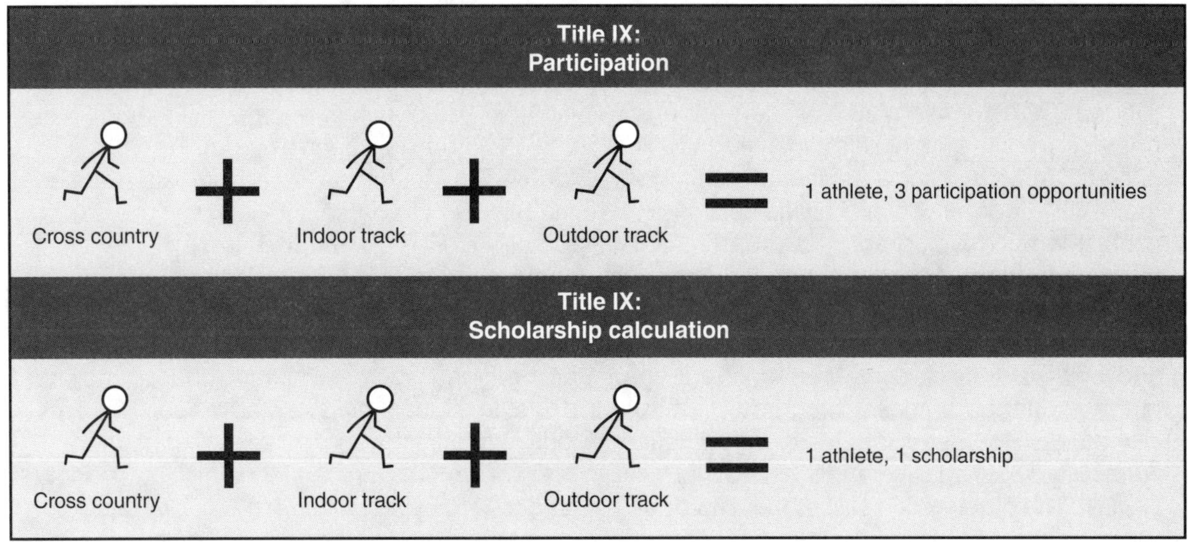

Figure 5.2 The Title IX participant.

Where a discrepancy greater than one percent exists, a school must demonstrate a nondiscriminatory rationale for financial disbursement based on gender-neutral policies or unforeseen events; such factors are evaluated on a case-by-case basis. Examples of potentially legitimate nondiscriminatory factors include the following:

- Differences between in-state and out-of-state tuition at public colleges
- Unexpected fluctuation in participation rates
- Phasing-in of athletics scholarships pursuant to a plan to increase participation
- Unexpected last-minute decisions by scholarship athletes not to enroll (U.S. Department of Education, 1996)

Inequities in providing financial aid are often influenced by the NCAA Division I financial aid designation as a "head-count" sport or an "equivalency" sport. In head-count sports, each athlete who receives athletics aid of any amount is figured into the head-count limit. Thus, it is common for each athlete in a head-count sport to receive a full scholarship to maximize competitiveness. In equivalency sports, on the other hand, limits are set on

Professional Development

Black AD Alliance, MOAA, and the John McLendon Foundation

Founded in 2020, the Black AD Alliance was established to advance the development of Black athletics administrators in Division I and elevate their voices. The alliance works with Black aspiring college athletics professionals through mentoring and building connections and networks. Additionally, the organization collaborates with the NCAA, the National Association of Collegiate Directors of Athletics (NACDA), and the Minority Opportunities Athletic Association (MOAA) to challenge racial and social injustices in college sports. Task forces of the alliance include those related to historically Black colleges and universities (HBCUs), social justice, athlete wellness, allyship and ambassadors, and Black administrator pipeline and recruitment.

The MOAA, formed in 2000, fosters opportunities for minorities in athletics under the umbrella of NACDA. MOAA holds its annual meeting at the NACDA convention and builds networking, professional development, resources, and research to improve diversity efforts in the industry. Membership services are intended to help minorities professionally, emotionally, financially, and physically in athletics. Members engage in the exchange of ideas through the MOAA community. Members also receive *Athletics Administration* magazine and the NACDA Daily Review. The organization utilizes the X (formerly known as Twitter) handle @MOAADiversity1 as an educational resource, and membership information can be found on the NACDA website. Student memberships are available.

The John McLendon Foundation also helps to develop diversity in intercollegiate athletics administration through educational resources and access to mentors. Established in 1999 through collaboration with NACDA, the foundation honors John McLendon, an iconic leader in athletics, basketball, and civil rights. Coach McLendon stressed integrity, education, leadership, and mentorship, and those values continue today as the foundation awards up to eight US$10,000 scholarships annually to minority candidates (known as McLendon Scholars) who aspire to graduate degrees in athletics administration or sport management. To date, over US$1,245,000 has been awarded in scholarship funds. The McLendon Foundation also created the Minority Leadership Initiative, in July 2020, to help young, aspiring minority coaches with strategic professional development, networking, and educational sessions. Over 80 coaches, from a wide range of sports, serve as mentors and funding sources, helping those who are newer to the coaching field advance to full-time jobs after participation in the year-long program. More information can be found at www.minorityleaders.org or by visiting the NACDA website.

the total value of financial aid that an institution may provide in any academic year. For example, under bylaw 15.5.3.1.1, the maximum equivalency for men's tennis teams is 4.5. Thus, if the value of a full scholarship is US$50,000, the men's tennis coach is allotted US$50,000 multiplied by 4.5—or US$225,000—to distribute among any or all of the athletes on the team. The coach may choose to give two full scholarships and numerous partial scholarships, or all partial scholarships, but in any case, the total amount spent must not be greater than the equivalency of 4.5 full scholarships. An institution can use either actual or average cost for determining equivalency calculations regarding room, board, tuition, fees, and cost of attendance as long as the same method is used for both the numerator and the denominator in individual calculations. Table 5.1 provides Division I head-count and equivalency limits.

Other Benefits

The third area of compliance outlined by the 1979 policy interpretation is equity in "other" athletics benefits and opportunities. This category is commonly referred to as "the laundry list" because it addresses equality in a multitude of program component areas, including the following:

- Provision and maintenance of equipment and supplies
- Scheduling of games and practice times
- Travel and per diem allowances
- Opportunity to receive coaching and academic tutoring
- Assignment and compensation of coaches and tutors
- Provision of locker rooms and practice and competitive facilities

Technology Tools

Online Reports: EADA and NCAA Financial Reports and Demographics Database

Passed in 1994, the Equity in Athletics Disclosure Act (EADA) requires that coeducational colleges and universities that receive Title IX funding and have varsity athletics submit annual reports to the Department of Education. In these reports, institutions must provide revenue and expenses for men's and women's teams, staffing information, and data on participation rates and scholarships for men's and women's teams. The goal of these EADA reports is to give current and prospective students and the public the ability to examine the equity within a school's athletics department. Through the EADA website, http://ope.ed.gov/athletics, users can retrieve information about individual schools, compare data across institutions, and customize data reports. Data collected by the Department of Education from the EADA reports may be used by the OCR to determine which institutions are not compliant with Title IX. Athletics departments also submit annual reports to the NCAA via the association's Financial Reporting System. Data in these reports also include information related to gender equity. However, EADA and NCAA data often do not match. While the focus of EADA reports is to show whether the components of a department support the principle of gender equity and uphold Title IX legislation, NCAA financial reports have more to do with fiscal integrity. Gender equity is a primary principle in the current NCAA constitution (Article 1.G, 2022). Article 6.C of the constitution reminds institutions it is the responsibility of each member institution to comply with federal and state laws regarding gender equity. Still, the information in these reports is beneficial for scholars and practitioners alike who advocate for equity in intercollegiate athletics.

Additionally, the searchable NCAA Demographic Database is another online tool that can assist in research and gauge representation in college sport leadership and participation numbers. This enables even greater analysis and exploration into race and ethnicity in intercollegiate athletics.

Table 5.1 Division I Equivalency and Head-Count Limits

HEAD-COUNT LIMITS	
FBS football	85 (with an additional limit of 25 initial counters* per year)
Men's basketball	13
Women's basketball	15
Women's gymnastics	12
Women's tennis	8
Women's volleyball	12
EQUIVALENCY LIMITS	
MEN'S SPORTS	
Cross country and track and field	12.6
FCS football	63 (with an additional limit of 30 initial and 85 total counters*)
Fencing	4.5
Golf	4.5
Gymnastics	6.3
Lacrosse	12.6
Rifle	3.6
Skiing	6.3
Soccer	9.9
Swimming and diving	9.9
Tennis	4.5
Volleyball	4.5
Water polo	4.5
Wrestling	9.9
WOMEN'S SPORTS	
Acrobatics and tumbling	14
Bowling	5
Cross country and track and field	18
Equestrian	15
Fencing	5
Field hockey	12
Golf	6
Lacrosse	12
Rowing	20
Rugby	12
Skiing	7
Soccer	14
Softball	12
Swimming and diving	14
Triathlon	6.5
Water polo	8
Wrestling	10

*"*Counters*" are individuals who receive financial aid and are countable against the aid limitations in the sport. FCS schools are allowed 63 scholarships among no more than 85 individual players, whereas FBS schools are allowed 85 players, all of whom may receive full scholarships.

From 2022-2023 Division I Manual (2023).

- Provision of medical and training services and facilities
- Provision of housing and dining services and facilities
- Publicity
- Recruiting
- Support services

In addressing compliance, and particularly in considering the intricacies of Title IX, it is easy to get bogged down in details because individual components of the legislation's interpretation can appear complicated. At the root of every test and every court case, however, is a simple question: Is it equitable? Describing gender equity in collegiate athletics, the NCAA Gender Equity Task Force has written the following:

> *An athletics program can be considered gender equitable when the participants in both the men's and women's sports programs would accept as fair and equitable the overall program of the other gender. An athletics program is gender equitable when the men's sports program would be* **pleased to accept for its own** *[emphasis added] the overall participation, opportunities, and resources currently allocated to the women's program and vice versa. (DeJulio et al., 2008)*

This sentiment lies at the heart of each "laundry list" element. The men's and women's programs do not need to look exactly the same, but the treatment of the entire men's and women's programs needs to be equitable. If disparities exist, they are assessed individually. For each program component, the men's program as a whole is compared to the women's program as a whole. When disparities are identified, further examination is required to determine whether the differences result in a student-athlete experience that is unequal. We will now explore two of these "other benefit" categories in depth to demonstrate how compliance with each of the laundry list issues might be demonstrated.

Provision and Maintenance of Equipment and Supplies

Equitable provision and maintenance of equipment and supplies requires institutions to provide equal uniforms, other apparel, sport-specific equipment and supplies, instructional devices, and conditioning and weight-training equipment. In monitoring these factors, a review should consider equipment quality, amount, suitability, maintenance and replacement schedules, and availability. Ideally, an institution should adopt a consistent and uniform policy based on the evaluation factors that ensures equity based on the specific and unique needs of each sport.

In this area of compliance, financial expenditures are not measured; rather, the criterion is overall equity. For instance, minimum necessary equipment for a hockey or football player is considerably more expensive than that for a cross country or soccer athlete. The cost of these uniforms, however, is not the primary concern, as long as the athletes are treated in an equitable manner in regard to the quantity and quality of their equipment and clothing.

It is important to understand Title IX analysis related to spending and the potential presence of funds raised. A common misconception about external funding is that it supersedes Title IX equity requirements and therefore that any inequities resulting from contributions are acceptable. This is inaccurate. All funds—regardless of a coach's popularity or ability to attract fundraising dollars to a unique project, endowment, or supply fund—are viewed as institutional funds. As a result, they need to be used equitably. If several coaches are outstanding fundraisers and are able to provide benefits that create an imbalance between the sexes in the department, the department may need to

Key Concepts of Title IX, Simplified

- Is it fair?
- Are the benefits provided to students equally available?
- Is a benefit being provided to one sex but not the other? If so, why?
- Is the underrepresented sex denied or limited any benefit provided to the other sex? If so, why?

allocate budgetary funds to balance the discrepancy created by the fundraising effort.

Travel and Per Diem Allowances

The 1979 policy interpretation outlines five areas to be examined in assessing travel and per diem allowances. Specifically, an institution should be able to demonstrate equivalence for men and women in (1) modes of transportation, (2) housing furnished during travel, (3) length of stay before and after competitive events, (4) per diem allowances, and (5) dining arrangements. As with each of the laundry list components, formal nondiscriminatory policies can help administrators make good decisions and

Transgender NCAA Athletes

Transgender athletes have received increased attention in recent years as more states pass laws preventing transgender athletes from competing for teams that do not match their assigned gender at birth. However, such laws directly conflict with NCAA policies. The NCAA's transgender policies for competition note that athletes can compete in the sport corresponding with the gender with which they identify. However, the association's policies do require testosterone suppression for transgender women (male to female) if they wish to compete on a women's team. Additionally, transgender policies impact the NCAA's rules on banned substances. NCAA bylaw 31.2.3 notes that testosterone is a banned substance; however, athletes transitioning from female to male may have an exemption to take testosterone-boosting medicine. In this instance, the institution must submit a medical exemption prior to the athlete beginning competition. Additionally, if the athlete is transitioning from male to female and requires medicine for testosterone suppression, the school must provide documentation to the NCAA. The NCAA has modeled these rules after the policies established by the International Olympic Committee and the U.S. Olympic and Paralympic Committee. The NCAA notes that, with these rules, it is trying to balance inclusion, fairness, and competitive equity (National Collegiate Athletics Association, 2023). What do you think?

Though not directly related to Title IX requirements for compliance in scholarship allocation, "tiering" is a common practice for dividing an institution's athletics offerings into differing levels of equal treatment. The top tier—which might include, for instance, football, men's basketball, women's basketball, soccer, volleyball, and gymnastics—would likely have the largest budgets, the nicest facilities, and the most comprehensive scholarship offerings. This practice enables an institution to treat different sports equitably within a tier, while recognizing that not all sports will be fully funded or treated equally.

This practice has been used for years, but budget cuts have spurred an increase in formalized practices over the past decade. When tiering is practiced, it is important for officials to be open about the process with departmental stakeholders so that they are aware of the reasons for the total differences on expenditures for men's and women's sports. Any tiering should also be done with equal opportunity in mind. For Title IX purposes in equal opportunity and "other benefits" components of the law, each tier should contribute to equal spending on men's and women's sports.

The OCR views equity both from the perspective of the student-athlete and from a broader look at the women's program as compared with the men's program. Therefore, sport-to-sport comparisons, and even overall budget comparisons, may not highlight overall equity. One common misconception in athletics departments is that expenditures on the women's basketball team need to mirror expenditures on the men's basketball team because they are equivalent sports. This is not necessarily the case. For example, a school might choose to highlight its men's basketball team and its women's soccer team, which could mean that both of those teams have equipment far superior to that of the women's basketball team. As long as the overall men's and women's programs are equivalent, a school can decide to elevate certain sports to top-tier status or to treat all sports equally. When tiering is practiced, the philosophy should be expressed to coaches and student-athletes so that they understand the department's overall gender-equity strategy and fair practices.

demonstrate equitable treatment. Specifically, it is helpful to outline departmental travel policies based on team size, distance traveled, and conflicts with class schedules.

Differences may exist for larger teams related to access to appropriate transportation and nourishing meals. Traveling with a group of 80 involves different logistical needs than traveling with a group of 20. The larger group may need chartered transportation, a larger hotel that has a sufficient number of rooms as well as large meeting spaces, and catered meals, whereas a smaller group may have significantly more travel, housing, and meal options. Necessary differences do not justify differences in quality or quantity. The amount of travel time, the number of athletes in each room, the number of meals provided, and the quality of accommodations must all be consistent. Overall, policies and procedures should be formulated in a gender-neutral manner so that all student-athletes' experiences are similar regardless of sex.

Permissible Differences

Because not all sports are created equal, it often makes sense and is not discriminatory to treat some sports differently than others. In particular, because of the large roster sizes of football teams, they often have unique needs that can create sex-neutral discrepancies in treatment. The OCR investigation manual outlines the following nondiscriminatory differences that may be deemed appropriate in an investigation.

- Differences inherent in the operation of specific sports because of rules of play, the nature or replacement of equipment, rates of injury resulting from participation, the nature of facilities required for competition, and the maintenance or upkeep requirements of those facilities
- Differences caused by sex-neutral factors arising out of special circumstances of a temporary nature, such as fluctuations in recruiting activities based on a team's annual needs and desires
- Differences directly associated with the operation of a competitive event in a single-sex sport that creates unique demands or imbalances that may be associated with large-event management issues
- Differences resulting from an institution's voluntary affirmative actions to overcome effects of historical differing treatment

As long as these factors are addressed equivalently for men and women and do not reduce the opportunity for equality when comparing the women's program as a whole to the men's program as a whole, the differences can be acceptable.

The Senior Woman Administrator

The designation of senior woman administrator (SWA) has evolved since 1981, when the NCAA first established the position (then referred to as primary woman administrator) to help with the transitional merger of the NCAA and the Association for Intercollegiate Athletics for Women (Tiell & Dixon, 2008; Wilson, 2017). The SWA has evolved into a position generally held by the highest-ranking female in each athletics department or conference.

The designation of SWA is intended to encourage and promote the meaningful involvement of female administrators in the decision-making process in intercollegiate athletics. The representation of women administrators with the SWA designation at the institutional, conference, and national levels supports women's interests but also provides a different perspective that enhances the overall experience for all involved. The SWA's daily responsibilities can include any departmental tasks and must include senior management responsibilities. When an institution has a female director of athletics, the AD should designate a different woman to assume the designation of SWA (NCAA, 2013a).

Employing Critical Theories

Administrators can use critical theories to better understand college athletics and improve experiences for those from traditionally marginalized groups. Critical race theory (CRT) is a useful analytic tool for understanding, problematizing, and reconstructing intercollegiate athletic cultures. Introduced into the sport management field in 2005 by Dr. John Singer, CRT centralizes the impact of race, racism, and other forms of oppression on the structures of society and the experiences of those who exist within a given milieu (Singer, 2005). The key tenets of CRT include the permanence of racism, whiteness as property norm, critique of liberalism, interest convergence, counter-storytelling and experiential knowledge, and intersectionality (DeCuir & Dixson, 2004). "Permanence of racism" is a concept that refers to the foundational ideology of the United States and its social institutions, whereby white Eurocentric ways of doing, being, and thinking are deemed superior and all nonwhite cultures—particularly Black African culture—are viewed as inferior. "Whiteness as property" refers to reservation of ownership and enjoyment of citizenship rights for whites. "Critique of liberalism" refers to the challenging of ostensibly "colorblind" meritocratic rationales for racialized disparities in society—the belief that white people achieve success due to merit and Black people fail to achieve due to a lack of merit. "Interest convergence" refers to the notion that any advancement by a disadvantaged group only occurs insofar as it benefits the dominant group. "Counter-storytelling" and "experiential knowledge" are terms that refer to the importance of centering the voices of those who have experienced distinct types of oppression. Intersectionality is a theoretical concept that centers the concurrent oppressions certain individuals and groups experience as a result of multiple disadvantaged identities in a given milieu; for example, a Black woman from a working-class background in the United States is disadvantaged by racism, sexism, and classism.

Several sport scholars have used CRT to examine college athletes' perceptions of activism (Agyemang et al., 2010); the intersection of racial, athletic, and academic identities (Bimper et al., 2012); racialized experiences of college athletes (Carter-Francique et al., 2013; Cooper & Hawkins, 2014; Singer, 2005, 2019) and athletics administrators (McDowell & Carter-Francique, 2017; Price et al., 2017); the impact of culturally responsive mentoring programs (Bimper, 2016, 2017; Carter-Francique, 2017; Carter-Francique, Dortch, & Carter-Phiri, 2017; Comeaux, 2010; Cooper et al., 2019); and the exploitative structures within the NCAA (Cheeks & Carter-Francique, 2015; Cooper et al., 2017; Donnor, 2005; Hodge et al., 2008). From a diversity standpoint, CRT has birthed numerous subtheories, including Asian critical race theory (AsianCrit), Latinx critical race theory (LatCrit), Indigenous critical race theory (TribalCrit), whiteness studies (WhiteCrit), Black critical theory (BlackCrit), feminist critical race theory (FemCrit), and critical disability studies (dis/abilityCrit)—to name a few (Annamma et al., 2017; Dumas & Ross, 2016; Yosso, 2005). Beyond CRT, additional critical theories, such as the internal colonization model (Hawkins, 2010), settler colonialism theory (Chen & Mason, 2019), world systems theory (Smith, 2009), race-centric ecological systems theory (Cooper, 2019), culturally responsive programming framework (Jolly et al., 2020), and antiracist culturally responsive transformational leadership approaches (Cooper et al., 2020), have also been useful in disrupting the ideology of whiteness embedded in college sport research. Hence, the use of critical theories and frameworks provides a reorientation of how college athletics have evolved over time and space and explores who is privileged and disadvantaged by established systems and norms. In practical terms, CRT can inform how practitioners reflect upon their department mission statements, vision statements, policies, and practices (i.e., data-driven approaches grounded in disparate access, treatment, and impact assessments); recruitment; position descriptions (i.e., Athletic Diversity and Inclusion Designee and staff); hiring, retention, and promotion practices; culturally responsive programming; and overall organizational culture (e.g., basic assumptions, espoused beliefs, and artifacts).

Idea: Sarah Fuller's Kickoff and Title IX

Sarah Fuller achieved a historic milestone when she was tasked with executing the kickoff during a Vanderbilt Commodores' game against the University of Missouri on November 28, 2020. Title IX regulations include a "Contact Sport Exemption," which allows schools to treat the underrepresented sex differently based on the classification of the sport as a contact sport or noncontact sport. If a sport is designated as a contact sport and the institution does not offer that sport for both sexes, the institution does not have to allow a member of the underrepresented sex to try out for that sport. Under this regulation, contact sports include "boxing, wrestling, rugby, ice hockey, football, basketball and other sports the purpose or major activity of which involves bodily contact" (U.S. Department of Education, n.d.). Under the Contact Sport Exemption, schools do not have to let female athletes try out for football. However, the school may allow a female to try out for a men's contact sport, and in that situation, the school must treat the athletes the same. Sarah Fuller's competition in 2020 was significant because it marked a step forward for gender equality and representation in college football. It challenged traditional gender norms and barriers in a male-dominated sport and served as inspiration to many aspiring female athletes. Administrators, coaches, and practitioners in college sports must wholeheartedly embrace their roles as resolute and unyielding advocates for women's participation in a wide-ranging spectrum of sports.

FEMINIST THEORY

Feminism is an "intellectual commitment and a political movement that seeks justice for women and the end of sexism in all forms. Motivated by the quest for social justice, feminist inquiry provides a wide range of perspectives on social, cultural, economic, and political phenomena," (McAfee, 2018, para. 1). Examining the structure of intercollegiate athletics through a feminist lens reveals conspicuous gendered power systems that dictate values, culture, and knowledge production (Naples, 2013; Patton et al., 2016). With this in mind, the purpose of feminist theory in sport is to center women in athletics and highlight their experiences to create more equitable opportunities (Brabeck & Brown, 1997; Bruening et al., 2005; Patton et al., 2016). Indeed, this theory is used to challenge gender roles and stereotypes, counter patriarchy, and change oppressive practices in athletics.

Previous scholarship has used feminist theory in sport to explore female athletes' and female administrators' experiences and Title IX, highlight discrepancies in funding for women's and men's teams, and investigate marketing and communication surrounding women in sport (e.g., Bruening et al., 2005; Kane et al., 2013; Oseguera & Goldstein, 2015; Toffoletti & Thorpe, 2018). Additionally, feminist theory intersects with CRT, most notably with FemCrit theory. FemCrit is increasingly used to explore and better understand the experiences of Black women in college athletics, since research has shown that this population of athletes receives little attention (Hughes, 2015; Pickett et al., 2019).

CONCLUSION

As we seek to facilitate equity and access to participation and leadership opportunities in intercollegiate athletics, the best place to start is through education. We hope the content of this chapter will empower you as a future leader to be an ally, to work toward improving representation of and equitable treatment for groups that have historically been marginalized, and to facilitate cultures of empowerment and advocacy.

Case Study

The NCAA Emerging Sport List

In 1994, the NCAA Gender Equity Task Force recommended the creation of a list of emerging sports for women to help athletics departments increase athletics opportunities. The list was soon established, and it included nine emerging sports: archery, badminton, bowling, ice hockey, rowing, squash, synchronized swimming, team handball, and water polo. After 10 years (in 2014), only four of these sports emerged as championship sports (bowling, ice hockey, rowing, and water polo), and the other five were taken off the list due to insufficient interest to fulfill the requirements to become championship sports. Six additional sports have been added to the list since the initial nine: acrobatics and tumbling, beach volleyball, equestrian, rugby, triathlon, and wrestling. Beach volleyball was adopted as a championship sport in 2014 (see figure 5.3).

In order for a sport to rise to "emerging sport" status, it must meet the NCAA definition of a sport; cite 20 or more existing varsity or competitive club teams on college campuses; and demonstrate governing-body support at the high school, professional, coach association, conference, or Olympic level. Finally, a minimum of 10 letters of commitment must be submitted by the athletics director and president of institutions intending to sponsor the sport. Once on the list, an emerging sport has 10 years to demonstrate steady progress toward championship status or meet the championship status requirement of being sponsored by 40 programs.

If a sport is removed from the list, it may be reinstated after 12 months through the same process; however, 15 letters of support are needed, and they must address how conditions have changed since the initial trial period.

Questions to Consider

1. Which sport currently on the emerging sport list do you think has the best chance of being elevated to championship status? Why?
2. If you were an athletics administrator who needed to increase participation numbers for women in your athletics department by adding a new sport, how might you determine which sport to add?

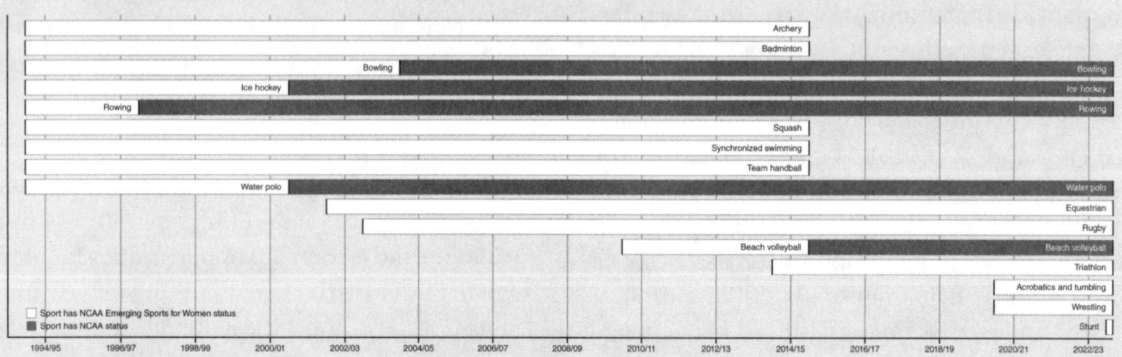

Figure 5.3 Timeline of emerging sports for women.

Reprinted by permission from "NCAA Emerging Sports for Women," Wikipedia, accessed September 12, 2023, https://en.wikipedia.org/wiki/NCAA_Emerging_Sports_for_Women. Distributed under the terms of the Creative Commons Attribution 4.0 International License (http://creativecommons.org/licenses/by/4.0/).

DISCUSSION QUESTIONS

1. Title VI of the Civil Rights Act, which prohibits discrimination in federally assisted programs on the basis of race, color, and national origin, was passed in 1964, which predates Title IX by eight years. The language in Title IX mirrors Title VI, yet the application and interpretation of Title IX in athletics programs has become far more robust. Why do you think there is so much more detail in the regulation of sex discrimination than in discrimination based on race, color, and national origin? How might the landscape be different if similar regulations were in place for Title VI? (See figure 5.1 for a graphic overview of Title IX regulations.)
2. How can athletics leaders establish better career pipelines for administrators of color and women administrators in athletics?
3. As a sports administrator, how would you manage your department's football players if they came forward expressing feelings of exploitation?
4. How can administrators use one of the critical theories presented in this chapter to better work with college athletes from historically marginalized communities?
5. Do you agree with the definition of a sport for Title IX purposes? Why or why not? How might the equation of proportionality change on your campus if current "nonsports" were accepted as sports under the umbrella of Title IX? What would be the implications of this change?
6. Discuss potentially legitimate nondiscriminatory factors that might explain a discrepancy in financial aid allocations between male and female athletes.

LEARNING ACTIVITIES

1. Building on the first discussion question comparing Title IX and Title VI, create an enforcement mechanism similar to (or different than) that shown in figure 5.1 that prohibits discrimination based on race in education.
2. In this chapter you learned about the underrepresentation of people of color and women in intercollegiate athletics leadership positions. On your own, do some research to find a current athletics director who is a woman and person of color. Consider what obstacles this leader might have had to overcome to become the athletics director.
3. Explore the NCAA Demographics Database (www.ncaa.org/about/resources/research/ncaa-demographics-database) and explain some participation or leadership trends.
4. Explore the TIDES Racial and Gender Report Card (www.tidesport.org) for college sport. How does Division I leadership and overall college sport compare to other leagues? Why do you think there are differences?
5. Create your own graphic overview of Title IX that demonstrates the intricacies of the legislation as it relates to intercollegiate athletics.
6. Examine Title IX through a feminist lens. How does this legislation achieve or not achieve the purpose of feminist theory? Pay particular attention to how Title IX challenges gender roles and stereotypes, patriarchy, and women's oppression in sport.
7. If possible, evaluate an element of the "other" or "laundry list" athletics benefits and opportunities that should be provided equitably to male and female student-athletes at your high school, college, or other athletics program. Based on your analysis, how is the program doing in this area of Title IX compliance?

Academics, Eligibility, and Student-Athlete Development

Sally R. Ross, Grand Valley State University
Lisa M. Rubin, Kansas State University
Erianne A. Weight, University of North Carolina at Chapel Hill

In this chapter, you will explore

- initial academic eligibility standards for first-year students and recruits,
- regulations related to NCAA visits and letter-of-intent process,
- academic standards for continuing student-athlete eligibility,
- resources and practices for athletics academic advisors, and
- examples of student development programming.

NAVIGATING THE WORLD OF STUDENT-ATHLETE SERVICES

A young former Division I athlete is hired as the student-athlete career development coordinator at a large Big Ten institution. During a typical week, she handles day-to-day advising and eligibility demands for student-athletes as they navigate the intercollegiate athletics experience. She also provides leadership for student-athletes in 26 sports as they work toward professional careers in life after sport. Charged with improving the experiences of 800 student-athletes, she must keep up with trends in the challenging 21st-century job market, understand the demands of each individual sport, and establish rapport with a departmental staff of more than 300 people, including 10 senior staff members and 70 coaches.

As this young professional navigates the leadership demands of her new role, her success will depend in large part on programming aimed at helping student-athletes balance their student role with their athlete role. However, efforts to promote holistic programming for this higher education population are not always appreciated by campus administrators who are skeptical of athlete-specific programs. As a result, this young professional often feels that she is working under a microscope, especially in light of media upheaval about commercialization, academic scandal, and exploitation of student-athletes. Some of her athletes have a difficult time imagining life after athletics, skeptics continually question the legitimacy of her job, and NCAA eligibility standards loom as hurdles for athletes who come to the department academically underprepared. As she begins her work, she wonders how best to press forward in developing, sustaining, and justifying the work she does with this unique population.

The six challenges confronting student-athletes identified by Parham (1993) continue to exist: (1) balancing athletic and academic endeavors, (2) balancing social activities with the isolation of athletic pursuits, (3) balancing athletic success or lack of success with maintenance of mental equilibrium, (4) balancing physical health with a need to keep playing, (5) balancing the demands of various relationships, and (6) dealing with the termination of a collegiate athletic career. For administrators in intercollegiate athletics, it is critical to understand these and other experiences and challenges faced by student-athletes. Toward this purpose, this chapter focuses on regulations, standards, and programs designed to facilitate optimal educational experiences for students who pursue intercollegiate athletics. Although each of the national governing bodies has its own set of rules and regulations, the NCAA is by far the most regulated. As such, the majority of our attention throughout this chapter will be specific to regulations adopted by NCAA member schools.

STANDARDS FOR INITIAL ACADEMIC ELIGIBILITY

In an effort to protect high school students, create competitive parity, and limit the time and effort spent on recruiting, the NCAA has developed numerous stipulations on permissible recruitment behavior for campus personnel and boosters. Bylaw article 13 in the NCAA manual outlines these guidelines and rules for Division I, II, and III institutions, and some of the stipulations are outlined in chapter 4 of this book. Building on the concepts introduced in chapter 4, this section focuses on the academic considerations and processes the NCAA has established to help ensure that student-athletes are prepared for the rigors of college.

First-Year Recruits

The NCAA Eligibility Center was created to evaluate and certify the initial eligibility of prospective first-year student-athletes. Registration with the Eligibility Center is required for students from

U.S. high schools, those who are homeschooled, and international student-athletes wanting to play sports in NCAA Division I or Division II programs. Eligibility requirements for Division III athletes are determined and certified by the school for which they choose to compete.

Minimum academic requirements must be met to compete in either Division I or Division II athletics in the first year. The minimum academic requirements to compete during the first year in either Division I or Division II have changed over time and were most recently amended for student-athletes who enrolled during the 2021-2022 academic year. Disruptions in testing centers due to the COVID-19 pandemic prompted the NCAA to waive the requirement of standardized test scores (i.e., SAT, ACT) to determine initial eligibility. Amended policies require incoming student-athletes to achieve a minimum grade point average (GPA) in 16 NCAA-approved core courses during high school in order to be an academic qualifier. Division I athletes must have a GPA of at least 2.3 to be eligible for competition, and Division II athletes must have a GPA of 2.2.

Between 1996 and 2021, the NCAA used a sliding scale to determine initial eligibility in Division I—as a student's GPA increased, the required standardized test score decreased. Therefore, a student with a lower GPA would need a higher test score than one with a higher GPA. For Division II, eligibility required at least a 2.0 GPA, and there was no sliding scale; there was, however, a required minimum test score. The NCAA testing requirement was also waived for student-athletes enrolling in 2022-2023.

The limited capacity for testing during 2020 did not only affect student-athletes. Many academic institutions became test optional for all new students in 2021. Seventy-six percent of four-year institutions in the United States are continuing to waive standardized test scores for students entering in 2022 and more than half are planning to eliminate the SAT or ACT requirement in the 2023-2024 academic year as well. A number of institutions have permanently eliminated the SAT and ACT testing requirement for admission. The NCAA is continuing to examine its initial eligibility criteria, and in 2021, the NCAA Standardized Test Score Task Force suggested the NCAA follow the lead of member institutions that are no longer using standardized test scores in admissions decisions.

Meeting NCAA eligibility standards does not guarantee admission to any university. Therefore, prospective students should also be aware of university admission standards.

Special Admits

Applicants being recruited to participate in college sports who are not admitted through the academic institution's regular admissions process, or whose application becomes complete after the published deadlines, may be considered for special admission by the university. The NCAA allows university presidents, or their designee, to make an exception for some student-athletes who do not meet the university's admission criteria. For example, at the University of Illinois, the Committee for the Admission of Student-Athletes (CASA) consists of senior admissions officers who review the admission criteria of potential student-athletes who would not be admitted under regular circumstances. The goal of this committee is "to determine whether students' academic records and demonstrated academic motivation, together with available support services, will combine to give them a reasonable chance for academic success on our campus" (University of Illinois Office of the Chancellor, 2021, para. 3). A desire to be competitive in athletics may prompt some college presidents to support the admittance of talented but underprepared student-athletes. Once these special exemption students arrive on campus, it is likely they will need more support to succeed and maintain their eligibility.

The public learned about a misuse of special admissions policies at a number of universities in 2019, during an FBI investigation code-named "Operation Varsity Blues." In exchange for payment, a private admissions consultant worked with parents, coaches, and university administrators to fraudulently present children of affluent and celebrity parents as student-athletes. Gurney and colleagues (2020) reviewed a number of scandals in athletics and asserted, "College presidents are acutely aware of potential athletic academic fraud scandals both for securing admission to the university and for maintaining eligibility" (p. 16).

International Student-Athletes

With an increase in global recruiting, more international students are participating in U.S. college athletics than ever before. In order to participate in NCAA competition, students who have completed all or part of their education outside of the United States are required to register with the NCAA Eligibility Center and meet academic and amateurism standards outlined by the association. International student-athletes must arrange to have standardized test scores and a number of academic documents sent to the Eligibility Center and, if necessary, translated into English. To help with this process, the Eligibility Center publishes an online (and downloadable) document called the Guide to International Academic Standards for Athletics Eligibility.

Transfer Student-Athletes

The NCAA also publishes a transfer guide that is available for download through the Eligibility Center website. This guide assists student-athletes who wish to transfer from one four-year school to another, as well as those looking to attend a four-year college or university after attending a two-year school. The guide outlines the "basic transfer rule" for Division I and Division II schools, which states that any transfer student must spend one academic year in residence at the new school before becoming eligible to compete. As of April 2021, transfers meeting special exception guidelines may be able to play right away at their new school. A transfer student must also meet all NCAA, conference, and institution rules. The student's athletics eligibility is also affected by their initial eligibility (qualifier) status as certified by the NCAA Eligibility Center and the division (I or II) of the school to which they are interested in transferring.

STANDARDS FOR RECRUITMENT

The NCAA (2021) defines a prospective student-athlete as a student who has started classes for the ninth grade. Although an institution is not allowed to provide recruiting materials to a prospect until the beginning of the student's junior year in high school, the recruiting process for many athletes and coaches often unofficially begins much earlier. Bylaw 13 in the NCAA manual details NCAA recruiting regulations and should be reviewed if recruiting becomes a major part of your responsibilities. This is especially true as it relates to the continuous evolution of name, image, and likeness (NIL) and its future impact on recruiting. Two elements of the recruiting process that involve many athletics department personnel are the campus visit and the National Letter of Intent (NLI), which we will now explore.

Campus Visits

The campus visit is an integral part of the process through which high school students choose an institution. Students can explore their options in one of three general ways: through camps, unofficial visits, and official visits. Camps are a good way to get to know the coaching staff, facilities, and team members early in the recruiting process—even as a youth. Students can attend as many individual camps as permitted by high school regulations (limits often apply to team camps); the camps are, however, generally costly. For student-athletes able to make them, these unofficial visits offer a way to explore as many programs as they like, on their own time and with their own agenda. Again, these visits must be paid for by the student, though the university can provide up to three complimentary admissions to campus athletic events.

Prior to a rule change in 2019, official visits were not allowed until an athlete's senior year of high school. Official visits may now begin during the junior year in high school, which can allow more time to assess schools and make a thoughtful decision. Official visits are initiated and paid for by the recruiting institution to indicate strong interest in attracting the recruited student. The recruiting institution is allowed to provide transportation, meals, lodging, and entertainment to prospects in their senior year of high school, as well as transportation, meals, and lodging for the student's parent(s) or legal guardian(s). Official visits are limited to 48 hours but still offer an excellent way to learn about an institution's priorities based on how time is allocated during the visit. Only five official visits are allowed per athlete to Division I and II schools (with no more than one visit per school regardless of the number of sports in which the athlete is involved); there is no limit for Division III schools. Division I institutions are also limited in the number of overall official visits that can be provided—for example, 56 annually for football, 25 annually for baseball, 28 in a rolling two-year period for men's basketball, and 24 in the same period for women's basketball (NCAA, 2021). In Division I and Division II, a prospect cannot be offered an official visit without receiving initial clearance from the NCAA Eligibility Center.

For students with many recruiters, it can be difficult to choose which five schools to include in official visits. Some students and families will spend a great deal of time and money on unofficial visits prior to making a college commitment. It is plausible that a highly ranked basketball recruit could travel throughout the United States taking five official and several unofficial visits with their family in a single month.

National Letter of Intent

Once a student-athlete recruited in NCAA Division I or Division II decides which institution to attend and is offered an athletics-based scholarship, they are sent a National Letter of Intent (NLI) and an accompanying athletics aid agreement from the recruiting university or coach. Once signed by the athlete and their parent or legal guardian, the letter of intent serves as a legal document of commitment to the university that signifies the end of the recruiting process. The NLI process was first created in 1964 by seven conferences and eight independent institutions in an effort to curb the cutthroat recruiting that had characterized football throughout the late 1940s and the 1950s. During that time, coaches had tried tirelessly to outdo each other in attracting top recruits to their programs, which were increasing in notoriety due to television exposure. Signifying the fervor of the process, accounts surfaced of coaches who attempted to lure recruits to their programs even after the students were enrolled at other institutions (Hosick, 2011).

Although the NLI program is completely voluntary for both recruits and universities, it provides certainty and finality to the recruiting process. Recruits, who are offered athletics-based financial aid, are assured of their financial package by the recruiting university for one academic year, and coaches who offer the athletics aid are assured that the recruit will in fact participate in their program for one academic year. Therefore, competing coaches can continue recruiting a "verbally committed" player, but the NLI legally concludes the recruitment process. Despite this general finality, however, even an NLI can be declared null and void if any of the following conditions occur:

- A recruit is denied admission to the university
- A recruit does not meet NCAA, institutional, or conference eligibility requirements
- A recruit does not enroll for at least one academic year and the scholarship (in its original amount) is no longer available
- A recruit serves in the military or on a church mission for one year
- The institution discontinues the sport
- The institution violates recruiting rules

Based on NCAA, *National Letter of Intent*, (2013). Available: national-letter.org.

Though originally intended for football, the NLI is now used across all Division I and Division II sports, and each sport has specific signing periods. In addition, when recruits choose a school, the coach cannot talk about them before a valid NLI is on file; as a result, national signing days have become akin to national holidays as the media and fans eagerly await announcements from universities about newly signed players (Emmons & O'Hallarn, 2019). NLIs bind the recruit with the institution, not the coach, which means that the agreement remains in effect if a coaching change occurs. Staurowsky (2017) emphasized that "the letter itself is also suggestive that the document is weighted to the benefit of the athletic establishment, not the athlete. Once athletes receive the NLI, they confront two options—accepting the terms as they are and signing, or not signing. There is no opportunity for negotiation" (p. 29).

CONTINUING ELIGIBILITY STANDARDS

Once initial eligibility has been secured and an athlete begins the collegiate experience, they must continue to meet amateurism regulations and academic benchmarks to remain eligible. NCAA academic benchmarks are often referred to as "progress toward degree" or "continuing eligibility" rules. The rules were set up to encourage athletes to stay on track toward graduation and ensure that schools in the same division apply equal academic requirements. In a memo outlining a proposed new NCAA Constitution (2021, December 6), the NCAA Constitution Committee addressed "the primacy of the academic experience," proposing, "It is the responsibility of each member institution to establish and maintain an environment in which a student-athlete's activities are conducted with the appropriate primary emphasis on the student-athlete's academic experience" (p. 1).

Collegiate administrators must understand the eligibility standards specific to their division of competition to create optimal experiences for the athletes in their programs. Institutions are responsible for determining and certifying the academic eligibility of athletes and for withholding academically ineligible students from competition. This responsibility, paired with pressure from often-overzealous coaches for their athletes to be "kept eligible," has led to heightened NCAA regulation, criticism, and preventive measures. We will now address minimum academic standards and progress-toward-degree requirements, then turn our attention to amateurism rules and other concerns related to all of these continuing eligibility regulations.

Academic Standards and Progress Toward Degree

Minimum academic standards are established to encourage students to commit to pursuing a degree rather than focusing solely on athletics. Division I athletes experience the highest level of regulation, which includes minimum GPA requirements, a "40-60-80 rule" known as Progress Toward Degree (PTD) that sets milestones for moving along in their academic work, and the academic progress rate (APR). Minimum GPA requirements are based on the institution's minimum overall GPA required for graduation. Athletes must earn a GPA that is at least 90 percent of the institution's minimum required for graduation at the beginning of their second year, 95 percent at year 3, and 100 percent at year 4. If, for instance, the minimum GPA required for graduation is 2.0, as it is at Florida State University, an athlete must have at least a 1.8 at the beginning of the sophomore year, a 1.9 at the beginning of the junior year, and a 2.0 at the beginning of the senior year to be eligible for competition. Institutions in some conferences may collectively agree to increase the minimum GPA standard and require that additional hours be completed for an athlete to remain eligible. Such conference-wide eligibility requirements must not fall below the NCAA requirements.

The 40-60-80 rule provides an eligibility standard for Division I athletes based on their progress

Technology Tools

Debating "Class Checkers"

To protect their athlete "investments," many football and men's basketball programs concerned for their athletes' eligibility have employed "class checkers" to track whether athletes are attending their classes. Traditionally, these class checkers have been friends of the program, people who stick their heads into classrooms or hang out in the hallway outside a class to see whether the athletes are in attendance. Athletics departments have justified this behavior as an effort toward early intervention, because poor attendance is an early warning sign of academic trouble. SpotterEDU is an automated attendance platform developed by a former Division I basketball coach "to not just identify truant students, but to alert a student's support network in real time[,] opening lines of communication to help change a student's behavior before it's too late" (Spotteredu.com, 2022). Critics have bemoaned the practice of class checking and the use of SpotterEDU as offensive, nonconsensual surveillance that infantilizes students who play sports.

toward earning a degree. Student-athletes are required to earn a minimum of 6 credit hours per term in order to remain eligible for the following term, and they must also complete 40 percent of the coursework required for a degree by the end of their second year, 60 percent by the end of their third year, and 80 percent by the end of their fourth year. Thus, if an athlete's degree requires completion of 120 credits, 48 credits must be completed by the end of the second year. Because of this flexibility, many Division I athletes choose to take a lighter course load during the competitive season, and those who can also take summer classes to remain on track for graduation. In 2011, however, the NCAA imposed a rule mandating that football players pass at least nine (increased from six) credits in the fall semester or face a four-game suspension. Additionally, baseball athletes ruled ineligible in the fall semester retained ineligible status to compete in the spring baseball season; thus, their focus on academics out of season is crucial.

The APR was instituted in 2004 in response to low Division I graduation rates in football (51 percent) and basketball (41 percent) based on a six-year graduation timeline. The APR is used to gauge and enforce student-athletes' academic progress (LaForge & Hodge, 2011). It serves as an early indicator of eventual graduation rates based on term-by-term measures of Division I scholarship athletes. The measure is calculated by giving each scholarship athlete per team one point for remaining in school and one point for remaining eligible. The point total earned by the team is divided by the total number of possible points and then multiplied by 1,000. An APR of 1,000, therefore, would be a perfect score. It is important to note that the NCAA excludes athletes who are not receiving athletic scholarships but includes any athlete who receives a partial or full scholarship in the APR and graduation success rate (GSR) metrics (Rubin & Rosser, 2014).

Provisions exist by which athletes who choose to transfer or play professionally before exhausting their eligibility do not count against the team's APR as long as the athlete leaves in good academic standing. If, for example, the men's basketball team fulfills the maximum scholarship allotment of 13, then 26 points are possible. If two players remain enrolled but are academically ineligible (–2 points), one player drops out due to being academically ineligible (–2), and one player joins the NBA but is in good academic standing at the time of his departure (0), the team's score would be 26 – 2 – 2 = 22. The APR, then, would be 846 (see the following calculation).

Sample 1-semester Team APR Calculation

$$APR = (22 \div 26) / 1000 = 846$$

Fortunately, the team's APR is based on a four-year rolling average, and the team in our example has had perfect APR scores (1,000) over the other seven semesters in a four-year period, thus their overall APR would be 980.75. Teams with a four-year average APR below 930 are banned from postseason play. An APR of 930 is equivalent to a 50 percent graduation rate. Teams that score below 930 can lose scholarships and forfeit participation in postseason competition.

Academic requirements for Division II athletes are quite similar to those for Division I athletes. To remain eligible for competition, Division II athletes are required to earn a 1.8 GPA after 24 semester hours (or 36 quarter hours), a 1.9 GPA after 48 semester hours, and a 2.0 GPA after 72 and 96 semester hours. In addition, Division II athletes must complete at least 24 hours of degree credit per year, at least 18 of which are taken during the traditional fall-to-spring academic year, and 6 credit hours per full-time term.

Maintenance of eligibility for Division III and NAIA athletes is determined based on individual institutional standards of academic good standing and satisfactory progress toward degree completion. Division III athletes are required, though, to enroll in at least 12 credit hours per term regardless of an institution's definition of "full time." Overall, however, it is clear that the level of academic (and other) regulations is significantly decreased in Division III, NAIA, and institutions under other governing bodies. This difference is a factor to consider as one chooses which type of athletics department to work in.

Academic metrics can be helpful for student-athletes as they research institutions. The NCAA maintains a searchable database that reports APRs for Division I and Division II institutions, along with GSR, federal graduation rates (FGR), and other indicators of academic performance. Whereas the APR is a term-by-term measure, the FGR and GSR are based on a percentage of first-time, full-time students who graduate in a six-year time frame. The FGR is compiled by the U.S. Department of Education, and the GSR is compiled by the NCAA.

The GSR was developed in response to criticism that the FGR understates graduation rates because transfer students are not taken into account. The GSR reflects the unique nature of student-athletes by considering transfer students who come to a university from a two-year school or another four-year school, as well as students in good academic standing who leave an institution to pursue additional playing time, a different major, or a professional career. The GSR and FGR are simply informational tools, whereas the APR can be used as a basis for punitive measures. Examples of GSRs and FGRs are listed in tables 6.1 and 6.2.

Concerns About Continuing Eligibility Measures

NCAA measures to enhance the academic focus and graduation rates of its members' athletics programs have led some to believe athletes "major in eligibility" (Newman, 2014). Though academic reform measures may be well intended, they have produced several unfortunate by-products. For instance, NCAA officials have claimed the rules regulating an athlete's course load, GPA, and progress toward a degree have led to higher graduation rates. However, critics contend that higher graduation rates do not necessarily indicate higher levels of academic focus or enhanced educational experiences (Grasgreen, 2012).

The practice of "academic clustering"—in which a number of athletes choose or are advised to choose a course of study representing the path of least resistance toward eligibility—is one consequence of academic standards and pressure for athletes to remain eligible. When the NCAA announced higher standards in 2012, academic advisors voiced concern that additional clustering would result. Athletics academic advisors are challenged with supporting students in their pursuit of the degree of their choice while working within restrictive academic rules (Navarro et al., 2020).

Because of the penalties associated with aca-

Table 6.1 2015 Graduation Success Rates and Federal Graduation Rates at the University of North Carolina at Chapel Hill

MEN'S SPORTS			WOMEN'S SPORTS		
Sport	**GSR (%)**	**FGR (%)**	**Sport**	**GSR (%)**	**FGR (%)**
Baseball	86	34	Basketball	100	58
Basketball	100	92	Cross country and track	94	80
Cross country and track	91	83	Fencing	100	100
Fencing	100	100	Field hockey	93	85
Football	71	59	Golf	83	57
Golf	100	100	Gymnastics	100	91
Lacrosse	91	84	Lacrosse	100	93
Soccer	100	81	Rowing	94	89
Swimming	100	95	Soccer	100	89
Tennis	100	88	Softball	92	64
Wrestling	75	63	Swimming	100	100
			Tennis	100	88
			Volleyball	100	89

GSR denotes graduation success rate; FGR denotes federal graduation rate.

Created from NCAA Education and Research Database (2022).

Table 6.2 2015 Graduation Success Rates and Federal Graduation Rates for Atlantic Coast Conference Men's Basketball

Institution	GSR (%)	FGR (%)
Boston College	83	33
Clemson University	100	64
Duke University	100	40
Florida State University	100	62
Georgia Institute of Technology	75	70
North Carolina State University	63	17
Syracuse University	86	31
University of Louisville	100	27
University of Miami	100	56
University of North Carolina at Chapel Hill	100	92
University of Notre Dame	83	77
University of Pittsburgh	73	44
University of Virginia	100	58
Virginia Polytechnic Institute and State University	100	46
Wake Forest University	90	47

GSR denotes graduation success rate; FGR denotes federal graduation rate.
Created from NCAA Education and Research Database (2022).

demic ineligibility, many coaches are now given incentives related to their team's academic performance. Ideally, strict academic standards coupled with financial incentives for coaches might alter the type of player that a coach chooses to recruit. This mindset might even filter down to emphasize the importance of academics in youth sport. Unfortunately, some evidence suggests "the reforms designed to open access to higher education to more athletes came at the expense of the integrity of the academy" (Gurney & Southall, 2013, p. 1).

In addition to academic clustering and pressures from athletics academic advisors and coaches to "just stay eligible," a growing number of fraudulent behaviors is littering the landscape of NCAA institutions. Among these are admissions scandals, academic fraud, and "gaming the system" to fudge APR numbers. In these circumstances, the values on which intercollegiate athletics is ostensibly founded can get washed away in a torrent of unethical pressure. Often caught in the middle of this torrent are the athletics academic advisors whose responsibility it is to help student-athletes achieve optimal educational experiences. This can be a challenging role that often requires them to juggle expectations from demanding coaches, academically underprepared athletes, rigorous university professors, and powerful university officials. Such pressure and responsibilities have led many athletics academic advisors to experience burnout and consider leaving the profession (Rubin, 2017; Rubin & Moreno-Pardo, 2018). Rubin's (2017) survey of the profession revealed that 91 percent of athletics academic advisors noticed colleagues in the profession burning out, and 60 percent had considered leaving the profession. In a follow-up study, Rubin and Moreno-Pardo (2018) explored the dimensions of burnout that student-athlete services professionals faced, including athletics academic advisors, learning specialists, student-athlete development staff, and administrators. The themes related to burnout or considering leaving the profession included a lack of career advancement in the field, stress-related health issues, the expectation to be available at all times, low salaries, and lack of recognition for their work (e.g., a coach gets a bonus higher than the athletics academic advisor's annual salary) (Rubin & Moreno-Pardo, 2018).

Academic Services for College Athletes

The NCAA offered academic enhancement funds to help establish academic centers for athletes on member campuses in the late 1980s and early 1990s. Stand-alone facilities sprang up on campuses around the country, showcasing another set of resources specifically for college athletes (Rubin & Moses, 2017). No NCAA bylaws require academic facilities, but just about every Division I athletic program has one. Due to the challenging schedules college athletes have, they often cannot access academic support services and offices during typical daytime hours (Navarro et al., 2020). Thus, these centers offer athletes advising, tutoring, learning support, and programming (e.g., career development) at hours that fit their schedules, such as in evenings and on weekends. They tend to divide athletes from the rest of the student population, who cannot access the athletics academic center (Rubin & Moses, 2017).

In their study on athletics subculture in athlete academic centers, Rubin and Moses (2017) conducted focus groups with three sets of athletes: revenue-sport male athletes, non-revenue-sport male athletes, and female athletes. The consensus among participants was that they needed a separate facility from the rest of the student body so they could have one-on-one tutoring instead of sharing tutors. Some athletes felt they would be distracted in a library or other general gathering place on campus because non-student-athletes might want to talk to them while they studied.

Several participants expressed that they can relate to other athletes with similar schedules and shared pressures. Thus, they might sit with other athletes and be competitive with grades in the same courses. This suggests some unintended positive effects from academic clustering, when athletes are put in the same classes or majors (Rubin & Moses, 2017). Rubin and Moses (2017) concluded, "Student-athlete academic centers have an integral role in building a positive team academic subculture," especially since athletes prefer to study in their academic center (p. 326).

Former College Athletes in Athletics Academic Advising Positions

The staff directories of intercollegiate athletics programs are filled with academic support staff members who were once college sport participants themselves. Former athletes possess in-depth understanding of the demands faced by student-athletes, and they can serve as effective athletics academic advisors because they themselves have graduated and in many cases obtained an advanced degree. As a result, both student-athletes and coaches view them as credible sources of information. They can also be inspiring and share messages of balance, persistence, and the value of higher education. Rubin (2017) discovered that about half of athletics academic advisors were former college athletes and half were not.

Former athletes working in student-athlete support services may also face some challenges. Young professionals who are not far removed in age from the student-athletes with whom they work must take care to develop professional relationships rather than friendships. In addition, former student-athletes have often developed into "team players" who are willing to sacrifice for the team and are eager to please coaches. People working in student-athlete support services, however, need to practice a high level of integrity in order to respect and understand the pressures faced by coaches and athletes without sacrificing their own professionalism.

Though many former athletes pursue careers in student-athlete support and development, it is not necessary to have a background as a college athlete in order to successfully provide support services to athletes. Persons interested in working with student-athletes should review job descriptions for positions they might like to pursue in order to identify the knowledge and experience required for the job.

Among the plethora of criticisms levied at the NCAA over a variety of practices, none has gained more momentum and traction than the movement against amateurism. Sack and Staurowsky (1998) led the modern attack on the NCAA's version of amateurism in their powerful book *College Athletes for Hire: The Evolution and Legacy of the NCAA's Amateur Myth*, wherein they outline the evolution of rules that transformed college athletes into college employees who are not accorded workers' rights. A class action lawsuit was initiated by former UCLA basketball star Ed O'Bannon (*O'Bannon v. National Collegiate Athletic Association*, 802 F.3d 1049 [9th Cir. 2015]), challenging the NCAA's right to profit in perpetuity from the names, images, and likenesses of college athletes without compensating them. As the lawsuit progressed, Pulitzer Prize winner Taylor Branch (2011) published an article in *The Atlantic* titled "The Shame of College Sports," wherein he compared participation in intercollegiate athletics to indentured servitude. Additionally, Lemons (2017) argued that the NCAA operates like a cartel, as it controls the market for college sports and fixes the compensation athletes can receive.

Though the NCAA has relentlessly argued that the value of a college education provides fair compensation for athletic performance, the services performed by some athletes are estimated to be worth more than US$1 million per year—far above the value of an athletics scholarship (Huma & Staurowsky, 2011). This mounting criticism of the amateurism notion in big-time intercollegiate athletics catalyzed changes in name, image, and likeness rules, but most likely, as long as intercollegiate athletics remains within the academy, it will remain a collegiate educational experience. We will now turn our attention to the athletics structures that support athlete education: athletics academic advising.

ATHLETICS ACADEMIC ADVISING

The field of athletics academic advising, sometimes called athletics academic counseling, student-athlete support services, or student-athlete development, has greatly expanded since the turn of the 21st century. These services are now characterized by a great deal of diversity both in the services provided and in the number of staff members involved. The size and scope of services depends largely on the size, institutional philosophy, and budget of the athletics program.

Just a few decades ago, even the largest Division I universities had small academic counseling staffs of two or three people. Athletic advising surfaced as a formal practice at colleges in the 1970s, in response to NCAA minimum academic standards for athletes to be eligible for competition (Rubin, 2017). Athletics academic support staff have grown for several reasons, including the expansion of NCAA rules, comprehensive eligibility certification procedures, and the perception that placing coaches in charge of academics creates a potential conflict of interest. In the largest programs, it is now common for an academic support unit to employ 8 to 10 academic counselors who each work closely with a few teams, as well as 2 or 3 learning specialists dedicated to helping students who are at risk, have a learning disability, or have come to college underprepared. The staff may also include individuals who specialize in student-athlete development.

Athletics academic advisors typically work with academic advisors and faculty in a variety of departments on campus to ensure that student-athletes are taking the correct classes. Because academic curricula are frequently updated, it is critical that athletics academic counselors develop collaborative relationships with others across campus to support student-athletes in navigating college and eligibility rules. In addition to athletics academic advisors, student-athletes often have access to university academic advisors who work with all students in a given major or specialization. Establishing relationships between athletic and campus advisors is critical to supporting athletes' academic success (Rubin & Lewis, 2020). Administrators should encourage advisors in all units to meet each other, come to staff meetings, get involved in a campus advising council, and serve on search committees across units. Additionally, athletics academic advisors and compliance staff should provide rules education for faculty and primary-role advisors so all campus advisors are aware of continuing eligibility requirements (Rubin & Lewis, 2020). Athletes face challenging stereotypes on campus, and it benefits athletics academic advisors and athletics departments to have a positive rapport with college faculty and staff (Rubin & Lewis, 2020; Stokowski et al., 2020). For example, the athletics department might have athletes share a "day in the life" program so campus stakeholders might know what athletes are really doing to represent the institution through their full-time athletic and academic commitments (Rubin & Lewis, 2020).

Athletics academic advisors must possess a breadth of knowledge about classes and requirements. They also need knowledge of student development theory to help students with current challenges and planning for the future. Collaboration between athletics academic advisors, faculty, and other advisors on campus can help inform student-athletes of all advising resources available to them.

Learning Specialist

Prior to the 1990s, few athletics departments employed learning specialists. In more recent years, however, the position has often become a necessary part of athletics academic support units due to increasing recognition and admission of athletes who are academically "at risk of not reaching graduation" (Steinberg et al., 2018, p. 78). Individuals who work in this position possess specialized training in student development and are hired to work independently with students who need extra help and support because they are underprepared for the challenges of college and in some cases have been diagnosed with learning disabilities. Learning specialists typically develop individualized learning strategies and connect athletes with relevant resources on and off campus to help them succeed academically and achieve a good life balance amid the rigorous demands of being a student-athlete. Learning specialists promote self-advocacy in their students while also providing valuable organizational and learning skills (Steinberg et al., 2018).

Organizational Structure and Related Challenges

A University of Washington (2009) study found three reporting structures used in academic support units for student-athletes: some units reported solely to the athletics department; others reported to someone outside of athletics (e.g., the university provost or dean of student affairs); and still others had dual reporting structures, reporting to individuals both inside and outside of the athletics department. When the unit is situated in the athletics department, the athletics director is ultimately responsible for directing staff and allocating resources to aid in the academic performance of student-athletes. Because athletics participation depends on academic eligibility, it is not difficult to surmise that this configuration—in which the athletics director controls academic support—constitutes a conflict of interest. As a result, some believe it necessary to use an administrative structure that requires athletics academic support units to exist under the control of administrators who are not part of the athletics department. More recently, Rubin and Lewis (2020) interviewed 28 advising professionals, 17 of whom worked exclusively with college athletes. Among the 17 athletics academic advisors, 9 reported to provosts or vice provosts, 4 to athletics directors, 2 to the centralized advising unit director, 1 to student affairs, and 1, with a dual reporting line, to a provost and an athletics director (Rubin & Lewis, 2020). Nine of the athletics academic advisors who reported

Continuing Education and Graduate Work

Many individuals who work with student-athletes in academic support services have earned an advanced degree. In Rubin's (2017) study about the background and experiences of athletics academic advisors, she found that 87 percent of athletics academic advisors held master's degrees and 8 percent had a doctoral degree. Some of the degrees pursued by those working in student-athlete support include higher education leadership or student affairs, educational and counseling psychology, exercise science and kinesiology, and sport management. Some unique programs, such as one at Kansas State University, emphasize developing specific knowledge about advising the student-athlete population, but other programs focus more on overall student development.

"to an academic/administrative unit outside of the athletic department . . . were still housed in athletic facilities" (Rubin & Lewis, 2020, p. 109).

Donna Lopiano (2008), former athletics director and current president of the college sport consulting firm Sports Management Resources, discussed best practices in the development of athletics academic support services. According to Lopiano (2008), academic support units have commonly developed and expanded in response to major changes and crises rather than in more strategic, intentional ways that match up with university missions and values. Lopiano (2008) believes that it is not only practical but also essential for academic support units to be monitored by the institution—not by the athletics department.

Industry Profile

SHERESE PARKER

Director of Athletics for Kennedy-King College, City Colleges of Chicago

Everywhere Sherese Parker has worked has seen academic success of students in specialized populations, who often have had additional risk factors when it comes to academic achievement. She has supported students on academic probation, first-generation students, and students with disabilities. However, Parker has found her niche working with the student-athlete population in intercollegiate athletic programs.

Since her start in athletics administration, Sherese Parker has been a leader in identifying and implementing success strategies for student-athletes. She has built comprehensive academic support units for student-athletes and created opportunities for them to achieve academically while participating in sport. Parker started her higher education career in 2005, working in disability services, where she became well versed in different learning modalities of students and the available resources used to aid in learning. Utilizing her collaborative experiences through curriculum evaluation, academic intervention strategies, program development, and assessment, Parker has elevated athletic programs' student retention and matriculation success rates. While serving at Lincoln University (Pennsylvania), the student-athletes were recognized by the NCAA for having a graduation success rate in the top 10 percent of all Division II programs.

Parker, who has a master's degree in academic advising, has studied academic success strategic development and uses her knowledge to be a vital partner in decision-making for student-athletes. Understanding the direct correlation between athletic participation and academic attainment, Parker has progressed in her career, keeping the foundation of sport as an educational access point. She has served in various leadership positions at NCAA Division I, Division II, and Division III member institutions. Since 2019, she has been director of athletics at Chicago's Kennedy-King College, a member institution of the National Junior College Athletic Association (NJCAA).

Not only has Parker focused on the academic achievement of student-athletes but she also has been a longtime champion of diversity, equity, and inclusion. She serves as a NJCAA equity, diversity, and inclusion ambassador, speaking up and out on behalf of the underrepresented and silent voices in athletics. She has given presentations to the NCAA Dr. Charles Whitcomb Leadership Institute alumni on leading through a pandemic and the NJCAA Lead Her Ship series, and she was awarded a grant to start a women's flag football team to provide additional sport opportunities for female student-athletes.

Clearly, when an academic support unit for student-athletes is housed outside of athletics, it is easier to establish faculty oversight and operational transparency. Strategic design of academic support programs that focus on the educational mission of the university may result in less pressure on athletics academic support employees, coaches, and other athletics department employees. According to Rubin and Lewis (2020), what is most important is that both athletic and campus advisors "maintain the same aim to help students achieve their educational goals" regardless of physical location or reporting lines (p. 117).

> *The NCAA has promoted these five key areas (academic achievement, leadership development, personal development, career development and community engagement) for decades. It is up to each institution to determine how best to implement the programming. Making sure our student-athletes have a holistic experience is a core value for Virginia athletics.*
>
> Dr. Carla Williams, director of athletics, University of Virginia (Daves, 2021)

STUDENT DEVELOPMENT PROGRAMMING

In 1991, the NCAA Foundation and the Division I-A Athletic Directors Association initiated an effort to create a total development program for student-athletes. This effort was unveiled in 1994 in the form of the CHAMPS/Life Skills program (Challenging Athletes' Minds for Personal Success). This program has evolved over the years as individual components and NCAA support staff have developed, implemented, and shared resources (National Collegiate Athletic Association, 2008).

Currently, nearly every Division I school has a student-athlete development program of some kind, but the way in which the programs are run (and what they are called) can vary dramatically from one institution to another. Some programs are mandatory, whereas others are optional; some are for credit, whereas others are noncredit; some are for first-year students, whereas others are for seniors; and some involve coaches, whereas others do not. Most deliver programming through speakers, workshops, classes, socials, and orientations. Instructional guidance varies across institutions and can include a wide range of activities, such as mentoring and career networking with alumni, stress management guidance, study skill development, nutrition

Professional Development

The National Association of Academic and Student-Athlete Development Professionals (N4A)

The National Association of Academic and Student-Athlete Development Professionals (N4A), created in 1975, provides professional development opportunities to people who advise in the unique area of college athletics. Over the years, the organization has evolved considerably due to growth in the field. Most recently, it became affiliated with the National Association of Collegiate Directors of Athletics (NACDA). Other organizations under the NACDA umbrella support individuals who work in such departments as collegiate marketing, development, licensing, and compliance. Affiliation with NACDA provides members with economic support, opportunities for networking, research, and access to potential corporate sponsorship. N4A annually holds a national convention.

Most athletics academic advisors join N4A as their primary professional organization, but some also join the NACADA: The Global Community for Academic Advising, which supports general academic advising outside of athletics, and has both an Advising Student-Athletes Community and an NCAA Advisory Board. This organization links athletics academic advisors and departmental advisors to encourage professional academic advising conversations and initiatives throughout the college or university. Discounted rates apply for student memberships.

Leadership Lesson

Interdependence and the Win-Win Paradigm

Student-athlete services have been referred to as the heart of an athletics department. Whether for study tables, student-athlete advisory committee meetings, scheduling, tutoring, counseling, or leadership training, athletes from different sports come together through student services to learn and grow in their nonathletic pursuits. With this in mind, it is fitting that we now return to the beginning of our leadership lessons by revisiting the heart of any leadership quest—the paradigm. In the leadership lesson in chapter 1, we put forward the notion that leadership begins at the individual level. In the leadership lesson presented here, we add an understanding that leadership efforts are also inherently interdependent and can often be enhanced through a win-win paradigm.

Before we explore this paradigm, let's focus for a moment on the point that leadership is inherently interdependent. There is no way to lead in a vacuum; therefore, interpersonal communication and understanding are essential. Daniel Goleman (1995) has theorized that the differentiator between good and great leaders is what he calls emotional intelligence (EI), which consists of five components that can be strengthened through practice: self-awareness, self-regulation, motivation, empathy, and social skill. Through research, Goleman has found that when a leader possesses a critical mass of EI capabilities, their units outperform others in yearly earnings by 20 percent.

These capabilities allow a person to contribute to what Covey (1989) calls an "emotional bank account"—a balance of trust accumulated in a relationship. "Deposits" in the account are made through acts of courtesy, honesty, follow-through, and kindness. When a significant balance of trust has been built up, communication is most effective. The parties give each other the benefit of the doubt and accept communication at face value. However, the trust account can also get drawn down or overdrawn as a result of "withdrawals" in the form of disrespect, deception, lack of follow-through, or malice. In this case, communication is difficult, flexibility is scarce, and deeper, perhaps malicious, meanings are often attributed to even the simplest exchanges.

Covey outlined six methods of making deposits to build a strong balance of trust in the emotional bank account.

1. Understand the individual. Some deposits mean more than others, depending on the unique attributes and capabilities of each person. What one person considers a large deposit (e.g., spending time going to lunch) might be considered a withdrawal by someone else!
2. Attend to the little things. Small efforts at courtesy or attentiveness can translate into large deposits. Similarly, small discourtesies or acts of disrespect can translate into large withdrawals.
3. Keep commitments. Keeping promises and delivering on expectations are ways to make deposits. Failing to keep a commitment, on the other hand, makes a large withdrawal.
4. Clarify expectations. It can pay dividends to invest the time up front to make sure that each person partakes of a shared vision. Lack of clarity, however, leads to unfulfilled or differing expectations and reduces the account balance.
5. Show personal integrity.

> *One of the most important ways to manifest integrity is to* be loyal to those who are not present. *In doing so, we build the trust of those who are present . . . Integrity in an interdependent reality is simply this: you treat everyone by the same set of principles. As you do, people will come to trust you. They may not at first appreciate the honest confrontational experiences such integrity might generate. Confrontation takes considerable courage, and many people would prefer to take the course of least resistance, belittling and criticizing, betraying confidences, or participating in gossip about others behind their backs. But in the long run, people will*

(continued)

LEADERSHIP LESSON *(continued)*

trust and respect you if you are honest and open and kind with them. (Covey, 2004, pp. 196-197)

6. Apologize sincerely when you make a withdrawal. We will make mistakes—that is inevitable. When we do, if we can sincerely apologize, we may be able to mitigate the withdrawal. However, repeated apologies with no change in behavior add up to large withdrawals.

In effect, emotional bank account deposits boil down to being respectful and truly valuing those with whom you work. This sentiment is expressed in Thaler and Koval's *The Power of Nice: How to Conquer the Business World With Kindness* (2001), in which they suggest that nice people live longer, are healthier, and make more money—and that "nice" companies have lower turnover, lower recruitment costs, and higher productivity. We urge you to utilize this strategy by creating strong emotional bank accounts in order to cultivate a win-win paradigm. "Win/Win is a frame of mind and heart that constantly seeks mutual benefit in all human interactions. . . . [It is] based on the paradigm that there is plenty for everybody, that one person's success is not achieved at the expense or exclusion of the success of others" (Covey, 2004, p. 207).

Maturity is the ability to express one's own feelings and convictions balanced with consideration for the thoughts and feelings of others.

Hrand Saxenian, researcher and Harvard Business School professor

We can use this paradigm when we bring high school students to our university for recruiting visits, when we negotiate the contract for a new hire, and when we cultivate a corporate partnership. We should approach each situation with an abundance mentality—with the idea that we need to either find a solution that benefits both parties or "agree to disagree agreeably" (Covey, 2004, p. 213). When this approach becomes our standard operating procedure, we will find our emotional bank accounts overflowing, and we will be able to expand the benefits of each exchange.

education, media relations education, leadership training, and sometimes more.

Today, student-athlete development is evolving. More than ever before, student-athlete development positions appear among athletics senior staff. Experts in this area are also sport administrators and oversee other aspects of athlete well-being, health, diversity and inclusion, and other areas. N4A developed a standardized set of program components for student-athlete development professionals through its Steve McDonnell Professional Development Institute. These areas include leadership development, personal development, career development, social responsibility, community engagement, diversity and inclusion, and strategic planning. There are many nuanced positions available for professionals in this space, such as roles focused specifically on career development, leadership development, community engagement, and diversity and inclusion, among others. Navarro et al. (2020) suggested, "Job descriptions in this field are constantly evolving and changing, and administrators will play a big role in shaping the future of this field" (p. 165).

Leadership Programming

The Cameron Institute for Student-Athlete Development at the University of California, Berkeley (Cal), showcases excellent examples of leadership programming in college athletics. The institute serves both athletes (over 900) and coaches from 30 teams and is led by Dr. Marissa Nichols, associate athletics director, student-athlete development. The California Way is a framework that guides holistic development for athletes while enrolled at Cal and through their future. The institute has three pillars: career development, community engagement, and mental performance and leadership development (Cal Cameron Institute, 2020).

Leadership programming is guided by specific outcomes that are measured annually with different metrics and instruments (Avolio et al., 2018). The main leadership development objective is for Cal athletes to become purposeful leaders who live their core values. Within this core objective are three suboutcomes: (1) student-athletes have an awareness of self and others, (2) student-athletes understand leadership approaches and develop a personal, unique style, and (3) student-athletes cultivate meaningful relationships and empower others. Leadership development metrics demonstrated that Cal athletes were extremely confident or confident in developing a personal leadership style after participation in the programs.

Program Offerings

The Cameron Institute at Cal Athletics offers a variety of programs designed to reach athletes and coaches. One such program is the leadership series, which offers tailored sessions related to different leadership topics (e.g., growth mindset) throughout the academic year, culminating in a leadership showcase. The event provides athletes with a space to demonstrate the leadership skills they have learned to an audience beyond their teammates and coaches. Participants in the showcase are nominated by coaches, teammates, and athletics staff members.

Another program is designed for team captains and formal leaders nominated by coaches. This program helps students in building confidence as a leader, developing a team culture, improving purposeful communication, and handling the expectations of a formal leadership role. Students in the program role-play scenarios and learn from athletes on other teams who experience different leadership challenges. The Cameron Institute also holds sessions for coaches to prepare them to support captains and formal leaders. In these sessions, coaches are given reflection questions to engage with participants from their teams.

Students' holistic development includes mental performance and well-being. Dr. Graig Chow, director of mental performance and leadership development, leads this area of the Cameron Institute's programming. Mental performance and leadership development comprise one pillar intentionally, because athletes' development as leaders is directly connected with their performance, mindset, and well-being. In the area of mental performance, services cover leadership topics like team building (referencing culture and values), team leadership (referencing emotional intelligence and coachability), and team dynamics (referencing conflict resolution and communication).

In its first academic year, the Cameron Institute offered 97 workshops to 18 teams. Metrics indicated 100 percent positive evaluations on their high quality, effectiveness, and helpfulness to the athletes. Dr. Chow also provides one-on-one mental training sessions for students who are managing challenges such as motivation, stress, or anxiety. Within the first year of offering these services, Dr. Chow held 247 sessions with students, and these also received 100 percent positive feedback from participants.

Unique to this program is the Cameron Institute's inclusion of coaches in programming and leadership development. The institute's staff aims to equip and empower coaches so they are able to support athletes too, since they are often mentors who build strong relationships with their students. This allows athletes to engage with the content of Cameron Institute programming between structured offerings since students see coaches regularly and sessions may be offered only a few times each semester. Coaches also have access to executive coaching to support their own leadership challenges, such as communication and decision-making. In the first year of these programs, 39 sessions were offered to coaches and received positive feedback on their quality, relevance, and effectiveness.

More information about this program can be found on the institute's website at https://calbears.com/sports/2020/8/13/cameron-institute-about.aspx, on their X (formerly known as Twitter) feed at https://x.com/CalCameronInst, or on Instagram at https://www.instagram.com/calcameroninst/.

Student-Athlete Advisory Committees

One of the best ways to encourage leadership growth is to provide opportunities for people to lead. Student-athlete advisory committees (SAACs) provide this opportunity to selected student-athletes who contribute to the governance of intercollegiate athletics at the campus, conference, and national levels. Specifically, SAAC members provide insight into student-athlete experiences and offer input on rules, regulations, and policies that affect student-athletes' lives. The functions of campus SAACs are summarized in the following list as published on the NCAA website:

- Promote communication between athletics administration and student-athletes
- Disseminate information
- Provide feedback and insight into athletics department issues
- Generate a student-athlete voice within the campus athletics department formulation of policies
- Build a sense of community in the athletics program involving all athletic teams
- Solicit student-athletes' responses to proposed conference and NCAA legislation
- Organize community service efforts
- Create a vehicle for student-athlete representation on campus wide committees
- Promote a positive image of student-athletes on campus.

The NCAA recommends that campus SAACs be organized into executive committees with elected positions including a chairperson, a secretary, a treasurer, and chairs of standing subcommittees. Outstanding campus SAAC members are often selected to serve on the conference or national SAAC. National SAAC members are selected by the Division I, II, or III management council from a pool of conference nominees. National SAACs provide a student voice within the NCAA legislative process as national SAAC members recommend, review, and respond to proposed legislation. National SAAC members also serve as liaisons between their own campuses and conferences and the national governing body of the NCAA.

The organization and support of SAACs can differ from campus to campus; whatever their specific form, however, their potential effect is immense. It is wise for institutional SAACs to create an annual report covering initiatives, concerns, and other relevant topics to distribute to campus stakeholders. Through such efforts, leaders in training can help effect change on a broad scale.

Community Service

College and university athletics departments possess a great deal of social capital, which in its most simplistic form means college sport has the ability to use its "people power" to do admirable work—if people are inspired to do so. Even so, intercollegiate athletics is commonly critiqued as a single-minded money-making venture that operates in a "silo," isolated from the rest of campus. This does not have to be the case, nor should it be.

Many college athletics programs have a history of participating in some type of community service initiative. These efforts may be coordinated by any number of athletics department personnel and are sometimes programmed through the campus SAAC. NCAA Team Works is the community engagement branch of the NCAA, established in 2014. The NCAA Team Works Community Service Competition Award recognizes college athletic programs based on the number of service hours completed and by the number of student-athletes involved. In 2021, the University of Pittsburgh, a Division I institution, received the award for services that included virtual programming with youth, COVID-19 vaccine registration programs, and a breast cancer walk. Emporia State University, in Kansas, earned the Team Works Award for Division II, and New Jersey City University was the 2021 recipient in Division III. An award through NCAA Team Works is a point of pride for athletics departments, which commonly share their community service achievements on the athletics department website, social media accounts, and at competitions.

CONCLUSION

The intercollegiate athlete population faces unique pressure to represent their schools athletically, perform academically, balance time constraints,

Case Study

Division II and Division III Greatness

The LEARFIELD Directors' Cup is awarded annually by NACDA to the athletics program that has the greatest overall competitive success. The winner of the inaugural Directors' Cup, in 1993, was the University of North Carolina at Chapel Hill; Stanford University subsequently won the cup every year until the University of Texas broke the streak in the 2020-2021 season.

Directors' Cup rankings were initiated in 1995 for NCAA Division II, Division III, and the NAIA. These divisions did not score performances in the 2019-2020 or 2020-2021 seasons due to the COVID-19 pandemic. Michigan's Grand Valley State University, a Division II public university with 24,000 students, has finished first or second every year since the 2001-2002 season. NCAA Division III has been dominated by Williams College, a private liberal arts college with approximately 2,000 students in Massachusetts. Williams won the Division III Directors' Cup every year except 1998-1999 until the 2021-2022 season, when it finished sixth, with fellow New England Small Collegiate Athletic Conference (NESCAC) opponent Tufts University, another Massachusetts school, taking the top spot for the first time.

What makes Grand Valley State and Williams different? Grand Valley State offers a large number of opportunities for student-athletes, with 779 participants receiving US$4.5 million in financial aid. Its nearest competitor in the standings, West Texas A&M, which finished second, has 484 student-athletes and distributed US$2.6 million in financial aid. Grand Valley State prudently invests in its athletics program and manages to net a small profit annually. As Division III institutions do not offer athletics scholarships, Williams College's advantage appears to be the emphasis on athletics participation within the student body, with 60 percent of students competing on a varsity, junior varsity, or club sport team. Williams also sponsors one of the broadest-based programs in Division III, offering 32 varsity teams for their 750 student-athletes. The investment in athletics at Division III is strategic for many schools, as research shows that small private colleges strategically use their reputation and brand strength to manage or increase enrollment.

Questions to Consider

1. Analyze a Division II school and conference in your region. What are their greatest strengths and what are their greatest challenges? Then do the same for a Division III school and conference.
2. What are the pros and cons of being a student-athlete at the Division II level? At the Division III level?
3. What are the pros and cons of being a coach at the Division II level? At the Division III level?
4. What are the pros and cons of being an administrator at the Division II level? At the Division III level?

adjust to living on their own, and, for a few students, complete all of these tasks while academically underprepared for the rigors of a university education. Therefore, it is important to provide the necessary resources to allow all within this population to succeed. Departments that deliver academic and developmental support to student-athletes help them succeed both in the classroom and as individuals. These support programs have expanded in the past two decades and are now often responsible for advising, tutoring, developmental programming, and monitoring of academic performance. Student-athlete support units are configured in a variety of ways. They collaborate widely with other individuals and departments on campus, as well as with NCAA representatives, to evaluate eligibility, academic performance, and overall experience.

DISCUSSION QUESTIONS

1. What is the purpose of regulating the initial eligibility standards for NCAA athletes? Are the regulations accomplishing their purposes? What are the implications of higher or lower academic standards for athletes hoping to pursue NCAA intercollegiate athletics?
2. The term "special admit" refers to a student who falls below average university admissions standards but is admitted because of athletic ability. What issues are involved in allowing special admits? Why is it important for athletics administrators to be aware of these issues?
3. Regulation is significantly decreased in every area for NCAA Division III and NAIA institutions as compared with NCAA Division I and II institutions. Why do you think this is the case? Do you believe that NCAA Division I and Division II institutions are overregulated? Why or why not?
4. Some unintended consequences of academic reform in the NCAA are discussed in this chapter. Search the web and outline an example of one of these issues that has emerged in the past several years. What could the NCAA or the involved member institution have done to prevent the issue?

LEARNING ACTIVITIES

1. Take a moment to research the APR, GSR, and FGR of schools in your conference by using the NCAA Research Interactive Databases (www.ncaa.org/sports/2017/9/5/ncaa-research-interactive-databases.aspx). What trends do you discover?
2. Explore the resources provided on the NCAA Eligibility Center's website. Describe one of the areas about which you learned the most.
3. Search the web for athletics department service initiatives. What purpose is fulfilled by the initiatives you find?
4. Visit athletics department websites for a variety of institutions and search for the academic support unit. How many athletics academic advisors or counselors does the athletics department employ, and what are each person's duties? Do some of the athletics academic advisors work with a number of sports? Does the university have a football team? If so, how many athletics academic advisors are employed to work with football players? Does the unit have learning specialists who work with at-risk or underprepared students? Does the unit offer assistantship, study-hall monitor, and tutoring opportunities for current students?

Media Relations

Robert H. Zullo, Slippery Rock University

In this chapter, you will explore

- why publicity is important,
- how to produce media,
- how to work with media outlets,
- the evolution of media,
- media training,
- the difference between forecasting and speculation,
- crisis management strategies,
- social media concerns, and
- privacy issues related to students' academic and medical records.

THE FISHBOWL: ALL EYES ARE ON YOU

With their most recent win, the student-athletes had earned the opportunity to compete in the postseason and were excited to celebrate their hard work with a night out. Unfortunately, they were baited into a full-scale brawl after defending a restaurant patron who was being picked on by locals. Team members were attacked with a glass bottle and flying chairs, but the videos that captured the scene happened to show only the taller, bulkier team members defending themselves in the ensuing fistfight. Police were called to the scene, and both locals and student-athletes were arrested. The head coach was notified, as well as the athletics director (AD), and the videos found their way onto social media before sunrise.

Local media outlets quickly picked up reports of the fight and posted them on their websites. In response to those reports and to still pictures extracted from video footage—and before the facts were presented to the public by the police or the AD—public opinion began to settle on the idea that the student-athletes had been "looking for trouble." As a result, the team's reputation was sullied, and fans and critics deluged news websites with comments about who should be suspended and calling for the head coach to be fired. The institution's board of trustees was embarrassed and demanded answers from the president.

How does a sports information director proactively control a crisis such as this one in a day and age when technology allows inaccurate or incomplete stories to be distributed to thousands of people at a moment's notice?

In intercollegiate athletics, media relations and public relations are generally blended together in the function known (depending on the school) as sports information, sport communication, or athletics media relations. This branch of intercollegiate athletics administration is typically handled by a sports information director (SID), who may be supplemented by associate and assistant directors, as well as graduate assistants, interns, and student workers, when the school can afford such resources (Stoldt et al., 2000).

The sports information department is vital to the athletics department because it deals with the mass media, which possess the greatest reach to the general public (Stoldt et al., 2006). Media outlets shape opinions about an athletics department by affecting what people see, hear, and read. The role of the sports information department is to help shape the information distributed (Andrews, 2005). It does so in part by proactively disseminating information, which requires it to maintain statistics and create media releases, media guides, game notes, programs, and other documents (Johnston, 2022; Stoldt et al., 2000). The department also holds media conferences, facilitates media training, and educates members of the athletics department about how media outlets function and what "sells."

> *Regardless of size or resources, irrespective of title—we are all storytellers.*
>
> *We tell the stories of our teams and coaches, and most importantly, our student-athletes. In whole, we are telling the unique tale of college athletics—its people and its impact—where lessons learned through sports are interwoven with our system of higher education.*
>
> *Whether managing a crisis, producing podcasts or writing press releases, advising a fellow administrator on messaging, mapping out a social media plan or updating a record book, we are telling a story.*
>
> Herb Vincent, associate commissioner of communications, Southeastern Conference (qtd. in CoSIDA Corner, 2019, p. 56)

Another important function of the sports information department is to oversee the athletics department's website and social media platforms so that fans and other stakeholders can access information about their favorite teams 24 hours a day, 7 days a week, 365 days a year. Proper control of the website can foster greater coverage of women's athletics and Olympic sport programs that traditional, for-profit media outlets tend not to cover (Cooper & Cooper, 2009; Cooper et al., 2009; Cunningham et al., 2004). The sports information office also helps other branches of the athletics department develop their online reach. For example, the website can be used to publicize upcoming promotions (for the marketing department), educate fans about NCAA rules (for the compliance office), provide directions and behavior policies for events (for facilities and event management), sell tickets (for the ticket office), procure donations (for the development office), and provide fans with their favorite merchandise (Menaker & Connaughton, 2010; Salas, 2022).

In addition, sports information directors must be able to handle the inevitable highs and lows of the athletics department with calmness and integrity while leveraging the department's publicity through various human interest stories, awards, honors, and other unique angles (Barrow, 2022). They must also strike a balance between understanding what the media expects and trying to put their department in the best light, whether in terms of a national championship or a reading program implemented through a local community service project. For most athletics departments, this obligation requires a heavy time commitment from the SID, who must be on call even while at home for the night or away on vacation.

PUBLICITY AND GOOD PUBLIC RELATIONS

Publicity is a no-cost alternative to advertising (Stoldt et al., 2006); in order to get it, however, as stressed by Leland Barrow, senior associate sports communication director for the University of Georgia, personal relationships are vital (2022). The key is to present information to the mass media—print, television, radio, and web outlets—in a manner that is edifying and will not be construed as a manipulated version of advertising. Ries and Ries (2002) stress that, through the continuous release of such information, high-quality public relations can be used to build stakeholders' trust in an organization. Consider the broad range of stakeholders for an intercollegiate athletics department as summarized in the following list.

Stakeholders in an Athletics Department

- Students in general
- Student-athletes
- Parents
- Alumni
- Coaches
- Athletics department staff
- Athletics department administrators
- School staff
- School faculty
- School administrators
- Fans
- Donors to the school
- Donors to the athletics department
- Sponsors of the athletics department
- Sponsors of the athletes (through name, image, and likeness)
- School's athletics conference
- School's peers in the athletics conference
- School's athletics governing body
- School's accrediting body
- Local community
- State community

Communicating effectively with each of these constituent groups must be a high priority for the department. The preferred methods and content for such communications continue to evolve in order to best address the diverse issues that arise (Jackowski, 2007).

PRODUCTION OF MEDIA

As noted by Mike Montoro, assistant athletic director for football communications at West Virginia University, helping the media and meeting their information needs in a timely manner is vital (2022). Sports information departments create press releases and media guides, oversee the athletics department website and social media, maintain historical records (including statistics, photos, and videos), and produce other publications (e.g., pro-

Industry Profile

KYLE MCMULLIN

Director of Athletics, Christopher Newport University (Virginia)

Kyle McMullin has served as the assistant director for advancement and communications since June 2010, overseeing the athletics department's messaging and communication to various stakeholders through athletic publications and the department's website. He also helped to oversee the athletics department's new brand identity, as well as the trademark licensing program. McMullin was named the school's director of athletics in May 2016, assuming responsibility for all of the athletic programs. The Christopher Newport University Captains annually contend for conference and national championships in all sports and often finish near the top of the Division III LEARFIELD Directors' Cup, a testament to their well-rounded excellence in athletic play.

Many of McMullin's athletic programs compete in the New Jersey Athletic Conference (NJAC), but some compete in the Coast-to-Coast Athletic Conference, whose member institutions are in California, Maryland, Michigan, New York, North Carolina, Virginia, and Wisconsin. A graduate of the University of Richmond and Ohio University, McMullin was active in helping the Capital Athletic Conference evolve into the Coast-to-Coast Athletic Conference, with meetings at the 2019 NCAA Convention and in Denver, Chicago, and Indianapolis before the conference was launched at the 2020 NCAA Convention in Anaheim, California. McMullin enjoys seeing students exposed to various different institutions and places. "Taking student-athletes from Newport News, Virginia, to Brooklyn, New York, or to Santa Cruz, California, truly is a unique cultural exchange that the schools lean into." The Coast-to-Coast Athletic Conference competes in limited regular-season competition but offers destination-based championships with the winner advancing to the NCAA Championships.

How did you get into your current field of work?

Serving as the director of athletics at Christopher Newport is one stop on a professional journey where I have sought out opportunities to learn and grow at every step. While an undergraduate at the University of Richmond, I asked to help with everything from selling tickets to managing game-day promotions. I found ways to volunteer at Virginia Tech when I went home over the holidays and during the summer to experience other aspects of the industry. Years later, while serving in a development and sales position, I was happy to chip in and help with media relations, broadcasting, and athletic communications, when colleagues were short-staffed. All of these experiences broaden my perspective of intercollegiate athletics and reinforce the fundamental tenet that as leaders in intercollegiate athletics, we are here to serve—serve our students, our staff and our alumni, family and friends.

Courtesy of CNU Athletics.

What are the most enjoyable aspects of your position?

Seeing the commitment and sacrifice required each day of our students to succeed at a championship level makes the moment you see them achieve their dreams so powerful. There is a small army of people that stand behind our students with the hope that we all play our role in supporting them and providing them with the opportunity to live out their dreams. Watching their dreams come true is the ultimate reward for working in college athletics.

What are the most challenging aspects of your position?

The director of athletics on a college campus must be able to seamlessly move throughout their day and know when they need to be a mentor, a teacher, a chief executive, a development professional, a human resources expert, or the department housekeeper. This position requires flexibility and acceptance that each day is a fluid experience that will test every aspect of your skill set. In this era of instant availability, the job demands your attention in ways that can be difficult to manage. As with most things in life, that which challenges us the most has the greatest reward and this role provides plenty of both.

To stay informed on current trends and issues I read . . .

The best resource for staying informed and on the leading edge of our industry is the network of professionals around you. I make a point to speak on the phone each day with at least one other director of athletics or commissioner. While I read daily newsletters like *D3 Ticker* or *NACDA* or *D3 Playbook*, I learn about what is happening in our industry by building relationships with my peers and constantly communicating with them. Whether discussing NCAA governance, conference membership, or championships, I believe strongly that this is not a zero-sum industry and that the more we work together, the better we all are at serving our students. Maintaining a healthy network of peers is a powerful tool to ensure our students and staff are positioned to succeed. Visiting other campuses, attending the NCAA Convention or NACDA's annual convention provides opportunities to strengthen relationships and add to your knowledge base.

Advice for students and others seeking to work in this field?

Never be too proud to do any job. Making a career in college athletics is about serving others and sometimes that may mean standing on the sideline at a championship game with donors. Other days it may mean that you literally need to take the trash to the dumpster. If you seek ways to learn and grow as a professional, find ways to add value to your organization and remain focused on serving your students while doing so, you will be amazed at the opportunities that come your way. Work ethic and selflessness are powerful skills that you can develop within yourself. (McMullin, 2022)

Kyle McMullin

grams and annual reports). They also host media conferences and handle some game-day duties at sporting events.

Amid these various duties, Battenfield and Kent (2007) suggest that sports information staffers are primarily "producers of information." With sufficient staff, the department may even be able to publish a magazine, produce its own videos, and handle sport photography (Salas, 2022).

WEBSITE INTERACTIVITY AND INNOVATION

Many athletics directors use the athletics department website to speak to fans en masse. In this setting, they have complete control of the message they want to convey, whether in stressful times or in times of celebration. Another benefit of the athletics department website is that the sports information department controls the message without fear of editing or omission by a media outlet (Stoldt et al., 2006). Examples include sharing community relations or academic success stories that might not be deemed sufficiently dramatic by the mass media. Georgia Southern University AD Jared Benko interacts with fans on his school's athletics website, providing pictures, videos, and updates. Similarly, Carla Williams, director of athletics at the University of Virginia, proactively promotes upcoming events and posts illustrations and explanations of facility construction plans.

Websites also provide interactive options where fans can engage with the athletics program by, for example, voting for their favorite teams and registering to win contests (Schultz, 2005). Sports information staffers can be heavily involved in creating both the appearance and the content of material designed for fans' consumption (Reichart-Smith, 2011). Some schools develop their websites in-house for greater control, whereas others outsource their websites to a sport marketing company (Salas, 2022). A viable athletics department website has "stickiness"—the quality of keeping visitors on the site for extended periods of time.

For example, fans of Mississippi State University (MSU) athletics can see who won a basketball game by visiting the school's website, the ESPN site, the Fox Sports site, or any number of other sport

Technology Tools

Graphic Design, Live Stats, and Streaming

Students aspiring to work in sports information are well advised to pursue courses in communications or journalism. In addition, duties such as creating media guides and other publications require sports information staff to be knowledgeable about tools and technologies such as Photoshop, Illustrator, InDesign, Procreate, and Adobe's Creative Suite and Acrobat Professional (Johnston, 2022; LaRiccia, 2022). Some smaller schools may use companies that build templates for social media that require you only to add photos and text. Students should also be comfortable using live stats and streaming tools such as StatCrew software, NCAA LiveStats, BlueFrame Technology, and SIDEARM Sports. Students can gain experience using these tools through volunteering in the sports information department.

websites. To stand out in this crowd, MSU's sports information department makes its website "sticky" by including live statistics from games and posting sound bites and video clips that competing websites might not have (Andrews, 2005). The school also created an appealing website domain—www.hailstate.com—to appeal to MSU Bulldogs fans through their well-known rallying cry used at sporting events. The shortness and simplicity of the domain's address make it easy to remember (Bruno & Whitlock, 2000).

These efforts are intended to maximize the number of unique visitors to the website. Unique visitors are people who visit a website; regardless of how many times they return to the website, each visitor only counts once. Another measurement tool for web traffic is the "hit," which is defined as a single request from a browser to a server (Stoldt et al., 2006). One valuable tool for assessing such metrics is Google Analytics. SkullSparks also provides analytics, segmented by social media platform, by athletics department, by sport, by coaches, by conference, and more.

In addition to providing information to departmental stakeholders, athletics websites can also serve as revenue generators (Schultz, 2005). Possible ways to generate revenue through the website include pursuing sponsorships, selling tickets or merchandise, offering a secondary ticket exchange, hosting online auctions, giving donors the opportunity to log in and make a contribution, and providing specific subscription content. Thus the website is not merely a publicity tool but has many beneficial aspects for an athletics department (Cooper & Pierce, 2011; Menaker & Connaughton, 2010).

GENERATING PUBLICITY

Producing media is important, but the information itself is relatively useless unless properly disseminated. Therefore, in order to generate effective publicity, sports information professionals must understand media channels. The mass media, taken together, constitute a highly competitive business that supplies people with information and entertainment (Schultz, 2005). Economic theory indicates that media outlets look to increase their market share of consumers, and this affects what is carried in the news, in what order, and in what quantity (Cooper et al., 2009). The media have evolved to interpret the news, thus shaping society's views and influencing ideology for the masses (Stoldt et al., 2006).

To give readers, listeners, and viewers an exciting "you are there" experience, media outlets often present not only the specifics and details of the event but also the associated histrionics. Andrews (2005) observes that media traditionally blends information, opinions, analysis, and criticism. The result can prove entertaining for many viewers, as evidenced by such sport-oriented television shows as *First Take* and *The Herd*.

The sports information department must work with various types of media and recognize that the media are a business. Consequently, the director

Division II and Division III Production of Media

With fewer resources, some Division II and Division III schools are forced to be more creative in their media production efforts. Seton Hill University, a Division II school in Greensburg, Pennsylvania, and a member of the Pennsylvania State Athletic Conference, outsources its media production to the Westmoreland Sports Network (WSN). The Westmoreland Sports Network staff, led by Dan Flickinger, helps to provide dedicated coverage of high school and college athletics in Westmoreland County. Live broadcasts include 30-minute pregame shows, half-time shows, and a postgame show with interviews of players and coaches. Games are archived so fans can access them on phones, tablets, and laptops. The Westmoreland Sports Network also helps to secure area sponsors, enabling Seton Hill University, a school of approximately 2,000 students, to focus on day-to-day operations in its athletics department and prepare to compete with multiple national Division II sports powers, including Slippery Rock University of Pennsylvania, Indiana University of Pennsylvania, and West Chester University (also in Pennsylvania).

Westminster College, a Division III school of approximately 1,000 students, competes in the Presidents' Athletic Conference against such schools as Washington and Jefferson University and Thiel College. Carnegie Mellon University and Case Western Reserve University compete in the conference as football-only members. Westminster has a broadcasting and sports communication academic major in which students, under the guidance of Gary Swanson, the technical operations manager and media systems engineer, and long-time distinguished faculty member David Barner, cover Titan athletics using the school's broadcast facilities and equipment, which include digital cameras, replay, audio and graphics systems, television and radio studios, remote truck, and remote transmission. Students work on podcasts, coaches' television shows, and the school newspaper, all of which are available through one centralized website. Many of the broadcasts are then funneled into the Presidents' Athletic Conference Digital Network, which consolidates all the schools' broadcasts.

Colleges and universities with fewer resources may wish to emulate these schools' efforts at media production because students, alumni, fans, and family now expect to see their athletic events streamed via YouTube and other platforms. It is not enough to provide live stats; some schools may provide straight video without commentary (if not enough personnel are available to produce audio play-by-play). Media production may require outsourcing or collaborating with the school's internal resources, as in the example of Westminster College.

must be a forward thinker who can identify stories that will sell (Andrews, 2005). The director must also formulate strategies about which stories should be directed to which media outlets, each of which has its own rhythm and deadlines (Howard & Mathews, 2000).

It is a wise practice for athletics department personnel to consider available content through the lens of how it might increase newspaper readership or website visitors for a media company seeking to generate revenue. What will raise ratings on a television or radio show looking to add sponsors through commercials? As relationships are built with media outlets by providing them with marketable content, the outlets may be more willing to highlight the program in a positive light or fact-check with the department before running misleading stories such as the one in the chapter-opening scenario.

At many Division I schools, the sports information department works with a "beat writer" who is assigned to cover athletics (Schultz, 2005) and focuses on the daily happenings of the athletics department. The department must also contend with columnists, who write to foster discussion and debate over their opinionated views in print or online articles (Andrews, 2005). The beat writer is traditionally hesitant to critique the athletics department harshly, since his or her access might be restricted, but the columnist is not subject to such restriction and strives simply to create the greatest impact.

To understand what it takes to "sell" a story, consider the acronym TIPCUP, which refers to news that is *t*imely, *i*mportant, *p*rominent, *c*onflict oriented, *u*nusual, and *p*roximate (close) to the audience (Thompson, 1996). In terms of timeliness, sport news from two years ago seems outdated compared to something that happened last weekend, yesterday, or perhaps an hour ago. In terms of importance, a team winning a national championship is obviously far more important than a team winning a scrimmage. Prominence comes into play, for example, when a head coach gets arrested and makes the headlines, whereas a graduate assistant in the same situation might go unnoticed. Conflict can take many forms, such as a decision about who will start in the conference championship game—something that fans will want to weigh in on, even though the decision rests, of course, with the head coach. The unusual can also take many forms, such as a student-athlete on a football team who served in the military prior to enrolling in college. And proximity dictates, for example, that the athletics department at the state's major public institution will get more media coverage than a conference rival from four states away.

Coaches and student-athletes sometimes assert that negativity is all that "sells" in the media; however, the TIPCUP acronym provides a more informative look at what the media tend to find worthy of coverage. Journalists write about what passionate fans want (Wigley & Meirick, 2008). Regardless, some coaches and staff continue to decry sportswriters and the media as wielding a "poison pen"—thus the importance of educating athletics department members about media relations.

Despite the need to cultivate good media relations, Howard and Mathews (2000) observe that media requests for information are sometimes rejected. Here are some reasons that sports information directors can use strategically.

- The issue in question simply cannot be discussed (e.g., a personnel matter, legalities, or privacy issues such as details of an injury or a player's academic situation).
- The time required to gather the information is unavailable due to the broad nature of the request.
- The reporter does not know what he or she wants.
- The host or interviewer has a record of asking "loaded" or unfair questions.
- The request asks someone in athletics to appear on a scandal-driven program.
- The request cannot be confirmed as coming from a reporter on assignment.
- The request comes from someone with a clear bias or a careless approach to journalism.

In similar fashion, strategy can be implemented in the way in which a story is released. Many SIDs acknowledge that releasing a story on Monday generates more attention, whereas Tuesday is traditionally a slow media day (Johnston, 2022). Along the same lines, releasing a story on a Friday afternoon helps bury it, because many media outlets have already established the storylines for their weekend sport coverage (Howard & Mathews, 2000).

EVOLUTION OF THE MEDIA

There was an era when the news was reported primarily through the morning newspaper and the evening newscast. Today's news is brought to the consumer at a much faster pace. Joe Hernandez, former associate athletics director for media and alumni relations at Ball State University, in Indiana, observed in 2005 that "media demands have changed dramatically. With the advent of the fax machine, email, and the Internet, the world wants news faster and faster. The technology has caused more and more media outlets to arise and require information" (qtd. in Schultz, 2005, p. 210). Since then, social media has only increased that challenge.

Indeed, in the 24-7 news cycle, media outlets demand immediate attention and assistance (Stoldt, 2000). This reality includes the mass media's use of X (formerly known as Twitter) to promote breaking news before a complete story is written (Schultz & Sheffer, 2010). In addition, websites overseen by traditional outlets must compete with team-specific fan sites, thus affecting the revenue streams gained through advertising and subscriptions (Butler & Sagas, 2008). Even the profiles of message board users are broken down by demographics for the benefit of online advertisers interested in details about factors such as gender, race, age, and income (Clavio, 2008).

The commercial nature of the media also affects

the framing of information. According to Bobby Parker, former associate athletics director for communication at Bradley University, "the growth of sports talk radio and the Internet [has] created a more negative approach to coverage. The Internet has provided another avenue for the media to get information, but it's not always reliable" (qtd. in Schultz, 2005, p. 210). This environment leads to increasing concern about credibility and accuracy and makes it difficult to police the information available to the general public (Andrews, 2005). An example of this occurred at the 2022 NCAA Division I Women's Swimming and Diving Championships, where a transgender student-athlete competed in and won the 500-meter freestyle. Three competitors took a photo together near the podium after the race and many fans and media were quick to surmise on social media that the photo was a protest of the transgender student-athlete. In actuality, it was a photo of three competitors who were previously teammates on the United States Olympic Team, two of whom were openly supportive of the transgender student-athlete (Berman, 2022). When errors do occur, Howard and Mathews (2000) suggest the following steps for rectifying the situation.

1. Acknowledge the difference between what is incorrect and what you don't *like* about the story.
2. In most cases, be charitable and do nothing.
3. In some cases, contact the reporter to request that the item be corrected for the record.
4. In a few cases, write a letter to the editor.
5. In rare cases, ask the publication to print a correction.
6. In no case contact a competing media outlet to tell them of the incident and ask them to set the record straight.
7. In case of a significant error, post the correction on the athletics department's website.

Many sports information departments have embraced proactive approaches to solving the problem of inaccurate reporting (Ruihley & Fall, 2009). In this regard, the athletics department's website and social media platforms are important tools for the athletics department to convey its message to the public. Such approaches illustrate the evolution of sports information's role from information provider to strategic adviser, and duties will continue to change as new issues and media emerge (Ruihley & Fall, 2009).

SENSATIONALISM

Today's journalism has broadened from local newspaper, radio, and television outlets to Internet coverage by investigative journalists (Andrews, 2005; Howard & Mathews, 2000). Howard and Mathews asserted in the early 2000s that this trend would not change, and they were right. Yahoo Sports and USA Today Sports, for example, have established a strong niche in their ability to research and uncover hidden stories (Fisher, 2011). TMZ Sports, following TMZ's gossipy approach to covering celebrities, spotlights athletics figures.

In this context, newspapers and radio and television stations also operate websites that enable breaking news coverage, and fan sites are dedicated to specific teams (Butler & Sagas, 2008). Butler and Sagas observe that while such sites provide information to fans about their favorite teams, they are not traditional media in the sense that fans are able to use them to create forums or message boards and other communities where they offer their unfiltered views, opinions, and feedback. Though fans flock to such websites, their parent companies may not adhere to industry ethics because they are newer forms of media operated independently of traditional sites (Yanity & Edmondson, 2011). The accuracy of fan-generated content can also be questionable (Butler & Sagas, 2008).

At the same time, comments posted on fan sites and online columns can make it easier for athletics administrators to gauge the mood of the fans (Andrews, 2005). Many newspapers now also permit fans to comment on articles (Butler & Sagas, 2008). These practices further the "soap opera" aspect of sports, and they also help journalists shape future stories (Andrews, 2005; Wigley & Meirick, 2008). Sensationalism will likely continue to grow with the development of more online media that allow for increased fan participation. As a result, sports information professionals must develop the needed skill set to both shape and learn from these activities.

MEDIA POLICY

Though one of the SID's core duties is to get information out to the media, the department also must identify "guiding principles and behaviors to ensure consistent, fair, and ethical communication with all constituents" (Mathews, 2004, p. 46). To this end, it is essential to develop and implement a media policy for the following reasons:

- The media policy designates who will serve as a calm and credible spokesperson in times of crisis (Barrow, 2022; Ruihley & Fall, 2009).
- It helps the athletics department staff be aware that members of the media should work with the sports information department to obtain official quotes, interviews, and comments.
- It conveys a firm message to the media that student-athletes are students first and are not to be disrupted during classes or while studying (Montoro, 2022).

For example, Yanity & Edmondson (2011) found that many high school recruits were frequently contacted by recruiting websites at all times of the day. A media policy establishes that this is not acceptable practice in intercollegiate athletics by informing the media of the proper procedures for setting up an interview with a student-athlete.

The media policy should also specify when and how to contact head coaches, who may be occupied with recruiting, watching films, or preparing for a game (Bratton, 2022; Lovings, 2022). The policy informs members of the media that student-athletes and coaches could be unavailable for interviews at certain times (Schultz, 2005). Possible reasons for limiting media access range from keeping the team focused on academics during exams to a coach's desire to better monitor a team that has spoken too freely with the media, perhaps making inflammatory comments about opponents (Bratton, 2022; Lovings, 2022; Thompson, 2022). An example of this occurred when three student-athletes from the Kent State University men's basketball team missed the first half of the 2022 conference championship game and an additional player was suspended, all because their Snapchat video with profanity about their next opponent was uncovered on X (formerly known as Twitter) (ESPN News Services, 2022). In addition, the policy should warn the media against conducting "ambush" interviews, such as questioning coaches or student-athletes during community service appearances outside of prearranged interview times (Andrews, 2005).

The media policy should specify cool-down periods after practices and especially after competition to enable coaches and student-athletes to control their emotions and get their thoughts together before speaking with the media (Johnston, 2022). A coach or student-athlete caught up in passionate feelings may speak without thinking rationally, thus making it harder to control the message delivered to the media. For example, shortly after being hired as head football coach at Louisiana State University, Brian Kelly spoke to the crowd in Baton Rouge at a home basketball game. Kelly, a former Notre Dame coach and a Boston native, shifted into a southern accent that was widely mocked on sports radio and other social media platforms as fake and disingenuous.

In addition, the media policy may provide for using teleconference calls to expedite the interview process and avoid redundancy in questions (Masteralexis et al., 2008). The policy should also establish priorities for postgame interviews; for example, the television or radio broadcast partner should have priority in interviewing the star player or head coach on the playing surface before the team departs to the locker room. This partnership is arranged through the media rights deal in place with the school, conference, or governing body (Gale, 2022).

MEDIA TRAINING

Sports information departments use media training to help coaches, administrators, and student-athletes avoid debacles (Stoldt et al., 2006). Media training can help these individuals find a more effective way to interact with the media and help eliminate the fallout that comes with negative interviews (Johnston, 2022). The media are capable of fueling stereotypes, such as the "dumb jock" stereotype, of college athletes (Harrison et al., 2009). Media training assists in combating such stereotypes and promoting a more positive image.

Members of the media may build mutual trust and respect with coaches and student-athletes, but it remains wise to avoid becoming friendly with media representatives, simply because mass media is a business (Schultz, 2005). Media training helps coaches and student-athletes anticipate questions and best formulate, in advance, the messages they would like to get across. Media training also informs coaches and student-athletes about how their behavior and reactions on the playing field, court, or other surface may be interpreted by the media, even if such interpretations are inaccurate (Earnheardt, 2010). Regardless of all these issues, the media plays a significant role in shaping fans' opinions of coaches, student-athletes, and athletics programs.

Media training helps educate those in the athletics department about not only what can go wrong when interacting with the media but also how it might be fixed (Johnston, 2022). Certain members of the media have a particular story angle in mind before they start talking with a coach or student-athlete, but proper training helps interviewees redirect the conversation or eliminate the angle completely if it portrays the team or athletics department in a negative light (Andrews, 2005). Here are two examples of such slanted questions and cautionary responses by a coach or student-athlete.

Question: Did your teammates' poor shooting cause you great frustration?

Answer: It is a team game, and collectively we did not play well enough to win.

Question: Did the cautious play calling from the coaches hinder your ability to win the game?

Answer: Our coaches put us in position to be here tonight, but the other team just played better.

Howard and Mathews (2000) highlight the fact that some reporters, in their effort to build their audience, may resort to trickery during interviews. Examples include needling, falsehoods or twisted "facts," misinterpretation of responses, and putting words into someone's mouth. Coaches and student-athletes can defuse such situations by calmly sticking to the key message, kindly correcting the interviewer, avoiding loaded responses, and steering clear of arguments (Howard & Mathews, 2000).

Members of the media are trained to notice if a respondent's body language gives any messages that could be used negatively (Andrews, 2005). For example, a roll of the eyes, an unwillingness to look someone in the eye, or increasing sweat on the forehead can be portrayed negatively in the media, even though each of these mannerisms could simply be a function of being interviewed in a hot locker room after a lengthy game or being tired from studying the previous evening. Therefore, proper training should provide examples of the media taking liberties based on body language to emphasize the importance of the respondent's expression, attire, and posture at all times.

Media training also helps remind interviewees that they cannot predict the future (Johnston, 2022). The media are capable of asking the same question in many different ways; therefore, media training prepares respondents to answer consistently, even in times of crisis. Everyone questioned must be comfortable acknowledging that they lack information, are looking into something, or cannot answer a question, perhaps due to privacy laws or personnel matters (Johnston, 2022). Media training can also help athletics administrators express sympathy if someone is injured at a sporting event without expanding on their answer to the point that their response can be used against them in a court of law (Braun, 2022).

In media training it is moreover important to stress that "off-the-record" answers simply do not exist (Howard & Mathews, 2000; Schmidt, 2022). The media is a business, and businesses and their employees typically operate in their own best interest. Therefore, if a supposedly off-the-record comment can help create better business for the media outlet, chances are that it will be used even if the interviewee indicated that the conversation was not for official release.

Regardless of whether an SID implements formal media training, the SID is obliged to guide student-athletes and coaches, especially those who are in the media spotlight or are subject to regular public scrutiny (Johnston, 2022). Using the analogy of a fishbowl, the sports information staff can advise a star student-athlete or coach that members of the media are watching their every move, both on and off the playing surface. For example, after a reporter called Deion Sanders, the former head football coach at Jackson State University, by his first name twice at the 2021 SWAC Media Days, the coach ended the phone call. Preferring to be addressed as Coach, Sanders stressed that Nick Saban would not be addressed as Nick (Associated Press, 2021; ESPN, 2021). In the following days, the media's focus was on the telephone hang-up, not football, and the reporter was quoted as saying he calls many interviewees by their first name, regardless of whether it is the first interview or after several interviews.

SPECULATING VERSUS FORECASTING

Forecasting is another element of media training that can help administrators control the messages relayed to the public. In this approach, the SID uses familiarity with the media's strategies for finding an appealing story angle to predict questions that may be asked. From time to time, for example, media personnel ask speculative questions related to events that *could* happen in the future. For instance, a reporter might ask a head coach about a player's eligibility for an upcoming season when grades have not yet been submitted. Similarly, an athletics director might be asked about forthcoming sanctions immediately after the announcement that violations have been submitted to the NCAA. In these scenarios, neither the coach nor the athletics director possesses enough information to make an informed response.

Forecasting allows administrators, coaches, and student-athletes to examine impending issues behind closed doors in an effort to identify potential scenarios and prepare desired responses in advance (Braun, 2022; Howard & Mathews, 2000). In the case of the student-athlete's eligibility, for example, if their forthcoming grades determine whether they can play during the next semester, the SID can help athletics department members forecast what type of question will be asked by the media regardless of whether or not the student-athlete ends up eligible to compete. Here are some specific examples.

If eligible, the student-athlete could be asked the following questions:

- How were you able to improve your grades?
- Were you motivated to get better grades in order to maintain your eligibility?
- What role did your teammates play in supporting you?
- What will keep the academic problems from reoccurring in the future?
- What role did your family play in this process?

If ineligible, the student-athlete could be asked the following questions:

- Have academics been a continuous issue for you?
- Do you feel that you were offered enough academic support by your coach, team, or athletics department?
- Now that you are ineligible, what is your next step?
- Will you consider transferring?
- How disappointed are you?

Although forecasting helps SIDs prepare for many potential scenarios, it is an imprecise science. Despite attending conferences and keeping up with the news, no SID is immune to crisis, and all will face an unanticipated issue at some point. In times of duress, the sports information director is the face that many administrators, coaches, and student-athletes look to for calmness and direction (Barrow, 2022). In being mindful of what sells in the media, a good SID can take some solace in the limited shelf life of today's negative news; however, the best preparation is to avoid such issues in the first place through regular education (Montoro, 2022).

CRISIS MANAGEMENT

By definition, a crisis is disruptive; it may also be unexpected, and it is frequently characterized by allegations that are not completely founded or proven, which can lead to erroneous assumptions (Connaughton et al., 2001). Crises can happen due to injury, improper recruiting, arrests, fights, academic improprieties, and other reputation-damaging issues. They can occur on campus, at off-site events, or even overseas during international goodwill trips. They can involve any number of departmental stakeholders—fans, donors, alumni, parents, coaches, student-athletes, cheerleaders, cheerleading coaches, and even mascots. Crises can take place in season, out of season, during the academic year, and throughout the summer. As a result, sports information departments are never immune to the concerns of crisis management (Barrow, 2022).

Seitel (2010) suggests that when a crisis occurs, administrators should adhere to the following guidelines.

- Speak early and often.
- Don't speculate.
- Go off the record at your own peril.
- Stay with the facts.
- Be open and concerned, not defensive.
- Make your own point and repeat it.
- Don't fight with the media.
- Establish yourself as the most authoritative source.
- Stay calm, and be truthful and cooperative.
- Never lie.

Dealing with a crisis has become more difficult with the growth of the Internet and, as mentioned earlier, the emergence of online tabloid journalism outlets such as TMZ Sports, independent fan sites, and chat rooms (Andrews, 2005; Butler & Sagas, 2008). In past generations, journalists traditionally verified their sources to ensure the accuracy of their reporting. Power has now shifted, however, from the mainstream media to uncontrolled information intermediaries who often possess sensationalist agendas or ulterior motives (Howard & Mathews, 2000). The race to break stories, and thereby boost an organization's ratings or readership, has reduced the importance of credibility (Howard & Mathews, 2000; Stoldt et al., 2006). Unnamed sources may be less credible, but they are still sources that help shape a story (Andrews, 2005). Thus it is important to develop an ample crisis management team and a plan that alerts all involved to possible tripping points.

As cited in Stoldt et al. (2006), a crisis can grow if the athletics department is not prepared to avoid the following pitfalls: stalling (Helitzer, 2000), telling lies (Stoldt, Miller et al., 2000), withholding negative news (Helitzer, 2000), ignoring tough questions (Stoldt et al., 2000), stating "no comment" (Stoldt et al., 2000), downplaying a crisis (Cutlip et al., 2000), going off the record (Cutlip et al., 2000), estimating monetary damages or medical diagnoses, shifting blame (Public Relations Society of America, 2000), or adding inappropriate humor (Schmidt, 2022). All are valuable points about which to educate the athletics department members well in advance. As Earnheardt (2010) observed, even the most zealous fans can become unfairly judgmental; thus, it is critical to take all crises seriously.

Despite the best efforts to educate and forecast, crises will inevitably occur. When they do, issues management is essential. Issues management is "the process of prioritizing and proactively addressing public policy and reputation issues that affect an organization's success" (Pinkham, as qtd. in Stoldt et al., 2006). With this in mind, administrators should be familiar with the following four-step process for managing any issues that arise:

1. Anticipate and analyze the issue.
2. Develop the organization's position.
3. Identify key publics.
4. Specify the desired behavior of these groups.

During such times, an SID who is viewed with trust and credibility by local media outlets is generally the person they turn to for answers (Masteralexis et al., 2008). "The ideal relationship is based on trust," according to Maxey Parrish, former SID at Baylor University. "The media have to trust the SID to be fully factual, whether the news is good or bad. The SID has to trust the media to treat [the] school fairly" (qtd. in Schultz, 2005, p. 210). As a result, it is the SID who traditionally advises senior administrators about what to do when a crisis reduces the available reaction time from hours to minutes (Johnston, 2022).

Crisis Management Plan

Because of the tendency to rush to reaction by key publics—fans, alumni, sponsors, ticket holders, students, and others—athletics departments stress a proactive approach to controlling the media and their story angles. The idea is to maximize reaction time and minimize clean up (Stoldt et al., 2006), and this requires careful creation of a detailed crisis management plan. Such a plan is analogous to a fire evacuation route in one's home. You hope you never need it, but if you do, you want it be as efficient as possible and to include a proactive step for every circumstance.

Examples of Recent Crises and Scandals in College Sport

- *Admissions scandal.* Georgetown University, Stanford University, University of Southern California, University of Texas, Yale University, and many other schools were found to admit "recruited" student-athletes (who were not actually recruited) after the parents funneled money through William Singer, a self-described "college counselor," as part of the bribery scandal that federal investigators called Operation Varsity Blues.
- *Canceled basketball tournaments.* March 2020 marked the beginning of the COVID-19 pandemic, halting conference basketball tournaments.
- *ESPN.* ESPN draws the ire of University of South Carolina Gamecocks women's basketball coach Dawn Staley and Gamecock fans after failing to invite Aliyah Boston, a unanimous first-team All-American and national Player of the Year who led her team to a national title, to the ESPY Awards.
- *Sarah Fuller and social media.* Vanderbilt University's Sarah Fuller makes history on the football field for her kicking but faces lewd and misogynist comments on social media.
- *Coach Gundy's T-shirt.* Oklahoma State University football coach Mike Gundy apologizes after a picture surfaces of him wearing an OAN T-shirt, causing the football team to organize a protest against racism.
- *University of Iowa financial issues.* Iowa cuts men's and women's swimming, men's tennis, and men's gymnastics but offers football coaches raises.
- *Kentucky stadium controversy.* Faculty members at the University of Kentucky call on the school to rename Rupp Arena, named after former coach Adolph Rupp, whom they view as a racist.
- *Liberty University allegations of racism.* Black student-athletes depart the school, claiming racist behavior toward nonwhite students on campus.
- *Cheating in men's basketball.* Accusations of cheating hang over programs at Arizona, Auburn, Kansas, Louisiana State, Louisville, Memphis, Miami, North Carolina State, Oklahoma State, Southern California, and other institutions in the aftermath of a 2017-2018 corruption scandal involving the FBI, Adidas, and numerous basketball coaches.
- *Gymnastics team physician convicted of sexual assaults.* Larry Nassar, the long-time Michigan State University gymnastics team physician, is sentenced to prison for sexually abusing girls and young women.
- *NCAA.* Participants in the women's NCAA basketball championship embarrass the association by making social media posts showing the meagerness of women's weight rooms, food, and other considerations compared to men's.
- *Professor faked grades for student-athletes.* Julius Nyang'oro, a long-time professor at the University of North Carolina, is at the center of a scandal involving faked class records and grades for student-athletes.
- *Ohio State University wrestling charges of sexual assault.* Numerous former wrestlers accuse U.S. Representative and former Ohio State wrestling coach Jim Jordan of covering up a sexual assault by a former team physician.
- *Razorbacks football overextended.* University of Arkansas football loses two games for which it paid US$3 million in guarantees to opposing schools while also being financially obligated to pay three football head coaches at once.
- *Saban.* Nick Saban's daughter posts COVID-19 conspiracy theories relating to Ohio State University Buckeyes football, delaying their appearance in the national championship game due to allegedly hoping to allow the Buckeyes' quarterback more time to get out of the coronavirus protocol prior to their matchup versus the University of Alabama.
- *Rolovich and COVID vaccine.* Washington State University head football coach Nick Rolovich is removed from his position after failing to comply with the state's coronavirus vaccine mandate.
- *Improper recruitment at Duke.* Former Duke University basketball star Zion Williamson faces allegations that he was paid during the recruiting process.

A crisis management team, frequently led by an SID in conjunction with other senior administrators, is established to explore potential worst-case crisis scenarios (Braun, 2022). The sports information director can be instrumental as a "problem-solving process facilitator" and catalyst in the communication effort (Ruihley & Fall, 2009). For each scenario, the crisis management team identifies response outcomes and needed support. Does the president or chancellor need to be informed? Is legal counsel necessary? If the crisis does in fact arise, the plan is then implemented to keep all involved parties consistent in working with the media.

Afterward, the plan's implementation is assessed to see what worked and what did not. Crises can arise unexpectedly, but the crisis management team can prevent them or prepare to manage them effectively through practices such as observation, discussion, and analysis of organizational crisis management tactics (Braun, 2022). In addition, in a crisis that could damage an entire university's reputation, the institution's general department of media and public relations may step in to assist or oversee media relations because the central administration wants greater control over the response to prevent further damage (Montoro, 2022).

REPUTATION

Reputation has been defined as the "ability of an organization to meet the expectations of its publics and the strengths of the relationships [that] various stakeholders have with the organization" (Stoldt et al., 2006, p. 35). Depending on the scale of a crisis and the institution's reputation, the institution may be able to withstand a damaging blow to its reputation quotient (Fombrun et al., 2000). The reputation quotient accounts for various factors that may be affected by a scandal: emotional appeal, products and services, vision and leadership, workplace environment, social responsibility, and financial performance.

SOCIAL MEDIA AND CONTINUOUS SURVEILLANCE

The evolution of online technology has forced sports information directors to assume a new role as social media police. Because the media can now pull information from a student-athlete's or coach's social media accounts, the athletics department's message has become more difficult to monitor (Gregory, 2009; Sanderson, 2011). All members of the department should be continuously educated about how the media can use details from any social media outlet at any time (Sanderson, 2011). Because of the rapid growth of social media, many athletics departments lack applicable policies, management plans, and oversight procedures for social media crises (Syme, 2012).

Similarly, many departments are unsure of how to use their own social media outlets in a time of crisis. Syme (2012) recommends that schools embrace the following five strategies:

The Athletics Department: Front Porch or Window to the World?

When an athletics department is flourishing on the field, it can build excitement among alumni and fans. Home sporting events and extensive media coverage of athletics can offer uplifting experiences and memories to many supporters. Replicating this success on the academic side of campus can prove more difficult despite the quality of research, education, and job placement.

T.K. Wetherell, former president of Florida State University, has referred to athletics as a school's "window to the world" (Hyland, 2010). Other leaders, including University of North Texas president Neal Smatresk and former University of Central Arkansas president Allen Meadors, have suggested that athletics can be viewed as the "front porch" of an institution, implying that athletics is the first thing that people see at the school (McCollum, 2009; Smatresk, 2011). When athletics momentum is positive, the school's donors and supporters can embrace the excitement. Those moments can be fleeting, however, in times of crisis, especially a crisis that threatens to harm the reputation of a great academic institution.

1. Implement a social media monitoring system to track what is being said about your organization.
2. Develop a social media policy to help provide guardrails.
3. Implement a social media management policy to enhance monitoring, tracking, and measurement.
4. Establish registration of department social media accounts to minimize unofficial accounts and lost passwords.
5. Establish a community manager for department social media to have a contact person or department for questions, guidance, and continuity.

Sports information staff must also strongly emphasize to coaches and student-athletes that the audiovisual recording functions of mobile phones mean that their actions, both good and bad, can be captured by anyone at any time (Sanderson, 2009)—and that the media can use the results in their reporting. Video footage of a coach's or student-athlete's drunken behavior, drug use, physical violence, competition in an unauthorized sporting activity while rehabilitating an injury, or other dangerous or otherwise undesirable activities can result in an unwanted appearance on tabloid websites. In such cases, the sports information staff are forced to address issues reactively, since sports talk radio and websites will quickly frame the story for their own economic gain (Sanderson, 2009).

Student-athletes and coaches may express concern about invasions of their privacy, but sports information directors need to remind them of their heightened visibility due to the economic realities of the media (Sanderson, 2011). Therefore, whereas obscene or profane posts, provocative pictures, or evidence of alcohol consumption may be considered acceptable by some college students or staff members (Miller et al., 2010), the behavior of a student-athlete or coach is more visible and is held to a higher standard.

These cautions also apply to student-athletes who use social media to lash out at a coach or teammate (Ballouli & Hutchinson, 2010). Athletes who use social media platforms as a medium for sharing their personal life should be warned of the potential pitfalls (Pegoraro, 2010). Fans of rival schools have disguised their identities to lure student-athletes and then taunt them at a sporting event. In addition, stalkers, agents, and persons affiliated with gambling interests may also use social media to reach student-athletes (Sanderson, 2011).

Some coaches, including John Calipari of the University of Kentucky men's basketball team, have revoked student-athletes' social media privileges after their posts led to undesirable media coverage (Staples, 2011). The sports information director should emphasize that the time spent in strategically repairing a program's brand could be better used in proactively pushing positive messages, thus heightening the importance of media education in the athletics department (Sanderson, 2011). Preventive monitoring by coaches and sports information staff can include such measures as having student-athletes send social media friend requests to coaches and sports information staff members. It can also mean pointing out to student-athletes that social media is frequently used for procrastination and escape, which can be detrimental to academic success (Brougham, 2021).

Social Media as a Marketing Tool

Pitfalls notwithstanding, when social media are used strategically they can serve as critical elements of an athletics department's marketing toolkit (Pegoraro, 2010; Williams & Chinn, 2010). A captivating link or picture, for example, can stimulate fan avidity and draw traffic to the department's website (Pegoraro, 2010). Similarly, social media posts by student-athletes and coaches can be used to highlight charity work, off-season training, travel, and reflection on large-scale events, such as postseason competition. Posts and images can be used to enhance marketing efforts that boost ticket sales, merchandise retailing, donations, and other means of support (Williams & Chinn, 2010). In addition, Phua (2010) has found that fan identification is stronger among online media users than among fans who connect through print and broadcast media. This is particularly important since the expansion, in 2022, of student-athletes' right to use their name, image, and likeness (NIL).

Dos and Don'ts of Social Media

To avoid "making news" in a negative manner, social media posts should not comment on issues involving politics, religion, or military actions (Pegoraro, 2010). Departments should also be careful to properly balance their own posts. Reichart-Smith (2011) found that athletics departments have produced posts that publicize men's programs more than women's programs. This concern needs to be addressed throughout the sports information or sport marketing department given Title IX's application to intercollegiate athletics, as well as the potential for missed opportunities to promote Olympic sport programs (Cooper, 2008).

Despite all these caveats, social media provide a valuable way to highlight rivalries, give updates about facility construction, thank fans, share news about community goodwill efforts, and offer a look at past or current success stories—all of which can enhance the department's brand (Wallace et al., 2011). If communication is a two-way platform between the athletics department and its supporters, athletics department staff can answer questions posted online that are directed toward coaches or student-athletes. This practice increases efficiency and eases the time constraints faced by student-athletes.

STUDENT-ATHLETE PRIVACY: FERPA AND MEDICAL ISSUES

The Family Educational Rights and Privacy Act (FERPA) requires that students' records be protected from release. The law is not limited to student-athletes, but given the heightened scrutiny applied to this population, sport administrators must understand the law thoroughly because the media often inquire about related issues, such as academic eligibility and graduation rates (Montoro, 2022). The law also protects student-athletes from searches of their medical records and drug tests (Schmidt, 2022). As a result, if a student fails a drug test, sports information staff traditionally note merely that a violation of team rules has warranted a suspension. Even if anonymous sources attribute the suspension to the use of illicit drugs, the sports information department should stand by its response that the student-athlete was disciplined due to a violation of team rules, while neither confirming nor denying the allegation (Schmidt, 2022).

Medical records are also protected when a student-athlete is injured. Minor injuries may be disclosed as the reason that a student-athlete did not play or practice. In the case of severe injury, however, athletics departments traditionally have a media policy requiring that the sports medicine staff first notify family members, then ask their permission before sharing a diagnosis publicly (Barrow, 2022). However, it is not unusual for members of the media to ask medical practitioners for a diagnosis and a description of the recovery faced by a student-athlete, especially if the athlete is a star figure.

FREEDOM OF INFORMATION ACT

The sports information department must educate coaches and other athletics staff members (including administrators and central administrators) about the fact that documents, including email correspondence, are subject to request by the media (Montoro, 2022). This is particularly important at public institutions, although employees at private schools should act under the assumption that their words could be read by others, as well. The media can file requests through the Freedom of Information Act (FOIA), otherwise referred to as the Open Records Act or an Open Records Request, thereby compelling the release of such documents in a timely manner.

Some FOIA requests are broad and some are narrower, such as a request for all emails related to the firing of a head coach. The media can request all email correspondence within a designated time period, and reporters will then read through the emails and convey their findings. As a result, coaches and other members of the athletics department are advised to treat their correspondence as if the general public will read it. Phone records are also commonly requested by the media in order to find patterns of calls or text messages, as well as any communication that is perceived as out of the ordinary. For example, the media used FOIA to discover that a University of Arkansas head football coach had texted a female reporter 1,000 times during a 6-week period (Associated Press, 2007).

Leadership Lesson

Negotiation

Revenue generated from media contracts serves as the lifeblood of many intercollegiate athletics departments. As a result, the negotiation of these contracts has become vitally important. The need for negotiation skills also extends into nearly every facet of an administrator's duties—from day one as a new employee, to the annual budgeting cycle, to the allocation of facility space and practice time between antagonistic coaches, to multimillion-dollar facility naming and sponsorship opportunities. In each of these situations, savvy administrators can break out their negotiation toolkit and approach the opportunity with confidence and excitement.

Excitement? Absolutely. Each of these situations requires give and take, the understanding of moving parts, the ability to put together pieces of a puzzle, and the skill of uncovering value that can invigorate each person at the table. These moments can get your adrenaline pumping and simulate in your own work the game-day experience that you are trying to facilitate for your athletes. There is, however, one tremendous difference. Generally, the negotiation process should not be viewed as a competitive sport. Rather, it is helpful to view both parties as being on the same team and working toward a "win-win" result.

In the chapter 6 leadership lesson, "Interdependence and the Win-Win Paradigm," we discussed the win-win frame of mind, which is "based on the paradigm that there is plenty for everybody, that one person's success is not achieved at the expense or exclusion of the success of others" (Covey, 2004, p. 207). In other words, rather than dividing a fixed pie, both parties work to expand the pie. This win-win mentality is very different from the common image of hard-nosed bargaining sessions in which parties threaten to walk away, try to take advantage of each other, exaggerate concessions, and attempt to squeeze every ounce of value for themselves out of the negotiation. The "distributive approach," in which each party battles for the largest possible piece of a fixed pie, can be appropriate in situations where you will never work with the other party, but it is generally not appropriate in most ongoing working relationships.

This is not to say that you should not try to satisfy your interests. You certainly should, but you do so with an awareness of the context and the interests of both parties. Before beginning a negotiation, then, there is a tremendous amount of work to be done. As you prepare for and begin each phase of a negotiation, strive to do so with the vision framework discussed in chapter 3. Begin with the end in mind. The following steps will help you enter any negotiation full of confidence.

1. Recognize the type of issue involved. There are three types, and each calls for its own strategies.
   a. Distributive—This is the typical "divide the fixed pie" situation. A fixed amount of resources is equally valued by both parties, and a gain for one party is viewed as a loss for the other. The best strategy in this situation is to get as much information as possible from the other party while limiting what you share. Be willing to make concessions for a realistic outcome.
   b. Integrative—There is a fixed amount of resources, but the issue is differently valued by each party. Something might be very important to one party but minimally important to the other. Seek to maximize integrative issues for both parties. The only way to understand these preferences is through honest information sharing in an effort to "expand the pie."
   c. Compatible—Both parties want the same outcome. Emphasize this mutual commonality.

2. Research the issue. When you arm yourself with data, you bring additional power to the negotiation. If, for example, you have done a competitive analysis, know the standard industry rates, possess relevant testimonials, and are equipped with pro forma budgets for a set of possible scenarios, the person who is negotiating with you is also negotiating with the data (and associated experts) that you bring to the table.
3. Define your interests. Prioritize your interests related to the issues that will be discussed. Define your negotiating zone and set points where accepting an impasse will be the best outcome for both parties (win-win or no deal). One way to do so is by understanding your BATNA—an acronym for "best alternative to a negotiated agreement" (Fisher & Ury, 2011). The BATNA is a predetermined alternative action that will be taken if your interests are not met in the negotiation. A strong BATNA (e.g., an alternative partner, offer, product, or employer) can empower you as a negotiator.
4. Research their interests. The more you understand the driving factors behind the other party's interests, the more creative you can be in approaching the issues. Ask questions, seek alternatives, and research past negotiations and possible options that the other party could bring to the table in order to recommend trade-offs.
5. Focus on interests rather than positions. Asking "why" can reveal the underlying interests behind positions. Finding out the motives behind stated positions can reveal information that facilitates integrative win-win outcomes.

Completing a tough, multiround negotiation can be tremendously rewarding. When two parties come together armed with preparation and an understanding that compromise is not the ***desired*** outcome, it is possible to create tremendous synergistic value. This type of negotiation involves both parties seeking to maximize integrative interests, identify and highlight compatible issues, compromise on distributive issues, and dig deep to find alternative solutions.

Unfortunately, this often does not happen. As you may have noticed, the tactics for maximizing value on distributive issues are contrary to the tactics for maximizing value on integrative issues. This contradiction can foster negotiation approaches with minimal information sharing, minimal understanding of interests, and maximal likelihood of an impasse. If one party shares information with a "value creator" mind-set, and the other approaches the discussion with a "value claimer" mind-set, the claimer will likely crush the creator, since the claimer can use the information shared by the creator to their advantage while concealing their own interests. The long-term consequences of the "claimer" approach, however, include a lack of trust and merely average future outcomes as both parties withhold information.

Other Resources

Cialdini, R.B. (2006). *Influence: The psychology of persuasion.* New York: HarperBusiness.

Fisher, R., & Ury, W. (1983). *Getting to yes: Negotiating agreement without giving in.* New York: Penguin Books.

PUBLIC RELATIONS CAMPAIGNS

Although the sports information department focuses primarily on media production and relationships with media outlets, it must occasionally mount a public relations campaign (Stoldt et al., 2001). Such campaigns are designed to change behavior, affect attitudes, build knowledge, or generate awareness (Mullin et al., 2007). They typically pursue specific short-term goals and are targeted at selected publics (Smith, 2002). For example, a school may promote a student-athlete for national recognition such as the Heisman Trophy.

Despite the importance of such campaigns, Stoldt and Narasimhan (2005) have found that sports information directors lack proficiency in adequately measuring or assessing the effectiveness of their publicity efforts. Ballouli and Hutchinson (2010) conclude that many sports information directors view themselves more in the role of providing technical expertise than of providing the managerial expertise necessary for public relations campaigns.

More generally, assessment is a difficult task for many who work in public and media relations, regardless of whether sport is involved (Howard & Matthews, 2000). Website success can be evaluated in terms of quantifiable metrics, but traditional media may not offer comparable patterns of analytics (Ballouli & Hutchinson, 2010). Consequently, public relations campaigns seek assessments that measure the target audience's changes in attitude or behavior (Howard & Matthews, 2000). However, these goals are difficult to gauge and analyze accurately with the limited staffing typically found in sports information departments.

CURRENT ISSUES

Sports information continues to change rapidly, embracing progress and innovation, whether that means helping student-athletes with name, image, and likeness (NIL) or helping to promote diversity, equity, and inclusion (DEI). Sports information departments also work with other departments in athletics to further revenue generation opportunities.

Name, Image, and Likeness

During summer 2022, student-athletes were able to begin using their name, image, and likeness (NIL) to build their brand and profit. However, many student-athletes needed guidance on how to transition their social media posts from reports of their daily activities to those befitting a brand ambassador. The sports information director can assist with not only media training but also social media training (Johnston, 2022). Common social media errors can include missed posting opportunities or posting about a sponsor's competitor. For example, a student-athlete might endorse a local restaurant but inadvertently post about a social outing with friends at the restaurant's competitor.

Student-athletes can also work with sports information to utilize such services as INFLCR and Opendorse. These platforms provide a way for student-athletes to use their photos for brand enhancement, as in social media posts (Johnston, 2022).

Diversity, Equity, and Inclusion in Sports Information

Starting with the 2017-2018 academic year, CoSIDA, today known as College Sports Communicators after a rebranding effort in August 2022, inaugurated its Diversity and Inclusion Committee. The committee's three initial goals were to create a value statement on diversity and inclusion, to expand programming at the CoSIDA Convention and other CoSIDA areas for professional development, and to learn more about the membership demographics (Poole, 2018). The value statement reads:

> *As leaders in the intercollegiate athletics landscape, the College Sports Information Directors of America (CoSIDA) seeks to foster and encourage environments that embrace gender equity, diversity and inclusion. As an organization, CoSIDA is committed to education, discussion, advocacy and programming to establish and sustain an equitable, inclusive and diverse culture within the membership and the institutions it serves.*

The statement reflects both CoSIDA's and its member institutions' interest in pursuing diversity, equity, and inclusion.

The committee worked with a public relations professor from the University of Oregon to better learn about constituent demographics and to strategize about programming needs. The Diversity and Inclusion Committee also worked with the Continuing Education Committee to be aware of unconscious bias and to plan programming for annual conventions (Poole, 2018).

In 2019, the committee hosted a fireside chat at the NACDA Convention for CoSIDA members to attend, along with their colleagues in the National Association for Collegiate Marketing Administrators (NACMA). The guest speaker was the NCAA vice president of inclusion and human resources (Poole, 2020). The 2019-2020 academic year also saw educational components on LGBTQA+ and the Americans with Disabilities Act, and CoSIDA again collaborated with NACMA at the convention for diverse programming, expanding the audience to N4A members. In summer 2020, the #CoSIDA ForChange campaign was launched (Atkinson, 2020). The campaign promoted racial and social justice issues and featured multiple webinars.

Through 2020 and into 2021, CoSIDA furthered its campaign with podcasts, webinars, personal video testimonials, and more (Kowal, 2022). Then in 2022, CoSIDA began the Diversity and Inclusion Fellowship program, collaborating with the Knight Commission on Intercollegiate Athletics, to host live webinars with athletic leaders and national figures in DEI, creating a resource library in the process. Collectively, these efforts are strategically enacted to inspire membership to be agents of progress on their respective campuses, fostering diversity, equity, and inclusion in their own staffing and daily duties.

Revenue Generation

In addition to publicizing the athletics department, the sports information department contributes to revenue generation for athletics. Specifically, sports information staff can supplement vital revenue streams in the following ways:

- Producing game-day programs sold at sporting events
- Providing subscription-based services on the athletics department website
- Displaying backdrops at interviews and media conferences that exhibit athletics department sponsors' names and logos (Andrews, 2005)
- Working with the media at sporting events to determine awards affiliated with sponsor recognition (Andrews, 2005)—for example, the Dairy Queen MVP of the game, the Chili's student-athlete of the week, or any other similar award voted on by members of the media

Professional Development

College Sports Communicators

College Sports Communicators, formerly known as College Sports Information Directors of America or CoSIDA, provides its members with a strategic focus on the sports information niche. Originally part of the American College Public Relations Association, the organization holds an annual conference that allows members to network and engage in professional development. Members can attend educational sessions and webinars about current events in intercollegiate athletics, such as the monitoring of social media or the media's growth and evolution. The organization publishes *360*, a monthly report of best practices and current topics, to further assist in professional development. It also advocates efficiency, effective organization, and proactive approaches to the field (Stoldt, 2008).

College Sports Communicators links colleagues regardless of school or conference affiliation, ranging from schools in the National Association of Intercollegiate Athletics to NCAA Football Bowl Subdivision schools. It promotes education and connection of peers through committees and councils devoted to key issues that work on solutions, proposals, and recommendations (Stoldt, 2008). The group's signature program is the annual awarding of Academic All-American honors. College Sports Communicators offers student memberships for those interested in starting their professional affiliation early.

Students in communication, journalism, public relations, and comparable majors can also join the Public Relations Student Society of America (PRSSA). Doing so is a way to engage in professional development that is advantageous to persons interested in a career in sports information. Membership provides access to networking opportunities, strategic career plans, internship and job boards, competitions, and a national convention. You can visit the organization's website at www.prssa.org.

Case Study

Work/Life Balance in Sports Information

It is the fall semester and your institution, a small liberal arts Division III member, has scheduled home games for women's soccer on Tuesday night, volleyball on Wednesday night, and men's soccer on Thursday night. Each of these events has you, the school's sports information director, on site at 6 pm and done by 10 pm. There is also a home football game on Saturday that will have you on campus from 10 am all the way to 4 pm (at least). That is 18 hours beyond the traditional Monday through Friday 9 am to 5 pm workday. A recent study, according to Doug Vance, former executive director of CoSIDA, found one Division III staff worked 53 to 58 hours per week over a 30-week period from September through May (2019).

Your sports information office is composed of you, a graduate assistant limited to 20 working hours, and student helpers. Fortunately, your supervisor lets you come into work late each morning to offset the hours committed to home events. But that is not the case at all schools. Every coach expects more publicity and wants the latest in graphic design to stand out from their competition. Coaches can escape their office to drop in on the weight room, look at game or practice films, and visit the playing field. They might also be on the road recruiting, assisting the development office, fulfilling a corporate sponsorship obligation, or engaged in team travel. The same cannot be said for the sports information staff, who will work long hours, including nights, weekends, and holidays, on top of still more obligations. These might include photo requests from the development office, changes to the website, emails to answer, interviews to set up, media guides to finish, statistics to update, media relationships to cultivate, social media strategies to plan, and more. Escaping the office can be a challenge. With the changes to name, image, and likeness (NIL) rules in summer 2022, many senior administrators are also looking to sports information to advance the media training and social media training of student-athletes. Pleasing everyone is a challenge and the busy period can run from early August potentially through June, if spring sports advance to the postseason. Crisis management also keeps sports information staff on duty 24 hours a day, lest there be something brewing on social media, the police blotter, or some other source that ends up in the headlines. You love your job, but as investments are made in areas that generate revenue, more is expected of your office with limited resources.

Questions to Consider

1. Aside from salary increases, what innovative strategies could the school, and especially the athletics department, implement to keep the sports information staff fresh, their morale positive, and their emotional wellness strong? How would you, the sports information director, make the case for salary increases?
2. How would you help the department shift from traditional media duties (writing press releases, assisting the media, helping with interviews, creating media guides, updating statistics) to strategic communications where the staff could invest more time in meeting with student-athletes, uncovering feature stories, promoting community service initiatives, advancing storytelling, helping with campaigns, being innovative on social media, and similar "as time permits" tasks?
3. How could the sports information staff best partner with existing entities on campus including sports management or communication departments and the campus media to maximize opportunities?
4. How could this industry recruit the next generation of sports information directors as trends include more online content and less traditional journalism? What skill sets should the students pursue in addition to strong writing skills?

CONCLUSION

Sports information is a time-intensive field that requires a committed effort to help the athletics department communicate through the mass media and other avenues, including social media and the department's own website. The flow of information stems from interviews with administrators, coaches, and student-athletes, as well as the production and distribution of various pieces such as media releases, media guides, and game notes. Sports information directors must balance the needs and deadlines of the media with fostering publicity for women's athletics and Olympic sports that frequently lack media coverage. Media training and crisis management planning can greatly help athletics departments to maintain a strong reputation and credibility with various stakeholders. Those who work in sports information must continue to adapt to the evolution of media, including social media.

DISCUSSION QUESTIONS

1. As the sports information director for a small athletics administrative staff, you are charged by the new athletics director with generating publicity for your small Division I school, which is not distinguished on the playing field. What strategies would you implement? How would your strategies differ at a Division II or Division III school?
2. After a hard-fought sporting event that ended in a controversial loss, you as the sports information director find that the mandatory cool-down period has not helped the team or the head coach accept their loss. Would you let the student-athletes and the coach visit with the media? Defend your decision.
3. A star player is arrested in their hometown during the off-season. Local media in that area try to contact the student-athlete and family members for quotes. The media are unaware of the school's media policy, and time is of the essence. As sports information director, what would you do?
4. A controversial website continues to report inaccurate stories and run headlines that create negative publicity about your institution. Though you know the stories to be false, the website producers are excited about the growing popularity of their online content, especially with your fan base. How would you address this issue?
5. A student-athlete decides to transfer and takes to social media to bash the school, the athletics department, the coaches, and former teammates. What steps do you take to control the damage?
6. Are there students on your campus that would be good candidates for name, image, and likeness opportunities? Perform a SWOT (strengths, weaknesses, opportunities, and threats) analysis on them and discuss what you would prioritize for them in media and social media training.

LEARNING ACTIVITIES

1. Create a "hot seat" class exercise. Identify one student to be the athletics director and one to be the sports information director. The rest of the class acts as members of the media in a press conference. The instructor should explore national media outlets, pick a current event in intercollegiate athletics, and share it with the class. With the students playing their roles, see if the athletics director is properly prepared by the sports information director to navigate the questions that stem from the mock press conference. Repeat the exercise with new students assuming the roles of the SID and AD.
2. Imagine that you approach your athletics director with the recommendation that they make a monthly post on the website or regular posts on social media to communicate with fans. The athletics director, however, is not a big proponent of technology. You want

to share examples of this practice becoming more common. Examine Division I athletics websites and social media platforms of athletics directors to see which institutions use this technology to enable the athletics director to personally communicate with fans. In addition, locate common themes in their posts. Using your findings, discuss how best to educate an athletics director who is reluctant to embrace this technology.

3. At a senior staff meeting, the athletics director wants to discuss making certain portions of the athletics website subscription based. Look at Division I athletics websites to see which institutions offer subscription-based content to their followers, identify what type of content requires a subscription, and find out the rates charged for such content.
4. Student-athletes have come to you for guidance on creating a public relations campaign centered around Black Lives Matter and social injustice. Research the topic and other social justice movements, then devise your own recommendations for this group.
5. Use graphic design to make a special sports-related announcement, such as securing an internship, committing to a graduate program, earning sports-related, academic, or service honors, or offering a sports-related summer camp in a hometown. Discuss the various graphic design tools, then identify classes that can help students acquire or improve these skills.

Financial Operations

Stephen L. Shapiro, University of South Carolina
Brendan Dwyer, Virginia Commonwealth University

In this chapter, you will explore

- the current financial environment in college athletics, including trends in media rights revenue, conference realignment, and the growing financial disparity between athletics programs;
- the unique nature of financial operations in college sport, including its operating structure within higher education, the nonprofit status of college sport, and the tiered financial structure of the NCAA, conferences, and individual athletics departments; and
- general financial knowledge and skills in the context of college athletics, including financial operations, financial statements, planning, and budgeting.

THE CHALLENGE OF BALANCING AN ATHLETICS BUDGET

The athletics program at a Football Bowl Subdivision (FBS) school has just completed its annual budget review. Meanwhile, with a new fiscal year approaching, word is spreading across campus that the state legislature, which has a budgetary shortfall, has pulled back a considerable portion of university funding. In an effort to make up for the expected cut in state funding, the university president has chosen to take back US$750,000 allocated to athletics through student fees—amounting to 5 percent of the total athletics budget—to redistribute it across the university. The cut comes at a time when the athletics department is already operating at a slight deficit. In response, the athletics director (AD) faces the challenge of balancing the budget by properly managing financial operations and making decisions that could lead either to additional revenue generation or to budget cuts.

From humble beginnings as an extracurricular activity for college students in the mid- to late 19th century, college athletics has grown into a tiered business operation with an industry value estimated at well above US$40 billion. More than 1,000 member institutions compete in the National Collegiate Athletic Association (NCAA) (What is the NCAA?, 2021), and hundreds of additional schools compete in other associations, such as the National Association of Intercollegiate Athletics (NAIA) and the National Junior College Athletic Association (NJCAA). The large numbers of participants, coaches, administrators, officials, and spectators mean that substantial economic activity is developed through the operation of college athletics. This chapter provides an overview of financial operations in college athletics departments, as well as an overview of issues associated with the current financial landscape in this environment.

A glimpse into the revenues and expenses of the most visible athletics departments in the NCAA's Football Bowl Subdivision (FBS) provides insight into the finances at play in this industry. This financial information is available from such sources as the Trends in Finances and Archives of NCAA Revenues and Expenses Reports (Finances of Intercollegiate Athletics, 2021), the Equity in Athletics Disclosure Act annual report, and the *USA Today* college athletics finances database (USA Today Sports, 2021). Median total revenue in 2020 for FBS institutions was US$77.2 million (NCAA, 2021b), which constituted a 5.9 percent decrease from 2019 but a 6.2 percent increase from the period 2011-2019 ("10 Year Division I Financial Summary," 2021).

In terms of individual athletics departments, the University of Oregon tops the revenue chart. It generated nearly US$392.7 million in 2019-2020, and more than 20 other programs also generated more than US$100 million (USA Today Sports, 2021). At some institutions, the revenue growth has been staggering. For example, between 2015 and 2020, the University of Oregon and Central Michigan University saw revenue growth of 271 percent and 134 percent, respectively (USA Today Sports, 2021). Growth in college sport appears to be an ongoing trend, even during the COVID-19 pandemic.

However, the substantial growth at the highest level of competition presents a very slanted view of the industry as a whole. In fact, the vast majority of athletics programs struggle financially. Only 20 FBS institutions reported a surplus in 2019-2020, which represents only 15.3 percent of FBS programs. Most Division I programs operate at a deficit, with a median loss of approximately US$19.3 million in generated revenue (not including university allocations) for FBS competition and US$14.8 million in generated revenue for Football Championship Subdivision (FCS) competition (NCAA, 2021b).

In addition, the disparity continues to grow between the haves and the have-nots. For example, while the University of Oregon generated over US$391.4 million in 2019-2020, the University of Louisiana at Monroe (another public institution competing at the FBS level) generated just US$15.3 million (USA Today Sports, 2021). Table 8.1 lists the highest- and lowest-revenue-generating programs at the FBS level.

Table 8.1 Athletics Department Revenue at NCAA Division I Public Institutions (2020)

Institution	Conference	Total revenue in US$	Allocated %*	Profit (loss) in US$
HIGHEST REVENUE				
1. University of Oregon	Pac-12	391,769,609	<1	270,885,021
2. Ohio State University	Big Ten	233,871,740	0	15,220,475
3. University of Texas	Big 12	200,772,813	0	22,103,839
4. University of Michigan	Big Ten	192,403,168	<1	3,879,410
5. University of Alabama	Southeastern Conference (SEC)	189,282,549	2	16,141,424
LOWEST REVENUE				
1. Coppin State University	Mid-Eastern Athletic Conference (MEAC)	2,788,949	62	(1,358,023)
2. Mississippi Valley State University	Southwestern Athletic Conference (SWAC)	3,911,532	18	0
3. Savannah State University	MEAC	4,030,759	57	(1,037,559)
4. University of Maryland–Eastern Shore	MEAC	5,646,465	80	0
5. Alcorn State University	SWAC	5,790,810	22	(1,345,882)

*Allocated % indicates percentage of revenue generated through institutional allocations in the form of student fees.

USA Today Sports' College Athletics Finances (2021).

In the scenario described at the start of the chapter, then, the athletics director faces funding cuts that are not uncommon in today's college athletics environment. Many athletics departments operate at a deficit while attempting to compete with the small percentage of programs that enjoy significantly more resources.

FINANCIAL DISTINCTIVENESS OF INTERCOLLEGIATE ATHLETICS

The disparity in athletics department budgets results from a number of factors, including revenue generation opportunities, conference realignment, the need for resources to remain competitive, and the current economic climate in higher education. These factors create a complex financial environment for college athletics, in which athletics programs have to maneuver through financial challenges to remain competitive on the field and fiscally sound off the field. These factors are addressed in some detail in the following sections.

Television Broadcasting Deals

Although disparity in financial resources has existed in college athletics for decades, the gap between the haves and the have-nots has escalated in recent years, largely due to television broadcasting deals. Broadcasting contracts for the Power Five conferences—the Southeastern Conference, the Atlantic Coast Conference, the Big Ten, the Pac-12, and the Big 12—range from US$2.4 billion to US$3.6 billion. Contract lengths range from 6 to 20 years, and annual per-school payouts run from US$17 million to US$44 million (Here's a Look, 2021).

Trends indicate these numbers will continue to increase in the foreseeable future, because negotiating windows exist within all of these contracts, and schools continue to change conferences to position themselves for greater financial reward. In fact, the recent conference realignment has been attributed largely to the desire to maximize revenue from broadcasting rights. Major conferences can command more revenue in these contracts by increasing their number of member institutions, and individual schools are willing to change conferences in order

Technology Tools

College Athletics Department Finance Databases

Multiple platforms provide financial information for college athletics departments. Most NCAA public institutions are required by state public records laws to provide information. These databases are a valuable resource for public awareness, academic research, and industry benchmarking. Following is a brief guide to these platforms.

USA Today NCAA Finances: Revenue and Expenses by School

https://sports.usatoday.com/ncaa/finances

USA Today provides a database of financial information for most public NCAA Division I schools. This database breaks down revenues and expenses for each athletics department and allows categorization by conference and region. Access to this database requires a paid subscription to ***USA Today***.

Knight Commission on Intercollegiate Athletics: Knight-Newhouse College Athletics Financial Information Database

https://cafidatabase.knightcommission.org/

This database uses data collected from NCAA Division I institutions that are required by state public records laws to provide information. The financial data are organized to show "Where the Money Comes From" (revenue) and "Where the Money Goes" (expenses) for each public Division I institution, athletics conference, and each of the three DI subdivisions. This database is free to the public.

NCAA Finances

https://www.ncaa.org/finances

This NCAA web page offers an overview of financial components of the association as a whole and NCAA institutions at all three levels. It covers all NCAA institutions, not just Division I. However, the financial data is provided in aggregate, at the division level rather than the individual team level.

Equity in Athletics Data Analysis (EADA)

https://ope.ed.gov/athletics/#/

EADA is provided by the Office of Postsecondary Education (part of the U.S. Department of Education). Data can be examined for one school or for multiple schools that receive Title IX funding. Customized reports can be downloaded and side-by-side comparison of data for up to four schools is possible. Trends can be examined across time, by state, for public versus private institutions, and other variables.

to stake their claim to guaranteed annual payouts from television deals (Dodd, 2021). The University of Oklahoma and the University of Texas moving to the SEC started the most recent realignment, announcing their move in 2021. To offset the Big 12's loss of two staple athletic programs, the conference announced the addition of the University of Central Florida, Brigham Young University, the University of Houston, and the University of Cincinnati. In 2022, USC and UCLA announced their move to the Big Ten conference, and in 2023, the University of Oregon and the University of Washington announced they also planned to join the Big Ten. In the fall of 2023, Stanford University, the University of California, and Southern Methodist University were announced as the newest members of the Atlantic Coast Conference.

Conference realignment in 2010-2011 resulted in a new financial layer for conferences and member institutions in the form of the exit fee, charged to institutions that wish to leave a given conference. In response to the realignments, conferences increased their exit fees to deter schools from leaving. The Big 12 levies an exit fee equal to one year's worth of conference revenue. The Atlantic Coast Conference (ACC) also changed its exit fee from US$20 million to US$50 million in an effort to deter members from leaving (Smith, 2012).

However, these exit fees have not slowed down conference realignment because the financial benefits to the schools outweigh the cost of moving conferences.

Arms Race

The race to compete for conference and national championships has never been more competitive. Even though the University of Oregon and the University of Louisiana at Monroe have vastly different resources, they compete in the same NCAA category, illustrating the fact that many institutions in smaller conferences feel pressure to compete with financially larger programs. Areas of competition include building and renovating facilities, expanding recruiting budgets, acquiring top-of-the-line equipment, and hiring the best coaches. All of these strategies lead to significant debt service, and smaller institutions do not have the capacity to take on such debt.

> *It became obvious that standing pat would mean falling behind. It would mean putting our program in a precarious position, both competitively and financially. It would leave us to play catch-up with our competition.*
>
> Joe Castiglione, University of Oklahoma athletic director (Blinder & Draper, 2021)

The race to compete creates a spending frenzy, further separating the haves from the have-nots in college sport. Table 8.2 lists sample program spending for both large and small institutions.

Current Economic Climate in Higher Education

The COVID-19 pandemic, starting in March 2020, has had a major effect on higher education, including cuts in state funding for public colleges and universities. According to Hubler (2020), the pandemic has cost colleges and universities at least US$120 billion. For larger athletics programs, these cuts may not have a direct impact, because many of these athletics departments receive limited state funding. However, the majority of Division I and lower-division institutions rely heavily on allocated revenues from the university. These programs are affected greatly by funding cuts to higher education, which increases the gap between large programs and their smaller competitors.

ORGANIZATIONAL STRUCTURE WITHIN INTERCOLLEGIATE ATHLETICS

The organizational structure of intercollegiate athletics is unique as compared with those of its counterparts in professional and amateur sport. The primary point of distinction is that college athletics departments operate within the bureaucratic structure of higher education. For the most part, this setup is unique to U.S. sport, because higher education and sport are not connected directly in most of the world. This approach means that the mission of college sport in the United States should be driven by the overall academic mission of colleges and universities. This purported focus has been an overarching issue throughout the history of U.S. college sport, and it affects financial operations through public funding, student fees, and the ability of athletics departments to raise capital.

The NCAA is a governing body controlled by a portion of member institution presidents. Therefore, the president of the NCAA has no direct control over decisions about regulations, conference alignments, the media rights of conferences or individual programs, or other organizational components that affect athletics department finances. In addition, the NCAA, its member conferences, and individual institutions all operate as nonprofit organizations. Nonprofit status affords these organizations tax exemption and the ability to generate revenue through charitable contributions. The nonprofit status of college sport is discussed in more detail later in the chapter.

Revenue Theory of Cost

The organizational and legal structure of college sport as a nonprofit endeavor under the umbrella of higher education has considerable effects on the

Table 8.2 Athletics Department Expenses at NCAA Division I Public Institutions (2021)

Institution	Conference	Total expenses in US$	Allocated %*	Profit (loss) in US$
HIGHEST EXPENSES (POWER FIVE INSTITUTIONS)				
1. Ohio State University	Big Ten	218,651,265	0	15,220,475
2. University of Michigan	Big Ten	188,523,758	<1	3,879,410
3. University of Texas	Big 12	178,668,974	0	22,103,839
4. University of Alabama	SEC	173,141,125	2	16,141,424
5. Louisiana State University	SEC	164,026,005	0	(3,592,530)
HIGHEST EXPENSES (NON-POWER FIVE INSTITUTIONS)				
1. University of Connecticut	Big East	78,760,755	60	(2,804,545)
2. University of Cincinnati	American Athletic Conference (AAC)	74,043,985	40	7,661,372
3. University of Houston	AAC	66,370,147	69	1,012,834
4. University of Central Florida	AAC	64,226,899	49	4,638,196
5. U.S. Air Force Academy	Mountain West Conference (MW)	64,445,937	74	4,071,520

*Allocated % indicates percentage of revenue generated through institutional allocations in the form of student fees. The database reflects schools' conference affiliation at the time.

USA Today Sports' College Athletics Finances (2021).

financial operation of the industry. The continuing trend of expenditures increasing at a similar rate to revenues is not uncommon in a nonprofit setting. By their very nature, nonprofit organizations must spend all the revenue they generate. This phenomenon is the foundation of Bowen's (1980) revenue theory of cost, which states that in a nonprofit setting, expenditure increases are a direct result of increased revenue that must be spent by the organization in order to avoid a significant surplus. Martin (2009) refers to this spending environment as the revenue-to-cost spiral.

Bowen (1970, 1980) articulated five laws to explain cost in higher education (see figure 8.1). The primary goals of institutions are educational excellence, prestige, and influence. In the quest to achieve these goals, there is no limit on what an institution will spend. There are never "enough" resources. Since current resources are never acceptable, institutions always attempt to increase revenue and subsequently spend all that they raise. Following these laws leads to a consistent increase in expenditures. Limits are not set in this environment because there is no determination of the minimal amount needed to run a high-quality college or university. Therefore, a cycle is created wherein revenue increases are the source of increases in expenditures.

College athletics departments are unique segments of higher education, yet they operate in a similar environment. Due to their nonprofit nature, they must spend all of their revenue in a given year. Although the revenue theory of cost and the revenue-to-cost spiral concepts were not developed for college athletics, they provide a framework for understanding financial decisions made by athletics departments (Suggs, 2009). The primary goals for college athletics programs are success, prestige, influence, and, ultimately, a positive reputation. In pursuit of these goals, athletics departments will exhaust all resources, which is evident in the vast number of programs losing money (USA Today Sports, 2021). In addition, there is no limit on the amount of revenue that athletics departments attempt to generate, and any revenue generated by the departments is spent. Finally, this behavior is cyclical in college sport, which provides a continued motivation to win and garner a positive national reputation.

Thus Bowen's (1970, 1980) revenue theory of cost should be considered throughout this chapter as we

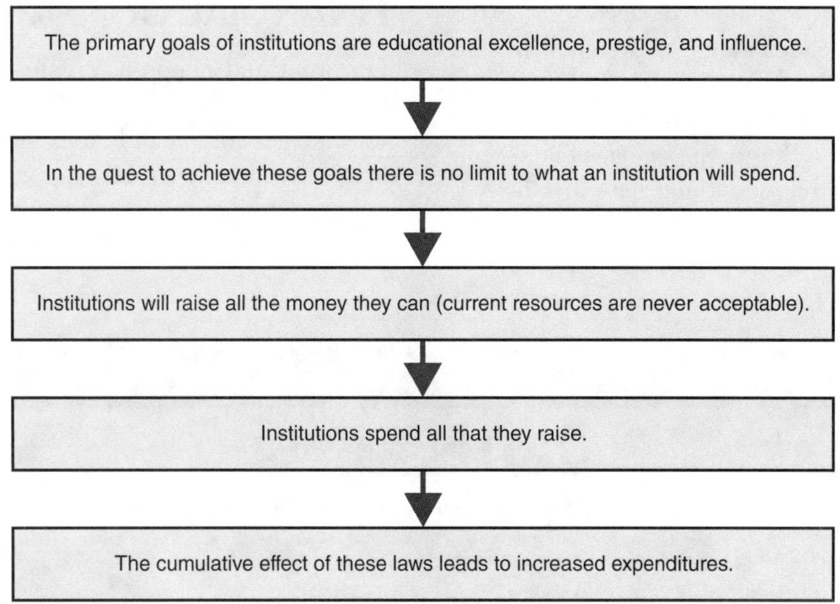

Figure 8.1 Bowen's Revenue Theory of Cost—Five "Cost Laws"
Adapted from H.R. Bowen, *The Costs of Higher Education* (San Francisco: Jossey-Bass, 1980).

dissect financial operations and decision-making in intercollegiate athletics. This theory plays out in a considerable number of athletics departments. In the chapter-opening scenario, the athletics director is already operating at a deficit due to the cyclical nature of spending in college sport. This situation becomes a challenge because generating additional revenue almost certainly leads to additional expenses, again leaving the athletics department with a similar deficit.

Sport Sponsorship

Another distinctive factor in college athletics is the operation of multiple sport programs under one umbrella, most of which generate limited or no revenue. For the vast majority of athletics departments, no programs are profitable, and in a select few departments one or two programs are profitable. These profitable sports are generally football and men's basketball. The revenue generated from these two sports often subsidizes the other sports in the department. Division I institutions must offer at least 14 sports (and Division II and Division III institutions must offer at least 10 and 5 sports, respectively), which adds to the department's overall operational costs (Our Three Divisions, 2022). From an economic perspective, it is not logical to continue to fund programs that are not self-sufficient, let alone to use revenue from profitable programs to subsidize programs that lose money. However, this is the unique nature of present-day college sport, and athletics departments must work successfully in this environment.

Title IX

The groundbreaking federal legislation known as Title IX of the Education Amendments of 1972 has had a tremendous effect in providing opportunities for women in sport by mandating equal opportunity based on sex in all federally funded educational settings. Since its inception in 1972, participation rates for women in college sport have increased by 400 percent (Pontz, 2020). Some would argue that this legislation has also created financial challenges for athletics departments. This argument is based on the financial reality that programs face if they have not demonstrated equality in opportunity and treatment. As discussed in chapter 5, if one sex is provided with greater facilities or opportunities, this federal law stipulates equality. As a result, many departments face financial challenges associated with equalizing their overall treatment of male and female athletes when discrepancies are evident.

Many facets of present-day college sport make it a unique and challenging environment from a financial operations perspective. The following section provides detail about financial structure and operations and how these components of finance in college sport can be used to navigate this distinct environment.

FINANCIAL CONFIGURATION

For-profit and nonprofit organizations are structured differently, and this difference affects both revenue generation and costs. When dealing with financial components of college athletics, therefore, we must understand the structure of nonprofit organizations and how it affects financial decisions.

Industry Profile

CATHY ROSSI

Deputy Director of Athletics, University of Wisconsin–Milwaukee

Balancing a budget is never easy, regardless of the task, program, or organization. However, at the University of Wisconsin–Milwaukee (UWM), the challenges are what keep the job exciting for Deputy Director of Athletics Cathy Rossi. UWM is an urban campus that is primarily funded by student fees. The athletics department has multiple athletics facilities spread throughout the city of Milwaukee, and it competes in the vast Horizon League, as UWM is one of only three Division I programs in the state of Wisconsin. As a result, revenue is often fixed and expenses variable.

Rossi's primary function is to manage the US$14 million overall budget and the 30 different budget areas within the department. There are 15 sports at UWM and 11 unique sport budgets, each with its own labor, operating and grant-in-aid components. In addition, there are 18 support function budgets such as marketing, administration, compliance, strength and conditioning, events, and academics. Labor and operating expenses are also components within each of these budgets. UWM has only one facilities and game operations budget, which is for minor improvements to the facilities and game operations expenses.

Rossi's job is to coordinate and oversee these budgets at the highest level. While coaches and program managers (e.g., marketing or compliance director) are responsible for their unit's forecasting and spending, Rossi is the individual who reconciles the current and previous year's spending and approves the upcoming year's annual budgets. She is also the individual who submits a budget request to the UWM student association and general campus each year.

Milwaukee Athletics

The above tasks, however, are just her business-related responsibilities. As deputy director of athletics, Rossi has also overseen facilities and game operations, ticket operations, and the baseball and women's tennis programs, and she is the sport supervisor for men's and women's track and cross country, and volleyball. Lastly, she is the athletics department's liaison with the general campus human resources, information technology, and business finance departments.

The workload is heavy but the work is important. According to Rossi, "The most rewarding aspect of the job is knowing that the work you do has a direct impact on the experience of the student-athletes that you serve. As a former student-athlete, I was incredibly grateful for my undergraduate experience and it is super rewarding watching our student-athletes graduate and go out and achieve great things in this world."

Nonprofit Status

Every sport organization has a business structure that influences operations from both a legal and a financial standpoint. Business structure dictates taxes, sources of funding, and personal and organizational liability. The NCAA, NAIA, NJCAA, and their respective member conferences and institutions all operate as nonprofit entities. Nonprofit organizations are established for civic, social, charitable, or educational purposes (Worth, 2019). In the case of college sport, organizations are a function of higher education, which affords them nonprofit status.

Nonprofits are driven by a civic cause to provide services to the community. Therefore, their organizational structure differs from that of a profit-seeking organization. Due to this social mission, the legal structure of nonprofits provides these organizations with specific benefits, including tax exemption, the ability to receive charitable contributions, lower prices and fees, and indemnification in certain situations for management (Bryce, 2017). These benefits make nonprofits distinct from for-profit organizations that have to deal with issues such as taxes and liability, which can play a significant role in the financial success of a business.

Tax Exemption and Legal Status

One of the main advantages enjoyed by nonprofit organizations is the ability to maintain a tax-exempt status, because taxes constitute one of the largest expenses for commercial organizations (Besley & Brigham, 2015). Colleges and universities (and affiliated departments and associations) operate under section 501(c)(3) of the U.S. Internal Revenue Code, which provides exemption for educational organizations. According to the Internal Revenue Service (IRS), organizations that meet the requirements of 501(c)(3) are exempt from federal income taxes, and donors who make charitable contributions to these organizations can receive a tax deduction (Internal Revenue Service, 2021). In order to receive exemption under 501(c)(3), an organization must meet two criteria. First, it must be established as a state-law nonprofit organization with a mission and goals that are charity focused (Columbo, 2010). Second, it must operate as a charitable entity, with the majority of its activities serving a charitable cause, while limiting resources spent on noncharitable purposes (e.g., lobbying or excessive employee compensation) (Columbo, 2010).

This second requirement has been a point of contention in college athletics due to some areas of substantial cash flow in major college athletics departments related to sports such as football and men's basketball. Columbo (2010) argues that the NCAA should fall into a category of its own, with certain components of operations having tax-exempt status and other operations being taxed under the unrelated business income tax (UBIT). This has been a point of debate because the NCAA and member institutions are provided with significant financial incentives through tax exemption. For example, if the University of Kansas' change in net assets for 2018 (US$53.1 million) was subject to the UBIT rate—the corporate tax rate of 21 percent—its tax expense would be approximately US$11.1 million (BKD CPA & Advisors, 2019).

Charitable Contributions

Not only does 501(c)(3) allow for tax exemption, which is one of the main organizational expenses, it also provides for a tax deduction for charitable contributions to the organization, which attracts many individuals and corporations looking to make donations. Fundraising is a key revenue source for nonprofits, so 501(c)(3) status is extremely valuable.

In 2020, college athletics programs charitable contributions accounted for 24 percent of generated revenues at NCAA Division I FBS institutions and 12 percent at Division I FCS programs (Finances of Intercollegiate Athletics Database, 2021). These substantial revenues highlight the significance of fundraising—and the importance of 501(c)(3) status—in college sport. The University of Florida generated more than US$52 million in charitable contributions in 2020, which amounted to 30 percent of its total athletics department revenue. This benefit is not exclusive to major athletics programs; for example, Wichita State University's athletics program raised more than US$9.2 million, which represented 31 percent of its revenue (College Athletics Financial Information, 2021a).

From a financial perspective, then, fundraising is an athletics department priority, particularly in times of slow economic growth (Brunette et al., 2017). In this environment, donations can increase or decrease based on the performance of major programs. For example, the University of Nebraska lost nearly US$20 million in charitable contributions from 2017 to 2019. It is estimated that a majority of this deficit is due to the poor performance of the football program.

When an athletics department relies heavily on fundraising, as most do, such shifts can have drastic effects on financial operations. Unlike ticket sales, where seating capacity limits sales, there is, at least in theory, no limit on the amount of revenue that can be generated through fundraising. There is also, however, no guarantee of consistent annual contributions. Development and the intricacies of athletics department fundraising are discussed in more detail in chapter 12.

In situations where additional revenue needs to be generated quickly, such as in the chapter-opening scenario, raising funds through additional contributions is a common strategy. In fact, many institutions use charitable contributions to directly fund the hiring of coaches or the building or renovation of facilities. In the scenario, this strategy could be used to overcome the substantial deficit created by the cut in allocated revenue.

Tiered Structure

College athletics operates according to a tiered structure in which an overarching association governs member institutions housed in conferences. The largest college sport association is the NCAA, which includes 1,104 active member schools, 352 of which are in Division I (130 FBS, 124 FCS, and 98 DI subdivision), 311 in Division II, and 441 in Division III (Membership Directory, 2021). Other associations include the National Association of Intercollegiate Athletics (NAIA) and the National Junior College Athletic Association (NJCAA); however, this section discusses only the NCAA. In terms of financial operations, the relationships between the NCAA, the conferences, and individual athletics programs can be complex. Some revenues and expenses are distributed from the association through the conferences to the programs. However, other revenues and expenses start at the conference or individual program level and are not associated with the NCAA. The following sections provide an overview of each tier.

NCAA

The NCAA is a large nonprofit entity whose 2020 assets totaled more than US$710 million. Total revenues during the 2019-2020 fiscal year were more than US$701 million. However, the figures were hampered greatly by COVID-19 (see the sidebar titled Impact of COVID-19). The 2018-2019 revenue totals were over US$1.1 billion. More than 80 percent of association revenue is generated through television and marketing rights—specifically, through the agreement with Turner/CBS Sports to broadcast the men's Division I basketball tournament. This broadcasting deal is worth US$10.8 billion over 14 years. While 2020 was a down year for revenue for the NCAA due the cancellation of the Men's and Women's Basketball Tournament, the organization increased in 2021 and is expected to continue to in the future.

The majority of NCAA revenue is distributed back to member institutions. More than 54 percent of revenue is distributed to Division I members, and 22 percent is used to run programs and championships at all levels. These distributions accounted for more than US$242 million in 2019 (Consolidated Financial Statements, 2020).

According to the NCAA, in 2021, nearly US$169 million was distributed to the basketball fund, which rewards long-term performance in the men's basketball tournament. Another US$222 million was distributed through the grant-in-aid fund, which provides more funding to schools with the most scholarship funding to student-athletes (Where does the money go?, 2021). The NCAA also distributes revenue based on the number of sports sponsored and the academic performance of student-athletes. Additional funding is provided for student-athletes with special financial needs. In total, the NCAA reports 14 different expense categories for the revenue generated from the Men's Basketball Tournament media contract and championships ticket sales (Where does the money go?, 2021).

Conferences

The majority of revenue generated by the NCAA is funneled down to conferences to be distributed to member institutions. Conferences have the authority to decide how this revenue will be distributed, and the approach varies from conference to conference. For example, the Southeastern Conference

Impact of COVID-19

For many college athletics administrators, the middle of March is one of the busiest times of the year. For the NCAA, it is certainly the most lucrative. Thus, when the COVID-19 pandemic reached North America during the second week of March 2020, it sent shock waves through college athletics. Arenas closed, sport seasons were canceled, and most students did not return to campus until fall 2020. Obviously, the impact on college athletics pales in comparison to the loss of human life and economic collapse caused by COVID-19; regardless, the pandemic has been devasting financially for the NCAA and its member institutions.

For instance, the 2020 Men's NCAA Basketball Tournament, which is the primary revenue source for the NCAA, was canceled. The organization lost a reported US$702 million in television and marketing rights fees compared to the year before; it was able to recoup US$270 million though an insurance policy, but the loss was substantial, and since this money is mostly distributed to the universities, this cancellation directly affected the bottom line of every Division I athletics department (Consolidated Financial Statements, 2020). Perhaps the biggest ramification of this trickle-down revenue loss was the sacrifices made by coaches and administrators. Layoffs and furloughs were the most common approach to offset the shortfalls (Whitford, 2020).

Operating an athletics department during a pandemic requires new protocols to ensure the health and safety of student-athletes, staff, and spectators. These new protocols are expensive. From daily testing to expanded cleaning procedures, athletics departments have had a whole new list of expenses since returning to athletic competition in August 2020. In addition, certain state and federal regulations have limited attendance at home games. For some schools, ticket sales, hospitality, food and beverage, and parking are important sources of revenue.

The NCAA also instituted additional years of eligibility for student-athletes affected by COVID-19. These additional years of eligibility have affected grant-in-aid numbers, as recruiting has not stopped. Thus, there has been the additional expense of athletes with a fifth and sometimes a sixth year of eligibility.

Fortunately, the primary source of revenue for the highest level of college athletics, television media rights, has not been affected since March 2020. The NCAA has been able to spread some of that revenue to lower levels to offset the additional costs of operating a department in these unprecedented times ("Where does the money go?," 2021). However, athletics administrators at every level are forced to deal with the day-to-day challenges of COVID-19, and keeping the focus on student-athletes and human resources requires sound financial decision-making.

(SEC) uses a multilevel financial distribution strategy (Goldkamp, 2021). It is not evident whether the revenue generated from media rights and the football conference championship is distributed equally among the 14 member institutions. However, the average amount distributed is US$45.5 million per school. The sources of revenue include television agreements, postseason bowl games, the College Football Playoff (CFP), the SEC Football Championship, the SEC Men's Basketball Tournament, and NCAA Championships. This total distributed to each school does not include US$6.1 million from the NCAA and a share of US$20 million to cover certain football bowl game travel expenses. A share of revenue is also kept by the conference office for general operations, marketing and advertising, and conference championship operations. It is likely a similar formula is utilized for each conference: Pool the revenue and disperse it relatively evenly.

Financial distributions vary significantly in smaller conferences. All conferences receive similar distributions from the NCAA (varying based on sports sponsored and postseason appearances), but compared with major conferences, midsize and small conferences do not receive significant media rights revenue to share. Most of the revenue they do receive through smaller media rights deals is split equally among member institutions, and some additional revenue is given to institutions with programs that compete in postseason play.

Athletics Departments

Although athletics departments rely on revenue distributions from the NCAA and conferences, these funds are not the most significant sources of revenue. Most athletics department revenue is generated through the athletics department or institution itself (as discussed in detail later in this chapter). For FBS programs, the median revenue distribution to athletics departments in 2019 was US$8.06 million, or 16.1 percent of total revenue. At the FCS level, these distributions are considerably smaller. In 2019, the median distribution for FCS programs was US$993,696, or 6.6 percent of total revenue (College Athletics Financial Information, 2021a).

Table 8.3 provides a summary budget for the University of Oregon athletics department. In fiscal year 2018-2019, Oregon projected just under US$35 million in conference distributions, which amounted to 29 percent of its total athletics revenue (including allocated revenue). However, this percentage is likely to increase as conference broadcast deals for football and men's basketball continue to escalate. Nearly US$25 million will be generated from spectator admissions and game guarantees. Interestingly, the university hopes to generate an additional US$3.5 million in ticket-related fees.

Table 8.3 University of Oregon Athletics Department Summary Projected Budgets for 2017-2018 and 2018-2019

REVENUE AND EXPENSE SUMMARY IN U.S. DOLLARS		
	2017-2018	2018-2019
Ticket sales and guarantees (men's sports)	25,891,553	24,141,553
Ticket sales and guarantees (women's sports)	512,500	632,500
NCAA/conference distributions	32,955,000	34,775,000
Broadcasting, sponsorships, and royalties	14,328,000	18,365,000
Fundraising contributions	28,150,000	31,273,607
Food and beverage	5,455,841	5,637,890
Ticket-related fees	3,425,000	3,425,000
Other revenue	2,491,200	2,334,200
Total revenue	**113,209,094**	**120,584,750**
EXPENSE SUMMARY		
	2017-2018	2018-2019
Operating expenses (men's sports)*	36,590,113	42,261,675
Operating expenses (women's sports)*	15,811,242	16,215,126
Salaries, wages, and benefits	8,474,948	8,842,700
Facilities/events/maintenance expenses	8,919,593	8,832,422
Food and beverage	3,339,072	3,532,370
Marketing/rally/band	2,056,201	2,027,773
Treatment center/strength and conditioning	3,776,509	3,362,389
Athletic and special events	3,752,539	3,920,779
Debt service	19,100,000	18,700,000
Other administrative expenses	11,388,877	12,889,516
Total expenses	**113,209,094**	**120,584,750**

Data from University of Oregon Department of Athletics, "Revenue Summary, Projected FY19 Revenues." Available: https://static.goducks.com/custompages/pages/athlfin/FY19Budget.pdf.

This pattern is generally consistent across the majority of athletics departments. However, athletics department revenue from conference distributions continues to grow at the highest level of competition. In 2020, the conference payout total for the CFP alone was nearly US$489 million, with the Power Five conferences receiving more than US$70 million each (Dosh, 2021). Expansion of the CFP is likely, and it was predicted that this could increase annual revenue by about US$2 billion (Associated Press, 2021).

Meanwhile, the vast majority of athletics departments are operating at a deficit and receive a limited amount of revenue from the football playoff system—around US$273,000, according to Dosh (2021). At the same time, expenses continue to increase at a faster rate than revenue. As a result, many schools face a challenging financial landscape as they move forward. Ways of dealing with the complex financial environment of college athletics are discussed in greater detail in the following sections.

FINANCIAL OPERATIONS

The disparity in revenue and expenses associated with college athletics is vast. In addition, the tiered distribution system and the diverse stakeholders contribute to a complex financial model. As a result, the financial operations form an essential component of an athletics department's organizational management. The NCAA, the conferences, and the individual athletics departments generally maintain a department of business and finance that is led by an individual at the deputy or associate director level who operates as the chief financial officer (CFO) and reports directly to the chief executive (i.e., the athletics director, president, or commissioner). In the NCAA, the CFO oversees financial resources, risk management, insurance, investments, travel management, physical plant operations, the NCAA Hall of Champions, purchasing and procurement, publications and printing, and information technology. For an example at the athletics department level, consider Ohio State University, which employs a senior associate athletics director who oversees planning and implementation of all aspects of the department's operating budget, the athletics business office, facility operations, event management, human resources, and information technology. This individual is also a liaison to other campus departments, such as central human resources and information technology. Each athletics organization has a business office whose personnel oversee daily business transactions, planning, accounting, investments, insurance, debt service, and travel.

This section introduces and defines an athletics department's most common streams of revenue and expenditures; it also provides examples of dollar figures and growing trends. From ticket sales and licensed merchandise to grant-in-aid funding and team travel, some of today's largest athletics departments manage tens of thousands of transactions per week in an attempt to become financially self-sustaining.

Revenues

For the purposes of this chapter, *revenues* are incoming monies or assets of an athletics department gained through a commercial transaction, charitable contribution, contractual agreement, transfer, or gift. This category includes income from capital assets, investment vehicles, and in-kind products and services. Two major categories of revenue are generated revenue and allocated revenue, which differ fundamentally in where they come from. *Allocated revenue* is defined as all support from noncommercial activity (e.g., student fees) that is directly assigned to athletics, as well as institutional support and government support. *Generated revenue* is broadly defined as income derived from commercial activities of the athletics department. These activities often involve actions in which a good or service is provided in exchange for a fee.

Government support, at both the federal and state levels, remains the most important source of revenue for colleges and universities, generally. However, each state has seen a different trend over the past 10 years. Some universities have seen a drop in state financial support, while others have seen a significant increase or remained constant. Regardless, since 1990, the difference between what the federal government provides a university and what a state provides has dropped 128 percent (Pew Charitable Trusts, 2019). As a result, institutions and certainly athletics departments have felt the pressure to become more self-sustainable, and thus, have paid greater attention to generating revenue. Strategies to increase revenue in the areas of sponsorship, donor relations, ticket sales, and media coverage have occupied more time and resources within departments than previously. From 2005 to 2020, median generated revenues for Power Five schools increased from just over US$40 million per year to US$100 million (NCAA, 2021b).

As a result, in the chapter-opening scenario, the athletics director could increase emphasis on activities related to revenue generation. For instance, the shortfall might be remedied at least in part by either a slight increase in the price of single-game tickets or an uptick in donations. Another way to bring in more revenue would be to creatively develop new sponsorship inventory. The challenge for the athletics director is to avoid upsetting fans, donors, or potential sponsors by gouging them too dramatically.

Many revenue sources exist for athletics departments. The following list includes the common sources of revenue in college athletics:

- Ticket sales—Advance ticket sales are an important source of revenue for an athletics department because they not only provide guaranteed income but also ensure an audience for the department's most important product—intercollegiate athletic competition. Stadiums and arenas filled to capacity create an exciting atmosphere, improve efficiency, and often provide the home team with an advantage. In general, while vital to the core sports service of intercollegiate athletics, ticket sales only account for 11 percent of the total revenue reported by all three divisions of the NCAA (2021). Interestingly, ticket sales to conference and national tournaments are typically excluded from institutional budgets, since these revenues go to directly to conferences or the NCAA.

  Season tickets are particularly important because they provide a steady, up-front revenue stream from the organization's most passionate fans. For many institutions—particularly those with demand equaling or exceeding supply—it has become customary for season ticket holders to provide a donation to the athletics department just to gain the right to purchase their yearly tickets. As with personal seat licenses at the professional level, a person who seeks a higher-quality seat is expected to make a larger donation. More information about priority seating and annual giving is provided in chapter 12.

- NCAA and conference distributions—Conference distributions include any revenue received from the conference's participation in tournaments, bowl games, and any other form of NCAA distributions (as discussed in the Tiered Structure section of this chapter). In addition, revenue from conference agreements with television and radio broadcasts (e.g., the Big Ten Network) is often received via distributions as well.

- Guarantees—These are contractual agreements between teams in which the home team pays the away team to participate. At some levels of football and basketball, guarantees represent a substantial revenue source for an athletics department. Although most guarantees are also intended to facilitate a guaranteed victory for the home team, visiting teams occasionally take both the money and the victory. Recent examples include Bowling Green State University (US$1.45 million and a win over the University of Minnesota), Howard University (US$600,000 and a win over 45-point favorite UNLV), and James Madison University (US$400,000 and a win over 13th-ranked Virginia Tech). A new trend has emerged whereby third-party locations or stadiums pay guarantees as well. Kansas State University originally signed a home and home contract with Stanford University in football stating that the two teams would play in 2016 and 2021. However, Cowboys Stadium, L.P., offered Kansas State (K-State) US$2.8 million to move the game to its facility (Hertel, 2021). On average, K-State generates US$1.7 million in tickets from hosting a home game, so this opportunity was certainly a net positive for the athletics department.

- Donations—Another growth area for athletics departments can be found in fundraising or donor relations. From major gifts such as bequests to small club membership fees, contributions are central to an athletics department's financial vitality. Donations are defined as revenue received directly from individuals, corporations, clubs, associations, foundations, or other organizations that are designated specifically for the operation of the athletics department. Examples of donations include cash, securities, and in-kind products and services. More information about annual donations is given in chapter 12.

- Third-party support—This category refers to all agreed-upon income from a third party that is not included on the institution's W-2 form. Examples of this kind of support include golf club memberships, vehicle allowances, clothing, entertainment, housing, money from speaking engagements, shoe and apparel contracts, and television appearances. As an example of the potential

The Financial Impact of NIL

The NCAA's name, image, and likeness (NIL) policy has the potential to bolster the financial position of individual student-athletes. Since the policy was passed in late June 2021, a number of high-profile deals and even some lower-level contracts have been made between student-athletes and corporate partners in exchange for money, equipment and apparel, and other in-kind services. But how does this policy affect the financial operations of an athletics department?

Theoretically, the policy should have no direct impact, either positive or negative, on the financial position of an athletics department, as NIL deals occur directly between a third party and a student-athlete. However, the following ripple effects of such transactions could affect revenue and expenses for an athletics department of any size.

- Decline in sponsorship revenue—The competition for corporate dollars is fierce, and oftentimes the student-athletes are the crown jewels (not including the head coaches). According to the Front Office Sports newsletter (2021), the majority of NIL deals come from football, men's basketball, and women's basketball. Therefore, if corporate partners can broker deals directly with student-athletes and cut out the athletics department, it may hurt the in-house sponsorship teams and the third-party sponsorship companies like LEARFIELD as they work to reach their yearly quotas.
- Increased compliance expenses—NIL rules differ between states and conferences. To receive benefits and remain eligible, student-athletes, coaches, and athletics departments need to know what they can and cannot do. This requires a professional staff that understands and can apply NIL policies in a dynamic environment.
- Additional NIL-related staff—Forward-thinking athletics departments understand the importance of educating their athletes about NIL. Therefore, they engage people to teach student-athletes branding strategies and contract negotiation skills, and aid in social media training. Bromberg (2021) reported in July that Nebraska, Colorado, St. John's, Florida State, Arkansas, and Duquesne would provide tools and education in these areas for their student-athletes. These services obviously cost money; however, they also are very inviting to prospective student-athletes.
- Potential decrease in sport camp revenue—Sport camps were specifically identified as a clear revenue source for student-athletes in the new NIL policy. However, in the past, camps have been a significant revenue generator for assistant coaches. This impact is purely hypothetical at this point as we have seen demonstrated research in this area, but there is certainly an opportunity for student-athletes to siphon some of the revenue away from assistant coaches.

In general, most of these hits to an athletics department's bottom line are minimal. Some are purely hypothetical at this point and others are in the best interest of student-athletes. Thus, they are hard to argue. The NIL policy received a great deal of media attention as a lightning rod in college athletics, but its effect on the day-to-day activities of an athletics department is still evolving. From a financial perspective, the greatest expense is in the investment in student-athlete education and compliance and the greatest threat is yet to be fully realized (e.g., forgone sponsorships).

magnitude of third-party support, the University of Michigan is being paid US$173.8 million, which comprises US$88.8 million in base compensation and US$85 million in Jordan Brand (Nike) apparel and gear (BCS guest writer, 2016). The deal runs from 2016 to 2027, and made UM the first football program to be outfitted with the Jumpman logo.

- Game-day inventory—This includes ancillary sales such as parking, program sales, merchandise, and concessions. For well-attended events, game-day inventory can represent a viable source of revenue for athletics departments. For smaller events, it provides an opportunity to offset costs. In 2018, US$97.4 million was generated from program sales, parking, and concessions, just from Division I football games (Novy-Williams, 2020).

- Media rights—Another category involves all the forms of media rights that athletics departments count on: contracted revenue received from television and radio broadcasts, television packages, program networks (e.g., Big Ten Network), Internet subscriptions, and e-commerce. For some programs, media rights have become a massive stream of revenue.

For example, in addition to the yearly conference payouts discussed earlier, the University of Texas athletics department garners an estimated US$22 million from its Longhorn Network contract with ESPN (Davis, 2021). The Big Ten Network reportedly pays its member schools a projected US$54 million per year (Felzer, 2021).

- Royalties, advertising, and sponsorship—This category includes all revenue from licensing, advertising sales, trademarks, corporate sponsorships, and royalties. Corporate sponsorship is becoming another essential source of revenue for athletics departments. Revenue from corporate partners can come in several forms, such as advertising sales, promotions, trademark usage, licensing, in-kind products and services, royalties, and naming rights. This remains a growth area of revenue for most programs as the inventory associated with sponsorship continues to grow. For instance, Allstate made a major splash in 2005 with its "Good Hands" field goal net sponsorship. Though the Good Hands net began at just a few schools and championship games, it is now being used at 75 Division I football stadiums (Allstate, 2021).

- Sport camps—Sport camps and clinics hosted by the university and conducted by team coaches and staff members provide an important source of revenue, especially for assistant coaches. These weeklong camps typically occur over the summer months and operate as an annual income generator and a low-level recruiting function.

- Investments—Some of the contributions listed earlier are rolled into investments or endowments for the athletics department, from which the organization generates revenue in the form of interest gained. In higher education, an endowment is either an organization's total investment from which it earns interest or a large investment earmarked to fund a specific purpose (e.g., a scholarship, a coach's salary, or a building maintenance fund) in perpetuity through interest earned from the investment.

- Miscellaneous—This encompasses other forms of departmental revenue, such as facility rentals. In the event that a stadium or arena is not being used by the athletics department, the opportunity exists to rent it to other sport organizations, live-entertainment companies, or convention organizers. In fact, not only does the rent provide a source of revenue, but also the event inventory itself is often up for negotiation (e.g., a percentage of ticket sales revenue). This category also includes anything and everything not specifically listed otherwise.

- Allocated Revenue—As mentioned earlier, allocated revenue represents all support from noncommercial activity, including but not limited to student fees, government funding, and institutional support. In 2014, 24 public institutions met the NCAA's benchmark for self-sufficiency in that they received no funding from student fees, the institution, or any other direct governmental agency (SI staff, 2015). In 2020, this number grew substantially; the average deficit among Power Five athletics departments was around US$2.6 million, whereas other Division I programs ranged from US$14 million for FCS and US$22 for non–Power Five schools (NCAA, 2021a).

- Direct institutional support—Most universities understand the importance of their intercollegiate athletics program in attracting and retaining students as well as media attention and public attention. As a result, institutions are willing to invest funds to keep the athletics department competitive—and in some cases solvent. Direct support from the institution can come in many forms, including money transfers, tuition waivers, and state appropriations.

• Indirect institutional support—This support also comes in many forms, and it is offset by an equal expense item. The most prominent sources include the value of facilities and services provided by the institution yet not charged. This indirect support may include an allocation for institutional administrative cost, facilities and building maintenance, grounds and field maintenance, security, risk management, utilities, depreciation, and debt service (College Athletics Financial Information, 2021a).

• Student fees—In addition to tuition, enrolled students pay a set of fees each semester that cover myriad administrative and overhead costs of the institution. In the majority of NCAA institutions, a portion of these fees is allocated to intercollegiate athletics. For departments receiving this support, it is most likely their largest source of revenue. For instance, James Madison University students pay more than US$2,300 in athletics fees each year, and these fees account for nearly 78 percent of the athletics department's revenue (Enright et al., 2020). Some large schools also use student activity fees to support their sport programs. For instance, according to the College Athletics Financial Information database (2021b), the University of South Florida used more than US$16 million in student fees, and the University of Virginia athletics program was allocated just over US$14 million. These amounts represented 27 percent of South Florida's athletics revenues in 2011 and 13 percent of Virginia's (College Athletics Financial Information, 2021b).

• Direct government funding—Government support can come from the municipal, state, or federal level. Funding from these entities is often marked explicitly for the operation of intercollegiate athletics. The notion of subsidizing major college sports has been a hot-button topic for decades, because critics believe this money should be used for academics. In general, the NCAA reported (2021b) that across the three divisions, 44 percent of all revenue was allocated from student fees, direct institutional support, or direct government support.

Expenses

Expenses are outgoing monies or assets that most often take the form of costs incurred in order to operate. As with revenues, costs in intercollegiate athletics can vary greatly from institution to institution. For the most part, the largest departmental expenses include salaries, capital projects, scholarships, and travel. In recent years, the cost of doing business in college athletics has garnered a great deal of attention. In 2021, the NCAA reported that median spending at the Division I level related to athletics operations increased 131 percent between 2005 and 2019 (College Athletics Financial Information, 2021a).

The following is a list of the more common expenses athletics departments deal with on a regular basis. A multitude of direct and indirect costs are associated with athletics department operations. It is imperative to consider these costs when assessing the financial well-being of the athletics department.

• Grants-in-aid—This expense includes the total amount of athletics-related student scholarship funding awarded for a given year, including the summer. It should account for tuition remission and waivers provided by the school. It should also include tuition expenses paid to nonathlete students such as graduate assistant coaches, managers, and training staff.

• Guarantees—For home teams looking to secure visiting opponents, guarantees can be an expense for an athletics department. In 2019, for example, Ohio State University paid US$9.54 million for its nonconference guaranteed games (College Athletics Financial Information, 2021a).

• Salaries and benefits—Salaries represent the largest expense for an athletics department. They include not only the wages paid to coaches, administrators, and support staff members but also bonuses and benefits. Benefits vary greatly between institutions and within departments. The more extravagant benefits include exclusive golf memberships, entertainment and clothing allowances, and private jet use. Coaches' salaries have skyrocketed over the past two decades. At the highest level of Division I athletics, Power Five, median coaching salaries have increased 192 percent since 2005 (College Athletics Financial Information, 2021a), and for the highest-paid population, football coaches, the average salary at these schools is US$4.4 million per year (Berkowitz & Shad, 2020). For some high-profile coaches and administrators, salary costs are partly subsidized by third-party entities, such as shoe and apparel companies, broadcast companies, and local businesses.

• Buyouts—While the practice of buying out an underperforming coach's contract has been around for decades, it has recently garnered a lot of attention as the amount of "dead money" schools are spending is adding up. A termination buyout is a sum of money paid to a coach or administrator upon severance of duties with the institution. A buyout can occur as a result of a provision in the contract when the coaches and their representation look to receive the amount of money promised to them when the coach is terminated without cause. Another name for this buyout provision is dead money, and according to a study done by Pistone (2021), Division I athletics departments paid US$533 million in dead money between 2011 and 2021.

• Team travel—Travel costs include air and ground transportation, lodging, and meals for teams, coaches, administrators, and other travelers related to preseason, regular season, and postseason competition. They also include lodging for many home teams staying in hotels before games. In addition, with the landscape of college athletics changing due to geographically illogical conference realignments, this expense will surely grow as conference members get farther apart. According to Bench (2019), in 2017, the average Big Ten school spent US$7.4 million in travel expenses.

• Recruiting—Recruiting expenses include transportation, meals, and lodging incurred throughout the recruiting process. Specific costs include fares and meals during recruiting trips, as well as costs incurred while hosting prospective student-athletes and their family members for official and unofficial visits. This category also includes expenses for other institutional personnel, telecommunications costs, and postage.

• Equipment—This expense includes team-related equipment, uniforms, and supplies that are not considered capital expenditures. It also includes materials for administrators and support staff that meet the same standard.

• Marketing and fundraising—Marketing and fundraising expenses include the costs associated with promoting athletic events and maintaining donor relations and corporate partnerships. Examples include hosting a golf outing, designing game-day programs, and evaluating the effectiveness of a sponsorship. The category also typically includes funding associated with spirit groups, such as bands, cheerleaders, and mascots.

• Game operations—This category includes all expenses required to run an intercollegiate athletics competition. Examples include security, event staff, ambulance services, officials, and food and beverage and catering services.

• Medical—This category includes both medical expenses and medical insurance premiums for student-athletes. This category has ballooned in recent years. For instance, the University of California, Berkeley, which provides very comprehensive medical coverage for its student-athletes, paid US$2.62 million in 2019 (College Athletics Financial Information, 2021a). Medical costs are increasing generally, as are the number of sports injuries (Ashmelash, 2021). In addition, the Supreme Court has questioned the legal standing of the high-value insurance policies for student-athletes, arguing the value undermines the amateur status the NCAA continuously advocates (Golembeski, 2021); thus, medical expenses are definitely an area of concern for the NCAA and its member institutions.

• Membership dues—This category includes all memberships and conference and association dues paid by an athletics department.

• Sport camps—This category includes all expenses paid by an athletics department related to the operation of an on-campus sport camp or clinic.

• Facilities and maintenance—These expenses include operating leases, utilities, rental fees, equipment repair, and building and grounds maintenance. In the athletics "arms race" mentioned earlier, first-rate athletics facilities form a key battleground. From stadium expansions to plush student-athlete living spaces, the costs of renovating and building on campus are excruciatingly high. While some expense categories are different across the three subdivisions of Division I, the median facilities spending between 2005 and 2019 increased by an average of 256 percent for each subdivision (College Athletics Financial Information, 2021a). Nevertheless, facility maintenance is an area that an athletics director could cut for a budget cycle or two if pressed to reduce expenses. In the chapter-opening scenario, for example, the AD might find a logical solution in postponing noncritical updates or stadium renovations until state funding returns to previous levels.

- Debt service—Debt service is the amount of money required to cover the interest and principal of a debt for a given period of time. These financial obligations for an athletics department are typically calculated annually and are most often related to major capital projects, maintenance, or renovations. Coffey (2020) reported that FBS schools had US$9.2 billion in debt in 2019, which accounted for US$744 million in expenses per year. Thirty-two teams at the FBS level had debt totals over US$100 million.
- Other—Other expenses include miscellaneous operating costs, such as printing, subscriptions, business insurance, utilities, postage, equipment leases, severance pay, and travel not related to competition.

FINANCIAL STATEMENTS

College athletics departments, like any other nonprofit entity, must account for all of their financial operations. In addition, financial managers must have a clear format for analyzing current and previous financial data and projecting revenue and expenses for budgeting purposes. These data help guide financial decisions regarding revenue opportunities, investments, and cost-cutting measures. Financial statements provide a record of all financial actions in an organization and are the primary source of data for financial planning, forecasting, reporting, and strategy.

Financial statements serve as the basis for planning and budgeting in both for-profit and nonprofit organizations. These statements are similar in the two types of organization but do include subtle differences in the data and reporting. Financial statements also serve as the basis for annual reporting to the government and other agencies in charge of monitoring nonprofit financial activity. In addition, from a nonprofit perspective, donors and certain stakeholders may have access to this information as part of efforts to evaluate the direction of the organization.

In terms of college athletics, financial statements provide a standard on all tiers of operation, including the NCAA, the conferences, and individual athletics departments. It is not mandatory for all college athletics data from financial statements to be made public. However, the U.S. Department of Education requires public institutions to provide financial data through the Equity in Athletics Disclosure Act (EADA). This act requires all postsecondary educational institutions that receive federal student financial assistance and have intercollegiate athletics programs to report specific information annually about their athletics programs, including some financial data (U.S. Department of Education, 2021). Various aspects of athletics department financial data are available through the EADA Report.

Three financial statements are commonly used in nonprofit operations: the statement of financial position, the statement of activities, and the statement of cash flows. The NCAA provides a public annual report that includes nonprofit financial statements (Consolidated Financial Statements, 2020). Therefore, the NCAA report is used in the following sections to further explain the three kinds of financial statement.

Statement of Financial Position

The *statement of financial position* displays the financial condition of a nonprofit organization at a certain point in time. It includes three parts: *assets* (tangible or intangible resources owned or controlled that produce value for a business), *liabilities* (obligations of a business entity arising from past transactions or events), and *fund balances* or *net assets* (assets minus liabilities). Total assets must always equal total liabilities plus net assets. This structure is similar to that of a commercial balance sheet. However, in for-profit companies, which have shareholders and owners who hold an equity stake in the business, shareholder equity is used instead of fund balances or net assets. Since nonprofits do not have such shareholders, net assets are used to detail the difference between a nonprofit's assets and liabilities.

Assets are listed from the most liquid to the least liquid. *Liquidity* refers to the time it takes for an asset to be converted into cash. Assets that can be converted into cash within a year are considered *current assets*, whereas assets that would take longer than a year to convert to cash are considered *fixed assets*. Liabilities for the organization are listed in the same manner, from short-term (must be paid in less than a year) to long-term (will take more than a year to pay off). Fund balance (net assets) indicates the remaining assets above liabilities that can be used for reserves. However, if an organization is in a poor financial position, liabilities could outpace assets, leaving a negative fund balance.

Table 8.4 shows the NCAA's statement of financial position for 2019 and 2020. Assets include cash, investments, prepaid expenses, and accounts and contributions receivable (bills expected to be paid in the short term). Commercial balance sheets include only accounts receivable, whereas nonprofits can also include contributions that have yet to be collected. The NCAA did not separate current from long-term assets in the statement, but assets are listed in order of liquidity. Total assets for 2020 were approximately US$701.2 million, which was a US$90 million increase from 2019. Liabilities include accounts payable (outstanding short-term debt to be paid), distributions payable (payments to conferences), deferred revenue (revenue received but spread over a period of time), and deferred deposits (deposits made but not immediately reported on an income statement). Total liabilities were approximately US$307 million for 2020.

Table 8.4 NCAA Statement of Financial Position (in USD)

	2020	2019
ASSETS		
Cash and cash equivalents	23,957,204	15,150,504
Investments	588,574,087	473,713,892
Prepaid expenses	9,649,659	4,920,944
Accounts receivable	28,336,646	61,465,921
Goodwill (including trademarks)	5,600,000	6,300,000
Intangible assets	650,000	780,000
Properties	44,011,075	43,478,741
Other assets	729,671	5,083,949
Total assets	701,508,342	610,893,951
LIABILITIES		
Accounts payable and accrued liabilities	249,386,357	100,682,159
Deferred revenue and deposits	49,713,144	48,147,363
Bonds payable—net	8,064,289	11,922,422
Total liabilities	307,163,790	160,751,944
NET ASSETS		
Without donor restrictions	393,244,754	447,799,739
With donor restrictions	1,099,798	2,342,268
Total net assets	394,344,552	450,142,007
Total	701,508,342	610,893,951

Data from National Collegiate Athletic Association, *Consolidated Financial Statements, August 31, 2020 and 2019*. Available: https://ncaaorg.s3.amazonaws.com/ncaa/finance/2019-20NCAAFIN_FinancialStatement.pdf.

The difference between assets and liabilities is reported as net assets. Net assets are broken down by restriction, because assets can be either unrestricted, temporarily restricted, or permanently restricted. (See the following sections for more about restrictions.) The NCAA appears to be financially sound in the period for which the statement of financial position was created. There is a significant discrepancy between 2019 and 2020, mainly due to the COVID-19 pandemic. However, this statement tells you only part of the organization's financial status.

Statement of Activities

The statement of activities shows a nonprofit organization's revenue and expenses over a period of time, usually one year. This statement is similar to the income statement for a commercial business. The difference between revenues and expenses over a period of time is reported as a change in net assets. This change can be broken down as a total fluctuation in net assets or as a change at the beginning or end of a given period, thus providing more detailed information about financial position throughout that period. Statements of activities generally provide information about the current and previous period of interest to offer detail about changes from one period to another. One component missing from the statement of activities is taxes. This is a distinguishing factor between for-profit and nonprofit sport, and it is a considerable advantage for nonprofits, since taxes are a primary expense for commercial firms.

> *Maintenance of facilities is the primary thing that we'll do away with this year. That entails upkeep on Washington-Grizzly Stadium and other facilities that we have, like Dornblaser Field and the soccer fields.*
>
> Kent Haslam, athletics director, University of Montana (qtd. in Green, 2013)

Table 8.5 provides the NCAA's statement of activities from 2019 and 2020. The majority of revenue in 2020 was generated through television and marketing rights (US$167.2 million). However, this was a substantial decrease from 2019, where television revenue totaled US$867.4 million. This dramatic decrease was due to the cancellation of the NCAA 2020 Men's and Women's Basketball Tournaments. Additional revenues are generated through other postseason tournaments, investments, and charitable contributions at the individual and corporate level. In terms of expenses, the primary cost is distribution, totaling approximately US$246.2 million in 2020. Similarly, distributions were significantly less than in 2019 (US$ 610.9 million) due to decreases in revenue as a result of the COVID-19 pandemic. Additional expenses include association programs provided to institutions and the general operations of the association.

The impact of the COVID-19 pandemic is evident in the change in net assets. In 2020, there was a negative change in net assets (US$54.5 million), compared to an increase in net assets in 2019 (US$70.5 million).

Not all revenues are free flowing in nonprofit organizations. Some revenues are permanently or temporarily restricted, either by donors or by grant-funding agencies. For example, donors can designate that their contribution be used for a specific sport. All nonrestricted revenues are available for use by the organization as it sees fit (Bryce, 2017).

It appears from the NCAA statement of activities that the pandemic had a considerable negative impact on net assets in 2020.

Statement of Cash Flows

The *statement of cash flows* provides sources and uses of cash during a specified period of time. The statement is usually broken down into three categories: operating activities, investing activities, and financing activities. Operating activities include net assets, changes in assets and liabilities, and gains or losses from investments. Investing activities include acquisition of property, land, and equipment, as well as changes in overall investments.

Examples of investing activities for the NCAA include the costs associated with purchasing the NIT for men's and women's basketball and the revenue generated from this investment. Financing activities include payments on bonds and revenue accumulated through dividends. Examples of financing activities for the NCAA include distri-

Table 8.5 NCAA Statement of Activities

	2020			2019		
	Without Donor Restrictions	With Donor Restrictions	Total	Without Donor Restrictions	With Donor Restrictions	Total
REVENUES						
Television and marketing rights fees	165,230,167	-	165,230,167	867,527,070	-	867,527,070
Championships and National Invitation Tournaments	15,799,943	-	15,799,943	177,872,026	-	177,872,026
Investment income—net	40,488,047	-	40,488,047	14,566,001	-	14,566,001
Sales and services	21,756,945	-	21,756,945	55,395,739	-	55,395,739
Loss of revenue insurance	270,000,000	-	270,000,000	-	-	-
Contributions—facilities	3,207,260	-	3,207,260	3,134,709	-	3,134,709
Total revenues	519,184,062	-	519,184,062	1,118,495,545	-	1,118,495,545
RECLASSIFICATIONS						
No donor restriction resources used for program services	1,242,470	(1,242,470)	-	112,672	(112,682)	-
Total reclassifications	1,242,470	(1,242,470)	-	112,672	(112,682)	-
EXPENSES						
Distribution to Division I members	246,279,339	-	246,279,339	610,911,851	-	610,911,851
Division I championships, programs, and National Invitation Tournaments	56,234,414	-	56,234,414	153,777,866	-	153,777,866
Division II championships, distributions, and programs	38,286,548	-	38,286,548	53,313,095	-	53,313,095
Division III championships and programs	22,199,542	-	22,199,542	35,179,996	-	35,179,996
Association-wide programs	171,171,083	-	171,171,083	149,966,362	-	149,966,362
Management and general	40,810,591	-	40,810,591	44,808,669	-	44,808,669
Total expense	574,981,517	-	574,981,517	1,047,957,839	-	1,047,957,839
Change in net assets	(54,554,985)	(1,242,470)	(55,797,455)	70,650,378	(112,672)	70,537,706
Net assets—beginning of year	447,799,739	2,342,268	450,142,007	377,149,361	2,454,940	379,604,301
Net assets—end of year	393,244,754	1,099,798	394,344,552	447,799,739	2,342,268	450,142,007

Data from National Collegiate Athletic Association, *Consolidated Financial Statements, August 31, 2020 and 2019*. Available: https://ncaaorg.s3.amazonaws.com/ncaa/finance/2019-20NCAAFIN_FinancialStatement.pdf.

butions to conferences and principal payments on bonds.

Cash flow from these activities is compared at the beginning and end of a specified period, thus illustrating a net change in overall cash flow. In the NCAA statement of cash flows (table 8.6), you can see a breakdown of cash flow from 2019 and 2020, including components from both the statement of financial position and the statement of activities. The NCAA has significant cash flows from operations but is limited in investing and financing, because these are not core components of the association's business model.

In practice, financial statements highlight areas of potential growth and areas where cost cutting would be beneficial. Although these are financial statements for the NCAA, an athletics director (such as the one in the chapter-opening case) also uses financial statements to forecast revenue and establish the need for resources in the upcoming fiscal year. In the case study, financial statements could be used to highlight areas that could be adjusted to account for the budget shortfall. Possibilities might include delaying planned facility renovations, increasing resources to help raise charitable contributions, and adjusting scheduling to limit travel expenses.

BUDGETING

At its core, a budget is nothing more than a planning document. Whether creating a yearlong, multimillion-dollar operating budget or managing a monthly household budget, the process of budgeting is merely planning that requires organization, forethought, and, most importantly, communication. A *budget* is a financial document that involves the strategic allocation of organizational funds to operations, activities, projects, or capital resources. The document itself and the budgeting process should provide a department, program, or unit with guidance, clarity, and direction. However, without good communication and a shared vision, budgets often create confusion and frustration.

Budgets come in all shapes and sizes. Regardless, the potential benefits of proper budgeting in intercollegiate athletics are numerous. A well-organized and well-communicated budget offers the following benefits:

- Allows decision-makers to better control and monitor spending
- Offers a clearer picture of organizational priorities
- Alerts management to revenue shortfalls
- Prevents rash financial decisions
- Provides a working document for strategic planning
- Proffers a precise measurement source for financial performance
- Motivates stakeholders to meet important goals and objectives

Another reason that budgets are essential in departmental operations is that, like consumers, athletics departments are constrained by time and money. As a result, managers are required to make strategic decisions about how much to allocate and for how long. For example, a given team's travel budget is often set at a specific amount (e.g., US$150,000) at the beginning of the fiscal year (July 1) and is available to finance the team's travel for only one year. A good budget should also provide an accurate projection of revenue and expenses detailing the projected costs of each planned trip. Thus, it can provide a source of stability in unpredictable times.

Planning, Forecasting, and the Budgeting Process

The budgeting process typically consists of three stages: data collection, planning, and budget development. *Data collection* for budgeting is the process of gathering internal and external financial information that may affect the planning, forecasting, and ultimate development of an organization's budget. Internal sources typically involve private data from previous operations within the organization. Another common data source for an athletics department is primary research in the form of fan or consumer surveys. External sources might come in the form of industry trends, local or regional economic data, or competitor analyses. Data collection must be a systematic and comprehensive process; most importantly, the sources must be valid and reliable.

Planning is a vital financial activity for any organization, particularly in conjunction with budg-

Table 8.6 NCAA Statement of Cash Flows in USD

	2020	2019
CASH FLOWS FROM OPERATING ACTIVITIES		
Change in NCAA net assets	(55,797,455)	70,537,706
ADJUSTMENTS TO RECONCILE CHANGE IN NET ASSETS TO NET CASH PROVIDED BY OPERATING ACTIVITIES		
Depreciation and amortization	5,835,811	6,764,850
Amortization of bond premium	(283,133)	(326,230)
Change in unrealized gain on investments	4,727,763	2,941,518
Change in realized gain on investments	(29,806,019)	(85,110)
CHANGES IN CERTAIN ASSETS AND LIABILITIES		
Receivables	33,129,275	6,875,766
Prepaid expenses	(4,728,715)	(858,855)
Other assets	1,514,753	(965,023)
Accounts payable and accrued liabilities	148,283,822	(10,264,721)
Deferred revenue and deposits	1,565,781	10,259,046
Net cash provided by operating activities	104,441,883	84,878,957
CASH FLOWS FROM INVESTING ACTIVITIES		
Purchases of capital assets	(5,538,144)	(3,379,050)
Notes receivable	2,839,524	-
Purchases of investments	(383,180,368)	(173,905,223)
Proceeds from sales of investments	293,818,805	97,973,050
Net cash used in investing activities	104,441,883	84,878,957
CASH FLOWS FROM FINANCING ACTIVITIES		
Proceeds from lines of credit	100,000,000	-
Repayments of lines of credit	(100,000,000)	-
Principal payments on bonds payable	(3,575,000)	(4,580,000)
Net cash from financing activities	(3,575,000)	(4,580,000)
Net increase (decrease) in cash and cash equivalents	8,806,700	987,734
Beginning of year	15,150,504	14,162,770
End of year	23,957,204	15,150,504
Supplemental cash flow information—cash paid for interest	482,755	711,244
Noncash transactions—purchases of property, plant, and equipment	-	-

Data from National Collegiate Athletic Association, *Consolidated Financial Statements, August 31, 2020 and 2019.* Available: https://ncaaorg.s3.amazonaws.com/ncaa/finance/2019-20NCAAFIN_FinancialStatement.pdf.

Leadership Lesson

Feed the Opportunities

As we pursue the tasks that fill our days, it is very easy to become busy—very, very busy. You may recall the anecdote from *Alice's Adventures in Wonderland* in the chapter 4 leadership lesson. The main idea was that if you do not know where you want to go, it does not matter which path you take. We might work from sunup to sundown, trudging along a path, only to realize when we reach the end that we took the wrong one. If we do not know where we hope to go, it is extremely difficult to get there.

It may seem like a pretty straightforward idea that we should manage our time based on importance. But how do you determine *importance?* We hope that by this point in the text (building on previous leadership lessons), you have crafted your personal mission statement. If you have, simply ask yourself whether a given task helps you get closer to your vision or to high-priority goals associated with your various roles. If it does, then it is important (Covey, 2004). As discussed in chapter 3 (Leadership and Management), Covey describes a four-quadrant grid (recall figure 3.3) for categorizing the various tasks we encounter, and he urges leaders to strive to live their lives primarily in quadrant II (addressing matters that are important but not urgent). Certainly, many matters arise that are both urgent and important (quadrant I), but habitually spending a majority of time in crisis management mode leads to stress, burnout, and ultimate inefficiency. Planning and carving out maximal time in quadrant II, on the other hand, creates a life led by vision, control, balance, and perspective. Therefore, effective leaders are advised to delegate all matters that are urgent but not important to trusted support staff and to avoid doing activities that are neither important nor urgent, since they result in irresponsible use of time (Covey, 2004).

> *Even when the urgent is good, the good can keep you from your best, keep you from your unique contribution, if you let it. . . . It's almost impossible to say "no" to the popularity of Quadrant III or to the pleasure of escape to Quadrant IV if you don't have a bigger "yes" burning inside . . . [O]nly then will you have sufficient independent willpower to say "no," with a genuine smile, to the unimportant.*
>
> Covey, 2004, pp. 157-158
>
> *In every area of effectiveness within an organization,* one feeds the opportunities and starves the problem.
>
> Drucker, 1967, p. 98, emphasis original

This vantage point differs from viewing your time in terms of efficiency. Crossing tasks off of a list may provide a temporary sense of accomplishment, but if the achievements are quadrant III or IV tasks—not driven by importance—then you are just spinning your wheels. In fact, Covey writes, "efficient scheduling and control of time are often counterproductive. The efficiency focus creates expectations that clash with the opportunities to develop rich relationships, to meet human needs, and to enjoy spontaneous moments on a daily basis" (Covey, 2004, p. 150). In order to balance the need for efficiency and focus on importance, Covey recommends scheduling your week based on one or two important goals in each role you play. When you allocate time to these goals throughout the week, you improve your flexibility, allow time for the quadrant I activities that are bound to pop up, and enable yourself to proactively balance the roles you play.

Such clarity is equally important in organizational priorities. The following questions are included in an exercise that consultant Patrick Lencioni (2000) has recommended for executive teams to do as they engage in strategic planning. Employees in a healthy organization should be able to unambiguously answer the following questions:

(continued)

LEADERSHIP LESSON *(continued)*

- Why does the organization exist, and what difference does it make in the world?
- What behavioral values are irreplaceable and fundamental?
- What business are we in, and against whom do we compete?
- How does our approach differ from that of our competition?
- What are our goals for this month, this quarter, this year, next year, and the next five years?
- Who has to do what in order for us to achieve our goals for this month, this quarter, this year, next year, and the next five years? (Lencioni, 2000, p. 154-155)

As you strive to become more effective on the individual and organizational levels, ask yourself what quadrant you're spending the majority of your time in. Do your individual weekly planning sessions or organizational meetings emphasize tasks focused on what is most important? In an organization, does the department allocate finances based on a clear organizational vision, or is there tremendous imbalance between the stated values and the priorities that are funded? It is very easy to forget about the big picture and get sucked into a quadrant I mentality, both in departmental budget management and in life.

eting. In finance, *planning* is the process of creating strategies, based on recent history and on forecasts, to guide the development and implementation of the budget. Given that a budget is nothing more than a component of the overall financial plan, it makes sense that the plan must be implemented first (Bergeron, 2002). Most often, the planning process is broken down into short-term planning and long-term planning. However, forecasting revenues and expenses is the primary aspect of planning that is used in the budgeting process.

Forecasting is the process of using financial data to predict and quantify future events. In particular, forecasting involves using statistical methods of prediction based on the relationships of various factors in an economic environment. In intercollegiate athletics, some of these factors, including most forms of revenue, lie outside of the organization's control (Brown et al., 2016). For instance, an athletics department may use forecasting techniques to predict the number of single-game tickets that will be bought or the major gifts that will be donated. Forecasting can be a powerful tool for an organization if the data analyzed are correct and the organization's financial plan has been clearly communicated. Forecasting should go hand in hand with strategic planning, yet often does not, if those tasked with developing the forecast are not tuned into the broader strategic vision (Hagel, 2014).

Finally, it is vital to develop a progressive yet realistic budget, aiming for conservative growth based on sound planning and data-driven forecasting. In particular, revenue estimations should be crafted with the idea of pushing the organization forward as a means of goal-oriented action. Likewise, expense forecasting should be carefully devised to include general inflation as well as the increased cost of developing new revenue.

Budget Types

This section highlights two main budget types commonly used in intercollegiate athletics: operational budgets, which affect the day-to-day functions of an organization, and capital budgets, which reflect one-time, financed expenses. Several types of operational budgets exist and are discussed in this section. In addition, formats, strategies, and implications associated with each type are provided.

Operational Budgets

An operational budget is a statement that anticipates revenues and expenses required for the day-to-day functions of a unit over a given period of time. The time period for an operational budget is typically one year, but the budget may also be segmented by quarter or month to provide benchmarks. At the beginning of a budget cycle, the figures in the budget are estimates; as the time period elapses, these estimates are compared with the actual amounts. The difference or variance between the two figures provides vital information about potential revenue shortfalls or overspending. This process is called *variance analysis*, and it provides a mechanism for monitoring and controlling revenue collections and spending. Table 8.7 provides an example of variance analysis for an athletics department over four quarters.

Returning to the chapter-opening scenario, the athletics director would certainly benefit from conducting a variance analysis in order to find expenses to cut for the upcoming fiscal year. Identifying quarterly shortfalls, for example, would help the department identify sources of wasteful spending or inefficient programming; meanwhile, a surplus could identify a potential area to revise in the budget.

Line-Item Budget A *line-item budget*, or object-of-expenditure budget, is a document in which individual financial items (revenues and expenses) are grouped by department and itemized by function. For instance, revenue generated from website subscriptions would be itemized as such and grouped under digital media. Line-item budgeting is often considered to be traditional budgeting, and it is implemented for a number of reasons, including simplicity, flexibility, and the ability to measure over time.

As shown in table 8.8, a line-item budget allows a manager to quickly populate a budget by looking at the previous year's line. It can be used by a wide range of programs and organizations, and it can also be as detailed as necessary because it is relatively easy to add or subtract a line during the planning process. Finally, line-item budgeting optimizes the control feature of budgeting, because it is easy to monitor from one period to the next but difficult to transfer money from one line to another.

However, this type of budget also has its drawbacks. Although simplicity is a strength of line-item budgeting, it is also a weakness, because it does not require much managerial analysis. In other words, the process of incrementally adjusting the previous year's budget puts focus on the cost of a function but does not oblige the manager to analyze the need for it. This drawback can produce a disconnect between strategic planning, efficiency, and line-item budgeting.

Program Budget A *program budget* is a document in which funds are allocated directly to a program. The unit then has the freedom to spend the money as it chooses so long as it does not exceed the allocated amount for the program. This is a top-down approach as compared with line-item budgeting. It allows an organization to evaluate the efficiency of a given activity without the control afforded through other budgeting formats.

For example, in line with an athletics department's goals and objectives, it may have several ongoing yet clearly delineated programs, such as a campaign to sell more season tickets or a promotion to attract more youth to home games. The use of a program budget system with these programs would entail creating and maintaining a separate budget document for each program. In the end, then, a program budget assesses the effectiveness of the department's pursuits by assessing each program separately, whereas the next type, the performance budget, evaluates the efficiency of management.

Performance Budget *Performance budgeting* links allocated funds to measurable objectives; therefore, it is the most result-oriented budgeting process. A performance budget typically consists of three sections: the result, the strategy, and the activity (National Conference of State Legislatures, 2021). The information gained from these elements is intended to aid in the decision-making process for allocating budgetary funds. Within specific programs of an athletics department (e.g., marketing or the men's golf team), this type of budgeting allows for a more comprehensive evaluation of actions. It tends to focus more on changes in funding rather than the base amount, and allows organizations to reallocate funds based on merit or success (National Conference on State Legislatures, 2021).

For example, if a golf coach invests US$800 in access to an online recruiting database that leads to four additional offers and one additional recruit, the detail of a performance budget provides an opportunity for the coach to weigh the benefits and costs of the action. In general, then, this approach should result in budgeting that is more in line with

Table 8.7 Example of Variance Analysis at XYZ Athletics Department

	Q1: JULY 1-SEPTEMBER 30			Q2: NOVEMBER 1-DECEMBER 31			Q3: JANUARY 1-MARCH 31			Q4: APRIL 1-JUNE 30			
	Budget	**Actual**	**Variance**	**Budget**	**Actual**	**Variance**	**Budget**	**Actual**	**Variance**	**Budget**	**Actual**	**Variance**	**Total variance**
REVENUE IN USD (THOUSANDS)													
Ticket sales	117	118	1	215	211	(4)	195	207	12	47	48	1	10
Conference distributions	900	900	0	900	900	0	900	900	0	900	940	40	40
Donations	220	206	(14)	400	418	18	300	288	(12)	220	215	(5)	(13)
Sponsorships	650	656	6	13	18	5	13	13	0	650	623	(27)	(16)
Institutional support	1,200	1,200	0	0	0	0	0	0	0	10	25	15	15
Other	50	51	1	25	27	2	25	24	(1)	50	54	4	6
Total	**3,137**	**3,131**	**(6)**	**1,553**	**1,574**	**21**	**1,433**	**1,432**	**(1)**	**1,877**	**1,905**	**28**	**42**
Total revenue	**8,000**	**8,042**	**42**										
EXPENSES IN USD (THOUSANDS)													
Grants-in-aid	325	329	(4)	0	0	0	325	311	14	195	201	(6)	4
Guarantees	125	125	0	75	75	0	0	0	0	0	0	0	0
Salaries and benefits	1,200	1,210	(10)	1,200	1,215	(15)	1,200	1,205	(5)	1,200	1,216	(16)	(46)
Team travel	185	196	(11)	400	421	(21)	250	279	(29)	150	166	(16)	(77)
Recruiting	45	46	(1)	65	64	1	59	68	(9)	45	49	(4)	(13)
Medical	110	116	(6)	190	188	2	85	88	(3)	40	41	(1)	(8)
Maintenance	88	96	(8)	88	85	3	88	85	3	88	98	(10)	(12)
Other	37	34	3	41	43	(2)	41	40	1	60	62	(2)	0
Total	**2,115**	**2,152**	**(37)**	**2,059**	**2,091**	**(32)**	**2,048**	**2,076**	**(28)**	**1,778**	**1,833**	**(55)**	**(152)**
Total expenses	**8,000**	**8,152**	**(152)**										
Total variance	**(110)**												

Table 8.8 XYZ Athletics Department, Line-Item Budget

	Last Year	Q1	Q2	Q3	Q4	Total
REVENUE IN USD (THOUSANDS)						
Ticket sales	600	188	220	225	46	679
Conference distributions	3,500	900	900	900	910	3,610
Donations	1,250	250	450	350	220	1,270
Sponsorships	1,360	650	13	13	650	1,326
Institutional support	1,200	1,200	0	0	10	1,210
Other	90	25	25	25	25	100
Total	8,000	3,143	1,608	1,513	1,861	8,125
EXPENSES IN USD (THOUSANDS)						
Grants-in-aid	830	325	0	325	180	830
Guarantees	225	150	75	0	0	225
Salaries and benefits	4,750	1,200	1,250	1,200	1,200	4,850
Team travel	1,064	190	450	283	166	1,089
Recruiting	205	45	65	50	45	205
Medical	425	110	190	85	40	425
Maintenance	352	88	88	88	88	352
Other	149	37	41	41	30	149
Total	8,000	2,145	2,159	2,072	1,749	8,125

the program's mission and strategies. At the highest level of the department, however, this budgeting process may not work, because eliminating programs due to performance may not be possible (due to Title IX and NCAA rules on minimum number of sponsored sports). This type of budgeting is also more time consuming and requires more detail than other forms.

Capital Budgets

Capital budgeting is a much different process than operational budgeting and requires separate documentation due to the unique nature of the items being financed. Depending on the subject, capital can be defined in many ways. For the purposes of this chapter, *capital* refers to money or assets put to use for productive gain. In most instances, forms of capital are costly one-time investments that are not fully consumed within a year yet provide some sort of financial return or public benefit. Typical examples in college athletics include an air-conditioning unit for the football locker room, a scoreboard for the hockey rink, and a cargo van for the golf team.

Given the high cost of most capital projects, it is logical to separate capital from the operational budget so as not to burden a recurring budget with a high-cost nonrecurring item. In addition, most capital projects are financed; as a result, capital purchasing decisions must consider the factors of time, interest rate, and rate of return. Several methods are available for deciding between capital projects, including the payback rule, net present value, internal rate of return, and discounted cash flow methods.

Financial Reporting for Institutions

The NCAA requires institutions to report athletics revenue and expenses in order to monitor the financial health of intercollegiate athletics departments (see the NCAA Bylaw 3.2.4.16 Operating and Capital Financial Data Report sidebar). The dashboard indicators provided by this standardized reporting also provide university decision-makers

NCAA Bylaw 3.2.4.16 Operating and Capital Financial Data Report

An institution shall submit financial data detailing operating revenues, expenses, and capital related to its intercollegiate athletics program to the NCAA on an annual basis in accordance with the financial reporting policies and procedures. The required data shall include, but is not limited to, the following: (Adopted: 1/17/09 effective 8/1/09)

a. All expenses and revenues for or on behalf of an institution's intercollegiate athletics program, including those by any affiliated or outside organization, agency, or group of individuals;
b. Capital expenditures (to be reported in aggregate for athletics facilities), including capitalized additions and deletions to facilities during the reporting period, total estimated book value of athletically related plant and equipment net of depreciation, total annual debt service on athletics and university facilities, and total debt outstanding on athletics and university facilities;
c. Value of endowments at fiscal year-end that are dedicated to the sole support of athletics;
d. Value of all pledges at fiscal year-end that support athletics; and
e. The athletics department fiscal year-end fund balance.

3.2.4.16.1 Verification and Certification. The report shall be subject to annual agreed-on verification procedures approved by the membership (in addition to any regular financial reporting policies and procedures of the institution) and conducted by a qualified independent accountant who is not a staff member of the institution and who is selected by the institution's chancellor or president or by an institutional administrator from outside the athletics department designated by the chancellor or president. The independent accountant shall verify the accuracy and completeness of the data prior to submission to the institution's chancellor or president and the NCAA. The institution's chancellor or president shall certify the financial report prior to submission to the NCAA. (Adopted: 1/17/09 effective 8/1/09)

Professional Development

Collegiate Athletic Business Management Association (CABMA)

CABMA is devoted to people who oversee business or fiscal matters in intercollegiate athletics. Its annual symposium, held during the convention of the National Association of Collegiate Directors of Athletics (NACDA), brings members together to share ideas, policies, and procedures related to efficient fiscal management in college sport. The group also facilitates problem-solving through continuous dialogue between members aimed at achieving greater cost efficiency in daily operations, strategic planning, and other areas of business management. Online resources available throughout the year, including *Athletics Administration* magazine and the NACDA Daily Review email, address current events, explore new strategies, and provide educational webinars. Reduced-price memberships are available to help students engage in professional development early in their career.

Case Study

The Student Fee Debate

Among the many sources of funding for college athletics departments, student fees are commonplace at all levels of competition. Approximately 80 percent of NCAA Division I public universities include some form of athletics fee within their student fee structure. These annual fees range from US$100 to over US$3,300 (Enright et al., 2020). In 2018, student fees accounted for US$1.5 billion in athletics department funding, approximately 8 percent of revenue (Baker, 2020). The practice varies widely. For instance, some athletics departments, such as the University of Texas, do not collect student fees to support athletics, but in 2020 James Madison University allocated over US$45.6 million in student fees earmarked for athletics (College Athletics Financial Information, 2022).

These fees fall under the category of allocated revenues, which are provided by institutional support rather than generated through goods and services provided by the athletics department. This is an important distinction, as many athletics departments claim to be self-sufficient while relying heavily on allocated revenues, such as institutional support and student fees. Another issue associated with student fees is transparency. In many cases student fees are lumped together in tuition and fees payments, so students cannot delineate between student fees for athletics versus fees for other support services such as the student recreation center or tutoring services (Enright et al., 2020).

College athletics administrators have made an argument for university financial support, including student fees, based on the return on investment (ROI) they believe athletics provide to the university. Many conference commissioners, athletics directors, and university administrators have justified allocations to athletics by arguing that college sport is the "front porch" to the university. The mass exposure of major college sport can open the door for additional student applications, charitable contributions, and university-wide sponsorship opportunities. Recently, Pac-12 Commissioner George Kliavkoff claimed:

> *We need to invest in coaches and facilities. That leads to better recruiting, which leads to winning, which leads to direct and indirect revenue and alumni engagement. And we've seen that it leads to more applications, which allow universities to become more selective in admissions. I can't imagine a more obvious ROI than investing in football.*

The financial claims have been questioned in the literature (Jones & Rudolph, 2020), but some studies have identified college sport as a point of attachment to the university, which is of particular interest to lower-level college sport programs (Katz, Dixon, Heere, & Bass, 2017).

Costs continue to rise within college athletic programs, resulting in the need to explore all revenue options, including student fees. As universities explore the use of student fees as a source of revenue, it is important to understand the arguments for and against allocating fees toward athletics.

The state of Utah recently conducted an audit to examine the amount of fees that a Utah college student pays to support college athletics (Jones & Pflaum, 2021). In 2020, college sport programs in Utah had US$202 million in revenue, but 43 percent of this revenue came from student fees and subsidies. The audit found that, on average, a Utah college student paid approximately US$742 in fees directed toward college athletics departments. Students at Southern Utah University paid US$1,500 in these fees annually. This is a significant percentage of overall tuition and fees paid by students. Utah State Auditor John Dougall contends that

> *one of the questions is, to what extent are athletics critical to that core college experience. And for some students it might be very crucial, and for other students who are working and are trying to just put themselves through school, it may be an extravagance they [cannot] really afford.* (Jones & Pflaum, 2021)

However, many athletics administrators believe students desire college sport as part of the

(continued)

CASE STUDY *(continued)*

overall university experience, and student fees are necessary to provide this service.

Questions to Consider

1. What are the pros and cons of using student fees to support college athletics?
2. What level of transparency should universities provide regarding student fee amount and usage as it relates to college athletics?
3. Based on the information provided regarding college athletics programs in the state of Utah, what are the key factors that should be considered when implementing a student fee allocation plan? How does that differ for various public institutions within the state?

with a potentially powerful set of metrics for benchmarking and strategic planning. The U.S. Department of Education also requires institutions to file annual financial and participation reports to comply with the EADA.

Both of these reporting functions are a step in the right direction for an industry that went without regulation for nearly a century. However, a good deal of the NCAA data are not available to the general public—for example, departmental financial statements from individual institutions. In addition, no standardized accounting principles are required (e.g., generally accepted accounting principles, or GAAP), and the data required for reporting are allowed to be broadly categorized.

For instance, common incomparable financial aspects include the reporting of coaches' salaries subsidized by shoe and apparel companies and the reporting of tuition waivers for grant-in-aid athletes. Each university may have a different approach to classifying these substantial expenses, which leads to significant inconsistencies between institutions. For example, institutional support in the form of new facility construction or rent is a significant expense for an athletics department, but given similar pursuits and shared property, it is easy to see how expenses between a university and an athletics department can be interchanged. To illustrate the level of interpretation available to general accountants, the 2011 Federal Accounting Standards Advisory Board's handbook, which serves as the clearinghouse for GAAP, is more than 2,000 pages long.

CONCLUSION

The current growth in college athletics emphasizes the need, now more than ever, for financial responsibility and accountability in athletics departments. The unique nature of this industry entails challenges and opportunities for sport managers because athletics departments operate both under the umbrella of higher education and under intense commercial pressures. As a result, today's college athletics administrators must have the ability to generate revenue, raise capital, and budget effectively to help provide an optimal educational experience for the student-athletes for whom the organizations exist.

This chapter provides an overview of the financial landscape of college sport and some challenges for the future. It also discusses in detail the nonprofit status of college athletics to provide an understanding of the unique nature of the industry. Finally, it covers financial concepts (e.g., business structure, financial statements, planning, and budgeting) in the context of this unique environment. It is critical to understand and implement these concepts as college athletics departments continue to increase costs and are forced to find creative methods for operating in a fiscally prudent manner.

DISCUSSION QUESTIONS

1. Scheduling guaranteed games is a hot-button topic for both teams involved. Why would an organization guarantee revenue to an opponent? What issues should be considered by an athletics department before offering a game guarantee?
2. What are the potential benefits and drawbacks of each of the following budget types: line-item, program, and performance? As a senior associate athletics director, which budget type would you choose, and why? As a head coach in charge of your team's budget, which budget type would you prefer, and why?
3. Bowen's revenue theory of costs is discussed in the chapter as a framework for spending in college athletics. Explain how the additional revenue generated through new television broadcasting deals might affect athletics department spending based on the cycle proposed in Bowen's theory.
4. In situations where athletics departments are out of compliance with Title IX, cutting nonrevenue male sports has been a common but unpopular strategy used to comply with the legislation. From a financial perspective, how might athletics departments comply with Title IX without necessarily cutting sports? What financial strategies could be used in an effort to maximize student-athletes' participation opportunities?
5. Currently, coaches' salaries for revenue-generating sports such as football and basketball are whatever the market will bear. As a result, these salaries have become a primary expense for Division I athletics departments looking to remain competitive. Do you believe that the current salary structure for coaches in revenue-generating sports is sustainable? Why or why not? What strategies could be used to reduce the expenses associated with coaches' salaries in football and basketball?

LEARNING ACTIVITIES

1. Suppose that you work in an athletics department in which a few teams outperformed expectations this year for tournament results and home-game attendance. As a result, your department is heading toward your first year of posting a profit (revenues have reached US$48 million and expenses have reached US$39 million). There are only a few weeks until the end of the fiscal year, and you cannot roll forward the difference; thus, you must spend it. Work in small groups to determine the best expense categories to which the US$9 million surplus could be allocated. Be ready to defend your decisions.
2. Interview an administrator who oversees financial operations in a Division I athletics department. What is the overall budget for the department? How much of the budget involves generated revenue versus allocated revenue? What are the main points of emphasis for generating revenue and controlling costs? Where does the athletics department budget rank in the conference? What is the general expectation for revenue growth each year?

Marketing

Tickets and Promotions

David J. Shonk, James Madison University

Alyssa T. Bosley, James Madison University

In this chapter, you will explore

- the five Ps of sport marketing,
- differences between online and traditional advertising,
- licensing and why colleges and universities use licensees,
- how atmospherics affect a consumer at an intercollegiate sporting event,
- community relations initiatives at various institutions,
- the secondary ticket market and the effect of dynamic ticketing in intercollegiate athletics, and
- various types of promotion in intercollegiate athletics.

THE CHANGING NATURE OF MARKETING INTERCOLLEGIATE ATHLETICS

Jennifer Johnson is hired as the new director of athletics marketing at a large public institution in Ohio. She is excited about returning to her alma mater after graduating 12 years earlier. However, she notices that the process of delivering the product to fans has changed considerably since she interned with the athletics department at the end of her senior year. One of the first items on her agenda is to hire a new marketing and fan experience director. Along with marketing responsibilities, the duties for this position will involve planning the game-day experience for fans and will involve coordinating public address scripts, videoboard, music, sponsorship fulfillment, national anthem, halftime acts/on-court promotions, band, and the spirit squad. But hiring for this position will be easy in comparison to some of the other issues on her plate. The landscape for intercollegiate athletics has changed considerably over the years. While a marketing director like Jennifer must be aware of issues surrounding conference realignment, a larger issue on her plate is understanding issues surrounding name, image, and likeness (NIL). In addition to her duties with placing social media advertisements and creating dynamic ticket promotions, Jennifer works with Opendorse, an agency that helps student-athletes market their name, image, and likeness.

Marketing, ticketing, and promotion are vital functions for intercollegiate athletics programs. The marketing of athletics programs is big business, and athletics departments use both traditional and online forms of advertising to sell tickets and multiple forms of social media to reach their target audiences. Intercollegiate sport marketers also use various licensees to create products bearing the name of the university. In addition, in an effort to market the appeal of the physical setting and sensory elements, colleges and universities are constantly building and renovating sport facilities. Athletics programs also use the celebrity status of their athletes and coaches to connect with their local communities through various community relations initiatives. Many athletics programs are now working with their student-athletes to also assist with NIL.

MARKETING INTERCOLLEGIATE ATHLETICS

Marketers of intercollegiate athletics use a variety of methods to appeal to their audience. This section discusses how advertising, social media, licensing, atmospherics, and community relations are used to promote intercollegiate athletics. First, however, it examines how marketers appeal to fans through five primary factors—product, price, promotion, place, and public relations—commonly referred to as the five Ps of sport marketing. The five Ps can be applied to highly identified fans in the following ways.

- Product—The core product in sport is the sporting contest itself. Some fans are highly identified with a particular sport (e.g., basketball) or a particular team (e.g., the University of Louisville Cardinals).
- Price—A fan may be willing to pay more to attend a marquee game, such as Duke versus North Carolina in basketball or Alabama versus Auburn in football.
- Promotion—Fans at Penn State University may be motivated to attend a game against a rival team when the athletics program promotes a whiteout (in which spectators wear white shirts to the game) or offers a bobblehead giveaway featuring a popular player.
- Place—Appealing venues can attract visitors to attend simply because of the atmosphere. Examples include the Palestra basketball arena in Philadelphia and classic football stadiums, such as the Horseshoe at Ohio State University.
- Public relations—The media attention given to certain celebrity student-athletes (e.g., quarterback Johnny Manziel) or teams (e.g., Notre Dame football) can be a primary motivator for some individuals to attend a sporting event.

ADVERTISING

Advertising has been defined as "any paid form of non-personal presentation of ideas, goods, or services by an identified sponsor" (Irwin et al., 2008, p. 4). However, advances in technology, including the rise of social media, have created opportunities to advertise at little or no cost. Most collegiate sport marketers use a combination of both traditional and online advertising to effectively reach their entire fan base.

Traditional advertising in intercollegiate athletics usually consists of print, outdoor, and broadcast media. Although these types of media are thought to be declining in popularity due to the growth of social media, many institutions continue to use them to reach older fans. At James Madison University, the athletics marketing department places advertisements in local newspapers and magazines, rents billboards along the interstate, mails season-ticket brochures, places flyers in locations around the community, and creates commercials for local radio and television stations. Each of these types of advertising, of course, carries a purchase or rental cost.

These efforts notwithstanding, in recent years a majority of advertising has been shifted online to try to capture a portion of the 4.26 billion people using social media (Dixon, 2022). In particular, many intercollegiate athletics programs use online advertising to appeal to their younger demograph-

Technology Tools

Name, Image, and Likeness

College athletes were first offered the opportunity to cash in on their name, image, and likeness (NIL) beginning on July 1, 2021. This meant athletes could now be compensated for third-party endorsements related to athletics without school or conference involvement, and for other student-athlete opportunities, such as social media, new businesses, and personal appearances, without institutional involvement or the use of trademarks or logos (Ivie, 2021). As this new source of revenue generation opened up for athletes in 2021, a number of digital platforms began operating that connected student-athletes with sponsorship opportunities. Some of these platforms included Opendorse, Icon Source, Altius Sports Partners, INFLCR, PWRFRD, Blue Wire, Cameo, and ConnectNIL.com, to name just a few (Gregory, 2021). In fact, Dellenger (2021) reports that more than 150 different platforms exist.

But it is not only digital platforms but also event operators who are looking at the lucrative nature of NIL. As noted by Christovich (2021), as long as the event operator is not a school or conference, it is eligible to offer NIL deals. In November 2021, the Roman Main Event, a nonconference men's basketball tournament held at T-Mobile Arena in Las Vegas, Nevada, in addition to having athletes playing in the tournament, also hired five athletes to serve as "ambassadors" to promote the event. Marketers of other events, like the Hula Bowl, arranged for athletes who were not playing in the event to do in-person appearances, such as autograph signings.

College athletics departments are also involved with NIL and can be expected to change their services to the student-athletes as NIL evolves. Bromberg (2021) highlights the University of Nebraska's #NILbraska initiative, announced on June 3, 2021. The initiative is a three-pronged plan for assisting Nebraska athletes with the Accelerate campus program, Husker Advantage Life Skills program, and Ready Now Opendorse program. The Accelerate campus program helps athletes identify talents, strengths, and entrepreneurial attributes, along with providing mentors, workshops and speakers, and pop-up classes. The Husker Advantage Life Skills program offers a personal-strengths assessment for athletes and a brand-building and brand-value assessment. The Ready Now Opendorse program helps the athlete build their personal brand, along with analyzing their social media accounts and identifying areas for improvement.

Social Media and Intercollegiate Athletics

A 2000 study by AthleticDirectorU of 292 Division I institutions using X (formerly known as Twitter), Facebook, Instagram and YouTube revealed the following (Boettger, n.d.):

- Of the 292 institutions, all of them have a primary athletics X (formerly known as Twitter) account; 291 a primary athletics Facebook account; 289 a primary athletics Instagram account; and 273 a primary athletics YouTube account with public settings.
- Institutions averaged a total of about 205 thousand [sic] followers over the four social media platforms, with 51% of followers on Facebook, 28% from X (formerly known as Twitter), 17% from Instagram, and 4% from YouTube.
- Trends from the most engaged universities suggest their social media accounts are thoughtful and strategic, using high-quality photos and video, crisp and attractive graphics, engaging tone, and a variety of athletes, coaches and teams.
- A total of 74 percent of the athletics websites had a dedicated social media directory page.
- A total of 30.1 percent of the websites had social media icon links in either the site's header or footer.

ics. The LEARFIELD Intercollegiate Fan Report (2021) suggests that college sport fans engage with both social and digital media throughout the entire year. In fact, according to the report, fans are consistently engaging with their favorite teams throughout the week despite the fact that website engagement is 23 percent higher on Saturdays. This is why most athletics programs use Facebook, X (formerly known as Twitter), and Instagram; some also use Snapchat and TikTok.

According to Fugere (2013), online advertising and social media are replacing traditional forms of advertising for a number of reasons.

- They are cost effective—unless you opt to pay for promotions, social media are free.
- They go viral.
- They live forever—what happens on the Internet stays on the Internet.
- They foster relationships—social media provide two-way communication channels.
- They generate leads—social media are trackable and make it possible to measure the exact impact that a social campaign has on a company's success.

Depending on the size of the college or university, as well as the particular needs of its athletics department, day-to-day management of a website may either be outsourced to a multimedia company or be handled in-house. When it is handled in-house, the marketing department often designates an employee responsible for maintaining the site. Increasingly, however, the trend is to outsource the function of producing and managing website content to multimedia companies. Many colleges and universities also realize the value of streaming content, which allows students, fans, parents, and alumni to watch various sporting events that they would otherwise not be able to see in person. The cost for streaming video is relatively inexpensive for most colleges and universities, and it meets the needs of providing content to these numerous stakeholder groups.

One of the challenges of marketing in intercollegiate athletics is appealing to the many stakeholder groups. Consider for a moment how perceptions of athletics on campus can differ between faculty, administrators, students, student-athletes, coaches, parents, alumni, local fans, and corporate sponsors. For example, many faculty perceive athletics as an intrusion into the academic mission of the university and are therefore not interested in the success of the athletics program. In contrast, alumni often demand winning performance and view their affiliation with the university through the lens of the athletics program's level of success. For some students, their very choice of a university depends on the success of the athletics program.

With all of this in mind, athletics has been described as the "front porch" of the university—it can be someone's first impression of the school. As a result, the various social media platforms are used not only as a way to provide information about the athletics program but also to extend the university brand. One example is the website of the University of Arkansas, recognized by *Sports Business Journal* as one of the best in sports social media. Arkansas' site is deemed outstanding because of its authenticity and creative content that uses coaches and athletes as influencers, and through the use of humor by poking fun at other teams in the Southeastern Conference (*Sports Business Journal*, 2022).

LICENSING

How often do you see someone wearing a shirt or cap bearing the name of a college or university? The answer is probably quite often. Colleges and universities use licensing as a way to extend their brand. More specifically, licensing is a contractual method that universities use to develop and exploit their intellectual property by transferring the rights of use to third parties without transferring ownership. For example, you can purchase a lamp and various other accessories bearing the UCLA Bruins logo that are manufactured by a company called CSI International in Niagara Falls, New York. In order to use a school's logo, the licensee (e.g., CSI International) may pay an initial licensing fee or a royalty fee, and it assumes the risks inherent in making the product. In turn, the licensor (e.g., UCLA) looks for potential licensees and polices the marketplace for anyone selling products bearing its name or marks without permission.

The advantage of licensing for most colleges and universities comes in the form of increased awareness of the institution's name. In some cases, licensing also allows the university to expand into new markets while assuming little risk. For example, a university that wants to popularize its image among high school students could put its name on a product that appeals to the high school market.

The potential disadvantage of licensing hinges on the fact that the school can lose control when another party makes a product bearing the university's name. To minimize problems, the Collegiate Licensing Company (CLC) was formed in 1981 to help schools protect and control the use of their logos through trademark licensing. CLC currently works with more than 200 colleges and universities, various bowl games, athletics conferences, the Heisman Trophy Trust, and the NCAA. CLC was purchased in 2007 by IMG Worldwide and operates as an affiliate of IMG College (Collegiate Licensing Company, 2014).

MARKETING AND ATMOSPHERICS

For students, alumni, and other fans, the atmosphere at a stadium or arena can offer an exciting escape from the worries of the day. In fact, game-day environments at various universities can be very interesting. For example, television cameras at Cameron Indoor Stadium in Durham, North Carolina, often capture Duke University students with painted faces, who are referred to by television announcers as the "Cameron Crazies." For many fans, the emotional appeal of being part of the game-day atmosphere is a motivational factor, and this motivation can be used as a tool through which collegiate sport marketers generate excitement.

Atmospheric management refers to intentional control and structure based on environmental cues, and it starts with an understanding of the target market (Schwarz et al., 2013). It is considered part of the promotional mix in sport, focusing in particular on the "place of purchase," and may include elements of the physical setting as well as sensory elements. Although a sport marketer has little if any control over the outcome of an athletic competition itself, he or she can influence the physical setting of athletics facilities.

Higher education institutions spent over US$11.5 billion on facilities upgrades and built 21 million square feet (almost two million square meters) of new facilities in 2015, and the largest and most expensive facilities are in the name of intercollegiate athletics (Huml, Pifer, Towle, & Rode, 2019). Both smaller and larger institutions are continuously revamping their facilities or building new stadiums, arenas, and practice facilities. For example, California University of Pennsylvania spent an estimated US$40 million on a new 142,000-square-foot (13,000-square-meter) convocation center, which it boasts is the largest indoor venue between Morgantown, West Virginia, and Pittsburgh, Pennsylvania. In 2017, Duke University, in Durham, North Carolina, completed a three-year US$140 million multiphase renovation of Wallace Stadium (Athletic Business, 2019). In November 2021, Vanderbilt University, in Nashville, Tennessee, announced the school would invest US$100 million along with another US$100 million from donor gifts to expand its basketball operations center and upgrade the north end zone of the football stadium, among other projects (Mojica, 2021). While many schools were cutting athletics programs during the COVID-19 pandemic, Colby College, a private liberal arts school in Maine, completed its new US$200 million Harold Alfond Athletics and Recreation Center in 2020 (Novy-Williams, 2021).

Such upgrades allow sport administrators to exercise greater control over the physical environment and further expand various sensory elements—components of the game-day atmosphere that appeal to spectators' five senses—sight, hearing, touch, taste, and smell. These components involve a wide range of factors, from the smells generated by concession stands, to seating for the band members who provide music at the event, to improved public address systems, along with numerous other amenities.

Sight

The core product on the court or field is the contest itself; therefore, much of what consumers watch is, of course, the athletes. Granted, most athletics programs at colleges and universities highlight the importance of academics and use the term "student-athlete" when referring to an athlete. The NCAA even runs a commercial noting that more than 400,000 student-athletes are "going pro in something other than sports." At the same time, athletics is a drawing card, and the athletics department at Ohio State University was one of the first to recognize the entertainment value of sport in its mission statement. Today, many intercollegiate sport events include some form of entertainment.

Universities recognize that athletes serve as entertainers on the court or field. With this entertainment function in mind, intercollegiate sport marketers also schedule various performers to entertain during intermissions, timeouts, and other breaks in the athletic action. Performers range from mascots to impersonators of superstars (e.g., Michael Jackson or Elvis) to local acts (e.g., school jump rope teams, jugglers, or animal performers).

Hearing

Auditory elements, such as the public address system and music, are key factors in providing

Cheer Squads

Promoting an exciting game-day atmosphere is an important marketing component. Cheer squads can significantly enhance excitement and atmosphere at a sport event. Various elements, such as marching bands, in-game promotions, and cheer squads quickly reveal to spectators how the game becomes an event. You may have been at a sporting event where the cheer team was not fully engaged with what was happening on the field or court but seemed more like a spectator. For some smaller schools that do not have the finances for giveaways or large videoboards, the cheer team may not be as engaged. However, perhaps you have seen cheer squads that are fully engaged with the game and are very engaged with the crowd. At Virginia Tech's Lane Stadium, in Blacksburg, Virginia, the crowd is highly engaged. You will often find the cheer team leading half of the crowd in screaming, "Let's go," and the other half screaming, "Hokies!" Some of the best-known performances by cheer squads happen at historically Black colleges and universities. For example, Virginia State University's iconic Woo Woo Cheerleading squad deploys its cheer and dance talent to the fullest extent for everyone's enjoyment and engagement with the game. Founded in the early 1970s by the inspirational Dr. Paulette Walker Johnson, the three core values of the Woo Woo have always remained as academics, athletics, and attitude (Hall, 2021).

Top Stadium Songs in College Sports

1. Virginia Tech Football: "Enter Sandman"
2. Ohio State Football: "Hang On Sloopy"
3. Wisconsin Football: "Jump Around"
4. West Virginia Football: "Take Me Home, Country Roads"
5. Florida Football: "I Won't Back Down" (DeCourcy, 2021)

spectators with information and adding entertainment value. The public address announcer serves as the master of ceremonies and keeps the audience informed about the latest happenings during the event. Music is also used by sport marketers to excite the crowd and set the scene, and computer technology now gives event personnel access to hundreds of songs.

In collegiate sport, of course, music is also played by marching bands and pep bands. Fight songs played by marching bands often appeal to the pride and emotion of university alumni. The alma mater is sung after football games at places like the University of Notre Dame and Ohio State University. Thus music can be used by collegiate sport marketers as a form of entertainment, but it also appeals to memories of days gone by and to the attachments of alumni and current students to their college or university.

Touch

Perhaps the most difficult of the five senses for sport marketers to appeal to is the sense of touch. At the University of Central Florida football games, it is not uncommon for the student section to pass a 900 square foot (about 84 square meters) "Welcome to the Knightmare" banner over their heads after each touchdown the Knights score. Unlike the athletes, spectators are normally passive during the athletic contest itself. However, sport marketers can engage spectators through the sense of touch by using creative in-game promotions. Examples include basketball shooting contests, kick for cash and prizes, and football throws, as well as songs played over the public address system that encourage coordinated clapping or stomping. This type of in-game promotion allows for hands-on involvement by spectators.

Taste and Smell

Taste and smell are widely used by marketers of intercollegiate sport. Of the five senses, smell is the most strongly connected to an individual's emotions, and therefore it is used to create lasting connections with fans. Key smells can include natural elements, such as newly cut grass in baseball or the smell of sweat in a gymnasium. The most notable smells, however, come from concession foods. For example, spectators attending a football game at Northwestern University may enjoy Wildcat Nachos or a breaded steak sandwich, while Sooner fans at the University of Oklahoma chew on a bone-in ribeye steak with caramelized cippolini onions, black pepper steak sauce, horseradish, grilled sweet peppers, and multigrain rolls (Sands, 2019). Many athletics departments outsource their concession operations to companies such as Aramark, Sodexo, and Levy Restaurants.

The sport industry is a service-related industry, and the experience that a fan undergoes at a sporting contest is intangible. In contrast, most consumer products (e.g., computers, automobiles, office products) are tangible in the sense that they can be touched. Despite the intangible nature of the sport product, however, atmospherics allow the sport consumer to have some tangible experiences in the process.

COMMUNITY RELATIONS

Athletics programs around the country understand the importance of community relations initiatives. Athletes in these programs are involved in initiatives such as reading to school groups, visiting hospitals, running youth league clinics, and coordinating canned food drives. The traditional idea of community relations is that an organization will "give back" and serve as a "good citizen" in its community. This notion derives from corporate public relations, which encompasses all non-sales-oriented public relations activities designed to reach target audiences (Irwin et al., 2008).

Larger athletics departments include at least one employee devoted to handling what is called

Industry Profile

SARAH RATCHFORD

Assistant Director of Athletics, Marketing, and Fan Experience, Fairfield University

How did you break into the sport industry?

My first full-time role in the sports industry was at the Eastern College Athletic Conference as a championships assistant. In that position I had an opportunity to work with students and administrators from Division I, II, and III institutions, which broadened my network and led me to my next opportunity, at Loyola Marymount University, where I received my master's degree and worked in the athletics department.

Describe your role at Fairfield and what a typical day looks like for you.

As the assistant director of athletics, marketing, and fan experience, my role is to lead marketing campaigns for the department that generate revenue and increase attendance and fan engagement. This includes ticket sales campaigns, sponsorship activations, and community outreach. What is most exciting about college athletics is that the day-to-day is never quite the same. However, on a weekly basis the beginning of the day is typically for planning for upcoming games and events as well as reviewing revenue and attendance goals that need to be met. Throughout the week I meet with student groups and campus partners as well as sponsors and community partners to further our reach in the campus and local community. That time is also used to implement our current marketing and advertising campaigns, with goals always in mind to generate revenue, increase engagement with our community and fans, and increase our brand recognition nationally. The highlight of the week or day is always game day, when you see the fans in the house cheering on our teams and I am actually executing our game presentation.

What has been your biggest professional accomplishment?

Being named the Fairfield University Student Association's Staff Member of the Year was one of my biggest accomplishments. Throughout the academic year, our team worked directly with the university's student association to cosponsor events and giveaways at home soccer, basketball, and lacrosse games. The ongoing partnership led to increased student engagement and boosted attendance. At the end of the academic year, the student association votes on the annual award, so it was nice to be acknowledged, but most importantly to know I impacted those students' experiences on campus through the course of the entire year.

Joe Adams

What has been the greatest challenge in your sport marketing career? How did you overcome it?

The greatest challenge in my career was the 2020-21 basketball season when no fans were permitted to attend games due to COVID-19 restrictions. Our marketing team was tasked with generating revenue and keeping our fan base engaged, but we were unable to sell any actual game tickets. Our team had to come up with creative alternative ways to generate revenue. We created a campaign to engage with our fans called the "Virtual Red Sea"—a play on the Fairfield student section [at games] being called the "Red Sea"—which included selling fan cutouts and having fans submit videos of themselves watching from home to play as our live audience during ESPN broadcasts. We sold out the entire section behind the team benches with fan cutouts to create a "packed house" environment for the student-athletes and filled seats on the broadcast. We broadcast the pregame shoot-arounds and included a link to the team's pregame playlist each day so fans felt like they were still a part of the game. For the final game that season, we sold tickets to a "virtual sellout" where fans received a commemorative ticket in the mail. Despite having few people in the building on game-days, we were able to keep our fans engaged on social media with this campaign. It was great to see them so excited about the cutouts of their families and pets showing up on the broadcasts as "fans of the game." We also were able to drive revenue to our department in a time most people were not.

What is one story you are continuing to watch in the world of sport today?

The conversation about mental health in both college and professional athletics. The demand on student-athletes becomes greater every year to fulfill their academic and athletic commitments while also attending a number of public events and participating in community service. Although mental health has been mentioned many times, the shortage in time and resources is still preventing some athletes from getting the attention they need. As more professional athletes publicly address mental health, I hope it will lead to an increase in resources and the understanding that athletes cannot always do it all on their own. It is encouraging to see more funds being allocated towards mental health initiatives and I look forward to seeing how athletics departments and organizations best support their athletes in the coming years and meet those needs.

As more sporting events continue to be broadcast on television or live-streamed, how do you attract fans to attend in-person games at Fairfield?

The key to getting fans in the venue is to build a personal connection with them. Finding out what our fans value and then incorporating that into our game presentation is our focus to drive attendance. On our campus I found students attend because they want to see their peers—whether it is the athletes competing in the game, their organization being recognized at the game for their accomplishments, or a giveaway they helped design. Families come because they want to see their children play a scrimmage at halftime or be recognized on the videoboard for their birthday. Some of our most successful events have been when we recognized other championship teams on campus or entire youth leagues in our community. Once we identify those interests and make the outreach, it is our job to maintain those relationships to keep them coming back by providing an engaging in-game experience.

The sport industry can be very competitive. What are three essential skills that someone needs to succeed in this industry?

Adaptability—learn to expect the unexpected and shift your plans accordingly. Creativity—the world of sports is constantly evolving, so it is essential to create new content and campaigns that appeal to what your fans want now. Organization—you will manage a lot of projects and sports simultaneously so organization is key.

What advice would you offer to people considering a career in college sport marketing?

If you are considering a career in college sport marketing, my advice is to gain as much experience as you can by attending sporting events at other institutions or professional organizations. Volunteer with other areas in your current organization or university to see what works, what you enjoy, and how you can apply those skills in your current or future roles. As you are searching for jobs, do not limit yourself to one institution or location.

community affairs or community outreach. For example, bilingual student-athletes at Ohio State University have helped promote literacy by reading to primary school students at the Columbus Spanish Immersion Academy. The celebrity of athletes provides sport organizations with advantages over other businesses in providing inspiration in areas such as education, health care, environmental concerns, and other social or cultural issues.

Intercollegiate athletics programs recognize the need to partner with the community to maintain a good relationship between "town and gown." For example, South Georgia State College, in Douglas, Georgia, seeks to build relationships, encourage participation, and solicit the support of local civic groups, local businesses, community leaders, and local citizens through community relations efforts ("Mission Statement," 2013). Athletes in all athletic programs at Pennsylvania College of Technology, an NCAA Division III institution in the United East Conference, participate in at least one event in their community ranging from to walkathons to support Alzheimer's disease awareness and bring attention to the problem of sexual assault, cleaning up the Susquehanna River Walk, and hosting a youth soccer clinic (Pennsylvania College of Technology Athletics, n.d.). The University of Miami (Florida) participates in various outreach projects with Boys and Girls Club, Best Buddies, and Holtz Children's Hospital, and some Miami athletes are pen pals with students at local elementary schools (NCAA, 2018). While these community outreach programs gained some publicity, it is worth pointing out that members of many collegiate athletic programs, especially in nonrevenue sports, volunteer regularly and receive little to no recognition.

Such programs highlight the fact that the college or university seeks to serve the local community. As athletics programs expand, institutions buy new land for building additional facilities, and local residents sometimes question the institution's motives. However, most institutions want to be perceived as contributing to the community. In a similar manner, the sponsor wants to give back to the local community and form partnerships with those affiliated with the institution.

Community relations differs from marketing in important ways. Marketing involves an organization's efforts to meet the needs and wants of its consumers, whereas community relations involves an obligation on the part of the organization to give back to the local community. Therefore, students interested in cause-related initiatives should consider a career in community relations. Many sport organizations have departments dedicated to public and community relations. In intercollegiate sport, the majority of athletics departments carry out this function through the marketing department. Responsibilities in a community relations position may include coordinating charitable donation programs, athletes' appearances, and pregame and on-field activities. Most job descriptions for community relations positions require someone with excellent communication, organizational, and interpersonal skills.

OUTSOURCING AND SECONDARY TICKET MARKET

Ticket sales make up an important part of the overall revenue for athletics departments. According to NCAA statistics in 2021, Division I athletics departments generated US$239 million in ticket sales, comprising roughly 1.8 percent of total revenues (National Collegiate Athletic Association, 2022). Traditionally, revenue sports (e.g., football, basketball, hockey) subsidize nonrevenue sports at most institutions.

Many colleges and universities have staff members handle internal ticket sales, but outsourcing is still a popular practice. Popp (2018) outlines many of the reasons why universities outsource ticket operations. Many colleges and universities are simply not set up to train and compensate ticketing professionals. Outsourcing these jobs means an institution can have the benefits of experienced staff and deal with a company that may be less bureaucratic than most institutions in higher education.

Though many fans get their tickets directly from the institution's athletics ticket office, athletics departments are increasingly becoming aware of the secondary ticket market. Individual athletics departments and their respective conferences, as well as the NCAA, have all recently started signing revenue-sharing deals with online secondary ticket companies such as StubHub (Cozart, 2010).

LEARFIELD Intercollegiate Fan Report

In August 2021, LEARFIELD launched a fan report that provides marketers with demographic and sociographic data from fans. The report provides intercollegiate athletics marketers with information concerning fan affluence, gender, mobility, and geography (Cision PR Newswire, 2021). Some of the interesting findings from the inaugural report suggest the following:

- At 182 million, college sport fans represent the largest group of sport fans in the United States.
- College sport fans are more likely to be in the 35- to 64-year-old age range than the general population in the United States.
- Of social media followers for college sport teams, 48 percent are female.
- Almost 50 percent of college sport fans have an income over US$100,000.
- College sport fans live in all 50 states, 210 designated market areas, and 93 percent of all counties.
- Up to 45 percent of persons purchasing college football tickets live within 30 miles of campus, compared with 64 percent of those purchasing college basketball tickets.
- College sport fans are engaged year-round.

Sport marketers find this report useful because it allows them to see how college sports audiences can be addressed at both the national and local levels.

Institutions such as Michigan State University, the University of Maryland, and the University of Pittsburgh work with StubHub to offer a place for fans to buy and sell tickets to their sporting events. In this way, athletics officials can refer ticketless fans to a website that helps ensure the legitimacy of the marketplace. The outsourced companies share their profit from resold tickets with the athletics department.

The secondary ticket market, also known as the resale market, exists between fans and brokers of event tickets after they have been purchased from the primary market (Burgess, 2012). The primary ticket market means tickets sold by a sport team, an outsourced ticket agency (e.g., Ticketmaster), or an artist. The secondary market includes the person-to-person resale market (e.g., buying from a friend); the scalper market, in which tickets are resold in the vicinity of the sport venue; and the secondary ticket websites (e.g., StubHub, TickPick, and SeatGeek) that provide access to ticket deals and sold-out tickets.

Although the traditional marketplace for intercollegiate athletics departments has been the primary market, more institutions are realizing the value of the secondary market. Burgess (2012) notes the following benefits of the secondary ticket market:

- Exhaustive inventory (tickets generally available for whatever event you want to attend)
- Aggregate prices that provide consumers with a comprehensive picture of what is available
- Detailed analytics and price forecasts, which ensure that the consumer gets the best deal
- Possibility of purchasing tickets below face value
- Transparent fees

In 2020, the global secondary ticket market was estimated to account for US$5240.1 million (Sharma, 2022) and leading websites included StubHub, Ticketmaster Entertainment, RazorGator, Ace Ticket Worldwide, Alliance Tickets, Coast to Coast Tickets, Tickets.com, Gotickets.com, Viagogo, Vivid Seats, TicketCity, TicketIQ, and eBay Tickets.

Secondary ticket websites are valuable to sport teams but have also been criticized. The secondary market does allow sport teams to offer additional value to season-ticket holders. For example, season-ticket holders at the University of Texas may find comfort in knowing that they can resell a ticket on StubHub if they are unable to attend a football game. Secondary ticket websites offer consumers the option of buying or selling tickets, but some have been criticized for underselling tickets and for allowing large brokers to purchase tickets in bulk, thus precluding individual consumers from buying them.

In college football, secondary ticket markets have affected supply and demand for Division I College Bowl games. In particular, low prices charged by secondary ticketing sites have reduced the number of tickets that athletics departments have been able to sell. This ticketing dilemma is described further in the case study sidebar.

DYNAMIC TICKET PRICING

The prices of season, miniplan, and single-game tickets for intercollegiate sporting events are typically set months before a team begins play. Preseason ticket sales for revenue sports are important to most athletics departments because they indicate expected attendance for the upcoming season. Ticket sales prior to the start of the season also help spur excitement about the upcoming season

Professional Development

National Association of Collegiate Marketing Administrators (NACMA)

As with many fields in the sport industry, sport marketing has its own professional development association. The National Association of Collegiate Marketing Administrators (NACMA) is home to more than 1,200 members and "provides the tools, training and network for collegiate sports marketers to successfully generate revenue, manage brands, and develop fans" (NACMA, n.d.). NACMA is an affiliate of the National Association of Collegiate Directors of Athletics (NACDA). Founded in 1965 and headquartered in Ohio, NACDA has more than 15,700 individual members: athletics directors, associate and assistant athletics directors, conference commissioners, and affiliated individuals or corporations from more than 1,700 institutions throughout the United States, Canada, and Mexico (NACDA, n.d.).

NACMA members share promotional ideas and marketing strategies. NACMA offers membership to students and to active employees working for an athletics department, on-campus property, corporation, or outsourced marketing agency (e.g., LEARFIELD). Benefits of a NACMA membership include the following:

- Members can register as mentees and mentors in NACMA's professional development mentoring program.
- Mentees have the opportunity to learn from veteran collegiate athletics administrators.
- Members can attend the annual convention at a discounted rate to learn about industry trends, participate in interactive breakout sessions, and network with peers.
- Members enjoy access to an online library of resources and best practices for marketing, ticketing, and promotions.
- Discounted membership pricing is available for students.

Intercollegiate administrators working in ticketing departments also have a professional development organization, called the National Association of Athletic Ticket Sales & Operations (NAATSO). The mission of this organization is to improve the overall understanding and effectiveness of selling, management, operations, pricing, and development while upholding the ideals of higher education. Likewise, those working in collegiate licensing can join the International Collegiate Licensing Association (ICLA). With a mission of promoting the collegiate licensing industry through education and development, the ICLA seeks to not only improve the understanding of the industry but to also develop licensing professionals and increase collaboration (International Collegiate Licensing Association, n.d.).

Mobile Ticketing at Notre Dame University

Although mobile ticketing has been gaining traction for years, the COVID-19 pandemic accelerated the number of organizations using these systems. Mobile ticketing means fans do not need to worry about losing a paper ticket. Instead, the mobile ticket is on the fan's smartphone, which helps to protect against ticket fraud and reduces the risk of stolen tickets. Another advantage is that fans can easily transfer the tickets to another user's digital wallet instead of having to physically hand them over in person to another user. The University of Notre Dame adopted mobile ticketing in fall 2021. Notre Dame Athletics (2021) officials highlighted the flexibility offered to their fans to manage their tickets anytime and anywhere.

and build momentum for additional sales during the season. For ticket holders, buying tickets prior to the start of the season offers the advantage of reduced prices.

In recent years, however, teams have begun to realize that ticket prices have not truly reflected fair market value and that additional revenue could be made. As a result, institutions have begun adopting the model of dynamic ticket pricing that has become increasingly popular in professional sport. At the forefront of this move in college sport have been such prominent institutions as the University of California, the University of Washington, and the University of South Florida. As perfected by the secondary ticket market, dynamic ticket pricing allows fan demand, or the lack thereof, to set the ticket prices for each sporting event. Specifically, dynamic pricing is defined as a "pricing strategy in which prices change either over time, across consumers, or across product/service bundles" (Kannan & Kopalle, 2001, p. 63). In the context of sport, ticket prices may change based on factors such as the day and time of the contest, the strength of the opponent, the weather, or overall demand for tickets.

The athletics department at the University of California (Cal) offers a good example of dynamic ticket pricing. Prior to the football season, athletics staff may deem their in-conference contest against the University of Oregon to be a premium game; in other words, they anticipate a sellout. As a result, the dynamic ticket pricing model allows ticket prices to increase as the game draws closer and ticket inventory decreases. In contrast, Cal staff might view the home game against FCS Eastern Washington as one that will not draw as well. As a result, the dynamic ticket pricing model lowers prices below face value to drive attendance. The Cal staff will not, however, drop the price below the season-ticket holder price per ticket (University of California, 2013). The Cal athletics department also uses dynamic pricing to encourage fans to purchase early or become season-ticket holders. At the same time, fans who do hold season tickets are not affected by the school's dynamic pricing structure; they are still guaranteed to pay the best possible price.

While dynamic ticket pricing started slowly in college athletics, it is now commonplace and schools use it adjust prices on an almost daily basis, based on market conditions. However, schools must be careful, because by definition, dynamic ticket prices fluctuate throughout the season, and fans may become upset or offended if they find out they paid more for a ticket than someone else sitting in the same section at the same game. To compensate, teams need to increase overall communication with fans and encourage preseason ticket sales. In addition, the process of moving to a dynamic ticketing solution can present challenges for an athletics department in the form of adopting new technology, training employees, and educating consumers about how ticketing will change.

Here are some suggestions for athletics administrators who are considering the transition to dynamic ticketing. First, consult with other institutions that have adopted dynamic ticketing and take into account the strengths and weaknesses of implementing such a system at your institution. Second, contact dynamic ticketing companies to learn more. Third, develop a plan and a timetable for launching dynamic ticketing. Once you have

Leadership Lesson

Meetings and Movies

One of the most common problems in athletics departments is that of "silos." Functional units accomplish the tasks they are charged to fulfill without realizing the synergistic potential of collaboration. Blaszka, Cianfrone, and Walsh (2018) noted that social media maximization is a continuous challenge in intercollegiate athletics. There are numerous teams, each with numerous student-athletes and numerous coaches and numerous support staffs. A conclusion of the study was that many teams utilizing X (formerly known as Twitter) are not capitalizing on its promotional potential. The sports information account managers provide information to fans, but they do not appear to interface with those who might hope to market the programs. This chapter merges two functions, ticketing and internal marketing, that many universities find problematic if there is a lack of communication. In this leadership lesson, we focus on meetings as a way to improve interdepartmental communication and combat "siloing."

In chapter 3 we presented best practices for traditional meetings. These are helpful and can be relevant in many organizations. If meetings drag, if passionate debate is lacking, or if participants leave the meeting feeling enervated rather than energized, it might be time to take a different approach. Business consultant Patrick Lencioni has compared bad meetings to movies. He finds it baffling that most executives seemingly would rather spend two hours "sitting in a movie"—an inherently passive experience—than sitting in a meeting that should be collaborative and directly relevant to our lives (2004). He has urged executives to learn from screenwriters. For a meeting to be captivating, there must be a hook, a conflict that is nurtured so participants are engaged from action to credits, and a clearly defined contextual structure.

- *The hook.* Meeting participants should be given a reason to care—a reason to believe that what transpires during the meeting is important to their lives. "The key to injecting drama into a meeting lies in setting up the plot from the outset. Participants need to be jolted a little during the first ten minutes of a meeting, so that they understand and appreciate what is at stake" (Lencioni, 2004, p. 228).
- *Nurtured conflict.* Meetings exist to share information, discuss alternatives, and ultimately make decisions and action plans. When intelligent and invested people come together to discuss relevant issues, it is important and natural for disagreement to arise. A meeting leader can prompt debate by expecting and encouraging conflict. In a moment of tension, for instance, a leader might interject, "Before you continue, and I definitely want you to continue, I just want to say that this is *exactly* the kind of thing I was talking about when I said we need to start engaging in more conflict" (Lencioni, 2004, p. 231). When conflict is not addressed—when team members are not encouraged or even allowed to defend their position and ideological passion—resentment can ensue and issues that could be resolved openly can fester and manifest themselves in interpersonal tension.
- *Defined contextual structure.* One of the problems with agenda-driven weekly or monthly staff meetings is they often create "meeting stew" wherein issues are discussed but not necessarily in order of importance; rather, attendees may jump from strategic issues to tactical issues and attempt to cover everything in between. To avoid the lack of productivity associated with meeting stew, Lencioni (2004) recommends four separate meetings:

1. *The daily check-in (or huddle).* The purpose of this meeting is for executive teams to report on their activities of the day, facilitate synergy, and avoid duplication of effort. This meeting is to last a maximum of five minutes, with all participants standing.
2. *The weekly (or biweekly) tactical.* The purpose of this meeting is to discuss issues of immediate concern. It should last 45-90 minutes, progressing as follows:

a. *The lightning round.* A quick reporting session in which each participant spends a maximum of 60 seconds reporting on two or three of their priorities for the week.

b. *Progress review.* No more than five minutes is spent discussing progress toward key organizational metrics.

c. *Real-time agenda.* Based on the issues raised in the lightning round and the progress review, this meeting's focus naturally evolves, but all participants must acknowledge that only issues of immediate concern are discussed (long-term, complex, or policy-related discussions require additional preparation and can take the wind out of many real-time discussions).

3. *The monthly strategic meeting.* This meeting is for wrestling with critical issues that determine the fundamental direction of the organization. The length of the meeting will vary depending on the number of topics considered, but at least two hours per topic should be allocated. Members should come prepared to discuss, defend, and challenge other perspectives about the issues.
4. *The quarterly off-site review.* This meeting steps away from regular issues and routines to review the organization from a holistic perspective. Topics should include comprehensive strategy, team, personnel, and competitive or industry reviews.

Meetings should be viewed as time-savers that can facilitate team-building and organizational synergy. The cohesive, proactive, passionate, and confrontational approach established in meetings will help to prevent office politics and foster productivity throughout the organization. To illustrate this, imagine the different outcomes of two athletics departments: In one, the sports information, marketing, ticketing, media, and development teams work together in constant communication. In another, the department heads meet, but very little cross-functional cooperation exists. In the first department, you can imagine the energy and creative approaches to improve fan involvement, and in the second department, you might find a sports information director generating a tremendous number of posts but communicating only one perspective in a broad organizational mission.

The final step to maximize meeting productivity has been labeled *cascading communication* (Lencioni, 2004). Teams should take a moment to identify key messages that need to be communicated. It can be helpful to review the progress made throughout the meeting, clarify any confusion among the executive staff, and emphasize the information that should (or should not yet) be communicated to the lower levels of the organizational hierarchy. When executive teams are on the same page, other staff within the organization will sense and reflect that unity.

developed a plan, the athletics department should begin to educate its consumer base about the benefits of dynamic ticketing. It should also start the process of training employees about these benefits and the technical aspects of using the dynamic ticketing software.

PROMOTION

Attending a sporting event provides a form of entertainment in exchange for an individual's time and money. Due to the large number of entertainment options available to potential consumers, sport marketers develop promotions to attract people to a game and provide entertainment throughout the event. With this context in mind, sport promotion is defined as "a fully integrated set of communication activities intended to persuade consumers toward a favorable belief or action as a tactical component of the overall marketing campaign" (Irwin et al., 2008, p. 3).

In-Game Promotion

Many institutions at every level of intercollegiate athletics implement some form of in-game promotional activity during sporting events. These promotions usually take place before play or during breaks in play—for example, in pregame and postgame time slots, at halftime, and during inning changes and timeouts. Some in-game promotions, such as tossing a T-shirt into the crowd when a baseball player hits a home run, extend for the entire season. Others, such as Boy Scout Day or a performance by a celebrity musical act, take place perhaps a few times a year. Another popular promotion in many arenas is the scoreboard "kiss cam," which pans the crowd looking for a couple who will provide a "smooch" (Steinberg, 2013).

Since in-game entertainment is designed to turn people into repeat buyers, most institutions include information about it on their athletics website and in collateral material. For example, George Mason University describes its in-game promotional activities, and the respective sponsors, on its athletics website (In-Game Promotions, 2012).

In addition to running in-game contests, 94 percent of college marketing directors hire local and national acts to perform at games, usually during halftime (Martin et al., 2011). The following list gives a small sample of popular acts that travel the country every year to perform at professional and intercollegiate sporting events.

- Extreme Team (dance team)
- ZOOperstars (inflatable entertainment)
- Red Panda (unicycle and ceramics balancing act)
- Tom Silver (hypnotist)
- AcroDunk (trampoline performers)

The process of formulating a strategic promotional schedule begins several months before a season begins to ensure that all details can be carefully developed and implemented. To begin brainstorming, marketing teams examine the previous year's promotions and decide which were popular enough to carry into a new season. Marketers can also research and observe peers' promotions and decide which would be enjoyable for their own fans. Once all promotions have been determined, marketers plug the information into the team's home schedule.

Some promotions, such as Girl Scout Day, are typically planned for a weekend game, when members of the target group are most likely to attend. Other promotions, such as ZOOperstars, might be scheduled for televised games or against nationally ranked opponents. Most national acts cost several thousand dollars per game, and sport marketers want to spend that money on premium games. In fact, these performances often increase attendance at the event. They can also generate additional revenue, because many athletics marketing departments solicit corporate sponsorship to cover the cost of booking such acts.

There has been some debate among both professional and collegiate marketers about which games should be given increased promotion. Due to budget constraints, most teams cannot mount maximum promotions for every game, and they are therefore faced with two options: focus on weekday games, which typically bring in lower attendance, or

In-Game Promotions at the University of South Carolina

- *Dollar Dog Day.* Fans can buy $1 hot dogs during the entire game.
- *Active Gamecocks Day.* Students between kindergarten and eighth grade who participate in a 2-week, 30-minute a day exercise regimen become eligible to receive two complimentary tickets to a future men's basketball game.
- *South Carolina Cheer Clinic.* Boys and girls between the ages of 5 and 14 are invited to participate in a cheer clinic, where they receive instruction from the University of South Carolina cheer team along with a photograph and photo opportunities, a clinic shirt, the opportunity to perform as pregame entertainment at a future men's basketball game, and a ticket to a future home game.
- *Legends Game.* Fans can welcome back former South Carolina basketball greats for a "Legends weekend," where there will be special halftime recognition of the players and staff and the players will wear their throwback uniforms.

on weekend games, when a larger crowd is expected. The idea behind using promotions for weekday games is to encourage fans to attend nonpremium games. Some marketers, however, would rather create the ultimate game-day experience when a nearly sold-out venue is anticipated. Fans at such games will have an enjoyable social experience and therefore will be motivated to attend more frequently. Either way, athletics marketers ultimately use promotion because of its potential to give them a return on their investment. Although a promotion adds to expenses, the cost is often outweighed by the additional revenues generated through corporate sales and the chance to incentivize new consumers and reach new markets.

To ensure the promotion runs smoothly, marketers of collegiate sporting events often use a timing sheet. A timing sheet simply provides the details of what is happening on the field or court during the course of the event. The timing chart can be distributed to everyone involved in running the event and it helps to ensure that everyone knows what they are doing and when. A sample is shown in the Sample Basketball Timing Sheet sidebar.

> *Fans are craving a return to normalcy [after a global pandemic] and the sense of pride and nostalgia they feel while cheering on their favorite teams in person. A key aspect of the fan experience is offering exclusive amenities and finding new ways to make the most of the game day experience.*
>
> Brian Cockerham, vice president, on location

Sales Promotion

Whereas in-game promotions provide entertainment value during a game, sales promotions provide incentives to stimulate sales and increase attendance. According to Irwin et al. (2008), sales promotion seeks to influence buyers' behavior and generally comes in the form of reduced prices, premium giveaways, contests, free samples, and other add-ons.

There are many useful giveaway items in sports. These include items like T-shirts, caps, fireworks, pocket schedules, lightbulbs, free general admission tickets for the next season, hand fans, insulated lunch bags, pot holders and oven mitts, calculators, rain slickers, basketball or baseball card sets, sweat rags, rally towels, key chains, jerseys, balls, pucks, toy footballs, reusable grocery bags, posters, "#1" foam fingers, bobbleheads and gnomes, stadium models or replicas, mini hockey sticks, water bottles, and drawstring bags. Of course, these items will vary based on the sport, budgets, geography, and local wants and needs.

The Indiana University Purdue University Indianapolis (IUPUI) athletics department offers a variety of giveaway items and ticket discounts to entice people to attend home basketball games. This list is a sampling of IUPUI's sales promotion offerings (Holdaway, 2022):

- Military Appreciation Day / Faculty and Staff Appreciation Day
- NCAA Readers Become Leaders Day
- Teacher Appreciation Night
- First Responders and Healthcare Appreciation Night
- Indianapolis Public Library Night
- Cram the Coliseum
- Non-Profit Day

Another form of sales promotion used to increase attendance is the student reward program, which has become increasingly popular in recent years. It is important to most institutions that students attend athletic events. Student attendance enhances the game-day atmosphere and contributes to the pride that students take in the institution. As a result, in many cases, the athletics department allocates a certain number of tickets for student use. When these tickets are not claimed by students, however, they are often returned to inventory and in some cases go unsold. One way of addressing this issue is through student reward programs.

At the University of Tennessee, students can participate in the Rowdy Rewards program. All current University of Tennessee undergraduate and graduate students who have paid their activity fees are eligible to participate in the Rowdy Rewards program. Rewards are allocated at designated events, typically once a month, and students can use the Rowdy Rewards app to find out when the rewards pick-up dates are scheduled. Rewards are based on points and the more students earn, the more they can win items like merchandise, autographed footballs, caps, and water bottles.

Sample Basketball Timing Sheet

James Madison University Basketball 2021-2022

Pregame/Halftime Format

James Madison University Dukes vs. University of Virginia Cavaliers

Tuesday, December 8, 2021, at 7:00 p.m.

Game Clock	EST	Activity
60:00	5:55 p.m.	Start countdown
55:00	6:00 p.m.	Court available for warm-up
30:00	6:25 p.m.	Teams leave floor
20:00	6:35 p.m.	Teams reenter arena
0:00	6:55 p.m.	National anthem by Brittany Young Recognition of Dawn Evans Team introductions UVA (starters and coaches) JMU (starters and coaches)
	7:00 p.m.	Tipoff

First Half

There will be official media timeouts after the 16-, 12-, 8-, and 4-minute marks, each with the duration of 105 seconds. Teams will each be entitled to four 30-second timeouts and one 60-second timeout for the game. Three 30-second timeouts may be carried over to the second half. Two 30-second timeouts may be called in succession but must be indicated by the coach or player when the timeout is called.

Halftime

15:00	Clear court
14:30	ZOOperstars!
6:00	Clear court and public address announcements
5:00	Floor available for warm-up

Second Half

To allow for radio and television to run commercial advertisements without missing the action on the court, media timeouts are built into every game. There will be official media timeouts following a dead ball after the 16-, 12-, 8-, and 4-minute marks in both halves. In addition, the first called 30-second team timeout in the second half will automatically become a full-length media timeout and will not replace the next scheduled media timeout.

Case Study

Declining Overall Attendance

One of the big challenges facing intercollegiate athletics marketers is declining overall attendance. Trends in football in particular are of concern. Dodd (2020) reports that NCAA statistics suggest that college football attendance hit a 24-year low in 2019, with FBS teams averaging 41,477 fans per game. Every Power Five conference except for the Big 12 had a decline in attendance in 2019. Dodd emphasizes that these declines are worrying because football ticket revenue is the second largest source of income for most athletics departments after media rights. At this time, not only did FBS schools experience declines in attendance, but FCS institutions also saw a 4.5 percent decline, with average attendance below 8,000 fans per game (Burton, 2019).

There are a number of reasons for the decline in attendance. One big factor is the cost of attending versus simply watching a game on television. As noted by Evans (2019), it can be stressful and expensive to drive to a game, fight with traffic, determine where to park on a college campus, walk to the stadium, and buy high-priced concessions. In comparison, fans can watch the game at a sports bar or from home in a comfy seat, not worry about waiting in line for the bathroom, and enjoy instant replay and high-definition television. And for students, there are numerous competing entertainment options plus a busy schedule.

Declining Attendance Dilemma

Another issue that intercollegiate athletic marketers must understand are differences in fan behavior and motivation between the levels of sport. For example, fan motivations for attending a Division I football game between Ohio State and Michigan is different than those motivations for fans attending a Division III game between Christopher Newport University and Kean University. Research by Mayer (2021) indicates that fan enjoyment for Division III fans has less to do wins and losses and more to do with the game-day atmosphere and social connections. Intercollegiate athletics marketers working at the Division III level should focus on how fans are connected to players, the team, and the school. Division III fans are more likely to be parents, classmates, or local supporters. For Division III athletics programs without large media rights deals, ticket revenues are particularly important. Another issue for Division I programs is how fans may feel when a Power Five team plays against Group of Five team. For example, will Alabama fans care enough to see their team play against a team like Akron University's?

Questions to Consider

1. What do you believe is the biggest reason why college students do not attend games?
2. What type of impact does not releasing kickoff times until a week before the game have on ticket sales and attendance? What about moving an on-campus home game to a neutral site location?
3. How might you promote an away game in close proximity to campus to students?

CONCLUSION

Intercollegiate athletics marketers can gain a competitive advantage by leveraging the newest technology to increase revenue from ticket sales and conduct promotional campaigns. Marketers now use various types of social media to connect with their fans. In addition, new and improved athletics facilities across the country continue to raise sport consumers' expectations. Sport marketers must be aware of these expectations and find ways to create a game-day atmosphere that meets them. Finally, intercollegiate athletics programs are increasingly looking for ways to connect with their community. Community relations programs should not only target the campus and community but also simply remember that people everywhere connect through sports.

DISCUSSION QUESTIONS

1. How do the primary and secondary ticket markets differ?
2. What main factors affect ticket pricing for colleges and universities that use dynamic ticket pricing?
3. Describe the differences between in-game promotion and sales promotion.
4. How can a sport marketer use atmospherics to appeal to a spectator's sense of hearing?
5. Describe some ways in which athletics programs advertise their products and services.
6. Why do intercollegiate athletics programs emphasize community relations initiatives?

LEARNING ACTIVITIES

1. *Secondary ticket market.* First, view the website of your favorite college or university and see if it offers an opportunity for season-ticket holders to sell unused tickets. Second, choose a large Division I team and compare the price of a ticket purchased on its website with the price on StubHub.com. Write a one-paragraph summary of your findings.
2. *In-game promotion.* Attend a local college or university athletic event and make a list of the in-game promotions during the event. Chart their purpose and when they occur (e.g., halftime, timeouts).
3. *Community relations.* Choose a social problem related to education, poverty, or the environment. Then develop a community relations program that addresses your chosen problem. Describe the program in detail.

Virginia Tech Athletics

Corporate Sponsorship

Robert H. Zullo, Slippery Rock University

In this chapter, you will explore

- various platforms that businesses can use to market themselves;
- different types of inventory available to businesses that become corporate partners;
- how the sales process operates, including some challenges specific to intercollegiate athletics; and
- how to assess sponsorship effectiveness, including strategies to offset ambush marketing efforts.

SUSTAINING SPONSORSHIP

After a highly successful basketball season that included capacity crowds and a postseason bid, the head coach announced his plan to depart your program for a higher-paying job. Students, fans, and alumni are concerned about the effect of his departure because the program had been underperforming for a long time prior to his arrival. In addition, sponsors are concerned that the loss of the head coach will result in less attendance at games and therefore less exposure. As an account executive responsible for securing sponsorships, how would you convince your sponsors to sustain or even increase their financial commitment to your school's sporting events during this time? How can you save this vital revenue stream?

Depending on the size and scope of an institution's athletics department, a sport marketing director may handle a tremendous variety of responsibilities. In larger institutions, the position generally entails promoting the athletics department's brand to loyal patrons in an effort to drive ticket sales. This work often involves crafting and implementing promotional efforts and creating exciting game-day experiences by organizing event progression and managing the music, cheer squad, videoboard, announcers, officials, and everything in between. At a smaller school, the sport marketing director may be the licensing liaison for organizations interested in using the school's athletics-related intellectual property, as well as the driving force behind community relations efforts and sponsorship sales. This chapter focuses on an important aspect of these responsibilities—the development of corporate partnerships.

The word *sponsor* can be used interchangeably in this context with *partner*, because businesses can support the athletics department either through financial support that increases revenue or through in-kind gifts that reduce expenses. Either way, this support is offered in return for the opportunity for the sponsor to be affiliated with the department's teams in hopes of garnering support from the organization's fans (Donavan et al., 2005). Viewing corporate sponsors as partners fits well with a relationship marketing mindset, which is built on the idea that sport patrons themselves are more than consumers and should be viewed as partners for the long run rather than as a mere source of immediate financial gratification (Capulsky & Wolf, 1990). Relationship marketing can enhance a school's competitive advantage over its peers through sustainable partnerships that outlast negative developments such as losses or poor off-the-field behavior (Morgan & Hunt, 1999). Corporate partnerships offer the sport marketing director the chance to forge a long-term relationship based on equal interactive and personal communication (Shani, 1997).

PLATFORMS

Businesses can promote themselves to prospective customers in many ways, such as direct mailing of coupons as well as advertising online, in newspapers, on radio and television, and posting billboards. The company can also promote itself or its products through the formation of a corporate sponsorship or partnership. Sponsorship is a two-way exchange between a sport organization and a corporate partner. The business pays a rights fee or offers in-kind remuneration for the opportunity to promote itself. Even a single business and a single sport organization can find a variety of avenues through which to engage in mutually beneficial exchanges. Indeed, using a variety of platforms can add complexity to the sponsorship process, and a large business has many options for forming corporate partnerships in college sport alone (Irwin et al., 2008).

PROPERTY

For sponsorship purposes, the athletics department is known as the *property or rights holder*, which means that it controls its property and determines how it can be used (Lynde, 2007). An athletics department's property typically extends to include its website, radio broadcasts of games,

Examples of College Sport Sponsorships

School. Virginia Lottery sponsors Virginia Tech athletics.

Team. Federal Taphouse sponsors Penn State University Wrestling.

Facility. Capital One sponsors the Capital One Arena, home of the Georgetown University Hoyas basketball team.

Conference. Food Lion is a sponsor of the Atlantic Coast Conference.

Governance level. Coca-Cola is a sponsor at the Corporate Champion level of the National Collegiate Athletic Association (NCAA Corporate Champions and Corporate Partners, 2022).

Coach. Eljo's (a local men's clothing store) sponsors University of Virginia head basketball coach Tony Bennett.

Media. Home Depot partners with ESPN's College GameDay.

Social Media. Athletics departments, teams, facilities, conferences/governing bodies, coaches, media, events, and student-athletes can utilize platforms such as X (formerly known as Twitter), Instagram, TikTok, and others to promote corporate partners.

Event. Jimmy V Week includes sponsors through the Jimmy V Foundation and through ESPN to raise funds that support cancer research in honor of the late iconic men's basketball coach Jim Valvano.

Student-Athletes. University of Iowa national champion wrestler Spencer Lee is sponsored by Ironside Apparel (Goodwin, 2021)

coaches' shows, and facility signage. Some schools secure sponsors through their in-house staff, but many Division I schools outsource their media rights management to companies that specialize in forming corporate partnerships, such as LEARFIELD (formerly Learfield/IMG College), JMI Sports, Playfly Sports, and Legends (Johnson, 2005; Maestas, 2020).

Whether this function is handled in-house or by an outside firm, the athletics department must identify its assets so that it can inform potential business partners about the inventory available to them for gaining exposure. Traditional inventory includes signage at athletics facilities (e.g., LED videoboards, scoreboards, ribbon boards, and permanent signage), videoboards, print options (e.g., media guides, ticket backs, and game programs), commercials during broadcasts of sporting events and during broadcasts of coaches' shows, website options (e.g., contests, rotating banners), game-day promotions, and premium giveaways that include recognition of the corporate partner (Johnson, 2005; Maestas, 2020). Football and basketball generate 70 percent of the value in multimedia rights deals as intellectual property and hospitality have increased as valuable inventory items for the companies. Schools earn an average gross revenue of US$6 million annually through the financial guarantees from the third-party firm (Maestas, 2020).

In addition to the traditional properties used by corporate sponsors to promote their messages and products, a growing number of nontraditional inventory items are also being offered, including the use of a school's athletics logo (which is the school's intellectual property), naming rights (discussed later in this chapter), experiential marketing opportunities, and access to hospitality opportunities (Smith, 2011b). Though a sign at an athletics facility may promote a corporate partner's message, experiential marketing is based on the growing belief that consumers want to use their senses to engage firsthand with a brand, product, or service (Experiential Marketing Forum, 2012).

For example, instead of a fitness facility promoting its massage service through a radio or television commercial, it might offer free massages to stressed fans at a home sporting event. At the conclusion of the massage, the company could offer a coupon designed to drive traffic to the fitness facility. Fans who join the facility could then receive a t-shirt bearing the athletics department's logo. (This arrangement is also an example of intellectual property use.)

Providing hospitality-related inventory for corporate sponsors can mean simply offering tickets and parking privileges to suites and club areas or providing access to a corporate village, to name only two examples. Schools have expanded the concept of access assets to include sideline passes, postseason trips, and the opportunity to travel with the team on charter planes. Access options can also include allowing corporate partners greater time with the athletes or head coaches of successful teams (Chelap, 2022).

A corporate village can enable businesses to offer food and beverages to invited guests in a relaxed environment before and after a game. To enhance the game-day experience of the corporate village, many hospitality areas are situated close to a football stadium, and they may host visits from the band, cheer squad, or mascot. Some schools even broadcast a live pregame radio show from the corporate village. These options give businesses access to premium assets that typical fans cannot enjoy.

Another nontraditional avenue of corporate partnership involves business-to-business exchanges (Lynde, 2007). The topic of business reciprocity is a big driving factor, especially for marquee-level partnership (Morales, 2022). For instance, Delta Airlines sponsors many schools and is the exclusive provider of charter flights for many athletic programs (Chelap, 2022). Another example of business-to-business exchange involves the upkeep of an athletic field, stadium, or arena. Because this typically requires the purchase of considerable quantities of maintenance products and equipment from a local home improvement store, the sales team for the athletics department might form a partnership with the store that gives the department lower prices if it pledges to make its purchases strictly from the sponsoring store (Smith, 2011a). The deal could include a performance-based renewal clause that depends on the athletics department to hit certain benchmarks in its purchases. For example, the corporate partnership deal could automatically renew annually at a certain level based on how much the department spends at the store. The corporate partner will be happy with this deal because of the guaranteed business; thus it will continue renewing its status as a partner of the athletics program (Morales, 2022).

COMPATIBILITY AND THE SALES PROCESS

Many businesses have a close affiliation with sport due to the relevance of their products to athletic endeavors (Lynde, 2007). Examples of such products are Gatorade and Powerade sports drinks, and Aquafina and Dasani bottled water. These, naturally, relate to sport because athletes need to hydrate frequently. Other good fits include apparel and equipment providers (e.g., Nike, Adidas, and UnderArmour), as well as regional health care

Professional Development

Industry Reads for Best Practices

In addition to joining the National Association of Collegiate Marketing Administrators (NACMA) referenced in the previous chapter, athletics administrators in intercollegiate athletics keep current by reading such industry publications as *Sports Business Journal*, Front Office Sports, Athletic Business, and AthleticDirectorU. These resources inform readers about current events, headlines, benchmarks, and research. *Sports Business Journal* offers an affordable student rate and both Front Office Sports and Athletic Business email headlines to the inboxes of students and administrators each day. AthleticDirectorU features articles, case studies, events, and additional resources for current and aspiring athletics administrators. Each of these platforms also features social media and podcast components.

providers (especially sports medicine providers).

Some sponsor relationships, on the other hand, may not be appropriate. Consider, for example, the possibility of a funeral home sponsoring an intercollegiate athletics department. In this case, the question of compatibility has to be raised. Does the business "fit" with the athletics department and its stakeholders? Are both the athletics department and the business pursuing the same target audience (Lynde, 2007)? The answer is clear. By contrast, a less obvious example of a good fit is Werner Ladder, designated as the official ladder sponsor of NCAA basketball tournaments, because the tradition of the championship team cutting down the nets atop a ladder offers the company great visibility for its products.

Brainstorming ideas for companies that might be a good fit can be done during the initial stages of prospecting. Prospecting is simply the first stage of sales, wherein the sales team identifies organizations that are potential sponsors (Fullerton, 2007). Prospecting can be done in many ways. Members of the sales team can review current and past sponsors. They can also look at competitors' sponsors. They can examine sponsors of other events in the area, ranging from concerts, festivals, and fairs to sporting events, including professional sports, high school athletics, golf tournaments, races, and more (Fullerton, 2007). Sales team members can also prospect by networking, such as with the local chamber of commerce.

In pursuing any of these strategies, the sales staff must consider compatibility in light of the fact that some schools place certain businesses off limits due to ethical concerns. Certain categories need to be handled carefully or may require prior approval from school administrators before approaching as they may not be considered appropriate sponsors for the school and its many stakeholders. Examples of this include lottery, gambling, and sports betting (including casinos); cannabis, alcohol, and tobacco; pharmaceutical companies; guns; and sensitive or politically charged topics such as religion, abortion, or sexuality. If the school is hesitant to consider sponsors from these categories, the limitations or restrictions could extend to the student-athletes trying to maximize on their name, image and likeness (Chelap, 2022; Thomas, 2021). The staff should also remember that the more compatible a business is with the athletics department, the easier it will be to secure a potential sponsorship with that business. As a result, it is critical for the sales team to thoroughly research potential sponsors (Chelap, 2012).

Potential sponsors can be grouped into categories, and exclusivity can be given to those who are willing to pay more to ensure that their competitors will not be affiliated with the athletics department (Fullerton, 2007). For example, PepsiCo may be the exclusive "pouring rights" provider for an athletics department, thereby preventing Coca-Cola from sponsoring that department's athletic events. Such categories can be either narrow or broad (Fullerton, 2007). Defining categories narrowly could mean, for example, putting McDonald's in the category of fast food, Subway in the category of sandwich

Determining Whether a Sponsorship F-I-T-S an Athletics Department

F—focus area. Where is the company located, and who does it want to affect? What advertising options in the area can help it create that effect?

I—intangibles. Is there a similarity of values and beliefs between the athletics department and the business? Is the product a natural for college sport? Are the sponsorship rates for this property affordable as compared with other options in sport? Are both the athletics department and the business interested in a comparable charitable tie-in?

T—target audience. Who is the business trying to reach, and who are the stakeholders of the athletics department (fans, students, alumni, etc.)?

S—seasonality. For example, do athletics events present the opportunity to promote gym memberships to the masses when people are making New Year's resolutions to lose weight? Are the athletics department and the potential sponsor interested in a holiday-themed tie-in?

Adapted from Lynde (2007).

shops, Pizza Hut in the category of sit-down pizza restaurants, Papa John's in the category of pizza delivery, and DiGiorno Pizza in the category of pizza available in the grocery store. Chipotle and Panera Bread would be examples of fast casual restaurants, versus traditional fast food establishments like McDonald's (Chelap, 2022). Defining a category broadly, on the other hand, could involve creating a single category for insurance, rather than breaking it down into life insurance, car insurance, health insurance, and other forms of insurance.

It can be tempting to create narrow categories in an effort to secure a high volume of corporate partners, but doing so also runs the risk of generating sponsorship clutter (Irwin et al., 2008). In this context, "clutter" refers to the process of inundating consumers with advertising messages, thereby rendering the messages ineffective. This mistake can lead corporate partners to spend their advertising dollars elsewhere instead of with your athletics department.

On the other hand, creating a category that is too broad in an effort to offer fewer sponsors more exposure runs the risk of losing potential sponsors and therefore leaving potential revenue untapped. A cost-benefit analysis can help the athletics department and the sales team decide which approach to take.

Prospecting is a continuous process, but the sales progression begins with the development of rate cards that include a description of the event, who attends it, available inventory, key benefits available to sponsors, and contact information for the salesperson (Irwin et al., 2008). Rate cards can also include current sponsors' testimonials or evaluative metrics demonstrating success in order to promote the effectiveness of corporate partnerships. After preparing its rate cards, the sales team begins to

Name, Image, and Likeness (NIL)

July 1, 2021, was the beginning of the opportunity for student-athletes at all levels to benefit from their name, image, and likeness (NIL). This opportunity is not merely for the star players of College Football Playoff teams within the Football Bowl Subdivision; many student-athletes of Division I Olympic sports or those who compete in Division II or Division III strategically utilize their social media platforms. In 2021, Swaylytics indicated that Shareef O'Neal, then a basketball player at Louisiana State University (LSU), had over 2.7 million followers on Instagram. Behind O'Neal was another LSU athlete, Olivia Dunne, a member of the gymnastics team, with 1.1 million Instagram followers (Swaylytics, 2021). Dunne, who also reportedly has more than 5.6 million followers on TikTok, has earned over US$1 million through NIL (Fleming, 2022). Student-athletes can now receive money and in-kind opportunities from numerous sponsorship categories, among them restaurants, automobiles, even a hair salon near their college campus. They can also benefit if their likeness is used with opportunities like summer camps and modeling, an opportunity that was previously not afforded. Craig Brommer, chief marketing officer of the American Eagle clothing company, said of NIL, "We're still learning as we go, but a few of these kids have really cut through in a big way and it moves the needle of social engagement" (Fleming, 2022). Through public appearances and social media platforms, student-athletes are now able to capitalize and monetize in a way that many of their coaches had been for years.

Name, image, and likeness does present challenges for both student-athletes and athletics departments. Student-athletes need to balance team obligations and academics. The addition of public appearances, negotiations and signing contracts, social media maintenance, and being a brand ambassador consumes even more of a student-athlete's time (Thomas, 2021). Businesses are not accepting of typos on X (formerly known as Twitter) or a sponsored student-athlete pictured utilizing a competitor brand, mistakes that a professional player's agent might prevent. Student-athletes are in the process of becoming adults in college and NIL development adds responsibility. For athletics departments, NIL presents certain concerns, as when high school or transfer recruits are bribed to attend a school. Athletics departments must also balance assisting their student-athletes with NIL issues while not affecting the sponsorship revenue of the greater athletics department (Thomas, 2021).

build relationships with businesses by setting up meetings to discuss the value of a corporate sponsorship (O'Brien, 2012).

Many businesses designate a gatekeeper to slow down or stop a sales team. As a result, the sales process requires persistence and determination. Research can also be helpful by yielding insight into the best time to approach the business, the individuals who make the key decisions, the business's current marketing strategies and advertising outlets, and any other information that helps open the doors (Irwin et al., 2008).

Many people in sales invite decision-makers from a potential business partner to a game in order to whet their appetite and demonstrate what options are available to the business as a corporate partner (O'Brien, 2012). Other sales strategies include the simple use of visual images or video recordings to bring the inventory directly to a potential corporate partners in their own offices. Though some sponsorships may be secured on the first sales visit, most require both an introductory meeting and follow-up meetings, in which the sales team presents detailed and personalized sponsorship options to effectively meet the needs and goals of the business (O'Brien, 2012). These options are frequently tiered, thereby enabling the salesperson to come in with a customized sponsorship package at one price but also showcase another, more attractive option in hopes that the business is willing to spend more. Many sales team members earn a commission on their sales, which means that upselling, or getting the business to spend a little more, increases both the corporate partner's exposure and the salesperson's pay.

After the proposals have clearly been laid out and defined, the sales team should make an offer to the business and close the deal, thereby securing the partnership. A contract detailing the specifics of the partnership is a requirement because contracts eliminate ambiguity about matters such as when payment is due or who covers which costs.

A corporate partner pays a rights fee for the opportunity to promote its business, brand, product, or service. But if the sponsor wants to leverage its sponsorship further, it should be willing to spend money on sponsorship activation, which means bringing the sponsorship to life—creating an active form of sponsorship (Chelap, 2012). An example of this would be Home Depot sponsoring the College GameDay on ESPN, which includes a three-hour pre-game show during football season but is strategically hosted on a college campus each week and welcomes fans and students to the festive site that features live music, cheerleaders, and giveaways. Passive forms of sponsorship include, for example, hanging a banner or creating signage. For a business wanting to hang a banner at a soccer game, it could be noted in the contract that the business will incur the cost of producing the banner.

Sponsors may also seek more aggressive sponsorships that require more complexity and work. If, for instance, a sponsor wants to provide a premium giveaway at a sporting event, it would incur the cost of producing the giveaway item. Assistance would also be needed in distributing the giveaway. If the sponsor wants to provide a booth where fans can sample the product or engage in experiential marketing, the sponsor would pay that activation cost (Chelap, 2012). Costs may also be incurred through hospitality expenses. A contractual activation fund can also assist by helping with such expenses as merchandise, food, and coach appearances (Chelap, 2022). The process of "eduselling," or carefully walking corporate partners through every step of the partnership process, makes sponsors aware that for every dollar they spend on the right to promote themselves, they should be prepared to spend at least another dollar in activation, thus increasing the potential for measurable success (Irwin et al., 2008).

Businesses value the return on investment and return on objectives, but many partnerships do not have a direct revenue that can be attributed to the relationship (Morales, 2022). While metrics and analytics exist, many larger brands, such as an AT&T or Coca-Cola, engage in "passion projects" where there is less concern with maximum exposure to a particular audience and more focus on alignments with how people feel about the brand and its connection to an artist, a cause, or a movement. This might include the use of niche platforms to facilitate the advancement of women's athletics, the fight for social equality, and similar projects that are less about traditional marketing and exposure and more about feeling (Morales, 2022).

In closing a deal, therefore, salespeople should not focus only on earning their commission but

Red Flag in Sales

Head coaches frequently have their own relationships with area businesses as part of the team's operations or summer camps. Although this practice is acceptable, the sport marketing department should establish a clear written policy about the process for soliciting money or in-kind support from businesses. In the absence of such a policy, a coach may ask a restaurant or hotel for its support at a time when a member of the sales team is also approaching the business with a larger sponsorship proposal (Hoch, 2009). This lack of coordination is frequently referred to as nickel-and-diming a business, and it gives the impression that the athletics department is not communicating effectively (O'Brien, 2012). It may also reduce the financial magnitude of a potential partnership if the business is already spending money directly through a coach without the sport marketing director's knowledge or consent.

should use eduselling to help their corporate partners see how best to use the partnership to the full advantage of both the business and the athletics department (Irwin et al., 2008). Salespeople should also be willing to blend in smaller, low-cost inventory items, such as public address announcements and program advertising, to add value to the partnership. Corporate sponsors can then truly view themselves as partners in supporting the athletics department.

> *If you make a sale, you make a commission. If you make a friend, you make a fortune.*
>
> Jeffrey Gitomer, *The Little Red Book of Selling*

MEASUREMENT AND AMBUSH MARKETING

Sponsorships may go unrenewed for many reasons, including a poor return on investment, a decision to go in a different corporate direction, budget cutbacks, poor execution by an event organizer, increased sponsorship costs, or conflict with an organizer (Copeland et al., 1996). One additional reason is simple inability of a salesperson to prove quality aftermarketing efforts. After the contract is signed and the sponsorship is activated, sales team members are encouraged to continuously communicate with their business partners to ensure their happiness (Titlebaum & Watson, 2001). A happy corporate partner can yield renewals.

Because businesses have many options for their advertising dollars, sales staff must provide both tangible and intangible measurements of corporate partnership success with the athletics department. After an initial visit with a potential corporate partner, a salesperson develops ideas to best promote the business in a manner consistent with the inventory that the business wants to use. Both the inventory items and the ideas for using them should be in line with what the corporate partner is looking to spend. In delivering the idea, it is not enough for it to be tailored; it should also be measurable, so that it can evaluated in the end (Irwin et al., 2008).

Thus, in activating a sponsorship, the sales team needs to be prepared to provide evidence of fulfillment of the sponsorship. Did the sponsorship accomplish what it was intended to accomplish? If so, how? If not, why not? Examples of intangible measures include photo or video evidence of a partnership generating pride among participants competing in a halftime event or of students wearing premium giveaway T-shirts in the student section at a game. Such evidence illustrates that sponsors are reaching their target audience.

Quantitative measurements might include the attendance total at a sporting event, the number of people who purchased a game program and therefore might see the partner's ad, or the duration of air time or the number of impressions that a sign at an athletics facility yields during the course of a sporting event or season based on analysis of actual attendance and televised viewership numbers. In fact, though these are all quantifiable measurements, today's sales teams strive to generate even greater detail in their sponsorship measurements (O'Brien, 2012). Examples include the number of visitors to fan fests, as well as their demographics; the number of new email addresses generated through a contest; and the number of coupons passed out at an event to drive traffic to the business partner.

Sponsors seek differentiation because they want their brand, their business, their product, and their services to be remembered by the patrons supporting the athletics department. Spending time on content development prior to activation helps to strengthen the assessment process (Morales, 2022). Although some corporate partners may prefer simple signage at the stadium or an ad placed in a game program, even these basic inventory options present the opportunity for differentiation. An ad in a game program can be turned into a coupon for fans to use, thereby making it more measurable. A videoboard commercial can be turned into a trivia contest in which fans text answers, thereby actively engaging the audience while garnering a database of phone numbers.

> *Simply knowing a sponsor has been on board for a number of years does not ensure the company's continued support.*
>
> Titlebaum & Watson, 2001

Businesses today have more advertising options than ever before for developing high-quality, effective, and measurable returns on their investment, which of course heightens the likelihood of renewal. Creativity in activation design helps sponsors stand out as more traditional kinds of inventory grow outdated (Bynum, 2006). Today's sponsors are no longer impressed with a thank-you letter from a head coach. Instead, business decision-makers need to demonstrate to their superiors that corporate sponsorship with athletics helps their bottom line (Chelap, 2012). In this environment, a banner recognizing the sponsor is less attractive than a creative opportunity such as a contest that puts a lucky fan on the field for the coin toss of a football game while also producing a database of names and contact information (generated through contest entries) and therefore yields a greater return on investment for the corporate partner. Emerging media, especially social media, requires that the content must not resemble advertising but still reach the desired audience because high-quality content drives dollars spent in rights fees (Morales, 2022).

Similarly, though college sport fans are passionate about their schools, simple affiliation is no longer enough for corporate partners to justify expenditures. However, continual assessment of sponsorship effectiveness helps renew sponsors' trust (O'Brien, 2012). Innovation and creativity in the differentiation process can also yield a larger rights fee for the sales team.

Throughout the entire sales process, attention must be given to the possibility of *ambush marketing*, in which a business tries to profit from the assets of an athletics department without paying a rights fee. This practice might take the form of a business passing out coupons or samples of its product in a parking lot where fans are tailgating or arriving for an event. It might also be implemented as fans exit an athletics facility after a sporting event.

To minimize ambush marketing, the sport marketing department must communicate to the entire athletics department the identity of the department's official corporate partners (Norcross, 2011). In this way, all members of the department will act as an enforcement team because they all realize the value of a corporate partner to the financial well-being of the athletics program (Irwin et al., 2008). Education enables each member of the marketing department to help protect corporate partners who have paid for the right to associate with the athletics program and its events.

FACILITY NAMING RIGHTS AND FAIR MARKET VALUE

Athletics departments may also use corporate sponsors to help with the cost of facility development or renovation through the purchase of corporate naming rights (Muret, 2011). Whether the naming right involves an entire facility or sections of it (e.g., parking lot, premium seating level, food court), this type of sponsorship offers corporate partners

Technology Tools

SponsorUnited, SponsorPitch, and LinkedIn

SponsorUnited is a "global sports and entertainment intelligence platform" (SponsorUnited.com, n.d.) that gathers data from the National Basketball Association, European football (soccer), National Football League, auto racing, and Major League Baseball, among others. To help facilitate benchmarking and best practices, particularly in revenue generation, the company explores venues, teams, events, and more, focusing on brand partnerships. A subscription-based service, SponsorUnited provides in-depth reports for athletics administrators while also providing current events and news for casual readers. This might include updates on NIL deals, brand reports from the Men's Final Four or College Football Championship, the expansion of categories, and progress on women's endorsement deals. Schools can utilize this platform to enhance creativity in their own sponsorship activation, borrowing from their peers. It can also provide innovative sponsorship inventory ideas and details on contracts, so that schools or their third-party marketing firms know their worth during negotiations. Knowing the fair market value of sponsorship deals helps schools to maximize revenue.

A similar company, SponsorPitch offers a sponsorship database to help those in the industry augment their marketing partnerships. Finally, LinkedIn is another great resource for students, since marketing firms like IMG, Octagon, GMR, Momentum, Genesco, CAA, and Wasserman often share innovations and news about their sponsorship deals on their respective pages (Morales, 2022). This path is an affordable option for those schools that might not otherwise be willing to pay for the services of a SponsorUnited or SponsorPitch.

Adapted from SponsorUnited, accessed October 12, 2022, www.sponsorunited.com.

broader exposure, particularly at multipurpose facilities that also host events such as concerts, stage shows, speakers, and meetings. Naming rights can also broaden exposure for corporate partners through media coverage when the affiliated team plays on regional or national television. In determining a rights fee, the school should conduct sound market research to identify the *fair market value*. This research might include communicating with other schools in the conference or the region about comparable partnerships, exchanging information at conferences and professional meetings, and reading industry publications, such as *Sports Business Journal*.

As with other forms of sponsorship, the sales team must be able to measure the return on investment for naming rights. To do so, 21 Marketing, a firm that specializes in maximizing sponsorship activation, cites the following 11 key metrics (Do Naming-Rights Deals Pay Off?, 2011):

1. National and international TV exposure
2. Exterior exposure (e.g., a facility located next to an interstate highway that results in exposure for anyone passing by)
3. On-site exposure for attendees
4. Ad campaigns
5. Local TV and radio broadcasts
6. Editorial coverage
7. Team publications
8. Collateral material
9. Direct mail, Internet, community, and partner promotions
10. Image association in ad campaigns
11. Hospitality

Though effective in revenue generation, corporate naming rights may not be an option on every campus, because some schools use a traditional naming-rights approach to honor individual donors or sizable contributors to the school itself. Affiliating with a corporate entity can also prompt greater public examination and even complaints about the corporate partner. This risk played out in recent years in the form of critics scrutinizing corporate naming-rights deals involving the banking industry at a time when the U.S. government was bailing out many of those businesses (Steinbach, 2009).

OUTSOURCING AND UBIT TAXES

Some schools use their in-house sport marketing staff to secure sponsorships. As mentioned earlier, however, there is a growing trend at the Division I level to outsource the sales effort. Outsourced marketing firms traditionally work with Division I schools because their larger fan base enables the firm to generate greater revenue and thus a profit for the parent company.

The benefits of partnering with an outsourced marketing firm include expertise specific to sales and revenue generation (Johnson, 2005). This know-how enables the in-house sport marketing staff to focus on promoting ticket sales and creating or boosting the in-game atmosphere (McKindra, 2005). The outsourced firm can also provide financial support in purchasing new equipment, such as scoreboards, that the school might not otherwise be able to afford on its own.

Generally, the outsourced firm represents several schools; therefore, when its account executives represent the firm in talks with a potential sponsor, they can highlight the increased exposure that the sponsor would receive. For example, if an account executive talks with a rental car company about a sponsorship that would affect all schools represented by their company, the executive might stress that the rental agency's services could be targeted to fans at schools in a certain part of the country. The downside of outsourcing the rights is that the school relinquishes the control that comes with keeping the sales effort in-house (Robinson, 2004). The school must also split the sponsorship revenue with the outsourced firm.

Outsourced marketing firms, frequently known as third-party marketing firms, typically pay a school in one of three ways. The firm may pay a

Industry Profile

DAN JANKOSKI

Vice President, Collegiate Partnerships, Legends

Dan Jankoski is the vice president of the collegiate division for Legends, a multimedia rights holder. Legends is well known in professional sports, and is extending its reach into intercollegiate athletics. A graduate of James Madison University, Jankoski started his career as an intern for Nelligan Sports Marketing and IMG before working for the New York Red Bulls as an inside sales representative and an account executive. Next, he joined the Jacksonville Jaguars as an account manager. He then transitioned into intercollegiate athletics, working at the University of Notre Dame as a premium sales and inside sales manager. He was then general manager at Villanova University and the University of Wisconsin before becoming senior director and then vice president of collegiate partnerships. Jankoski assists collegiate sports organizations with developing and executing strategic plans to drive incremental capital, corporate hospitality, and ticket sales revenue (Jankoski, 2022).

Leadership Lesson

Seek First to Understand, Then to Be Understood

As we prospect for and seek to confirm corporate partners, it is tempting to create a one-size-fits-all approach. Indeed, it certainly might save printing costs or pitch preparation time if each presentation were identical! The problem with this approach is that each corporate partner is different; as a result, prefabricated package deals are unlikely to maximize the potential benefits that can be achieved through a personalized partnership.

Even after you research a company and feel that you will be able to convince it to sign on, think again—dig a little deeper. Until you understand the organization's unique needs and goals, you will not be able to form an optimal partnership. "The amateur . . . sells products; the professional sells solutions to needs and problems" (Covey, 2004, p. 244). In order to find those solutions, you must first take the time to listen—to really understand the other party's goals. Once you understand those needs, it is much easier to craft a synergistic partnership.

The single biggest problem in communication is the illusion that it has taken place.

George Bernard Shaw

The most important thing in communication is to hear what isn't being said.

Peter F. Drucker

We have two ears and one mouth so that we can listen twice as much as we speak.

Epictetus

This principle is as true and important in day-to-day interactions as it is in corporate sponsorship meetings. Communication experts estimate that only 10 percent of our communication is derived from the words that are spoken. The rest happens through body language (60 percent) and sounds and intonation (30 percent) (Covey, 2004).

Given the critical nature of communication in organizational and personal life, it is troubling that this skill is often taken for granted. Though most of us have the physical ability to hear, very few have taken the time to develop the transformative skill of listening. When you demonstrate a true desire to learn from and understand people, you are able to communicate on a new level, and through this process make them feel valued. As Henry David Thoreau said, "The greatest compliment that was ever paid me was when one asked me what I thought, and attended to my answer" (qtd. in Rosenblum, 2000, p. 103).

To illustrate the point, Stephen Covey uses the example of going to the optometrist. After listening to you briefly, the optometrist hands you her glasses and says, "Put these on. I've worn this pair of glasses for 10 years now and they've really helped me. I have an extra pair at home; you can wear these" (2004, p. 236). Once you put the glasses on, you can see even less—everything is a blur—because, of course, the glasses don't correct *your* vision impairments. They might work well for the doctor, but not for you.

As in this illustration, when we listen to others, we often prescribe before we diagnose. We judge before we truly understand. We see another's issues through our own paradigm rather than seeking first to understand the other person's paradigm. It is a lot easier to hand someone a pair of glasses than to make time to understand their unique viewpoint. In conversation, most people listen with the intent of replying rather than the intent of understanding. We do this because we hope that others will understand us; however, when little true listening takes place between parties, very little communication or understanding occurs.

So what can we do? Seek first to understand, then to be understood. A good place to start is to practice active listening, in which you strive to understand the complete message being sent by the other person. Once this is mastered, Covey recommends empathic listening, in which you strive to occupy another person's frame of reference and see through their lens. Both of these skills start with actively choosing to give the speaker your undivided attention. Look at the speaker directly, consider their body language, block out distracting thoughts and noises, and avoid forming a response until the speaker has finished their thought and your understanding is complete.

Empathic listening involves four developmental stages.

1. Mimic the content to demonstrate that you heard what the other person said. This is the least effective technique but the easiest.
2. Rephrase the content to ensure you have correctly understood the speaker. Sometimes clarifying questions might be needed before you are able to rephrase the content, but avoid the pitfall of asking too many questions and creating the feeling that you are "grilling" the speaker.
3. Reflect the feeling you observe. There is always emotion behind words, and understanding this emotion will help you understand the content more fully.
4. Rephrase the content and reflect the feeling. Once you have mastered steps 2 and 3 in a situation, you can reflect true understanding by interlacing both the core content and the feeling of the person with whom you're communicating. (Covey, 2004)

To solidify your gains, use the following ground rules for listening as you strive to develop this critical skill.

- Don't interrupt.
- Don't change the subject or move in a new direction.
- Don't rehearse in your own head.
- Don't interrogate.
- Don't teach.
- Don't give advice.
- Don't discount the speaker's feelings by using stock phrases such as "it's not that bad" or "you'll feel better tomorrow."
- *Do* reflect back to the speaker what you understand and how you think the speaker feels. (Burley-Allen, 1982; Salem, 2003)

Covey (2004, p. 253) says, "As you learn to listen deeply to other people, you will discover tremendous differences in perception. You will also begin to appreciate the impact that these differences can have as people try to work together in interdependent situations. Referring back to figure 1.4, you see the young woman; I see the old lady. And both of us can be right." Whether you are striving to close a multiyear, multimillion-dollar partnership agreement or resolve a disagreement with a coworker, seeking first to understand, and only then to be understood, will release illuminating dialogue that can turn a difficult situation into a tremendous opportunity for relationship development.

guaranteed fee to the school, the two parties may share the revenue generated, or the school and the firm may create a payment option that combines both the guaranteed fee and a revenue-sharing element beyond an established threshold (Smith, 2011b). A larger Division I school debating whether to keep its sales effort in-house or outsource it would typically send out a request for proposal, inviting firms to bid on the opportunity to work with the athletics department.

If the athletics department chooses to use an outsourced firm, the firm then sells sponsorships as an extension of the department (McCarthy, 2006). This is a risk-for-reward proposition, because the firm needs to meet its financial obligations to its schools. In trying to meet its quota, an outsourced marketing firm sells aggressively, thereby requiring the school to be in continuous communication with the firm in order to maintain a sense of control (McKindra, 2005). In addition, because school presidents, fans, and alumni frequently disapprove of excessive commercialization at sporting events in higher education, it is important to clearly establish a win-win approach in the request-for-proposal (RFP) stage of the process. (Refer to chapters 6 and 7 for more about the win-win paradigm.)

Case Study

Division III and the Town and Gown Sponsors

In Division III intercollegiate athletics, the NCAA's largest division of college sports, athletics can assist as an enrollment tool for many schools (Segura & Willner, 2019; Weatherall, 2006; Willner, 2019). Athletic intensity and fierce competition are still present for the coaches and student-athletes despite the absence of athletic scholarships and significant television coverage. Teams compete regionally, before smaller crowds, and in some departments, coaches also serve in administrative roles (Barr, 2018).

Coaches working in a dual capacity can find it challenging to maximize the event experience and increase corporate sponsorship revenue because of obligations to recruiting, coaching, and retention. Division III athletics departments face fiscal challenges and limited ticket and licensing revenue (Sparvero & Warner, 2013). Yet ignoring the lucrative sponsorship revenue stream hinders the athletic budget. Division III athletics administrators, continuously pursuing creative revenue streams, must realize that schools and athletics departments can benefit from a "town and gown" relationship with community businesses like hotels, restaurants, and coffee shops that benefit from the presence of students, family, alumni, faculty, staff, and fans (Katz & Clopton, 2014).

This case study challenges you, the aspiring athletics administrator, to think critically about how to do more with less at the Division III level, for the greater good of the entire athletics department.

Questions to Consider

1. How would you develop a corporate sponsorship program that balances the staff's coaching with their pursuit of businesses to become sponsors? Should every staff member be able to pursue sponsors? Why or why not?
2. Explain how you would ensure that communication is prioritized among coaches and staff, as well as other fundraising entities on campus, that are prospecting potential sponsors, in order to avoid overlap or undervalued sponsorships.
3. What are your potential inventory options and what strategies would you take to ensure fair market value with your inventory items? What inventory items exist on campus that may not be directly tied to athletics?
4. What are your prospecting strategies, including those for "town and gown"? Aside from "town and gown" collaborations, how do alumni and families of student-athletes factor into prospecting?
5. If staff and coaches are facing rejection in the sales process and the message from the businesses is that you are only a small Division III athletics department, what counterargument would you make to secure the sponsorship?
6. In pursuing businesses in the community, what competitors might you and your staff face, both from within sports and outside of sports?
7. How would your department evaluate the corporate sponsorships and what type of deliverable measurements would be provided to the businesses to bolster their return?
8. How would you balance maximizing revenue for the department versus the concern of overcommercialization—the presence of the sponsor's name, image, and branding everywhere on your campus?

Because outsourced firms work with many schools in a region or even across the United States, they are well versed in the fair market value of various inventory offerings. Though rights fees may vary from region to region, the expertise and depth of an outsourced firm's research can bring to light the fact that some corporate partnerships have been financially undervalued. As a result, a change in the sales team can frequently yield "sticker shock" when an outsourced firm tells a corporate partner that the price of being a sponsor is going to increase (O'Brien, 2012). In such cases, the firm thoroughly details why the rights fee has increased, but the explanation is not likely to be well received by the business, regardless of how undervalued the previous contractual arrangements may have been for the athletics department.

Another value of using an outsourced marketing firm is the presence of UBIT taxes. UBIT stands for unrelated business income tax, which can be involved in sport sponsorships. Higher-education institutions are mindful of their tax-exempt status and of the potential for losing this status through excessive UBIT taxes (Graham et al., 1995). Through affiliation with an outsourced marketing firm, the school can shift that concern from itself to a third party.

CONCLUSION

Corporate partnerships can play a vital role in generating revenue or offsetting expenses in intercollegiate athletics. Businesses have many platforms for advertising and promoting themselves, including corporate sponsorships in intercollegiate athletics. In trying to maximize such opportunities, sport marketing staffs must exercise caution in light of concerns about overcommercialization in higher education. Athletics departments can promote their corporate partners in various ways: through signage, multimedia options, hospitality, naming rights, and other options that can be sold either by in-house staffers or outside firms. The sales process begins with prospecting and stresses the fact that today's corporate partners seek robust measurable value and differentiation in their sponsorship activation.

DISCUSSION QUESTIONS

1. A new president takes over at the university and expresses concern about athletics facilities resembling a professional sports arena due to the heavy presence of sponsorships. The president wants a "cleaner" look, but the athletics department needs the revenue. How would you create a win-win scenario?
2. A local business has sponsored the athletics department for decades. Recently, however, the department has outsourced its multimedia rights to a third-party firm, which, in light of fair market value, has raised the rates for certain inventory items, causing the business to feel alienated. The owner of the business carries a great deal of clout in the community. How would you appease the business owner and try to retain the business as a sponsor?
3. Your athletics department has a partnership with a pizza delivery business. The pizza business's competitor learns that students are camping out for a highly anticipated game and delivers free pizza to the happy recipients. What concerns emerge in this situation?
4. A corporate sponsor calls at the last second and requests extra tickets for a sold-out event. The sponsor already has tickets but stresses the urgency of the matter. How would you handle this situation? Would your response change if the sponsor were deciding whether or not to renew their deal? Would your response depend on the level of financial support provided by the sponsor?
5. In building a new athletics facility, prominent alumni have indicated that they will contribute major gifts to begin the construction only if the venue is kept free of sponsorships. Knowing that this limitation will negatively affect annual revenue, how would you address this situation?

6. A potential sponsor is eager to support the athletics department, but only if its product is carried in the dining hall in place of a competitor's product. How would you approach the dining services department about replacing one of its products with this potential sponsor's product?
7. With the advancement of name, image, and likeness, what concerns might your athletics department or multimedia rights holder face with respect to balancing support for student-athletes versus revenue generation for the department, and how might such concerns be alleviated?

LEARNING ACTIVITIES

1. The athletics department is building a new basketball arena. What opportunities exist for new inventory options that could benefit corporate partners? To find inventory ideas, visit athletics department websites and those of sports marketing firms.
2. Fair market value dictates that sponsors pay a rights fee consistent with what the market will bear. Call the following parties to ask for their advertising rates: a local newspaper, a local television station, a local radio station, a local direct mailer, and a local billboard manager. Explore online and social media options as well.
3. A potential sponsor wants to support the athletics department, but only if its sponsorship includes supporting a local nonprofit. Using online resources, identify local sport-related nonprofits that could be tied into the sponsorship proposal. Repeat the exercise, assuming that the business wants the sponsorship to support cancer prevention and treatment, antibullying efforts, social equality, or the promotion of health and fitness among youth.
4. Research the nominees for *Sports Business Journal* Agency of the Year, then explore some of their partnerships in intercollegiate athletics, sharing their innovations and success stories.
5. Many students utilize the NCAA Market to find and apply for their job opportunity. Visit some third-party firms' websites and explore what experience they seek in hiring. How might students gain that experience on their own or on nearby campuses?

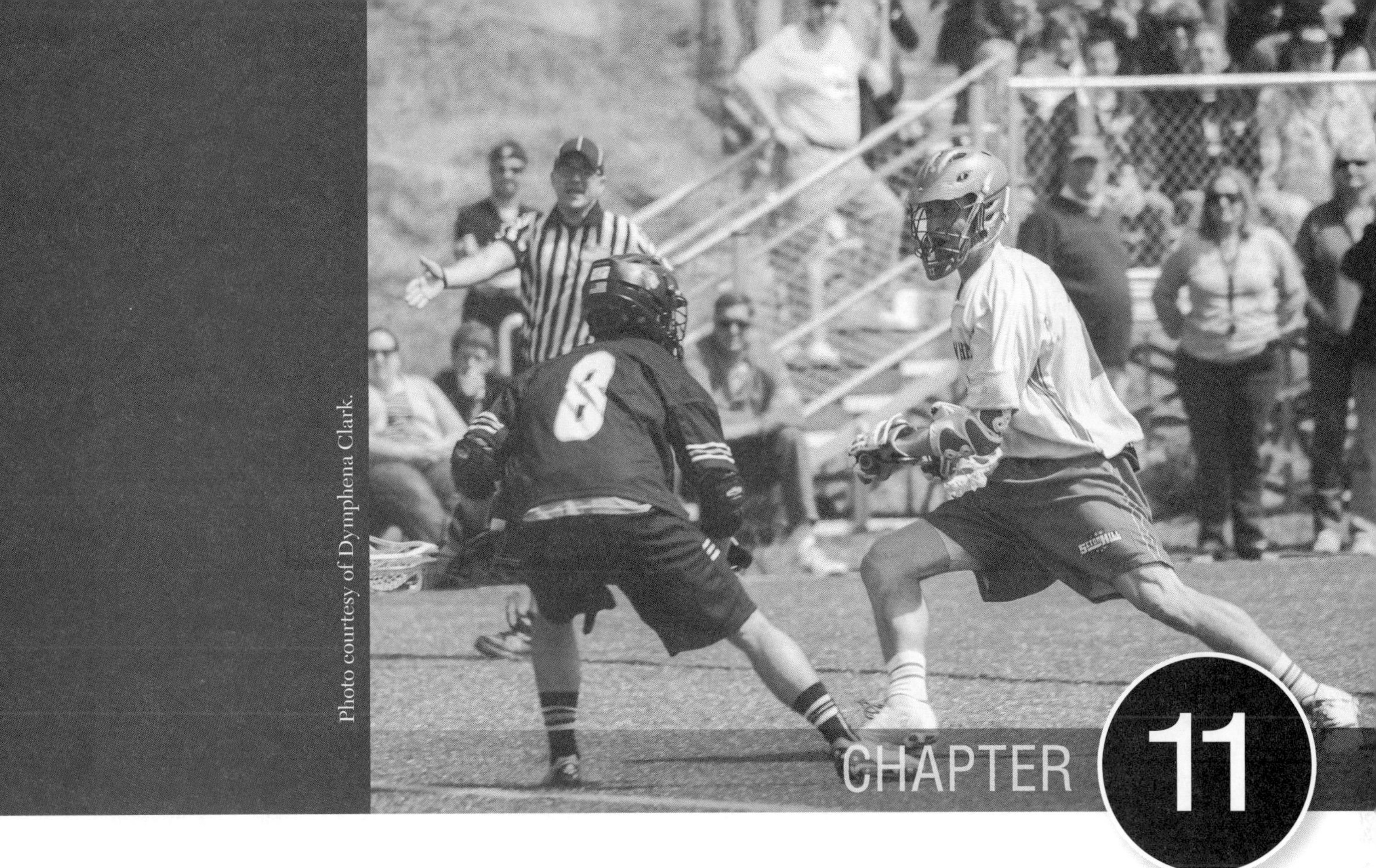

Facility and Event Management

Robert H. Zullo, Slippery Rock University

In this chapter, you will explore

- fundamentals of event management,
- safety measures and risk assessment,
- fans' increasing assertion of what they perceive as their rights at games,
- facility planning and funding, and
- current issues in facility and event management.

BALANCING STUDENT EXCITEMENT WITH SAFETY

In the final two minutes of a highly contested basketball game, the home team is on the verge of upsetting the top-ranked team, and the student section is eager to celebrate the momentous occasion on the court. The head coach of the visiting team has previously indicated his discontent with people storming the court due to his concern for his players' safety. However, keeping the students confined to the stands is going to be difficult, because those in the upper rows have started to move closer to the court, flooding into the aisles. As athletics director, what are your concerns about this situation, and how can you proactively address these concerns? Have your facility and event management staff prepared in advance for this moment—if so, how? How will you assess the effectiveness of your game-day preparation?

In intercollegiate athletics, facility and event managers face the challenge of ensuring that facilities are prepared for a wide range of athletic and nonathletic events, each of which has its own facility needs. Whether the institution is hosting a tennis tournament or a football game, certain specifications need to be met in order to adhere to regulations. Facility and event staff must also meet the requirements of people working in sports information, development, and marketing in order to best service the media, donors, and corporate sponsors. Adequate staffing is essential, especially for large-scale events, which may require extra support in terms of parking, ticket taking, ushering, and concessions. Event managers must also accommodate sports medicine and strength and conditioning staff who are there to meet the game-day needs of the athletes (Steinbach, 2005d). These diverse challenges typically go unnoticed by casual fans, but meeting them is essential to game-day operations.

Facility management also entails working with senior athletics and university officials on short- and long-term strategic planning for capital needs and improvements. In addition, the increasing emphasis on naming rights and premium seating requires facility managers to collaborate with staff members involved in sponsorship, development, and ticket sales. Facility structure and use must comply with federal legislation, including the Americans With Disabilities Act and Title IX. Facilities may also be shared with professional sport teams or used for concerts and other special events, such as convocations.

On game days, fans' behaviors can present an escalating concern if unsporting activities get out of hand. In particular, concerns have grown about alcohol consumption during tailgating at or before intercollegiate athletic events. In addition, in the aftermath of the 9/11 and the Boston Marathon tragedies, threats of terrorism are also a concern. Other, less volatile challenges may occur with an increase in the use of athletics facilities for nontraditional events.

For most people who work in event operations, the duties require long hours, because most events are held on weekends, nights, and holidays. At the same time, administrators need balance in their lives in order to be able to meet the demands of the role (Meiser et al., 2011; Steinbach, 2005d). To efficiently meet this challenge, they must have a firm understanding of facility and event management.

EVENT MANAGEMENT AND OPERATIONS

When sport fans attend an event, they generally pay little regard to the tremendous behind-the-scenes effort that makes the event possible. Directors of facilities and events coordinate the logistics with little fanfare. This work includes scheduling facilities and ensuring that each detail is properly handled to enable a successful event (Palmero et al., 2011). The work involves three stages—preevent planning, event implementation, and postevent analysis—that address factors such as space usage, timing, and staffing to maximize efficiency, accountability, and fiscal responsibility. Events are detailed to the minute in order to ensure that they run smoothly for all stakeholders, including participants, officials, and spectators.

Industry Profile

ROBYN FELTON

Chief Operating Officer, Knight Eady

Numerous companies have emerged that offer outsourced management of game-day hospitality. These companies supply amenities like tents, chairs, generators, satellite televisions, food, beverages, and coolers, and some offer to expand revenue opportunities by proposing use of sport facilities as meeting spaces or for receptions, proms, or movie nights, to name a few (Dosh, 2021). Among these companies is Knight Eady, for which Robyn Felton is the chief operating officer. Felton was previously the senior vice president, talent acquisition and human resources, at REVELxp.

What are some of the best parts of your job?

Generally speaking, the best part about working in our industry is that even though skill sets vary and roles are diverse, we get to have sports as a backdrop to everything we do. I might be able to do what I do in a hotel, or a retail store, or a bank, but doing it in an environment with the energy of college sports all around us, it's invigorating!

How does Knight Eady find good fits in terms of which schools to collaborate with?

Our first filter is, who has a need? Fortunately for us, college athletics has a wide range of needs, and we have a wide portfolio of service offerings, so collaborating with most anyone is possible. The best fits, though, are where a potential client approaches third-party relationships as partnerships, rather than transactional vendor relationships.

How can students find out about careers like yours in the business of college sports?

Be curious! When you find companies that look intriguing, reach out on LinkedIn to people in the company and see if they'll spend 30 minutes with you. If there are student organizations on your campus that relate to sports business careers, get involved and start volunteering. If there are not events to work, start networking. Conversations you have in college could lead to jobs down the road—it does not cost a dime to have an impactful conversation.

What social media, periodicals, conferences, and organizations do you follow for best practices in your area?

I follow CollegeAD on Twitter for a daily recap of headlines in our industry. I read articles of interest in *Sports Business Journal*. I listen to podcasts on leadership and business (Harvard Business Review Ideacast is a regular listen). And, I will follow a few industry leaders who I admire, all on Twitter.

What advice would you give to students wanting to work in college sports?

Be ready to grind—this industry is not for the faint of heart. Be ready to move—opportunities will not always come in your favorite city, and you will miss opportunities if you aren't [flexible] about your location. Be ready to make connections—our industry is a small world, and you never know whose paths yours will cross.

Facility Scheduling and Setup

The facility and events department works with the athletics program to schedule practices and game usage, including setup and breakdown. Multipurpose facilities may also require the staff to change the setup from one event to another—for example, converting a basketball arena from a basketball practice setup to a wrestling or volleyball venue. Space must be provided for such essentials as benches, coolers, and fitness equipment (Steinbach, 2005d). However, equipment cannot be left in place; instead, it needs to be stored when not in use in order to lower the risk of injury (Borkowski, 2006).

Game-day needs may also include a variety of tech tools, like headsets for coaches and specific scoreboard formats for sports as diverse as wrestling and basketball. This factor can be complicated when an athletics program, such as the Georgetown University men's basketball team, competes for a "home" game at an off-campus venue, thus requiring communication with the staff of a separate facility. In Georgetown's case, the team plays at the Capital One Arena, which is also home to a National Basketball Association team and a National Hockey League team. It is easy to see how this can complicate scheduling and event management.

Game-Day Preparation

For game days, facility and event managers work with the sports information department to ensure that their colleagues can adequately support the needs of members of the media. This aspect may include setting up the press box and issuing credentials to certified media members (Purvis, 2022). Credentials may be all-access or site-specific, the latter of which limits an individual to the press box, sideline, locker room, or interview room.

At large-scale events, game-day preparation also requires staff to have maintenance support available to repair scoreboards, elevators, escalators, heating and cooling units, refrigeration units, and power supplies (Purvis, 2022). At the conclusion of a sporting event, custodial services and cleaning crews are necessary to return the facility and its environs to their original state.

Game-day preparation must also secure adequate staffing for concessions, ticket taking, and ushering. Personnel support extends to the premium seating areas, such as suites and club levels. Because many of these staff members are the first people to interact with fans, it is vital that they possess high-quality customer service skills. Toward this end, some schools use Disney theme parks as an example to educate and prepare their game-day staff members, sometimes including everyone from the vendors outside the stadium to the ushers inside (Steinbach, 2013). Disney considers every theme park worker to be a performer who contributes to attendees' experience, and this philosophy extends to those selling food and merchandise and even the custodial staff. Colleges can borrow this philosophy to good effect, since most fans do not interact with the athletics director (AD), the head coach, or student-athletes on game day, but they do interact with support staff (Steinbach, 2013).

Personnel needs vary by sport and game. Large-scale sporting events require additional personnel, especially if fans have been eagerly anticipating the contest (Steinbach, 2006d). Students can overcrowd a seating area and present safety issues by sitting on the rails or in the aisles, thus drawing concern from police and fire marshals. Inadequate staffing in such situations not only leaves potential hazards unaddressed but also casts the school in a bad light (Steinbach, 2006d). First responders, such as police, fire, and emergency medical personnel, need to be onsite in sufficient proportion to the crowd size.

Staff must also ensure that designated parking areas are kept available for important donors, which requires additional security officers who can also oversee orderly tailgating. Campus and area police can help, but some schools or athletics departments are billed for the presence of this additional security support. Tailgating also creates a need for intensive trash clean-up, particularly after large events (Johnston, 2009). Unlike a professional sport facility, an institution of higher education must return to its primary objective of educating and developing students immediately after the sporting event, and schools can incur tremendous costs and publicity concerns if the campus is littered or damaged (Diamond, 2009). Viable solutions include encouraging student organizations to pass out trash bags or enlisting them to help with clean-up. School and athletics officials, and those in public safety roles, must continue to evaluate, communicate, and adjust tailgating policies as needed (Gillentine et al., 2010).

Staff Motivation

Some staffing needs may be met through positions that pay an hourly wage, but many support personnel are volunteers. Because events tend to involve long hours on nights, weekends, and holidays, facility and event managers must be mindful of boosting the morale and customer-service focus of their game-day staff (Bang & Ross, 2009). Examples of employee morale boosters that a manager can deploy include knowing everyone's name, recognizing employees when they do something good (e.g., through a wall of fame or employee-of-the-month award), arranging pep talks by coaches or student-athletes, setting up a suggestion box, hosting an end-of-year dinner, and implementing an incentive program with prizes (e.g., merchandise discounts, promotional giveaways, or gift certificates). Holly Stalcup, former assistant athletic director for event management at the University of Illinois, and current director of stadium and game operations for the College Football Playoff, stresses the "power of praise" to staff who may be required to work through heat, snow, and rain (2016). Each staff member can affect a fan's experience at an event, and high-quality service maximizes repeat customers and boosts game-day revenues.

Parking

Large-scale sporting events held on campus can have a tremendous effect on the daily routine of many school constituents. Although college football games are traditionally held on Saturdays, some programs play home games during the week. In addition, more schools are embracing the idea of Saturday classes, which are held while games are being played. Thus, solid partnership is needed among school officials to determine who is in charge of what areas and when (Palmero et al., 2011).

COVID-19 and Flexibility

Beginning in spring 2020, the COVID-19 pandemic fundamentally altered society. Students began to take classes remotely and Zoom meetings became the new normal. The sports world was no exception. Athletics facilities and the events the facilities hosted had to modify their operations. Were they masking or not masking? Did case spikes in a region affect that decision? Were patrons required to social distance? How would fans who disagreed with the policies be handled? Policies evolved and were revised rapidly as medical experts and local and national authorities continuously updated information.

Facilities also needed modifications like touchless fixtures in the bathrooms and locker rooms. Automatic valves in toilets, sinks, soap dispensers, paper towel dispensers, and sanitizer dispensers are updates that the average fan, staff member, or student may not recognize as a risk management adjustment. Some athletics facilities installed sneeze guards and safety barriers to protect fans, staff, and participants (Purvis, 2022).

Travis White, an athletics facilities and events coordinator for the Duquesne University Athletics Department, stressed that two strategies were important in the school's approach to the pandemic. First, flexibility was key. That might mean updating a sign in a facility or modifying a message to the fans that correlated with the latest science-based information. Second, consistency was significant. Everyone is entitled to their own belief, but not adhering consistently to a policy is unprofessional and can be concerning for people at home events (White, 2022). If, for instance, maintenance and custodial staff, public safety personnel, athletic staff, and the game-day support staff (e.g., ushers, ticket takers, parking lot attendants, and concession workers), are all communicating different messages about the pandemic, confusion can result, potentially leading patrons to seek other entertainment options. Flexibility and consistency during the global health crisis can help schools adapt to best serve their students, staff, and fans.

Campuses with large stadiums must also arrange for ample parking or shuttle services, which requires collaboration between school and community officials to support the parking needs of students and fans alike. Many institutions use parking lots close to the stadium as a VIP benefit for donors, which may require students and staff to vacate the lots in the late hours on the day before a game (Purvis, 2022).

Consideration for persons with disabilities can be challenging if spots usually reserved for such persons are converted into donor parking on game day. It is essential to comply with the Americans With Disabilities Act and maintain sufficient accessible parking for all patrons (Pate et al., 2010). Information about parking for persons with disabilities should be included in ticket brochures and on the departmental website. In addition, staff members in the development, ticketing, and parking offices should be educated about accessible seating and parking. The Americans With Disabilities Act is discussed in further detail later in this chapter.

SAFETY AND RISK ASSESSMENTS

Facility and event managers have an obligation to protect the individuals who participate in, attend, and work at an event. Preserving the safety of everyone involved requires a high standard of care. Meeting this standard requires managers to conduct risk assessments to examine potential sources of injury, from the moment someone arrives on campus to the moment they depart. The assessment should consider participants, spectators, staff, the facility itself, and equipment used at the event (Borkowski, 2010; Steinbach, 2005d). An organizational chart can be used to indicate who oversees what, thus increasing efficiency and accountability (Palmero et al., 2011).

Risk assessment is a continuous process in facility and event management, and it should address such areas as participant safety, terrorism threats, student behavior, alcohol consumption, and tailgating. The assessment process (Westerbeek et al., 2006) itself should include the following steps.

1. Identifying specific potential risks
2. Establishing policy and procedures
3. Documenting all incidents
4. Executing the policy and procedures
5. Evaluating continuously

Facilities that are not in use should be secured, because unsecured facilities are subject to damage or may even cause harm to visitors—a possible source of lawsuits (Borkowski, 2006). When legal matters do arise, for this or any other reason, schools may use either in-house or third-party legal counsel to advise administrators (Scholand, 2011).

Participant Safety

A primary area of concern for event managers is ensuring participants' safety around the playing surface. Of course, an adequate standard of care must be provided to coaches and participants; the standard of care is what would be consistent at other athletic events as determined by a court of law. Close attention must be paid to the fact that players' momentum can carry them off of the playing surface and into the stands. As a result, a buffer zone should be established around the playing area to protect student-athletes. Filling the buffer zone with extra seats or media tables invites an accident (Borkowski, 2006).

Care must also be taken regarding cheer squad, photographers, and band equipment and members near the playing surface (Associated Press, 2010a; Dodd, 2009; MU's tab, 2012, Steinbach, 2008b). With such risks in mind, officials are obligated to do a pre-event inspection in and around the competition area, and any concerns should be addressed with the event manager and rectified.

Safety measures can extend into the event itself, as demonstrated by the COVID-19 pandemic. Beginning in spring 2020, the pandemic continued to affect sports into the fall semester. Some Division I schools tried to play modified schedules, but games were canceled due to student-athletes, coaches, and staff falling ill or obeying COVID-19 protocols. Previously, inclement weather or an unplayable field or court may have been officials or referees' greatest game-day challenge, but the pandemic made last-moment cancellations the norm.

Protective measures must also be taken in the postgame phase of an event, as student-athletes, coaches, and referees frequently find themselves swarmed by fans who have rushed the playing surface (LaVetter & Choi, 2010; Steinbach, 2006a). Fans may be energized by a game being televised or seeing their school play a rival or nationally ranked opponent, thus requiring event managers to anticipate fans storming the playing surface. Public address announcements can be used to encourage fans to stay in their seats, but many will not listen to the messages. In some cases, public safety officials may simply be unable to hold the fans off the court or field, in which case it is vital to first secure the officials and the visiting team and escort them to their locker rooms (Steinbach, 2006a).

For the same reason, it is also advisable to use collapsible goalposts at football stadiums to help protect student-athletes, officials, coaches, and spectators (LaVetter & Choi, 2010). More generally, facility and event managers must adopt and strictly follow standard operating procedures consistent with the expectations of each respective sport. Given the numerous sports included in intercollegiate athletics, the many procedures are not addressed individually in this chapter, but they can be found by consulting with governing bodies at the conference and national levels. Following such standards reduces an institution's liability.

Terrorism Threats

Another area of concern centers on threats of terrorism. A large-scale sporting event gives terrorists a potential opportunity to attack at a time when sport fans are in a relaxed but highly visible state (Cohen, 2001; Hall et al., 2010; Miller & Dunn, 2011). To counter this risk, continuous education must be provided to facility and event management personnel to reinforce procedures, identify vulnerable areas, and foster ongoing evaluation of threat assessment (Hall et al., 2010).

In fact, this area of concern is grave enough that the University of Southern Mississippi has created a research center focused on it. The center recommends the adoption of certain pre-event strategies, including policies and procedures that address facility access, game-day activity monitoring, and video surveillance (Marciani & Hall, 2007). Tactics

Technology Tools

Texting and QR Codes

Fans attend sporting events for a variety of reasons. They might be supporting a loved one or friend. They might want to support the team or enjoy school spirit. They might want to have fun or escape from other obligations. What fans do not attend games for is to see fights break out, to see projectiles cause potential harm, to hear profanity, or to see drunk fans vomit. To help prevent or minimize these and other disorderly behaviors, many athletics departments have implemented a texting system. Police officers and security personnel are unable to see every incident that may require their attention, so they rely on fans to help. For example, if a fight breaks out at a tailgate hours before a game or as fans exit parking lots after the game, fans can text for assistance. The benefits of this are threefold: concerned fans can remain anonymous, police or security can directed to a precise location, and the emergency can be precisely described. If police are directing traffic off campus after a heavily attended game, a simple text from a fan can alert the proper authorities to an emergency that might require immediate medical attention or notify security to come toward the exiting traffic. It is important to inform fans of this texting system. Game-day announcements, videoboards, social media, the athletics department website, and even information printed on tickets can all help in the education process.

Additionally, some schools have begun to use QR codes that patrons can scan to send in game complaints, needs, problems, and facility issues (Purvis, 2022). Some codes may be designated to alert maintenance and custodians if a light is out or a soap dispenser is empty. This can help to ensure timeliness in repairs and regular facility upkeep. Schools adopting technology systems as best practices and to communicate with fans about their concerns can only improve the game-day experience.

to lower the risk of terrorism include bag checks, bomb-sniffing dogs, trained security, and barriers to keep vehicles at a distance from the facility (Steinbach, 2006b). Additional security practices can include the following:

- Central command to coordinate security responses
- Venue lockdown prior to any event
- Prohibition of concession deliveries within 90 minutes of the event
- On-premises security personnel 24/7
- Restrictions on access to critical areas of the facility
- Photo identification and zone passes for employees
- Creation of a formal risk management plan
- Pre-event training program for all event staff
- Coordination with local and state police agencies
- Preparation of a formal evacuation plan
- Awareness of potentially explosive or otherwise dangerous facilities nearby
- Undercover surveillance with radio equipment dispersed throughout the building
- No-fly zones over and around the building
- Mobile emergency room vehicle on standby
- One crowd observer per 250 people in all sections of the venue
- Security patrols in the parking lot
- Periodic announcements to spectators regarding security practices and restricted items
- Ban on carry-in backpacks and other large bags
- Postevent debriefing for all personnel

These security practices are recommended in the Springfield College Security Study (Pantera, Accorsi, Winter, Gobeille, Griveas, Queen, et al., 2003). In addition to preventive measures, facility and event managers should establish a security action plan to be activated if a terrorist attack does occur (Miller & Dunn, 2011).

Student Behavior

A third area of concern involves student behavior. Though most student sections provide a positive home-court or home-field advantage, it takes only a few individuals to cause concern with negative behavior (Steinbach, 2008a). Bad behavior can take place at any type of contest, as demonstrated by a football game in Knoxville, Tennessee, in 2021. A game was delayed for 20 minutes as fans, predominantly in the student section, threw bottles, cans, and other projectiles onto the field. Despite there only being 54 seconds left in the close game, the Tennessee cheer squad and the school band had to move to avoid the projectiles. Eighteen people were arrested, 47 fans were ejected from the facility, and the school had to pay a fine of US$250,000 (Low, 2021).

Whether a problem involves chanting, clothing choices, or other behavior, facility and event managers should have a policy in place for addressing problematic situations when they arise. Often, a warning to a student is enough to stifle the issue, but ejection from the facility is another option when fans behave in a way that reflects poorly on the school and the athletics department. Schools have also used their own coaches to encourage students to cheer loudly but tastefully (Steinbach, 2001). Failing to proactively curtail students' poor behavior can result in negative attention through the media and potential fines levied by governing bodies.

Alcohol at Sporting Events

One highly debated question of risk is whether schools should serve alcohol at their sporting events. Among schools that do sell alcohol, many restrict alcohol consumption to their premium seating areas to foster greater contributions by donors in return for this benefit. The NCAA and other governing bodies have remained neutral on the issue, choosing to grant institutional control over pouring choices (Steinbach, 2004b).

Critics of alcohol sales during events note that binge drinking is a sizable problem on college campuses and argue that serving alcohol sends the wrong message to students (Popke, 2005). By contrast, proponents of allowing alcohol consumption inside stadiums and arenas point out that it can generate considerable revenue. They also argue that many patrons consume alcohol prior to the event while tailgating (Steinbach, 2005c). Indeed, West Virginia University came under scrutiny due to alcohol consumption during tailgating before home football games. For years, fans would binge-drink before kickoff and try to sneak alcohol inside the facility. Season-ticket holders grew upset about the behavioral issues inside the stadium and threatened not to renew their tickets.

In an effort to combat the complaints, West Virginia took a different approach—it brought the alcohol inside the stadium. Specifically, for the 2011 season, West Virginia implemented two major changes at home football games. First, alcohol was sold inside the university's Milan Puskar Stadium. Second, fans who exited the stadium during the game could no longer gain readmission (Novy-Williams, 2011; Steinbach, 2011; WVU approves, 2011), because the athletics department believed that some fans were using halftime as a chance to return to their tailgating areas in order to binge-drink. The sale of alcohol inside the stadium includes several provisions:

- Strict enforcement of ID checks
- Purchase limits
- No alcohol point of sale near the student section
- No alcohol sales in seating areas
- No alcohol sales after the midpoint of the third quarter
- Designated driver program

The third-party concession group assumed responsibility for training its staff, managing intervention procedures, and procuring the alcohol license. The adoption of alcohol sales was implemented in conjunction with the TEAM (Techniques for Effective Alcohol Management) Coalition, a nonprofit organization that addresses alcohol consumption in stadiums and arenas. The coalition works with beer distributors, traffic safety authorities, concessionaire groups, and facility managers to identify solutions for offering a more respectful, fan-friendly atmosphere at events in professional sport, entertainment, and intercollegiate athletics. In 2015, there were 34 Division I Football Bowl Subdivision schools that permitted alcohol sales at their stadiums (Malone, 2015). Prior to the 2018 season, the number of schools was 40 and prior to 2019, the number increased to 78 (Hayes, 2019).

Alcohol-related safety measures can include restricting how early fans can tailgate, limiting the duration of tailgating, and banning kegs and other large alcohol containers (Steinbach, 2003b). Fans can be educated in advance about alcohol policies through the athletics and school websites (Menaker & Connaughton, 2010). Some schools also designate certain drinking areas, and others clear the school's property of tailgaters once the game begins. Earlier kickoff times also reduce the amount of time available for alcohol consumption prior to the game.

Tailgating Concerns

For many fans, the game-day experience begins long before tipoff or kickoff with tailgating on campus. Setting up chairs, tables, grills, and tents increases the fans' time on campus but also comes with concerns. The possession and consumption of alcohol is difficult to monitor, but it needs to be addressed in order to ensure patrons' safety. In addition, donor parking spaces should be numbered to assign ownership to each space. Doing so prevents problems such as exceeding parking lot capacity or having fans tailgate in multiple parking spaces. Campus and local police officials can help prevent such problems through continuous presence, particularly at large events.

With such issues in mind, event managers must foresee risks and oversee tailgate areas as potential liabilities. For a tailgating management plan to succeed, each of the following topics and rules must be addressed and communicated to all constituents (Gillentine et al., 2010):

- Enforcement procedures
- Cooperative agreements
- Designated tailgating areas
- Tailgating hours
- Parking
- Grilling
- Glass containers
- Trash receptacles
- Stadium reentry
- Alcohol consumption
- Evaluation and monitoring

This is particularly important for schools that outsource their premium tailgating location to third-party firms. Research has shown that many schools lack alcohol policies and trained security staff for patrons in the tailgating areas outside the facilities (Miller et al., 2019).

FAN RIGHTS

The back side of many tickets includes a statement that fans are subject to removal from the venue at the discretion of facility managers or the athletics department (Nagel, 2011). Event organizers do have the legal right to eject patrons due to the fact that tickets are revocable licenses (Nagel). Of course, ejecting fans is not a desirable outcome, but it can be difficult to know where to draw the line. Many fans attend college events to physically support their team. Some fans argue that they have the right to freedom of speech, but when cheering crosses into vulgarity or profanity, facility managers seek ways to indulge the passion of the fan base without the vulgarity or profanity.

> *Sports is life with the volume turned up. People don't like to be told anything today. "I bought my ticket, and I can do whatever the hell I want to do. So what if a guy makes an announcement?"*
>
> Barry Mano, president, National Association of Sports Officials (qtd. in Steinbach, 2001, para. 11)

An example of fans attempting to assert their perceived rights occurred at the University of Maryland. The athletics department tried to improve student behavior at home basketball games by creating a student task force designed to identify strategies for reducing offensive behavior. At the request of the state attorney general, the committee took care not to violate First Amendment rights. The task force met 12 times in 3 months, held an open town hall forum, and surveyed more than 200 students. The task force ultimately recommended a number of initiatives to encourage voluntary compliance with guidelines for positive fan behavior:

- A T-shirt exchange at athletics venues to provide free T-shirts to students who turn in profane ones
- Head coaches addressing incoming first-year students during convocation at the beginning of each school year on the importance of avoiding offensive speech and behavior
- An open practice with the head basketball coach prior to a marquee game to discuss with students the value of good sporting behavior
- A lighthearted game-day newspaper (featuring nonprofane but creative, witty cheers created by students) for basketball fans to continue the tradition of shaking the papers while the opposing team is introduced
- A best-sign contest on the videoboard at football and basketball games to encourage creative and appropriate signs and banners
- Additional signage discouraging profanity at athletics venues

FACILITY PLANNING

Optimal facility planning involves all stakeholder groups that may use or be involved with the facility, including participants, administrators, sports information staff, sports medicine staff, strength and conditioning staff, members of the media, hospitality providers, concession providers, and others (Browne et al., 2008; Bynum, 2007; Klein, 2019). Money is generally a primary consideration, and sharing space and choosing certain materials (e.g., artificial turf rather than grass) can reduce both construction and operational costs (Steinbach, 2006c). At the same time, cost-saving measures should be balanced with administrative considerations, such as scheduling and fiscal oversight.

In the planning stages of facility development and renovation, project managers should invest the time and energy to identify specific facility needs. This process includes conducting thorough feasibility studies and benchmarking. In choosing a firm to serve as an architectural, engineering, or construction partner, managers should balance cost efficiency with demonstrated success and testimonials from other schools to ensure timely construction.

Adding Esports and Your Facility Needs

According to the website AthleticDirectorU, an increasing number of schools have developed esports programs to help with student recruitment and retention. With the first program starting at Robert Morris University (Illinois) in 2014, the tally grew to 125 programs in 2019 and over 200 programs a year later (Staff, n.d.). Scholarships can be allocated to esports participants, and these grew from US$2.5 million in 2015 to US$15 million by 2019. Esports has a high participation rate but offers such advantages as a low barrier to entry in terms of participation and ease of maintenance from a logistical and fiscal standpoint (White, 2022).

However, obtaining a facility can be a significant hurdle due to technological needs and the ability to secure thousands of dollars of equipment. It could be as simple as converting an old computer lab or developing a new arena dedicated to esports. Collegiate governing bodies for esports vary in their facility requirements, with such criteria as power sources, horsepower of individual personal computers, dedicated individualized Internet access, lag-free environments, and more (White, 2022). There is also the need to ensure separate space for competitive varsity gamers versus recreational student gamers seeking communal space (Singaby, 2019).

While these may seem trivial to the common observer unfamiliar with esports, these expectations should not be trivialized. After all, one would not play baseball at night without lights or play basketball without regulation rims. The technology associated with esports requires frequent updating and comes with significant cost (Miller, 2020). Maintenance is not as simple as cutting a field's grass and painting new lines. More varsity esports teams are emerging and scholarships are available for competitors, but as with other sports, recruits expect to see a school's commitment reflected in top-quality facilities and continuously updated resources.

Needs Assessment

A facility's stakeholders include not only coaches and student-athletes but also recruits, support staff, and fans. Athletics facilities may also be shared with the school's student body for recreational purposes. In addition, consideration must be given to the needs of the media, concession operators, and hospitality providers, which may call for premium seating. For the media, camera sightlines are not enough; multimedia needs, bandwidth, and future technological advances are other concerns (Klein, 2019). Including constituents from this wide range of stakeholders provides more robust dialogue to help with facility needs assessment early in the process (Westerbeek et al., 2006).

Feasibility Study

A feasibility study can help with facility renovation and construction by bringing objectivity to the process (Seifried, 2012). Feasibility studies typically comprise an affordability analysis, steps to decrease the risk of failure, a best-fit examination of the facility in relation to users, an exploration of budget issues, and an initial game plan for marketing and public relations (Westerbeek et al., 2006). The study should thoroughly examine such considerations as the following:

- Historical issues
- Facts
- Goals
- Stakeholders
- Timelines
- Market research

This process enables objective scrutiny of proposed locations, weather implications for construction, legal issues, and financial concerns, especially hidden costs (Westerbeek et al., 2006).

Benchmarking

Benchmarking enables school officials to research other facilities in order to glean ideas and develop comparisons. Benchmarking can be done through initial on-campus research followed by trips to other schools. These trips provide a firsthand perspective on new resources and technology, such as upgrades in LED scoreboards that can improve the game-day experience and increase revenue (Dahlgren, 2000). Similarly, exposure to other facilities' amenities, such as banners, wall murals, floor graphics, and wall padding, can stimulate ideas for visual additions to augment the facility experience for staff, recruits, student-athletes, and patrons (Steinbach, 2005a). These trips can also foster discussion of programming, structural systems, safety concerns, turf and flooring needs, and appropriate HVAC and lighting systems (Browne et al., 2008).

Requests for Proposals

After the needs assessment, feasibility study, and benchmarking steps have been completed, it is time to solicit proposals from architects, engineers, and construction firms (Westerbeek et al., 2006). Schools put out a request for proposal (often referred to by the acronym RFP) inviting firms to submit bids detailing their capabilities for consideration by the school. Some firms may be invited to campus for further discussion. The construction or renovation process can involve a large number of contractors and subcontractors, and checking references and examining their past facility projects can lower the risk of failure.

Environmentally Friendly Facilities

Facilities are generally constructed with sustainability, multipurpose functionality, and operational flexibility in mind to maximize the investment (Baker, 2019). Sustainability emerges, for example, in sensor-activated lights or natural lighting to reduce power usage, renewable energy sources, and waste reduction programs such as recycling and other environmentally friendly programs. Schools can also reduce stormwater runoff or use the water for other purposes. In addition, facilities can recycle construction material or expect building materials to come from a regional supplier, thereby reducing carbon emissions from transportation (Funk, 2007). Some schools use solar panels and wind power for greater energy efficiency (Cohen, 2000; Cohen, 2007). Even bike racks and priority parking for carpoolers and electric vehicles can help the environment (Funk, 2007). Commitment to change is becoming more prevalent with the advent, in 2016, of the United Nations' Sports for Climate Action Framework. Through this pledge by senior school officials, the athletics department commits to undertake systematic efforts to promote greater environmental responsibility, reduce overall climate impact, educate for climate action, promote sustainable and responsible consumption, and advocate for climate action through communication (Berg, 2020).

Facilities can also earn LEED (Leadership in Energy and Environmental Design) certification if they meet certain criteria as evaluated by the U.S. Green Building Council (Cohen, 2010). The four LEED tiers are platinum, gold, silver, and certified. Many schools perceive efforts to go green as cost prohibitive, but this assumption may be erroneous and these expenses are declining annually.

Americans With Disabilities Act

Facility and event managers must be knowledgeable about the Americans With Disabilities Act and how it affects not only spectators but also student-athletes who may be injured. This is especially true in regard to new facility construction (Dethlefs, 2007) and facility alterations (Steinbach, 2007). Seating for persons with disabilities should include a variety of options, provide sightlines comparable to those of other seats, and be easy to access from the parking area, concession stands, and restrooms. In addition, staff working in disability seating and parking areas need to be knowledgeable about the principle of accessibility in event management, thus ensuring high-quality customer service in an area that is frequently neglected (Grady, 2010).

Providing such options can entail additional construction costs but ensures compliance with the federal legislation requiring that one percent of seating be appropriate for persons with disabilities (Steinbach, 2007). Noncompliance can carry its own costs.

Title IX

Title IX is another piece of federal legislation that requires adherence, in this case with respect to equitably scheduling events and practice times, determining locker room sizes, and providing resources for both men's and women's programs. Complaints regarding noncompliance, which can

Professional Development

Collegiate Event and Facility Management Association (CEFMA)

In order to succeed, facility and event administrators need to take advantage of professional development opportunities while providing the best and most up-to-date service to their school. They can do so by joining an organization such as the Collegiate Event and Facility Management Association (CEFMA). CEFMA provides educational programs, professional development and networking opportunities, and best practices to develop the field of event and facility management. In conjunction with the National Association of Collegiate Directors of Athletics (NACDA), CEFMA promotes the growth, leadership, integrity, and success of administrators and professional staff involved in collegiate athletics. Student rates are available for membership and for the professional conference held each summer. Benefits of CEFMA include the following:

- Complimentary copy of NACDA's magazine, *Athletics Administration,* published quarterly and featuring the CEFMA Corner, which highlights current information about intercollegiate facility and event management submitted by CEFMA members
- Reduced registration rates for the annual CEFMA convention, which is held in conjunction with the NACDA convention
- Opportunity to belong to the CEFMA email list to communicate directly with CEFMA members
- Opportunity to receive the NACDA Daily Review email, which compiles web links to articles related to intercollegiate athletics
- Opportunities for networking and resource sharing with the diverse group of professionals who make up CEFMA and NACDA's other affiliate associations

Additional professional development resources for those working in facility and events include the International Association of Venue Managers and Stadium Managers Association.

Additionally, *Facility Manager* is a magazine dedicated to the public assembly building business. It identifies trends, introduces readers to other professionals in the industry, and covers new developments. *Athletic Business* also offers current information on new facilities and best practices. There are also peer-reviewed publications in this area, including *Sport and Entertainment Review* (formerly *Journal of Venue and Event Management*), *Event Management Journal, International Journal of Event Management Research*, and *International Journal of Event and Festival Management*, in addition to peer-reviewed journals in the related fields of hospitality and tourism. Additionally, industry journals such as *Sports Travel* and *SportsEvent* can be helpful to schools that wish to host concerts and other events not directly affiliated with the school's athletics department.

come from coaches or student-athletes, are handled by the U.S. Office for Civil Rights (Funk, 2010). In terms of facilities, administrators should foster equity in all areas of construction, upgrades, resources, and operations. Title IX is addressed in greater detail in chapter 5.

FACILITY BUDGETING

Despite the bleak financial realities faced by most intercollegiate athletics departments, administrators have escalated expenditures on facility construction and renovation to seek a competitive advantage in recruiting. This phenomenon has come to be known as the "arms race of expenditures." In this race, schools adopt the mentality that if they spend a bit more than their conference rival (e.g., on a practice facility, locker room, player lounge, weight room, coach's salary, or sports medicine facility), the investment should translate into better recruits and ultimately a higher winning percentage. However, because this competitive mentality is shared by many institutions, each school spends more and more in an effort simply to keep up with its rivals (Bennett, 2012; Bynum,

2007; Steinbach, 2003a). This tendency is most common at Division I schools found in the ACC, Big Ten, Big 12, Pac-12, and SEC conferences, where coaches particularly aspire to occupy facilities that are welcoming to recruits in terms of size, amenities, and personal touches (Mead, 2007).

Institutions that generate less revenue must plan strategically to assess their facility needs with a limited budget. Stressed budgets can cause adjustments in staffing, including split shifts, seasonal staffing, the use of contracting services, and a reliance on volunteers (Sports Turf Managers Association, 2011). When budgets are reduced, emphasis should also be placed on minimizing utility costs and maximizing the efficiency of staff (Gioglio, 2011; Palmero et al., 2011). Fiscal matters and budgeting are discussed further in chapter 8.

FACILITY FUNDING

Schools use a wide range of financing mechanisms for facilities, including naming rights, bonds, institutional support, student fees, and funding from local governments (Myers, 2008).

The selling of facility naming rights is becoming more prevalent in intercollegiate athletics but is still not as widely accepted as it is in professional sport (Chen & Zhang, 2012). At this point, it is a more common practice for schools to honor individuals affiliated with the school, including donors. In another area of difference with professional sport venues, it is less common for institutions of higher learning to rely on taxpayers to help fund intercollegiate athletics facilities, as politicians face other pressing fiscal burdens in their regions (Brown & Nagel, 2010).

One growing trend in new facility construction in intercollegiate athletics is the inclusion of premium seating (e.g., suites, club levels, and courtside bunkers) due to the considerable long-term revenue-generating capabilities of these amenities (Lawrence & Titlebaum, 2010; Steinbach, 2005b). Premium seating areas can provide an environment in which businesses want to host clients, reward employees, conduct business, and offer hospitality in a fun atmosphere (Lawrence et al., 2009; Titlebaum et al., 2012). Through collaborative planning with targeted businesses, the development and ticketing offices can maximize funding capabilities, as these groups can best assess the market demand for various kinds of seating.

CURRENT ISSUES

Although the fundamental principles of facility and event management are consistent, new issues continue to arise, and administrators must be prepared to meet these challenges. Emerging issues include, for example, the process for bidding to host a postseason event, decisions about whether to outsource concessions or facility management to third-party firms or to play games at a neutral site. There are numerous ways of thinking outside the box, preparing for the unexpected, and doing more for fans to enhance the game-day experience. Each of these areas is discussed in the following sections.

Bidding to Host NCAA Postseason Events

When a school bids to host a postseason event, it typically responds to a request for proposals (RFP) in which the NCAA (or other governing organization) sets forth its minimum expectations. For example, the bidding process might require potential hosts to provide a specified number of seats in a facility, ample nearby hotels, experience in hosting comparable events, and a leadership team with demonstrated knowledge in this realm (Bilsky, 2007). Because many athletic teams participate in postseason events, a school can make its bid more attractive by forming partnerships with local hotels, restaurants, and transportation and sport commissions. In addition, they can analyze past hosted events to develop projected expenses and revenues, including an anticipated budget for providing the resources needed for media relations, sports medicine, and sport marketing (publicity).

In putting forth a bid, Steve Bilsky (2007), former athletics director at the University of Pennsylvania, challenges administrators to ask the following questions.

- First, do you have the support of the entire community? You should consider whether being a championship host would benefit only your institution or if the community would benefit through added tourism dollars and positive publicity. The easiest way to answer this question is to discuss your ideas with tourism officials and other local agencies. Do not hesitate to ask the mayor or even your state's governor for financial support.

- Second, can you put on a championship-caliber event? The student-athletes competing are the very best at their sport and deserve a venue worthy of the occasion. If you will not be hosting the event at your own site, make sure the event managers know what they are doing and have a proven record of accomplishment. Nothing spoils an event like spectators spending an inordinate amount of time parking, waiting in line for tickets, and searching for concessions and restrooms, or teams arriving and not knowing where to be at what times.

- Third, can you make a competitive bid? Make sure that facilities are up to snuff and that the infrastructure is there to support the event. And be realistic about your customer base—large events like the lacrosse championships are highly sought after, and one of the criteria is whether a venue can offer the right amount of revenue.

After earning the bid, communication is key, according to Cass Ferguson, former director of championships for the Atlantic 10 Conference and current associate athletic director for facilities and events at the University of North Carolina at Charlotte (2016). It is crucial for a school to communicate regularly with the sport's governing body so there are no surprises at the event. This helps ensure event manuals, visitor guides, and policy handbooks are current and, in turn, allows postseason play to reach its fullest potential for the participants, coaches, staff, fans, media, and all other stakeholders.

> *You only get ONE chance to make a first impression. Everyone in college sports can look at the facility itself on a year-to-year basis, whether that is on the field/court, sidelines, offices, etc. When it comes to operating a new facility, though, you only have one home opener. This gives you major reason to reassess and take stock of what the actual operations and protocols of the venue look like and how logistically positive they are. What needs improvement in terms of how the facility is operated? How can we maximize safety and cleanliness for our fans? From a logistical standpoint, how can we stand out and give our fans an impactful experience when they are at the facility? Transitioning to a new facility provides schools and administrators the chance to create new best practices and not be stuck in the paradigm of status quo.*
>
> Travis White, athletic facility and events coordinator, Duquesne University (2022)

Outsourcing Facility Operations

Many schools outsource facility operations to a third party to benefit from their expertise and maximize cost efficiency. Such companies help manage larger arenas in the areas of booking, sales, marketing, concessions, public relations, and risk management (Palmero et al., 2011; Steinbach, 2004a). In addition, schools can generate revenue by having the company book nonathletic events at their facilities. This may have the added bonus of saving money, because the third-party firm might receive a bulk discount on purchases of items needed for facility management. Hosting additional events can also add value in naming rights and sponsorship agreements for the venue.

Other third-party firms specialize in crowd management, security, guest services, and event traffic and parking. Still others offer expertise in hospitality management and oversight of premium seating inside and outside facilities.

These potential benefits notwithstanding, using a third-party firm to manage a facility can also be problematic because the school exercises less control over the venue. For example, if an athletic team is not communicating directly with a school official to schedule practices at the game-day facility, there might be a conflict if an outside event is scheduled for the same time slot (Steinbach, 2004a).

The decision about whether to outsource facility management involves several factors. First, at some schools, there is no decision to make, because school policy requires in-house management. For schools without such a policy, the decision should be revisited periodically by examining the current level of satisfaction with the facility's management, as well as its staffing capabilities. Another consideration involves risk. Outsourcing management operations may not only enable a school to host more events and generate greater revenue but also transfer the financial and legal risks to the third-

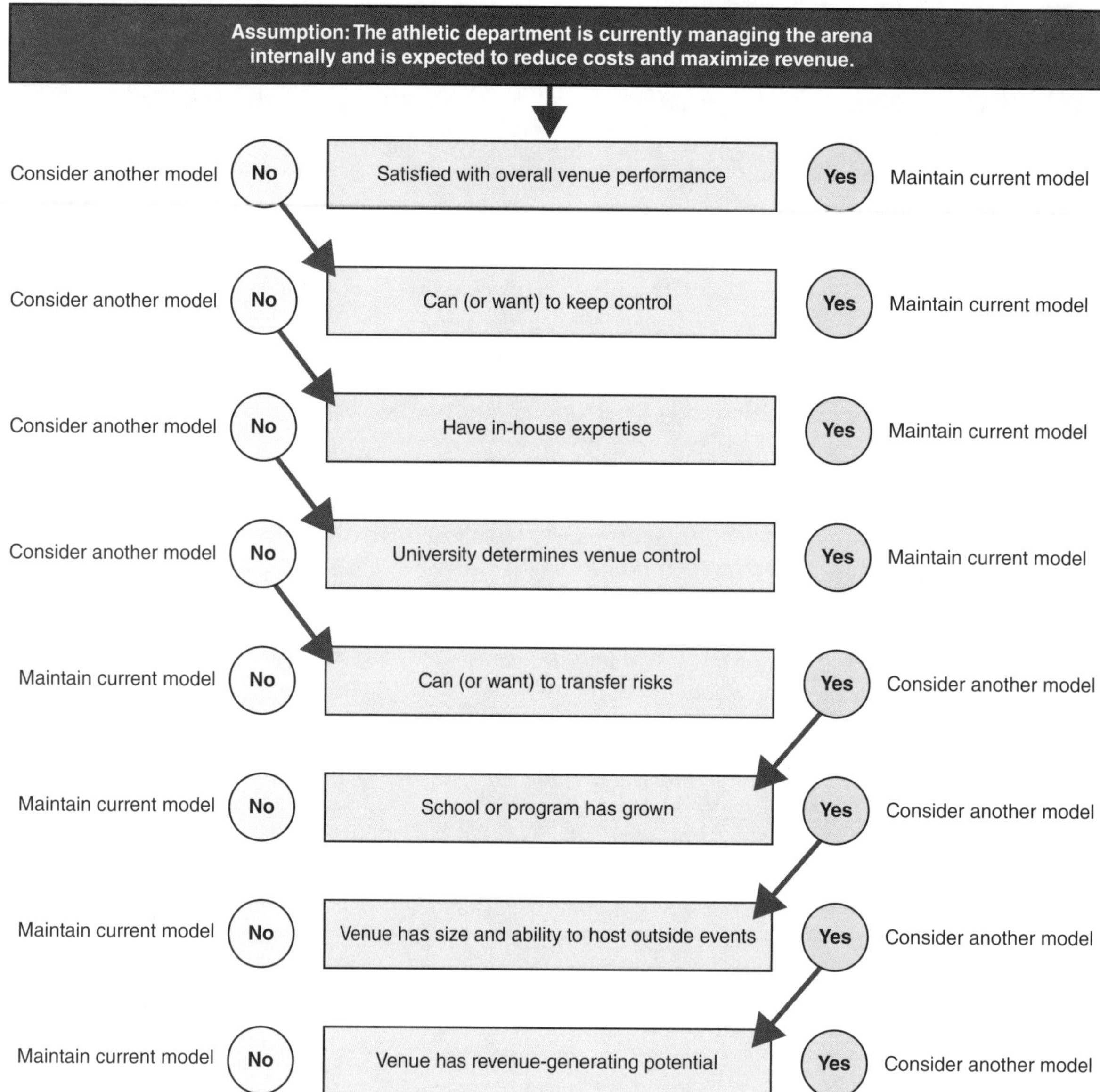

Figure 11.1 Decision framework for determining an arena management model.
Reprinted by permission from M. Palmero et al., "Who is in Charge? An Analysis of NCAA Division I Arena Management Models," *Journal of Venue and Event Management* 3, no. 2 (2011): 18-32.

party company (Palmero et al., 2011). One way to determine an arena management model is to use the decision framework presented in figure 11.1.

Coordinating Concessions

More than half of Division I athletics departments outsource their concessions in order to take advantage of specialized firms' expertise, add revenue opportunities, and stay current with industry trends (Steinbach, 2000). Schools choosing to keep concessions in-house tend to do so in the interest of greater control.

Some schools' concession contracts are tied into the school's dining service contract, whereas others are specific to athletics. The contract may also indicate whether the parent concession company can include vendors local to the area (Steinbach, 2008c).

Planning Neutral-Site Games

In Division I college football, established neutral-site rivalries have led athletics administrators to ponder whether their school should play in such a format. Some famous contests, such as the Georgia–Florida game (played in Jacksonville) and the Texas–Oklahoma game (played in Dallas), are well known in their traditional cities, but programs such as Notre Dame's have ventured into neutral-site games. These games can help coaches recruit in a selected area or give the school a chance to play in an area with a heavy alumni presence.

However, neutral-site games also have to make sense fiscally, as the host facility is traditionally responsible for assuming event management duties through contractual obligations (Dougherty, 2008). The host school may also have to educate the facility's staff and administrators about standards and expectations, particularly if the facility is not familiar with hosting an event in a certain sport. In addition, coaches and student-athletes want a neutral-site game to feel like a home game in terms of scheduling practice, arranging transportation, and enjoying other resources comparable to those of their home facility. Fans also expect that the event should meet the same professional standards expected at an on-campus home event. These standards include high-quality ticketing, parking, security, concessions, and other aspects of the game-day experience.

Thinking Outside the Box

Creative thinking has taken more college sporting events outside. In one particularly dramatic example, in 2011, Michigan State University played the University of North Carolina in men's basketball on a U.S. aircraft carrier and these games continue each year (Michigan State University and Gonzaga University played on the USS *Abraham Lincoln* on Veterans Day in 2022) (Moore, 2011). Another example is a women's basketball game in 2000 between Arizona State University and the University of Tennessee played at Chase Field (then known as Bank One Ballpark), home of the Arizona Diamondbacks (Metcalfe, 2016). And Michigan State University hosted the University of Michigan in a men's hockey match played at Michigan State's football stadium and attended by more than 74,000 fans (Associated Press, 2010b). In August 2023, the University of Nebraska women's volleyball team played a match inside the school's football stadium, setting a new attendance record with over 92,000 patrons (Schmidt, 2023). These events are gradually becoming more common.

Of course, outdoor games can be affected by the weather. Low temperature, low visibility, and high wind will hamper play, but adaptations can be made in the playing surface, the lighting, the stands, and the locker rooms. A provisional facility can also be made available. For the game on the aircraft carrier, contingency plans included a second basketball court below decks in case of inclement weather (Bishop, 2011). These uniquely sited games are also common in college football postseason, as when bowl games are held at historic baseball venues such as Fenway Park in Boston and Yankee Stadium in New York.

Expecting the Unexpected

When revenue streams are challenged, be it through a global pandemic or significant changes in college sports such as a modification to a taxation law or through the addition of name, image, and likeness (NIL), athletics administrators must pinpoint new revenue streams. The sponsorship categories of gambling and liquor once were shunned, although state lotteries and beer brands were embraced as corporate partners. Beer and wine sales used to be restricted to premium seating, helping to serve as tool to increase fundraising. Now, with changes in U.S. state laws, cannabis use and sports gambling are becoming more commonplace. In the quest for additional revenue streams, schools are now more accepting of sponsors in the categories of sports gambling, liquor, and cannabis (Higgins, 2021).

Doing More for Fans to Heighten the Game Experience

The "arms race" in college sports is the idea of spending more in areas such as facilities, travel, and other resources to attract the best recruits to your campus. The concept is starting to extend to the game-day experience as customers become more selective with their entertainment dollars. Just as coaches want a recruit to choose their school over a competitor school, the game-day experience has a major competitor in the fan's home. A fan could set up a high-definition big-screen television in their backyard and enjoy their favorite college football game with cheaper food and beverage options in their refrigerator. There are no traffic or parking

Leadership Lesson

Motivation 3.0

Event operations staff are those who organize experiences, coordinate vendors, greet visitors, welcome longtime supporters, and provide hospitality for the competitors—even fierce rivals. If collegiate athletics is the "front porch" of the university, facility and event operations staff are the friendly neighbors who wave on the front lawn. Event staff may work at conference tournaments, summer camps, simultaneous home-team competitions, and endure back-to-back-to-back-to-back late nights and early mornings, so these jobs can be draining. Some institutions, however, have mastered the art of hosting. They maintain an events staff composed of people who are eager to go out of their way to facilitate optimal experiences for their guests and who find great fulfillment in completing their jobs well. They do this through what Daniel Pink refers to as "Motivation 3.0."

According to Pink, at one point, humans were driven by biological needs (Motivation 1.0), but they evolved to respond to rewards and punishments—the carrot-and-stick method of motivation. This was Motivation 2.0, and it can still be an effective extrinsic motivator, particularly for algorithmic or repetitive tasks (those that follow a set of established instructions toward a single conclusion) and for activity that brings a baseline reward (for instance, a salary). However, for heuristic tasks—those that require experimentation, creativity, artistry, and novel solutions—extrinsic "if-then" rewards can actually foster negative behavior. Specifically, rewards can

- extinguish intrinsic motivation;
- diminish performance;
- crush creativity;
- crowd out good behavior;
- encourage cheating, shortcuts, and other unethical behavior;
- become addictive; and
- foster short-term thinking (Pink, 2009, p. 59).

> *Throughout my athletics career, the overall goal was always to be a better athlete than I was at the moment—whether next week, next month, or next year. The improvement was the goal. The medal was simply the ultimate reward for achieving that goal.*
>
> Sebastian Coe, Olympic silver medalist, British politician, and successful sport administrator

Pink argues that it is time for a societal upgrade to Motivation 3.0—an approach founded on three elements that facilitate intrinsic motivation: autonomy, mastery, and purpose. These three elements must work in concert to encourage professional success and foster personal fulfillment in ourselves and in our colleagues.

Autonomy

We are innately self-directed, but this internal drive is often suppressed by outdated notions of organizational management. Several studies have demonstrated that companies outperform their competitors when they foster autonomy in the work environment (Baard et al., 2004; Deci & Ryan, 2008). One way to foster autonomy is by creating a "results-only" mind-set. In this approach, individuals are accountable for their work, but what they do (task), when they do it (time), who they do it with (team), and how they do it (technique) are all up to them.

Mastery

Autonomy alone cannot create motivation, but it helps. Whereas earlier management methods attempted to enforce compliance through control, autonomy can lead to mastery, which is the second element necessary to foster intrinsic motivation. Mastery abides by three rules (Pink, 2009).

1. Mastery is a mind-set: It requires believing that one's abilities are infinitely improvable and that learning goals are valued over performance goals.
2. Mastery is pain: It demands relentless effort, steady perseverance, and disciplined practice.
3. Mastery is an asymptote: That is, it can never be fully realized, which makes its pursuit alluring, joyful, and frustrating.

To enable mastery in your team members, give them tasks that continually challenge and stretch their skill set. In addition, emphasize collaboration. Facilitate task shifting and cross-training, and allow diverse groups to work with one another to stimulate new ideas and processes.

Purpose

The final element of the three-part formula for Motivation 3.0 is purpose, which provides an overarching context within which people can pursue mastery autonomously. As emphasized throughout the leadership lessons in this book, "the most deeply motivated people—not to mention those who are most productive and satisfied—hitch their desires to a cause larger than themselves" (Pink, 2009, p. 133). In this mind-set, purpose maximization and profit maximization are equally important.

One cannot lead a life that is truly excellent without feeling that one belongs to something greater and more permanent than oneself.

Mihaly Csikszentmihalyi, psychology professor and researcher

The desire to do something because you find it deeply satisfying and personally challenging inspires the highest levels of creativity, whether it's in the arts, sciences, or business.

Teresa Amabile, Harvard Business School professor and researcher (best known for research on creativity)

The University of North Carolina at Chapel Hill (UNC) has become known for its event operations. Walk into any event, and you will likely be greeted with a smile from helpful staff members who take pride in the particular element of the event operations plan with which they are tasked. Much of this success derives from the work of Ellen Culler, the former assistant athletics director of event operations. She led and trained her team with care and passion, allowed them autonomy in their work, created an environment that fostered mastery, and above all emphasized that it is a privilege to play a part in hosting events at UNC. She empowered those around her to do better, continually challenged them, and reminded them that they are part of something great. In other words, the event operations unit at UNC is fueled by Motivation 3.0.

hassles and if inclement weather arrives, the television and tailgate party can be moved inside. If another game is more competitive or desirable to watch, then the channel can simply be changed. Staying at home also ensures an opportunity to watch multiple games versus just one contest.

Schools formerly viewed the game itself as the product, thinking that the band, the cheer squad, the mascot, the videoboard, and the crowd were great secondary benefits. However, administrators have no control over an opponent's ranking and whether the game is competitive. Schools now must regularly assess their game-day atmosphere and determine what is missing and how new attractions could be added (Privitera, 2018; Purvis, 2022). One example of this is Mississippi State University introducing a bonus known as the Balconies in the 2022 college football season. Instead of the

Case Study

Outsourcing Your Premium Tailgating

Fans have long tailgated at home athletic events. Whether it is football, soccer, baseball, softball, or other sports, grills have been fired up and food and beverages have been enjoyed by students, alumni, and fans near athletics venues. In recent years, outsourced tailgating companies have emerged. Fans place their order with and pay one of the companies, and the tailgate will be waiting for them on game day. This means that fans no longer have to race to a prime campus location, carry chairs and coolers, or set up a tent. For a premium price, some tailgating companies will even set up a generator and satellite television at the tailgating site. Food and beverages are provided at the tailgate location so fans can enjoy pregame and postgame hospitality without the preparation and cleanup. These companies typically partner with Division I schools that have a culture of tailgating. The companies purchase tents, tables, chairs, coolers, generators, and televisions in bulk, storing them in warehouses or storage units when they are not in use.

For this case study, research these companies. Then imagine that your school, or a school of choice, adopted premium tailgating reservations as a revenue stream.

Questions to Consider

1. For what sports would you offer premium tailgating? Where would these tailgating spots be located?
2. What would fan and student reaction be to paying to reserve premium tailgating space?
3. What would pricing strategies be? How would this change if tables and chairs were provided? What about tents and cooler(s)? Are there other amenities that could affect pricing?
4. How would the reservation and payment system work?
5. Who would provide the labor for tailgating setup and breakdown, including trash removal?
6. Could premium parking be a consideration in the packaging options?
7. How would these answers vary at a smaller Division I school in your region? What about at a Division II or Division III school?

traditional "nosebleed" upper decks, the school allocates certain sections inside the stadium for tailgating. The new seating experience allows fans to continue their tailgating throughout the game, but enables fans to choose their food, beverage, and alternate entertainment options. To secure these prime locations, a minimum donation to the athletics department is required, along with the purchase of a minimum number of tickets. Each tailgate area varies in size, but all feature a shaded area, a field-facing drink rail, electrical outlets, and a storage area for food and beverages (Keen, 2022). Fans can bring in their own table, chairs, fans, and refrigerators but are prohibited from grilling.

CONCLUSION

This chapter examines the foundation of facility and event management. Athletics administrators in this area help ensure that coaches, student-athletes, fans, media, sponsors, sports medicine practitioners, donors, and others have what is needed in order to succeed, whether in practice or on game day. Facility management involves handling both short-term and long-term planning, budgeting, and funding while striving (in the United States) to meet the standards required by such legislation as the Americans With Disabilities Act and Title IX. Facility managers are also responsible for scheduling, setup, and staffing, including everyone from custodians to ushers to workers overseeing the parking lots.

Game-day preparation and management are detailed processes that ensure the safety not only of event participants but also of spectators. Administrators continuously assess risks while trying to respect the rights of fans, including students. Continuing education is required as administrators strive to implement best practices regarding diverse issues, including the threat of terrorism, alcohol-related concerns and rowdy fan behavior, environmental concerns, concession offerings, decisions about outsourcing facility management, decisions about playing at neutral sites, and handling the various other expected and unexpected issues that arise in this line of work.

DISCUSSION QUESTIONS

1. Your school is set to play a bitter rival in a televised Saturday-night game at your home court. Coaches and student-athletes have played up the rivalry in recent years through unflattering comments about each other in the media. In addition, there is no love lost between the two schools' fans, students, and alumni. At past games, objects have been thrown onto the court and profanity has been chanted at the visiting team. The president of your institution wants to know what steps you are taking to ensure the safety of everyone at the game. She does not want an embarrassment on national television. What is your answer?
2. The institution's board of trustees has asked for a report identifying the pros and cons of permitting alcohol sales at home sporting events. What schools would you consult with to address this request? What pros and cons would you point out?
3. At a nationally televised season-opening football game, multiple storms in the area have affected play. What factors need to be considered in deciding whether to continue the game, reschedule it, or cancel it?
4. Your athletics facility is booked for two sporting events on one day. A basketball game will take place at noon, followed by wrestling at 7:00. What needs to be done to ensure that both events are successfully held? What are your concerns?
5. Your facility is hosting a conference basketball championship over the span of several days. The last game on one particular day extends to eight overtime periods, sending your support staff home well after midnight. The staff, including ticket takers, ushers, and security officers, must return the next morning to continue operating the tournament. Given their lack of sufficient sleep, how would you boost their morale?
6. Your school is hosting an outdoors NCAA tennis tournament that features a team championship, singles championship, and doubles championship for both men and women. Weather has affected play, leaving you to determine the options for ensuring that the tournament is completed in good time. Assuming that you have an indoor facility, explore all of your options, identifying the pros and cons of each scenario.
7. Does your school embrace sustainability practices on campus? What about in athletics facilities and at home athletic events? If yes, share how. If not, how might this be rectified?

LEARNING ACTIVITIES

1. Examine the NCAA's website for postseason bid specifications. Pick a Division I sport and determine what facilities in your area meet the NCAA's expectations. Repeat the exercise for various sports and at the Division II and Division III levels.
2. Draft a game-day timeline and a checklist of what is needed to host a sporting event at your school. Invite an athletics administrator to class and compare your timeline and checklist with those used by the school.

3. Go to an on-campus athletics facility and conduct a risk assessment. Repeat the assignment with other athletics facilities on campus. Repeat the assignment again during live sporting events.
4. Go to an on-campus athletics facility and identify ways in which it could be upgraded to benefit student-athletes, coaches, administrators, and fans. Discuss which is more feasible—renovation or new construction. Repeat the assignment with other athletics facilities on campus.
5. Use online resources (e.g., YouTube) to examine new facilities, including locker rooms, practice facilities, and game-day venues. Identify trends resulting from the arms race in collegiate sports and discuss what amenities could be seen in the near future.
6. The baseball team has done very well, and its ranking indicates that it is likely to play a game at home in the opening rounds of the postseason tournament. However, the NCAA requires schools to bid if they have an interest in hosting. Find the NCAA postseason bid specifications and identify a particular school's strengths for putting a bid forward.
7. Research Disney and its approach to customer service. What Disney attributes could your school or schools in your conference adopt in their event management strategies?
8. Some schools have utilized esports as an enrollment strategy. Research what colleges and universities offer competitive esports. What investments, including facilities, were necessary to launch the program? What events are held on college campuses, and how are they organized?

University of South Carolina.

Alumni Relations and Athletics Development

Robert H. Zullo, Slippery Rock University

In this chapter, you will explore

- the importance of fundraising in intercollegiate athletics;
- how to identify, qualify, cultivate, solicit, and steward donors;
- ways in which donors can contribute to intercollegiate athletics departments;
- ways to thank donors for their support; and
- concerns that can arise with fundraising.

WHO IS IN CHARGE?

Your basketball coach has won many conference championships and consistently reached postseason play until the past three years. However, attendance at home games is dropping and a significant number of student-athletes have transferred. Changes were made in the coaching staff, but results have not materialized in recruiting or in winning percentage. Both the fans and the media are suggesting it is time to make a change in leadership. The issue delaying any change is that the coach has a significant contract buyout. Some donors remain loyal to the coach and believe the program can be turned around with investments elsewhere in the program, but others have expressed a willingness to assist with the buyout. Your experience with agents tells you that new hires also tend to bring additional expenses in the form of facility upgrades and assistant personnel salaries.

Some of the bigger donors have provided names of coaching candidates for you to consider. They are willing to help with the buyout if their candidate is hired. Your short list of candidates does not include any of your donor's candidates. However, the donors have indicated that either the next head coach comes from their list or their contributions to the athletics department and the university come to an end. How do you find a solution that identifies the best candidate for your school while retaining the support of your top donors?

As discussed in chapter 8, athletics departments build the revenue portion of their budget through a variety of sources, which can include (to name a few) ticket sales, sponsorship revenue, allocations from conferences and governing bodies, state appropriations, student fees, and concessions. For the vast majority of institutions, however, expenses heavily outpace revenues (NCAA revenues and expenses report, 2012). Therefore, in order to meet the growing financial demands of athletics administration, it is imperative for most institutions to seek financial support from athletics donors through fundraising efforts.

In intercollegiate athletics, fundraising is frequently referred to as development. As Kirk Gatlin, assistant athletics director for annual giving at Tulane University, noted, "college athletics is in a perpetual arms race and successful development work is vital to consistent revenue streams for programs supporting student-athletes and coaches." (2022) Donors' contributions help offset, for example, the expense of scholarships, facilities, and salaries. Thus, fundraising is a priority of for all athletics directors today. In fact, Zack Lassiter, vice president for athletics at Abilene Christian University, emphasizes the importance of fundraising by noting that "everyone's a fundraiser," which means that the development skill set is needed in each athletics staff member (Lassiter, 2022). This includes such development positions as alumni relations, annual giving, major gifts, letterwinners' clubs, and event planning.

According to J Batt, director of athletics at Georgia Tech and former senior deputy athletics director and chief operating officer for revenue and development at the University of Alabama, these positions can be evaluated by financial and activity metrics, both individually and as a group, on monthly and annual visits. Fundraisers can have specific dollar goals they need to reach in gift types of capital, planning giving, endowments, and other areas. Weekly or biweekly meetings can help assess the staff's advancement with leads and donors, while overall progress to goal evaluation can be held biennially (Batt et al., 2020). Face-to-face visits, calls, and actual solicitations are quantified and assessed as well as outreach to new or past donors. Additional metrics could include frequency of contact, average gift, unique visits, event attendance correlation, and donor retention. Staff accountability must be balanced realistically to encourage strong staff productivity and teamwork as well as long-term relationships with donors.

Fundraising involves identifying, cultivating, soliciting and stewarding donors. Brian Thornburg, an associate athletics director for major gifts at the University of Maryland, emphasizes that listening to prospects and donors and relationship building are key tools to being successful in development (2022). Fundraising is not simply transactional, since donors like their input to be heard in both good times and bad. Ben Ross, a vice president for development with the Tiger Athletic Foundation at Louisiana State University, challenges fundraisers to talk less and listen more (2016). In other words, skillful execution is needed in order to build relationships, request a donation (known as an "ask"), and gain a donor's financial support.

Fundraising 101: Donor Cultivation

Identification, qualification, cultivation, solicitation, and stewardship are frequent terms utilized in fundraising. *Identification* is the process of pinpointing who should be on a list of potential prospects that could eventually become donors (Wanless et al., 2017). Some of this involves looking at existing data, such as season ticket holders, frequent ticket purchasers, or people who attend campus events (see the technology tools sidebar to learn more about data collection). Existing data can also include databases of alumni, former letterwinners, and friends of various athletics programs. The more touchpoints there are, the more data there is to identify those who could support athletics. Referrals to prospective donors from active donors are another valuable source (Wanless et al., 2017).

Qualification is the process of prioritizing names from the data that could be viable donors. Qualification involves looking at ability, interest, and link (Newman, 2017). For example, a recent graduate might be a candidate for annual giving with the idea that they could eventually become a candidate for a major gift. In theory, young alumni's ability to give strengthens as their income increases. Qualification also includes the interest of the individual—for instance, a database might have the name of a student-athlete's parent who is interested in giving only until the student-athlete graduates. Qualification also includes link because it important to note how the individual aligns with the organization. Someone giving to the biology department may not have an alignment with giving to athletics. Someone interested in supporting women's basketball may not have an alignment with giving to other athletics programs.

Cultivation involves meeting with the prospect or lead and moving them toward solicitation. This includes getting to know the potential donor, inviting them to special events, and generally building a relationship (Thornburg, 2022). Through this process, athletic development staff can share current or upcoming projects and opportunities, while the potential donor might share their areas of interest for potential contributions (Wanless et al., 2017).

Solicitation involves asking for a certain amount for a specific project or opportunity. Information has been shared with the potential donor about various projects and the money necessary for the project. The project might be a new facility, a facility renovation, a major gift for operations or endowments, or a multitude of other giving opportunities. The ask aligns with past conversations with the potential donor and their capability so that there are no surprises in the amount requested. The solicitation also includes continued education to the potential donor about the benefits to the student-athletes, the program, the athletics department, and the school, relative to peer institutions. Finally, the solicitation enumerates the benefits to the potential donors, like naming opportunities and recognition (Wanless et al., 2017).

Stewardship is the continuous process of thanking the donor, reminding them of the gift's impact, and updating them about future athletics donor opportunities (Newman, 2017). It means continuing to strengthen the relationship with the donor so that the gift does not appear purely transactional. Stewardship could entail inviting them to games or special events, taking them to lunch, sending them thank-you notes, or introducing them to coaches and student-athletes.

One significant change to this process as the result of the COVID-19 pandemic is that communication with donors moved online. As in other areas, virtual meetings are becoming more common, increasing the efficiency of initial communications (Murphy, 2022). Furthermore, this increased the opportunity for remote work since development officers could work from home or on the road instead of coming to campus.

Development work also requires flexibility. As described by Gene Smith, athletics director at Ohio State University, "Fundraising is critical in today's business model within athletics departments. Great organizations are able to be agile and innovative with their development planning and solicitations" (Convention preview, 2010).

With expenses in intercollegiate athletics escalating, robust donor support is critical. Cultivating lifelong donors helps offset annual costs over the long term. Personalized cultivation and stewardship enable donors to feel that they are part of the athletics department's success, both on the playing surface and in the classroom.

All donors want to think they're the only donor you have. Whether they're $50-a-year donors or $50,000-a-year donors, they think they're just as important as everybody else.

Kevin Hansen, development manager, Lutz Software (qtd. in Steinbach, 2003)

CULTIVATING DONORS: CLUBS, ASSOCIATIONS, FOUNDATIONS, AND SOCIETIES

Fundraising successfully requires support from many people. As Tsiotsou (2007) notes, development entails establishing long-term relationships with both current and prospective donors. This goal is achieved in part by forming clubs, foundations, associations, and societies in conjunction with the athletics department. Such groups make it easier to identify more donors, establish contact with them, and solicit them for donations (Humphreys & Mondello, 2007).

The solicitation message can even be communicated in the name of the organization, as demonstrated by Clemson University. Supporters of the Clemson Tigers belong to IPTAY, which stands for "I pay ten [dollars] a year." It can also be helpful to identify inspirational keywords, such as *champion, legacy, innovation, rebrand, initiative,* and *team,* to create an optimistic atmosphere of success in pursuing a fundraising goal.

One of the appealing aspects of fundraising is the fact that its possibilities are endless. As noted by Tim McMurray, former athletics director at Texas A&M–Commerce University, "There are only so many tickets that you can sell and only so many sodas that you can pour. But the one area in our profession where there's no ceiling is the number of private dollars you can bring into your program" (qtd. in Steinbach, 2009). In contrast, other sources of funding may be limited. Businesses, for example, allocate only a certain amount of funds to corporate sponsorship; they may also pursue other promotional options. Similarly, facilities have set seating capacities, thus putting a firm limit on the number of people who can attend an event. But individual donors may be willing to contribute for various reasons, in varying forms and amounts, to support an athletics department.

By joining an athletics-related club, donors can obtain various benefits based on their level of giving. Depending on the institution, benefits may include tax breaks, priority seating and parking, professional and social contacts, invitations to members-only functions, access to coaches and student-athletes, hospitality, publications (e.g., media guides, programs), decals, tickets to away games and postseason competition, and travel with the team. For example, when the University of Alaska Anchorage created the Seawolf Athletic Association to carry out fundraising for its athletics department (Northcutt, 2010), the department reaped the following benefits.

- Fundraising for athletics as a whole versus sport-specific donations
- Streamlined fundraising process
- Collective growth of volunteer support
- Conversion of sport-specific fans into Seawolf Athletics fans
- Creation of a scholarship endowment program
- Establishment of a database of potential donors, particularly alumni
- Engagement with alumni through season recaps, newsletters, and special events
- Development of a phonathon with participation by student-athletes

A development club should not single out only graduates but should be open to both alumni and nonalumni, because both groups are invaluable to athletics fundraising efforts. Indeed, Tsiotsou (2007) found that alumni and nonalumni donors do not differ in their motivation, involvement, income, or contributions. Instead, research has found that the level of a donor's contribution depends on income and on the donor's involvement with the athletics program (Tsiotsou, 2004).

A donor's giving behavior can also be affected by demographic factors, such as age, gender, residency, and education (Tsiotsou, 2004). Solicitation of donors should include such previously underrepresented sectors as women and members of minority groups (Robinson, 1998; Shapiro & Ridinger, 2011; Staurowsky, 1996; Tsiotsou, 2006). Great prospects can also be found in the fan base of nonrevenue sports (Bernat, 2010).

Relationship building helps increase trust, and when donors have confidence in the reliability and integrity of the university, they are likely to be more motivated to give. In these conditions, they believe in the leadership and want to be involved (Hanson & Peachey, 2022; Tsiotsou, 2007). Toward this end, development officers can help donors learn about the athletics department by hosting social events where speeches are given by campus and athletics leaders (Tsiotsou, 2007). For example, schools may have luncheons with student-athletes, coaches, and senior administrators. The development staff can also offer donors early opportunities to learn about potential projects or see newly completed facilities. Staff can also invite donors to special events like the student-athlete awards banquet or end-of-year recognition ceremonies.

It is also important, as emphasized by Aaron Epstein, executive senior associate athletics director for championship resources and assistant vice president for philanthropy and alumni engagement at Western Kentucky University, to find the right voice in which to talk with donors. Sometimes this effort means having student-athletes personalize the experience by sharing their success stories. This is especially true in Division II and lower levels, where donors can better appreciate the effect they have on a student-athlete's education (Gardiner, 2009; Hanson & Peachey, 2022). Donors can also be informed through emails, traditional mailings, newsletters and other publications, and social media. Such materials provide opportunities to indicate donor contributions via narratives or lists (Tsiotsou, 2007).

> *To accomplish longitudinal bonds, athletic fundraising needs to keep donors motivated, build trust, enhance their loyalty, and increase their involvement with the athletic programs of the university.*
>
> Tsiotsou, 2007, p. 87

Personnel resources in athletics development vary by school. At a larger Division I school, the department may include senior staff, major gift facilitators, support staff, gift processing personnel, interns, and graduate assistants (Kirinovic & Milliron, 2009). Smaller schools and schools in Division II or lower may require personnel to perform multiple roles (Hanson & Peachey, 2022).

Fundraising is relationship driven, and in some cases a particular development staffer has an exceptionally strong one-on-one relationship with a donor. Even these relationships, however, need support in the stewardship process. This is particularly true because development offices strive to maintain relationships with donors regardless of changes in personnel. Thus fundraising always requires skillful collaboration as a team, the word serving as a useful acronym to remind us that "*t*ogether *e*veryone *a*ccomplishes *m*ore." For all schools, but especially those with a smaller development staff, volunteers are also vital in the cultivation and stewardship process (Hall, 2009).

BROADENING THE DONOR BASE

Broadening the donor base can be as simple as pursuing referrals from current donors, but it also entails researching alumni databases, former letter-winners, parents/family of students, ticket holders, and members of the community (Barber, 2007). It can also include the fans not directly affiliated with the school (Epstein, 2022). In 2017, the University of Alabama released a 17-page document known as the Standard, a strategic plan outlining

Branding in the Development Office

Anthony Henderson Sr. is a veteran senior athletics administrator, with stints at Old Dominion University (Virginia), the University of Akron (Ohio), the College of William & Mary (Virginia), and Yale University (Connecticut). He stresses that branding is vital in philanthropy to separate your organization from others (2018). He calls branding "a promise to your donors," noting that it reflects what donors can expect. The assessment of branding involves significant self-discovery in your department but can yield the opportunity to better control your organization's narrative. This is particularly important because development staff cannot control wins and losses, the players, injuries, transfers, coaching changes, or other sports-related variables. Some of this reflection on development includes examining the following questions:

- What is your department's mission?
- What are the benefits to the donor who contributes to your department?
- What do donors or prospects already think of your department?
- What qualities do you want them to associate with your department?

After these questions have been answered and you have pinpointed your brand, Henderson stresses that getting the message out is vital. He recommends these strategies (2018).

- It all begins with a great logo. Place it everywhere.
- Write down your brand messaging and make sure everyone internally is speaking the same language when it comes to how it is communicated.
- Integrate your brand into every aspect of your department, how you answer the phone, voicemail, email signatures, etc.
- Develop a tagline—be memorable, meaningful, and concise.
- Develop templates and create a brand guide for your marketing materials so the look and feel are consistent throughout.
- Be true to your brand—deliver on the promise to the donor.
- Be consistent. If not, the establishment of your brand will not happen.

Nick Popplewell, an assistant vice president for institutional advancement at the University of Texas at El Paso, adds that branding includes positive storytelling about the student-athletes, coaches, athletics programs, and school to donors. He emphasizes that "people will donate more to an entity that is organized, genuine, has a professional appearance and approach, engages at a high level, and has a compelling case for philanthropy" (2019). The Miner Athletic Club, the fundraising arm for UTEP Athletics, embraced a rebrand to increase relationships with fans and donors alike. The name of the fundraising arm was retained since it connected with the school's mascot, and the word "club" imparted the feeling that fans could belong to something unique. However, the logo was modified to better connect with the school mascot and school spirit. The mission statement and tagline of the club were also updated to align with the new core values and mission statement of the athletics department. Development staff then turned these updates into a brief elevator pitch, making it easier to educate donors about the cause. To push these changes externally, a new website was launched and a social media strategy was implanted (2019).

Continuous reflection on an organization's brand helps to maximize the stakeholders' perception of the entity and the team. External perception is crucial in fundraising. People can give and make a difference in many places. Keeping that passion aligned with athletics is a perpetual process through relationships and continuous brand assessment.

the mission statement and core values of Alabama athletics. Part of the Standard included doubling the number of scholarship club donors (Alabama Athletics, 2022) to, among other things, deepen the pool of donors who might be solicited for larger contributions.

Young Alumni

Complications arise when premium seating for donors is limited. This creates a waiting list. A similar problem can arise when students graduate and no longer have access to sold-out sporting events. One option, of course, is to expand premium seating areas, resulting in greater contributions. In another approach, some schools have enabled undergraduate students to earn "priority points" for attendance at sporting events. For example, the University of South Carolina offers a "young alumni" ticket option whereby recent graduates can purchase season tickets at a discounted rate for up to four consecutive years after graduation, earning benefits to the Gamecock Club (Gamecock Club, 2022). This move heightened recent graduates' affinity for the program and built their point level so that they did not have to make a substantial contribution to gain access while their earning power was still low.

Former Student-Athletes

Great donor prospects can also be found among former student-athletes (Bernat, 2010). Giving by former student-athletes is influenced by the potential donor's importance to, connection with, knowledge of, and experience with the athletics program (Brown et al., 2008; Shapiro et al., 2010). Strategies for engaging former student-athletes in giving include inviting them to serve on volunteer committees, hosting reunions and alumni weekends, and communicating actively with them, especially when changes are made in the coaching staff (Gimbl, 2010; LaPlante, 2011). Many schools also create a letterwinner's club specifically for former student-athletes and managers.

MOTIVATING DONORS

As ample research indicates, donors give for a variety of reasons (Billing et al., 1985; Gladden et al., 2005; Mahony et al., 2003; Staurowsky et al.,1999; Strode & Fink, 2009; Tsiotsou, 1998). For example, they may want to receive personal recognition, memorialize a friend or family member, influence decisions, socialize or affiliate with the university or other supporters (e.g., attend sport events with friends and family members), receive tangible benefits (e.g., priority ticketing, parking, and access), satisfy their philanthropic motives, or enhance the program's athletics success. Indeed, Strode and Fink (2009) found that donors believe their support of an athletics department could yield success for a team. In turn, such success heightens a donor's affiliation with the program.

Development staff members should consider these various motivations. Simply providing access to premium tickets is not sufficient. In a cautionary example, Arizona State University's Sun Devil Club consisted of 12,500 active donors in 2008. By 2010, however, membership was down to 4,000, and the drop cost the organization almost US$4 million (Steinbach, 2012). Self-analysis by the organization found that the group had relied too heavily on premium seating as its primary means for raising funds. Additionally, sports enthusiasts now enjoy big-screen, high-definition televisions at home, meaning more football games can be watched at a fraction of the cost with cheaper food and beverages, a cleaner restroom, and less parking hassle (Gatlin, 2022). Moreover, donors may not see their donation as a generous gift but rather as transactional extension of the cost of a season ticket.

To achieve healthy department–donor relations, it is crucial to understand the motives that drive giving. Tim McMurray, former athletics director at Texas A&M–Commerce University, indicates that "what really separates a good development officer is if you can get to the root of the *no.* Is it no to timing? Is it no to the amount? Or is it no to the cause? If it's one of the first two, that's forgivable. We can work around that—we can get into payment plans or we can lower the amount of the ask. If it's no to the cause, then we've got work to do internally. People have to feel good about your cause" (qtd. in Steinbach, 2009).

In addition, the cause itself can vary. For some donors, the cause is team success, whereas for others it is helping student-athletes get an education. Research on Division II donor motives indicated vicarious achievement, philanthropy,

Ten Ways to Blow the Ask

If you've been in this profession for long, you've probably stumbled in some attempts to secure a donor—and have learned lessons to improve for the next time. Prior to your next prospect meeting, check to see if you're committing any of these common mistakes before you blow the ask.

Mistake 1: You don't present the "right" project.

We've all been there. The athletics director sets a priority, and there's pressure to meet the fund-raising goal.

This might seem obvious, but you must do your homework on every prospect to ensure that the project you're presenting really speaks to that individual. If a prospect gets excited about programmatic support, presenting a bricks-and-mortar facility project—even if it's the priority of your athletics department—can really be off-putting to the prospect. It shows you haven't taken the time to get to know him or her. Be sure that the project you're presenting is something the prospect has a genuine interest in, and you'll be much more likely to secure a commitment.

Mistake 2: You don't ask for the right amount.

Asking for the right amount is just as important as finding the right project.

Prospects rarely get offended if you ask for too much. Most people are flattered that you think they're capable of such a gift. And a high ask can raise someone's sights. But asking for too little shows you haven't prepared properly, which can derail the development process.

Mistake 3: You didn't sufficiently prepare the prospect for the ask.

No one likes to be caught off guard by someone making an unexpected request—and that goes double for solicitations.

Be sure to lead your prospects to a point where they know you're going to ask for a significant gift. Make sure they're ready to seriously consider such a request. When the time for the solicitation comes, you might not even have to ask for the gift; the prospect will understand why you are there, what size gift you are seeking, and what the gift will support.

Mistake 4: You exclude important people from your request.

Although you might be more comfortable making an ask during a one-on-one meeting—less of an audience, right?!?—be sure that you don't exclude someone who might play an important role in the donor's decision-making process.

Does your prospect consult with a partner, an attorney, or an accountant? If so, ask if that individual might be included in the meeting. It can be very frustrating to finish a solicitation only to learn that someone who is part of the decision was not present.

Mistake 5: You "wing it" during the solicitation meeting.

When you, your athletics director, and the prospect get together and start talking, you hope the ask might just "naturally" happen. But there's a good chance it won't, especially if the dollar amount is very significant.

Before the meeting, be sure to map out a plan for how the conversation will unfold. Determine in advance who will state the need, put the ask on the table, and outline next steps at the end of the meeting.

Mistake 6: You waffle when making the ask.

You've put a great deal of time and energy into developing a positive relationship with the prospect. When the time comes for an ask, don't back down. If you don't ask, the prospect won't give.

Think of it this way: you're offering the prospect an opportunity to invest in your program. Prospects often appreciate having interesting ideas brought to them for their consideration. So move forward with confidence and conviction—seasoned with humility—and you'll see positive results.

Mistake 7: You stick blindly to your agenda.

Despite your best preparations, sometimes the ask meeting will veer in an unexpected direction. If you're thrown a curveball, be flexible and try to salvage the meeting as best you can.

But don't be so determined that you steamroll past the issue at hand, potentially offending your prospect and damaging the chance of a gift in the future. If you can't get back on track, you might say to the prospect, "You know, I came here today to discuss a significant commitment to the athletics department. Why don't I address (the immediate concern) today, and then we can schedule a time to talk further about the campaign."

Mistake 8: You pressure the donor for a commitment.

When you make an ask, know when to stop talking and patiently wait for a response.

Your prospects are successful, educated people. They gather information, process it, and make careful decisions. When you ask for a significant investment in your institution, they're going to need time to think it over. If you insist on walking out the door with a signed pledge agreement, you may find yourself leaving empty-handed. Instead, put a proposal on the table and give the prospect time to mull it over. This approach might even yield a greater gift than one he or she can agree upon immediately.

Mistake 9: You promise donors things you can't deliver.

It's easy to get carried away when describing the recognition or special treatment a donor might receive in appreciation for a gift. If you can't get the donor on the team plane for the Rose Bowl, don't offer it. It's better to underpromise and overdeliver.

Mistake 10: You announce the gift prematurely.

You've just received a commitment, and you're bursting with excitement! But be sure everything is in place before you announce the gift, lest the news travel back to the prospect prematurely. This could not only upset the prospect and jeopardize his or her commitment; it could also create a problem for the campus if for some reason the gift does not materialize.

Reprinted by permission from M. Pientka, *Best Practices: 10 Ways to Blow the Ask* (National Association of Athletic Development Directors, 2009). Available: http://www.nacda.com/sports/naadd/spec-rel/101609aak.html.

commitment, and power (Kim et al., 2019). Therefore, it is vital to listen to donors, because giving is not a one-size-fits-all endeavor. More specifically, segmenting donors based on motivation can benefit fundraisers in the following ways (Tsiotsou, 2007):

- Provides the base for targeted fundraising
- Helps develop more effective marketing mixes in order to motivate specific donor segments
- Facilitates cause differentiation
- Enables marketing strategies targeted toward specific motivational groups
- Enables shaping of fundraising tactics to optimize results
- Provides easier identification of fundraising opportunities and threats

BENEFITS OF GIVING: PRIORITY SEATING AND PARKING

Ideally, demand for premium seating is greater than availability, thus creating a "tough ticket" and heightening donors' urgency to contribute (Steinbach, 2005c). With this potential motivation in mind, athletics departments often tie giving to the privilege of purchasing premium seating or reserved parking.

Supporters of the athletics department also may receive benefits that resemble a retail store's "loyalty program." Benefit points can be based on the contribution amount and on the number of years for which a contributor has given, thus rewarding loyalty (Berman, 2011). Development software can be used to help development officers and donors evaluate the benefits that accompany various levels of donation while also preserving the integrity of the process such that it becomes more transparent to staffers and donors alike (Steinbach, 2003).

Donors frequently ask, "Who gets better seats—those who give more or those who give longer?" It is vital for development offices to remember the long-term value of a season-ticket holder who contributes annually but not substantially (Mahony et al., 2003). Annual contributions from such donors open the door to continuous revenue through ticket sales, parking fees, and concession and merchandise sales at sporting events. Thus it is important for athletics departments to recognize not only amount but also longevity in annual giving.

> *Sitting courtside at University of Georgia basketball is the closest thing to being a part of the game without playing or coaching in it. Unless you are sitting on the bench with the team, it is the best way to feel and see all the energies, efforts, and emotions of the players and coaches before, during, and after each game.*
>
> Frank Beltran, men's basketball courtside seat holder (qtd. in Center, 2010)

Fans who desire reserved parking or premium seats can be encouraged to donate at a higher level and to keep giving annually in order to retain their benefits. Contributions for premium seating (e.g., suite, club level) may also give donors access to areas that allow alcohol consumption at sporting events and invitations to private dinners with team and staff members (Center, 2010), while premium

Big Tax Changes in 2018

If someone donated US$5,000 for the opportunity to purchase 2017 college football season tickets, 80 percent of the donation was tax deductible. The cost of the tickets themselves was not. That opportunity ceased to exist January 1, 2018, as tax laws changed. To help donors with deductions, some athletics departments tried to ask donors to donate for multiple upcoming seasons by December 31 (Uhler, 2018). The University of South Carolina (USC) and the University of Oklahoma took prepayment contributions for the upcoming 3 football seasons, the University of Georgia 5 seasons, and the University of Notre Dame 10 seasons. Oklahoma State University had no limit on how many upcoming seasons a donor could pay in advance for (Novy-Williams & Lorin, 2017).

> *"It remains to be seen, the overall implications from the loss of the tax-deductible status for donations to college sports programs," University of South Carolina Athletic Director Ray Tanner said in a statement. "We do know that there will be an impact with how some of our supporters filed their taxes. Our fans are very passionate about the Gamecocks, though, so I hope they will continue to buy tickets and give to our program." (Gay, 2018)*

According to Jesse Marks, deputy director of athletics for development at Northwestern University (and previously a senior administrator at the University of Miami), and Chad Weiberg, athletics director (and former deputy athletics director) at Oklahoma State University, the change in the tax law required development officers to focus their attention on philanthropic giving to athletics, though many top athletics programs are able to keep the "donation or giving for premium seating" plan in place, minus the benefit of tax deductions (Batt et al., 2020). Tom McMillen, the chief executive of the LEAD1 Association, indicated his concern that millions of dollars in donations that benefit student-athletes would be lost and that nonrevenue sports would be hurt the most. However, Dave Ridpath, a professor at Ohio University and a former president of the Drake Group, remains hopeful that the loss of revenue could lead to a market reset of exorbitant and unnecessary athletic spending (Wingerter, 2018).

parking privileges allow fans to tailgate nearer to the event and to arrive closer to the starting time of a game.

Contributions also offer tax benefits, because institutions of higher education are considered nonprofits, which means that donations are fully deductible at their fair market value (Howard & Crompton, 2003). Deductions can total up to 50 percent of an individual's adjusted gross income, and donations beyond that level can be allocated to the individual's adjusted gross income over the next five years (Bittel, 2022).

WAYS TO GIVE

When donors think about supporting athletics, they may initially believe that cash is the only way to contribute. In fact, however, donors can support athletics in various ways, including donations of real estate, investments, employee contributions, and more. Contributions can be part of a major gift, a capital campaign effort to raise a substantial amount of funds, or an endowment program that funds a scholarship or other expense item. Additional forms of giving are deferred giving, matching gifts, purchasing a brick toward a building project, participating in a silent auction, or even taking part in a camp held by an athletic team. Development officers should work diligently to ensure that all types of contribution are encouraged.

Major Gifts

Fundraising involves building relationships with donors who believe in a cause; it takes time and involves an extensive process (Lindahl, 1995). By cultivating a relationship with a donor, the development office can gauge whether the donor wants to support a specific athletics program or athletics in general. In other words, donors have the option of contributing either restricted or unrestricted gifts. Unrestricted giving, which is preferred by a development staff, enables a school to use the funds for any purpose (Humphreys & Mondello, 2007). Restricted gifts, on the other hand, are earmarked for a specific purpose.

Major gifts can be used to reduce the expenses associated with facility construction or renovation. For example, the University of Virginia received a major gift of US$40 million in April 2022 from a former student-athlete, its largest commitment ever (Newton, 2022); Valparaiso University used two gifts, totaling US$550,000, to help with adding turf to the baseball field (Valpo News, 2020).

Stadium and arena construction and renovation are the most visible projects, but major gifts can also be used for locker rooms, weight rooms, training tables, and academic facilities, thus supporting student-athletes in their wellness and their studies. In other examples, a significant lead or "first" gift enabled Georgia Southern University to start construction on an indoor practice facility (Grice, 2022) and a lead gift enabled a former baseball letterwinner to help modernize an exercise room at Cornell College (Iowa) and honor his wife who had died a few years before (Cornell College, 2022). Similarly, Virginia Tech used a lead gift of US$15.2 million to help with a new student-athlete performance center (Moris & Vosburgh, 2017).

Endowment Programs

Endowment programs enable development offices to cultivate funds from donors, invest the principal, and use the interest to cover annual operating expenses in perpetuity (forever). Given a five percent interest rate, an endowment donation of US$250,000 would yield an average of US$12,500 per year. Endowment funds can grow more quickly in a bull market, thus providing considerable interest. Covered expenses can include, for example, the cost of scholarships, coaches' salaries, facility upkeep, and operational budgets. In return for the donation, the donor may be recognized in various ways, depending on the expectation set by the school, but it often includes a naming opportunity for the endowment.

One example of a successful scholarship endowment program can be found at Boston College, where the cost of an athletics scholarship exceeded US$60,000 in 2022, up from US$53,500 in 2011. With 272 scholarships committed to student-athletes, the school needs to generate funds targeted for this considerable expense (Foley, 2011). To meet this need, Boston College uses an endowment fund supported by an annual donor luncheon on a home football weekend where student-athletes, coaches, and school administrators meet the donors who support them. The personal interaction continues with thank-you notes and updates from student-athletes coordinated through the development office. The program enabled Boston College to increase its total of endowed scholarships from 31 in 2005 to 162 by 2011 with an end goal of endowing every scholarship.

Capital Campaigns

Athletics departments work with their school's academic departments via capital campaigns to address capital, operating, and endowment efforts within a limited time frame. Establishing a board of supportive donors initiates the process, which also includes the recruitment of other donors in a private or "silent" phase. This silent phase allows time to solicit major financial commitments that build fundraising momentum for a more public phase (Heil, 2019).

The University of Virginia launched a US$5 billion capital campaign titled "Honor the Future" as part of a concerted effort to create a prosperous future from an operational and competitive standpoint. Although the campaign targets overall enhancement of the university, the fundraising arm of the school's athletics department was expected to raise US$500 million as part of the larger campaign. According to Dirk Katstra, former executive director of the Virginia Athletics Foundation, a US$40 million campaign gift in April 2022, from a former student-athlete, came as a result of the donor's continuing support of the school's annual fund effort (Wendel, 2022).

As Tsiotsou (2007) has stressed, campaigns centered on increasing a university's prestige can help build donors' motivation. Prestige can be measured

Boston College Endowed Athletics Scholarships

Donors making a commitment to an endowed athletics scholarship have the opportunity to name the fund according to their wishes. This can be in honor or memory of a loved one or to establish a family legacy. They also have the option to personalize the fund to match their interests—perhaps to a specific sport or for a student-athlete enrolled in a particular school.

Types of Endowments at Boston College

Endowed Athletic Scholarships

Each year Boston College funds 272 full athletic scholarships through a combination of the endowment and Flynn Fund annual support. The greater we can grow the scholarship endowment, the greater the opportunity to utilize Flynn Fund dollars for strategic initiatives and improve the overall financial stability of the athletics department.

Your Student-Athlete and Fund Updates

Your endowed fund lives in perpetuity at BC and provides support to a student-athlete. You will have the opportunity to meet the recipient of your fund each year at our annual gathering and watch them as they grow as a student and athlete at BC.

Athletics Financial Aid Endowments

A named financial aid fund may also be established with a commitment of $100,000. These funds are not able to be restricted to a specific sport nor assigned to a specific student-athlete. Instead, it adds much needed funds to the general athletics endowment in support of scholarships.

Operating Endowments

Funds to help alleviate operating expenses may be established with a commitment of $100,000 or more and can be designated toward any of BC's 31 varsity sports. For example, a soccer operating endowment could enhance the program annually by funding a special project such as updated film analytics software.

Adapted by permission from *Ways to Give: Endowed Scholarships.* (Chestnut Hill, MA: Boston College). Available: http://www.bceagles.com/boosters/bc-endowment-current-winners.html.

both quantitatively (e.g., in terms of winning percentages, championships, and graduation rates) and qualitatively (e.g., through placement of alumni and other personal success stories) (Tsiotsou, 2007). Campaign themes should also emphasize the fact that donors' gifts help the school build resources that are comparable to, if not better than, those of their counterparts—both academically and athletically (Ford, 2009; McGinniss, 2011; O'Brien, 2010; Stanley, 2009).

Industry Profile

DR. MAURA MURPHY

Senior Associate Athletic Director for Development, Ohio State University

Dr. Murphy is a senior athletics administrator engaged in major gifts, including endowments and capital projects, at Ohio State University. An outstanding fundraiser, Dr. Murphy started as director of development in June 2010, before advancing to assistant and then associate athletic director. Prior to Ohio State, Murphy was at the University of Central Florida (UCF), where she was the assistant athletics director for development, providing leadership in annual giving, the premium-seat programs, and helping with major gifts. Additionally, she was the head of the Golden Knights Club (the fundraising arm of UCF Athletics).

Dr. Murphy was previously at Ohio University as assistant athletic director for development, working on the annual giving program, capital projects, endowments, and special events. She has also worked with the Orange Bowl Committee, facilitating Orange Bowl Festival ancillary events, including team site visits, welcome receptions, beach parties, kickoff receptions, and coaches' luncheons.

Hailing from Greensburg, Pennsylvania, Dr. Murphy studied education at Saint Mary's College in Notre Dame, Indiana. While an undergraduate student, she worked for four years as a student assistant in the football office at Notre Dame, helping to plan and manage official recruiting visits, creating information for mailings, and maintaining the Fighting Irish recruiting database. She also spent a summer as an operations intern for the Cleveland Browns, assisting the team's marketing, new media, and operations departments and helping with the general public's viewing of training camp. She then earned her master's degree in Sports Administration from Ohio University while working full time. Her doctorate, from Ohio State University in 2018, examined development effectiveness in intercollegiate athletics.

Ohio State Athletics

Stanford University has used the endowment model to generate a substantial revenue stream when the economy is sound. According to the Stanford Giving website, the school's endowment paid out US$1.33 billion at the beginning of the 2020-21 fiscal year, or 4.6 percent of the endowment's value of US$28.9 billion, helping with 21 of the university's operating costs (2022). Because endowment investments are prone to the same volatility that characterizes investments in general, they can be affected by an economic downturn.

Another issue that arises in endowment programs hinges on the fact that donors tend to support highly visible sports, such as football and men's basketball, which offer a widely desired affiliation with high-profile athletes and coaches. Even so, targeted cultivation and stewardship can yield positive fundraising results for all sport teams. A former volleyball letterwinner at the University of North Carolina contributed a million-dollar gift to celebrate women's athletics (University Development, 2022).

To add to a campaign's chance of success, a school can divide the campaign into phases (Terrell, 2010). Doing so enables the school to prioritize its needs and reassess the level of contributions. At the University of Virginia, for example, phase I included building two natural grass fields where a past basketball arena existed. Phase II emphasized construction of a new football operations center (Newton, 2022).

Matching Gifts and Employee Giving

The process of employee giving can be simplified through payroll deduction, and employees who give can be recognized at an annual luncheon. Many employers will match an employee's charitable donation, though certain employers will not match a donation to an athletics department; some of these, however, can be persuaded to match donations earmarked strictly for scholarship purposes (Howard & Crompton, 2003).

Real Estate and Investments

Donations of real estate and investments offer the donor relief from long-term capital gains taxes (Howard & Crompton, 2003). The tax reduction depends on how long the donor held the asset before donating it. The maximum capital gains tax rate is 20 percent of the increase in the value of the real estate or investment from the point of original purchase to the point of selling it for those in the highest tax bracket, 37 percent (Bittel, 2022). It is 15 percent for taxpayers in the 22 percent, 24 percent, 32 percent, and 35 percent tax brackets, and 0 percent for taxpayers in the 10 percent and 12 percent marginal tax brackets. However, by donating the asset rather than selling it, the donor eliminates the tax completely.

Deferred and Planned Giving

Deferred giving, accomplished through contributions that take effect after one's death, is a common form of donation, particularly among passionate supporters who want to leave a lasting legacy (Kegler, 2010). Planned giving can include wills, trusts, insurance policies, and annuities. Because the athletics department, a nonprofit entity, is named as the recipient, the donor's estate does not have to pay state or federal inheritance taxes on the donated assets (Howard & Crompton, 2003). Life insurance policy gifts also offer value to an athletics department, provided that the premiums are paid in full and the athletics department is listed as the sole beneficiary. Trusts can be used to provide a fixed annuity to the donor until his or her death, at which time the remainder of the trust benefits the athletics department.

Auctions, Bricks, and Camps

Smaller contributions can also be garnered through targeted events or campaigns, including auctions, building bricks, and camps. Auctions, either online or in-person, can feature such items as access to special events, coaches, and game-worn apparel. The University of Indianapolis also includes merchandise from sponsors, ranging from oil changes to condo rentals, to deepen its online auction offerings (Riley, 2010). Some athletics departments outsource auctions to a third-party firm, which may charge a fee for its services, take a portion of the generated revenues, sell banner advertising around the auction, or implement an entry fee for donors who want to participate (Popke, 2008).

Brick campaigns draw funding by enabling donors to personalize a brick for a walkway or plaza to commemorate their contribution. Louisiana State University uses a brick campaign in which donors' bricks are placed near the home of Mike the Tiger, the school's mascot, a Bengal tiger that lives on campus (Brick and Paver Program, 2013). In this way, a brick that costs the school US$10 or US$20 can be marked up in value, thus earning the school considerable revenue through a cost-effective commemoration (Bynum, 2004).

Additional revenue can be generated through special events, such as fantasy camps. Many fans will pay to play side by side with past greats or to be coached by a well-known head coach. Offerings include football camps for women, parent-and-child camps, and alumni outings such as golf tournaments (Zullo, 2011).

GROWING AFFINITY: CLUBS AND ORGANIZATIONS BEYOND CAMPUS

For larger athletics departments with a significant fan base, local chapters of booster clubs can be formed throughout a state or geographic region. These organizations give fans a place to share their passion while enhancing the regional, national, and, in some cases, global reach of the athletics department. Groups may gather to watch nationally televised games, arrange outings to home sporting events, and develop other social activities, such as golf tournaments. During the summer, an athletics department can have its coaches travel to meet fans in a given region, knowing that the local chapters can arrange the facility and food for the event.

One downside to local chapters is that their operational expenses are passed on to the area fan base, which can dilute development efforts focused on major gifts. For example, a donor paying for a local membership may construe that contribution as focusing on athletics development, whereas in fact membership dues may be used to offset operational expenses for the local chapter's events. Thus the development staff needs to communicate regularly with local chapters to avoid donor confusion regarding local contributions perceived to be earmarked for the athletic development office.

Concerns can also arise about control between the athletics department and any outside organization supporting athletics. For example, a representative of the Quarterback Club backing the Notre Dame football team embezzled more than

Technology Tools

Data Analytics for Development

Customer relationship management (CRM) tools utilize data analytics to bring constituent data together in a single application for use in athletics development and other kinds of fundraising across campus. Technology makes it easier to identify and vet potential donors, focusing on those most likely and most able to give.

Development offices use CRM tools such as Salesforce and EverTrue to identify new donor prospects (Epstein, 2022). Both help to identify and assess potential donors, thereby creating a pipeline of leads. For example, alumni can be potential contacts, but if an alum is returning to campus for homecoming, attending events, opening emails, downloading documents, or completing surveys, this can help to discern more data that reflects stronger connection to the school. Individuals who engage in these activities may not be alumni but could be supporters of the schools, family members of students, or others who have shown interest. The leads can then be assigned to individual gift officers who follow up with the leads. Research on the leads can include employer size, employer industry, location, job title and department. Thus, a lead is stronger than a general contact.

For example, at the University of Texas, stakeholders were involved in a multitude of ways, reporting to various campus entities (Garcia, 2017). There were former letterwinners in diverse sports, season ticket holders, single-game ticket purchasers, donor to athletics programs, nonathletics donors, students, recent graduates, older alumni, and more. Information was available, but analyzing the data was challenging without a shared technology system. The popular CRM software Salesforce was implemented in 2014 (Garcia, 2017). Reports on demographics, segments, behavior, donations, website traffic, transactions, ticket scans, donations, loyalty points, degrees, biographical data, and more could be generated for strategic pursuit of potential leads who could become donors. Duplicate records could be minimized, data could be "cleaned," and rankings could be established. Overall data collection increased in efficiency, tying together ticket purchases to commitments and donations, helping to better segment and prioritize leads. CRM automates the collection of marketing data from high-value web links, online activity, and emails (Garcia, 2017). This results in improved data analysis, stronger data tracking, better-quality data, utilization of a single platform, and other shared benefits that increase efficiency and staff productivity while reducing administrative costs, information search costs, and time spent on multiple systems (Garcia, 2017).

US$1 million (Morant, 1999). The funds were spent on lavish gifts and trips for members of the football team. The NCAA determined that the club was affiliated with the University of Notre Dame, effectively making club members representatives of the school. As a result, gifts from the members constituted impermissible extra benefits, and the school was sanctioned with scholarship losses and probation (Dufresne, 1999). With these issues in mind, proactive education about rules and regulations should extend to all clubs and organizations associated with the athletics department in order to maintain compliance with governing body requirements.

CONCERNS WITH FUNDRAISING

Although fundraising provides an athletics department with a crucial revenue source, working with donors can also create issues of concern. For one thing, each institution must decide whether academic needs or athletic needs come first in fundraising. In addition, an economic downturn affects all giving, including fundraising efforts in intercollegiate athletics (Brown, 2011). Another potential issue involves donor influence, which can affect both the operations and the image of an athletics department, as in the case of rogue boosters who hinder an athletics department's compliance with NCAA rules and regulations.

Although a successful athletics program can increase a school's visibility, some observers initially believed that athletics success was detrimental to collective fundraising efforts because of a negative effect on the academic mission of the institution (Stinson & Howard, 2004). However, as Stinson and Howard (2008) later found, donors who contribute to both academics and athletics give larger gifts than athletics-only donors and are retained as donors longer than those who donate only to academics. Still, faculty members may express concern when fundraising efforts appear to be misaligned with the mission of the institution.

In this context, development offices have to prioritize the projects that need donor support. This process has drawn scrutiny, as reform groups—including the Drake Group, the Coalition on Intercollegiate Athletics, and the Knight Commission on Intercollegiate Athletics—have offered recommendations for quelling the "arms race" of spending that exists in NCAA Division I athletics.

Institutions have to decide what approach they will take to the greater fundraising efforts, which may result in a centralized or decentralized approach between the institution development and athletics development (King et al., 2010). Some of the benefits of having a centralized approach between the institution and athletics include the potential for more development staff working together in a clear and coordinated effort with the donors. The downside of this approach is that, depending on the institution, athletics stakeholders may believe that athletics are not a priority in the school's fundraising. However, at some institutions, the opposite may be true: the perception may be that athletic fundraising exceeds academic fundraising (King et al., 2010).

In a decentralized approach, athletics development staff focus solely on fundraising for athletics; the university development staff focuses on fundraising for academics. However, this can result in confusion about who approaches which donors (King et al., 2010). The institution can suffer if its fundraising goals are not clearly stated and tensions develop between athletics development and fundraising for academics. Communication and teamwork are key to efficiency, effectiveness, and trust, because athletics and academics should not be seen as adversarial (Hanson & Peachey, 2022; Penry, n.d.). Communication can be as simple as text messages, emails, phone calls, meetings and/or data reports. Home athletic events, tailgating, and postseason play provide opportunities for the entire institution to be successful in fundraising, producing future campus visits which can heighten the opportunity for gifts that benefit university goals and not simply athletics.

Donor Influence

Fundraising enables the athletics department to find additional revenue, but that revenue can come with outside influence. Donors sometimes feel that substantial contributions give them the right to weigh in on the hiring and firing of coaches and other issues affecting the department (Staurowsky et al., 1999). For example, the late T. Boone Pickens (Oklahoma State University), Phil Knight (University of Oregon), and Bobby Lowder (Auburn University) have donated substantially to their schools and are heavily influential in personnel-related decision-making (Evans, 2009; Greenhouse, 2000; Thamel & Whitmire, 2011).

In addition, financial conditions can change quickly in intercollegiate athletics due to factors such as dwindling attendance or a lack of faith in a revenue sport's future. In such cases, head coaches can be bought out of their contracts to change the direction of a program, but doing so often requires the support of donors (Doughty, 2011). When donors provide funds to remove a coach, they may also want to influence the hiring of the new coach. In one dramatic case, the University of Connecticut parted ways with an athletics director after an unhappy donor—who disagreed with recent personnel decisions regarding the football program—asked for his US$3 million contribution to be returned (Associated Press, 2011).

Donors can also influence a department's philosophy in other ways. At the University of North Carolina at Chapel Hill, key donors long believed that the Dean Smith Center, home of the basketball program, should not feature sponsor advertising (Steinbach, 2005a). As a result, the donors' decision to support the facility honoring the coach came at the price of lost sponsorship revenue for decades. On a very different matter, donors at San Jose State University voiced their collective opinion about in-game dance performances being too provocative, thus leading the school to modify the performances to suit supporters' wishes (Steinbach, 2005b). Development officers need to be mindful of the fact that, in addition to these case studies, research reiterates the reality that donors' contributions may be accompanied by their desire to exert influence and psychological commitment (Gladden et al., 2005; Mahony et al. 2003; Staurowsky et al., 1999).

The University of Notre Dame uses two policies to preclude issues from arising about donors' expectations regarding influence, as well as premium seating. The first policy hinges on the establishment of an athletics affairs committee. Acting on behalf of the school's board of trustees, the committee enables fans, including big donors, to voice their opinions (Rovell, 2013). It also enables the director of athletics to act on issues without undue influence from a major donor. In regard to seating, donors have to enter a lottery for seats at prominent events, and this requirement even applied to the 2013 national title game (Rovell, 2013). As a result, Kevin Compton, an alumnus of Notre Dame and

Name, Image, and Likeness Versus Fundraising

The summer of 2022 saw name, image, and likeness (NIL) take effect. This enabled student-athletes to receive money and in-kind opportunities from local, regional, and national businesses, organizations, and causes. Although this benefits the student-athletes, there is concern among development staff that donors may give fewer philanthropic dollars to development and more to NIL efforts, thus "cannibalizing" philanthropic giving (Epstein, 2022; Gatlin, 2022). It also creates the possibility of miscommunication with athletics program supporters. Instead of a two-party relationship between athletic development staff and donors, student-athletes and coaches may now be at the fundraising and revenue generation table, and in some cases, there also might be an in-house representative or third-party firm specializing in NIL.

Ryan Day, the head football coach at Ohio State University, indicated in early June 2022 that he would need US$13 million in NIL funding to keep his roster intact (Athletic Staff, 2022). Greg Schiano, the head football coach at Rutgers, the State University of New Jersey, echoed that sentiment a month later, indicating that without millions in NIL support, the best players on his roster would be poached by other schools (Dyer, 2022). In a speech to a group of Rutgers football boosters, Schiano indicated donors had four months before student-athletes would depart for more lucrative opportunities. It was a rare public display of a head coach prioritizing money for players over building facilities—the latter being a more traditional reason for fundraising.

substantial donor to the school's new hockey arena, had to secure his tickets through the lottery like everyone else.

Naming Rights

Concerns can also arise when naming rights are implemented to recognize donors and their contributions (Chen & Zhang, 2012). Individuals interested in the naming rights for a facility can expect to cover one-third to one-half of the funds for the facility's construction (Steinbach, 2004). This form of naming rights differs from corporate naming rights, in that there is no marketing relationship between the school and a business entity. As a result, naming a facility after an individual donor eliminates the factor of commercialism that accompanies corporate naming rights, but it can still present problems. Unlike a corporate naming-rights deal, naming a facility after a donor or a donor's request comes with no expiration date. Yet there is no guarantee that the association will remain a positive one.

In one dramatic example, Villanova University had planned to call its basketball arena the du Pont Pavilion to recognize John Eleuthère du Pont, a major donor to the facility. However, du Pont later murdered Olympic wrestling gold medalist David Schultz (Crompton & Howard, 2003). In the aftermath, the school dropped the du Pont name.

In a less dire example, the University of Missouri opened a new basketball arena named the Paige Sports Arena in honor of the daughter of two prominent donors who contributed US$25 million to the project. Supporters of the university were disappointed to learn, however, that Paige Laurie did not attend the University of Missouri but rather the University of Southern California (Associated Press, 2004). The scandal grew larger when media outlets reported that she had paid college roommates US$20,000 to do her coursework. The facility was renamed.

NCAA Compliance

Other potential problems involve donors who break NCAA rules. In bringing donors close to the athletics department for their support, the department may become vulnerable to rogue donors who make payments or provide other benefits to influence recruits or reward current student-athletes (Steinbach, 2002). Staff can use continuing education forums and up-to-date online information to instruct donors about what is permitted and what is not in their interactions with prospective or current student-athletes, especially as NIL becomes more prevalent. The vital theme of compliance can also be emphasized in media guides and game programs, and on social media and the athletics website.

In an example of what can go wrong, the University of Miami athletics department engaged with a negligent football booster, Nevin Shapiro, who jeopardized student-athletes' eligibility, teams' eligibility for championships and bowl games, and recruiting efforts by providing improper benefits to student-athletes (Robinson, 2011). Specifically, the donor provided meals, nightclub outings, yacht trips, Miami Heat tickets, cash, travel, and other items. When asked why he did so even though he knew it could jeopardize the football program, he said, "I did it because I could. And because nobody stepped in to stop me" (Robinson, 2011). A recent booster of the athletics department, billionaire John Ruiz, continues the compliance dilemma with the University of Miami through his aggressive pursuit of name, image, and likeness opportunities for Hurricanes student-athletes (Al-Khateeb, 2023).

Coaches Fundraising Without Direction

It is a traditional fundraising tool to have coaches share their enthusiasm and vision for an athletics program with donors (Hanson & Peachey, 2022). Problems can arise, however, if coaches solicit donations without communicating with the development office. This practice is problematic because the development staff may be simultaneously building a relationship in preparation for asking a donor to make a substantial contribution. That preparatory work can go to waste if a coach asks for a smaller donation to cover a program-specific need and the donor then refuses the development office's request because he or she has already contributed to the coach. To avoid working at cross-purposes and possibly leaving money on the table, coaches and development offices must communicate continuously about program needs, prospective donors, and planned asks so that a coach does not undercut or limit the process (Thornburg, 2022).

CURRENT ISSUES

As budgets have gotten tighter, some schools have eliminated sports in order to reduce expenses. This practice creates a tremendous amount of stress and negative publicity for an athletics department. At the same time, development offices are trying to identify tomorrow's donors and encourage them to become supporters of athletics at an earlier age than was typical in the past. This focus means that development offices are tapping into the student body to build students' awareness of the importance of long-term giving. These competing trends—pressure to cut expenses and pressure to increase fundraising—mean that people working in development must carefully manage relationships amid the reality that some stakeholders may face disappointment when their sport is cut.

Eliminating Sports

According to the Business of College Sports website tracker, athletics programs have been cut at a number of schools during COVID-19, including the University of Connecticut, East Carolina University, the University of Minnesota, Appalachian State University (North Carolina), Wright State University (Ohio), Fresno State University (California), and the University of Iowa (Pert & Harringer, 2021). Over 75 Division I programs were cut and not reinstated, with men's sports like tennis, baseball, tennis, golf, track and field, and swimming and diving affected substantially. The elimination of a sport can lead student-athletes, coaches, and supporters to feel alienated and conclude that their sport is not viewed as important (Rheenan et al., 2011). To minimize such occurrences, administrators must work with coaches of nonrevenue sports early on to identify donors. Proactive efforts to procure private donations can help coaches and student-athletes understand that cutting sports is a last resort due to budgetary issues and is not related to such issues as Title IX, academics, or other concerns (Weight & Cooper, 2011).

In some cases, a certain sport—for example, baseball at the University of California—is asked to fund itself, meaning that the school does not assist in fundraising. In the case of Cal baseball, a nonprofit organization called the Cal Baseball Foundation was responsible for fundraising. An all-volunteer group, it reported to the school's officials to ensure communication, efficiency, and sustainability (Phelps, 2012). For such sports, administrators must continuously educate coaches to help them understand that their fundraising role may be crucial to the long-term viability of their program (Berkowitz, 2011).

Creating Student Donors

McClung (2010) emphasizes the fact that solicitation of donors can start as early as students' undergraduate years. This type of fundraising can be carried out through the creation of a student supporters group. Students who attend more sporting events and already display great pride in their school's athletics program may require less marketing in order to appreciate the benefits of joining such an organization, whereas their peers who are not active athletics supporters may require more persuading (McClung). Such nonsupporters will need greater education about the value and perks of being a student booster, including stronger school allegiance, affordability, and social contacts.

Westminster College created a student-focused sports promotion program in which students gave their input about how to enhance the game-day atmosphere and facilities. The students' inclusion helped enhance the school's relationship with these prospective donors. In addition to giving input on game themes and music selection, student supporters enjoyed various perks, such as the following:

- Free admission to all athletics contests
- Better seating at select home athletic events
- Free giveaways at select home athletic events
- Free food and tailgates at select home athletic events
- Recognition on athletic social media platforms
- Inclusion in charitable event opportunities
- Input on premium giveaway items

Development offices that engage with undergraduate students, particularly through student groups and activities tied to athletics, are more likely to benefit in the long run if athletics and institutional development objectives focus on valuable, socially validating, and integrated experiences that create broader and deeper university relationships

Leadership Lesson

Your Authentic Leadership Style

People trust you when you are genuine and authentic, not a replica of someone else.

George et al., 2007, p. 129

Imagine sitting across from a donor who has deep pockets and an affinity for your women's soccer program. If you can convince her to donate, you will make a name for yourself in the department and make the soccer coach very happy. For a moment, you feel a twinge of self-doubt—you have never been in this situation before. You watched your predecessor close deals in her charismatic and somewhat brash style, and you concluded that her approach must be what donors like. She was worshiped in the department and brought in millions. So you do your best to channel her style, even though it is not entirely natural for you. The lunch ends early, you do not get the donation, and the potential donor reports back to the department that she just did not trust you and does not feel comfortable giving at this time.

So often, we believe that in order to fit the mold of a leader, we must act in a certain way. In this leadership lesson, we will debunk that myth and help you discover your own authentic leadership style.

During the past 50 years, more than 1,000 studies have been conducted by leadership scholars seeking to pin down the profile of a leader. So far, no one has identified definitive characteristics. Some overarching conclusions, however, have been drawn. Leadership is not about charisma, personality, or even talent. Instead, it is about vision, principles, passion, discipline, and purpose (Collins & Porras 1994; Covey, 2004; Drucker, 2005; George & Sims, 2007; Goleman, 2000; Kotter, 2001). A leader is not someone who gets by on quick-fix personality alterations learned at the latest seminar but a person who is genuine and authentic—who has what Covey calls the "character ethic" (2004). Indeed, George et al. (2007) have argued that authentic leadership emerges through our individual life stories.

As a result, as you work to become a leader in intercollegiate athletics, it is important for you to gauge where you have been, where you are, who you are, where you hope to go, and who you hope to be. As you do so, George et al. (2007) suggest that you ask yourself the following questions.

- Which people and experiences in your early life had the greatest effect on you?
- What tools do you use to become self-aware? What are the moments when you say to yourself, "This is the real me"?
- What are your most deeply held values? Where did they come from? How do your values inform your actions?
- What motivates you extrinsically? What are your intrinsic motivations? How do you balance extrinsic and intrinsic motivation in your life?
- What kind of support team do you have? How can your support team make you a more authentic leader? How should you diversify your team to broaden your perspective?
- Is your life integrated? Are you able to be the same person in all aspects of your life—personal, work, family, and community? If not, what is holding you back?
- What does being authentic mean in your life? Are you more effective as a leader when you behave authentically? Have you ever paid a price for your authenticity as a leader? Was it worth it?
- What steps can you take today, tomorrow, and over the next year to develop your authentic leadership?

One of the most dangerous myths that can trap you in your professional progression is that of the "complete leader"—the idea that in order to be credible you must be flawless and know everything. This notion can lead you to present yourself as a contrived version of what you think a leader should look like. However, a growing body of literature supports doing the opposite. Specifically, scholars have urged leaders to do the following.

- Accept that you're human, with strengths and weaknesses (Ancona et al., 2007).
- Blend deep personal humility with intense professional will (Collins, 2005).
- Show that you're human, capitalize on your uniqueness, and care passionately about your employees (Goffee & Jones, 2000).
- Be self-aware—know your strengths, weaknesses, drives, and values (Goleman, 2000).

(Brunette et al., 2017). Another example of this involves San Diego State University's development office working with the Student-Athlete Academic Support Services through a "Senior Suit-Up" program that connected graduating seniors with former student-athletes, current donors, university alumni, and the business community (Huiras, 2016). Donors were asked to make an impact through volunteering their time, contributing to scholarships and becoming a mentor, assisting with career preparation, business etiquette, and relationship building. Despite these efforts for development to connect personally, Popp, Barrett, and Weight (2016) stress that the concern of declining student attendance should facilitate stronger external family/youth marketing, beyond offering a traditional "kids club," to build a stronger pipeline of future donors to annual giving efforts.

Increasing Diversity, Equity, and Inclusion (DEI)

In June 2020, the University of San Diego's (USD) athletics administrative team and coaches met to make changes to systemic behaviors and failures. USD was a predominantly white school, so the group established a fundraising initiative wherein donors could invest in their list of diversity and inclusion ideas. Honoring one of their distinguished alumni, the Bernie Bickerstaff Diversity and Inclusion Fund was created to foster inclusion and improve the racial climate at the university, helping coaches, staff, and most importantly, students. As of June 2022, over US$100,000 in private funds was raised (Lanoue, 2022).

In similar fashion, Johns Hopkins University (Maryland), the University of North Texas, and the

Professional Development

National Association of Athletic Development Directors (NAADD)

NAADD provides professional development through an annual conference and online resources. Membership provides networking opportunities and access to educational sessions, such as best practices education and roundtables at the summer conference. Officers and committees steer NAADD and select annual award winners and keynote speakers. The leadership also holds question-and-answer sessions and advances the demographic diversification of professionals working in the industry. Online resources available throughout the year include *Athletics Administration* magazine and the NACDA Daily Review email, which address current events, explore new strategies, and sponsor educational webinars. Reduced-price memberships are available to help students engage in professional development early in their career.

Case Study

Where Are the Students?

As entertainment options for college students increase, fewer students are attending home athletic events and many students are picky about which games they attend. On many campuses, the facilities have been updated to include the state-of-the-art videoboards and upgraded WiFi to attract more students. The music selection also is geared toward students. Tailgating is still strong for late Saturday afternoon and evening football games, but can be minimal for early weekend kick-offs. Outcomes for some Power Five games can also be more predictable, especially with guarantee games on the home schedule of these schools. Students are better educated in what matchups must be seen live versus those that can be seen via streamed or televised highlights. College football, for all of its culture and tradition, faces an attendance issue, especially with students (Popp et al., 2016).

For generations, college students were lucky if they had three channels on television and a local radio station that played music they liked. Cable, streaming, and satellite options would not be invented for decades. The stadium was the place to be for fun and fellowship on a Saturday afternoon. This concentrated campus atmosphere created a strong pipeline of future donors to the athletics program, since alumni wanted to see athletics be successful and joined with other fans who felt the same way. Families would tailgate, and Saturday was the only day for college football. As times have changed, even historic programs like Duke Men's Basketball and Alabama Football have seen their student sections at less than 100 percent capacity for less attractive games. Students are still passionate, but the entertainment options on and around campus are stronger. Students can watch home, neutral-site, or away games on high-definition television, especially if the weather is bad. Students are also more selective in how to utilize their time, especially if a football game is played on a Tuesday, Wednesday, Thursday, or even a Friday night on campus. This case study challenges aspiring athletics administrators to tackle the issue of dwindling student attendance and the concern of losing future athletic donors (Popp et al., 2016).

Questions to Consider

1. How do you best articulate the value of midweek televised football and basketball games to students and donors who prefer games to be played on the traditional Saturday?
2. How do you best articulate to students and donors why games may start before noon or run late into the evening?
3. What are the short-term and long-term benefits of televised games? What are the short-term and long-term drawbacks of such games?
4. By the late 1980s and into the 1990s, cable television became more prevalent in homes across the United States. What are some of today's additional entertainment options that might affect student and donor attendance?
5. How could scheduling be improved to better attract students, donors, and fans to home games? Include neutral-site games in your discussions.
6. How can development offices be mindful of the dilution of passionate student fan bases and create strategic options to make these students into future donors? What options would involve marketing and game operations departments?
7. What efforts could be made to better attract students to home athletic events? How could students be enticed to stay for the entire game? Present tiered rewards options as one of your strategies.
8. With students paying student fees to support athletics, make a case for the value of a student discounted season package for home football games. What are the counterarguments?
9. How would your answers change at the Football Championship Subdivision, Division II, and Division III levels?

University of Louisville (Kentucky) have strengthened diversity, equity, and inclusion with efforts from their development offices. North Texas established nine initiatives focused on social justice to spark conversations between student-athletes, staff, and supporters: Fund, Vote, Read, Honor, Educate, Facilitate, Pledge, Listen, Empower (Littleton & Lopez, 2021). Johns Hopkins collaborated with the Black Student Athlete Association, created in summer 2020, to give them a platform to speak, network, and connect with alumni. This included a virtual 5K (where supporters run on their own time and location of choice) to generate awareness and foster a mentoring program (Littleton & Lopez, 2021). The University of Louisville empowers its female student-athletes by connecting them to female alumnae, donors, and season ticket holders through a Women of Influence program that offers internships, networking, leadership retreats, brand workshops, and other benefits (Edwards, 2019).

Preserving Continuous Trust

The University of Kansas suffered a scandal surrounding its priority seating plan that centered on tickets to its sold-out home men's basketball games. In the scandal, five former staff members were sentenced for their involvement in a five-year, US$2 million scheme in which 17,000 basketball tickets and 2,000 football tickets allocated for donors were instead sold to ticket brokers. In addition, two staff members were sentenced to probation for failure to report a crime (Fagan, 2011).

The scandal forced school officials to heighten the transparency of the priority seating program. Interim athletics director Sean Lester noted, "I think our donors appreciate the enhancements we have made in transparency, accountability, and the fact that so many of their seating locations have improved. We are unwavering in our continued commitment to our student-athletes, donors, and fans" (qtd. in Fagan, 2010). To restore confidence, the university made changes in the athletics department's leadership—on the athletics board, among senior administrators, and in the director of athletics position. The school also hired an independent auditor. In an effort to prevent such problems, some schools, such as the University of Washington and the University of Texas, rely on internal and external auditors plus risk management assessors to preserve trust in their ticket sales and distribution policies (Associated Press, 2010).

CONCLUSION

Athletics departments use fundraising as a revenue stream to supplement funds earned through other means, such as ticket sales, sponsorship revenue, allocations from conferences and governing bodies, state appropriations, student fees, and concessions. Funds raised can be used to support scholarships, facilities, salaries, operating costs, and other rapidly growing expenses. Donors have to be identified and cultivated so that relationships can be built to ensure the donor's financial support over the long term. Motivated donors provide support through such varied means as major gifts, endowment programs, capital campaigns, and planned giving. However, fundraising personnel must be mindful of potential problems, such as when donors become overzealous or coaches attempt to solicit funds without proper direction. Scandals and crises can also affect the credibility of fundraising efforts.

DISCUSSION QUESTIONS

1. Why do people give money to worthy causes? What are some reasons for which people might give specifically to intercollegiate athletics?
2. A very generous donor is willing to contribute at a level that surpasses any other donor. However, this donor wants significant influence in personnel decisions, especially with respect to the hiring and firing of head coaches. Identify the pros and cons of accepting the donor's contribution.
3. A prospective donor is excited about supporting the athletics department and interested in securing naming rights for a proposed facility. The naming rights would honor a deceased family member who graduated from the school. However, the donor's intended level of giving does not meet the standard set by the development office for receiving naming rights. How would you handle this situation?

4. The president of the school has made it very clear that the capital campaign is to focus on academic programs. However, donors continue to indicate an interest in making athletics-specific contributions in order to support the continuing success of the school's football program. The school's development office is growing more resentful of the athletics development office. How would you rectify the situation?
5. The head coaches of certain sports want to engage in their own fundraising efforts, separate from the efforts of the development office. The coaches perceive that their sports are viewed as unimportant as compared with revenue-generating sports. How would you address their concerns and work toward an amicable solution?
6. After much scrutiny and consideration, the school's governing body has accepted a recommendation to move forward with eliminating certain sport programs. Donors are furious about the decision. How would you address their concerns by using the school's decision as an opportunity to educate people about the finances of intercollegiate athletics?
7. You are trying to build a relationship with a potential donor, who asks why they should give to the athletics department when some of their peers are giving directly to student-athletes through name, image, and likeness (NIL). How would you best answer this question?
8. Imagine that you are fundraising for a Division III college or university with a small enrollment and limited athletic success. How would you best promote your school and athletics department to prospective donors?

LEARNING ACTIVITIES

1. A new donor is very excited about supporting the athletics department and believes that his contributions should entitle him to greater benefits. Pick one of the five major athletics conferences (ACC, Big Ten, Big 12, Pac-12, SEC) at the Division I level and examine each school's website to find information about benefits provided to big donors. Share your findings with the class. Do the assignment again with a Division I conference outside the Power Five, a conference at the Division I FCS level, or a Division II conference.
2. After much scrutiny and consideration, the school's governing body has accepted a recommendation to move forward with eliminating certain sport programs. Students, especially student-athletes, are angry about the decision. Using your research skills, find examples of where this has occurred and how schools dealt with the backlash from students and alumni, especially letter winners. Share your examples with the class.
3. Your athletics department is moving up to a new conference and a new level of competition, and greater expenses are anticipated. As a result, the donor base needs to be increased, starting with current students. Examine athletics department websites and use your findings to formulate a student supporter group that balances a focus on home-team spirit with creating future athletics donors.

Support Services

Robert H. Zullo, Slippery Rock University

In this chapter, you will explore

- the operations of support services, including sports medicine;
- digital media services, equipment staff, and holistic development personnel; and
- challenges associated with resource allocation in support services.

A DAY IN THE LIFE OF AN INTERCOLLEGIATE ATHLETE

As an intercollegiate varsity athlete currently in season, your next contest is a few days away, and you're settling into your weekly routine. Last night you spent the evening at study hall until 10:00 p.m., so it's especially difficult this morning to wake up for your 6:00 a.m. workout and lift. After your training session with the strength and conditioning staff, you make time to eat a hearty breakfast before sitting in your first lecture class, which begins at 8:00 a.m. Once classes conclude in the early afternoon, you report for practice. You change clothes and go to the athletic training room to have your ankles and wrists taped in preparation for practice.

After practice, you are on your way back to the locker room when your team's sports information director approaches and asks you to take part in a new video that will be highlighted on the athletics department's website and shown during your next home game. You take time to shower, then get ice wrapped on your elbow before heading to the cafeteria, where you are scheduled to meet with the sport nutritionist to discuss weight management strategies. You have a five-page paper due tomorrow, so you plan to go to study hall tonight, but that will have to wait until after you watch 30 minutes of video from practice, 30 minutes from your previous competition, and an hour of your upcoming opponent.

In reading the opening scenario, you may have noticed that a collegiate student-athlete comes into contact with a variety of athletics department staff members. As an aspiring intercollegiate administrator, it is important for you to understand the various ancillary groups that play a vital role in an athletics department's operation—and in a student-athlete's daily pursuit of excellence.

HOLISTIC DEVELOPMENT STAFF AND SERVICES

Student-athletes are the center of athletics departments, and it is necessary to consider the ancillary services provided to optimize their holistic—physical, mental, spiritual, social, and emotional—development (Hirko, 2009; Howard-Hamilton & Sina, 2001; Pascarella & Blimling, 1996; Watson & Kissinger, 2007). In the not-too-distant past, the head coach was the individual responsible both for student-athletes' physical development and for their health and safety—for example, a coach might supervise weightlifting, tape ankles and wrists, and provide first aid. However, at most institutions, these duties have evolved, and the resources provided have become more specialized in order to address the various dimensions of student-athletes' development.

Physical Resources

The services provided for athletes' physical development are arguably the most familiar because of their history in athletics and their obvious implications for performance, health, and safety (Dzikus et al., 2012; Powers, 2007). For instance, the introductory scenario shows the student-athlete beginning the morning with a workout supervised by strength and conditioning staff. Whether in season or out of season, student-athletes must maintain or improve their conditioning and strength. With this in mind, the strength and conditioning staff may structure their sport-specific programs to push athletes to be bigger, faster, and stronger for the sake of competition. The "athletics arms race" is not only in the salaries of Division I head coaches and assistants but in strength and conditioning coaches as well. The annual salary of some of these staff members reaches the high six figures at many Power Five schools' football programs (see table 13.1.)

A well-planned strength and conditioning program reduces the likelihood of sport-related injury (Nadelen, 2012; Thacker et al., 2004). As a result, athletics administrators hiring strength and conditioning professionals would be wise to recruit individuals who possess a background in an academic discipline such as physiology, kinesiology, and exercise science.

Suicide Prevention

Thomas Cole, a four-star recruit, did not play football for the University of California, Los Angeles (UCLA), in 2021, his first season as a UCLA Bruin. The early January enrollee announced his retirement from the game in July 2022, disclosing a suicide attempt and mental health challenges. Cole received help from the UCLA hospital, residential treatment, and a therapist, and he mentioned the support he felt from his teammates, especially his fellow offensive linemen, during his struggles (Scott, 2022). In a post announcing his retirement, he reminded people that it is okay to ask for help. Earlier in the academic year, Ohio State University football student-athlete Harry Miller, a redshirt junior, also retired from the sport, citing mental challenges. Miller, an engineering student with a 4.0 GPA and recognition on the Allstate American Football Coaches Association Good Works Team for his community service, posted on X (formerly known as Twitter) that mental health issues can affect anyone (Lind, 2022). Stanford University soccer player Katie Meyer helped her team win the national championship in fall 2019. On March 1, 2022, she took her own life in her dorm room.

All students face the challenges of academics, being away from home, time management, and assimilation with peers socially, but student-athletes can also face the challenges of practice and competition, optimizing health and fitness, traveling, and scrutiny of their athletic performance through traditional and social media (Chen & Andone, 2022). A panel of athletes on *The Today Show* discussed how they are expected to be tough, push through pain, hide weakness, and fight to play, suppressing feelings (Holohan, 2022). Treatment is sought from an athletic trainer for a physical injury, but not a mental one. These and other high-profile student-athletes speaking out have helped to lessen the stigma that people who pursue counseling or help are "weak."

Mental health struggles took the lives of University of Northern Michigan freshman track and field student-athlete Jayden Hill (North Wind Staff, 2022), University of Wisconsin junior track and field student-athlete Sarah Shulze (Brockington, 2022), and James Madison University sophomore softball student-athlete Lauren Bernett, each in April 2022 (Vivinetto, 2022). Bernett had just been named her conference's player of the week and was the starting catcher for the team that reached the Women's College World Series in her freshman year. In May 2022, freshman Arlana Miller, a cheerleader at Southern University and A&M College, also took her life (Holohan, 2022). Colleges, universities, and athletics departments continue to invest resources into year-round mental health awareness, educating staff and encouraging student-athletes to seek help.

Note: If you or someone you know is having thoughts of suicide or is in emotional distress, utilize the resources within your community or contact the 988 Suicide and Crisis Lifeline (formerly the National Suicide Prevention Lifeline, at 1-800-273-TALK(8255)) via text or phone call or visit suicidepreventionlifeline.org.

Another ancillary resource offered to optimize physical development is sport nutrition. From the perspective of athletic performance, specialized instruction from a sport nutritionist is appropriate for optimal eating strategies and for meeting goals such as losing weight and body fat and gaining muscle mass (American College of Sports Medicine, American Dietetic Association, & Dieticians of Canada, 2000; Rodriguez et al., 2009). However, the sport nutritionist and the strength and conditioning coach should not operate independently of each other. Instead, they should collaborate to construct individualized, comprehensive programs that help athletes reach their goals.

Sport nutritionists also advise athletes about eating a balanced, nutritionally efficient diet. Student-athletes are subject to strenuous athletic, academic, and social demands. Like other college students, however, they may be tempted to skip breakfast, rely on convenient fast foods, or replace water with unhealthy beverages. If their diet is consistently deficient in vitamins, minerals, proteins, fats, or carbohydrates, they will not have the necessary nutrients or energy to meet their responsibilities.

Table 13.1 2022 Salaries of FCS Football Strength and Conditioning Coaches

Name	School	Amount (USD)
Rob Glass	Oklahoma State University	$1,000,000
Mickey Marotti	Ohio State University	$821,179
Mark Hocke	University of Florida	$750,000
Raimond Braithwaite	University of Iowa	$710,000
Aaron Wellman	Indiana University	$710,000
David Ballou	University of Alabama	$700,000
Ben Herbert	University of Michigan	$700,000
Jerry Schmidt	University of Oklahoma	$650,000
Joey Batson	Clemson University	$625,000
Ron McKeefery	University of Washington	$600,000
Jason Novak	Michigan State University	$541,667
Torre Becton	University of Texas	$525,000
Dave Andrews	Iowa State University	$525,000
Brian Hess	University of North Carolina	$500,000
Jay Butler	Rutgers University	$500,000
Tyson Brown	Mississippi State University	$500,000

Data from "College Football Strength Coach Salaries," USA Today, last modified December 7, 2022, https://sports.usatoday.com/ncaa/salaries/football/strength.

Arguably the most prominent ancillary resource catering to the physical needs of student-athletes is that of sports medicine. However, due to the complexities and legal implications of sports medicine in an athletics department, it is addressed after the following discussion of other types of holistic care personnel.

Mental Health Resources

First and foremost, student-athletes are students in a higher education setting. As they pursue their education, they must juggle the demands of athletics as a prominent component of their daily schedule. In light of the considerable time they invest in their practice, competition, and travel schedules, they may benefit from specialized academic support services. Academic support services for student-athletes can vary from university to university; generally, however, they may include subject tutors, academic mentors, study groups, learning specialists, and academic advisors (Broughton & Neyer, 2001; Comeaux, 2013; Covell & Barr, 2010; Wolverton, 2008). Academic support personnel for student-athletes are critically important because they help these uniquely situated students navigate their educational experience, balance the demands of academics and athletics, and prepare themselves for life after their playing career ends. These personnel also help student-athletes meet academic eligibility requirements.

There is another dimension of the mental aspect of the student-athlete experience, and this one goes beyond the pursuit of an academic skill set. This dimension is addressed by sport psychology, which focuses primarily on strengthening performance by equipping athletes with strategies to help their mental self-talk work for them rather than against them (Weinberg & Gould, 2011). An athletics administrator may hire a sport psychology consultant (SPC) as a part-time or full-time member of the holistic care team.

For example, let's imagine that the student-athlete described in the introductory scenario consistently experiences extreme frustration or anxiety upon perceiving that they have made a mistake. An SPC is trained to help the student-athlete manage such feelings through appropriately individualized measures. The consultation can extend to helping the student-athlete manage mental self-talk relating to technique. Thus, when a student-athlete experiences a slump in performance, an SPC can provide an alternate perspective and voice that may help the student-athlete internalize the situation more effectively in order reach to their greatest athletic potential.

Sport psychology entails much more than what is briefly mentioned here. It is an academic discipline with stringent professional standards and credentialing (Association for Applied Sport Psychology, 2013a, 2013b). The current trend is to integrate sport psychology professionals into intercollegiate athletics departments to facilitate holistic care for student-athletes. The University of Southern California is a national leader in sports psychology. Its athletics department has 10 trained professionals providing individual therapy, team meetings on dynamics and performance, educational sessions with coaches and staff (on such topics as depression, anxiety, suicide prevention, substance abuse, body image, eating disorders, healthy relationships, and the psychological effects of an injury) and addressing urgent issues (Lindberg, 2021). Empowering student-athletes is a goal because peak performance in life starts with good mental health.

> *Within the wider field of mental health, there is a growing trend toward developing personalized approaches to prevention and care. Rather than assuming that everyone would benefit from lying on a couch for 45 minutes free-associating about dreams, there is a strong move toward adapting mental health interventions that are more reflective of the diverse experiences and backgrounds of the people seeking treatment.*
>
> Ivan Tchatchouwo, CEO, The Zone, and Dr. Adam Brown, clinical psychologist and associate professor of psychology, The New School for Social Research (2022)

Spiritual Resources

Whereas many people are comfortable with the more tangible outcomes of physical and mental development, spiritual care for student-athletes seems more likely to be questioned. However, as discussed in this chapter's leadership lesson, many leadership experts advocate caring for the spiritual dimension of our lives. Spiritual care in this sense does not necessarily refer to anything religious; rather, it involves value clarification, value commitment, study, and meditation.

Although students are encouraged to engage in self-reflection during their college years, this broader sense of spirituality (which can manifest

Student-Athletes and Mental Health

A 2022 study by the NCAA indicated that student-athletes continue to face challenges with mental health, including mental exhaustion, anxiety, and depression at levels higher than before the COVID-19 pandemic (Johnson, 2022). Responses from nearly 10,000 student-athletes indicated knowledge about where to go on campus for mental health support, but almost 50 percent of the respondents said they felt uncomfortable doing so. Continuing outreach to student-athletes and their athletics programs is important to bridge the gap between knowing where resources are located and a willingness to utilize those resources. This outreach begins with the athletics department's top administration and continues to coaches embracing conversations about student-athlete's mental well-being. Coaches aspire for their team to achieve peak performance in competition, but that can be difficult if team members feel mentally exhausted, are sleep deprived, face overwhelming anxiety or sadness, or have a sense of loss or hopelessness. Coaches and their support staff can play an important role in helping student-athletes as mental health awareness becomes more commonplace at all levels of intercollegiate athletics.

itself through adhering to a particular faith tradition) (Astin et al., 2011; Delaney & Madigan, 2009; Galli & Reel, 2012; Hales, 2007; Koenig, 2009; Koenig et al., 1997; Shaw et al., 2005) is often ignored. In order to address this important element of holistic development, some athletics departments partner with a sport chaplain to help student-athletes engage their spirituality. Although the broader profession of chaplaincy promulgates professional standards, the specialized nature of sport chaplaincy is continuing to emerge. In fact, no standardized model for sport chaplaincy exists in intercollegiate athletics departments, which makes this ancillary service a challenge to implement (Dzikus et al., 2012). Nonetheless, aspiring athletics administrators should be aware of the trends and challenges, because these ancillary resources continue to grow and evolve in order to better serve student-athletes holistically.

Social and Emotional Resources

Have you ever noticed a student-athlete development coordinator in an athletics department's staff directory and wondered about his or her job duties? Broadly, the responsibilities of this position include planning, organizing, and implementing leadership, interpersonal, and life skills initiatives for student-athletes. Examples include community service projects, ropes course challenges, résumé and interview workshops, dinner etiquette sessions, and motivational and leadership seminars (Covell & Barr, 2010; Wolverton, 2008). These events are structured to foster social and emotional competencies by exposing student-athletes to culturally diverse programs.

In light of increased emergence of mental and emotional health issues among active and retired athletes, some athletics departments have begun integrating licensed social workers and licensed mental health professionals into their holistic care team (Hayden et al., 2013). These individuals can be employed either part-time or full-time to assess, diagnose, and treat psychological and emotional issues and disorders. This relatively new development in intercollegiate athletics addresses the social and emotional dimension of human beings as framed by Covey (2004) in this chapter's leadership lesson.

As you may have observed, the holistic services discussed here are not exclusive to a single dimension of personhood—that is, physical, mental, spiritual, social, or emotional. Rather, the dimensions are interconnected. Consequently, the staff members who make up the holistic care team should recognize the value of all areas of expertise and collaborate to best promote student-athletes' holistic personal development.

Before shifting gears to discuss additional prominent support services outside of the holistic care team, we focus now on the role of sports medicine. Athletics administrators must have a working knowledge of the complexities involved in sports medicine so that they can proactively serve student-athletes, operate in a fiscally sound manner, and avoid negligence claims.

SPORTS MEDICINE

Given the increasingly high financial stakes in intercollegiate athletics, sports medicine emphasizes providing exemplary physical care to injured athletes to get them back to optimal performance as soon as possible without compromising their health and safety. In addition, the use of performance-enhancing drugs and the increase in knowledge about concussions and other head injuries have put a spotlight on the professionals who confront these controversial issues. Sports medicine personnel are capable of providing exceptional care, but they face challenges that athletics administrators should be aware of—for example, resource allocation, facility management, liability mitigation, and organizational structure, which all affect the treatment that student-athletes receive.

Athletic Training

Although you may have heard the terms *sports medicine* and *athletic training* used interchangeably, the first step in better comprehending this ancillary service is to understand the difference between these terms. Sports medicine involves all members of the sports medicine staff, which can include athletic trainers, physicians, orthopedic surgeons, physical therapists, dentists, and masseuses, to name a few. Athletic training specifically involves personnel who are certified according to professional standards set forth by the National Athletic Trainers' Association (NATA) (2014a),

Industry Profile

MIKE CURTIS

Strength and Conditioning Head Coach for Men's Basketball, University of Virginia

Mike Curtis is the head strength and conditioning coach for the University of Virginia (UVA) Men's Basketball team, winners of the 2019 national championship. Curtis graduated in 1998 from UVA after studying sports medicine, then earned his master's degree in exercise physiology in 2000. He was previously the head of strength and conditioning at the University of Michigan, overseeing 20 athletic teams, 5 assistant coaches, and 2 training facilities. Additionally, he was the head strength and conditioning coach for the NBA's Memphis Grizzlies for six years and also served as the basketball strength and conditioning coach for the men's basketball program at the University of South Carolina. He is a certified strength and conditioning specialist (CSCS), USA Weightlifting (USAW) certified, a performance enhancing specialist (PES), corrective exercise specialist (CES), Functional Movement Systems Level 1 (FSM-1) certified, Exos performance specialist (XPS) certified, and Functional Range Conditioning (FRC) certified, and is pursuing his doctorate in sports medicine at the University of Virginia.

Could you describe the many hats that a strength and conditioning coach wears?

It varies dependent on the institution and/or program. Inherently, a strength and conditioning coach is involved in pedagogy, as teaching the practical skills related to strength, power, and endurance development are the principal job demands. However, it is often forgotten that psychology is an additional responsibility. A strength and conditioning coach is perpetually managing [athletes'] physical stress in addition to promoting the supporting behaviors (e.g., sleep, nutritional adherence, coping mechanisms) that allow for positive physical adaptations. Today the need for some level of competency in utilizing data derived from the many technologies associated with training is also a prerequisite. This leads to the additional need to be a great communicator to relay inferences and intervention guidance to sport coaches.

Mike Riley/UVA Athletics

Could you discuss the relationship between a strength and conditioning coach and a head coach?

This varies across institutions and programs. I would say that in the revenue-generating sports, the strength and conditioning coach is a more integrated member of the staff. This affords that individual more influence and latitude in helping the head coach make decisions related to the training process. Itis important in these sports that the strength and conditioning coach is also an extension of the head coach. This means conveying the principles and cultural approach for the program at the athlete level. This is an important piece of culture building, because the student-athlete often is more receptive to members of the staff who do not control playing time in receiving that messaging. In non-revenue-generating sports, the strength and conditioning coach is more of a peripheral support system, given these individuals are spread thin due to multiple sport assignments.

How do you motivate student-athletes from various backgrounds, building toughness that maybe they do not see in themselves?

I believe that meeting the athletes where they are is paramount to terminal outcomes and positively affecting social and emotional growth. [Gathering] information about that athlete's history provides clues to nurture and nature, which ultimately allows "good" coaches to formulate a communication strategy specific to the athlete.

(continued)

INDUSTRY PROFILE *(continued)*

Once the most effective strategy has been identified, it allows for deficits in "toughness" or other limiting behaviors to be addressed in a way the athlete can understand and process. I will say that in collegiate strength and conditioning, the nurture element can be daunting to overcome if the athlete has 16-18 years of life in a home environment lacking responsibility, accountability, process, resilience, and a growth mindset.

How did you work with student-athletes during the peak of the COVID pandemic?

During the early stages of the pandemic, many of my interactions were virtual, through Zoom or app-based platforms, as everything shut down and people were sent home. That consisted mostly of check-ins and follow-ups on training prescriptions. Obviously, basketball is a revenue-generating sport, so there was a priority to get back to competition. During the early return to play, we tried to operate with some level of normalcy, but the safety measures were often a reminder of what we were facing and the risks. At that stage, the psychological responsibilities of managing the stoppages and the unknown short- and long-term effects of contracting COVID were a high priority.

Student-athletes are still college kids who can indulge in unhealthy late-night meals, parties, and inconsistent eating. How do you get students to look at a bigger picture of the importance of nutrition?

Education! Unless they have an understanding of how those things impact performance, they cannot make informed decisions when they are tempted by the short-term gratification of what most other students are doing. For those who aspire to be a professional athlete, I have often painted a picture in the following way: "Say you have the potential, from a physical make-up and sporting talent standpoint, to earn $50 million in your career, and each time you make a poor decision you must subtract a million from your career earnings—would that deter you or make you think twice?"

What has changed the most in the past decade in strength and conditioning and what can we expect in the future?

The use of technology and data has increased with the responsibilities of the practitioner. In terms of the student-athletes, I would say I have observed a decrease in attentiveness and resilience. I think changes in the transfer rules and NIL have shifted what used to be important about getting an education through athletics. Improving long-term financial wellness has now shifted to improving what will probably be short-term financial wellness. Instant gratification related to financial gain has impacted work ethic and patience. This changes how we have to coach and interact with student-athletes.

What technology does your industry use that students interested in this field should research or learn about?

In my opinion data science is a knowledge base that will open doors, as big data is part of every aspect of athletics (from team or competition level to the business of sport). The technologies will come, go, and evolve. What's important is the ability to analyze, visualize, and interpret the metrics they produce.

What advice would you offer students interested in this field?

In general, sport and strength and conditioning are about problem solving. Any course or learning pathway that promotes critical thinking is essential for anyone interested in this field. There is a lot of noise and bad information in this field and ability to objectively assess information helps to find signals in all the noise that is out there.

Board of Certification for the Athletic Trainer, and the individual state in which they practice. Please note also that the professional title of these individuals is not simply "trainer" but "athletic trainer."

Of the various members of the sports medicine team, athletic trainers have the most interaction with student-athletes and are the most likely to be full-time employees of a college or university. Therefore, this section primarily addresses issues regarding their role in the athletics department. It is understandable that athletics administrators may not be familiar with all of the standards required to become an athletic trainer; however, it is critical that administrators appreciate the daily role that athletic trainers play in virtually every student-athlete's life.

Daily Operations of a Certified Athletic Trainer

As with any occupation, certified athletic trainers' daily operations in collegiate athletics can vary widely, both from sport to sport and from institution to institution. Duties can also vary depending on the athletics department's organizational structure and its ratio of athletic trainers to student-athletes. Amid these variations, however, intercollegiate athletic trainers share common responsibilities.

In a broad sense, a typical day for a certified athletic trainer (ATC) involves administrative duties, rehabilitation and treatment, staff and coach meetings, prepractice preparation and treatment, practice responsibilities, and postpractice treatment. These duties can include, but are not limited to, injury prevention, clinical evaluation, diagnosis, immediate care of injuries, and rehabilitation of injuries. ATCs may also be involved in reconditioning athletes after an injury to ensure that they can successfully return to preinjury levels without rushing the rehabilitation (S.D. Halverson & K. King, personal communication, January 2013).

In addition, each of these obligations includes its own list of responsibilities. For example, administrative duties include maintaining health records, complying with safety and sanitation standards, managing inventory, budgeting, organizing the facility, cleaning, and maintaining equipment. Providing this level of detail for all areas of the job, however, goes beyond the scope of this chapter. Therefore, we now turn our attention to understanding the critical decisions that an athletics administrator must make regarding the commitment to sports medicine at his or her institution (S.D. Halverson & K. King, personal communication, January 2013).

Resource Allocation

As in any organization, budgeting and resource allocation deserve much attention. At an NCAA Division I Football Bowl Subdivision (FBS) institution, the budget for sports medicine could be greater than US$1,000,000 annually, as compared with a couple of hundred thousand dollars at NCAA Division III schools. This budget line item includes ATCs' salaries, compensation for student assistants, facility debt service, purchase and maintenance of equipment, insurance premiums, and outsourced medical treatment (e.g., from professionals who are not on staff, which might include physicians, orthopedic surgeons, chiropractors, physical therapists, optometrists, cardiologists, neurologists, dentists, and dermatologists) (S.D. Halverson & K. King, personal communication, January 2013).

The majority of the dollars allocated to sports medicine in athletics departments depends largely on athletics administrators' commitment to injury prevention. For example, athletics administrators must decide how many ATCs and student assistants to hire for appropriate sport coverage. They must also decide whether or not to invest in modern equipment intended to reduce the likelihood of sport injuries. Hiring more ATCs and acquiring state-of-the-art equipment are calculated investments that may decrease liability, health care bills, and rehabilitation time and increase the performance of student-athletes (S.D. Halverson & K. King, personal communication, January 2013).

These are just a few of the considerations that an administrator must ponder when allocating resources for sports medicine. The NATA document "Recommendations and Guidelines for Appropriate Medical Coverage of Intercollegiate Athletics" (NATA, 2014b) offers universities a well-developed tool for evaluating their current level of coverage for student-athletes (S.D. Halverson & K. King, personal communication, January 2013).

Facility Management

Also in the interest of injury prevention, administrators and ATCs are wise to thoroughly discuss facility management. Facility space on college campuses comes at a premium, and it can be a challenge to acquire or construct the square footage necessary to effectively meet the needs of hundreds of student-athletes. In addition, if possible, it is logical for the athletic training room to be near the strength and conditioning area because medical staff may use strength training and agility equipment in this area, and proximity between the two facilitates collaboration between ATCs and strength and conditioning staff as well as enables a quick medical response in an emergency. To ensure that such concerns are understood and addressed, athletics administrators should seek advice from sports medicine staff regarding how to make the facility as practical and functional as possible before attempting to secure space (S.D. Halverson & K. King, personal communication, January 2013).

As an aspiring athletics administrator, you should be aware that there is an "arms race" in collegiate athletics regarding sports medicine facilities and equipment. For example, athletic training facilities at major NCAA Division I FBS institutions can range from 1,000-square-foot (93-square-meter) facilities constructed in the mid-1990s to modern facilities that can exceed 8,000 square feet (740 square meters) (S.D. Halverson & K. King, personal communication, January 2013).

The arms race also involves state-of-the-art equipment used by ATCs, which, on the high end, can include an underwater treadmill (e.g., HydroWorx) that costs approximately US$100,000 and requires thousands of dollars' worth of annual maintenance. In this context, spending millions of dollars to provide superior treatment may be justified not only for the health, safety, and welfare of student-athletes but also for attracting prospective student-athletes (S.D. Halverson & K. King, personal communication, January 2013).

Liability Mitigation

Because we live in litigious times, it is critical to briefly discuss liability and risk management in relation to sports medicine. Once again, resource allocation plays a role. For example, if an athlete suffers a traumatic injury, who is responsible for paying for the medical services—the student-athlete's health insurance provider or the university's insurance provider? What if the student-athlete does not have health insurance?

The answer will depend on decisions that have been made by the school's athletics administrators. Some universities deem student-athletes to be 100 percent responsible for their health insurance—or lack thereof. Without insurance, paying for surgery

Professional Development

Professional Organizations in the Support Services

While many athletics administrators further their knowledge of best practices through joining organizations under the auspices of the National Association of Collegiate Directors of Athletics (NACDA) or through College Sports Communicators, there are professional organizations for support staff that fall outside these two umbrellas.

- *Strength and Conditioning.* National Strength and Conditioning Association (NSCA)
- *Sports Medicine and Athletic Training.* National Athletic Trainers' Association (NATA)
- *Video Services.* College Sports Video Association (CSVA)
- *Equipment Service.* Athletic Equipment Managers Association (AEMA)

In addition, sports psychology staff may further their professional development through such organizations as the American Psychological Association (APA), Division 47: Society for Sport, Exercise, and Performance Psychology; the Association of Applied Sport Psychology (AASP); and the Clinical/Counseling Sport Psychology Association (CCSPA).

caused by a sport injury would be the responsibility of the student-athlete. On the other end of the spectrum, an athletics department may commit to covering 100 percent of the costs of medical treatment for injuries sustained during sport participation. This approach, of course, results in increased insurance premiums and medical expenses for the athletics department. In order to avoid potential grievances, it is vital for athletics administrators to have discussions with the sports medicine staff and with student-athletes and their families to clearly outline policies and procedures (i.e., financial liability) should an injury occur (S. D. Halverson & K. King, personal communication, January 2013).

Another common concern for athletics administrators in liability management relates directly to human resources. If an athletics department has 15 sport teams but only 4 full-time ATCs, where does additional needed support come from? The answer usually involves undergraduate students aspiring to be ATCs and sometimes graduate students who may or may not already have their ATC certification. Student assistants may be eligible to receive compensation in the form of tuition reimbursement, room and board, free meals, and free gear, which constitutes another budget consideration (S.D. Halverson & K. King, personal communication, January 2013).

Student assistants provide much-needed support for ATCs and are allowed to perform limited athletic training duties at the discretion of their supervising ATC. They must not, however, practice any athletic training duties outside of the direct supervision of an ATC. Student assistants who overstep their permitted responsibilities, whether intentionally or unintentionally, could cause harm or trouble for themselves, a student-athlete, a supervising ATC, or the athletics department overall. Consequently, it is important for athletics administrators to communicate clearly with ATCs, students, and legal counsel to ensure that everyone is aware of, and held accountable for, ensuring that student assistants stay within their proper role in athletic training settings (S.D. Halverson & K. King, personal communication, January 2013).

Another legal consideration involving the health and safety of intercollegiate athletes focuses on traumatic brain injuries, such as concussions. Sports medicine professionals are often the first line of defense in diagnosing and properly treating athletes who may have suffered head trauma. If the proper standard of care is neglected, there is a risk of legal consequences—as well as the risk of a debilitating injury to the athlete.

Organizational Structure

Another important issue directly related to resource allocation and liability management involves the organizational and reporting structure of a sports medicine unit in an athletics department. Ancillary staff are housed in a variety of functional areas in athletics departments, but sports medicine is unique. Athletics administrators are wise to deliberate on the reporting lines (i.e., the chain of command) involving sports medicine professionals because strict legal standards apply to medical reporting and decision-making. Therefore, special attention is devoted here to the organizational structure of sports medicine in athletics departments; in particular, we focus on two prominent models, which we refer to as model A and model B.

Model A

The majority of institutions assume this model, in which sports medicine is housed in the athletics department like any other athletics-related functional area (e.g., media relations, sport marketing, compliance). In this model, the director of sports medicine is a full-time employee of the athletics department and may be a physician or ATC. The director of sports medicine oversees all ATCs involved with the athletics department and reports to the athletics director.

Those instituting this model are likely to use outsourced medical personnel (e.g., physicians, orthopedic surgeons, chiropractors, physical therapists, dentists). As a result, athletics administrators need to be prepared to pay private clinic fees to secure these services. Although outsourcing may be expensive, one advantage is that the arrangement protects the athletics department from a liability standpoint, since the burden falls on the contracted third party (S.D. Halverson & K. King, personal communication, January 2013).

Another concern with this model is a possible conflict of interest in decision-making by the sports medicine staff. Since the director of sports medicine and ATCs can be hired and fired at will by the athletics director, these personnel must, unfortunately, manage the expectations of coaches. This possibility raises ethical considerations because it can jeopardize the health and safety of student-athletes. For instance, an ATC may feel pressured to appease a coach by clearing a player to return to competition prematurely, rather than making a medically sound decision in favor of the student-athlete's health, safety, and well-being. The pressure derives from the fact that in this model, the athletics director signs the payroll checks, and ATCs may feel that if they anger a powerful coach they may be fired (S.D. Halverson & K. King, personal communication, January 2013).

With this potential pitfall in mind, athletics administrators must foster an environment that allows sports medicine staff to feel comfortable making decisions in the best interest of the welfare of student-athletes instead of the outcome of a competition. Figure 13.1 outlines a hypothetical model A organizational structure (S.D. Halverson & K. King, personal communication, January 2013).

Model B

The main difference between model A and model B is that model B situates sports medicine outside the athletics department, most likely as a division of the campus health department. Therefore, the director of sports medicine reports to the director of campus health, who in turn reports to the institution's chancellor or vice chancellor—not the athletics director. In this model, the director of sports medicine still hires and supervises all ATCs but under the guidance of the director of campus health. As a result, ATCs in this model are technically employed by campus health rather than by the athletics department; however, the athletics department reimburses campus health to distribute the salaries (S.D. Halverson & K. King, personal communication, January 2013).

As you may have deduced, this structure of reporting buffers ATCs from potential pressure exerted by coaches, since accountability is dictated by the campus health department rather than the athletics department. In addition, sports medicine units that operate according to this model are more likely than those in model A to use the services of other campus health employees (e.g., physicians, surgeons, physical therapists) instead of outsourcing to professionals in private practice (S.D. Halverson & K. King, personal communication, January 2013). Figure 13.2 outlines a hypothetical model B organizational structure. Notice the difference in reporting lines between model A and model B.

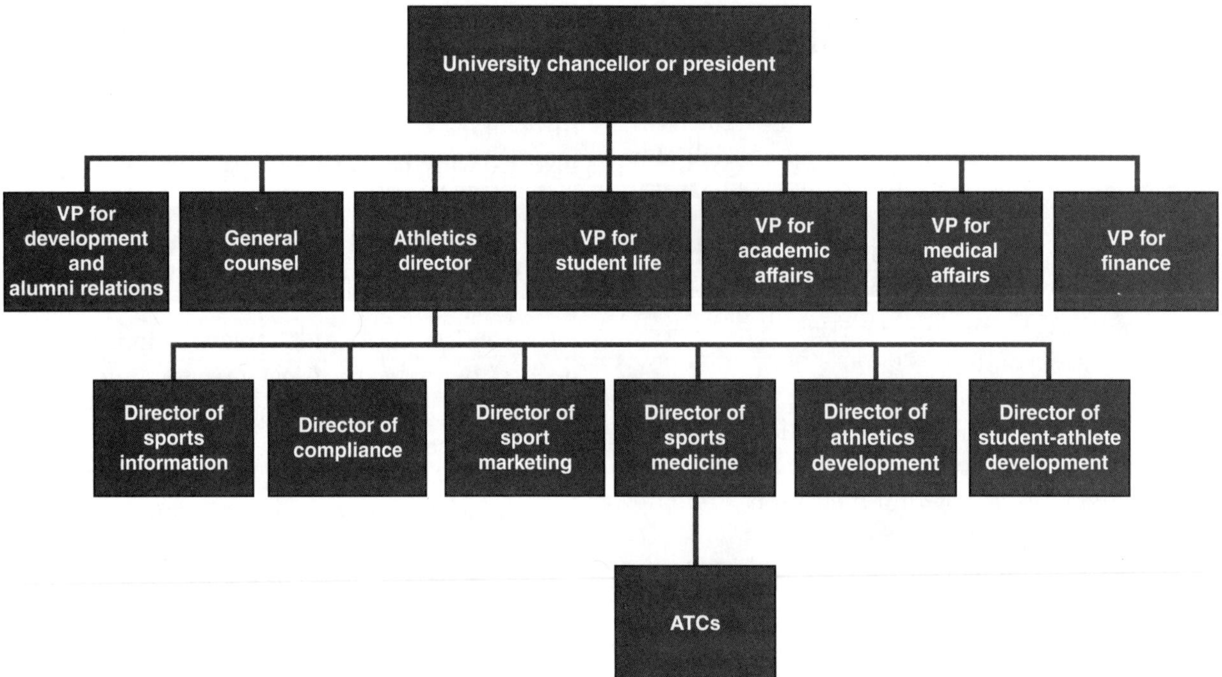

Figure 13.1 Hypothetical university organizational structure—model A.

Clearly, sports medicine's role in an athletics department involves many moving parts. In addition, sports medicine personnel, particularly ATCs, have daily interaction with student-athletes and coaches. Therefore, gaining a better understanding of their daily operations and decision-making processes can help administrators make informed decisions to prevent litigation and practice fiscally sound resource allocation. In pursuing the profession of athletics administration, you take on the obligation of protecting the holistic wellness, health, safety, welfare, and integrity of student-athletes. Comprehending the sports medicine support group is a critical step toward meeting that responsibility.

The ancillary groups discussed thus far engage in considerable direct interaction with student-athletes on a day-to-day basis, particularly regarding their personal holistic wellness. Athletics departments also include other support services that bear less responsibility for student-athletes' wellness but still have a substantial effect on the student-athlete experience. A few of these prominent support services are discussed in the following sections.

DIGITAL MEDIA SERVICES

Digital media services, which generate products such as graphics and videos, have become an essential element of athletics departments' branding and operations. As discussed in various other chapters, websites have become an essential technological medium for brand-building initiatives (Wallace et al., 2011). When websites are crafted properly and filled with creative content, they provide a unique opportunity to house informational and promotional materials in a manner that reinforces the athletics department's brand (Cooper & Weight, 2011). Websites provide a platform to market the personnel and programs housed in the department. In fact, they often include a themed video section offering feature stories, highlight clips, coach and player interviews, and other promotional pieces.

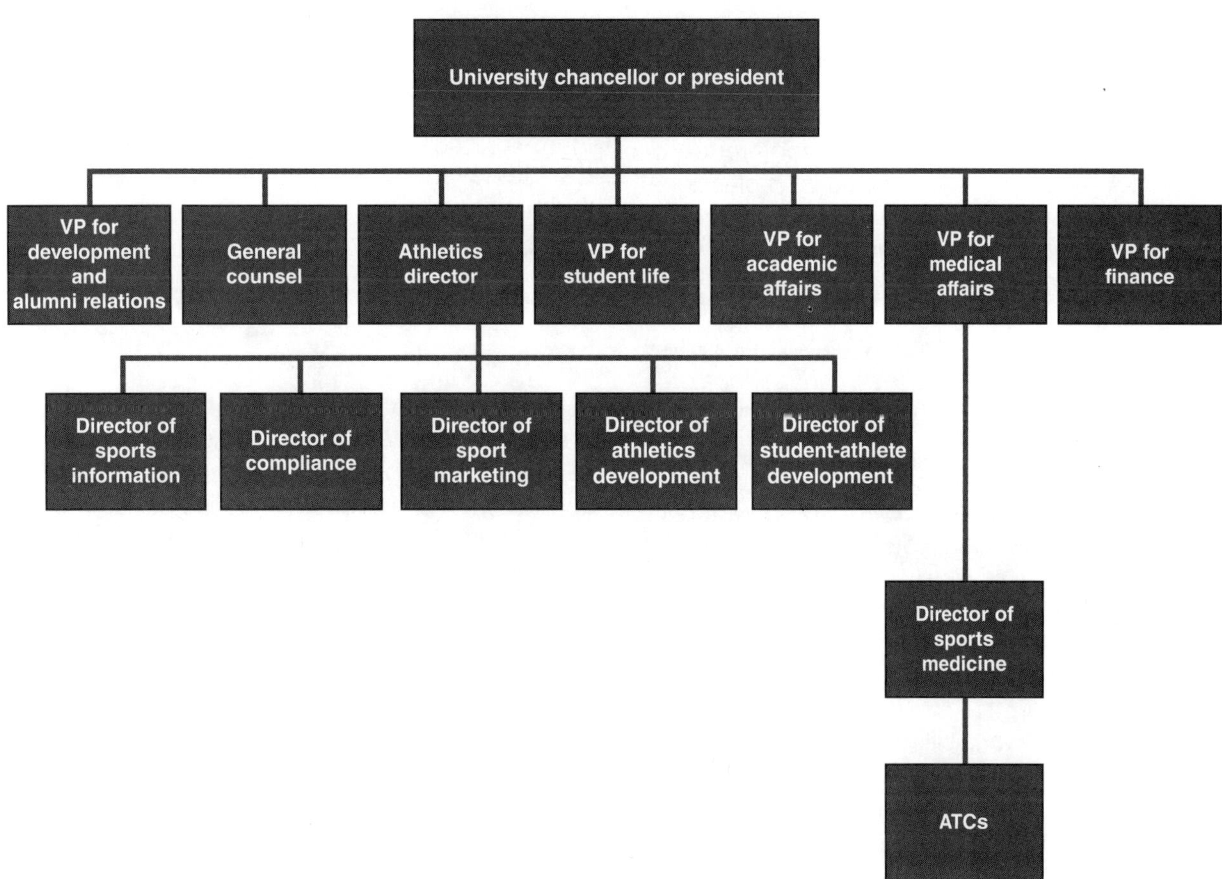

Figure 13.2 Hypothetical university organizational structure—model B.

Leadership Lesson

Sharpen the Saw

This chapter explores daily operations and challenges associated with a variety of functional areas that work in concert with the other units discussed throughout this book. It is critical to take a step back to review each of the working parts that function independently to facilitate optimal athletics department operations. Now that we have discussed the complex issues, processes, and oversight needed in the administration of intercollegiate athletics, it may not surprise you to hear of the 80-hour week that many athletics department staff members commonly work.

> *Show me a man who cannot bother to do little things, and I'll show you a man who cannot be trusted to do big things.*
>
> Lawrence D. Bell, founder of Bell Aircraft Corporation (manufacturer of the first supersonic aircraft)

Indeed, the typical 8-to-5 workweek is often just the beginning of an administrator's schedule. The evening fundraising events, home athletic contests, and awards ceremonies pile up, in addition to road trips, conference or NCAA meetings, and occasional professional development conferences. As a result, it is often said that working in athletics is not a job but a lifestyle and that in order to succeed you must have a passion for the industry and the work you do. We believe this is true. We also believe that in order to achieve success *and balance,* you must proactively do what Stephen Covey calls "sharpening the saw."

Covey (2004) shares an example illustrating this principle in *The 7 Habits of Highly Effective People.* Imagine that you see someone in the woods who is zealously working to saw down a tree. You can see the tremendous effort the person is putting into each movement of the saw, but little progress is being made. You comment to the person, "It looks like you're working very hard to cut down this tree! Why don't you take a few minutes to sharpen the saw?!" The person responds "Yes, I've been working for five hours, but I don't have time to sharpen the saw. I'm too busy sawing!"

A few minutes spent refining the instrument could have saved a lot of time, but instead the determined worker chose to pour all their energy into feverishly extending and retracting a dull blade. How many times have you sat down to get something done and, because you were feeling a bit hazy, you ended up reading the same paragraph over and over or you were sidetracked from the task you initially set out to accomplish? These outcomes might be symptomatic of trying to work with a dull saw.

Sharpening the saw, according to Covey (2004, p. 288), involves "preserving and enhancing the greatest asset you have—you." Covey outlines four dimensions that need attention.

1. Physical (exercise, nutrition, stress management)
2. Mental (reading, visualizing, planning, writing)
3. Spiritual (value clarification and commitment, study, meditation)
4. Social and emotional (service, empathy, synergy, intrinsic security)

Taking time to renew and refresh yourself is crucial. There will always be something that seems more important or more urgent, but spending time on these dimensions is "the single most powerful investment we can ever make in life" (Covey, 2004, p. 289). Take time to work out, read, ponder, pack a healthy lunch, attend professional development conferences, and spend time with your family. Take time to sharpen your saw. If you question the time spent on any of these investments, just think of the hours wasted by the person in the woods!

This concept offers many applications for organizational renewal. We focus here on the importance of feedback. Eliciting feedback from those you work with can help you focus your self-improvement efforts—and sharpening the saw is all about self-improvement. Arguably the most effective method of feedback is 360-degree (or multi-rater) feedback because of its comprehensive nature. In essence, you receive feedback from everyone you work with (i.e., from 360 degrees around you)—your peers, your boss, anyone you supervise, yourself, and sometimes even your customers. Generally, the feedback should be relatively simple, allowing those participating in the process to share their perceptions of your strengths and "developmental needs" or "opportunities for improvement." The most effective 360-degree feedback programs are confidential, constructive, and part of a developmental plan wherein feedback is supported with follow-up and coaching.

As you manage the variety of tasks and issues discussed in this chapter and throughout this book, you will inevitably learn and grow. Each on-the-job experience can bring unique insights and can contribute to your skill set, thus enhancing your competencies and marketability. When you also choose to proactively develop your greatest asset—yourself—your abilities increase exponentially. Time will pass, you will get older, and the job will get done. But whether you enjoy the journey, and whether you squeeze everything you can out of your experiences, is up to you.

It's the little things that make the big things possible. Only close attention to the fine details of any operation makes the operation first class.

J. Willard Marriott, founder of the Marriott Corporation and Marriott International (one of the largest hotel companies in the world)

In terms of staying on the cutting edge of marketing endeavors, the creation of unique digital content also provides innovative materials to be circulated via social media. This is a primary reason for the trend of athletics departments investing in digital media. High-quality digital media make it likely that revenues will increase because more visitors to the site provides an enticing sponsorship opportunity. At a minimum, an increase in web visitors allows athletics departments to build and publicize their brand. Therefore, it is important to become aware of the personnel who contribute to digital media services.

The demand for multimedia services is increasing in our society in general, and, as illustrated in the scenario at the beginning of the chapter, the demands of video services routinely affect student-athletes' schedules. Consequently, athletics departments are allocating more resources to video technology and management that extends beyond traditional website content. To better understand how video technology is managed and integrated into athletics departments, it is helpful to approach this ancillary group from two perspectives—external production and internal services. These two groups share similar tasks, technology, equipment, and footage, but their job responsibilities and operations differ.

External Video Production

One of the first things that many spectators notice upon entering a stadium or arena is the animation on a videoboard (e.g., jumbotron, LED ribbon board). This content is managed by dedicated ancillary staff, and due to its high visibility it is vital to understand how these services operate and function.

Video and multimedia services can be housed in a variety of functional areas in an athletics department. For instance, staff who produce video content intended for the public (e.g., for website, videoboard, or ribbon board use) could be directly supervised by the media relations staff, the sport marketing staff, or the multimedia and new media staff. These roles could also be outsourced to an organization outside of the institution. Some of these departments stand alone and some might be connected to the broadcasting department, especially if the school belongs to a conference with its own television network. Video produced for these functions is intended to be professional and stimulating to the audience, and staff members hired to produce content for external presentation must have expertise in video editing and video production (Castro, 2022).

Although an employee or student assistant may be trained in the use of video editing software, there is often a learning curve before one can properly operate videoboards, scoreboards, and ribbon boards due to their unique graphic user interface. In contrast, external video services staff who are trained to use certain equipment and software can communicate with the manufacturer directly (Castro, 2022).

Challenges for administrators related to external production include resource allocation and infrastructure. As demand increases for multimedia on a variety of platforms and devices, administrators must reflect on their mission, vision, goals, and objectives to determine the amount of resources to invest in external multimedia production. For example, these services can be outsourced, but doing so creates a new set of challenges, including access to coaches, student-athletes, and facilities, as well as ensuring the outsourced technology's integration and compatibility with the athletics department's hardware and software. However, if administrators decide to maintain in-house video production, they must make a substantial financial investment to hire full-time staff and secure the needed infrastructure to produce high-quality multimedia content.

In addition, there is no typical slot for external video production in the athletics department organizational chart. The trend is to place external video production in media relations, but some departments place it in sport marketing. Another alternative is to create a new functional area, commonly referred to as digital media, which can also oversee social media initiatives. With all of this in mind, it is critical for you as an aspiring administrator to reflect on the technology and management challenges inherent to external video production in an intercollegiate athletics department.

Internal Video Services

In contrast to external video production, internal video services manage video and digital media not shown to the public. This work primarily involves managing video from competitions and practices, and video used in team meetings. Internal video operations also help the coaching staff with game analysis software. A secondary responsibility of internal video services is to produce video that can be used to benefit the team in other ways, such as game highlights or pregame motivational segments, and for recruitment (Castro, 2022).

Most athletics departments include a video coordinator who works closely with coaching staff. This person may double as an assistant coach or be a graduate student assistant. The video coordinator's responsibilities vary from team to team and school to school, but they most likely entail coordinating internal digital media services for the football and basketball teams. To help you learn about internal digital media services in their most complex setting, the following discussion uses the scenario of a major NCAA Division I FBS institution.

Daily Operations

The fundamental purpose of internal digital media services is to record, edit, catalog, and maintain a video library from practices, competitions, and opponents' competitions. The purpose of this extensive library is to provide the coaching staff with tools to evaluate and analyze their team and their opponents. In many programs, staff members shoot every practice throughout the season, using multiple cameras to capture a variety of angles (Castro, 2022).

In football, for example, cameras may be used at the following angles: (1) high, wide, sideline-to-sideline view of the full field for both offense and defense, (2) angle from the end zone from hash mark to hash mark for both offense and defense, (3) individual cameras to shoot position drills, and (4) any other perspectives the coaches desire. This variety of angles requires the staff to shoot from a variety of heights, as well as on the ground. Not all practice fields have a press box, so teams may use a scissor lift or scaffolding for recording. Due to liability and risk management issues, however, new game analysis technology offers remote shooting to remove the need to climb to these heights (Castro, 2022). Additionally, the use of cameras mounted to hand-cranked poles on the field level has become more prevalent. These allow operators to remain safely on the ground while raising the camera high above the practice field.

Each play is shot from these multiple angles with the intent of providing as much information as possible for performance analysis. Thanks to advancements in technology, the process of editing and cataloging clips and getting them ready to view takes only 25 to 30 minutes once practice ends (Castro, 2022).

Now that you are aware of the many cameras and angles used on a daily basis, the next step is to understand how the technology is used to construct and maintain the robust digital media library.

Technology

Collegiate athletic teams use several brands of game analysis technology, including DVSport and Catapult. Each brand has its strengths and weaknesses, but they all serve the same basic purpose. Ultimately, a team chooses a technology provider based on the coaching staff's preferences about aspects such as the user interface. The financial investment for these services—including the initial cost of hardware, software, training, and support—can run to about US$500,000, and the annual cost of maintenance and support can reach about US$50,000 (Castro, 2022). It is considered worth the cost because it facilitates game analysis by enabling staff to catalog the tens of thousands of clips accrued throughout the season, thus aiding both organization and efficiency.

With this technology, each recorded play can be assigned any combination of attributes and codes according to the coaches' preferences. For instance, GPS trackers attached to the players can measure speed, distance covered, acceleration, calories burned, and other data, and can be integrated into the video through the editing software (Castro, 2022). In football, for example, each clip can be assigned any of about 40 attributes, such as down, distance, yard line, run or pass, play action, motion, offensive or defense formation, personnel, time, or hash mark. The coaching staff can then use the software to create a series of clips (often referred to as "cut-ups") filtered for any combination of the attributes (Castro, 2022).

Imagine that a coach or defensive player wants to prepare for the next opponent by analyzing the opponent's passing tendencies with a two-tight-end formation inside the 20-yard line on the second or third down in the fourth quarter. Since the video coordinator has already uploaded the opponent's game videos (previously acquired through the conference's exchange policy) and tagged each play, a few simple commands produce a collection of clips from the entire season that meet all of the selected criteria. The coaching staff or player can then quickly evaluate those plays and prepare for the opponent's tendencies in that specific game situation before moving on to the next chosen situation (Castro, 2022).

As you might imagine, the chosen attributes vary from sport to sport, and different software companies may target different sports. In addition, a given brand may offer particular versions of software to meet the particular needs and preferences of a given sport or coaching staff. For instance, in track and field, it is more appropriate to analyze and improve one's personal performance than to analyze an opponent's performance. Therefore, a coach or athlete might call for cut-ups of personal acceleration out of the blocks (Castro, 2022).

Other options offered by digital media technology providers include resources such as recruiting databases, mobile apps, and replay services. Altogether, this powerful capability to sort and filter video on demand for efficient game analysis helps justify the fiscal investment in ancillary staff and resources in the high-stakes world of elite intercollegiate athletics (Castro, 2022).

Personnel and Staff

The operating budget for internal digital media services varies from school to school, depending on the overall athletics department budget, but a typical budget for internal video services at a major NCAA Division I FBS football program is approximately US$250,000 per year. The number of full-time staff, part-time staff, and student assistants who work with internal video services varies, but the salary pool for staff totals approximately US$170,000. Student assistants can be compensated through a salary, an hourly wage, tuition reimbursement, free equipment, or free meals (Castro, 2022).

For individuals interested in pursuing internal video management, no specific academic program or credential is required. Many video coordinators pursue a major in sport management, sport communication, communication, or journalism. However, the primary qualification is experience in working with a video staff that stresses experiential learning with leading technology. It is also helpful to become a member of the Collegiate Sports Video Association and attend the group's annual conference, where professionals and aspiring professionals network and participate in sessions to learn improved techniques for capturing, editing, and securing footage for their databases. Ultimately, internal digital media services strive to enable the coaching staff and student-athletes to improve their performance through video analysis (Castro, 2022).

Digital media services are more prominent than ever in intercollegiate athletics departments. Whether digital media products are generated to entertain fans or edited to serve as teaching and learning tools for coaches and players, athletics administrators need to familiarize themselves with video management and technology in order to more efficiently serve their internal and external stakeholders.

EQUIPMENT SERVICES

Another ancillary area that directly affects the student-athlete experience is equipment services. The role of equipment in intercollegiate athletics has recently surpassed its core function as apparel and objects needed to pursue a sport, extending into branding and marketing. The University of Oregon's athletics department, particularly its football program, has embraced innovative graphics and apparel, amplifying its teams' national visibility in the media. As Oregon's approach illustrates, equipment's role in a collegiate athletics department goes beyond outfitting student-athletes to include marketing and revenue generation (Meshad, 2022). The University of North Carolina's association with Michael Jordan's Jumpman brand is another example of this (Greenberg, 2017).

The dominant official equipment providers in collegiate athletics are Adidas, Nike, and UnderArmour, but each school is free to enter into contract negotiations with any equipment provider. Furthermore, each sport likely has some latitude to negotiate with multiple brands regarding sport-specific equipment for its teams. For example, brand A may provide equipment for the football and basketball teams but be unable to provide soccer balls, swimwear, wrestling shoes, or field hockey equipment. As an athletics administrator, you will be tasked with negotiating equipment contracts, which have implications for virtually every member of the athletics department and for external stakeholders as well.

Equipment Contracts

Contracts with equipment providers can take a variety of forms. One element they typically include involves value-in-kind (VIK), which means that the company agrees to provide a certain amount of equipment for student-athletes, coaches, and staff; in return, the apparel company's brand receives exposure in the local, regional, or national media. Once the maximum VIK is reached, the contract

Technology Tools

Equipment Inventory Simplified

Numerous inventory management tools are available to help athletics departments organize gear for practices, games, weather, and travel. Within equipment services, Front Rush is a leading inventory management tool. When new equipment arrives it can be scanned in and then distributed. This technology can also prove useful when there are taxes involved. For example, the state of Georgia requires documentation of fringe benefits, including athletic gear (Meshad, 2022). Full-time staff members and coaches can be taxed on any item or apparel they receive. An inventory system enables an accurate account of every item the Georgia Athletic Association orders, receives, and issues. Items can be scanned in as they are received, then scanned out as they are distributed. Employees can then return the item to avoid any fringe-benefit taxation (Meshad, 2022).

usually provides for more equipment to be purchased at a fraction of the wholesale price. The company may also agree to pay a dollar amount to the athletics department. It is not uncommon to use this subsidy to supplement head coaches' base salaries, which can affect the quality of head coach that an athletics director can hire.

So how does millions of dollars' worth of athletics apparel and equipment get distributed to hundreds of athletes, dozens of coaches, and athletics department staff members? Enter equipment managers.

Equipment Managers

As you might imagine, it can be overwhelming for a coach to meet the inventory requirements of managing equipment shipments and distributions. Therefore, full-time equipment managers are hired to handle these needs in virtually every athletics department. There may be four to six full-time equipment managers in a major NCAA Division I FBS athletics department, and one-half to two-thirds of them likely work with football, whereas the others are responsible for all other sports. In fact, some major FBS athletics departments have only one full-time equipment manager outside of the football program (Meshad, 2022). Football staff and support staff have grown significantly in football since the 1990s, requiring more apparel and equipment orders and distribution (Greenberg, 2017).

Full-time equipment managers are primarily responsible for inventory and for communicating with apparel company representatives. It is critical to store, organize, and document incoming and distributed equipment efficiently so that no NCAA rules are violated in the form of extra benefits for student-athletes. Full-time equipment managers are also responsible for communicating with an individual team's equipment representatives to distribute each team's gear and equipment (Meshad, 2022).

The method of equipment distribution differs for football teams as compared with virtually every other kind of team because football teams have large rosters, complex equipment requirements, and large budgets. In sports other than football, coaches may receive equipment from the equipment manager and then distribute it to their student-athletes. There has, however, been a recent trend toward streamlining the inventory and equipment distribution processes. For example, student-athletes will go to the equipment storeroom, where the full-time equipment manager will scan the equipment and the student-athlete's identification card to keep accurate records of who receives what gear. Nonetheless, in sports other than football, coaches and student-athletes assume the primary responsibility of managing equipment for both practice and competition, including laundering and transporting equipment. Football, however, requires a great deal of attention to equipment management, and the following sections are more pertinent to football programs than to other sports.

Since there are relatively few full-time equipment managers, athletics departments enlist the help of student equipment managers to help with the day-to-day operations of individual teams. Not surprisingly, football programs employ the most student assistants. As with student video assistants, student equipment managers can receive compensation in the form of an hourly wage, a salary, tuition reimbursement, free meals, or free equipment (Meshad, 2022).

Student equipment managers are often responsible for preparing equipment for practices and competitions. On a daily basis, this work entails providing athletes and coaches with their practice gear (i.e., setting it up in their individual lockers), getting equipment ready on the practice field per the coaches' requests, storing equipment after practice, and doing laundry to prepare for the next day. On game day, student equipment managers' roles are similar. They set game equipment in lockers for athletes and coaches and organize equipment near the competition site so that replacement pieces are readily available and players miss as little playing time as possible (Meshad, 2022).

Equipment managers or student assistants are also responsible for packing equipment to be transported to away games. Athletics administrators may be involved in this process, because transporting equipment can be costly and time consuming. For example, do you invest in buying a tractor trailer or lease a truck for each road game to haul equipment? Can the equipment be transported by plane on a commercial flight? These are just a few of the relevant considerations, and though they may

Case Study

Tragedy on the Gridiron in College Park

On May 29, 2018, Jordan McNair, a 19-year-old offensive lineman for the University of Maryland, collapsed during a team workout that began at 4:15 p.m. He had trouble standing after running sprints the length of the field during voluntary workouts with the strength and conditioning and sports medicine staff. A call to emergency services was placed at 5:58 p.m., with reports of hyperventilating and difficulty breathing. McNair was transported to Washington Adventist Hospital before being moved to Cowley Shock Trauma Center in Baltimore, where he died on June 13 (Dinich, 2018). An investigation indicated McNair had had a body temperature of 106 degrees and suffered heatstroke, and no significant efforts were made to immediately cool him down.

In 2021, the University of Maryland agreed to a settlement of US$3.5 million with McNair's family as school officials admitted a failure by their sports medicine team to properly assist McNair (Fornelli, 2021). Despite reports of a "toxic culture" created by the head coach, D.J. Durkin, and strength and conditioning coach Rick Court, both staff members received buyouts as the program transitioned to a new football staff after players walked out of a Durkin-led meeting (Fornelli, 2021). Court received over US$300,000 in 2019 (Oyefusi, 2021) and Durkin, who had signed a five-year, US$12.5 million contract, received US$3.2 million in the 2019-20 fiscal year and then an additional US$2.1 million (Barker, 2020). Durkin's contract indicated he would receive the full US$2.1 million even if he took another coaching job. Durkin became an assistant coach at the University of Mississippi, earning US$700,000 (Barker, 2020). According to an open records request from the *Baltimore Sun,* eight assistant coaches at the University of Maryland also received buyouts ranging from US$43,365 to US$1.2 million. The school, already paying a US$2.6 million buyout for previous head coach Randy Edsall, eliminated seven sports teams in 2012, including men's tennis, men's cross country, men's indoor track, men's swimming, women's swimming, and women's water polo, as well as acrobatic and tumbling (formerly competitive cheer), in an effort to better balance the budget (Barker, 2020).

Questions to Consider

1. What checks and balances should be in place for an athletics department, especially as it relates to player safety, risk management, and communication between sports medicine, strength and conditioning, coaches, and athletics administrators?
2. How can benchmarking play a role in best practices and policy updates in sports medicine?
3. How can current events, such as the case study, help to develop safer practices, games, and workouts for student-athletes, coaches, athletic trainers, and athletics administrators?
4. How might your answers vary to the first three questions if this scenario occurred at the Division II, Division III, NAIA, or junior college level, where resources vary from those afforded to Division I schools?

seem minor in the grand scheme of the decisions faced by athletics administrators, they are essential nonetheless.

Equipment managers can also be involved in the setup and breakdown of wireless communication for the coaching staff (Meshad, 2022). Recruiting and photo shoots are additional time commitments throughout the year that require creativity and potentially long hours. Mishaps in either area can hinder game-day operations or recruitment of future players.

Equipment can easily be taken for granted, but dozens of individuals help operate this multimillion-dollar ancillary group. Can you imagine competing for a national championship with a key piece of equipment malfunctioning? Equipment managers are proficient at handling inventory and organization so that spare equipment is close by to ensure that athletes and coaches can perform at their optimal level.

CONCLUSION

As an athletics administrator, you will find that various functional areas in an athletics department demand your time and attention. Among these areas are a number of seemingly minor ancillary groups that actually play a major role in the day-to-day operations of an athletics department. To be a successful administrator, you must be familiar with the details of these groups' operations. To that end, this chapter outlines a few of the ancillary groups commonly found in athletics departments, and it is now your responsibility to develop your awareness and educate yourself about these groups' functions so that you can make informed, efficient, effective decisions that ultimately benefit hundreds of individuals.

DISCUSSION QUESTIONS

1. The athletics department's operating budget has been cut 10 percent from last year's level, and you are charged with making recommendations about which services and personnel on the holistic care team should be retained. What recommendations do you make?
2. Student-athletes are indicating that stress levels are rising and mental health challenges are increasing. Some students are concerned that discussing mental health would lead peers, coaches, or family to perceive them as "weak" or "soft." What steps would you take to allay their concerns?
3. The athletics department in which you work is restructuring its sports medicine unit. Describe three or four considerations that are critical to efficiently integrate sports medicine in an athletics department.
4. As an administrator, what key areas of digital media should you consider when evaluating your digital presence?
5. Digital media services, including creative graphics and video production, can be housed in a variety of functional areas in an athletics department. What do you think is the best strategy for incorporating these services into an athletics department? What is the best strategy for working with third-party entities such as multimedia rights holders?
6. Discuss the direct and indirect effects that a partnership with an apparel equipment provider can have on an athletics department.

LEARNING ACTIVITIES

1. Determine who makes up the holistic care team at your institution. Are there any gaps in coverage or responsibility area? What resources have been allocated to assist in students' mental health?
2. Interview a video coordinator at your university's athletics department and discuss daily operations.
3. Conduct an internet search to review equipment contracts at a variety of institutions and compare their similarities and differences.
4. Talk to a senior athletics administrator to determine what insurance policies are necessary to lower the school's risk and protect students, staff, and patrons in sports medicine.

References and Resources

Chapter 1

About ND. (2013). University of Notre Dame. www.nd.edu/about/.

Allmendinger, D.F. (1973). The dangers of ante-bellum student life. *Journal of Social History* 7(1), 75-85.

Athletic Communications Staff. (2022). Candice Storey Lee: Vice Chancellor, Athletics and University Affairs, and Athletic Director. *Vucommodores.com*. https://vucommodores.com/staff/candice-storey-lee/.

Barr, C.A. (1998). *The faculty athletics representative: A survey of the membership*. Overland Park, KS: National Collegiate Athletic Association.

Bear, C. (2008, May 12). American Indian boarding schools haunt many. *National Public Radio*. www.npr.org/templates/story/story.php?storyId=16516865.

Birdseye, C.F. (1907). *Individual training in our colleges*. New York: Macmillan. http://books.google.com/books?id=B-v7ZFGz9MCYC&printsec=frontcover&source=gbs_ge_summary_r&cad=0#v=onepage&q&f=false.

Blinder, A. (2021, December 4). Big contracts, big buyouts, big pressure: College football coaches hit the jackpot. *New York Times*. www.nytimes.com/2021/12/04/sports/ncaafootball/college-football-coaching-changes.html.

Brooks, A. (2021, July 12). ESPN preps for 2021 college football season with comprehensive coverage of conference media days. *ESPN Press Room*. https://espnpressroom.com/us/press-releases/2021/07/espn-preps-for-2021-college-football-season-with-comprehensive-coverage-of-conference-media-days/.

Byers, W. (1995). *Unsportsmanlike conduct*. Ann Arbor, MI: University of Michigan Press.

Carlson, S. (2013, January 28). What's the payoff for the "country club" college? *Chronicle of Higher Education*. http://chronicle.com/blogs/buildings/whats-the-payoff-for-the-country-club-college/32477.

College Ranker. (2021, October 10). Colleges as country clubs: Today's pampered college students. *Collegeranker.com*. www.collegeranker.com/features/colleges-as-country-clubs/.

Chu, D. (1989). *The character of American higher education and intercollegiate sport*. Albany, NY: SUNY Press.

Crowley, C. (2006). *In the arena: The NCAA's first century*. Indianapolis: National Collegiate Athletic Association.

Dellenger, R. (2021, December 9). The ties that divide: Expanding the college football playoff has become increasingly difficult. *SI.com*. www.si.com/college/2021/12/09/college-football-playoff-expansion-disagreement-12-team-8-team.

Desrochers, D. (2013). *Academic spending versus athletic spending: Who wins?* Washington, DC: American Institutes for Research.

Dober, R.P. (2007). *Old Main*. Ann Arbor, MI: Society for College and University Planning.

Dodd, D. (2021, November 1). Group of athletic directors suggests sweeping changes to NCAA enforcement model. *CBSSports.com*. www.cbssports.com/college-football/news/group-of-athletic-directors-suggests-sweeping-changes-to-ncaa-enforcement-model/.

Dunnavant, K. (2004). *The 50-year seduction: How television manipulated college football, from the birth of the modern NCAA to the creation of the BCS*. New York: St. Martin's Press.

Elfman, L. (2012, December 9). Football is king. *Inside Higher Education*. http://diverseeducation.com/article/50011/.

Gerber, E.W., Felshin, J., Berlin, P., & Wyrick, W. (1974). *The American woman in sport*. Reading, MA: Addison-Wesley Publishing Company.

Grant, C. (1981). Statement opposing the NCAA motion to offer women's championships in Division I. Statement presented at the NCAA Convention, Miami, FL. Courtesy of the Sharon Taylor Association for Intercollegiate Athletics for Women (AIAW) Archives in the Department of Sport Management at Drexel University.

Grundy, P. (2001). *Learning to win: Sports, education, and social change in the twentieth century*. Chapel Hill, NC: University of North Carolina Press.

Harris, R. (1932). *King football: The vulgarization of the American college*. New York: Vanguard Press.

Heitner, D. (2022, January 7). Will the NCAA intervene on NIL deals tied to enrollment? *Abovethelaw.com*. https://abovethelaw.com/2022/01/will-the-ncaa-intervene-on-nil-deals-tied-to-enrollment/.

Holland, J. (1974). AIAW handbook of policies and operating procedures. Washington, DC: American Alliance for Health, Physical Education, Recreation, and Dance.

Hosick, M. (2011, February 2). Equal opportunity knocks. *NCAA News*. www.ncaa.com/news/ncaa/2011-02-02/equal-opportunity-knocks.

Ingrassia, B. (2012). *The rise of gridiron university: Higher education's uneasy alliance with big-time football*. Lawrence: University of Kansas Press.

Intercollegiate Athletic Association of the United States. (1906). *Proceedings from the first annual meeting*. New York, NY. https://archive.org/details/proceedingsannu-14assogoog.

Ireland, C. (2012, April 19). Harvard's long-ago student risings. *Harvard Gazette*. http://news.harvard.edu/gazette/story/2012/04/harvards-long-ago-student-risings.

Jacob, B., McCall, B., & Stange, K. (2018). College as Country Club: Do Colleges Cater to Students' Preferences for Consumption? *Journal of Labor Economics*, 36(2), 309–348. https://doi-org.ezproxy.ithaca.edu/10.1086/694654.

Jenkins, S. (2007). *The real Americans: The team that changed a game, a people, a nation*. New York: Random House.

Johnson, R. (2017, September 21). Jerry Falwell Jr. says the Sun Belt only turned down Liberty's money because of politics, but the Sun Belt says differently. *SBNation.com.* www.sbnation.com/college-football/2017/9/21/16339764/liberty-football-fbs-conference-jerry-falwell-sun-belt.

Jordan, D.S. (1905, December 9). The future of football. *Collier's Weekly. 36:* 19–20.

Kiernan, J. (1932, November 13). King football: Racket or sport? *New York Times,* p. BR3.

Lederman, D. (2019, February 1). NCAA punishes Missouri in blatant academic fraud case. *Inside Higher Education.* www.insidehighered.com/news/2019/02/01/ncaa-punishes-missouri-blatant-case-academic-fraud.

Libit, D., & Cyphers, L. (2019, November 19). Tom McMillen's "dark side" shuffle. *Newsletter of Intent.* https://theintercollegiate.substack.com/p/tom-mcmillens-dark-side-shuffle.

McQuilkin, S.A., & Smith, R. (1993, Spring). The rise and fall of the flying wedge: Football's most controversial play. *Journal of Sport History, 20*(1), 57–64.

Mendenhall, T.C. (1993). *The Harvard-Yale boat race and the coming of sport to the American College: 1852-1924.* Mystic, CT: Mystic Seaport Museum.

Miller, S. (2021, May). Academic clustering and intercollegiate baseball programs: Do national rankings matter? *Journal of Issues in Intercollegiate Athletics.* Retrieved from http://csri-jiia.org/wp-content/uploads/2021/09/RA_2021_14.pdf.

Moran, M. (1989, August 27). College football '89; Defining the 80's? No Easy Task. *New York Times.* www.nytimes.com/1989/08/27/sports/college-football-89-defining-the-80-s-no-easy-task.html.

National Collegiate Athletic Association. (1916, December 28). Proceedings from the Eleventh Annual Convention. New York: National Collegiate Athletic Association.

National Collegiate Athletic Association. (2013, January 21). Chronology of enforcement. Indianapolis: http://archive.today/Ea1B.

OH Predictive Insights. (2021, November). ASU GSI Q4 National Sports Public Opinion Pulse Update. *Global Sports Matter.* https://globalsport.asu.edu/sites/default/files/resources/global_sport_institute_national_snapshot_poll_december_2021_takeaways.pdf

Oriard, M. (2001). *King football: Sport and spectacle in the golden age of radio and newsreels, movies and magazines, the weekly and daily press.* Chapel Hill: University of North Carolina Press.

Oriard, M. (2009). *Bowled over: Big-time college football from the sixties to the BCS era.* Chapel Hill: University of North Carolina Press.

Oxendine, J. (1988). *American Indian sports heritage.* Lincoln, NE: University of Nebraska Press.

Rittenberg, A. (2013, February 20). Spartans blended race in 1960s. *ESPN.* http://espn.go.com/espn/print?id=8970293&type=story.

Rudolph, F. (1990). *The American college and university: A history* (Rev. ed.). Athens, GA: University of Georgia Press.

Sack, A.L., & Staurowsky, E.J. (1998). *College athletes for hire: The evolution and legacy of the NCAA amateur myth.* Westport, CT: Praeger.

Savage, H. (1929). *American college athletics, Bulletin no. 23.* New York: Carnegie Foundation for the Advancement of Teaching.

Schad, T., & Berkowitz, S. (2021, December 1). Brian Kelly's contract with LSU tops list of 10 biggest deals in college football history. *USA Today.* www.usatoday.com/story/sports/ncaaf/2021/12/01/brian-kelly-contract-lsu-largest-college-football-history/8808802002/.

Schuster, B. (2019, October 9). Report: NCAA chose not to adopt recommended academic fraud reforms in the wake of the UNC scandal. *Yahoo! Sports.* www.yahoo.com/now/report-ncaa-chose-not-to-adopt-recommended-academic-fraud-reforms-in-wake-of-unc-scandal-214909491.html.

Seidentop, D., & Vandermars, H. (2011). *Introduction to physical fitness and sport.* East Windsor, NJ: McGraw-Hill.

Shapiro, M. (2021, June 10). Source: College Football Playoff Committee recommends 12-team field. *SI.com.* www.si.com/college/2021/06/10/college-football-playoff-12-team-expansion-recommended.

Smith, R. (1988). *Sports and freedom: The rise of big-time college athletics.* New York: Oxford University Press.

Smith, R. (1994). *Big-time football at Harvard, 1905: The diary of coach Bill Reid.* Champaign, IL: University of Illinois Press.

Smith, R. (2001). *Play-by-play: Radio, television, and big-time college sport.* Baltimore: Johns Hopkins University Press.

Soares, W.G. (1979). *A history from 1820 to 1890 of two theories of physical training: The collegiate gymnastics movement and the rise of intercollegiate athletic teams at Amherst, Harvard, Princeton, and Yale.* Unpublished doctoral dissertation. New York: Teachers College, Columbia University.

Sperber, M. (1993). *Shake down the thunder: The creation of Notre Dame football.* New York: Henry Holt.

Staff. (2021, November). Candice Storey Lee uses her platform to inspire. *HarpethHall.com.* www.harpethhall.org/news/p/~board/n/post/candice-storey-lee-uses-her-platform-to-inspire.

Staurowsky, E. (2005). *Reclaiming our inheritance as faculty: Understanding academic freedom in relationship to college sport.* Paper presented at the meeting of the North American Society of Sociology and Sport Conference (Greensboro, NC).

Staurowsky, E.J. (2011, December 1). Urban and me: We're almost twins . . . except for that six-year $26.6 million contract. *College Sports Business News.*

Staurowsky, E.J. (2012). A radical proposal: Title IX has no place in college sport pay-for-play discussions. *Marquette Sports Law Review, 22*(2), 575-595.

Stephenson, C. (2020, February 4). Vanderbilt AD Malcolm Turner resigns; Alabama native Candice Storey Lee takes over as interim AD. *Al.com.* www.al.com/sports/2020/02/vanderbilt-ad-malcolm-turner-resigns-alabama-native-candice-storey-lee-takes-over-as-interim-ad.html.

Stevens, M. (2007). *Creating a class: College admissions and the education of elites.* Cambridge, MA: Harvard University Press.

Suggs, W. (2005). *A place on the team: The triumph and tragedy of Title IX.* Princeton, NJ: Princeton University Press.

Sweet, W. (2011, August 29). 150 years ago: Amherst established nation's first college health program. *Amherst News.* www.amherst.edu/aboutamherst/news/news_releases/2011/08/node/337711/.

The Athletic Staff. (2021, November 3). NCAA rejects Oklahoma State's appeal, bans men's hoops team from 2022 postseason. *The Athletic.* https://theathletic.com/news/ncaa-rejects-oklahoma-states-appeal-bans-mens-hoops-team-from-2022-postseason/8taw61AHP2o8/.

Thelin, J. (2021, August 20). Where are the presidents? *Inside Higher Education.* www.insidehighered.com/views/2021/08/20/presidents-have-been-largely-silent-about-issues-college-sports-and-commercialism.

Tucker, T. (2004). *Notre Dame vs. the Klan: How the Fighting Irish defeated the Ku Klux Klan.* Chicago: Loyola Press.

UPI (1981, January 14). Dramatic move by NCAA gives women 20 national title events. *Lodi News-Sentinel.* http://news.google.com/newspapers?nid=2245&dat=19810113&id=ReMzAAAAIBAJ&sjid=ajIHAAAAIBAJ&pg=6996,1427102.

Vecsey, G. (2011, November 8). The dangerous cocoon of King Football. *New York Times,* p. B16.

Watterson, J.S. (2000). *College football: History, spectacle, controversy.* Baltimore: Johns Hopkins University Press.

Weinstein, R. (2021, November 14). Vanderbilt athletic director Candice Storey Lee on Vandy United projects. *247sports.com.* https://247sports.com/college/vanderbilt/LongFormArticle/Vanderbilt-athletic-director-Candice-Storey-Lee-on-Vandy-United-projects-175314847/#175314847_1.

West, G. (2021, March 5). LSU releases report on sexual misconduct investigation from Husch Blackwell. *SI.com.* www.si.com/college/lsu/football/lsu-husch-blackwell-report-findings.

Whiton, J. (1901, June). The first intercollegiate regatta. *The Outlook, 18*(5), 286-289.

Wilson, W. (1909, November). What is a college for? *Scribner's,* 570-577. www.unz.org/Pub/Scribners-1909nov-00570.

Chapter 2

Adelson, A., Bonagura, K., & Rittenberg, A. (July 11, 2022). Inside the stunning USC-UCLA move to the Big Ten—and the chaos that followed. *ESPN.com.* www.espn.com/college-football/story/_/id/34217498/inside-stunning-usc-ucla-move-big-ten-chaos-followed.

Bandre, M.A. (2011). The impact of financial aid on the enrollment and retention of student athletes at National Collegiate Athletic Association (NCAA) Division III colleges and universities: A review of the literature. *Journal of Student Financial Aid, 41*(1), 4.

Beaver, W. (2014). The changing nature of Division III athletics. *College and University, 89*(3), 34.

Bruder, H.J. (2017). *Athletics Programs as Facilitators of Enrollment at Private NCAA Division III Institutions in the Midwest.* [Doctoral dissertation, North Central University]. Dissertation published on ProQuest, available at https://eric.ed.gov/?id=ED579861.

Covey, S.R. (2004). *The 7 habits of highly effective people: Restoring the character ethic.* New York: Free Press.

Dodd, D. (2022, January 14). Jim Phillips details ACC's opposition to College Football Playoff expansion calling for reform. *CBS Sports.* https://cbssports.com/college-football/news/jim-phillips-details-accs-opposition-to-college-football-playoff-expansion-while-calling-for-reform/.

Duderstadt, J.J. (2003). *Intercollegiate athletics and the American university: A university president's perspective.* Ann Arbor, MI: University of Michigan Press.

Elmore, T. (2010). *Habitudes: Images that form leadership habits and attitudes.* Duluth, GA: Growing Leaders, Inc.

Feezell, T. (2009). Adding football and the "uses" of athletics at NCAA Division II and Division III institutions. *New Directions for Higher Education, 2009*(148), 65-72.

Finances of Intercollegiate Athletics Database. (2022). NCAA Revenues & Expenses Report. *NCAA.* https://www.ncaa.org/sports/2019/11/12/finances-of-intercollegiate-athletics-database.aspx.

Forde, P. (2010, June 13). Swarbrick focused on ND's interests. *ESPN.* http://sports.espn.go.com/ncf/columns/story?columnist=forde_pat&id=5267138.

Frankl, V.E. (1963). *Man's search for meaning.* New York: Washington Square Press.

Knight Commission on Intercollegiate Athletics. (2009). Quantitative and qualitative research with Football Bowl Subdivision university presidents on the costs and financing of intercollegiate athletics: Report of findings and implications. www.knightcommissionmedia.org/images/President_Survey_FINAL.pdf.

Knight-Newhouse College. (2022). Knight-Newhouse College Athletics Database. www.knightnewhousedata.org.

Maxwell, J.C. (2011). Leading a life of intentional influence. www.johnmaxwell.com/cms/images/uploads/ads/Leading_a_Life_of_Intentional_Influence.pdf.

Media Center. (2022, January 20). NCAA members approve new constitution. *NCAA.* https://www.ncaa.org/news/2022/1/20/media-center-ncaa-members-approve-new-constitution.aspx.

Miller, P.S., & Kerr, G. (2002). The athletic academic and social experience of intercollegiate student-athletes. *Journal of Sport Behavior,* 25(4), 346-365.

Minor, J.T., & Perry, L. (2010). Faculty involvement in athletic decision making: A review of three athletic major conferences. *Academia.edu*. www.academia.edu/1119307/Faculty_Involvement_in_Athletic_Decision_Making_A_Review_of_Three_Athletic_Major_Conferences.

National Association of Intercollegiate Athletics. (2023). About us. https://www.naia.org/about/about-us.

National Christian College Athletic Association. (2023). About us. www.thenccaa.org/tournaments/?id=567.

National Junior College Athletic Association. (2022). 2021-2022 NJCAA Annual Report. https://d2o2figo6ddd0g.cloudfront.net/h/z/x5oxckgwtzxf4r/2021-22_NJCAA_Annual_Report_09-28-22.pdf.

National Collegiate Athletics Association. (2022). Division III 2022-23 Facts and Figures. https://ncaaorg.s3.amazonaws.com/about/d3/D3_FactsandFigures.pdf.

National Collegiate Athletics Association. (2020). Our Three Divisions. https://ncaaorg.s3.amazonaws.com/about/ncaa/101/NCAA101_Our3Divisions.pdf.

NCAA Constitution. (2022). NCAAGov_Constitution121421.pdf (ncaaorg.s3.amazonaws.com).

Stancill, J. (2013, April 18). Holden Thorp says athletics "can overwhelm" chancellor. *Raleigh News and Observer*. www.newsobserver.com/2013/04/18/2834890/holden-thorp-says-athletics-can.html.

Todd, M., & Brown, C. (2003). Characteristics associated with superstitious behavior in track and field athletes: Are there NCAA divisional level differences? *Journal of Sport Behavior*, *26*(2), 168.

United States Collegiate Athletic Association. (2023). www.theuscaa.com.

Weight, E., Weight, M., & Schneider, R. (2013). Confronting the arms race: Conference commissioner perspectives on spending within intercollegiate athletics. *The International Journal of Sport Management*, 14(4), 1-21.

Chapter 3

Abreu, A., Macedo, P., & Camarinha-Matos, L.M. (2009). Elements of a methodology to assess the alignment of core values in collaborative networks. *International Journal of Production Research*, *47*(17), 4709-4934.

Ammons, D., & Glass, J. (1988, May). Headhunters in local government: Use of executive search firms in managerial selections. *Public Administration Review*, *48*(3), 687-693.

Bass, B.M. (1985). *Leadership and performance beyond expectations*. New York: The Free Press.

Benko, J., director of athletics, Georgia Southern University. (2022). Interview by R. Zullo.

Bennis, W.G. (1984). Good managers and good leaders. *Across the Board*, *21*(10), 7-11.

Berings, D., De Fruyt, F., & Bouwen, R. (2004). Work values and personality traits as predictors of enterprising and social vocational interests. *Personality and Individual Differences*, *36*, 349-364.

Berkowitz, S., & Upton, J. (2011, October 6). Demands on college ADs resemble CEO challenges. *USA Today*. www.usatoday.com/sports/college/story/2011-10-18/athletic-director-salaries-cover/50671214/1.

Berry, L.L. (1999). *Discovering the soul of service: The nine drivers of sustainable business success*. New York: Harper Business.

Bolon, D.S. (2005). Comparing mission statement content in for-profit and not-for-profit hospitals: Does mission really matter? *Hospital Topics*, *83*, 2-9.

Branch, T. (2011, October). The shame of college sports. *The Atlantic*. www.theatlantic.com/magazine/archive/2011/10/the-shame-of-college-sports/308643/.

Brennan, C. (2022, February 2). Carla Williams on breaking boundaries at UVA's athletic director. *Justwomenssports.com*. https://justwomenssports.com/carla-williams-on-breaking-boundaries-as-uvas-athletic-director/.

Brown, W.A., & Yoshioka, C.F. (2003). Mission attachment and satisfaction as factors in employee retention. *Nonprofit Management Leadership*, *14*, 5-18.

Burns, J.M. (1978). *Leadership*. New York: Harper and Row.

Collins, D. (2009, July 5). Big man on campus: Ron Wellman refuses to let the size of the school inhibit the size of its dreams. *Winston-Salem Journal*. www2.journalnow.com/sports/2009/jul/05/campus-ron-wellman-refuses-to-let-the-size-of-the--ar-156459/.

Collins, J. (2001). *Good to great: Why some companies make the leap . . . and others don't*. New York: Harper Business.

Collins, J.C., & Porras, J.I. (1994). *Built to last: Successful habits of visionary companies*. London: Random House.

Conger, J.A., & Kanungo, R.N. (1987). Toward a behavioral theory of charismatic leadership in organizational settings. *Academy of Management Review*, *12*, 637-647.

Cooper, C.G., & Weight, E.A. (n.d.). Division I, II, & III administrator values. Unpublished manuscript.

Cooper, C.G., & Weight, E.A. (2012). Maximizing organizational effectiveness: NCAA Division III administrator core values and departmental culturization. *Journal of Issues in Intercollegiate Athletics*, 5, 339-353.

Cooper, C.G., Weight, E.A., & Pierce, D. (2014). The leader–value continuum: NCAA Division I core values and transformational leadership. *The International Journal of Sport Management*. *15*(2) 151-171.

Covey, S.R. (1989). *The 7 habits of highly effective people*. New York: Simon & Schuster.

Dean, Z. (2017, July 17). After two-year provisional period, Embry-Riddle officially NCAA member. *The Daytona Beach News-Journal*. www.news-journalonline.com/story/sports/2017/07/17/after-two-year-provisional-period-embry-riddle-officially-ncaa-member/20136932007/.

Deford, F. (2011, September 14). The NCAA and the so-called student-athlete. *National Public Radio*. www.npr.org/2011/09/14/140433661/the-ncaa-and-the-so-called-student-athlete.

Earley, P.C., & Mosakowski, E. (2000). Creating hybrid team cultures: An empirical test of transnational team functioning. *Academy of Management Journal, 43,* 26-49.

Earnest, G.W., & Cugliari, C.W. (2009). Making meetings manageable. *Ohio State Leadership Center.* http://ohioline.osu.edu/lc-fact/0001.html.

Ely, R.J., & Thomas, D.A. (2001). Cultural diversity at work: The effects of diversity perspectives on work group processes and outcomes. *Administrative Science Quarterly, 46,* 229-273.

Estes, G. (2021, January 20). Ugly as Jeremy Pruitt's firing is for Tennessee football, it'd be worse in court. *Nashville Tennessean.* www.tennessean.com/story/sports/college/ut/2021/01/21/jeremy-pruitt-fired-tennessee-football-michael-lyons/4218032001/.

Floridagators.com. (2010, June 24). Gator athletics program finishes second in the nation. https://floridagators.com/story.aspx?filename=18360&file_date=6-24-2010.

Ferguson, J., & Milliman, J. (2008). Creating effective core organizational values: A spiritual leadership approach. *International Journal of Public Administration, 31,* 439-459.

Frenette, G. (2010, December 11). Florida AD Jeremy Foley makes gutsy call by hiring Will Muschamp. *Florida Times-Union.* http://jacksonville.com/opinion/blog/400617/gene-frenette/2010-12-11/gene-frenette-florida-ad-jeremy-foley-makes-gutsy-call.

Gordon, J. (2009, July 27). Get the right people on the bus. Jon Gordon blog. www.jongordon.com/blog/2009/07/27/get-the-right-people-on-the-bus-2/.

Graeff, C.L. (1983). The Situational Leadership Theory: A Critical View. *Academy of Management Review, 8,* 285-291.

Harmon, F.G. (1996). *Playing for keeps.* New York: Wiley.

House, R.J. (1971). A Path-Goal Theory of Leader Effectiveness. *Administrative Science Quarterly, 16,* 321-339.

Ind, N. (2007). *Living the brand* (3rd ed.). London: Kogan Page.

Kotter, J.P. (1996). *Leading change.* Boston: Harvard Business School.

Lencioni, P.M. (2002, July). Make your values mean something. *Harvard Business Review,* 113-117.

Lencioni, P. (2006). *Silos, politics, and turf wars: A leadership fable about destroying the barriers that turn colleagues into competitors.* San Francisco, CA: Jossey-Bass.

Maxwell, J. (2005). *Developing the leader within you* (Rev. ed.). Nashville: Thomas Nelson.

Mayfield, K. (2022, June 17). ERAU grabs highest finish ever in Division II LEARFIELD Directors' Cup; Places 26th with 472 points in 2021-22. *Embry-Riddle Athletics.* https://erauathletics.com/news/2022/6/17/general-erau-grabs-highest-finish-ever-in-division-ii-learfield-directors-cup-in-2021-22-places-26th-with-472-points.aspx.

Meyer, J.D. (2008). *Scoring points online: College athletics departments' brand positioning through communications on the World Wide Web.* Unpublished master's thesis, University of North Carolina at Chapel Hill.

Milliman, J., & Clair, J. (1995). Environmental HRM best practices in the USA: A review of the literature. *Greener Management International, 10,* 34-48.

Mondello, M. (1997, February). Meet Jeremy Foley: Athletic director, University of Florida. *Coach and Athletic Director.* www.thefreelibrary.com/Meet+Jeremy+-Foley%3A+Athletic+Director,+University+of+Florida.-a019266603.

Murray, P. (2018, March 23). Texts, emails outline Vols coaching search, downfall of John Currie. *WBIR.* www.wbir.com/article/sports/texts-emails-outline-vols-coaching-search-downfall-of-john-currie/51-531210325.

NCAA Division I Manual. (2022). *2022-2023 NCAA Division I manual.* Indianapolis, IN.

Newell, K. (2008, February 1). The best in the business: University of Florida athletic director Jeremy Foley. *Coach and Athletic Director.* www.highbeam.com/doc/1G1-175526847.html.

Ouchi, W.G. (1979). A conceptual framework for the design of organizational control mechanisms. *Management Science, 25,* 933-948.

Pattakos, A.N. (2004). The search for meaning in government service. *Public Administration Review, 64*(1), 106-112.

Rafferty, A.E., & Griffin, *M.A. (2004).* Dimensions of transformational leadership: Conceptual and empirical extensions. *The Leadership Quarterly, 15*(3), 329-354.

Ridpath, D., Yiamouyiannis, A., Lawrence, H., & Galles, K. (2008, December). Changing sides: The failure of the wrestling community's challenges to Title IX and new strategies for saving NCAA sport teams. *Journal of Intercollegiate Sport, 1*(2), 255-283.

Rittenberg, A. (2017, December 1). Every move of a Tennessee coaching search that is already infamous. *ESPN.* www.espn.com/college-football/story/_/id/21630892/line-tennessee-volunteers-bungled-coaching-search-butch-jones-john-currie-firing.

Roby, P. (2012). *Values-driven leadership in the 21st century.* Presentation given at the 2012 NCAA Convention, Indianapolis, IN.

Schein, E.H. (2010). *Organizational culture and leadership.* San Francisco: Jossey-Bass.

Simon, H.A. (1977). *The new science of managerial decision making.* Englewood Cliffs, NJ: Prentice Hall.

Smith, M. (2011, December 5). Help with high-stakes hires: Colleges turn to search firms to find coaching, AD candidates. *Sports Business Journal.* www.sportsbusinessjournal.com/Journal/Issues/2011/12/05/In-Depth/Lead.aspx.

Smits, G. (2016, June 13). Florida athletic director Jeremy Foley retiring after 25 years. *The Florida Times Union.* www.jacksonville.com/story/sports/college/uf-gators/2016/06/13/florida-athletic-director-jeremy-foley-retiring-after/15713567007/.

Splitt, F.G. (2011, March 8). "Academically adrift" in a sea of sports. *Chronicle of Higher Education.* http://chronicle.com/article/article-content/126643.

Staples, A. (2019, March 5). After his messy exit at Tennessee, John Currie gets a fresh start. *SI.* www.si.com/college/2019/03/05/john-currie-wake-forest-ad-tennessee-phillip-fulmer.

Sull, D. (2010, March). Are you ready to rebound? *Harvard Business Review,* 71-74.

Sull, D.N., & Spinosa, C. (2007). Promise-based management. *Harvard Business Review, 85,* 79-86.

Swann, W.B., Jr., Kwan, V.S.Y., Polzer, J.T., & Milton, L.P. (2003). Fostering group identification and creativity in diverse groups: The role of individuation and self-verification. *Personality and Social Psychology Bulletin, 29,* 1396-1406.

The Happy Manager. (2012). *Rational decision making model.* https://the-happy-manager.com/article/rational-decision-making-model/.

Tichy, N., & Charan, R. (1989, September-October). Speed, simplicity, and self-confidence. *Harvard Business Review,* 171-222.

Toppmeyer, B. (2021, January 18). Phillip Fulmer shows somber mood as he steps aside to let successor pick next Tennessee football coach. *Knoxville News Sentinel.* www.knoxnews.com/story/sports/college/university-of-tennessee/football/2021/01/18/phillip-fulmer-tennessee-football-jeremy-pruitt/3980292001/.

University Athletic Association. (2017, June 19). Dick Rasmussen: "Mr. UAA." https://uaasports.info/sports/general/30for30/rasmussen.

Van Rekom, J., Van Riel, C.B., & Wierenga, B. (2006). A methodology for assessing organizational core values. *Journal of Management Studies, 43*(2), 175-201.

Vedder, R. (2011, August 29). Intercollegiate sports: Have they no shame? *Chronicle of Higher Education.* http://chronicle.com/blogs/innovations/intercollegiate-sports-have-they-noshame/30217?sid=pm&utm_source=pm&utm_medium=en.

Vroom, V.H., & Yetton, P.W. (1973). *Leadership and Decision Making.* Pittsburgh, PA: University of Pittsburgh Press.

Ward, Jr., R.E., & Hux, R.K. (2011). Intercollegiate athletic purposes expressed in mission statements: A content analysis. *Journal for the Study of Sports and Athletes in Education, 5,* 177-200.

WBIR Staff. (2021, January 18). Fulmer to receive $37,500 per month through end of 2023 after retiring from Athletics Director position. *WBIR.* www.wbir.com/article/sports/college/vols/phillip-fulmer-to-retire-as-ut-athletics-director-after-three-years-on-the-job/51-07b62fcf-22ad-430a-b3d2-61e1f12c5394.

Weight, E.A. & Walker, M. (2012). Ensuring strategic sport marketing success. In B. Turner et al. *Sport marketing: Winning strategies for sport business success. Dubuque, IA:* Kendall Hunt.

Welch, J., & Welch, S. (2005). *Winning.* New York: HarperCollins.

West, J. (2021, January 27). Tennessee hires UCF's Josh Heupel as next head coach. *SI.* www.si.com/college/2021/01/27/josh-heupel-hired-tennessee-head-coach.

Woronoff, B. (2013, June 20). Embry-Riddle eyes move to NCAA Division II. *The Daytona Beach News-Journal.* www.news-journalonline.com/story/news/2013/06/20/embry-riddle-eyes-move-to-ncaa-division-ii/30626763007/.

Wykes, T. (2022, May 28). First Person: Time winding down for interim Dartmouth AD Peter Roby. *Valley News.* www.vnews.com/Peter-Roby-q-and-a-46534830.

Yiamouyiannis, A., & Lawrence, H.J. (2009, May 29). *Sport opportunities in intercollegiate athletics: Using ethical theory and structured models to assist in responsible decision making.* Presentation for the North American Society for Sport Management Conference, Columbia, SC.

Yukl, G. (1989). Managerial leadership: a review of theory and research. *Journal of Management, 15*(2), 251-289.

Chapter 4

Carroll, Lewis. *Alice's Adventures in Wonderland.* (1865). New York: Macmillan.

Collins, J.C., & Porras, J.I. (1994). *Built to last: Successful habits of visionary companies.* London: Random House.

Covey, S.R. (2004). *The 7 habits of highly effective people.* New York: Simon & Schuster.

Daniels, T. (2022, May 19). Jimbo Fisher says Nick Saban's comments on NIL, Texas A&M recruiting are "despicable." *Bleacher Report.* https://bleacherreport.com/articles/10036280-jimbo-fisher-says-nick-sabans-comments-on-nil-texas-am-recruiting-are-despicable.

Division I Compliance. (n.d.). Division I. *NCAA.* https://www.ncaa.org/sports/2021/5/11/division-i-compliance.aspx.

Division II Compliance. (n.d.). Division II. *NCAA.* https://www.ncaa.org/sports/2021/5/24/division-ii-compliance.aspx.

Division III Compliance. (n.d.). Division III. *NCAA.* https://www.ncaa.org/sports/2021/5/11/division-iii-compliance.aspx.

Drucker, P. (1967). *The effective executive.* New York: Harper & Row.

Durham, M. (2022, August 31). Division I Board of Directors modernizes infractions process. *NCAA.* www.ncaa.org/news/2022/8/31/media-center-division-i-board-of-directors-modernizes-infractions-process.aspx.

Feldman, B. (2007). *Meat market: Inside the smash-mouth world of college football recruiting.* New York: ESPN Books.

Fricke, J. (2022, December). NAAC Corner. *Athletics Administration.* https://digital.learfield.com/nacda-december-issue.html.

Hemminger, A., & Bensch, D. (2007). *Destination basketball: A once in a lifetime adventure to meet the best coaches in college hoops.* Oak Harbor, OH: Oak Town United.

Hosick, M.B. (2013, January 19). Division I streamlines rulebook. www.ncaa.org/about/resources/media-center/news/division-i-streamlines-rulebook.

Infante, J. (2011, July 10). Ohio State, Oregon, and West Virginia plotting the future of compliance. NCAA Bylaw Blog. https://www.athleticscholarships.net/bylaw-blog.htm.

Kotter, J.P. (1996). *Leading change.* Boston: Harvard Business School.

Ludlow, R. (2011, June 23). Trustees may change how Ohio State oversees athletics. *The Columbus Dispatch.* www.dispatch.com/content/stories/local/2011/06/23/ohio-state-trustees-athletics.html.

McGavic, M. (2021, February 24). Your guide to the Independent Accountability Resolution Process. *FanNation.* www.si.com/college/louisville/basketball/guide-to-the-iarp.

NCAA Division I Manual. (2022). *2022-2023 NCAA Division I manual.* Indianapolis, IN.

NCAA Rules Enforcement: For the Good of the Game (2014). The National Collegiate Athletics Association. www.ncaa.org/about/resources/media-center/ncaa-rules-enforcement-good-game.

NIL Interim Policy (2021). NIL interim policy. *NCAA.* https://ncaaorg.s3.amazonaws.com/ncaa/NIL/NIL_InterimPolicy.pdf.

Rhoden, W.C. (2009, April 11). University compliance officers: Good cop, bad cop. *New York Times*, p. D2.

Smith, R.A. (2021). *The myth of the amateur: A history of college athletic scholarships.* University of Texas Press.

Tait, M. (2022, August 31). NCAA votes to dissolve IARP path as part of infractions overhaul; IARP still expected to handle Kansas basketball case to completion. *KU Sports.* www2.kusports.com/news/2022/aug/31/ncaa-votes-dissolve-iarp-path-part-infractions-ove/.

Wallgren, J., of University of Akron. (2022). Interview by R. Zullo.

Witz, B. (2022, January 20). N.C.A.A. reorganizes around new constitution that shifts power to universities. *The New York Times.* www.nytimes.com/2022/01/20/sports/ncaafootball/ncaa-constitution-transgender-athletes.html.

Chapter 5

Adelson, A. (2020, November 12). Through the groundskeepers, Virginia football team aims for lasting change in Charlottesville. *ESPN.* https:// espn.com/college-football/story/_/id/30219536/through-groundskeepers-virginia-football-team-aims-lasting-change-charlottesville.

Agyemang, K., Singer, J.N., & DeLorme, J. (2010). An exploratory study of black male college athletes' perceptions of race and athlete activism. *International Review for the Sociology of Sport*, *45*(4), 419-435.

Annamma, S.A., Jackson, D.D., & Morrison, D. (2017). Conceptualizing color-evasiveness: Using dis/ability critical race theory to expand a color-blind racial ideology in education and society. *Race, Ethnicity and Education*, *20*(2), 147-162.

Ashe, A.R., Jr. (1988). *A hard road to glory: A history of the African-American athlete 1619-1918.* New York: Warner Books.

Au, W. (2016). Meritocracy 2.0: High-stakes, standardized testing as a racial project of neoliberal multiculturalism. *Educational Policy*, *30*(1), 39-62.

Beamon, K.K. (2008). "Used goods": Former African American [sic] college student-athletes' perception of exploitation by Division I universities. *The Journal of Negro Education*, 77(4), 352-364.

Bimper, A.Y. (2016). Capital matters: Social sustaining capital and the development of Black student-athletes. *Journal of Intercollegiate Sport*, 9, 106-128.

Bimper, A.Y. (2017). Mentorship of Black student-athletes at a predominately [sic] White American university: Critical race theory perspective on student-athlete development. *Sport, Education and Society*, 22(2), 175-193.

Bimper, A.Y., Harrison, L., & Clark, L. (2012). Diamonds in the rough: Examining a case of successful Black male student athletes in college sport. *Journal of Black Psychology*, 1-24.

Brabeck, M., & Brown, L. (1997). Feminist theory and psychological practice. In J. Worell & N. G. Johnson (Eds.), *Shaping the future of feminist psychology: Education, research, and Practice* (pp. 15-35). Washington, DC: American Psychological Association.

Branch, T. (2011). The shame of college sports. *The Atlantic.* www.theatlantic.com/magazine/archive/2011/10/the-shame-of-college-sports/308643/.

Brooks, D.A., & Althouse, R.C. (2007). *Diversity and social justice in college sports: Sport management and the student athlete.* Morgantown, WV: Fitness Information Technology.

Brown v. Board of Education of Topeka, Kansas 347 U.S. 483 (1954).

Bruening, J.E., Armstrong, K.L., & Pastore, D.L. (2005). Listening to the voices: The experiences of African American female student athletes. *Research Quarterly for Exercise and Sport*, *76*(1), 82-100.

Buford, K. (2010). *Native American son: The life and sporting legend of Jim Thorpe.* New York: Knopf.

Carter-Francique, A.R. (2017). Is excellence inclusive? The benefits of fostering Black female college athletes' sense of belonging. *Journal of Higher Education Athletics & Innovation*, *1*(3), 48-73.

Carter-Francique, A.R., Dortch, D., & Carter-Phiri, K. (2017). Black female college athletes' perception of power in sport and society. *Journal for the Study of Sports and Athletes in Education*, *11*(1), 18-45.

Carter-Francique, A., Hart, A., & Steward, A. (2013). Black college athletes' perceptions of academic success and the role of social support. *Journal of Intercollegiate Sport*, *6*(2), 231-246.

Cheeks, G., & Carter-Francique, A.R. (2015). HBCUs versus HWCUs: A critical examination of institutional distancing between collegiate athletic programs. *Race, Gender & Class*, *22*(1-2), 23-35.

Chen, C., & Mason, D.S. (2019). Making settler colonialism visible in sport management. *Journal of Sport Management*, *33*, 379-392.

Clotfelter, C.T. (2019). *Big-time sports in American universities*. New York: Cambridge University Press.

Comeaux, E. (2010). Mentoring as an intervention strategy: Toward a (re)negotiation of first year student-athlete role identities. *Journal for the Study of Sports and Athletes in Education, 4*, 257-276.

Comeaux, E. (2018). Stereotypes, control, hyper-surveillance, and disposability of NCAA Division I Black male athletes. *New Directions for Student Services, 2018*(163), 33-42.

Cooper, J.N. (2019). *From exploitation back to empowerment: Black male holistic (under)development through sport and (mis)education*. New York: Peter Lang.

Cooper, J.N. (2022). Race matters in sports. In E. Staurowsky & A. Hart (Eds.), Diversity, Equity, and Inclusion in Sport (pp. 55-76). Champaign, IL: Human Kinetics.

Cooper, J.N., Cavil, J.K., & Cheeks, G. (2014). The state of intercollegiate athletics at historically Black colleges and universities (HBCUs): Past, present, and persistence. *Journal of Issues in Intercollegiate Athletics, 7*, 307-332.

Cooper, J.N., Corral, M.D., Macaulay, C.D.T., Cooper, M.S., Nwadike, A., & Mallery, M., Jr. (2019). Collective uplift: The impact of a holistic development support program on Black male former college athletes' experiences and outcomes. *International Journal of Qualitative Studies, 32*(1), 21-46.

Cooper, J.N., & Hawkins, B. (2014). The transfer effect: A critical race theory examination of Black male transfer student athletes' experiences. *Journal of Intercollegiate Sport, 7*(1), 80-104.

Cooper, J.N., Newton, A.C.I., Klein, M., & Jolly, S. (2020). A call for culturally responsive transformational leadership in college sport: An anti-ism approach for achieving equity and inclusion. *Frontiers in Sociology, 5*(65), 1-17.

Cooper, J.N., Nwadike, A., & Macaulay, C. (2017). A critical race theory analysis of big-time college sports: Implications for culturally responsive and race-conscious sport leadership. *Journal of Issues in Intercollegiate Athletics, 10*, 204-233.

Cunningham, G.B. (2007). Opening the black box: The influence of perceived diversity and a common in-group identity in diverse groups. *Journal of Sport Management, 21*(1), 58-78.

Davis, T. (2008). Race and sports in America: An historical overview. *Virginia Sports & Entertainment Law Journal, 7*, 291-311.

DeCuir, J.T., & A.D. Dixson. (2004). "So when it comes out, they aren't that surprised that it is there": Using critical race theory as a tool of analysis of race and racism in education. *Educational Researcher 33*, 26-31.

DeJulio, M., Grant, C., Judge, J., Morrison, K., O'Brien, T., & Sweet, J. (2008). Teaching Title IX PowerPoint presentation. *The NCAA Title IX Resource Center.* www.ncaa.org/gender_equity.

Dent, G. (2020). New designees set to champion diversity and inclusion. *NCAA*. https://www.ncaa.org/news/2020/8/10/new-designees-set-to-champion-diversity-and-inclusion.aspx.

Donnor, J.K. (2005). Towards an interest-convergence in the education of African-American football student-athletes in major college sports. *Race, Ethnicity and Education, 8*(1), 48.

Dumas, M.J., & Ross, K.M. (2016). "Be real black for me": Imagining BlackCrit in education. *Urban Education, 51*(4), 415-442.

Fay, T., & Wolff, E. (2009). Disability sport in the twenty-first century: Creating a new sport opportunity spectrum. *Boston University International Law Journal, 27*, 231-248.

Flowers, C.L. (2015). Legal issues and the Black female athlete's collegiate experiences at HBCUs. In B. Hawkins, J.N. Cooper, A.R. Carter-Francique, & J.K. Cavil (Eds.), *The athletic experience at Historically Black Colleges and Universities: Past, present, and persistence* (pp. 129-144). Lanham, MD: Rowman & Littlefield.

Franks, J.S. (2016). Asian Americans and Sport. In L.J. Borish, D.K. Wiggins, G.R. Gems (Eds.), *The Routledge history of American sport* (pp. 205-216). New York: Routledge.

Frey, W.H. (2018, March 14). The US will become "minority white" in 2045, Census projects. *Brookings Institution*. www.brookings.edu/blog/the-avenue/2018/03/14/the-us-will-become-minority-white-in-2045-census-projects/.

Garrison, M.J. (2009). *A measure of failure: The political origins of standardized testing*. Albany, NY: SUNY Press.

Gayles, J.G., Crandall, R., & Morin, S. (2018). Student-athletes' sense of belonging: Background characteristics, student involvement, and campus climate. *International Journal of Sport & Society: Annual Review, 9*(1), 23-38.

Harper, S.R. (2018). *Black male student-athletes and racial inequities in NCAA Division I college sports*. Los Angeles: USC Race and Equity Center.

Harrison, C.K., Ochoa, V., & Hernandez, M.S. (2013). From turf to the top: Access to higher education by Latino male college football players. In D. Brooks & R. Althouse (Eds.), *Racism in college athletics* (pp. 365-378). Morgantown, WV: Fitness Information Technology.

Hawkins, B. (2010). *The new plantation: Black athletes, college sports, and predominantly White NCAA institutions*. New York: Palgrave Macmillan.

Hawkins, B., Baker, A.R., & Brackebusch, V.B. (2015). Intercollegiate athletics and amateurism. In E. Comeaux (Ed.), *Introduction to Intercollegiate Athletics*, pp. 312-325. Baltimore, MD: Johns Hopkins University Press.

Hill, E., Tiefenthäler, A., Triebert, C., Jordan, D., Willis, H., & Stein, R. (2020, May 31). 8 minutes and 46 seconds: How George Floyd was killed in police custody. *The New York Times*. https://nytimes.com/ 2020/05/31/us/george-floyd-investigation.html.

Hodge, S., Burden, J., Robinson, L., & Bennett, R. (2008). Theorizing on the stereotyping of Black male student-athletes: Issues and implications. *Journal for the Study of Sports and Athletes in Education, 2*(2), 203-226.

Hughes, C. (2014). *American Black women and interpersonal leadership styles*. Rotterdam: Sense.

Jolly, S., Cooper, J.N., & Chepyator-Thomson, J.R. (2020). An examination of culturally responsive programming for Black student-athletes' holistic development at Division I historically White institutions (HWIs). *Journal of Issues in Intercollegiate Athletics, Fall Special Issue*, 73-90.

Kane, M.J., LaVoi, N.M., & Fink, J.S. (2013). Exploring elite female athletes' interpretations of sport media images: A window into the construction of social identity and "selling sex" in women's sports. *Communication & Sport, 1*(3), 269-298.

KCIA. (2021). Achieving racial equity in college sports. *Knight Commission on Intercollegiate Athletics.* www.knightcommission.org/wp-content/uploads/2021/05/KCIA-Racial-Equity-Report_5.12.21.pdf.

Keaton, A.C.I. (2021). The emergence of athletic diversity and inclusion officer positions in Division I collegiate athletics. *Journal of Higher Education Athletics & Innovation, 1*(8), 82-112.

King, C.R. (2015). *Native Americans in sports.* New York, NY: Routledge.

Lussier, R., & Kimball, D. (2013). *Applied Sport Management Skills (With Web Study Guide).* Champaign, IL: Human Kinetics.

Mattheessen, C. (2016). A brief overview of the Association for Intercollegiate Athletics for Women. 147-151. www.eiu.edu/historia/Clara%20Mattheessen%20historia%202016.pdf.

McAfee, N. (2018). Feminist philosophy. *Stanford Encyclopedia of Philosophy.* https://plato.stanford.edu/entries/feminist-philosophy/.

McDowell, J., & Carter-Francique, A. (2017). An intersectional analysis of the workplace experiences of African American female athletic directors. *Sex Roles, 77*, 393-408.

Naples, N. A. (2013). *Feminism and method: Ethnography, discourse analysis, and activist research.* New York: Routledge.

National Collegiate Athletic Association v. Alston 958 F. 3d 1239 (9th Cir. 2021). California Senate Bill 206.

NCAA (2021a). Inclusion. www.ncaa.org/inclusion.

NCAA (2021b). NCAA student-athlete activism and racial justice engagement study. *NCAA Research. Survey Results.* www.ncaa.org/ncaa-student-athlete-activism-and-racial-justice-engagement-study.

National Collegiate Athletics Association (2023). Transgender Student-Athlete Participation Policy. https://ncaa.org/sports/2022/1/27/transgender-participation-policy.aspx.

NCAA Student Athletes and NIL Rights: Hearings before the U.S. Senate Committee on Commerce, Science, and Transportation. 117th Congress. (2021).

Newton, A.C.I. (2020). Race, sports, and education: Improving opportunities and outcomes for black male college athletes. *Journal of Sport Management, 34*(5), 504-505.

Nocera, J., & Strauss, B. (2016). *Indentured: The inside story of the rebellion against the NCAA.* New York: Portfolio.

O'Bannon v. National Collegiate Athletic Association, 802 F.3d 1049 (9th Cir. 2015).

Office for Civil Rights. (1996). Clarification of intercollegiate athletics policy guidance: The three part test. Washington, DC: U.S. Department of Education.

Office of Civil Rights (2020). *The Final Rule.* www2.ed.gov/about/offices/list/ocr/docs/titleix-overview.pdf.

Oseguera, L., & Goldstein, A. (2015). Theoretical tenets of higher education and college athletes. In E. Comeaux (Ed.), *Introduction to intercollegiate athletics*, (pp. 61-80). Baltimore, MD: Johns Hopkins University Press.

Patton, L.D., Renn, K.A., Guido, F.M., & Quaye, S.J. (2016). *Student development in college: Theory, research, and practice.* San Francisco: Jossey-Bass.

Pickett, M.W., Dawkin, M.P., & Braddock, J.H., II. (2019). Challenges to Title IX: A critical race perspective. *Negro Educational Review, 70* (1-4), 78-99.

Price, T., Dunlap, R., & Eller, J. (2017). An exploration of Black women's intersectionality in athletic administration. *Journal of Issues in Intercollegiate Athletics, 10*, 57-77.

Rietmann, T. (2017, October 18). Franklin recognized for championing diversity. *National Collegiate Athletic Association.* www.ncaa.org/about/resources/media-center/news/franklin-recognized-championing-diversity.

Roessner, A., & Whiteside, E. (2016). Unmasking Title IX on its 40th birthday: The operation of women's voices, women's spaces, and sporting myth narratives in the commemorative coverage of Title IX. *Journalism, 17*(5), 583-599.

Sage, G. (2007). Introduction. In D.D. Brooks & R.C. Althouse (Eds.), *Diversity and Social Justice in College Sports: Sport Management and the Student Athlete* (pp. 1-20). Morgantown, WV: Fitness Information Technology.

Singer, J.N. (2005). Understanding racism through the eyes of African-American male student athletes. *Race, Ethnicity and Education, 8*(4), 365-386.

Singer, J.N. (2019). *Race, sports, and education: Improving opportunities and outcomes for Black male college athletes.* Cambridge, MA: Harvard Educational Press.

Smith, E. (2009). *Race, sport and the American dream* (2nd ed.). Durham, NC: Carolina Academic Press.

Spencer, H. (2018). *Summer of hate: Charlottesville, USA.* Charlottesville, VA: The University of Virginia Press.

SPLC (2005). NCAA rules against "Indian" mascots. *Southern Poverty Law Center.* www.splcenter.org/news/2005/08/11/ncaa-rules-against-indian-mascots.

Staurowsky, E. (2007). "You know, we are all Indian": Exploring White power and privilege in reactions to the NCAA Native American mascot policy. *Journal of Sport & Social Issues, 31*(1), 61-76.

Staurowsky, E.J., & Weight, E.A. (2011). IX Literacy: What Coaches Don't Know and Need to Find Out. *Journal of Intercollegiate Sport, 4*(2), 190-209.

Staurowsky, E., & Weight, E.A. (2013). Discovering dysfunction in Title IX implementation: NCAA administrator literacy, responsibility, and fear. *Journal of Applied Sport Management, 5*(1), 9.

Thelin, J. (1996). *Games colleges play: Scandal and reform in intercollegiate athletics.* Baltimore, MD: Johns Hopkins University Press.

Tiell, B., & Dixon, M. (2008). Roles and tasks of the senior woman administrator (SWA) in intercollegiate athletics: A role congruity perspective. *Journal for the Study of Sports and Athletes in Education, 2*(3), 339-361.

Title IX of the Education Amendments of 1972, 20 U.S.C. §§ 1681-1688.

Toffoletti, K., & Thorpe, H. (2018). Female athletes' self-representation on social media: A feminist analysis of neoliberal marketing strategies in "economies of visibility." *Feminism and Psychology, 28*(1), 11-31.

U.S. Department of Education. (n.d.). Title IX regulations. 34 C.F.R. § 106.41.

Van Rheenen, D. (2011). Exploitation in the American academy: College athletes and self-perceptions of value. *The International Journal of Sport & Society*, 2(4), 11-26.

Weight, E.A., & Staurowsky, E.J. (2014). Title IX literacy among NCAA administrators and coaches: A critical communications approach. *The International Journal of Sport Management.* 15(3) 1-29.

Weight, E.A., Lewis, M., & Harry, M. (2020a). Self-efficacy belief and the influential coach: An examination of collegiate athletes. *Journal of Athlete Development and Experience*, 2(3), 198-216.

Weight, E.A., Taylor, E., Huml, M.R., & Dixon, M.A. (2020b). Working in the sport industry: A classification of human capital archetypes. *Journal of Sport Management.* https://doi.org/10.1123/jsm.2020-0070.

Westerhaus, C. (2007). Prologue. In D.D. Brooks & R.C. Althouse (Eds.), *Diversity and social justice in college sports: Sport management and the student athlete* (pp. xi-xiii). Morgantown, WV: Fitness Information Technology.

Wetzel, D. (2022, December 8). *Can a woman coach men to be champions?* Yahoo Sports. https://sports.yahoo.com/can-a-woman-coach-men-to-be-champions-u-chicagos-julianne-sitch-proved-it-can-be-done-205421962.html.

White, J. (2020, July 13). Q&A: Carla Williams gives an update on UVA athletics. *UVA Today*. https://news.virginia.edu/content/qa-carla-williams-gives-update-uva-athletics.

Wilson, A. (2017). Optimization of the senior woman administrator designation. Retrieved from https://ncaaorg.s3.amazonaws.com/inclusion/swa/SWA_InclusionsSWAReport.pdf.

Wininger, S.R., & White, T.A. (2015). An examination of the dumb jock stereotype in collegiate

student-athletes: A comparison of student versus student-athlete perceptions. *Journal for the* Study of Sports and Athletes in Education, 9(2), 75-85.

Yosso, T.J. (2005). Whose culture has capital? A critical race theory discussion of community cultural wealth. *Race, Ethnicity and Education*, 8(1), 69-91.

Chapter 6

Avolio, B.J., Wernsing, T., & Gardner, W.L. (2018). Revisiting the development and validation of the authentic leadership questionnaire: Analytical clarifications. *Journal of Management*, 44(2), 399-411.

Branch, T. (2011). The shame of college sports. *The Atlantic.* www.theatlantic.com/magazine/archive/2011/10/the-shame-of-college-sports/8643/.

Cal Cameron Institute. (2020). Cameron Institute pillars. https://calbears.com/sports/2020/8/18/cameron-institute-pillars.aspx.

Covey, S.R. (1989). *The 7 habits of highly effective people.* New York: Simon & Schuster.

Covey, S.R. (2004). *The 7 habits of highly effective people.* New York: Simon & Schuster.

Daves, J. (2021, June). Preparing amazing citizens. *Cavalier Corner, 26*(3), 12-13. https://virginiasportsmp.com/assets/pdf/Preparing-Amazing-Citizens.pdf.

Emmons, B., & O'Hallarn, B. (2019). The public relations pseudo-event as cultural legitimacy: A study of National Signing Day. *Sport in Society, 24*(4), 629-645. https://doi.org/10.1080/17430437.2019.1703685

Goleman, D. (1995). *Emotional intelligence: Why it can matter more than IQ.* New York: Bantam Books.

Grasgreen, A. (2012, May 9). Tough choices for athletes' advisers. *Inside Higher Ed.* www.insidehighered.com/news/2012/05/09/ncaa-academic-rules-frustrate-advisers-athletes.

Gurney, G., & Southall, R.M. (2013, Feb 14). NCAA reform gone wrong. *Inside Higher Ed.* www.insidehighered.com/views/2013/02/14/ncaa-academic-reform-has-hurt-higher-eds-integrity-essay.

Gurney, G.S., Rubin, L.M., Stokowski, S.E., & Ridpath, B.D. (2020). The original sin of college sports: College presidents' ineffectual use of special admissions. *Journal of NCAA Compliance, 2020*(3), 3-4, 12-19.

Hosick, M.B. (2011, Feb 2). History of the National Letter of Intent. *NCAA.com.* www.ncaa.com/news/ncaa/2011-02-02/history-national-letter-intent.

Huma, R., & Staurowsky, E.J. (2011, September). *The Price of Poverty in Big Time College Sport.* Riverside, CA: National College Players Association.

LaForge, L., & Hodge, J. (2011). NCAA academic performance metrics: Implications for institutional policy and practice. *The Journal of Higher Education, 82*(2), 217-235.

Lemons, R.S. (2017). Amateurism and the NCAA cartel. In E. Comeaux (Ed.), *College athletes' rights and well-being: Critical perspectives on policy and practice* (pp. 32-42). Baltimore: Johns Hopkins University Press.

Lopiano, D. (2008) Key elements and best practices in the development of academic support programs. *Sports Management Resources.* www.sportsmanagementresources.com/library/key-elements-academic-support-programs.

National Collegiate Athletic Association (2002). NCAA Division I graduation success rate dashboard. https:// ncaa.org/sports/2017/12/12/division-i-graduation-rates-database.aspx.

National Collegiate Athletic Association (2008). CHAMPS/Life Skills Program [Brochure]. Indianapolis, IN.

National Collegiate Athletic Association. (2021). *Division I manual.* NCAA.

National Collegiate Athletic Association. (2021, December 6). *NCAA Constitution* [Draft]. NCAA.

NCAA National Letter of Intent. (2021). NCAA National Letter of Intent. Nationalletter.org

Navarro, K.M., Rubin, L.M., & Mamerow, G.P. (2020). *Implementing student-athlete programming: A guide for supporting college athletes.* New York: Routledge.

Newman, J. (2014, December 18). At top athletic programs, students often major in eligibility. *Chronicle of Higher Education.* www.chronicle.com/article/at-top-athletics-programs-students-often-major-in-eligibility/.

Parham, W.D. (1993). The intercollegiate athlete: A 1990s profile. *Counseling Psychologist, 21*(3), 411-429.

Rubin, L.M. (2017). Who are athletic advisors? State of the profession. *NACADA Journal, 37*(1), 37-50.

Rubin, L.M., & Lewis. W.A. (2020). Collaboration between campus and athletic advisors: Ensuring college athletes' success. *Journal of Issues in Intercollegiate Athletics, Special Issue*, 91-124.

Rubin, L.M., & Moreno-Pardo, M.D. (2018). Burnout among student-athlete services professionals. *Journal of Higher Education Athletics and Innovation, 1*(3), 1-25. http://doi.org/10.15763/issn.2376-5267.2018.1.3.1-25.

Rubin, L.M., & Moses, R.A. (2017). Athletic subculture within student-athlete academic centers. *Sociology of Sport Journal, 34*(4), 317-328.

Rubin, L.M., & Rosser, V.J. (2014). Comparing Division IA scholarship and non-scholarship student-athletes: A discriminant analysis. *Journal of Issues in Intercollegiate Athletics, 7*, 43-64.

Sack, A.L., & Staurowsky, E.J. (1998). *College athletes for hire: The evolution and legacy of the NCAA's amateur myth.* Westport, CT: Praeger.

Spotteredu.com. (2022). SpotterEDU. https://spotteredu.com/

Staurowsky, E.J. (2017). The National Letter of Intent: A symbol of the need for an independent college athlete players association. In E. Comeaux (Ed.), *College athletes' rights and well-being: Critical perspectives on policy and practice* (pp. 23-31). Baltimore: Johns Hopkins University Press.

Steinberg, M.A., Walther, C., Herbst, M., West, J., Zamagias, D., & Smith, J. (2018). Learning specialists in college athletics: who are they and what do they do? *Journal of Higher Education Athletics & Innovation, 1*(4), 77-118.

Stokowski, S.E., Rubin, L.M., Rode, C.R., Fridley, A., & Shkorupeieva, S. (2020). Separate kingdoms: Academic advisers' perceptions of college athletes and athletic departments. *The Mentor: Innovative Scholarship on Academic Advising, 22*, 16-32. https://doi.org/10.26209/mj2261353.

Thaler, L.K., & Koval, R. (2001). *The power of nice: How to conquer the business world with kindness.* New York: Random House.

University of Illinois Office of the Chancellor. (2021, October 20). *Committee on the admission of student athletes.* https://uofi.app.box.com/s/8et874927zdlfwmmuwf3iueuispdgq5x/file/881579601003.

University of Washington (2009, February 19). Report to the Advisory Committee on Intercollegiate Athletics: Survey of SAAS reporting structures. www.washington.edu/faculty/facsen/acia/saas_reporting_structure.pdf.

Chapter 7

Andrews, P. (2005). *Sports journalism: A practical introduction.* Thousand Oaks, CA: Sage.

Associated Press. (2007, April 18). Hogs' Nutt addresses text scandal. *Lubbock Avalanche-Journal.* http://lubbockonline.com/stories/041807/col_041807011.shtml.

Associated Press. (2021, July 20). "Don't call me Deion": Jackson State coach drops reporter at SWAC Media Day. *WVTM13.* www.wvtm13.com/article/dont-call-me-deion-jackson-state-coach-drops-reporter-at-swac-media-day/37084072.

Atkinson, S. (2020, September). CoSIDA Corner. *Athletics Administration,* 54. https://s3.amazonaws.com/nacda.com/documents/2020/9/1/Page_54.pdf.

Ballouli, K., & Hutchinson, M. (2010). Digital branding and social-media strategies for professional athletes, sports teams, and leagues: An interview with Digital Royalty's Amy Martin. *International Journal of Sport Communication, 3,* 395-401.

Barrow, L., senior associate sports communication director, University of Georgia. (2022). Interview by R. Zullo.

Battenfield, F.L., & Kent, A. (2007). The culture of communication among intercollegiate sport information professionals. *International Journal of Sport Management and Marketing, 2*(3), 236-251.

Berman, S. (2022, March 19). Erica Sullivan says that there was no podium protest after 500 freestyle at NCAA's. *Swim Swam.* https://swimswam.com/erica-sullivan-says-there-was-no-podium-protest-after-500-freestyle-at-ncaas/.

Bratton, T., assistant softball coach, Mississippi State University. (2022). Interview by R. Zullo.

Braun, A., director of athletics, University of Wisconsin-Milwaukee. (2022). Interview by R. Zullo.

Brougham, J.K. (2021). The impact of social media on the mental health of student-athletes across NCAA divisions. *Journal of Issues in Intercollegiate Athletics,* 14, 717-739. http://csri-jiia.org/wp-content/uploads/2021/12/RA_2021_34.pdf.

Bruno, R., & Whitlock, K. (2000). Nothin' but net. In M. Helitzer (Ed.), *The dream job: $port$ publicity, promotion and marketing* (3rd ed., pp. 429-441). Athens, OH: University Sports Press.

Butler, B., & Sagas, M. (2008). Making room in the lineup: Newspaper web sites face growing competition for sports fans' attention. *International Journal of Sport Communication, 1,* 17-25.

Cialdini, R.B. (2006). *Influence: The psychology of persuasion.* New York: HarperBusiness.

Clavio, G. (2008). Demographics and usage profiles of users of college sport message boards. *International Journal of Sport Communication, 1,* 434-443.

Connaughton, D., Spengler, J.O., & Bennett, G. (2001). Crisis management for physical-activity programs. *Journal of Physical Education, Recreation & Dance, 72*(7), 27-29.

Cooper, C.G. (2008). NCAA website coverage: An analysis of similar sport team gender coverage on athletic department home web pages. *Journal of Intercollegiate Sport, 1*, 227-241.

Cooper, C.G., & Cooper, B.D. (2009). NCAA website coverage: Do athletic departments provide equitable gender coverage on their athletic home web pages? *The Sport Journal, 12*(2). http://thesportjournal.org/article/ncaa-website-coverage-do-athletic-departments-provide-equitable-gender-coverage-on-their-athletic-home-web-pages/.

Cooper, C.G., Eagleman, A., & Laucella, P.M. (2009). NCAA March Madness: An investigation of gender coverage in *USA Today* during the NCAA basketball tournament. *Journal of Intercollegiate Sport, 2*, 299-311.

Cooper, C.G., & Pierce, D. (2011). The role of divisional affiliation in athletic department web site coverage. *International Journal of Sport Communication, 4*, 70-81.

Covey, S.R. (2004). *The 7 habits of highly effective people.* New York, NY: Simon & Schuster.

Cunningham, G.B., Sagas, M., Sartore, M.L., Amsden, M.L., & Schellhase, A. (2004). Gender representation in the NCAA news: Is the glass half full or half empty? *Sex Roles, 50*, 861-870.

Cutlip, S.M., Center, A.H., & Broom, G.M. (2000). *Effective public relations* (8th ed.). Englewood Cliffs, NJ: Prentice Hall.

Earnheardt, A.C. (2010). Exploring sports television viewers' judgments of athletes' antisocial behaviors. *International Journal of Sport Communication, 3*, 167-189.

ESPN. (2021, July 20). Jackson State Tigers coach Deion Sanders takes issue with reporter after being referred to by his first name twice. *ESPN*. www.espn.com/college-football/story/_/id/31851065/jackson-state-tigers-coach-deion-sanders-takes-issue-reporter-being-referred-first-name-twice.

ESPN News Services. (2022, March 12). Malique Jacobs to miss first half of MAC title game as four Kent State players disciplined for anti-Akron Snapchat video. *ESPN*. www.espn.com/mens-college-basketball/story/_/id/33485842/malique-jacobs-miss-first-half-mac-title-game-four-kent-state-players-disciplined-anti-akron-snapchat-video.

Fisher, E. (2011, September 19). Miami story reset bar for investigative work online, Fuchs says. *Sports Business Journal*. www.sportsbusinessjournal.com/Journal/Issues/2011/09/19/Media/Fuchs.aspx.

Fisher, R. & Ury, W. (2011). *Getting to yes: Negotiating agreement without giving in.* New York, NY: Penguin.

Fombrun, C., Gardberg, N., & Sever, J. (2000). The reputation quotient: A multi-stakeholder measure of corporate reputation. *Journal of Brand Management, 7*(4), 241-255.

Gale, D., president, LEONA. (2022). Interview by R. Zullo.

Gregory, S. (2009, June 5). Twitter craze is rapidly changing the face of sports. *Sports Illustrated*. http://sportsillustrated.cnn.com/2009/writers/the_bonus/06/05/twitter.sports/index.html?eref=sihpT1.

Harrison, C.K., Lawrence, S.M., Plecha, M., Bukstein, S.J., & Janson, N.K. (2009). Stereotypes and stigmas in college athletes in Tank McNamara's cartoon script: Fact or fiction. *Journal of Issues in Intercollegiate Athletics* [Special issue], 1-18.

Helitzer, M. (2000). *The dream job: $port$ publicity, promotion and marketing* (3rd ed.). Athens, OH: University Sports Press.

Howard, C.M., & Mathews, W.K. (2000). *On deadline: Managing media relations.* Long Grove, IL: Waveland Press.

Hyland, A. (2010, May 26). Biggest, longest-lasting impact of ticket scandal at Kansas University may have very little to do with tickets. *Lawrence Journal-World*. www2.kusports.com/news/2010/may/26/biggest-longest-lasting-impact-ticket-scandal-kans/.

Jackowski, M. (2007). Conceptualizing an improved public relations strategy: A case for stakeholder relationship marketing in Division I-A intercollegiate athletics. *Journal of Business and Public Affairs, 1*(1). www.scientificjournals.org/journals2007/articles/1016.htm.

Johnston, B., senior associate athletics director for communication and creative services, Georgia Southern University. (2022). Interview by R. Zullo.

Kowal, B. (2022, May) CoSIDA Corner. *Athletics Administration*, 70. https://s3.amazonaws.com/nacda.com/documents/2022/5/31/Page_70.pdf.

LaRiccia, N., assistant athletic director for media relations, Westminster College. (2022). Interview by R. Zullo.

Lovings, M., associate head coach for football, Arkansas State University. (2022). Interview by R. Zullo.

Masteralexis, L.P., Barr, C.A., & Hums, M. (2008). *Principles and practice of sport management* (3rd ed.). Burlington, MA: Jones & Bartlett.

Mathews, W. (2004, May-June). What should I tell them? Why every organization should have an official policy for communicating. *Communication World, 21*(3), 46-60.

McCollum, D. (2009, July 25). New UC president taking front-porch philosophy with athletics. *Log Cabin Democrat*. http://thecabin.net/news/local/2009-07-25/new-uca-president-taking-front-porch-philosophy-athletics#.UxnzUV5-Ufo.

McMullin, K., director of athletics, Christopher Newport University. (2022). Interview by R. Zullo.

Menaker, B.E., & Connaughton, D.P. (2010). Stadium alcohol policies: A comparison of policies available on college athletic department web sites. *International Journal of Sport Communication, 3*, 151-162.

Miller, R., Parsons, K., & Lifer, D. (2010). Students and social networking sites: The posting paradox. *Behaviour & Information Technology, 29*, 377-382.

Montoro, M., assistant athletics director for football communications, West Virginia University. (2022). Interview by R. Zullo.

Mullin, B.J., Hardy, S., & Sutton, W.A. (2007). *Sport marketing* (3rd ed.). Champaign, IL: Human Kinetics.

Pegoraro, A. (2010). Look who's talking—Athletes on Twitter: A case study. *International Journal of Sport Communication, 3,* 501-514.

Phua, J.J. (2010). Sports fans and media use: Influence on sports fan identification and collective self-esteem. *International Journal of Sport Communication, 3,* 190-206.

Poole, J. (2018, March). CoSIDA Corner. *Athletics Administration,* 55. https://s3.amazonaws.com/nacda.com/documents/2018/3/2/_nacda_cefma_2017_18_misc_non_event__CEFMACornerMarch18.pdf.

Poole, J. (2020, February). CoSIDA Corner. *Athletics Administration,* 54. https://s3.amazonaws.com/nacda.com/documents/2020/2/28/Page_54.pdf.

Public Relations Society of America. (2000). Tips and techniques: Crisis planning and management. *PPC Online.* www.prsa.org/ppc/68001.html.

Reichart-Smith, L. (2011). The less you say: An initial study of gender coverage in sports on Twitter. In A. Billings (Ed.), *Sports media: Transformation, integration, consumption* (pp. 146-161). New York: Routledge.

Ries, A., & Ries, L. (2002). *The fall of advertising and the rise of PR.* New York: HarperCollins.

Ruihley, B.J., & Fall, L.T. (2009). Assessment on and off the field: Examining athletic directors' perceptions of public relations in college athletics. *International Journal of Sport Communication, 2,* 398-410.

Salas, D., assistant athletics director of digital and Internet services, Virginia Tech University. (2022). Interview by R. Zullo.

Sanderson, J. (2009). Professional athletes' shrinking privacy boundaries: Fans, information and communication technologies, and athlete monitoring. *International Journal of Sport Communication, 2,* 240-256.

Sanderson, J. (2011). To tweet or not to tweet: Exploring Division I athletic departments' social-media policies. *International Journal of Sport Communication, 4,* 492-513.

Schmidt, T., sports information specialist, Jacksonville State University. (2022). Interview by R. Zullo.

Schultz, B. (2005). *Sports media: Reporting, producing and planning* (2nd ed.). Brentwood, TN: Focus Press.

Schultz, B., & Sheffer, M.L. (2010). An exploratory study of how Twitter is affecting sports journalism. *International Journal of Sport Communication, 3,* 226-239.

Seitel, F. (2010). *The practice of public relations* (11th ed.). Upper Saddle River, NJ: Prentice Hall.

Smatresk, N. (2011, November 11). A successful sports program benefits both the university and our community. *Las Vegas Sun.* www.lasvegassun.com/news/2011/nov/11/successful-sports-program-benefits-both-university/.

Smith, R.D. (2002). *Strategic planning for public relations.* Mahwah, NJ: Erlbaum.

Staples, A. (2011, March 21). Harrellson emerged from doghouse to become UK's steadiest player. *Sports Illustrated.* http://sportsillustrated.cnn.com/2011/writers/andy_staples/03/19/Kentucky.west.virginia.harrellson.

Stoldt, G. (2000). Current and ideal roles of NCAA Division I-A sports information professionals. *Cyber-Journal of Sport Marketing, 4*(1). http://fulltext.ausport.gov.au/fulltext/2000/cjsm/v4n1/stoldt41.htm.

Stoldt, G.C. (2008). Interview with John Humenik, executive director of the College Sports Information Directors of America. *International Journal of Sport Communication, 9,* 458-464.

Stoldt, G.C., Dittmore, S., & Branvold, S. (2006). *Sport public relations: Managing organizational communication.* Champaign, IL: Human Kinetics.

Stoldt, G.C., Miller, L.K., Ayres, T., & Comfort, P.G. (2000). Crisis management planning: A necessity for sport managers. *International Journal of Sport Management, 1*(4), 253-266.

Stoldt, G.C., Miller, L.K., & Comfort, P.G. (2001). Through the eyes of athletic directors: Perceptions of sports information directors and other PR issues. *Sports Marketing Quarterly, 10*(3), 164-172.

Stoldt, G.C., & Narasimhan, V. (2005). Self-assessments of collegiate sports information professionals regarding their public relations task expertise. *International Journal of Sport Management, 6*(3), 252-269.

Syme, C. (2012, February). Using social media in a crisis: higher education results. https://collegesportscommunicators.com/media/documents/2012/8/caseckssymehighered2012usingsocialmediainacrisis.pdf.

Thompson, J., head coach for men's tennis, Virginia Tech. (2022). Interview by R. Zullo.

Thompson, W. (1996). *Targeting the message: A receiver-centered process for public relations writing.* White Plains, NY: Longman.

Vance, D. (2019, December). CoSIDA Corner. *Athletics Administration,* 53. https://s3.amazonaws.com/nacda.com/documents/2019/12/4/Page_53.pdf.

Vincent, H. (2019, September). CoSIDA Corner. *Athletics Administration,* 56. https://s3.amazonaws.com/nacda.com/documents/2019/9/3/Page_56.pdf.

Wallace, L., Wilson, J., & Miloch, K. (2011). Sporting Facebook: A content analysis of NCAA organizational sport pages and Big 12 Conference athletic department pages. *International Journal of Sport Communication, 4,* 422-444.

Wigley, S., & Meirick, P.C. (2008). Interactive media and sports journalists: The impact of interactive media on sports journalists. *Journal of Sports Media, 3*(1), 1-25.

Williams, J., & Chinn, S.J. (2010). Meeting relationship-marketing goals through social media: A conceptual model for sport marketers. *International Journal of Sport Communication, 3,* 422-437.

Yanity, M., & Edmondson, A.C. (2011). Ethics of online coverage of recruiting high school athletes. *International Journal of Sport Communication, 4,* 403-421.

Chapter 8

Allstate. (2021). Allstate college football sponsorships. www.allstate.com/national-sponsorships/college-football.aspx.

Ashmelash, L. (2021, June 21). Across sports, athlete injuries are on the rise: A few factors are to blame. *CNN.* www.cnn.com/2021/06/21/us/sports-injuries-rise-trnd/index.html.

Associated Press. (2021, June 11). CFP expansion could increase annual revenue to $2 billion. *USA Today.* www.usatoday.com/story/sports/ncaaf/2021/06/11/cfp-expansion-could-increase-annual-revenue-to-2-billion/45662665/.

Baker, K. (2020, March 11). Inside the world of college sport financing. *Axios.* www.axios.com/college-sports-financing-student-tuition-costs-bd1d44b5-19c7-4d27-a374-cdbeb-54860fe.html.

BCS guest writer. (2016). The Jordan effect: The blueprint to Michigan's lucrative apparel deal with Nike. *Business of College Sports.* https://businessofcollegesports.com/football/jordan-effect-blueprint-michigans-lucrative-apparel-deal-nike/.

Bench, E. (2019, May 10). Here's how much athletic travel costs Ohio State. *Columbus Business First.* www.bizjournals.com/columbus/news/2019/05/10/slideshow-heres-how-much-athletic-travel-costs.html.

Bergeron, P.G. (2002). *Finance: Essentials for the successful professional.* Mason, OH: Thompson Education.

Berkowitz, S., & Shad, T. (2020, October 13). 5 surprising findings from college football coaches salaries report. *USA Today.* www.usatoday.com/story/sports/ ncaaf/2020/10/14/college-football-coaches-salaries-five-surprising-findings-data/5900066002/.

Besley, S., & Brigham, E.F. (2015). *Principles of finance* (6th ed.). Boston: Cengage Learning.

BKD CPA & Advisors. Kansas athletics, incorporated and subsidiary (2019). *KUathletics.com.* https://kuathletics.com/wp-content/uploads/2019/11/KAI-Audit-Report-2019.pdf.

Blinder, A., & Draper, K. (2021, August 4). Oklahoma and Texas to join SEC and add to a juggernaut. *New York Times.* www.nytimes.com/2021/07/30/sports/ncaafootball/oklahoma-texas-sec-college-sports.html.

Bowen, H.R. (1970). Financial needs of the campus. In R.H. Connery (Ed.), *The corporation and the campus.* New York: Academy of Political Science.

Bowen, H.R. (1980). *The costs of higher education.* San Francisco: Jossey-Bass.

Bromberg, L. (2021, July 1). In the NIL arms race, some schools are going the extra mile to help their athletes. *Sports Illustrated.* www.si.com/college/2021/07/01/name-image-likeness-programs-schools-ncaa.

Brown, M.T., Rascher, D.A., Nagel, M.S., & McEvoy, C.D. (2016). *Financial management in the sport industry* (2nd ed.). New York: Routledge.

Brunette, C., Vo, N., & Watanabe, N.M. (2017). Donation intention in current students: An analysis of university engagement and sense of place in future athletic, academic, and split donors. *Journal of Issues in Intercollegiate Athletics, 10,* 78-100.

Bryce, H.J. (2017). *Financial & strategic management for nonprofit organizations* (4th ed.). Boston: Walter de Gruyter.

Coffey, B. (2020, July 2). Debt-laden college football programs making muni market nervous. *Sportico.* www.sportico.com/business/finance/2020/debt-laden-college-football-programs-making-muni-market-nervous-1234608360/.

College Athletics Financial Information. (2021a). About the data. *Knight Commission on Intercollegiate Athletics.* https://cafidatabase.knightcommission.org/about-the-data.

College Athletics Financial Information. (2021b). Improve the understanding of finances in college athletics. *Knight Commission on Intercollegiate Athletics.* https://cafidatabase.knightcommission.org/about-the-data.

College Athletics Financial Information Database. (2022). *Knight Commission on Intercollegiate Athletics.* https://cafidatabase.knightcommission.org/reports/d7ff4f69.

Columbo, J.D. (2010). The NCAA, tax exemption, and college athletics. *University of Illinois Law Review,* 2010, 109-163.

Consolidated Financial Statements. (2020). *National Collegiate Athletic Association.* https://ncaaorg.s3.amazonaws.com/ncaa/finance/2019-20NCAAFIN_ FinancialStatement.pdf.

Covey, S.R. (2004). *The 7 habits of highly effective people.* New York: Simon & Schuster.

Davis, B. (2021, January 29). Texas athletics generates $200.7 million in revenue, $22.1 million profit in 2019-20 fiscal year. *Hook'em.com.* https:// hookem.com/ story/sports/football/2021/01/29/texas-football-longhorns-turn-22-1-million-profit-2020/4301655001/.

Dodd, D. (2021, November 18). With NCAA constitution changing, will powerful college football teams effort [sic] to formally divide FBS? *CBS Sports.* www.cbssports.com/college-football/news/with-ncaa-constitution-changing-will-powerful-college-football-teams-effort-to-formally-divide-fbs/.

Dosh, K. (2021). 2019-20 College Football Playoff Payouts. *Business of College Sports.* https://businessofcollegesports.com/2019-20-college-football-playoff-payouts/.

Enright, M., Lehren, A.W., & Longoria, J. (2020, March 8). Hidden figures: College students may be paying thousands in athletic fees and not know it. *NBC News.* www.nbcnews.com/news/education/hidden-figures-college-students-may-be-paying-thousands-athletic-fees-n1145171.

Felzer, D.J. (2021, May 23). Big Ten daily: Big Ten led all conferences in 2020 revenue. *FanNation.* www.si.com/college/indiana/football/big-ten-daily-big-ten-leads-all-conferences-in-2020-revenue-indiana.

Finances of Intercollegiate Athletics. (2021). *National Collegiate Athletic Association.* www.ncaa.org/about/resources/research/finances-intercollegiate-athletics-database.

Front Office Sports. (2021). The first six months of the NIL era. https://frontofficesports.com/newsletter/how-nil-money-is-being-spent/.

Goldkamp, T. (2021, February 5). SEC announces conference revenue distribution for 2019-20. *247sports.com.* https://247sports.com/college/florida/Article/Florida-Gators-Football-SEC-announces-conference-revenue-distribution-for-2019-20-160501486/.

Golembeski, D. (2021). College athletes often bear the cost of injuries and insurance. *Best Colleges.* www.bestcolleges.com/news/2021/09/10/college-athletes-ncaa-injuries-insurance/.

Green, A. (2013, January 26). Athletic department cuts over $150,000 from budget: Enrollment numbers thrash UM athletic departments' budget. *Montana Kaimin.* www.montanakaimin.com/news/article_17362212-67f1-11e2-a81e-001a4bcf6878.html.

Hagel, J. (2014). How to better connect planning, forecasting, and budgeting. *Journal of Accountancy.* www.journalofaccountancy.com/Issues/2014/ Apr/forecasting-budgeting-cgma-magazine-20149480.htm.

Here's a look at all the current conference TV deals (2021, September 12). *On3.* www.on3.com/news/conference-tv-deals-current-status-college-football/.

Hertel, A. (2021, September 1). Six cool facts about college football guarantee games, including Kansas State's $2.8m payout from Cowboys Stadium. *USA Today.* www.usatoday.com/story/sports/ncaaf/2021/09/01/college-football-six-cool-facts-guarantee-games/5610215001/.

Hubler, S. (2020, August 26). Colleges slash budgets in in the pandemic, with "nothing off limits." *New York Times.* www.nytimes.com/2020/10/26/us/colleges-coronavirus-budget-cuts.html.

Internal Revenue Service. (2021). Life cycle of a public charity/private foundation. www.irs.gov/charities/charitable/article/0,,id=136459,00.html.

Jones, C., & Pflaum, N. (2021, September 17). Students, taxpayers may overly subsidize Utah college sports, auditor says. *2KUTV.* https://kutv.com/news/beyond-the-books/students-taxpayers-may-overly-subsidize-utah-college-sports-auditor-says-09-17-2021.

Jones, W.A., & Rudolph, M. (2020). Are rising athletics allocations associated with student costs?: Evidence from public NCAA Division I universities. *Higher Education Politics & Economics*, *6*(1), 56-80.

Katz, M., Dixon, M.A., Heere, B., & Bass, J.R. (2017). Front porch, small house: A longitudinal study of team and university identification among incoming students at a Division III university. *Journal of Intercollegiate Sport, 10*(1), 103-125.

Lencioni, P. (2000). *The four obsessions of an extraordinary executive: A leadership fable.* New York: Jossey-Bass.

Martin, R.E. (2009). The revenue-to-cost spiral in higher education. *The John W. Pope Center for Higher Education Policy.* www.popecenter.org/acrobat/revenue-to-cost-spiral.pdf.

Membership Directory. (2021). *National Collegiate Athletic Association.* www.ncaa.org/membership-directory.

National Conference of State Legislatures. (2021). Performance Based Budgeting Fact Sheet. www.ncsl.org/research/fiscal-policy/performance-based-budgeting-fact-sheet.aspx.

NCAA. (2021a). More athletics departments in autonomy conferences are self-sufficient, but others in DI are increasingly subsidized. www.ncaa.org/champion/more-athletics-departments-autonomy-conferences-are-self-sufficient-others-di-are-increasingly.

NCAA. (2021b). Trends in Division I athletics finances. https://ncaaorg.s3.amazonaws.com/research/Finances/2021RES_D1-RevExpReport.pdf.

Novy-Williams, E. (2020, August 10). Breaking down the billions that are spent and made on college football. *Sportico.* www.sportico.com/leagues/college-sports/2020/college-footballs-billions-1234610808/.

Our Three Divisions (2021). *NCAA.* www.ncaa.org/about/resources/media-center/ncaa-101/our-three-divisions.

Pew Charitable Trusts. (2019). Two decades of change in federal and state higher education funding: Recent trends across levels of government. www.pewtrusts.org/en/research-and-analysis/issue-briefs/2019/10/two-decades-of-change-in-federal-and-state-higher-education-funding.

Pistone, A. (2021). College football's "dead money": Why fired coaches keep getting paid. *GMTM.* https://gmtm.com/articles/dead-money-is-alive-and-well-in-college-sports.

Pontz, M. (2020, February 5). Nearly 50 years after Title IX, girls and women in sports are still chasing equity. *Ms.* https://msmagazine.com/2020/02/05/nearly-50-years-after-title-ix-girls-and-women-in-sports-are-still-chasing-equity/.

Rossi, C., deputy director of athletics, University of Wisconsin-Milwaukee. (2022). Interview by B. Dwyer.

SI staff. (2015, May 27). Report: 24 public schools met NCAA's benchmark for self-sufficiency. (2015, May 27). *Sports Illustrated.* www.si.com/college/video/2015/05/27/report-24-public-schools-met-ncaas-benchmark-self-sufficiency.

Smith, C. (2012, September 19). ACC's new exit fee: Punitive or par for the course? *Forbes.* www.forbes.com/sites/chrissmith/2012/09/19/accs-new-exit-fee-punitive-or-par-for-the-course/.

Suggs, W. (2009). Making money—or not—on college sports. *New Directions for Institutional Research, 144,* 19-31.

USA Today Sports college athletics finances. (2021). *USA Today.* www.usatoday.com/restricted/?return=https%3A%2F%2Fsports.usatoday.com%2Fncaa%2Ffinances.

U.S. Department of Education. (2021). Equity in Athletics Disclosure Act. https://ope.ed.gov/athletics/#/.

What is the NCAA? (2021). National Collegiate Athletic Association. www.ncaa.org/about/resources/media-center/ncaa-101/what-ncaa.

Where does the money go? (2021). NCAA. https://ncaaorg.s3.amazonaws.com/about/ncaa/101/NCAA101_WheretheMoneyGoes.pdf.

Whitford, E. (2020, September 2). Fall brings wave of furloughs. *InsideHigherEd.com.* www.insidehighered.com/news/2020/09/02/colleges-furlough-more-employees.

Wilner, J. (2022, January 6). Pac-12 commissioner George Kliavkoff to the university presidents; Spend more on football, reap the rewards. *The Mercury News.* https://mercurynews.com/2022/01/06/pac-12-commissioner-george-kliavkoff-to-the-university-presidents-spend-more-on-football-reap-the-rewards/.

Worth, M.J. (2019). *Nonprofit management: Principles and practice* 5th ed. Thousand Oaks, CA: Sage.

10 Year Division I Financial Summary. (2021). *NCAA.* https://ncaaorg.s3.amazonaws.com/research/Finances/2021RES_D1-FinancesSummary.pdf.

Chapter 9

Athletic Business (2019, December 5). Building boom continues for collegiate sport facilities. www.athleticbusiness.com/facilities/stadium-arena/article/15158451/building-boom-continues-for-collegiate-sports-facilities.

Blaszka, M., Cianfrone, B.A., & Walsh, P. (2018). An analysis of collegiate athletic departments' social media practices, strategies and challenges. *Journal of Contemporary Athletics, 12*(4), 271-290.

Boettger, E. (n.d.). College Athletics Social Media Rankings. https://athleticdirectoru.com/articles/college-athletics-social-media-rankings/.

Bromberg, L. (2021, July 1). In the NIL arms race, some schools are going the extra mile to help their athletes. www.si.com/college/2021/07/01/name-image-likeness-programs-schools-ncaa.

Burgess, C. (2012). The expert series: Guide to the secondary ticketing market. *SeatGeek.* http://tba.seatgeek.com/articles/secondary-ticket-market-and-resellers.

Burton, C. (2019, June 6). The solution to declining college football attendance numbers is oversharing. www.college-sports-journal.com/the-solution-to-declining-college-football-attendance-numbers-is-oversharing/.

Christovich, A. (2021, November 22). College sports event operators invest in NIL. https://frontofficesports.com/college-sports-event-operators-invest-in-nil/.

Cision PR Newswire (2021, August 17). LEARFIELD Introduces Inaugural Intercollegiate Fan Report. www.prnewswire.com/news-releases/learfield-introduces-inaugural-intercollegiate-fan-report-301356341.html.

Collegiate Licensing Company. (2014). About CLC. www.clc.com/About-CLC.aspx.

DeCourcy, M. (2021, July 7). Dancing in the seats: The 15 best stadium songs in college and pro sports, ranked. *Sporting News.* www.sportingnews.com/us/ncaa-football/list/dancing-in-the-seats-the-15-best-stadium-songs-in-college-and-pro-sports-ranked/ksz2l048r9kn1dbyymhx93kab.

Dellenger, R. (2021. April 22). Inside the hidden industry of name, image and likeness and the changing world for college athletes. www.si.com/college/2021/04/22/ncaa-athletes-profit-nil-marketplace-july-1.

Dixon, S. (2022, September 16). Number of global social network users 2018-2027. www.statista.com/statistics/278414/number-of-worldwide-social-network-users/#:~:text=Social%20media%20usage%20is%20one,almost%20six%20billion%20in%202027.

Dodd, D. (2020, March 10). College football must innovate as FBS attendance dips for sixth straight year to lowest since 1996. www.cbssports.com/college-football/news/college-football-must-innovate-as-fbs-attendance-dips-for-sixth-straight-year-to-lowest-since-1996/.

Evans, N. (2019, August 24). Attendance drops for college football. www.npr.org/2019/08/24/753962604/attendance-drops-for-college-football.

Fugere, L. (2013). 5 reasons social media marketing has replaced traditional advertising. *Social Selling University.* www.socialsellingu.com/blog/5-reasons-social-media-marketing-has-replaced-traditional-advertising/.

Gregory, S. (2021, September 10). As college athletes finally start cashing in, entrepreneurs big and small also look to score. *Time.* https://time.com/6094842/college-sports-nil-operndorse/.

Hall, D. (2021, April 21). Soul of RVA: Legacy of Virginia State University's Woo Woo Cheerleaders. www.wric.com/community/soul-of-rva-legacy-of-virginia-state-universitys-woo-woo-cheerleaders/.

Holdaway, E. (2022, October 26). IUPUI announces 2022-2023 men's basketball promotions schedule: Single-game tickets to go on sale in the coming days. https://iupuijags.com/news/2022/10/26/mens-basketball-iupui-announces-2022-2023-mens-basketball-promotions-schedule.aspx.

Huml, M.R., Pifer, N.D., Towle, C., & Rode, C.R. (2019). If we build it, will they come? The effect of new athletic facilities on recruiting rankings for power five football and men's basketball programs. *Journal of Marketing for Higher Education,* 29(1), 1-18.

In-game promotions—Basketball. (2012). *George Mason Athletics.* www.gomason.com/ViewArticle.dbml?DB_OEM_ID=25200&ATCLID=205360471.

International Collegiate Licensing Association (n.d.). ICLA Membership. https://nacda.com/sports/2018/8/24/icla-membership.aspx#About.

Irwin, R.L., Sutton, W.A., & McCarthy, L.M. (2008). *Sport promotion and sales management.* Champaign, IL: Human Kinetics.

Ivie, N. (2021, July 1). The NCAA's NIL update: What it is and how it affects partner marketing. www.tune.com/blog/ncaa-nil-rule-update-what-it-is-and-how-it-affects-partner-marketing/.

Kannan, P.K., & Kopalle, P.K. (2001). Dynamic pricing on the Internet: Importance and implications for consumer behavior. *International Journal of Electronic Commerce,* 5(3), 63-83.

Lencioni, P. (2004). *Death by Meeting.* San Francisco: Jossey-Bass.

Martin, C.L.L., Miller, L.L., Elsisi, R., Bowers, A., & Hall, S. (2011). An analysis of collegiate athletic marketing strategies and evaluation processes. *Journal of Issues in Intercollegiate Athletics, 4,* 42-54.

Mayer, K.C. (2021). Attendance motivators and constraints: A Division III fall sports inquiry. *Journal for the Study of Sports and Athletes in Education*, 1-22.

Mission statement. (2013). *South Georgia State College.* http://168.20.183.97/athletics/mission.html.

Mojica, A. (2021, November 12). Vanderbilt University athletic facilities to see massive $300 million upgrade. *Fox17.com.* fox17.com/news/local/vanderbilt-university-athletic-facilities-to-see-massive-300-million-upgrade-football-basketball-baseball-commodores-ncaa-tennessee-sports.

NACDA. (n.d.) What is NACDA and what does it do? https://nacda.com/sports/2018/7/17/nacda-nacda-overview-html.aspx.

NACMA. (n.d.) About NACMA: Mission Statement. https://nacda.com/sports/2018/7/17/nacma-nacma-overview-html.aspx.

NCAA. (2018, April 6). 3 schools honored for community outreach. www.ncaa.org/about/resources/media-center/news/3-schools-honored-community-outreach.

NCAA. (2022, October). Finances of Intercollegiate Athletics Database. www.ncaa.org/sports/2019/11/12/finances-of-intercollegiate-athletics-database.aspx.

Notre Dame Athletics (2021, May 18). Notre Dame adopts mobile ticketing for athletic events. https://und.com/notre-dame-adopts-mobile-ticketing-for-all-athletic-events/.

Novy-Williams, E. (2021, June 30). How D-III Colby College built a $200 million athletics center during a pandemic. www.yahoo.com/now/d-iii-colby-college-built-095529485.html.

Pennsylvania College of Technology Athletics (n.d.). Penn College athletes give back to the community. https://pctwildcats.com/news/2017/1/18/general-penn-college-athletes-give-back-to-the-community.aspx/.

Popp, N. (2018) Ticket sales in college athletics. *NACDA.* http://nacda.com.s3.amazonaws.com/documents/2018/8/3/1771__nacda_2014_15_misc_non_event__dec14.pdf.

Schwarz, E.C., Hunter, J.D., & Lafleur, A. (2013). *Advanced theory and practice in sport marketing* (2nd ed.). New York: Routledge.

Sharma, R. (2022, August 19). Secondary ticket market to reach USD 9702.8 million, globally, by 2027 at 9.2% CAGR: Brandessence Market Research. www.linkedin.com/pulse/secondary-ticket-market-reach-usd-97028-million-globally-sharma/.

Sports Business Journal (2022, May 16). Best in sports social media. www.sportsbusinessjournal.com/Journal/Issues/2022/05/16/Sports-Business-Awards/Social-Media.aspx.

Steinberg, D. (2013, February 13). Kiss cam and unscripted close-ups usually make for a perfect match. *Washington Post.* www.washingtonpost.com/sports/kiss-cam-and-unscripted-close-ups-usually-make-for-a-perfect-match/2013/02/13/76b6fb68-7600-11e2-8f84-3e4b513b1a13_story.html?tid=pm_labs_sports_pop.

University of California. (2013). Cal introduces dynamic pricing for football, basketball. www.calbears.com/sports/m-footbl/spec-rel/072312aac.html.

Chapter 10

Barr, C.A. (2018). Collegiate sport. In L. P. Masteralexis, C. A. Barr, & M. A. Hums (Eds.), *Principles and practice of sport management* (6th ed. pp. 189-210). Burlington, MA: Jones & Bartlett Learning.

Burley-Allen, M. (1982). *Listening: The forgotten skill.* New York: Wiley.

Bynum, M. (2006, October). Marketing: Three keys to attracting sponsorships. *Athletic Business.* www.athleticbusiness.com/three-keys-to-attracting-sponsorships.html.

Capulsky, R.J., & Wolf, J.M. (1990). Relationship marketing: Positioning for the future. *Journal of Business Strategy, 11*(4), 16-26.

Chelap, M., of Octagon. (2012). Interview by R. Zullo.

Chelap, M., of Octagon (2022). Interview by R. Zullo.

Copeland, R., Frisby, W., & McCarville, R. (1996). Understanding the sport sponsorship process. *Journal of Sport Management, 10*(1), 32-48.

Covey, S.R. (2004). *The 7 habits of highly effective people.* New York: Simon & Schuster.

Do naming-rights deals pay off? Measuring ROI in naming-rights deals. (2011, September 19). *Sports Business Journal.* www.sportsbusinessjournal.com/Journal/Issues/2011/09/19/In-Depth/ROI-chart.aspx.

Donavan, D.T., Carlson, B.D., & Zimmerman, M. (2005). The influence of personality traits on sports fan identification. *Sports Marketing Quarterly, 14*(1), 31-42.

Experiential Marketing Forum. (2012). www.experientialforum.com/.

Fleming, K. (2022, July 18). College athletes score lucrative modeling contracts—here are the haute-est players. *New York Post.* https://nypost.com/2022/07/18/college-athletes-like-olivia-dunne-scoring-modeling-contracts/.

Fullerton, S. (2007). *Sports marketing.* New York: McGraw-Hill/Irwin.

Gitomer, J. (2005). *Little red book of selling.* Charlotte, NC: Buy Wisdom.

Goodwin, C. (2021, September 7). Iowa wrestler Spencer Lee's key to success in the NIL era: "If you want to make money, just start winning." *HawkCentral.* www.hawkcentral.com/story/sports/college/iowa/wrestling/2021/09/07/iowa-wrestling-spencer-lee-nil-deals-rudis-ironside-apparel-mgc-sports-agency-ncaa/5715911001/.

Graham, S., Goldblatt, J.J., & Delpy, L. (1995). *The ultimate guide to sport event management and marketing.* Chicago: Irwin.

Hoch, D. (2009, May). How to solicit sponsorships. *Athletic Business.* www.athleticbusiness.com/fundraising/how-to-solicit-sponsorships.html.

Irwin, R.L., Sutton, W., & McCarthy, L. (2008). *Sport promotion and sales management* (2nd ed.). Champaign, IL: Human Kinetics.

Jankoski, D., of Legends (2022). Interview by R. Zullo.

Johnson, K. (2005, February 21). A marketing slam dunk. *Sports Business Journal.* www.sportsbusinessjournal.com/Journal/Issues/2005/02/20050221/SBJ-In-Depth/Amarketing-Slam-Dunk.aspx.

Katz, M., & Clopton, A.W. (2014). Town & gown . . . & jerseys? NCAA Division III athletics as social anchors. *Journal of Issues in Intercollegiate Athletics, 7,* 285-306. http://csri-jiia.org/old/documents/publications/research_articles/2014/JIIA_2014_7_14_285_306_Town_&_Gown.pdf.

Lynde, T. (2007). *Sponsorships 101: An insider's guide to sponsorships in corporate America.* Mableton, GA: Lynde & Associates.

Maestas, A.J. (2022). Negotiating college sports multimedia rights deals. *AthleticdirectorU.* https://athleticdirectoru.com/articles/negotiating-college-sports-multimedia-rights-deals/.

McCarthy, M. (2006, November 16). Schools, coaches cash in on lucrative media deals. *USA Today.* www.usatoday.com/sports/college/football/2006-11-16-cover-coaches-media_x.htm.

McKindra, L. (2005, November 7). Marketing the mission. *NCAA News.* http://fs.ncaa.org/Docs/NCAANewsArchive/2005/Division+I/marketing%2Bthe%2Bmission%2B-%2B11-07-05%2Bncaa%2Bnews.html.

Morales, C., of Genesco Sports (2022). Interview by R. Zullo.

Morgan, R.M., & Hunt, S. (1999). Relationship-based competitive advantage: The role of relationship marketing in marketing strategy. *Journal of Business Research, 46*(3), 281-290.

Muret, D. (2011, October 10). Illini offer naming rights to finance arena renovation. *Sports Business Journal.* www.sportsbusinessjournal.com/Journal/Issues/2011/10/10/Facilities/Illinois.aspx.

NCAA Corporate Champions and Corporate Partners (2022, January 5). *National Collegiate Athletic Association.* www.ncaa.com/news/ncaa/article/2011-02-25/corporate-champions-and-partners.

Norcross, L. (2011, February 28). Best defense against ambush marketing is a good offense. *Sports Business Journal.* www.sportsbusinessjournal.com/Journal/Issues/2011/02/28/Opinion/From-The-Field.aspx.

O'Brien, D., of IMG College. (2012). Interview by R. Zullo.

Robinson, M. (2004, February/March). Ready for a handoff? *Athletic Management, 16*(2).

Rosenblum, N.L. (2000). *Thoreau: Political writings.* Cambridge, UK: Cambridge University Press.

Salem, R. (2003). Empathic listening. In G. Burgess & H. Burgess (Eds.), *Conflict information consortium,* University of Colorado, Boulder. www.beyondintractability.org/essay/empathic-listening.

Segura, J., & Willner, J. (2019). Athleticism in NCAA D-III: It ain't only football that matters. *Journal of Sports Economics, 20*(7), 929-958.

Shani, D. (1997). A framework for implementing relationship marketing in the sport industry. *Sports Marketing Quarterly, 6*(2), 9-15.

Smith, M. (2011a, August 29). UPS, MillerCoors go in—and go big—on campus. *Sports Business Journal.* www.sportsbusinessjournal.com/Journal/Issues/2011/08/29/Marketing-and-Sponsorship/UPS-MillerCoors.aspx.

Smith. M. (2011b, September 5). IMG's reach creates big college platform for UPS. *Sports Business Journal.* www.sportsbusinessjournal.com/Journal/Issues/2011/09/05/Marketing-and-Sponsorship/IMG-UPS.aspx.

Sparvero, E.S., & Warner, S. (2013). The price of winning and impact on the NCAA community. *Journal of Intercollegiate Sport, 6,* 120-142.

SponsorUnited. (n.d.). *SponsorUnited.com.* Retrieved October 12, 2022.

Steinbach, P. (2009, February). Fundraising: Naming rights deals scrutinized by private and public sectors alike. *Athletic Business.* www.athleticbusiness.com/Fundraising/naming-rights-deals-scrutinized-by-private-and-public-sectors-alike.html.

Swaylytics (2021, July 7). Top 100 college athletes with the biggest Instagram followings. *Swaylytics.* https://swaylytics.com/top-100-college-athletes-instagram/.

Thomas, A., of University of Georgia (2021). Interview by R. Zullo.

Titlebaum, P., & Watson, S. (2001, January 1). After tackling a sponsorship, don't leave sponsors in the dirt. *Athletic Business.* http://athleticbusiness.com/articles/article.aspx?articleid=141&zoneid=35.

Weatherall, M.P. (2006). *How NCAA Division III colleges and universities use athletics as part of their strategic enrollment management plan: A case study of three institutions.* Philadelphia: University of Pennsylvania.

Willner, J. (2019). Private universities and NCAA Division III athletics as a general recruiting tool. *International Advances in Economic Research, 25,* 293-307.

Chapter 11

Associated Press. (2010a, August 31). Houston wide receiver Patrick Edwards sues Marshall, Conference USA over injury. *ESPN.* http://sports.espn.go.com/ncf/news/story?id=5516879.

Associated Press. (2010b, December 9). Michigan–Michigan State outdoor hockey game should set attendance mark. *ESPN.* http://sports.espn.go.com/ncaa/news/story?id=5903608.

Baard, P.P., Deci, E.L., & Ryan, R.M. (2004). Intrinsic need satisfaction: A motivational basis of performance and well-being in two work settings. *Journal of Applied Social Psychology, 34,* 2045-2068.

Baker, B. (2019, June 2). CEFMA Corner. *Athletics Administration.* 72. https://s3.amazonaws.com/nacda.com/documents/2019/6/2/Page_72.pdf.

Bang, H., & Ross, S.D. (2009). Volunteer motivation and satisfaction. *Journal of Venue and Event Management, 1*(1), 61-77.

Bennett, B. (2012, June 14). Arms race proves recession-proof. *ESPN.* http://espn.go.com/college-football/story/_/id/8047787/college-football-facilities-arms-race-proves-recession-proof.

Berg, A. (2020, July 17). Power Five ADs commit to action on climate. *Athletic Business.* www.athleticbusiness.com/operations/legal/article/15159753/power-five-ads-commit-to-action-on-climate.

Bilsky, S. (2007, April/May). The scoop on hosting. *Athletic Management.* www.athleticmanagement.com/2007/05/08/the_scoop_on_hosting/index.php.

Bishop, G. (2011, November 11). Season tips off in location unlike any other. *New York Times.* www.nytimes.com/2011/11/12/sports/ncaabasketball/unc-and-michigan-state-tip-off-on-an-aircraft-carrier.html?_r=0.

Borkowski, R. (2006, October/November). When good facilities go bad. *Athletic Management.* www.athleticmanagement.com/2007/01/15/when_good_facilities_go_bad/index.php.

Borkowski, R. (2010, April/May). A closer look. *Athletic Management.* www.athleticmanagement.com/2010/04/04/a_closer_look/index.php.

Brown, M.T., & Nagel, M.S. (2010). Public recreation financing trends: Taxpayer backlash causes new models to emerge. *Journal of Venue and Event Management,* 2(1), 30-36.

Browne, W.A., Briggs, J., & Strube, B. (2008, August). Non-revenue sports gaining access to sophisticated practice facilities. *Athletic Business.* www.athleticbusiness.com/Locker-Room/non-revenue-sports-gaining-access-to-sophisticated-practice-facilities.html.

Bynum, M. (2007, March). Basketball and football practice facility design. *Athletic Business.* www.athleticbusiness.com/gym-fieldhouse/basketball-and-football-practice-facility-design.html.

Chen, K.K., & Zhang, J.J. (2012). To name it or not name it: Consumer perspectives on facility naming rights in collegiate athletics. *Journal of Issues in Intercollegiate Athletics, 5,* 119-148.

Cohen, A. (2000, April). Solar panels installed at Vaught-Hemingway Stadium at Ole Miss. *Athletic Business.* www.athleticbusiness.com/solar-panels-installed-at-vaught-hemingway-stadium-at-ole-miss.html.

Cohen, A. (2001, October). Securing sports facilities, post-9/11. *Athletic Business.* www.athleticbusiness.com/securing-sports-facilities-post-9-11.html.

Cohen. A. (2007, March). College and universities committing to wind power. *Athletic Business.* www.athleticbusiness.com/college/colleges-and-universities-committing-to-wind-power.html.

Cohen, A. (2010, February). Who cares what building was the first to receive LEED certification? *Athletic Business.* www.athleticbusiness.com/rec-center/who-cares-what-building-was-the-first-to-receive-leed-certification.html.

Dahlgren, S. (2000, August). LED technology brings fans closer than ever to the action. *Athletic Business.* www.athleticbusiness.com/Stadium-Arena/led-technology-brings-fans-closer-than-ever-to-the-action.html.

Deci, E.L., & Ryan, R.M. (2008). Facilitating optimal motivation and psychological well-being across life's domains. *Canadian Psychology, 49*(1), 14-23.

Dethlefs, D. (2007, September). Championship-caliber seating configurations for spectator facilities. *Athletic Business.* www.athleticbusiness.com/stadium-arena/championship-caliber-seating-configurations-for-spectator-facilities.html.

Diamond, L. (2009, September 17). UGA news conference to detail tailgaters' destruction. *Atlanta Journal-Constitution.* www.ajc.com/news/news/local/uga-news-conference-to-detail-tailgaters-destructi/nQSjn/.

Dodd, D. (2009, June 11). Placing blame for Edwards injury a pain in itself. www.cbssports.com/collegefootball/story/11844867.

Dosh, K. (2021, September 11). Turnkey tailgating business booming as fans return to college football stadiums. *Forbes.* www.forbes.com/sites/kristidosh/2021/09/11/turnkey-tailgating-business-booming-as-fans-return-to-college-football-stadiums/?sh=68b78c034e27.

Dougherty, N. (2008, June/July). Home away from home. *Athletic Management.* www.athleticmanagement.com/2008/06/01/home_away_from_home/index.php.

Felton, R., of REVELxp (2022). Interview by R. Zullo.

Ferguson, C. (2016, December 16). CEFMA Corner. *Athletics Administration.* 60. https://nacda.com/documents/2016/12/1/_nacda_cefma_2016_17_misc_non_event__CEFMACornerDec16.pdf.

Funk, A. (2007, October/November). It's easy being green. *Athletic Management.* www.athleticmanagement.com/2007/11/03/its_easy_being_green/index.php.

Funk, A. (2010, November). Learning from Title IX. *Athletic Management.* www.athleticmanagement.com/2010/11/29/learning_from_title_ix/index.php.

Gillentine, A., Miller, J., & Crow, B. (2010). Essential components of a "best practice" model for tailgating events. *Journal of Venue and Event Management,* 2(2), 54-68.

Gioglio, T. (2011, October/November). Bringing out the axe. *Athletic Management.* www.athleticmanagement.com/2011/10/20/bringing_out_the_axe/index.php.

Grady, J. (2010). Accessibility doesn't happen by itself: An interview with Betty Siegel, J.D., director of the Kennedy Center Accessibility Program. *Journal of Venue and Event Management,* 2(2), 69-74.

Hall, S., Marciani, L., Cooper, W., & Phillips, J. (2010). Needs, concerns and future challenges in security management of NCAA division I football events: An intercollegiate facility management perspective. *Journal of Venue and Event Management, 1*(2), 1-16.

Hayes, D. (2019, August 18). College football programs that sell in-stadium beer and alcohol at game in 2019 NCAAF season. *Fan Duel.* https://www.fanduel.com/theduel/posts/college-football-programs-that-sell-in-stadium-beer-alcohol-at-games-in-2019-ncaaf-season-01dje257jj5d.

Higgins, L. (2021, September 16). The bar is now open at more college football stadiums. *Wall Street Journal.* www.wsj.com/articles/college-football-beer-gambling-cannabis-sponsorships-11631759264.

Johnston, L. (2009, September 26). More Georgia fans put their trash away. *Atlanta Journal-Constitution.* www.ajc.com/news/sports/college/more-georgia-fans-put-their-trash-away/nQXDC/.

Keen, E. (2022, June 22). Mississippi State introduces in-game tailgating experiences at Davis Wade Stadium. *Sports Illustrated.* https://www.si.com/college/mississippistate/football/mississippi-state-football-tailgating-experience-balconies.

Klein, K. (2019, March). CoSIDA Corner, *Athletics Administration.* 56. https://s3.amazonaws.com/nacda.com/documents/2019/3/1/Page_56.pdf.

LaVetter, D., & Choi, Y.S. (2010). Implications of toppling goal posts in college football: Managing institutional risk. *Journal of Sport Administration & Supervision, 2*(1), 52-62.

Lawrence, H., & Titlebaum, P. (2010). Luxury suite administrators: Essential to success. *Journal of Venue and Event Management, 2*(2), 42-52.

Lawrence, H.J., Kahler, J., & Contorno, R.T. (2009). An examination of luxury suite ownership in professional sports. *Journal of Venue and Event Management, 1*(1), 1-18.

Low, C. (2021, October 18). SEC fines Tennessee Volunteers $250K for fan behavior at end of loss to Ole Miss Rebels. *ESPN.* www.espn.com/college-football/story/_/id/32425051/sec-fines-tennessee-volunteers-250k-fan-behavior-end-loss-ole-miss-rebels.

Malone, C. (2015, October 16). Beer map shows list of college stadiums selling alcohol. *Saturday Down South.* www.saturdaydownsouth.com/sec-football/beer-map-shows-trend-stadiums-selling-beer/.

Marciani, L., & Hall, S. (2007, August/September). Home-field security. *Athletic Management.* www.athleticmanagement.com/2007/08/13/home-field_security/index.php.

Mead, D. (2007, August/September). Personalizing locker rooms. *Athletic Management.* www.athleticmanagement.com/2008/08/20/personalizing_locker_rooms/index.php.

Meiser, P., Tucker, T., & Abaray, C. (2011). Where the heart is. *Athletic Management.* www.athleticmanagement.com/2011/04/03/where_the_heart_is/index.php.

Menaker, B.E., & Connaughton, D.P. (2010). Stadium alcohol policies: A comparison of policies available on college athletic department web sites. *International Journal of Sport Communication, 3*(2), 151-162.

Metcalfe, J. (2016, March 15). ASU women 'forever in debt' to Tennessee's Pat Summit. *AZCentral.* https://www.azcentral.com/story/sports/college/asu/2016/03/16/asu-women-forever-debt-tennessees-pat-summitt/81816666/.

Miller, J., & Dunn, A. (2011). Perceptions of terrorist threat: Implications for intercollegiate basketball venue managers. *Journal of Venue and Event Management, 3*(1), 2-10.

Miller, J., Voigt, S., Scroggins, C., & Gillentine, A. (2019). A content analysis of tailgating alcohol policies at NCAA Division I football games. *International Journal of Sport Management.* 20, 109-124.

Miller, M. (2020, January 2). 3 factors to consider in developing your college esports program. *EdTech Magazine.* https://edtechmagazine.com/higher/article/2020/01/3-factors-consider-developing-your-college-esports-program.

Moore, D. (2011, November 12). UNC, Michigan State on flight deck. *USA Today.* http://usatoday30.usatoday.com/sports/college/mensbasketball/story/2011-11-11/Carrier-Classic-11/51171104/1.

MU's tab $250,300 in Houston WR suit. (2012, April 27). *Charleston Gazette.* http://wvgazette.com/Sports/201204270163.

Myers, J. (2008, February/March). Connecting the dollar signs. *Athletic Management.* www.athleticmanagement.com/2008/03/05/connecting_the_dollar_signs/index.php.

Nagel, M. (2011). Changing attitudes regarding ticket "rights." *Journal of Venue and Event Management, 3*(2), 34-38.

Novy-Williams, E. (2011, December 9). Football beer taps add safety, $700,000 to West Virginia University sports. *Bloomberg News.* www.bloomberg.com/news/2011-12-09/football-beer-taps-add-safety-700-000-to-west-virginia-university-sports.html.

Palmero, M., Li, M., Lawrence, H., & Conley, V.M. (2011). Who is in charge? An analysis of NCAA Division I arena management models. *Journal of Venue and Event Management, 3*(2), 18-32.

Pantera, M. J., III, Accorsi, R., Winter, C., Gobeille, R., Griveas, S., Queen, D., et al. (2003, Fall). Best practices for game day security at athletic & sport venues. *The Sport Journal, 6.* www.thesportjournal.org.

Pate, J.R., Bemiller, J., & Hardin, R. (2010). Reserved: Best practices for on-campus football parking for people with physical disabilities. *Journal of Venue and Event Management, 2*(1), 2-13.

Pink, D.H. (2009). *Drive: The surprising truth about what motivates us.* New York: Riverhead Books.

Popke, M. (2005, September). Drying agents. *Athletic Business.* www.athleticbusiness.com/drying-agents.html.

Privitera, S. (2018, March 18). CEFMA Corner. *Athletics Administration.* 55. https://nacda.com/documents/2018/3/2/_nacda_cefma_2017_18_misc_non_event__CEFMACornerMarch18.pdf.

Purvis, B., assistant athletic director for facility management, Mississippi State University. (2022). Interview by R. Zullo.

Schmidt, K. (2023, August 23). Nebraska volleyball breaks world record for women's sporting event attendance on 'Volleyball Day in Nebraska.' *NCAA*. https://www.ncaa.com/news/volleyball-women/article/2023-08-30/nebraska-volleyball-breaks-world-record-womens-sporting-event-attendance.

Scholand, G. (2011, April/May). A solid defense. *Athletic Management*. www.athleticmanagement.com/2011/04/03/a_solid_defense/index.php.

Seifried, C. (2012). The historic structure report: A tool for the renovation, reconstruction, restoration and rehabilitation of sport facilities. *Journal of Venue and Event Management, 4*(1), 14-28.

Singaby, R. (2019, December 4). CEFMA Corner. *Athletics Administration*. 53. https://s3.amazonaws.com/nacda.com/documents/2019/12/4/Page_53.pdf.

Sports Turf Managers Association. (2011, January 10). Weathering the economic downturn. *Athletic Management*. www.athleticmanagement.com/2011/01/10/weathering_the_economic_downturn/index.php.

Staff. (n.d.). The rise of collegiate eSports programs. *AthleticDirectorU*. https://athleticdirectoru.com/articles/the-rise-of-collegiate-esports-programs/.

Stalcup, H. (2016, June 16). CEFMA Corner. *Athletics Administration*. 60. https://s3.amazonaws.com/nacda.com/documents/2016/8/16/_nacda_cefma_2016_17_misc_non_event__June16CEFMACorner.pdf.

Steinbach, P. (2000, March). The benefits of outsourcing concessions. *Athletic Business*. www.athleticbusiness.com/Marketing/the-benefits-of-outsourcing-concessions.html.

Steinbach, P. (2001, April). Fan's mind-set fostered by rivalries can translate into acts of aggression. *Athletic Business*. www.athleticbusiness.com/fan-s-mind-set-fostered-by-rivalries-can-translate-into-acts-of-aggression.html.

Steinbach, P. (2003a, February). Locker room & laundry—Locked and loaded. *Athletic Business*. www.athleticbusiness.com/Locker-Room/locked-and-loaded.html.

Steinbach, P. (2003b, July). Party lines. *Athletic Business*. www.athleticbusiness.com/party-lines.html.

Steinbach, P. (2004a, July). Special operations. *Athletic Business*. www.athleticbusiness.com/special-operations.html.

Steinbach, P. (2004b, August). Sporting events and booze a volatile mix. *Athletic Business*. www.athleticbusiness.com/drugs-alcohol/drinking-games.html.

Steinbach, P. (2005a, July). Venue visuals. *Athletic Business*. www.athleticbusiness.com/Marketing/venue-visuals.html.

Steinbach, P. (2005b, August). Honeymoon suites. *Athletic Business*. www.athleticbusiness.com/stadium-arena/honeymoon-suites.html.

Steinbach, P. (2005c, December). Sideline supplies. *Athletic Business*. www.athleticbusiness.com/Stadium-Arena/sideline-supplies.html.

Steinbach, P. (2006a, March). Storm fronts. *Athletic Business*. www.athleticbusiness.com/athlete-safety/storm-fronts.html.

Steinbach, P. (2006b, April). Enemy at the gates. *Athletic Business*. www.athleticbusiness.com/Facility-Security/enemy-at-the-gates.html.

Steinbach, P. (2006c, October). A majority of Division I-A football programs now use synthetic turf. *Athletic Business*. www.athleticbusiness.com/Outdoor/a-majority-of-division-i-a-football-programs-now-use-synthetic-turf.html.

Steinbach, P. (2006d, November). Sectional healing. *Athletic Business*. www.athleticbusiness.com/sectional-healing.html.

Steinbach, P. (2007, March). Michigan Stadium is at the center of pending ADA litigation. *Athletic Business*. www.athleticbusiness.com/Stadium-Arena/michigan-stadium-is-at-the-center-of-pending-ada-litigation.html.

Steinbach, P. (2008a, April). Abusive student sections drawing attention from outside the arena. *Athletic Business*. www.athleticbusiness.com/Spectator-Safety/abusive-student-sections-drawing-attention-from-outside-the-arena.html.

Steinbach, P. (2008b, April). Can sidelines be made safer for athletes who tread out of bounds? *Athletic Business*. www.athleticbusiness.com/Outdoor/can-sidelines-be-made-safer-for-athletes-who-tread-out-of-bounds.html.

Steinbach, P. (2008c, July). Concession contracts capitalizing on consumers' brand loyalty. *Athletic Business*. www.athleticbusiness.com/Marketing/concessions-contracts-capitalizing-on-consumers-brand-loyalty.html.

Steinbach, P. (2011, May). Selling alcohol to fight alcohol abuse. *Athletic Business*. www.athleticbusiness.com/Drugs-Alcohol/selling-alcohol-to-fight-alcohol-abuse.html.

Steinbach, P. (2013, January). Athletic departments apply Disney principles to game day. *Athletic Business*. www.athleticbusiness.com/staffing/athletic-departments-apply-disney-principles-to-game-day.html.

Teall Capital to revolutionize premium game and event day experiences with launch of REVELxp, acquisition of Colonnade Group. (2020, December 15). *PR Newswire*. www.prnewswire.com/news-releases/teall-capital-to-revolutionize-premium-game-and-event-day-experiences-with-launch-of-revelxp-acquisition-of-colonnade-group-301193629.html.

Titlebaum, R., DeMange, C., & Davis, R. (2012). Professional versus collegiate facilities: Perceived motivations for luxury suite ownership. *Journal of Venue and Event Management, 4*(1), 2-12.

Westerbeek, H., Smith, A., Turner, P., Emery, P., Green, C., & van Leeuwen, L. (2006). *Managing sport facilities and major events*. New York: Routledge.

White, T., of Duquesne University. (2022). Interview by R. Zullo.

WVU approves alcohol sales in football stadium. (2011, June 3). *Pittsburgh Post-Gazette*. www.post-gazette.com/stories/local/region/wvu-approves-alcohol-sales-in-football-stadium-300506/.

Chapter 12

Alabama Athletics. (2022). The stand. *University of Alabama Athletics.* https://rolltide.com/documents/2017/11/9/The_Standard_11_7_17.pdf.

Al-Khateeb, Z. (2023, April 1). Who is John Ruiz? Meet billionaire booster behind Miami's NIL-driven Final Four roster. *The Sporting News.* https://www.sportingnews.com/us/ncaa-basketball/news/john-ruiz-billionaire-booster-miami-nil-final-four/supeffhqzbaac6ggf0txuh21.

Ancona, D., Malone, T.W., Orlikowski, W.J., & Senge, P.M. (2007). In praise of the incomplete leader. *Harvard Business Review, 85*(2), 92-100.

Associated Press. (2004, November 24). College removes name of Wal-mart heiress on area. *USA Today.* http://usatoday30.usatoday.com/money/industries/retail/2004-11-24-walmart-heiress-arena_x.htm.

Associated Press. (2010, May 28). KU scandal prompts universities to look at ticket rules. *KUSports.com.* www2.kusports.com/news/2010/may/28/ku-scandal-prompts-universities-look-ticket-rules/.

Associated Press. (2011, January 26). Connecticut donor wants $3 million back after athletic director dispute. *USA Today.* http://usatoday30.usatoday.com/sports/college/football/bigeast/2011-01-25-connecticut-donor_N.htm.

Athletic Staff. (2022, June 2). Ryan Day says Ohio State needs $13 million in NIL money to keep roster intact: Report. *The Athletic.* https://theathletic.com/news/ryan-day-ohio-state-nil-money/B5gAPd06FIwQ/.

Barber, A. (2007, February/March). Pass go: Collect new donor. *Athletic Management.* www.athleticmanagement.com/2007/03/19/pass_go_collect_new_donor/index.php.

Batt, J, Marks, J.H., McFarlane, C., & Weiberg, C. (2020), Experts' Roundtable: Key fundraising topics. *AthleticdirectorU.* https://athleticdirectoru.com/articles/experts-roundtable-key-fundraising-topics/.

Berkowitz, S. (2011, April 18). Program-specific donations at Cal may alter fundraising practices. *USA Today.* http://usatoday30.usatoday.com/sports/college/2011-04-18-college-sports-funding-california_N.htm.

Berman, M. (2011, March 3). Virginia Tech will reward donors with new seating assignments. *Roanoke Times.* http://roanoke-times.vlex.com/vid/virginia-tech-will-new-seating-assignments-255754926.

Bernat, J. (2010, June). *NCAA Division I athletic development: A model for donor management in non-revenue-generating sports.* Poster session presented at the North American Society for Sport Management Conference, Tampa, Florida.

Billing, J.E., Holt, D., & Smith, J. (1985). Athletic fundraising: Exploring the motives behind donations. Chapel Hill: University of North Carolina Press.

Bittel, K., assistant professor of business and certified public accountant, Westminster College. (2022). Interview by R. Zullo.

Brick and Paver Program. (2022). *LSU Tiger Athletic Program.* www.mikethetiger.com/pavers.

Brown, C., Clayborn, K., Hays, B., & Pritchard, Z. (2008). *Former collegiate athlete donor motivation study.* Paper presented at the College Sport Research Institute, Memphis, TN.

Brown, N. (2011, March). Economy affects fundraising for college athletic facilities. *Athletic Business.* www.athleticbusiness.com/fundraising/economy-affects-fundraising-for-college-athletic-facilities.html.

Brunette, C., Vo, N., & Watanabe, N.M. (2017). Donation intention in current students: An analysis of university engagement and sense of place in future athletic, academic, and split donors. *Journal of Issues in Intercollegiate Athletics, 10,* 78-100.

Bynum, M. (2004, July). Paving the way. *Athletic Business.* www.athleticbusiness.com/paving-the-way.html.

Center, C. (2010, November 16). Premium seating at the University of Georgia. *National Association of Athletic Development Directors.* www.nacda.com/sports/naadd/spec-rel/111610aaa.html.

Chen, K., & Zhang, J. (2012). To name it or not name it: Consumer perspectives on facility naming rights sponsorship in collegiate athletics. *Journal of Issues in Intercollegiate Athletics, 5,* 119-148.

Collins, J. (2005, July). Level 5 leadership: The triumph of humility and fierce resolve. *Harvard Business Review,* 136-146.

Collins, J.C., & Porras, J.I. (1994). *Built to last: Successful habits of visionary companies.* London: Random House.

Convention preview: Future of athletic development. (2010, March 1). *National Association of Athletic Development Directors.* www.nacda.com/sports/naadd/spec-rel/030110aag.html.

Slater provides major gift for athletic facilities. (2022, February 15). *Cornell College.* https://news.cornellcollege.edu/2022/02/slater-provides-major-gift-athletics-facilities/.

Covey, S.R. (2004). *The 7 habits of highly effective people.* New York: Simon & Schuster.

Crompton, J., & Howard, D. (2003). The American experience with facility naming rights: Opportunities for English professional football teams. *Managing Leisure, 8,* 212-226.

Doughty, D. (2011, March 11). Coaching changes possible for some ACC also-rans. *Roanoke Times.* ww2.roanoke.com/sports/notebookplus/wb/279735.

Drucker, P.F. (2005, January). Managing oneself. *Harvard Business Review,* 100-109.

Dufresne, C. (1999, December 17). Notre Dame penalty is deemed "major." *Los Angeles Times.* http://articles.latimes.com/1999/dec/17/sports/sp-44956.

Dyer, K. (2022, July 29). Greg Schiano: NIL, not a new facility, is the number one issue for Rutgers football right now. *Rutgers Wire.* https://rutgerswire.usatoday.com/2022/07/29/greg-schiano-nil-not-a-new-facility-is-the-number-one-issue-for-rutgers-football-right-now/.

Edwards, M. (2019, June). NAADD Corner. *Athletics Administration,* 78. https://s3.amazonaws.com/nacda.com/documents/2019/6/2/Page_78.pdf.

Epstein, A., executive senior associate athletic director for championship resources, assistant vice president for philanthropy and alumni engagement, Western Kentucky University. (2022). Interview by R. Zullo.

Evans, T. (2009, September 4). A playbook underwritten by deep pockets. *New York Times.* www.nytimes.com/2009/09/05/sports/ncaafootball/05okstate.html.

Fagan, M. (2010, November 18). Federal charges filed against five former Kansas Athletics officials accused of stealing tickets from KU. *Lawrence Journal-World.* www2.kusports.com/news/2010/nov/18/federal-charges-filed-against-five-former-kansas-a/.

Fagan, M. (2011, March 30). Former manager of KU athletics ticket office Kassie Liebsch sentenced to 37 months in federal prison. *Lawrence Journal-World.* www2.ljworld.com/news/2011/mar/30/former-manager-ku-athletics-ticket-office-sentence/?breaking.

Foley, J. (2011, February 24). Boston College's scholarship luncheon reiterates the importance of good stewardship. *National Association of Athletic Development Directors.* www.nacda.com/sports/naadd/spec-rel/022411aaa.html.

Ford, T. (2009, October 16). Capital campaigns in focus: Yale tomorrow. *National Association of Athletic Development Directors.* www.nacda.com/sports/naadd/spec-rel/101609aae.html.

Gamecock Club. (2022). Young alumni program. https://thegamecockclub.com/young-alumni-program/.

Garcia, J. (2017, April). Salesforce enhancing athletics donations and ticket sales. *Higher Ed Summit.*

www.slideshare.net/salesforcefoundation/salesforce-enhancing-athletics-donations-and-ticket-sales.

Gardiner, J. (2009, August/September). A strong drive. *Athletic Management.* www.athleticmanagement.com/2009/08/16/a_strong_drive/index.php.

Gatlin, K., assistant athletic director of development, Tulane University. (2022). Interview by R. Zullo.

Gay, M. (2018, April 6). Tax reform claims popular college sports deduction: Impact unclear but many enthusiasts unfazed. *Greenville Business Magazine.* www.greenvillebusinessmag.com/2018/04/06/170708/tax-reform-claims-popular-college-sports-deduction-impact-unclear-but-many-enthusiasts-unfazed.

George, B. & Sims, P. (2007). *True north: Discovering your authentic leadership.* San Francisco, CA: Jossey-Bass.

George, W., Sims, P., McLean, A., & Mayer, D. (2007). Discovering your authentic leadership. *Harvard Business Review, 85*(2), 129-138.

Gimbl, R. (2010, October 26). Engaging alumni athletes. *National Association of Athletic Development Directors.* www.nacda.com/sports/naadd/spec-rel/102610aab.html.

Gladden, J.M., Mahony, D.F., & Apostolopoulou, A. (2005). Toward a better understanding of college athletic donors: What are the primary motives? *Sport Marketing Quarterly, 14*(1), 18-30.

Goffee, R., & Jones, G. (2000, September). Why should anyone be led by you? *Harvard Business Review,* 63-70.

Goleman, D. (2000, March). Leadership that gets results. *Harvard Business Review,* 78-90.

Greenhouse, S. (2000, April 25). Nike's chief cancels a gift over monitor of sweatshops. *New York Times.* www.nytimes.com/2000/04/25/us/nike-s-chief-cancels-a-gift-over-monitor-of-sweatshops.html.

Grice, D. (2022, April 23). Anthony P. Tippins Family Indoor Practice Facility groundbreaking. *Grice Connect.* https://griceconnect.com/2022/04/anthony-p-tippins-family-indoor-practice-facility-groundbreaking/.

Hall, J. (2009, June/July). Up with volunteers. *Athletic Management.* www.athleticmanagement.com/2009/06/10/up_with_volunteers/index.php.

Hanson, A. & Peachey, J.W. (2022). Athletic fundraising: An in-depth analysis of the challenges faced and strategies utilized in the NCAA Division II athletic landscape. *Journal of Intercollegiate Sport, 15*(1). 101-122. https://doi.org/10.17161/jis.v15i1.15609.

Heil, R. (2019, December). NAADD Corner, *Athletics Administration,* 60. https://s3.amazonaws.com/nacda.com/documents/2019/12/4/Page_60.pdf.

Henderson, A., Sr. (2018, September). NAADD Corner. *Athletics Administration.* https://nacda.com/documents/2018/9/4/Page_61B.pdf.

Howard, D.R., & Crompton, J.L. (2003). *Financing sport* (2nd ed.). Morgantown, WV: Fitness Information Technology.

Huiras, M. (2016, December). NAADD Corner. *Athletics Administration.* 66. https://nacda.com/documents/2016/12/1/_nacda_naadd_2016_17_misc_non_event__NAADDNAATSOCornersDec16.pdf.

Humphreys, B.R., & Mondello, M. (2007). Intercollegiate athletic success and donations at NCAA Division I institutions. *Journal of Sport Management, 21*(2), 265-280.

Kegler, B. (2010, December 15). New deferred giving program leverages power of gifts. *National Association of Athletic Development Directors.* www.nacda.com/sports/naadd/spec-rel/121510aaa.html.

Kim, S., Kim, Y., & Lee, S. (2019). Motivation for giving to NCAA Division III athletics. *Sport Marketing Quarterly, 28*(2). 77-90. http://doi.org/10.32731/SMQ.282.062019.02.

King, E.H., Sexton, E.L., & Rhatigan, J.J. (2010). Balancing fundraising in academic programs and intercollegiate athletics. *New Directions for Higher Education, 2010*(149), 65-71.

Kirinovic, M., & Milliron, M. (2009, June 25). OU best practices and peer comparison analysis. *National Association of Athletic Development Directors.* www.nacda.com/sports/naadd/spec-rel/062509aac.html.

Kotter, J.P. (2001, December). What leaders really do. *Harvard Business Review,* 85-96.

Lanoue, M. (2022, June). Incorporating DEI in fundraising initiatives. *Athletics Administration,* 77. https://s3.amazonaws.com/nacda.com/documents/2022/5/31/Page_77.pdf.

LaPlante, M. (2011, February 28). Colorado State looks to create a culture of giving among its student-athletes. *National Association of Athletic Development Directors.* www.nacda.com/sports/naadd/spec-rel/022811aac.html.

Lassiter, Z., vice president for athletics, Abilene Christian University. (2022). Interview by R. Zullo.

Lindahl, W.E. (1995). The major gift donor relationship: An analysis of donors and contributions. *Nonprofit Management and Leadership, 5,* 411-432.

Littleton, S. & Lopez, A. (2021, July). NAADD Corner. *Athletics Administration,* 78. https://s3.amazonaws.com/nacda.com/documents/2021/7/15/Page_78.pdf.

Mahony, D.F., Gladden, J.M., & Funk, D.C. (2003). Examining athletic donors at NCAA Division I institutions. *International Journal of Sport Management,* 7(1), 9-27.

McClung, S. (2010, October 26-29). *Student booster programs: Marketing communication for the non-believers.* Presentation at the 8th annual conference of the Sport Marketing Association, New Orleans, LA.

McGinniss, K. (2011, January 25). University of Rhode Island's first athletics capital campaign proves to be a success. *National Association of Athletic Development Directors.* www.nacda.com/sports/naadd/spec-rel/012511aab.html.

Morant, M. (1999, June 4). Tawdry, twisted tale. *Chicago Tribune.* http://articles.chicagotribune.com/1999-06-04/sports/9906050005_1_kim-dunbar-notre-dame-institutional-control.

Moris, P., & Vosburgh, T. (2017, December 18). Virginia Tech receives $15.2M gift to construct student-athlete center. *Virginia Tech* . https://vtx.vt.edu/articles/2017/12/athlete-performance-center.html.

Murphy, M., senior associate director of athletics for development, Ohio State University. (2022). Interview by R. Zullo.

NCAA revenues and expenses report. (2012). *National Collegiate Athletic Association.* http://ncaapublications.com/p-4306-revenues-and-expenses-2004-2012-ncaa-division-i-intercollegiate-athletics-programs-report.aspx.

Newman, R. (2017, September 1). *The five phases of the donor cultivation cycle. Newman Consulting.* https://newmanconsulting.ca/2017/09/the-5-phases-of-the-donor-cultivation-cycle/.

Newton, M. (2022, April 20). Virginia Athletics receives $40 million gift from former student-athlete. *Sports Illustrated.* www.si.com/college/virginia/football/virginia-athletics-receives-40-million-dollar-gift-from-former-athlete.

Northcutt, T. (2010, December 15). Creation of Seawolf Athletic Association allows Alaska Anchorage to achieve success through streamlined structure. *National Association of Athletic Development Directors.* www.nacda.com/sports/naadd/spec-rel/121510aan.html.

Novy-Williams, E. & Lorin, J. (2017, December 22). College football teams mount blitz to lock in donors' tax breaks. *Bloomberg.* www.bloomberg.com/news/articles/2017-12-22/college-football-teams-mount-blitz-to-lock-in-donors-tax-breaks.

O'Brien, S. (2010, February 1). Capital campaigns in focus: University of California, Santa Barbara. *National Association of Athletic Development Directors.* www.nacda.com/sports/naadd/spec-rel/020110aaa.html.

Penry, J. (n.d.). Marrying athletics & institutional advancement: Arkansas State's Jason Penry. *Athleticdirectoru.com.* https://athleticdirectoru.com/articles/athletics-and-advancement-jason-penry-arkansas-state/.

Pert, A. & Harringer, D. (2021, June 22). Tracker: College sports programs cut during COVID-19 pandemic. *Business of College Sports.* https://businessofcollegesports.com/tracker-college-sports-programs-cut-during-covid-19-pandemic/.

Phelps, M. (2012, April/May). A pitch for survival. *Athletic Management.* www.athleticmanagement.com/2012/03/31/a_pitch_for_survival/index.php.

Pientka, M. (2009, October 16). Best practices: 10 ways to blow the ask. *National Association of Athletic Development Directors.* www.nacda.com/sports/naadd/spec-rel/101609aak.html.

Popke, M. (2008, October). Online tools becoming popular in fundraising. *Athletic Business.* www.athleticbusiness.com/Fundraising/online-tools-becoming-popular-in-fundraising.html.

Popp, N., Barrett, H., & Weight, E. (2016). Examining the relationship between age of fan identification and donor behavior at an NCAA Division I athletics department. *Journal of Issues in Intercollegiate Athletics,* 9, 107-123. http://csri-jiia.org/old/documents/publications/research_articles/2016/JIIA_2016_9_06_382.pdf.

Popplewell, N. (2019, September). NAADD Corner. *Athletics Administration,* 62. https://s3.amazonaws.com/nacda.com/documents/2019/9/3/Page_62.pdf.

Rheenan, D.V., Minjares, V., McNeil, N., & Atwood, J.R. (2011). The elimination of varsity sports at a Division I institution. *Journal for the Study of Sports and Athletes in Education,* 5(3), 161-180.

Riley, E. (2010, June 4). University of Indianapolis' Greyhound Club online auction. *National Association of Athletic Development Directors.* www.nacda.com/sports/naadd/spec-rel/060410aaf.html.

Robinson, C. (2011, August 16). Renegade Miami football booster spells out illicit benefits to players. *Yahoo Sports.* http://sports.yahoo.com/investigations/news?slug=cr-renegade_miami_booster_details_illicit_benefits_081611.

Robinson, M. (1998, March). An untapped market. *Athletic Management.* www.momentummedia.com/articles/am/am1002/untapped.htm.

Ross, B. (2016, September). NAADD Corner. *Athletics Administration,* 62. https://nacda.com/documents/2016/9/2/_nacda_naadd_2016_17_misc_non_event__NAADDNAATSOCornersSept16.pdf.

Rovell, D. (2013, January 7). Fighting influence. *ESPN The Magazine,* 32.

Shapiro, S.L., Giannoulakis, C., Drayer, J., & Wang, C. (2010). An examination of athletic alumni giving behavior: Development of the former student-athlete donor constraint scale. *Sport Management Review, 13*(3), 283-295.

Shapiro, S.L., & Ridinger, L.L. (2011). An analysis of donor involvement, gender, and giving in college athletics. *Sport Marketing Quarterly, 20,* 22-32.

Stanford Giving. (2022) What about the endowment? *Stanford University*. https://giving.stanford.edu/endowment/.

Stanley, K. (2009, November 16). Capital campaigns in focus: Utah State University. *National Association of Athletic Development Directors*. www.nacda.com/sports/naadd/spec-rel/111309aaa.html.

Staurowsky, E.J. (1996). Women and athletic fundraising: Exploring the connection between gender and giving. *Journal of Sport Management, 10*(4), 401-416.

Staurowsky, E.J., Parkhouse, B., & Sachs, M. (1999). Developing an instrument to measure athletic donor behavior and motivation. *Journal of Sport Management, 10*(3), 262-277.

Steinbach, P. (2002, September). Booster shots. *Athletic Business*. www.athleticbusiness.com/booster-shots.html.

Steinbach, P. (2003, October). New development. *Athletic Business*. www.athleticbusiness.com/new-development.html.

Steinbach, P. (2004, April). Open market. *Athletic Business*. www.athleticbusiness.com/open-market.html.

Steinbach, P. (2005a, April). Signs of the time. *Athletic Business*. www.athleticbusiness.com/marketing/signs-of-the-times.html.

Steinbach, P. (2005b, May). Dance fever. *Athletic Business*. www.athleticbusiness.com/College/dance-fever.html.

Steinbach, P. (2005c, August). Honeymoon suites. *Athletic Business*. www.athleticbusiness.com/stadium-arena/honeymoon-suites.html.

Steinbach, P. (2009, November). In uncertain economy, athletics development more critical than ever. *Athletic Business*. www.athleticbusiness.com/College/in-uncertain-economy-athletics-development-more-critical-than-ever.html.

Steinbach, P. (2012, June). Athletics development success hinges on broadening the donor base. *Athletic Business*. www.athleticbusiness.com/Fundraising/athletics-development-success-hinges-on-broadening-the-donor-base.html.

Stinson, J.L., & Howard, D.R. (2004). Scoreboards vs. mortarboards: Major donor behavior and intercollegiate athletics. *Sport Marketing Quarterly, 13*(2), 129-140.

Stinson, J.L., & Howard, D.R. (2008). Winning does matter: Patterns in private giving to athletic and academic programs at NCAA Division I-AA and I-AAA institutions. *Sport Management Review, 11*(1), 1-20.

Strode, J., & Fink, J. (2009). Using motivational theory to develop a donor profile scale for intercollegiate athletics. *Journal for the Study of Sports and Athletes in Education, 3*(3), 335-354.

Terrell, M. (2010, January 5). Capital campaigns in focus: New Kenan Stadium. *National Association of Athletic Development Directors*. www.nacda.com/sports/naadd/spec-rel/010510aaa.html.

Thamel, P., & Whitmire, K. (2011, January 8). Auburn's kingmaker isn't sharing in the moment. *New York Times*. www.nytimes.com/2011/01/09/sports/ncaafootball/09boosters.html?pagewanted=all&_r=0.

Thornburg, B., associate athletic director of major gifts, University of Maryland. (2022). Interview by R. Zullo.

Tsiotsou, R. (1998). Motivation for donations to athletic programs. *Cyber Journal of Sport Marketing 2*(2).

Tsiotsou, R. (2004). The role of involvement and income in predicting small and large donations to college athletics. *International Journal of Sports Marketing & Sponsorship, 6*(2), 117-123.

Tsiotsou, R. (2006). Investigating differences between female and male athletic donors: A comparative study. *International Journal of Nonprofit and Voluntary Sector Marketing, 11*(3), 209-223.

Tsiotsou, R. (2007). An empirically based typology of intercollegiate athletic donors: High and low motivation scenarios. *Journal of Targeting, Measurement, and Analysis for Marketing, 15*, 79-92.

Uhler, A. (2018, January 1). Athletic departments scramble as donors lose tax deduction for ticket rights. *Marketplace*. www.marketplace.org/2018/01/01/big-time-donors-losing-tax-deduction-ticket-rights-have-athletic-departments/.

University Development. (2022, June 16). Major gift to Carolina Volleyball supports FORevHER 50 years campaign. www.unc.edu/posts/2022/06/16/major-gift-to-carolina-volleyball-supports-forevher-50-years-campaign/.

Valpo News (2020, January 28). Bauer Field renovation off to strong start. *Valparaiso University*. www.valpo.edu/news/2020/01/28/bauer-field-renovation-off-to-strong-start/.

Wanless, L., Pierce, D.A., Lawrence-Benedict, H.J., & Kopka, N. (2017). Best practices in athletic donor relations: The NCAA Football Bowl Subdivision. *Journal of Applied Sport Management, 9*(3). 24-37. https://doi.org/10.18666/JASM-2017-V9-I3-8151.

Weight, E.A., & Cooper, C.G. (2011). Bridging the gap: The perceptions of athletic directors and coaches regarding nonrevenue program discontinuation decisions. *Journal of Sport Administration & Supervision, 3*(1), 61-73.

Wendel, K. (2022, April 19). UVA department of athletics announces largest single gift commitment in its history. *UVAToday*. https://news.virginia.edu/content/uva-department-athletics-announces-largest-single-gift-commitment-its-history.

Wingerter, J. (2018, January 7). Tax reform provision will affect donations to OU and OSU athletics. *The Oklahoman*. www.oklahoman.com/story/news/politics/2018/01/07/tax-reform-provision-will-affect-donations-to-ou-and-osu-athletics/60551070007/.

Zullo, R. (2011, February/March). On-field fantasy: Athletic departments looking to bring in new money and deepen connections with fans are turning to a fun new idea—fantasy camps. *Athletic Management*. www.athleticmanagement.com/2011/02/26/on-field_fantasy/index.php.

Chapter 13

American College of Sports Medicine, American Dietetic Association, & Dieticians of Canada. (2000). Joint position statement: Nutrition and athletic performance. *Medicine and Science in Sports and Exercise, 32*(12), 2130-2145.

Association for Applied Sport Psychology. (2013a). About AASP. www.appliedsportpsych.org/about/.

Association for Applied Sport Psychology. (2013b). Become a certified consultant. www.appliedsportpsych.org/certified-consultants/become-a-certified-consultant/.

Astin, A.W., Astin, H.S., & Lindholm, J.A. (2011). *Cultivating the spirit: How college can enhance students' inner lives.* San Francisco: Jossey-Bass.

Barker, J. (2020, March 2). University of Maryland is paying coaches $8.1 million not to coach—including some who were fired after football player's death. *The Baltimore Sun.* www.baltimoresun.com/news/investigations/bs-pr-sp-university-of-maryland-buyouts-20200302-6fda3vj23fatnb3tokep4g6qlm-story.html.

Brockington, A. (2022, April 24). Family mourns death of 21-year-old college star athlete: "Sarah was a power of good." *Today.* www.today.com/parents/parents/sarah-shulze-university-of-wisconsin-runner-obituary-rcna25757.

Broughton, E., & Neyer, M. (2001). Advising and counseling student-athletes. *New Directions for Student Services, 93*, 47-53.

Castro, J., of Virginia Tech University. (2022). Interview by R. Zullo.

Chen, N. & Andone, D. (2022, June 1). Suicides among college athletes have grieving parents and students calling for NCAA action. *CNN.* www.cnn.com/2022/06/01/us/college-athlete-suicides-ncaa-action/index.html.

Comeaux, E. (2013). Rethinking academic reform and encouraging organizational innovation: Implications for stakeholder management in college sports. *Innovative Higher Education, 38*(4), 281-293.

Cooper, C.G., & Weight, E.A. (2011). Participation rates and gross revenue vs. promotion and exposure: Advertisement and multimedia coverage of 18 sports within NCAA Division I athletic department websites. *Sport Management Review, 14*(4), 399-408.

Covell, D., & Barr, C.A. (2010). *Managing intercollegiate athletics.* Scottsdale, AZ: Holcomb Hathaway.

Covey, S.R. (2004). *The 7 habits of highly effective people.* New York: Simon & Schuster.

Curtis, M., of University of Virginia. (2022). Interview by R. Zullo.

Delaney, T., & Madigan, T. (2009). *The sociology of sports: An introduction.* Jefferson, NC: McFarland.

Dinich, H. (2018, August 10). Sources: Maryland OL Jordan McNair showed signs of extreme exhaustion. *ESPN.* www.espn.com/college-football/story/_/id/24343021/jordan-mcnair-maryland-terrapins-died-heat-stroke-team-workout.

Dzikus, L., Hardin, R., & Waller, S.N. (2012). Case studies of collegiate sport chaplains. *Journal of Sport & Social Issues, 36*(3), 268-294.

Fornelli, T. (2021, January 16). Maryland reaches settlement with family of Jordan McNair in relation to 2018 death of former Terps player. *CBS Sports.* www.cbssports.com/college-football/news/maryland-reaches-settlement-with-family-of-jordan-mcnair-in-relation-to-2018-death-of-former-terps-player/.

Galli, N., & Reel, J.J. (2012). "It was hard, but it was good": A qualitative exploration of stress-related growth in Division I intercollegiate athletes. *Qualitative Research in Sport, Exercise, and Health, 4*(3), 297-319.

Greenberg, J. (2017, August 30). Five questions with Jason Freeman. *North Carolina Athletics.* https://goheels.com/news/2017/8/30/football-five-questions-with-jason-freeman.aspx.

Hales, D. (2007). *An invitation to wellness: Making healthy choices.* Belmont, CA: Thomson Wadsworth.

Halverson, S.D., & King, K. (2013). Interview by C. Cooper & L. Huffman.

Hayden, E.W., Kornspan, A.S., Bruback, Z.T., Parent, M.C., & Rodgers, M. (2013). The existence of sport psychology services among NCAA Division I FBS university athletic departments and counseling centers. *The Sport Psychologist, 27*(3), 296-304.

Hirko, S. (2009). Intercollegiate athletics and modeling multiculturalism. *New Directions for Higher Education, 2009*(148), 91-100.

Holohan, M. (2022, May 31). "We're taught to push through pain": College athletes on mental health crisis. *Today.* www.today.com/health/essay/college-athletes-mental-health-suicides-rcna30381.

Howard-Hamilton, M.F., & Sina, J.A. (2001). How college affects student athletes. *New Directions for Student Services, 2001*(93), 35-45.

Johnson. G. (2022, May 24). NCAA student-athlete well-being study. *NCAA Research.* www.ncaa.org/news/2022/5/24/media-center-mental-health-issues-remain-on-minds-of-student-athletes.aspx.

Koenig, H.G. (2009). Research on religion, spirituality, and mental health: A review. *Canadian Journal of Psychiatry, 54*(5), 283-291.

Koenig, H.G., Parkerson, G.R., & Meador, K.G. (1997). Religion index for psychiatric research. *American Journal of Psychiatry, 154*(6), 885-886.

Lind, A. (2022, March 10). Ohio State offensive lineman Harry Miller medically retiring from football. *SI.* www.si.com/college/ohiostate/football/ohio-state-football-redshirt-junior-offensive-lineman-harry-miller-medically-retiring-mental-health.

Lindberg, E. (2021, Summer). Let's talk about the quiet crisis in college sports: Mental health. https://news.usc.edu/trojan-family/college-athlete-mental-health-usc-sports-psychologists/.

Meshad, J., of University of Georgia. (2022). Interview by R. Zullo.

Nadelen, M.D. (2012, January 10). *Basic injury prevention concepts. American College of Sports Medicine.* www.acsm.org/access-public-information/articles/2012/01/10/basic-injury-prevention-concepts.

National Athletic Trainers' Association. (2014a). Get certified. www.nata.org/get-certified.

National Athletic Trainers' Association. (2014b). Recommendations and Guidelines for Appropriate Medical Coverage of Intercollegiate Athletics. www.nata.org/appropriate-medical-coverage-intercollegiate-athletics.

North Wind Staff. (2022, April 22). Editorial—Our community is grieving. *The North Wind* https://thenorthwindonline.com/3892060/opinion/editorial-our-community-is-grieving/.

Oyefusi, D. (2021, June 16). Rick Court, former strength coach who resigned after reportedly abusing Maryland football players, hired by Michigan school district. *The Baltimore Sun.* www.baltimoresun.com/sports/terps/bs-sp-rick-court-strengh-coach-maryland-football-players-michigan-20210616-pitxk57akbdgldzn5lnh3yezpm-story.html.

Pascarella, E.T., & Blimling, G.S. (1996). Students' out-of-class experiences and their influence on learning and cognitive development: A literature review. *Journal of College Student Development,* 37(2), 149-162.

Powers, E. (2007, June 28). When prayer reaches the locker room. *Inside Higher Ed.* www.insidehighered.com/news/2007/06/28/faith.

Rodriguez, N.R., DiMarco, N.M., & Langley, S. (2009). Position of the American Dietetic Association, Dietitians of Canada, and the American College of Sports Medicine: Nutrition and athletic performance. *Journal of the American Dietetic Association, 109*(3), 509-527.

Scott, J. (2022, July 17). UCLA's Thomas Cole announces football retirement after suicide attempt. *SI.* www.si.com/college/2022/07/17/ucla-thomas-cole-football-retirement-suicide-attempt.

Shaw, A., Joseph, S., & Linley, P.A. (2005). Religion, spirituality, and posttraumatic growth: A systematic review. *Mental Health, Religion, and Culture, 8*(1), 1-11.

Tchatchouwo, I. & Brown, A. (2022, December). The future of mental wellness in college athletics. *Athletics Administration,* 57(4), 25-26.

Thacker, S.B., Gilchrist, J., Stroup, D.F., & Kimsey, C.D., Jr. (2004). The impact of stretching on sports injury risk: A systematic review of the literature. *Medicine & Science in Sports & Exercise, 36*(3), 371-378.

Vivinetto, G. (2022, April 27). College softball star Lauren Bernett died of apparent suicide, authorities say. *Today.* www.today.com/news/sports/softball-star-lauren-bernett-died-apparent-suicide-authorities-say-rcna26343.

Wallace, L., Wilson, J., & Miloch, K. (2011). Sporting Facebook: A content analysis of NCAA organizational sport pages and Big 12 Conference athletic department pages. *International Journal of Sport Communication, 4*(4), 422-444.

Watson, J.C., & Kissinger, D.B. (2007). Athletic participation and wellness: Implications for counseling college student-athletes. *Journal of College Counseling, 10*(2), 153-163.

Weinberg, R.S., & Gould, D. (2011). *Foundations of sport and exercise psychology* (5th ed.). Champaign, IL: Human Kinetics.

Wolverton, B. (2008, September 5). Rise in fancy academic centers for athletes raises questions of fairness. *Chronicle of Higher Education.* http://chronicle.com/article/Rise-in-Fancy-Academic-Centers/13493/.

Index

Note: The italicized *f* and *t* following page numbers refer to figures and tables, respectively.

O

P

About the Editors

Robert H. Zullo, PhD, is on the faculty of the sport management program at Slippery Rock University in Slippery Rock, Pennsylvania. He was the founding program director at Westminster College and Seton Hill College and previously taught at James Madison University and Mississippi State University. He has worked in intercollegiate athletics at the University of Georgia, Virginia Tech, and the University of North Carolina. He started his career in intercollegiate athletics administration through experiences with the University of Virginia athletics department and the Virginia Military Institute. He is a member of the North American Society for Sport Management (NASSM) and the National Association of Collegiate Marketing Administrators (NACMA).

Erianne A. Weight, PhD, MBA, is the director of Center for Research in Intercollegiate Athletics and a professor of sport administration at the University of North Carolina (UNC) at Chapel Hill. She is involved in a variety of Division I athletics consultancies through her role as a research consultant for Collegiate Sports Associates. She is a former president of the North American Society for Sport Management (NASSM) and is chair of the UNC Faculty Athletics Committee. It is her hope that through research, there will be an increase in the quantity and quality of opportunities for athletic participation and education for young people throughout the world.

Photograph by Peter Peets.

Photograph by Peter Peets.

Contributors

Alyssa T. Bosley, MS
James Madison University

Joseph N. Cooper, PhD
University of Massachusetts–Boston

Brendan Dwyer, PhD
Virginia Commonwealth University

Molly P. Harry, PhD
University of Arkansas–Fayetteville

Barbara Osborne, JD
University of North Carolina at Chapel Hill

Sally R. Ross, PhD
Grand Valley State University

Lisa M. Rubin, PhD
Kansas State University

Stephen L. Shapiro, PhD
University of South Carolina

David J. Shonk, PhD
James Madison University

Ellen J. Staurowsky, EdD
Ithaca College